33RD EDITION

STUDENTS WITH DISABILITIES AND SPECIAL EDUCATION LAW

Autism

Gifted Students

Mainstreaming

IDEA

Bullying

IEPs

Center for
Education & Employment Law

Center for Education & Employment Law
P.O. Box 3008
Malvern, Pennsylvania 19355

Copyright © 2016 by Center for Education & Employment Law
All rights reserved. No part of this publication may be reproduced by any means, electronic
or mechanical, including photocopying, without prior written permission from the publisher.
First edition 1984
Thirty-third edition 2016
Printed in the United States of America

"This publication is designed to provide accurate and authoritative information
in regard to the subject matter covered. It is sold with the understanding that the publisher
is not engaged in rendering legal, accounting or other professional services. If legal
advice or other expert assistance is required, the services of a competent professional
person should be sought."—from a Declaration of Principles jointly adopted by a
Committee of the American Bar Association and a Committee of Publishers and
Associations.

The Library of Congress has catalogued this book as follows:

Library of Congress Cataloging-in-Publication Data
Students with disabilities and special education. 32nd ed.
p. cm.
Includes index.
ISBN 978-1-933043-98-2

Cover design by Patricia Jacoby

1. Special education—Law and legislation—United States. 2. Handicapped children—
   Education—Law and legislation—United States. I. Center for Education & Employment Law
   (Malvern, PA)

LC4031.5875 1999
371.91'0973—dc20

Library of Congress Catalog Card Number: 93-13784

   ISBN 978-1-933043-98-2
   ISSN 1076-0911

Other Titles Published by Center for Education & Employment Law:

Deskbook Encyclopedia of American School Law
Deskbook Encyclopedia of Employment Law
Deskbook Encyclopedia of Public Employment Law
Higher Education Law in America
Keeping Your School Safe & Secure: A Practical Guide
Legal Update for Teachers: The Complete Principal's Guide
Private School Law in America

TABLE OF CONTENTS

CHAPTER ONE
Laws Protecting Students with Disabilities

CHAPTER TWO
Identification and Evaluation

CHAPTER THREE
Individualized Education Programs

TABLE OF CONTENTS

CHAPTER FOUR
Placement

CHAPTER FIVE
Changes in Placement and Student Discipline

TABLE OF CONTENTS

CHAPTER SIX
IDEA Procedural Safeguards

CHAPTER SEVEN
Private School Tuition

TABLE OF CONTENTS

CHAPTER EIGHT
Transition Services and Related Services

CHAPTER NINE
School Liability

CHAPTER TEN
Student Civil Rights

CHAPTER ELEVEN
Employment

TABLE OF CONTENTS

CHAPTER TWELVE
School District Operations

REFERENCE SECTION

INTRODUCTION

Federal law requires that school districts provide each child with a disability a free appropriate education. *Students with Disabilities and Special Education Law* has been published in response to the need of school administrators and others involved in providing special education services to have a reference available when confronted with any of the multitude of problems in the special education area. The 32nd Edition continues to group cases by subject matter and contains the full text of the Individuals with Disabilities Education Act as amended through July, 2005. The full legal citation is given for each reported case, and all cases have been indexed and placed in a Table of Cases following the Table of Contents.

Although the IDEA has undergone several major amendments – from the EHA to the EAHCA to the HCPA and finally to the IDEA – the book generally uses the abbreviation "IDEA" in place of the others for ease of readability and textual flow.

The intent of this volume is to provide professional educators and lawyers with access to important cases, statutory and regulatory law in the field of special education and disabled students' rights.

Thomas D'Agostino, Esq.
Managing Editor
Center for Education & Employment Law

ABOUT THE EDITORS

Carol Warner is the editor of *EducationTechNews.com* and two monthly newsletters: *School Safety & Security Alert* and *Legal Update for Teachers*. She is also a contributing editor for *HigherEdMorning.com* and *Higher Education Legal Alert*. Before joining the Center for Education & Employment Law, she was an editor for two employment law newsletters: *What's Working in Human Resources* and *What's New in Benefits & Compensation*. Ms. Warner is a graduate of The New York Institute of Technology and holds a Bachelor of Arts in English with an emphasis in professional writing.

James A. Roth is the editor of *Legal Notes for Education* and *Special Education Law Update*. He is a co-editor of *Students with Disabilities and Special Education Law* and an adjunct program assistant professor at St. Mary's University in Minnesota. Mr. Roth is a graduate of the University of Minnesota and William Mitchell College of Law. He is admitted to the Minnesota Bar.

Thomas D'Agostino is a managing editor at the Center for Education & Employment Law and is the editor of *Higher Education Legal Alert*. He is a co-author of *Keeping Your School Safe & Secure: A Practical Guide*. He graduated from the Duquesne University School of Law and received his undergraduate degree from Ramapo College of New Jersey. He is a past member of the American Bar Association's Section of Individual Rights and Responsibilities as well as the Pennsylvania Bar Association's Legal Services to Persons with Disabilities Committee. Mr. D'Agostino is admitted to the Pennsylvania bar.

Curt J. Brown is the Editorial Director of the Center for Education & Employment Law. Prior to assuming his present position, he gained extensive experience in business-to-business publishing, including management of well-known publications such as *What's Working in Human Resources, What's New in Benefits & Compensation, Keep Up to Date with Payroll, Supervisors Legal Update,* and *Facility Manager's Alert*. Mr. Brown graduated from Villanova University School of Law and graduated magna cum laude from Bloomsburg University with a B.S. in Business Administration. He is admitted to the Pennsylvania Bar.

HOW TO USE THIS VOLUME

We have designed *Students with Disabilities and Special Education Law* in an accessible format for both attorneys and non-attorneys to use as a research and reference tool toward prevention of legal problems.

Using Your Deskbook to Conduct Research

As a research tool, our deskbook allows you to conduct your research on two different levels – by topics or by cases.

Topic Research

◆ If you have a general interest in a particular **topic** area, our **Table of Contents** provides descriptive section headings with detailed subheadings for each chapter.

    ✓ For your convenience, we also include an individual chapter table of contents at the beginning of each chapter.

Example:
If you are seeking information on medical services, the Table of Contents indicates that a discussion of that topic takes place in Chapter Eight, under "Transition Services and Related Services," on page 238:

How to Use This Volume

♦ If you have a specific interest in a particular **issue**, our comprehensive **index** collects all of the relevant page references to particular issues.

> **Example:**
> For more information on individualized education programs (IEPs), the index provides references to all cases dealing with IEPs, including those cases dealing with their implementation:
>
> > Individualized education programs (IEPs), 45-90
> > > appropriateness, 61-76
> > > > maximizing potential, 69-71
> > > > methodology questions, 61-65
> > > > ➡ student progress, 65-69
> > > > transfer students, 71-73
> > > behavior intervention plans, 83-87
> > > functional behavioral assessments, 87-89

Case Research

♦ If you know the **name** of a particular case, our **Table of Cases** will allow you to quickly reference the location of the case.

> **Example:**
> If you wanted to look up the case *T.B. v. St. Joseph School Dist.,* you would look in the Table of Cases, which has been arranged alphabetically. The reference to the case is located under section T and directs you to page 209.
>
> **T**
>
> > T.B. v. Bryan Independent School Dist., 290
> > T.B. v. San Diego Unified School Dist., 240
> > ➡ T.B. v. St. Joseph School Dist., 209
> > T.F. v. Fox Chapel Area School
> > > Dist., 12, 257, 390
> > T.G. v. Baldwin Park Unified School Dist., 115

✓ Each of the cases summarized in the deskbook also contains the case citation that will allow you to access the full text of the case from a law library. See *How to Read a Case Citation*, p. 517.

How to Use This Volume

♦ If your interest lies in cases from a **particular state**, our **Table of Cases by State** will identify the cases from your state and direct you to the page numbers where they are located.

Example:

If cases from Arizona are of interest, the Table of Cases by State, arranged alphabetically, lists all of the Arizona case summaries contained in the deskbook.

ARIZONA

Cain v. Horne, 217
Deer Valley Unified School Dist. v. L.P., 75
Gallagher v. Tucson Unified School Dist., 306
Hance v. Fountain Hills Unified School Dist., 175
Niehaus v. Huppenthal, 220

✓ Remember, the judicial system has two court systems – state and federal – which generally function independently of each other. See *The Judicial System*, p. 513. We have included the federal court cases in the table of cases by state according to the state in which the court resides. However, federal court decisions often impact other federal courts within that particular circuit. Therefore, it may be helpful to review cases from all of the states contained in a particular circuit.

Reference Tool

As a reference tool, we have highlighted important resources that provide the framework for many legal issues.

♦ If you would like to see specific wording of the **Individuals with Disabilities Education Act Amendments of 1997**, refer to **Appendix A**.

♦ If you would like to review the **Table of Special Education Cases Decided by the U.S. Supreme Court** in a particular subject matter area, our topical list of U.S. Supreme Court case citations located in **Appendix B** will be helpful.

How to Use This Volume

We hope you benefit from the use of *Students with Disabilities and Special Education Law*. If you have any questions about how to use the deskbook, please contact Thomas D'Agostino at tdagostino@pbp.com.

OVERVIEW AND KEY TERMS

The Individuals with Disabilities Education Act (IDEA), 20 U.S.C. §§ 1400 – 1487 is the most important federal law regarding the education of students with disabilities. States also have special education laws that parallel the IDEA. Unlike Section 504 of the Rehabilitation Act and the Americans with Disabilities Act (ADA), the IDEA does not prohibit discrimination on the basis of disability. Instead, it imposes obligations on the states and requires them to comply with IDEA procedures as a condition of receiving federal funds.

Congressional findings in support of the IDEA tell a story about the lack of educational services for students with disabilities both before and after federal involvement began in 1975. Before the Education for All Handicapped Children Act of 1975 (Public Law 94–142) was enacted, the special educational needs of children with disabilities were not being fully met. Congress found that over half the children with disabilities in the U.S. did not receive appropriate educational services that would enable them to have full equality of opportunity.

An estimated one million children with disabilities in the U.S. were excluded entirely from the public school system and did not go through the educational process with their peers. Congress found in 1975 that disability is a natural part of the human experience and in no way diminishes the right of individuals to participate in or contribute to society.

Improving educational results for children with disabilities was declared an essential element of our national policy of ensuring equality of opportunity, full participation, independent living, and economic self-sufficiency for individuals with disabilities. Congress found student disabilities often went undetected. Because of the lack of adequate services within the public school system, families were often forced to find services outside the public school system. The IDEA provides federal funding to local education agencies through grants to the states. To receive IDEA funds, states must demonstrate that they maintain a policy assuring that all children with disabilities have access to a free appropriate public education (FAPE).

Local educational agencies receiving IDEA funds must include satisfactory assurances that they are identifying and providing special education services to all students with disabilities residing within the local jurisdiction.

The IDEA has been reauthorized periodically by Congress, with the most recent reauthorization taking place in 2004 in what was known as the Individuals with Disabilities Education Improvement Act. The 2004 IDEA amendments increased federal funding, adopted terms from the No Child Left Behind Act, and relaxed some student disciplinary provisions.

The IDEA was originally passed as the Education of the Handicapped Act of 1970 (EHA). It was intended to assist the states in providing a FAPE to children with disabilities by establishing minimum requirements with which the states had to comply in order to receive federal financial assistance. Congress amended the EHA in 1975 with the Education for All Handicapped Children Act (EAHCA) (P.L. 94–142), which contains many of the most important legal protections of the legislation now known as the IDEA.

The Handicapped Children's Protection Act of 1986 (HCPA) (P.L. 99–372), further amended the EHA by specifically authorizing awards of attorneys' fees to the families of students with disabilities who prevailed in EHA lawsuits. The HCPA also expressly allowed disabled students to cumulate their available remedies under Section 504 of the Rehabilitation Act of 1973 (29 U.S.C. § 794) and 42 U.S.C. § 1983. The HCPA is found in the present IDEA at 20 U.S.C. § 1415(i)(3) and Section 1415(l).

In 1990, Congress passed the amendment renaming the legislation the Individuals with Disabilities Education Act (IDEA) (P.L. 102–119), and added specific clauses to abrogate sovereign immunity and authorize remedies under both legal and equitable theories (20 U.S.C. § 1403). In 1994, Congress amended the IDEA as part of the Improving America's Schools Act of 1994 (P.L. 103–382). States and LEAs must have in place a number of statutory policies and procedures in order to ensure the receipt of IDEA funds.

School districts must comply with the general requirements of 20 U.S.C. § 1414(a)(1)(A), which requires a full and individual initial evaluation upon a parent request or its own initiative. Districts must comply with IDEA notice and procedural requirements. Parents who have not allowed an evaluation of their children, or who have refused special education, are barred from later asserting IDEA procedural protections in disciplinary cases.

Each IEP includes statements of annual goals, including benchmarks or short-term objectives, related to meeting the student's needs that result from the student's disability, to enable involvement and progress in the general curriculum. IEPs include a statement of the special education and related services to be provided to the student and a statement of the program modifications to be furnished, which will allow the student to advance appropriately toward attaining the annual goals, and be involved and progress in the general curriculum and participate with other students.

Each IEP must explain the extent to which a student will not participate with non-disabled students in regular classes and a statement of any individual modifications that are needed for the student to participate in state or local student achievement assessments. For students age 14 and over, a statement of the student's necessary transition services under the applicable components of an IEP focusing on courses of study must be included.

For those over 16, a statement of necessary transition services must be included which may describe interagency responsibilities. Beginning at least one year before the student reaches the age of majority under state law, the IEP must include a statement that the student has been advised of IDEA rights that will transfer to the student upon the attainment of the age of majority.

The following abbreviations are used in this edition of *Students with Disabilities and Special Education Law*:

ABA – applied behavior analysis

ADA – Americans with Disabilities Act

ADD – attention deficit disorder

ADHD – attention deficit hyperactivity disorder

ALJ – administrative law judge

ARD – admission, review and dismissal

AVT – auditory-verbal therapy

AYP – adequate yearly progress

CSE – committee on special education

CST – child study team

DTT – discrete trial training

EEOC – Equal Employment Opportunity Commission

ESY – extended school year

FAPE – free appropriate public education

FERPA – Family Educational Rights and Privacy Act

FIE – full and individual evaluation

FMLA – Family and Medical Leave Act

IDEA – Individuals with Disabilities Education Act

IEE – independent educational evaluation

IEP – individualized education program

IFSP – individual family service plan

IHO – independent hearing officer

OVERVIEW AND KEY TERMS

IU – intermediate unit

LEA – local educational agency

LRE – least restrictive environment

MDE – multidisciplinary evaluation

MDT – manifestation determination team

NCLB Act – No Child Left Behind Act

OG – Orton-Gillingham

OT – occupational therapy

PPT – planning and placement team

PT – physical therapy

RICO – Racketeer Influenced and Corrupt Organizations Act

TA – teaching assistant

TEACCH – Treatment and Education of Autistic and related Communication
   Handicapped Children

TABLE OF CASES

TABLE OF CASES

TABLE OF CASES

TABLE OF CASES

TABLE OF CASES

TABLE OF CASES

TABLE OF CASES

TABLE OF CASES

TABLE OF CASES

TABLE OF CASES BY STATE

TABLE OF CASES BY STATE

TABLE OF CASES BY STATE

TABLE OF CASES BY STATE

TABLE OF CASES BY STATE

TABLE OF CASES BY STATE

NORTH CAROLINA

TABLE OF CASES BY STATE

CHAPTER ONE

Laws Protecting Students with Disabilities

I. INDIVIDUALS WITH DISABILITIES EDUCATION ACT

A. Background

The Individuals with Disabilities Education Act (IDEA) imposes obligations on the states and requires compliance with IDEA procedures as a condition of receiving federal funds. To receive IDEA funds, states must maintain a policy assuring that all children with disabilities have access to a free appropriate public education (FAPE). "FAPE" refers to appropriate special education and related services provided at public expense that meet state educational agency standards in conformity with an individualized education program (IEP).

The individualized education program (IEP) is the IDEA's most important procedural protection. The IDEA requires adequate notice to parents and opportunities for parental participation in the development of a student's IEP. A school district "must include the parents of a child with a disability in an IEP meeting unless they affirmatively refuse to attend."

B. Minimum IDEA Standards Under *Board of Educ. v. Rowley*

♦ A Virginia student's IEP for kindergarten initially called for half of his education to take place in general education settings, but the IEP team gradually shifted his time away from general to special classrooms. After the student missed significant school time during grade one, new goals were proposed for his second-grade IEP and more time was planned for him to remain in general education classrooms. But the parents rejected the IEP proposal. The school district offered to revise the IEP, but the parents sought a 1:1 aide, extended school year services and assignment of a full-time nurse to the school. They filed a due process hearing request, challenging the IEP on six grounds. Based on their child's evaluations, the parents claimed he not only made no progress in school but regressed academically. A hearing officer issued a decision rejecting their argument and also found the IEP had been properly implemented. Later, a federal court affirmed the decision for the school board.

On appeal to the Fourth Circuit, the parents urged the court to find that a FAPE requires the provision of "meaningful" rather than "some" educational benefit. The parents argued the court should jettison the longstanding ruling from *Board of Educ. v. Rowley*, this chapter. The court interpreted *Rowley* to hold that **a FAPE requires schools to provide only "some" educational benefit to fulfill the intent of Congress. It rejected arguments that 1997 and 2004 IDEA amendments replaced the *Rowley* standard.** The court held a FAPE still described the provision of "some" educational benefit rather than a "meaningful benefit." The court refused to find Congress sought to overrule *Rowley*, since no language in the IDEA dictated this. Next, the court held the school district had adequately implemented the student's IEP. There was evidence that the student did not need 1:1 support for basic daily needs and did not require a school nurse to be safe in school. The court held for the school board. *O.S. v. Fairfax County School Board*, 804 F.3d 354 (4th Cir. 2015).

♦ A Colorado child with autism had significant behavior problems. Near the end of his fourth-grade school year, his behavior worsened and a new behavior intervention plan (BIP) was included in his IEP. But the parents withdrew him from the district and enrolled him in a private school. An ALJ denied their request for tuition reimbursement and a federal court later affirmed the decision. The parents appealed to the Tenth Circuit Court of Appeals, which held they did not show a failure to adequately report their child's progress denied them meaningful participation in his education. While his progress reports "could have been more robust," the court found evidence that they knew about his progress and were active participants in his education.

When developing an IEP for a child whose behavior impedes learning, the IDEA requires a school to "consider the use of positive behavioral interventions and supports and other strategies to address that behavior." In the court's view, the district was working to address the student's behavior when the parents rejected the IEP and privately placed him. The IDEA requires a BIP or a functional behavioral assessment only if there is a disciplinary change in placement, which was not the case here. **The court declined the parents' invitation to abandon the standard for assessing IEPs set by the Supreme Court in *Board of Educ. v. Rowley*,** this chapter. While the parents argued IEPs must be calculated to confer a "meaningful educational benefit" to satisfy the IDEA, the court disagreed. In ruling for the district, the court held **IEPs need only be reasonably calculated to provide "some educational benefit" to satisfy the requirements of the IDEA.** *Endrew F. v. Douglas County School Dist. RE 1*, 798 F.3d 1329 (10th Cir. 2015).

In Board of Educ. v. Rowley, *this chapter, the Supreme Court held the IDEA establishes only a basic floor of opportunity for students with disabilities, and imposes no requirement on school districts to maximize student potential.* **Rowley** *limits a court's inquiry to whether the district has complied with IDEA procedural protections and whether the IEP was reasonably calculated to enable the student to receive educational benefits. If a school district* *satisfies this two-part inquiry, the court's analysis is at an end. According to the U.S. Supreme Court in the leading case of* Board of Educ. of Hendrick Hudson Cent. School Dist., Westchester County v. Rowley, *458 U.S. 176, 102 S.Ct. 3034, 73 L.Ed.2d 690 (1982), below, the IDEA was not enacted to maximize the potential of students, but rather to open the door of educational opportunity.*

♦   In *E.L. v. Chapel Hill-Carrboro Board of Educ.*, 773 F.3d 509 (4th Cir. 2014), the U.S. Court of Appeals, Fourth Circuit, held a free appropriate public education is one conferring "some educational benefit" upon a child. The court held **"the IDEA is concerned with equality of access rather than equality of outcomes."** In finding a North Carolina school board complied with an autistic student's IEP, the court cited longstanding case law beginning with the *Board of Educ. v. Rowley* decision, which held that an IEP will be upheld if it is "reasonably calculated to enable the child to receive educational benefits." As long as an IEP provides a "basic floor of opportunity" for a student, a court is not to resolve disagreements about methodology.

♦   An Alabama student struggled in elementary school and had to repeat a grade. He was placed in special education in middle school. For grade nine, the student passed only two classes. But the IEP team granted his mother's request to place him on a regular diploma track. It also let him "double up" on his grade nine and 10 classes so he could remain with his peers. Asserting that the school board denied her child a free appropriate public education (FAPE), the mother filed a due process hearing request. A hearing officer held the school district provided the student a FAPE. When the case reached the U.S. Court of Appeals, Eleventh Circuit, it found the student's IEP reading goals were not adapted to address his individual needs. His reading skills were assessed at a first-grade level, but the reading goal for the IEP was derived from the state standard for ninth-graders. Moreover, the student's IEP goals remained largely the same from year to year. **The school used "boilerplate IEPs," with goals going far beyond his reading levels that did not provide him educational benefits.** Postsecondary goals and transition services stated in the IEPs did not meet relevant standards. Finding a lack of individualized planning and a program that denied the student a FAPE, the court held for the parent. *Jefferson County Board of Educ. v. Lolita S.*, 581 Fed.Appx. 760 (11th Cir. 2014).

♦   The parents of an eight-year-old New York student with profound hearing impairments disagreed with their local education board over the student's need for a sign-language interpreter. They insisted that the tutoring and hearing aid provided by the school district were insufficient, even though the student performed better than average and advanced educationally. The parents argued that because of the disparity between her achievement and her potential, she was not receiving a FAPE under the IDEA (then known as the EHA). An independent hearing examiner found the interpreter unnecessary because the student was achieving educationally, academically and socially without this service. A federal court held that because of the disparity between the student's achievement and her potential, she was not receiving a FAPE. The Second Circuit affirmed the decision, and the U.S. Supreme Court granted review.

The Court observed that in passing the IDEA, "Congress sought primarily to make public education available to [children with disabilities]. But in seeking to provide such access to public education, Congress did not impose upon the States any greater substantive educational standard than would be necessary to make such access meaningful." According to the Court, the IDEA imposed no requirement on states to provide equal educational opportunities and Congress recognized that educational opportunity differs among students of varying abilities. Because of the "wide spectrum" of abilities, the Court refused to establish a test to determine the adequacy of educational benefits provided by schools under the IDEA. Instead of imposing a general rule, the Court held:

> Insofar as a State is required to provide a handicapped child with a "free appropriate public education," we hold that it satisfies this requirement by providing **personalized instruction with sufficient support services to permit the child to benefit educationally from that instruction**. Such instruction and services must be provided at public expense, must meet the State's educational standards, must approximate the grade levels used in the State's regular education, and must comport with the child's IEP. In addition, the IEP, and therefore the personalized instruction, should be formulated in accordance with the requirements of the Act and, if the child is being educated in the regular classrooms of the public education system, should be **reasonably calculated to enable the child to achieve passing marks and advance from grade to grade**.

The Court ruled that the school board was not required to provide the sign-language interpreter. The IDEA required only the development of an IEP that was reasonably calculated to enable the disabled student to derive some educational benefit. **The IDEA created a minimum floor** for the provision of special education services but did not require states to maximize the potential of each disabled child. In this case, the child was advancing through school easily and was not entitled to an interpreter, despite evidence that this would remedy the disparity between her achievement and her potential. *Board of Educ. of Hendrick Hudson Cent. School Dist., Westchester County v. Rowley,* 458 U.S. 176, 102 S.Ct. 3034, 73 L.Ed.2d 690 (1982).

♦   A California preschool child with autism received private in-home applied behavioral analysis (ABA) therapy. His parents asked for a trans-disciplinary reevaluation (TRR) and IEEs at public expense. The school district requested a due process hearing and offered the child a special day preschool placement that included eight hours of weekly school-based ABA and six hours of in-home ABA with one-on-one adult support. The parents rejected the proposal, stating it dramatically decreased the services agreed upon in a prior mediated settlement. Another due process case was filed and consolidated with the TRR matter. The parents removed the child from district programs and stated they would seek a private program at the district's expense. Near this time, the parents declined district vision evaluation attempts. Meanwhile, the district continued to provide the child 20 hours of weekly in-home ABA therapy. After a hearing, an administrative law judge found the district's TRR was appropriate, and the IEP provided a free appropriate public education.

Appeal went before a federal court, which recited the general rule in IEP disputes from *Board of Educ. v. Rowley*, above. Under *Rowley*, **the IDEA does not require districts to maximize student abilities or offer the best education available**. According to the court, the parents relied on testimony pertaining to the student's performance after the time the IEP was drafted. **A "snapshot" rule for assessing IEPs requires that the IEP be assessed at the time of drafting the document, not at a later time.** While the parents sought "a total in-home ABA program," the court held the district's IEP offered educational benefits. In rejecting a claim that the district did not assess the child in all areas of suspected disability, the court found the parents had not consented to the district's offer to assess his vision. Their additional arguments were found meritless, and the court held for the school district. *B.M. v. Encinitas Union School Dist.*, No. 08cv412-L(JMA), 2013 WL 593417 (S.D. Cal. 2/14/13).

◆   When a California student transitioned from middle school to high school, an IEP meeting was held to discuss transcription services, among other things. Although the IEP included transcription services, the parents refused to consent to it because it didn't specify the word-for-word transcription known as CART. The district instead offered a meaning-for-meaning transcription known as TypeWell. The parents sought due process and won at the administrative level. A federal court, however, held that **the administrative law judge (ALJ) had examined the case under a standard more rigorous than *Board of Educ. v. Rowley***. It remanded the case so the ALJ could consider whether the district's proposed transcription services offered the student "some educational benefit" as opposed to the most meaningful accommodation. *Poway Unified School Dist. v. Cheng*, 821 F.Supp.2d 1197 (S.D. Cal. 2011).

◆   An Indiana school district created an IEP for a student with traumatic brain injury, incorporating the findings of the parents' neuropsychologist. The district placed the student in a half-day kindergarten. However, the parents wanted a full-day placement as their neuropsychologist had recommended. Eventually they placed their son in a Lindamood Bell Learning Center and sued the district for violating the IDEA. A federal court and the Seventh Circuit ruled against them, noting that **the district did not have to defer to the opinion of the neuropsychologist, and it did not have to provide the best possible education** to the student. He made notable gains in the half-day placement. *M.B. v. Hamilton Southeastern Schools*, 668 F.3d 851 (7th Cir. 2011).

◆   A Washington student with learning disabilities attended regular classes and progressed from grade to grade. Her parents became dissatisfied with her education and found an independent evaluator who suggested that no public schools in the state could provide an adequate education. The parents enrolled their daughter in a Massachusetts private school and sought tuition reimbursement. An administrative law judge ruled against them, but a federal court held the ALJ had improperly used the *Board of Educ. v. Rowley* standard, which had been superseded by amendments to the IDEA. The case reached the Ninth Circuit, which held **the *Rowley* standard was still the appropriate**

means for determining whether a child received an appropriate education. *J.L. v. Mercer Island School Dist.*, 575 F.3d 1025 (9th Cir. 2009).

♦   The parents of a Connecticut student disagreed with his IEPs for grades five and six. They placed him in a private school with smaller classes, then sought due process, asserting that the board did not fully evaluate him and did not base the IEPs on the recommendations of their experts. The case reached the Second Circuit, which ruled for the board. The IEPs for both grades provided the student with a **basic floor of opportunity** and "prescribed interventions that anticipated the suggestions of the [parents'] experts." *Mr. B. v. East Granby Board of Educ.*, 201 Fed.Appx. 834 (2d Cir. 2006).

♦   In 2002, Missouri amended its special education law to delete the requirement that special education programs maximize the capabilities of students with disabilities. When a disabled student and a public interest law center challenged the amendment as violative of the Missouri Constitution, the case reached the state supreme court. The court held that the amendment did not violate the state constitution. It did not amend the law in a way that changed its original purpose. As a result, **Missouri now uses the federal standard for determining the sufficiency of special education services**. *McEuen v. Missouri State Board of Educ.*, 120 S.W.3d 207 (Mo. 2003).

♦   A student struggled in his public school placement, but did not qualify for special education services. His parents obtained an independent evaluation, learned he had dyslexia and attention deficit disorder, and enrolled him in a private school. The student returned to public school before the end of the year and was referred to an admission, review and dismissal (ARD) committee. The ARD committee recommended 10 hours per week in a reading and language resource room with weekly speech therapy. The student continued to experience some difficulties in grade four and received extended-year services and compensatory speech therapy. His parents objected to the district's failure to implement certain IEP modifications. A hearing officer found that the district failed to consistently or appropriately implement the student's IEP. For the student's seventh-grade year, the parties failed to agree on an IEP, and the parents placed him in a private setting. A federal court held the student showed improvement and received educational benefit during the disputed time period.

The parents appealed to the Fifth Circuit, which noted that the test for appropriateness of an IEP includes assessment of whether education is provided in a coordinated and collaborative manner by key stakeholders and asks whether the student is receiving positive academic and nonacademic benefits. Here, the lower court properly determined that any shortcomings in the school district's implementation of the IEP were remedied by the compensatory services it offered. **It was unnecessary for the student to improve in every academic area in order to receive educational benefit.** Since he received a FAPE in his public school, the claim for private school reimbursement was rejected. *Houston Independent School Dist. v. Bobby R.*, 200 F.3d 341 (5th Cir. 2000).

C. U.S. Supreme Court Cases

◆   In 2016, the U.S. Supreme Court refused to review a lower court's decision that a Kentucky student's home behavior was not relevant to his special education status. In a decision by the U.S. Court of Appeals, Sixth Circuit, the court held that **to show a need for special education and related services, the parents had to show their child's autism adversely affected his "educational performance."** According to the parents, the term "educational performance" includes academic, social and psychological needs. But the court held the term suggested school-based evaluation. *Q.W. v. Board of Educ. of Fayette County, Kentucky*, No. 15-1043, 136 S.Ct. 1729 (cert. denied 4/25/16).

◆   In 2014, the Supreme Court denied review of a decision for two California students with hearing impairments who sought word-for-word transcription services from their school districts. In prior court activity, the U.S. Court of Appeals, Ninth Circuit, held a federal district court improperly held their valid IEPs automatically satisfied the Americans with Disabilities Act (ADA). The Ninth Circuit held ADA regulations created independent obligations for public schools. **In some cases, the ADA might require schools to provide different services to hearing-impaired students than what they have to provide under the IDEA.** Courts are to analyze IDEA and ADA claims separately. *Tustin Unified School Dist. v. K.M.*, 134 S.Ct. 1493 (cert. denied 3/3/14). *Poway Unified School Dist. v. D.H.*, 134 S.Ct. 1494 (cert. denied 3/3/14).

◆   A Maryland student with learning disabilities and a speech impairment attended private schools until the eighth grade, when his parents sought to place him in district schools. The district conducted an evaluation and drafted an IEP that would have placed him in one of two district schools. The parents rejected the offer, seeking a smaller classroom setting with more intensive services. They requested an IDEA due process hearing, where the administrative law judge ruled they had the burden of persuasion and did not meet it. Eventually the case reached the U.S. Supreme Court, which agreed that **parents who challenge IEPs have the burden of proving that the IEPs are not appropriate**. To do otherwise would force courts to assume that every IEP is invalid until the school district demonstrates that it is not. *Schaffer v. Weast*, 546 U.S. 49, 126 S.Ct. 528, 163 L.Ed.2d 387 (2005).

◆   The Supreme Court held that an Iowa school district had to provide a quadriplegic student with a full-time aide to assure his meaningful access to education under the IDEA. **Providing an aide amounted to a necessary related service and not an excluded medical service.** Using a "bright-line" rule, the Court limited medical services to those provided by a physician. *Cedar Rapids Community School Dist. v. Garret F.*, 526 U.S. 66, 119 S.Ct. 992, 143 L.Ed.2d 154 (1999).

◆   The U.S. Supreme Court held that a New York statute that created a special school district for a religious community (which had been incorporated as a village) had to be struck down as violative of the Establishment Clause. **The

special school district exceeded the bounds of religious neutrality required by the Constitution. *Board of Educ. of Kiryas Joel Village School Dist. v. Grumet,* 512 U.S. 687, 114 S.Ct. 2481, 129 L.Ed.2d 546 (1994).

◆ The Court held that the failure of a school district to propose an appropriate IEP and placement for a learning disabled student justified an award of private school tuition reimbursement by the district, even though the private school was not approved by the state of South Carolina. This was because the private school placement was appropriate and because South Carolina did not publish a list of approved schools. The IDEA requirement to provide a free appropriate public education did not apply to parental placements. **To recover private school tuition costs, parents must show that the placement proposed by the school district violates the IDEA and that the private school placement is appropriate under the act.** Federal courts have broad discretion in granting relief under the IDEA and may reduce tuition reimbursement awards found to be unreasonably expensive. The Court upheld the lower court decisions in favor of the parents. *Florence County School Dist. Four v. Carter,* 510 U.S. 7, 114 S.Ct. 361, 126 L.Ed.2d 284 (1993).

◆ The Establishment Clause of the First Amendment did not bar a public school district from **providing a sign-language interpreter to an Arizona student who attended a parochial school**. The provision of the interpreter was a neutral service that provided only an indirect economic benefit to the parochial school. *Zobrest v. Catalina Foothills School Dist.,* 509 U.S. 1, 113 S.Ct. 2462, 125 L.Ed.2d 1 (1993).

◆ In *Dellmuth v. Muth,* 491 U.S. 223, 109 S.Ct. 2397, 105 L.Ed.2d 181 (1989), the Supreme Court held Congress did not intend that the IDEA permit monetary damages against states in actions brought in federal courts. This permitted Pennsylvania to avoid liability in an IDEA damage suit brought by a learning disabled student. [In 1990, Congress responded by abrogating sovereign immunity (20 U.S.C. § 1403) in IDEA cases and authorizing both equitable (injunctive and declaratory) and legal remedies for IDEA violations.]

◆ The suspension or expulsion of a special education student constitutes a change of placement under the IDEA, according to the 1988 decision *Honig v. Doe.* School authorities may not unilaterally exclude a child from classes pending administrative proceedings. However, **the IDEA's stay-put provision (20 U.S.C. § 1415(j)) did not prevent school districts from imposing temporary suspensions of 10 school days or less** upon students who present a threat of harm to other persons. *Honig v. Doe,* 484 U.S. 305, 108 S.Ct. 592, 98 L.Ed.2d 686 (1988). The 1997 Amendments address suspensions for disciplinary reasons in 20 U.S.C. Section 1415(k) and allow removal from class for up to 45 days on a case-by-case basis under unique circumstances.

◆ A Texas **school district had to provide catheterization services for a disabled student while she attended school because it was a "supportive service" (related service)** under the IDEA, 20 U.S.C. § 1401(26). The Court held that the student's parents were also entitled to receive their attorneys' fees under Section 504 of the Rehabilitation Act. *Irving Independent School Dist. v. Tatro*, 468 U.S. 883, 104 S.Ct. 3371, 82 L.Ed.2d 664 (1984).

♦   A disabled Rhode Island student was not entitled to recover attorneys' fees despite prevailing in an IDEA lawsuit against his school district in *Smith v. Robinson*. The Court ruled that there was no evidence that the school district had violated any of the student's procedural safeguards under the IDEA. Congress responded to the *Smith* decision by passing the Handicapped Children's Protection Act of 1986 (P.L. 99–372), which **specifically authorized attorneys' fee awards to students with disabilities who prevailed in IDEA lawsuits**. The same legislation provided that disabled students may cumulate available remedies under Section 504 of the Rehabilitation Act (29 U.S.C. § 794) and 42 U.S.C. § 1983. *Smith v. Robinson*, 468 U.S. 992, 104 S.Ct. 3457, 82 L.Ed.2d 746 (1984). Because the Handicapped Children's Protection Act of 1986 substantially overruled *Smith v. Robinson*, there is no further summary of the case in this volume.

♦   The parents of a learning disabled Massachusetts student violated the IDEA's stay-put provision by unilaterally enrolling him in a private school. Because the proposed IEP was held appropriate, the parents were not entitled to tuition reimbursement and other costs. The Court noted that in some cases, parents may be reimbursed for unilaterally placing a student in a private school. A court must find the proposed IEP inappropriate to allow this. **Parents who unilaterally change their children's placement do so at their own risk**, because if the proposed IEP is upheld, the parents have to pay for it. *School Committee of the Town of Burlington, Massachusetts v. Dep't of Educ. of Massachusetts,* 471 U.S. 359, 105 S.Ct. 1996, 85 L.Ed.2d 385 (1985).

II. SECTION 504 AND THE ADA

The Americans with Disabilities Act (ADA), 42 U.S.C. Section 12101, et seq., and Section 504 of the Rehabilitation Act, 29 U.S.C. Section 794, prohibit discrimination based on a disability and require reasonable accommodations for qualified individuals with disabilities. While the ADA requires a person to define disability by reference to an impairment that substantially limits a major life activity, the IDEA instead requires that a student have a qualifying disability that creates a need for special education and related services.

While standards for required accommodations under the ADA and IDEA overlap where both laws apply, the IDEA does not require a party to have an impairment that substantially limits a major life activity. An IDEA-qualifying disability does not always involve substantial limitation of a major life activity.

The Rehabilitation Act is a federal law to promote employment training and habilitation for individuals with disabilities. Its key provision, Section 504 (29 U.S.C. Section 794) prohibits entities that receive federal funds from discriminating against individuals with disabilities in their programs or services. Since school districts, states and educational agencies receive federal funds, Section 504 complaints are commonly filed by students seeking educational benefits, by individuals seeking employment or benefits, and by employees claiming disability discrimination. Section 504 differs from the IDEA in scope, intent and coverage. The congressional objective of Section 504 is the elimination of discrimination against individuals with disabilities.

A. Section 504 Plans

Federal regulations interpreting Section 504 in the educational context specify that disabled students are entitled to a free appropriate public education (FAPE) and reasonable accommodations. Although an IEP is not required for an individual who is a student with a disability under Section 504, the regulations state that providing a student with an IEP is one way to meet Section 504 requirements to provide a FAPE.

In CTL v. Ashland School Dist., *743 F.3d 524 (7th Cir. 2014), this chapter, the U.S. Court of Appeals, Seventh Circuit, reviewed numerous federal cases and found the courts have held minor deviations from IEPs are not an automatic violation of law. It found Section 504 education requirements have been held to be less exacting than those of the IDEA. For a Section 504 plan violation to be disability discrimination, the Seventh Circuit held it must be significant enough to effectively deny a child the benefit of a public education.*

♦   A Pennsylvania high school student attended a rigorous, advanced program for gifted students. In her junior year, she was diagnosed with gastroparesis and was intermittently hospitalized. She received weekly homebound instruction, which her parents supplemented with private tutoring. Although she returned to school for her senior year, she had a relapse and remained at home. The school found the student eligible for a Section 504 service plan allowing her to attend school when her health allowed. Near this time, she was diagnosed with an anxiety disorder. Her parents questioned the effectiveness of homebound instruction, noting a school district instructor was unable to provide substantive guidance in advanced placement courses such as Japanese and Chinese. The student dropped some courses and completed others with tutoring. Although the district sought permission to evaluate the student for eligibility under the IDEA, the parents declined. A Section 504 plan was offered to her with "significantly more permissive accommodations" such as a lack of attendance penalties for medical absences and permission to enter and exit the school as needed. But the student soon fell behind in her classes and began taking refuge in the library.

After finishing the school year at home with the help of private tutoring, the student graduated 21st in her class of 336. But she had to withdraw from college in her second year. Her parents filed a due process complaint against the district. A hearing officer found the district had been careless, but did not act with deliberate indifference to the student's rights. The parents sued the school district in a federal court, claiming it did not properly implement the Section 504 plan. The court held for the district and the parents appealed. The U.S. Court of Appeals, Third Circuit, rejected the argument that state law entitled the student to accommodations that maximized her potential. It found that **virtually every interaction between the parents and school district had led to express**

action to address the student's concerns. Homebound services were never intended to be a substitute for in-class learning. On the whole, the district provided the student with a meaningful opportunity to pass advanced courses and allow her to gain admission to a prestigious university. As a result, the court found no discrimination. The parents rejected suggestions to evaluate the child for IDEA eligibility and to coordinate services from the district and her psychologist. **Since there had been no deliberate indifference to the student's rights, the court held for the school district.** *K.K. v. Pittsburgh Public Schools*, 590 Fed.Appx. 148 (3d Cir. 2014).

♦   Due to Klinefelter Syndrome and ADHD, a California student was eligible for Section 504 accommodations. He enrolled in an advanced placement (AP) calculus course, where he struggled and suffered from anxiety and weight loss. His mother asked for permission to drop the class but was told the three-day window for dropping classes had passed. An administrator said no exceptions could be made to the school policy. A hearing officer denied the parent's request for an order requiring the district to pay for a Section 504 evaluation and remove a failing AP calculus grade from the student's records. On appeal, a federal court dismissed the Section 504 claim. It held **the student was prohibited from dropping the AP class under a general rule of the school district, not because of a disability**. But the student had a plausible claim regarding a timeline and procedure to evaluate students who might need Section 504 accommodations. He could refile the claim to allege denial of a service or benefit solely due to a disability. But he could not show any deprivation of a protected interest in not being allowed to drop his AP course. As a due process right is implicated only when exclusion from the entire educational process is at stake, the court dismissed the constitutional claims. *S.M. v. San Jose Unified School Dist.*, No. 14-CV-03613, 2015 WL 1737535 (N.D. Cal. 4/13/15).

♦   Wisconsin parents of a child with Type 1 diabetes worked with their school to develop a Section 504 plan incorporating his doctor's orders to administer insulin doses and snacks at school. The plan required the school to train three employees as "trained diabetes personnel." Although the parents were mostly satisfied during the child's kindergarten year, they maintained only one school nurse had the training to be qualified under the "trained diabetes personnel" designation. Conflict grew when a school nurse supervisor banned the nurse from deviating from insulin dosages recommended by the personal diabetes manager on a "case by case basis." The supervisor believed state law required strict adherence to doctor's orders and did not allow school nurses to follow conflicting parental instructions. After filing an agency complaint, the parents sued the school district in a federal court. The court held for the school district.

On appeal, the Seventh Circuit Court of Appeals held that **for a Section 504 plan violation to be deemed disability discrimination, it must be significant enough to effectively deny a child the benefit of a public education**. As the lower court found, the district trained three people to serve as "trained diabetes personnel" in fulfillment of the 504 plan. Any violation of the plan by the school was minor. The school's refusal to employ the case-by-case approach urged by the parents amounted to a dispute over doctor orders. As the doctor's orders were confusing and the school's refusal to deviate from them was not unreasonable, the court found no discrimination. The court held for the school district. *CTL v. Ashland School Dist.*, 743 F.3d 524 (7th Cir. 2014).

♦   A Pennsylvania student with a severe nut allergy was deemed at risk of life-threatening allergic reactions. Although at least four meetings were held to develop a Section 504 accommodation plan for the student, no agreement could be reached. Believing the district's plan was not sufficiently detailed, the parents gave the school a 19-page proposed plan. The district rejected the plan because some items were already standard district procedures and because the plan was excessively long. Although the district offered new Section 504 plan proposals, the parents rejected them – even one that had been approved by the student's doctor. The parents then filed a complaint against the district with a state agency. A hearing officer found the district did not discriminate against the student or deny him a free appropriate public education. A federal court held for the school district, and appeal reached the U.S. Court of Appeals, Third Circuit.

The court found evidence that a Section 504 plan relating to food allergies had to be accessible and understandable to staff in the event of an emergency. District teachers and staff were trained to identify symptoms of anaphylaxis and to administer epinephrine. **The court held the failure to include each requested accommodation and detail requested by the parents was not a Section 504 violation.** There was evidence that the district worked diligently with the parents to ensure their child participated in school activities and had access to educational benefits. Since the parents did not show their child was denied program benefits or subjected to discrimination, the court held for the district. *T.F. v. Fox Chapel Area School Dist.*, 589 Fed.Appx. 594 (3d Cir. 2014).

♦   Due to a Michigan student's severe, life-threatening allergy to peanuts and tree nuts, his school district made his school nut free. The parent of another child attending the school claimed the school-wide ban on nuts infringed upon their rights. Although they had requested a Section 504 plan, the school declined to create one, and the parent did not appeal this decision. However, she sued the school district in a state court, seeking to overcome the school ban on nuts. When the case reached the Court of Appeals of Michigan, it held that neither the challenging parent nor her daughter had been parties to the Section 504 plan created for the allergic student. For this reason, neither of them had standing to challenge the allergic student's 504 plan. The court held **the district had authority to adopt a school-wide ban on nuts, given the finding that a ban was necessary for the allergic student's safety**. As there was no merit to any of the parent's claims, the court held for the district. *Liebau v. Romeo Community Schools*, No. 306979, 2013 WL 3942392 (Mich. Ct. App. 7/30/13).

♦   A New York City school worked with the parent of a diabetic student who was returning to school after a life-threatening onset of symptoms. After several options were explored, the district superintendent refused to grant the parent's request for staff members to warm up the student's lunch in a microwave oven. When the dispute reached a federal court, it found no evidence that diabetics are required to eat hot food. The school's accommodations included menu options and monitoring of the student's blood glucose level. **"Meaningful access" to school programs and benefits did not mean "equal access" or preferential treatment.** Neither Section 504 nor the ADA required the school to offer additional accommodations than those offered to the student. As he had meaningful access to school, there was no violation, even if he sometimes skipped lunch because he disliked the food. *A.M. v. NYC Dep't of Educ.*, 840 F.Supp.2d 660 (E.D.N.Y. 2012).

♦ A Missouri student with ADHD attended school under a Section 504 plan. His district determined that he did not qualify for special education under the IDEA because he performed at appropriate academic levels. As high school progressed, his academic performance declined. During his junior year, his mother asked the school to stop providing Section 504 supports because he was relying on them too much. The district conducted another evaluation, but it again found him ineligible for special education. He quit school and sued for disability discrimination. A federal court ruled against him, noting that **he was not substantially limited in the major life activity of learning** and that the district had offered him accommodations. *Schnelting v. St. Clair R.-XIII School Dist.*, No. 4:10-CV-01240-JAR, 2011 WL 5913483 (E.D. Mo. 11/28/11).

B. FAPE Under Section 504

Because Section 504 and the ADA define disability more broadly than the IDEA, some students are covered by Section 504 and the ADA but not the IDEA. A Section 504 regulation, 34 C.F.R. Part 104.33, mandates that schools provide qualified students with disabilities a free appropriate public education (FAPE).

In Mark H. v. Lemahieu, *513 F.3d 922 (9th Cir. 2008), the Ninth Circuit held a Section 504 free appropriate public education (FAPE) is not identical to FAPE under the IDEA. And in* K.M. v. Tustin Unified School Dist., *725 F.3d 1088 (9th Cir. 2013), the court held a valid IEP did not necessarily satisfy ADA Title II communication requirements. The court held that in some cases, the ADA might require schools to provide different services than under the IDEA.*

Revocation of consent to IDEA services does not eliminate the broader protections of Section 504 and the Americans with Disabilities Act. See Kimble v. Douglas County School Dist. RE-1, *925 F.Supp.2d 1176 (D. Colo. 2013), summarized in Chapter Two, Section II.B. of this volume.*

The following cases focus on Section 504 and ADA discrimination claims involving the provision of a free appropriate public education. For more cases involving monetary claims for damages based on bullying, discrimination, harassment and other liability issues, please see Chapter Ten of this volume.

♦ Due to Tourette's syndrome, ADHD and another condition, a New York student received special education. According to a federal court complaint filed after his suicide, the student was subjected to teasing, taunting, bullying, name-calling, violence, offensive touching, hitting and other forms of misconduct by peers. The estate claimed this conduct was minimized, dismissed and ignored by the school district. Among the estate's claims was that the student was disciplined and removed from the school baseball team as the result of a horseplay incident involving a teammate. It was claimed that the teammate was not disciplined and that coaches allowed the student to be ridiculed by teammates. In pretrial activity, the court found the estate failed to identify specific facts linking any action or inaction by the school district or its employees to the student's death. Although the estate was allowed to file an amended complaint, the court found the only specific facts to be found in the estate's papers pertained to isolated events taking place some seven months prior to the suicide. There was no special relationship or state-created danger in this case, precluding any exception to the general rule that the Due Process Clause does not require a state entity to protect one citizen from others.

Although the estate claimed there had been an equal protection violation, the court held it was not shown that the student was treated differently from his peers. Retaliation claims under the First Amendment and Section 504 also failed. Constitutional claims against the board of education failed because there was no showing of a district-wide policy or custom of due process violations. While the estate argued the district violated the ADA and Section 504, the court found no proof that the student qualified for disability law protection. The court held the "brief references to Gregory exhibiting 'disability related tics' fails to describe the impairment of a major life activity." According to the court, **the fact that the student received special education did not automatically qualify him for protection under Section 504 and the ADA**. As the federal claims all failed, the court dismissed them. The estate could pursue the state law claims in a state court. *Spring v. Allegany-Limestone Cent. School Dist.*, 138 F.Supp.3d 2820 (W.D.N.Y. 2015, 2d Cir. appeal filed, 12/4/15).

♦   A Texas student with cerebral palsy used a wheelchair and needed help with lavatory transfers. Two employees were supposed to accompany disabled children during lavatory breaks under a school policy, but they often made such transfers without help. An aide who was assigned to help the student at school accompanied him alone to the lavatory and sexually molested him there. After the student told his mother of the assault, she reported the aide, who confessed to the misconduct. In a federal court, the mother sued the school district under the ADA, Section 504 of the Rehabilitation Act and Title IX of the 1972 Education Amendments. In pretrial activity, the family settled its claims against the aide. After the court held for the school district on the remaining claims, the family appealed to the U.S. Court of Appeals, Fifth Circuit. Rejecting the ADA claim, the court held the evidence did not support claims by the student that the district denied him an accessible, safe lavatory. It found the lavatory had safety devices for disabled students and that several urinals were accessible. Two employees accompanied the student on the vast majority of his lavatory visits.

Attempts to accommodate a student with a disability, even if imperfect, do not support an intentional discrimination claim. **In order to pursue a Section 504 claim based on failure to provide a free appropriate public education (FAPE), the student had to show some evidence of bad faith or gross mismanagement by the school district.** But the student failed to show a denial of a FAPE. The school district held no less than 28 IEP meetings to formulate his program. Any flaws in his IEPs did not result in the loss of an educational opportunity. Finding insufficient evidence to show the district failed to provide the student with educational opportunities or grossly mismanaged his IEP, the court affirmed the judgment for the district. *Estrada v. San Antonio Independent School Dist.*, 575 Fed.Appx. 541 (5th Cir. 2014).

♦ A Maryland student had ADHD and was eligible for a Section 504 plan. Despite having accommodations, she had difficulty with her classes. By grade six, her parents obtained medical opinions suggesting she needed an IEP instead of a Section 504 plan. But the school system repeatedly declined their requests to consider an IEP. Team members instead discussed removing accommodations that had already been granted. The parents said that as her eighth-grade year went on, teachers did not consistently provide some Section 504 plan accommodations. After removing their child from school, the parents enrolled her in a private school for grade nine and requested a hearing. An ALJ dismissed the complaint. A federal court held **liability under Section 504 in the context of the provision of FAPE requires a showing of bad faith or gross misjudgment by the school system**. While this is a very high standard, the court found the parents set forth facts suggesting the school system denied accommodations it had agreed to provide without explanation. When the student was in eighth grade, the school's diligence in addressing her needs appeared to decline markedly. Teachers insisted that she advocate for her own accommodations even though her language difficulties significantly hindered her ability to do so. Near this time, evaluators were continuing to find the student had additional areas of weakness. Since the facts supported a finding that the district was no longer acting in good faith to fully address the student's needs, the court returned the case to the administrative level for a hearing. *K.D. v. Starr*, 55 F.Supp.3d 782 (D. Md. 2014).

♦ A California student who experienced seizures claimed her school did not allow her reasonable accommodations. When she entered high school, she had a number of seizures in class. She said teachers did not know what to do and often did not follow her seizure plans. By the end of the student's ninth-grade year, her parent said a vice principal told her the seizures "were too much for the school to handle" and that she should be kept at home. Although the school found the student eligible for a Section 504 plan, she was not found IDEA-eligible. After the student had a seizure in jazz choir class, her parent claimed she was required to reaudition. The school district found the student was not IDEA-eligible. The parent dismissed a due process complaint she had filed, based on the district's finding that the student was not IDEA-eligible. She sued the school district in a federal court for violating Section 504 and the ADA.

Although some of the student's discrimination claims involved denial of a FAPE and failure to accommodate a disability, the court found that there was no IDEA relief available for her. Next, the court held the student qualified for federal disability protection. She said she had been excluded from class, disallowed from making up work or compensating for missed class time and excluded from participating in the jazz choir. Since these actions denied the student the benefits of a full public education, the court held she could pursue her discrimination claims. In addition, **the student asserted intentional discrimination by the district, which was on notice that she needed**

accommodations to obtain the benefits of a public education. The court noted that the parents repeatedly provided the school with physician-approved seizure plans. She communicated with counselors, teachers and the vice principal. The court found it should have been obvious to the district that the student needed accommodations for her seizure disorder. It further found the district did not do enough to address the potential harm to her. As the student stated valid Section 504 and ADA claims, she also made out a case under the state civil rights act. The court denied the district's motion for dismissal and to strike parts of the complaint. *S.L. v. Downey Unified School Dist.*, No. CV 13-06050 DDP (PJWx), 2014 WL 934942 (C.D. Cal. 3/10/14).

♦ A Florida mother with a disability designated her hearing-impaired child's grandmother to represent him in school matters. Without input from the mother or grandmother, the school board devised an IEP that placed the child in a one-hour class for students with disabilities each day. As the mother felt this was unnecessary and detrimental, she withdrew her consent for the IEP. But at the same time, the mother requested services for her child under Section 504. This included assistive technology for his classes. The board refused to provide the requested services, and the mother sued the school district in a federal court.

In pretrial activity, the court held the parent's withdrawal of IDEA consent was not as extensive as the school board claimed. She had made a request for services, which "can hardly constitute a waiver of those services." **The court found no basis for the district's argument that withdrawal of consent to IDEA services constituted a waiver of services under other laws.** An IDEA regulation (34 C.F.R. Part 300.300) states that if consent is withdrawn by a parent, a school is not to provide special education to a child and it cannot be considered in violation of its duty to provide a FAPE. But the court found the same regulation is limited in that a school district cannot use parental refusal to consent to one service or activity to deny the parent or child any other service, benefit or activity of the school. A student's right to be free from discrimination is independent of eligibility or parental consent for IDEA services. The mother's refusal to provide IDEA consent did not authorize the district to deny her request to provide her child assistive technology under Section 504. As the mother stated an adequate Section 504 claim, the court refused to dismiss it. She also stated an adequate claim for retaliation for withdrawing consent to the IEP. *D.F. v. Leon County School Board*, No. 4:13cv3-RH/CAS, 2014 WL 28798 (N.D. Fla. 1/2/14).

♦ A Pennsylvania student was identified with learning disabilities in reading and math as a fourth-grader. Although she denied needing special education, her mother agreed with the school's recommended IEP. For grades 5-10, the student remained in special education, scoring above grade level on some tests but below average on others. A dispute arose during an IEP meeting held in her tenth-grade school year. As part of the resolution, the district agreed to the parent's request for an independent education evaluation (IEE). The school psychologist who conducted the evaluation found the student was not disabled and never had been. After the student completed her high school education, she filed a due process case. A hearing officer found she never had a disability.

The student's parent sued the school district in a federal court for disability discrimination. Appeal reached the U.S. Court of Appeals, Third Circuit, where she claimed the district did not accurately identify children with disabilities and did not ensure her child was properly evaluated. In addition, the parent argued the IDEA should be construed to protect African-American children such as her daughter because Congress identified a history of identifying minority students as having special education needs. In the court's view, the IDEA term "child with a disability" excluded non-disabled children who had been mistakenly identified. Nor did language from the IDEA's "child find" provision impose a duty on the district. **The school district had evaluated the student many times.** In assessing the discrimination claims, the court applied a "deliberate indifference" standard. There was insufficient evidence of any deliberate indifference to impose liability on the district. The parent relied mainly on her child's subjective disagreement with a special education placement. **The relevant inquiry was a "knowing violation of the law," not a mistaken diagnosis by the school district.** The district exited the student from special education as soon as it learned she was not IDEA-eligible, and the court held in its favor. *S.H. v. Lower Merion School Dist.*, 729 F.3d 248 (3d Cir. 2013).

♦   A Pennsylvania student with a learning disability obtained Title I remedial instruction and attended special education programs. When she was a high school senior, her father began to doubt the nature of her disability and her need for special education. He requested a hearing to seek her removal from special education, and later the parents sued the school district in a federal court for discrimination in violation of Section 504 and the ADA. After the court held for the district, the student appealed to the U.S. Court of Appeals, Third Circuit.

The court held a party seeking compensatory damages under Section 504 and the ADA must show intentional discrimination. While the student missed out on some general education classes, she did not complain about this while she was enrolled in special education. According to the student, her grade average was artificially lowered and her program was "pointless, a waste of time," and "hand-holding." The court found the evidence only showed she was unhappy with her program. Throughout the student's school career, her parents had opportunities to review her IEPs but never objected. No deliberate indifference by the district was shown. A defective evaluation would not prove the district had knowledge of harm, and an evaluation report did not indicate the student was erroneously placed in special education or improperly designated as a student with an other health impairment. As the facts did not show deliberate indifference, the court held for the school district. *A.G. v. Lower Merion School Dist.*, 542 Fed.Appx. 194 (3d Cir. 2013).

♦   A 17-year-old Maryland special education student began gambling at his high school with other students. The school district's code of student conduct included gambling as a form of "Level II misconduct." Early in a school year, the student told his special education teacher that a school security guard was extorting money from him and from other special education students. The principal responded by firing the teacher and threatening the student with discipline. When the student sued for discrimination under Section 504 of the

Rehabilitation Act, a federal court held that he failed to make out a case of intentional discrimination. **Even if the complaint to the teacher was protected activity, the student did not show any connection between the complaint and the later threats of discipline.** The court allowed him 10 days to amend his complaint. *Braswell v. Board of Educ. of Prince George's County*, No. 12-cv-02434-AW, 2012 WL 5511005 (D. Md. 11/13/12).

♦   A 27-year-old Pennsylvania student had autism and a severe developmental disability and suffered from seizures. From 1991 to 2005, her parents filed five due process complaints against her school district and two complaints with a state agency, charging the district with failure to provide services and comply with her IEPs. For two years, the student remained in a placement that was found inappropriate by a consultant because of a disagreement about evaluation. This led to a complaint to the state special education bureau, which found the district was not providing the therapy specified in her IEP. In the fifth due process case, a hearing officer found the district had denied the child a free appropriate public education (FAPE) for more than three years. She awarded the student 3,180 hours of compensatory education and ordered the district to place $209,000 in trust for her education expenses. In 2005, the parents sued the school district under the IDEA, the ADA and Section 504. After the court held for the district, the U.S. Court of Appeals, Third Circuit, sent the ADA and Section 504 claims back to the lower court for reconsideration. **The court clarified that the parents had to prove intentional discrimination to support the Section 504 and ADA claims.** The parents responded with hundreds of educational records. Finding the parents did not offer any new evidence that was not previously available, the trial court held for the school district. When the case returned to the Third Circuit, it held the lower court had properly analyzed the ADA and Section 504 discrimination claims under *S.H. v. Lower Merion School Dist.*, above.

While the trial court found no intentional discrimination, it still had to determine whether the school district was deliberately indifferent to providing a FAPE. There was evidence that the district ignored requests to provide services, provided inadequate services and allowed extended delays in requests for hearings. It was also claimed that the district failed to fund therapy it agreed to provide, and it could not confirm that it ever provided the student any compensatory education. Since many facts were still in dispute, the case was again returned to the lower court. *Chambers v. School Dist. of Philadelphia Board of Educ.*, 537 Fed.Appx. 90 (3d Cir. 2013).

CHAPTER TWO

Identification and Evaluation

I. CHILD FIND DUTY

The IDEA's "child find" duty requires states, through local educational agencies, to "identify, locate, and evaluate all children with disabilities residing within their boundaries." The child find obligation is triggered as an individualized duty to a child when an educational agency "has knowledge" that the child has a disability. When this individualized duty has been triggered, students who have not been identified as eligible for IDEA services may claim IDEA procedural protections when their schools seek to discipline them.

In G.M. v. Saddleback Valley Unified School Dist., this chapter, the U.S. Court of Appeals, Ninth Circuit, cited a Hawaii federal district court decision finding **the duty is triggered when a district has reason to suspect a disability and that special education may be needed to address it.** *In D.K. v. Abington School Dist., 696 F.3d 233 (3d Cir. 2012), the Third Circuit held the child find provision does not require a formal evaluation of every struggling student.*

♦ A Missouri student was found eligible for IDEA services while attending a Head Start preschool program, but was found ineligible for IDEA services as a kindergartener. After considering independent evaluations in several areas, the district issued a report which found the child was not eligible under the IDEA. After placing the child in a private school, her guardian filed a due process complaint. Her primary issues were the district's decision to offer only three Section 504 accommodations and the denial of door-to-door transportation. She sought private school tuition reimbursement and therapy for the student. A hearing panel held the enrollment of the child in a private school before the filing of the complaint barred the case. Appeal reached the Court of Appeals of Missouri, which held the failure to file a due process complaint before the child left the district barred any claim based on the provision of a free appropriate public education. While the guardian could no longer seek tuition reimbursement, she could still have requested a reevaluation of the child and asked for an IEP even after making a private school placement. Next, the court held the district's child find duty did not revive the tuition reimbursement claim.

According to the court, the child find duty is not a requirement that a school district provide special education to a particular private school child. Instead, school districts are required to spend proportionate amounts of federal funds they receive on special education for qualified children attending private schools. The IDEA specifies that no parentally placed private school child has an individualized right to receive special education and related services. **The child find duty creates no individualized right that a parentally placed child may enforce in a due process proceeding.** The court held the FAPE claims were barred because of the child's withdrawal from the district. As the child find duty claim failed, the court held for the school district. *A.H. v. Independence School Dist.*, 466 S.W.3d 17 (Mo. Ct. App. 2015).

♦   A California student with a long history of mental health difficulties began attending school in a new district. His parent said he had an "unnamed major depressive disorder," and she asked for a district evaluation. When the school district did not initiate a special education assessment according to a timeline set by the parent, she placed him in a private, non-profit facility and requested a due process hearing. An ALJ found the three-month time period during which the student attended school in the district did not allow the staff to distinguish his symptoms from the behavior of a typically developing child. A federal court held the child find duty was triggered only if the district had observed the child over a long period of time. Three months was not a long period of time. Other health impairment is the type of disability for which a child find duty is triggered "only if the District is aware of its chronic or acute nature." There was no such showing in the relevant three months. In addition to denying the parent relief, the court held the case was frivolous. It granted the district's motion to receive a part of the nearly $58,000 in attorneys' fees it sought from her.

On appeal, **the U.S. Court of Appeals, Ninth Circuit, upheld the lower court's finding that the school district had complied with its IDEA child find duties**. An IEP had been drafted that was found reasonably calculated to confer an educational benefit upon the child. However, the court questioned the lower court's solicitation of a request for attorneys' fees based on its conclusion that the parent's claims were frivolous. School districts that prevail in an IDEA case may obtain attorneys' fees awards from parents if the litigation is held frivolous, unreasonable, without foundation, or presented for an improper purpose. Finding the case involved a "close and novel question" of law regarding the district's IDEA child find duty, the court returned the case to the trial court for it to reconsider the request for attorneys' fees. *G.M. v. Saddleback Valley Unified School Dist.*, 583 Fed.Appx. 702 (9th Cir. 2014).

♦   In *W.H. v. Schuylkill Valley School Dist.*, 954 F.Supp.2d 315 (E.D. Pa. 2013), a federal court rejected arguments by Pennsylvania parents that their school district violated state and federal law by failing to timely identify their child's disability. According to the court, **neither state nor federal law established a deadline for evaluating a child suspected of having a qualifying disability**. And the U.S. Court of Appeals, Third Circuit, recently noted in *Ridley School Dist. v. M.R.*, 680 F.3d 260 (3d Cir. 2012), that "the IDEA does not require a reevaluation every time a student posts a poor grade."

♦   An Alabama student with ADHD was making progress at a math, science and technology magnet school. According to his parents, the school neglected to respond to red flags suggesting the need for a special education referral and evaluation. They did not request an evaluation but requested Section 504 accommodations. Later, the parents requested a due process hearing under the IDEA. A hearing officer held in the student's favor. The board appealed to a federal court, where it argued the IDEA child find provision did not impose any enforceable duty or obligation. But the court found the argument invalid on several grounds. One of these was that the claim arose under 20 U.S.C. § 1414(a)(1), which allows parents to request an initial evaluation. Even though the parents had initially sought services in the context of Section 504, the hearing officer found the board's response was inappropriate and denied the student a free appropriate public education (FAPE). Although the board claimed the student displayed no markers of a child in need of special education, the hearing officer found the student's disabilities were well known to the board.

In fact, **the claim for denial of FAPE rested on the board's failure to treat the requests for assistance as requests for an initial IDEA evaluation**. While the board insisted that the parents had no viable claim under the IDEA, the court held the language and structure of the act indicated a right of action on behalf of a child claiming to be denied a FAPE due to a school's failure to comply with its child find obligation. The court rejected the board's argument that the hearing officer had violated the IDEA's limitation period. The board failed to properly and timely respond to the parents' request for services for the child and denied him a FAPE by failing to timely evaluate him. The court held the student's academic record and performance gave rise to a duty by the board to initiate a special education referral. *J.Y. v. Dothan City Board of Educ.*, No. 1:12cv347-SRW, 2014 WL 1320187 (M.D. Ala. 3/27/14).

♦   A federal court action led to an agreement by Connecticut officials in 2002 to increase participation rates of students with intellectual disabilities in general education classes and take measures to reduce the discriminatory identification of such students. The agreement stated five goals to encourage compliance with the IDEA, including an increase in the percentage of students with intellectual disabilities in regular classes, a reduction in discriminatory identification of such students and an increase in the share of the school day students would spend with their non-disabled peers. The agreement sought to increase the placement of students with intellectual disabilities in neighborhood schools and to increase their extracurricular participation rates. By its terms, federal court oversight of the agreement would end in 2010. In 2009, representatives of the students asserted the state was out of compliance with the agreement. After the court held the students did not prove state officials frustrated essential purposes of the agreement, appeal reached the U.S. Court of Appeals, Second Circuit.

In the court's view, the agreement operated as a consent decree, which gave the lower court continuing authority to supervise it. There was no showing of "substantial noncompliance" with the agreement. The essential purposes of the agreement were limited to five identified areas, and its goals were quantitative, not qualitative. Each of the goals addressed numerical improvements in the integration and classification of students with intellectual disabilities. The court found nothing in the agreement covered the quality of education. **There was evidence that students made significant progress toward the goals of the agreement.** There was a marked reduction in the discriminatory identification of students. It appeared to the court that the state was trying to implement the agreement even after it was no longer bound to do so. Since it was not shown that the state failed to comply with the agreement, the court held for the state. *P.J. v. Connecticut Board of Educ.*, 550 Fed.Appx. 20 (2d Cir. 2013).

♦   A Connecticut student's parents expressed many concerns to school staff about his struggles. Through his fourth-grade year, the parents contested district evaluations while obtaining several private evaluations. At the end of the student's fourth-grade year, the board of education identified him as IDEA-eligible with a specific learning disability. But the parents rejected several offers of services and enrolled him in a private special education school. In due process proceedings, a hearing officer upheld the IEPs offered by the school system. On appeal to a federal court, the parents argued the hearing officer should have ruled on their IDEA child find claims relating to school years prior to their private placement. The parents also claimed discrimination under Section 504. Although the court agreed with the parents that there was a factual record referring to the years before the private placement, the parameters of the dispute had been confined to the student's private school years by agreement. **The court found there was no way of knowing whether there was a complete factual record as to the child find issues.** In the court's view, the parents ignored an important distinction between issues that were being contested and the relevant evidence. Moreover, the parents' approach would undermine the IDEA administrative exhaustion requirement by misleading the hearing officer and board as to what legal claims were being advanced. Since the parents did not exhaust their administrative remedies regarding violations of the IDEA and Section 504, the court dismissed the claims. *Mr. and Mrs. P. v. Greenwich Board of Educ.*, 929 F.Supp.2d 40 (D. Conn. 2013).

♦   In 2005, six students sued the District of Columbia for a systemic failure to identify, locate, evaluate and offer special education to disabled preschoolers. A federal district court certified a class of preschool students who were (or might be) eligible for special education. Included in the class were students ages three to five whom the district did not identify, locate, evaluate or make any offer of special education. An order was entered for partial judgment regarding liability under the IDEA, Rehabilitation Act and District of Columbia law. Appeal reached the U.S. Court of Appeals, District of Columbia Circuit, which found the "glue" binding the claims of the class members was the district's "systemic failures." The court found potential class representatives must assert a "common contention" that would be capable of providing a classwide resolution.

In this case, there was no common contention on behalf of the class members whose determination would resolve an issue central to the validity of each one of the claims in one stroke. Because the class was defined by reference to a pattern and practice of failing to provide a FAPE, the court held the class was too broad. **The harms being asserted involved different district policies and practices at different stages of the child find and FAPE process.** No single or uniform policy or practice bridged all the claims. Since the claimants challenged multiple and disparate failures to comply with the child find duty and not a truly systemic policy or practice, the court held the class certification had been improper. *DL v. District of Columbia*, 713 F.3d 120 (D.C. Cir. 2013).

◆ A Texas student with ADHD was found eligible for accommodations under Section 504 but not for special education under the IDEA. Despite the accommodations, he continued to exhibit disruptive behavior and truancy. A committee determined that his behavior was not a manifestation of his ADHD. His mother later claimed that the district had denied him a free appropriate public education and violated the IDEA child find provision by declaring him ineligible for special education until he developed rheumatoid arthritis. She sought compensatory education. The case reached the Fifth Circuit, which ruled against her. **The IDEA does not penalize school districts for not timely evaluating students who do not need special education.** And the student here was not IDEA-eligible until he contracted arthritis. *D.G. v. Flour Bluff Independent School Dist.*, 481 Fed.Appx. 887 (5th Cir. 2012).

II. ELIGIBILITY DETERMINATIONS

A. IDEA Eligibility Determinations

The IDEA, at 20 U.S.C. § 1414(a)(1)(A), requires a full and individual evaluation before the initial provision of special education and related services to resident students with disabilities. Evaluations may take place upon a parental request or the school's initiative. Each state must also demonstrate that each resident student with a disability is identified, located and evaluated under 20 U.S.C. § 1412(a)(3), and is provided with an IEP that meets IDEA requirements described at 20 U.S.C. § 1414(d).

In Z.H. v. Lewisville Independent School Dist., No. 4:12cv775, 2015 WL 1384442 (E.D. Tex. 3/24/15), a federal court explained that school districts are not required to classify students into a particular disability category. An IDEA provision (20 U.S.C. Section 1412(a)(3)(B)) states that classification by disability is not required, so long as each child who has a qualifying disability "and who, by reason of that disability, needs special education and related services is regarded as a child with a disability under this subchapter."

◆ A Virginia student had a specific learning disability. His behavior included aggression, hyperactivity and delinquency that was "clinically significant." His school classified him as having an "other health impairment." The student became involved in disciplinary incidents that led to a suspension. His parents filed a due process complaint, and the school district agreed to partially fund a private academy placement to settle the dispute. While at the private academy, a professional diagnosed the student with an autism spectrum disorder. Later, the student was hospitalized for a psychiatric evaluation as a result of an incident at the academy. The parents and the school district held IEP meetings to discuss the student's IEP and transition back to a public school. But he said "he would have to kill himself" if he returned to a public school. During this time, the academy advised the parties that he would not be readmitted.

A hearing officer found the district denied the student a free appropriate public education by improperly designating him as having an emotional disability. She found the student was a child with autism and ordered the emotional disability designation deleted. The student was to remain in the private academy until his graduation in 2019. A federal magistrate judge agreed that the student had autism. But there was no reason to delete the emotional disability designation, since there was overlap among the behaviors associated with the two conditions. **Nothing prevented an IEP from designating a child as having both disabilities.** Because the private academy was no longer available to the student, the magistrate judge held much of the relief ordered by the hearing officer was moot. The court vacated the order directing attendance at the academy and ordered the IEP team to develop a new IEP and a new placement reflecting the primary disability of autism. *School Board of the City of Suffolk v. Rose*, 113 F.Supp.3d 803 (E.D. Va. 2015).

♦   A bilingual California student with disabilities struggled in school. His parents hired a psychologist who tested the child and estimated his IQ at 104 on the Weschsler Intelligence Scale for Children and the Woodcock-Johnson Tests of Achievement-III (WISC). The parents supplied the results to the school district and asked it to evaluate the child. After administering two different tests, a school psychologist decided the most reliable measure of his intellectual ability was the WISC score. At the time of the testing, California law required a "severe discrepancy" between intellectual ability and achievement in order to qualify for special education with a learning disability. After their child was denied eligibility for special education, the parents requested a hearing. An ALJ held for the district. Both the district and the parents had the child retested, and he was declared eligible for special education. When the case returned to the ALJ, the school district again prevailed. A federal court held for the district, and the parents appealed. In 2011, the Ninth Circuit held **school districts have the discretion to select the diagnostic tests they use**. A district is to make a reasonable choice between valid tests when determining if a severe discrepancy exists. The case was returned to the lower court. *E.M. v. Pajaro Valley Unified School Dist.*, 652 F.3d 999 (9th Cir. 2011).

The district court approved the ALJ's use of the WISC score and the child's lowest academic standard score of 87. The court found an auditory processing order could not be both a specific learning disability and an other health impairment (OHI). By the time the case returned to the Ninth Circuit, the student had graduated. The court held the family did not show the district acted unreasonably by using the WISC score. It was reasonable to consider three test results and use the middle score. Testing in later school years did not undermine the student's testing scores for grade five, even though he was later found

IDEA-eligible. **The court rejected the finding that a particular disability could not qualify for special education under more than one IDEA disability category.** But the student did not show he was improperly denied special education under the OHI category. While recognizing that a child with an auditory processing disorder may qualify under the OHI category, the court held for the school district. *E.M. v. Pajaro Valley Unified School Dist. Office of Administrative Hearings*, 758 F.3d 1162 (9th Cir. 2014).

◆   The U.S. Court of Appeals, Fifth Circuit, upheld a lower court decision finding that **a Texas school district had significantly delayed identifying and diagnosing a child's disabilities.** As a result, the court held he went most of his school career without necessary accommodations. The child had a cortical visual impairment, cerebral palsy and attention deficit disorder. School employees were unaware of the nature of the student's visual impairment and had discounted it. They failed to create and implement an appropriate IEP for him. In a brief order, the Fifth Circuit upheld the judgment for the student. *Caldwell Independent School Dist. v. Joe P.*, 551 Fed.Appx. 140 (5th Cir. 2014).

◆   New Jersey parents asked a child study team (CST) to evaluate their two-year-old child. A CST report noted the child had significant delays in receptive communication and in social and cognitive skills. The CST classified her as "preschool disabled" and placed her in a half-day integrated preschool class. At a parent-teacher conference, district teachers "expressed serious concerns" about the child's social skills and communications. The parent then took the child to a pediatrician, who made an autism diagnosis. A private neurologist confirmed the diagnosis and recommended applied behavior analysis (ABA).

The parents later placed their child in a private autism learning institute and filed a due process petition. Finding the district did not test her in all areas of suspected disability, an ALJ awarded the parents tuition reimbursement and compensatory education. On appeal, a federal court found no reason to depart from the administrative findings. A review of the district's evaluations showed the child had clear signs of autism. Like the ALJ, **the court found that without the proper evaluative information about the child, the IEPs offered to her were inappropriate.** Multiple experts said the child needed an ABA program to meaningfully benefit, and the court held they were entitled to full reimbursement for their private tuition costs. *Millburn Township Board of Educ. v. J.S.O.*, Civ. No. 13-1208 (FSH), 2014 WL 3619979 (D.N.J. 7/21/14).

◆   A Connecticut mother claimed her son had to miss significant school time due to respiratory issues caused by mold at his school. Before he advanced to grade six, the mother asked the school district to declare him eligible for special education under the other health impairment (OHI) category due to asthma and allergies. The district removed carpeting from the student's school. But the mother placed him in a private school with no state-approved special education program for grade six. In a due process proceeding, she claimed the school district failed to identify her child as requiring special education and related services. A hearing officer ordered the parties to hold a planning and placement team (PPT) meeting to consider the child's eligibility. After the meeting, the student was found ineligible for special education. An allergist's report found no data indicating the public school was "the major culprit of M.A.'s problems."

When the case returned to a hearing officer, she found the student's chronic asthma and allergies did not adversely affect his educational performance. As a result, he was not IDEA-eligible. The parent sued the school district in a federal court. The court dismissed claims against the town for improperly maintaining district schools. It found the district did not abide by its duty to hold PPT meetings and develop IEPs after the student was placed at a private school. But he did not need special education during the years at issue. **Since he was not IDEA-eligible, the court found no merit to the reimbursement claims.** Although the parent sought monetary damages, the court found they were not available under the IDEA. But she was entitled to $55,950 in attorneys' fees. *M.A. v. Torrington Board of Educ.*, 980 F.Supp.2d 279 (D. Conn. 2014).

♦ A California student was referred to a child counseling center to address his anger and lack of self-control. Near this time, he was diagnosed with ADHD and began to take Adderall. For most of his third-grade year, he was assigned to a teacher who ultimately proved unable to control his behavior. For grade three, the school developed a behavioral support plan (BSP). But the teacher did not implement it with fidelity, and he had 16 incidents of discipline and 10 days of suspension. Following revisions to the BSP, the student was reassigned to a new teacher with a very structured classroom. She implemented the BSP with fidelity. By year end, the student achieved or neared mastery in most of his academic areas. His behavior improved. A school team found him ineligible for special education, and the parent requested a hearing. An ALJ found the student did not qualify as disabled under any of three categories proposed by the parent.

Appeal then went before a federal court, which held the ALJ had made erroneous findings with regard to each eligibility category. **A child is eligible for special education if he or she has a qualifying disability, and "by reason thereof, needs special education and related services."** But the ALJ merged this analysis by considering the effect of general education modifications when assessing impairment. Evidence indicated that with general education support in a structured general education class, the student was nearing grade-level standards. He did not show a need for specialized instruction, and there was no authority for the idea that the school had to provide special education support for his home behavior. *L.J. v. Pittsburg Unified School Dist.*, No. 13-cv-03854-JSC, 2014 WL 1947115 (N.D. Cal. 5/14/14).

♦ A Pennsylvania kindergartener struggled with reading and misbehaved regularly. He had to repeat kindergarten, but he made little progress even in a full-day program. His behavior problems continued in first grade. A school evaluation found that he had ADHD but that he did not need special education. In third grade, the district evaluated him again and found him eligible for special education. The parents sought compensatory education for the previous four years, but the Third Circuit ruled against them. It noted that there was **no unwarranted delay in the first evaluation and that the district did not have to jump to the conclusion that his misconduct indicated a disability**. Also, the student made academic progress despite his behavior problems, and he received substantial accommodations. The district did not violate its child find obligations. *D.K. v. Abington School Dist.*, 696 F.3d 233 (3d Cir. 2012).

♦ A learning-disabled student underwent a vocational evaluation that the district failed to review. When the student's parent challenged that failure as a denial of FAPE, a hearing officer held that the evaluation was invalid. Therefore, the district didn't deny the student a FAPE by failing to review it. A federal court then ruled that the school district denied the student a FAPE by its inaction. The school district asserted that it didn't have to provide compensatory education because the student had since graduated, but the court disagreed. It **ordered the district to determine what compensatory education was needed to make up for the earlier failure**. *Brooks v. District of Columbia*, 841 F.Supp.2d 253 (D.D.C. 2012).

♦ After teachers expressed concerns about a Minnesota elementary student's behavior, his mother asked the district to assess him. The district conducted an assessment, and a psychologist diagnosed him with ADHD, but the district found him ineligible because the ADHD diagnosis came from a psychologist and not a physician. Over the next three years, the student's behavior worsened. His mother finally provided an ADHD diagnosis from a doctor, claiming that she hadn't understood the special education process. The student was then deemed eligible for special education. When his mother asserted that the delay in identifying his disability led to the intensity of supports he required, a hearing officer ruled for the district, holding that it did not violate its child find duties under the IDEA. A federal district court reversed the administrative decision, holding that the student was entitled to an award of compensatory education for the school district's delay. **The child was obviously failing in school, and the district could not shift its responsibilities to the mother.** *M.J.C. v. Special School Dist. No. 1, Minneapolis Public Schools*, No. Civ. 10–4861 JRTTNL, 2012 WL 1538339 (D. Minn. 3/30/12).

♦ A Hawaii student struggled with reading. Her mother requested an evaluation using a response to intervention (RTI) model. The department of education instead used a classroom reading assessment report and a formal academic assessment. These found the student ineligible for special education because there was no "severe discrepancy" between the student's IQ and her achievement on standardized tests. A neuropsychologist diagnosed dyslexia, but the department still found the student ineligible because of the lack of a "severe discrepancy." Eventually the Ninth Circuit ruled that **the department violated the IDEA by relying on the "severe discrepancy" model**. Instead, the department should have used the RTI model. *Michael P. v. Dep't of Educ., State of Hawaii*, 656 F.3d 1057 (9th Cir. 2011).

♦ After an Ohio student's performance began to decline, his parents sought an evaluation for special education. **The principal allegedly refused to authorize the evaluation because it was too late in the school year**, so the parents obtained a private evaluation, which showed that the student had Asperger's, ADHD, anxiety and depression. When they gave the report to the district, it conducted a meeting without them and determined that the student did not have a disability. It continued to delay action on their requests for further evaluations, so the parents sued. While the district's delays were far from exemplary, they did not demonstrate that administrative remedies would be futile. *Doe v. Dublin City School Dist.*, 453 Fed.Appx. 606 (6th Cir. 2011).

B. Section 504 Eligibility

School districts have child find duties under both the IDEA and Section 504. Where a Section 504 claim is based on the provision of educational services for a disabled child, liability depends upon proof that school officials acted in bad faith or with gross misjudgment. To prove this, a student must show a substantial departure from accepted professional judgment. Section 504 and the ADA do not "create general tort liability for educational malpractice."

♦ Compton Unified School District (CUSD) students filed a federal case asserting they are so traumatized by violence and poverty that they should be deemed to have disabilities. According to the complaint, the neurobiological effects of complex trauma impairs the ability to perform essential activities of education such as learning, thinking, reading and concentrating. The students argued complex trauma amounted to a disability under the Americans with Disabilities Act (ADA), Section 504 of the Rehabilitation Act and Section 504 regulations. The students said CUSD did not properly train its teachers and staff to recognize and address the effects of complex trauma and did not provide staff with evidence-based trauma interventions. The restorative practices sought by the students were said to encourage healthy relationships, address conflicts and violence and permit students to self-regulate in high-stress or anxiety situations. CUSD was accused of subjecting traumatized students to punitive and counterproductive suspensions, expulsions, transfers and referrals to law enforcement that push them out of school and into the criminal justice system.

The court found it unnecessary for impairments to be listed in the Diagnostic and Statistical Manual of Mental Disorders (DSM) in order to state a preliminary case. Trauma was within the DSM definition of "mental disorder." It was claimed that if children repeatedly experience fear, areas of the brain can become over-sensitized, leading to hyperarousal or disassociation triggered by seemingly innocent stimuli. **The students made a valid preliminary claim by asserting they suffered substantial limitations on major life activities such as learning, reading, concentrating, thinking and communicating.** The court found the claims showed the students were denied the benefits of CUSD programs solely by reason of a claimed disability. A group of CUSD teachers could also pursue claims in their own right. *P.P. v. Compton Unified School Dist.*,135 F.Supp.3d 1098 (C.D. Cal. 2015).

♦ A Pennsylvania child with cerebral palsy and ADHD was found ineligible for special education. He earned As and Bs, and his behavior was satisfactory. The parents obtained evaluations diagnosing him with Asperger's syndrome. When the student began grade four, his parents again sought a reevaluation. This yielded a finding that he had a disability in math but still did not need special education. The parents removed him from the district and placed him in a cyber-charter school that found him eligible for special education. They then requested a hearing. A hearing officer upheld the district evaluations.

When the case came before a federal court, it held **school districts have a child find obligation under both the IDEA and Section 504**. Once the parents request an evaluation, the school district must evaluate the child in all areas of suspected disability, using a variety of technically sound assessment tools. A school may not rely exclusively on one assessment. The parents complained that the district's use of assessment tools known as DIBELS and GMADE was not sound. But the court found the psychologist used these tools appropriately. In most areas, the student's achievement not only matched his ability but was in the average range. Observations by a teacher and psychologist provided a sufficient basis to find he did not have an IDEA-qualifying disability. It appeared that the student performed at his best in a regular classroom. The cyber-charter school's later eligibility finding did not undermine the findings of the school district. In the short time between evaluations, the student's situation changed substantially. When he was diagnosed with Asperger's syndrome, the district updated his accommodations. He earned As and Bs, and his behavior was satisfactory. Finding the student meaningfully benefitted from his education under a Section 504 plan, the court held for the district. *Timothy F. v. Antietam School Dist.*, No. 12-2719, 2014 WL 1301955 (E.D. Pa. 3/31/14).

♦   Colorado parents agreed to their child's IEPs when she was in elementary school but rejected an IEP proposal as she entered middle school. They revoked their consent to continued provision of special education and related services under the IDEA. A district director of special education notified the parents that the student's "Section 504 plan would be her IEP." But the director also claimed the parental revocation of IDEA services cut off any district obligation to serve the student under the Rehabilitation Act. Later, the parties met and agreed that the child was a qualified individual with a disability under Section 504. But the district offered only to implement the same IEP services that had been rejected months earlier. The parents declined the Section 504 plan and sued the school district for violating the Americans with Disabilities Act and Section 504.

The court observed that without parental consent, special education cannot be provided. When the parents revoked consent under the IDEA, the district was required to cease providing special education, with no further obligation to develop an IEP for the student. But IDEA language clearly stated that nothing in the act was intended to interfere with or limit rights under other federal laws, including the ADA and Section 504. The court agreed with the parents that their rejection of an IEP devised under the IDEA was not an automatic rejection of a Section 504 plan. **Section 504 regulations suggested that satisfying Section 504 through an IEP offer was only an expediency to avoid a duplicate process and did not establish "a legal equivalency."** Parental revocation of consent for special education and related services under the IDEA did not eliminate the protections of Section 504 and the ADA. The student remained protected from disability discrimination after the revocation of IDEA consent. The court noted the school district had held a Section 504 meeting after the revocation of IDEA consent. At the meeting, a

Section 504 plan was proposed, albeit with the same accommodations described in the previously rejected IEP. Since Section 504 regulations permitted a school district to meet its Section 504 obligations through an IEP, the court refused to hold the district liable for denying accommodations. It held the Section 504 meeting and offer of accommodations was sufficient. *Kimble v. Douglas County School Dist. RE-1*, 925 F.Supp.2d 11176 (D. Colo. 2013).

♦   A Missouri parent declined several offers by her child's school district to conduct IDEA eligibility evaluations after he exhibited behavior problems in elementary school. She obtained private evaluations diagnosing her child with ADHD and depression. Early in the student's fourth-grade year, his mother requested a Section 504 evaluation. When the district said it must first hold an IDEA evaluation, the parent authorized one. When the district finally conducted an IDEA evaluation, the student was found ineligible. A Section 504 evaluation was promptly conducted, and a plan was implemented. But the mother objected to details of the plan and pulled her son out of school. She also filed a lawsuit.

A federal court rejected the parent's claims. On appeal, the U.S. Court of Appeals, Eighth Circuit, held that where ADA and Section 504 claims are based on educational services, **liability depends upon proof that officials acted in bad faith or with gross misjudgment**. To meet this requirement, the parent had to show officials substantially departed from accepted professional judgment. Most of the claims complained of simple noncompliance with the law. As the court found insufficient evidence to trigger liability under Section 504 or the ADA, it affirmed the judgment for the school district. *B.M. v. South Callaway R-II School Dist.*, 732 F.3d 882 (8th Cir. 2013).

♦   The Hawaii Department of Education provided Section 504 accommodations to a student with a central auditory processing disorder and ADHD. Her mother challenged the evaluation, claiming that it failed to assess her child in all areas of suspected disability and that her daughter should be eligible for special education under the IDEA. A federal court and the Ninth Circuit both found the student was able to perform successfully in general education classes. **The DOE discussed the disability categories in an eligibility meeting and reviewed school records, medical and psychological reports, teacher observations and student work samples, among other data.** Thus, the student was assessed in all areas of suspected disability. *C.M. v. Dep't of Educ., State of Hawaii*, 476 Fed.Appx. 674 (9th Cir. 2012).

C. Decertification or Change in Classification

A number of courts have observed that the IDEA is not concerned with "labels," but with whether a student is receiving a free appropriate public education. The IDEA does not provide a specific right for a student to be classified under a particular disability, but requires that the IEP be designed to suit the child's demonstrated needs. See 20 U.S.C. Section 1412(a)(3)(B).

♦   Hawaii school officials declared a high school senior ineligible for special education after many years of eligibility. His parents obtained a new private evaluation of their child and asked the state department of education (DOE) to reevaluate him. At an eligibility meeting, team members found the student did not meet the requirements for specific learning disability and was ineligible for special education. In response, the parents requested a hearing. A hearings officer found the student should have been found eligible for special education.

The hearings officer approved a private placement found by the parents and held they were entitled to tuition reimbursement. A federal court held for the DOE. On appeal, the U.S. Court of Appeals, Ninth Circuit, held the lower court did not commit an error by finding the student ineligible for special education. The court found two criteria for qualifying for special education services based on a specific learning disability. First, it had to be shown that the child had inadequate achievement or a severe discrepancy between achievement and ability. Next, the child had to have shown insufficient progress or a pattern of strengths or weaknesses in performance consistent with a specific learning disability. According to the court, the state DOE could show the child was ineligible for special education through evidence that he was achieving adequately and did not have a severe enough discrepancy between his achievement and ability. This showing was met, because the DOE presented evidence that the child performed well in his classes and was generally engaged while there. In addition, **the child was earning good grades at the private school despite receiving only "tier one" accommodations available to all students**. As he performed well academically, the court upheld the ruling that he was ineligible for special education. *Dep't of Educ., State of Hawaii v. Patrick P.*, 609 Fed.Appx. 509 (9th Cir. 2015).

◆ A Maine student qualified for an IEP with a specific learning disability from grade three year until high school. When she reached high school, the results of a triennial reevaluation included average or higher scores on a battery of tests. But some standardized test scores remained in the "low average" range. Although the student earned all As, her parents sought to preserve her program and placement. Using state learning disability factors, an IEP team concluded she was no longer eligible for special education. In response, the parents filed two due process petitions. After the first case settled, a hearing officer found the school evaluations of the student had been appropriate and there were no IDEA violations. A federal court found the IEP team's decision had been based upon evaluations, state standardized test scores, the testimony of teachers and the student's excellent grades. A Maine regulation stated that no specific learning disability could be found unless a student had taken a valid test of psychological processing and obtained low scores in two areas of psychological processing.

The parents claimed the state regulation imposed a duty not listed in federal law. But the court found the student was achieving at a more than adequate level for her age. It held the federal requirements for a specific learning disability were not met. Next, the court held the parents should not be reimbursed for the cost of private evaluations, as the district's evaluations had been appropriate. In sum, **the court held the district did not violate the IDEA by finding the student ineligible for special education and related services**. There was no violation of state special education regulations, and the court denied a request to be reimbursed for private evaluations. *Mr. and Mrs. Doe v. Cape Elizabeth School Dep't*, Civ. No. 2:13-cv-00407, 2014 WL 7369358 (D. Me. 12/29/14).

♦ A Maine student made progress on her IEP goals and performed at grade level in all her classes. Her IEP team reduced her daily time in special education from over one hour to 15 minutes. Teachers believed the student could be in a general education setting for grade four. At an IEP meeting, the parents agreed to a reevaluation but felt the school district was misrepresenting the child's progress. Evaluations indicated she was performing in the average range and no longer needed special education. Classroom observation and a speech/language evaluation corroborated these findings. When the IEP team completed its review, it determined the child did not have a specific learning disability. It dismissed her from special education with an exit plan to general education.

The parents filed an administrative challenge. A hearing officer found the child did not have a specific learning disability, and the parents appealed. A federal court referred the case to a magistrate judge, who found a student could be identified with a specific learning disability due to lack of adequate achievement for the child's age or failure to meet state-approved standards. Although the parents asserted the hearing officer and IEP team had used the wrong criteria for terminating their child's special education eligibility, the magistrate judge found this argument would prevent any student from ever losing eligibility. There was no evidence that the student was faltering in general education subjects by the end of third grade. **The IEP team justified its analysis and provided the student an extensive exit plan.** She achieved adequately for her age and met state-approved grade-level standards in all areas. As a result, the magistrate judge recommended judgment for the district. The court adopted the recommendation. *J.B. and A.B. v. Wells-Ogunquit Community School Dist.*, No. 2:13-CV-11-DBH, 2014 WL 4100903 (D. Me. 8/18/14).

♦ A Texas student with an emotional disturbance (ED) attended a behavior modification classroom. He passed most of his classes and was considered on track to graduate. Although the student's parents urged his school to change his eligibility classification from ED to autism, they repeatedly declined district requests for their permission to speak with his physician. The team concluded the student did not meet state eligibility criteria for autism. During his ninth-grade year, a professional who conducted an independent evaluation found the student did not have autism. The parents again denied a school request to speak with their child's physician and filed a due process complaint. They also refused to consent to an autism assessment. Although the school district offered the student compensatory homebound instruction, the parents declined and placed him in a residential facility without notice. A federal court later rejected their claim that the district should have found their child had autism. In the court's view, **the particular diagnosis noted for a child in an IEP will often be immaterial because the IEP will be tailored to the child's specific needs**.

The IDEA does not provide a specific right for a student to be classified under a particular disability, but instead requires that the IEP be designed to suit the child's demonstrated needs. It appeared to the court that the district had considered the services and strategies listed in state law for students with autism, implemented many of them, and asked the parents what else they wanted. The court found the school district focused on the needs of the student and tried to develop an IEP suited to his needs. As the district had properly conducted evaluations, held ARD committee meetings and devised IEPs that addressed the student's specific needs, the court held for the district. *R.C. v. Keller Independent School Dist.*, 958 F.Supp.2d 718 (N.D. Tex. 2013).

♦ A Missouri student with Down syndrome (and autism) attended school under an IEP that did not suggest any diagnosis of autism. For about five years, she progressed toward her goals and achieved some of them. At that point, her parents became concerned about her behavior, and an independent psychological evaluation determined that she had autism as well. The district then offered her an IEP that included services based on her autism. The parents instead placed her in a private school and sought tuition reimbursement, claiming that the failure to identify the autism was a violation of the IDEA. The case eventually reached the Eighth Circuit, which ruled that **the failure to specifically identify the autism did not deprive the student of educational benefits**. The IEP was highly customized to meet her needs. *Fort Osage R-1 School Dist. v. Sims*, 641 F.3d 996 (8th Cir. 2011).

♦ The parents of an Alaska first-grader became concerned about his reading skills and requested a special education evaluation. The district told them to wait until fall, but the district delayed an evaluation. The parents requested due process and hired a private neuropsychologist. They provided the results to the district, which used them to determine that the student was ineligible for special education. The Supreme Court of Alaska later ruled that they were entitled to be reimbursed for the cost of the private evaluations. **Even though the student wasn't eligible for special education, the district failed to conduct an evaluation within 45 days of notification** that he might have a learning disability. *J.P. and L.P. v. Anchorage School Dist.*, 260 P.3d 285 (Alaska 2011).

D. Uncooperative Parents

The IDEA requires school districts to reevaluate eligible students with a disability at least every three years. Parents must be informed about and consent to these evaluations, and a district may file a due process request if they do not. But a school district need not request a due process hearing or obtain an updated evaluation if a parent refuses consent for this.

♦ A New York parent refused to consent to evaluation of her child with Down syndrome for nine years. As the student advanced through elementary school, integration with her non-disabled peers became increasingly difficult. Her parent continued to withhold consent for reevaluation or cognitive testing. As a result, the committee on special education (CSE) had to prepare IEPs for grades six and seven without any current evaluations. An instructor recommended removing the student from mainstream social studies for grade nine. But the parent took the position that she should be mainstreamed in every class so she could earn a Regents diploma or local diploma credit. In the CSE's opinion, the student's cognitive and emotional deficits prevented her from participating in a Regents curriculum. The parent refused to consent to testing and evaluations and filed a hearing request. An impartial hearing officer held in her favor.

When the case reached a federal court, it held the parent could not assert the denial of a FAPE. She had withheld consent for evaluations and testing for nine years. **If a parent refuses to consent to special education and related services, or fails to respond to a request to provide consent, a school district is not considered to be in violation of the IDEA's requirement to make a FAPE available.** In any event, the court held the IEP would have provided the student a FAPE. The decision that she would not receive Carnegie credits and pursue a Regents diploma was not an IDEA violation. *V.M. v. North Colonie Cent. School Dist.*, 954 F.Supp.2d 102 (N.D.N.Y. 2013).

♦   The U.S. Supreme Court denied review of lower court decisions that declined to find a Virginia school district failed to evaluate a student for an auditory processing disorder. In prior activity, a federal district court held the district did not overlook any areas of disability and provided an appropriate IEP. On appeal, the U.S. Court of Appeals, Fourth Circuit, held the parents could not challenge the eligibility determinations since the case was untimely filed. In any case, **the parents had refused to consent to reevaluation of their son, undercutting any argument that the school failed to assess him in all his areas of suspected disability.** *Torda v. Fairfax County School Board*, No. 13-6908, 134 S.C. 984 (U.S. cert. denied, 12/2/13, reconsideration denied 1/13/14).

♦   An Ohio student with multiple disabilities attended an "EduCare" program for students with disabilities. Her parents opposed a school district proposal to remove her from EduCare and filed a due process hearing request. A hearing officer found the student's least restrictive environment for instruction was EduCare. But in disregard of this order, the parents did not enroll her in EduCare or any other school. The district set up several IEP meetings, but the parents refused to attend them, and the district eventually advised them that their child could be considered truant. The parents said they would neither return their child to school for an evaluation (necessary to create an interim IEP) nor return her to school without an IEP. The school district requested a due process hearing. The parents continued to object to conditions or times of IEP meetings.

When the case reached a federal court, it upheld the hearing officer. But the parents still refused to place the child in EduCare and filed a new due process complaint. A hearing officer found the district was not liable for denying the student a FAPE, and the case returned to a federal court. It noted that the student was 14 and had not attended school in the district for several years. The parents had disregarded the hearing officer's order and engaged in a lengthy pattern of "failure to cooperate and participate in" IEP meetings. In the court's view, **the parents did not fulfill their duty to participate in the IEP process and "impaired that process irredeemably."** Despite their "persistent non-cooperation," the court found they had no specific objections to the IEPs. It found no error in the hearing officer's decision and held the parents responsible for leaving their child without an IEP. Among other "obstructive tactics," they wrongfully conditioned an IEP on a non-existent "right" to record hearings. The court held for the school district. *Horen v. Board of Educ. of City of Toledo Public School Dist.*, 948 F.Supp.2d 793 (N.D. Ohio 2013).

♦   The father of a Minnesota student complained about the evaluation methods used on his son. He asserted that the district failed to consider a private evaluation he obtained and also failed to use a transitions planning test he preferred to the evaluation model used by the district. In the lawsuit that resulted, the Minnesota Court of Appeals held **state regulations required districts to use a variety of evaluation tools and not any single procedure**. The district evaluation was thorough and well-documented, and the father did not have a right to insist on evaluation methodology. *Heller v. Minnesota Dep't of Educ.*, No. A09-1720, 2010 WL 2035844 (Minn. Ct. App. 5/25/10).

♦   The parents of a New Hampshire student became concerned that she needed special education, and their school district found she had a learning disability in math. An IEP team suggested a private school placement, to which the parents agreed. The following year, the parents requested due process, claiming the district had denied her a free appropriate public education (FAPE) for the previous five years. They withdrew the student from school and began homeschooling her. The district threatened to file truancy charges against them unless they registered her as a homeschooled student. When the case finally reached a federal court, it held that **the parents acted unreasonably during the IEP process; thus, any delay in developing an IEP did not violate the IDEA**. Also, the truancy threat did not amount to a denial of FAPE. *Kasenia R. v. Brookline School Dist.*, 588 F.Supp.2d 175 (D.N.H. 2008).

E. Emotional/Behavioral Issues

In Munir v. Pottsville Area School Dist., *this chapter, the parents of a Pennsylvania student who made multiple suicide attempts could not recover the costs of residential placements that were made primarily in response to mental health needs and not for education.*

♦   The U.S. Court of Appeals, Sixth Circuit, agreed with Kentucky school officials that an autistic student's home behavior was not relevant to his special education eligibility status. To show a need for special education and related services, the parents had to show their child's autism adversely affected his "educational performance." According to the parents, "educational performance" includes a student's academic, social and psychological needs. They argued their child's problematic behavior at home was relevant to his "educational performance." The court held the term "educational performance" suggested school-based evaluation. Moreover, the court found the parents' argument would require schools to address all behavior flowing from a child's disability, no matter how far removed from the school day. As a result, **the court held the inquiry into the student's educational performance should be confined to classroom and school settings**. The court rejected the parents' attempt to discredit hearing testimony by the board. The student experienced academic success at school. Finding it was not entitled to discount the lower court's view of the evidence, the court held for the board. *Q.W. v. Board of Educ. of Fayette County, Kentucky,* 630 Fed.Appx. 580 (6th Cir. 2015).

♦   A Minnesota child had lymphoma and underwent chemotherapy. She had frequent illnesses, infections and asthma and was diagnosed with generalized anxiety disorder. When the child began kindergarten, she exhibited separation anxiety when being dropped off at school. Although the parents requested a special education evaluation, the school did not comply. After missing about 20% of her school days during kindergarten and first grade, the child missed 39 of the first 102 days of second grade. The parents requested a due process hearing, at which they asserted the school district should have identified their child as eligible for special education with other health disabilities (OHD). An ALJ held the district failed to follow its own child find procedures and ordered the district to verify a medical diagnosis of a chronic or acute health condition and assess the child's eligibility for services.

On appeal, **a federal court held a school must identify and evaluate all children who are reasonably suspected of having a disability, even if a parent does not request an evaluation**. State regulations required a medical evaluation of a child with a chronic or acute health condition meeting at least three of eight relevant OHD factors. The court found the district had observed and received reports that the child might have a health condition and knew she was struggling due to her absenteeism. Coupled with the parents' request to evaluate the child, the school district had reason to suspect that a medical evaluation might yield critical information. The court held the district committed a child find violation by failing to fully evaluate the child. It held the district had to get a medical assessment and reevaluate the child. *Independent School Dist. No. 413 v. H.M.J.*, 123 F.Supp.3d 1100 (D. Minn. 2015).

♦   A California student's behavior included pulling out her eyelashes, toenails and fingernails and screaming profanities. Due to her maladaptive behaviors, the student was often removed from classes. Her parents felt her program was too difficult and that bad behavior by classmates was harming her. The school district denied their request for a private placement, and they notified the district they intended to place her in a private school at public expense. The district requested an IEP meeting, but the parents responded that none of the suggested dates were acceptable. Although they expressly stated that they did not consent to an IEP meeting in their absence, the district held a meeting without them.

The parents initiated a due process hearing. An ALJ held for the school district. **A federal court found no merit to the district's argument that ongoing daily informal observations as part of the child's support services amounted to an assessment.** No formal tests had been administered, and the district did not assess the student's behavior despite many parental requests and ample evidence that she was becoming more aggressive. The court held the district's failure to assess the student's behavior and anxiety denied her a FAPE. In addition, the district deprived the parents of their rights by holding an IEP meeting in their absence. Since the district did not try to notify them of the date of the IEP meeting, there was an IDEA violation. The parents were due reimbursement for their private tuition, plus the costs of an independent educational evaluation. *M.S. v. Lake Elsinore Unified School Dist.*, No. 13-CV-01484-CAS (SPx), 2015 WL 4511947 (C.D. Cal. 7/24/15).

◆   A 13-year-old student was hospitalized after making suicidal threats. After his release, his school district found he did not meet IDEA eligibility criteria. Over the next few years, he attended district schools and generally had good grades. He attempted suicide. His father asked for an IEP, but the district offered a Section 504 plan instead. After another suicide attempt, his father placed him in a therapeutic/residential treatment center. The district found him IDEA-eligible and offered a public school placement. The father rejected the offer. A federal court held that the district was not delinquent in identifying the student as IDEA eligible. He generally had B and C grades, and **the primary purpose of the residential placement was for mental health treatment**.

When the case reached the U.S. Court of Appeals, Third Circuit, it stated that in cases seeking residential tuition, a court has to focus on whether a full-time residential placement was necessary for education. **No reimbursement is required if placement was a response to medical, social or emotional problems that were segregable from the learning process.** There has to be some "link" between the private services and the child's educational needs. As the district's IEP offer complied with the IDEA, the court held for the school district. *Munir v. Pottsville Area School Dist.*, 723 F.3d 423 (3d Cir. 2013).

◆   A Missouri student had behavior problems beginning when he first entered school. He was suspended many times for fighting and making threats, and he had a record of poor performance in class and on standardized tests. At the end of his fifth-grade year, his father sought special education for him. When the district found that he didn't qualify for special education, his father sought due process. The case reached the Eighth Circuit, which held that **the student was entitled to special education. His problems with other students and staff were not primarily social maladjustment** but rather emotional disturbance that qualified under the IDEA. He also qualified as "other health impaired" as his hyperactive and inattentive behavior severely impaired his ability to learn. *Hansen v. Republic R-III School Dist.*, 632 F.3d 1024 (8th Cir. 2011).

◆   A Texas ninth-grader began to have behavior problems after his parents divorced and his grandparents died. He was assigned to an alternative school, where his behavior did not improve. A private evaluation determined that he had ADHD, but the school district didn't evaluate him for special education even though he was failing at least four classes. An updated evaluation also found he had ADHD, but the district still didn't initiate an IDEA evaluation for more than a year. Eventually, the district found him eligible for special education as "other health impaired." A federal court ruled that the parents were entitled to a year of compensatory educational services as well as attorneys' fees because **the district's delay in evaluating the student was not reasonable. It had reason to suspect the student had a disability, and it failed to act.** *D.G. v. Flour Bluff Independent School Dist.*, 832 F.Supp.2d 755 (S.D. Tex. 2011).

◆   A New York seventh-grader began using marijuana heavily and also began failing classes. His parents grew concerned by his deterioration and requested a psychological evaluation, which resulted in a finding that his cognitive functions were average, his processing skills were borderline and his oral expression skills were superior. A committee on special education found him ineligible for special education, but he was given testing accommodations under Section 504. However, he continued to use marijuana and was later placed in a residential home. When his parents sought tuition reimbursement, it was denied. A federal court ultimately held that **his problems were associated with his drug use** and that he did not have an emotional disturbance under the IDEA. *P.C. v. Oceanside Union Free School Dist.*, 818 F.Supp.2d 516 (E.D.N.Y. 2011).

♦ A New York tenth-grader had a falling out with his hockey coach and began to suffer from depression. He used drugs and alcohol. Eventually he was expelled for disruptive behavior. His parents placed him in a Utah program for troubled teens, where he was diagnosed as having serious emotional problems. His parents then sought special education and related services as well as tuition reimbursement for the Utah placement. An independent psychologist found the student was in the average range of intellectual functioning and had a non-clinical level of depression. A hearing officer found the student eligible for special education, but a review officer reversed. A federal court then held that **the student's problems were the result of truancy, drug abuse and conduct disorders**, such that he was not eligible for special education under the IDEA. *W.G. v. New York City Dep't of Educ.*, 801 F.Supp.2d 142 (S.D.N.Y. 2011).

♦ A Rhode Island student with oppositional defiant disorder suffered bouts of extreme rage that eventually resulted in her hospitalization for suicidal and homicidal ideation. Her school district determined she was not eligible for special education and did not provide educational services to her during or after her hospitalization. A hearing officer awarded her 21 weeks of compensatory education, and a federal court agreed with that outcome. **The student's problems were so severe that they could not be segregated from the learning process.** *Linda E. v. Bristol Warren Regional School Dist.*, 758 F.Supp.2d 75 (D.R.I. 2010).

F. Reevaluation

After a student's initial eligibility determination, a school must reevaluate IDEA eligibility every three years, unless the parties agree otherwise. See 34 C.F.R. Part 300.303. In Phyllene W. v. Huntsville City Board of Educ., below, the Eleventh Circuit Court of Appeals found an Alabama school board had to assess a student's hearing, even though her parent waived her right to a reevaluation based on concerns that the child would test out of IDEA eligibility.

♦ An Alabama student had seven ear surgeries by age 16 and had significant difficulties in reading, math, organizing her schoolwork and taking standardized tests. Her mother paid for a private tutor for her throughout her K-12 career. Near the end of the student's second-grade school year, she was found to have a specific learning disability that qualified her for special education. At an IEP team meeting during the student's fifth-grade year, the parent notified the team that her child had tubes implanted in her ears and that her hearing loss was worsening. But the team did not schedule an evaluation. The next year, a triennial reevaluation was due, but the team recommended that no evaluation take place due to fear that she would test out of special education eligibility. The parent consented to this. The student was promoted from grade to grade despite failing to meet state content standards in reading and math. Prior to grade 10, the parent informed IEP team members that her child was being fitted for a hearing aid. But the team still did not evaluate her or consider whether her hearing loss affected her progress. As the student entered grade 10, her reading was assessed at a grade 3.6 level and her math abilities were found to be at a 2.6 grade level. The parent placed her in a private school and requested a hearing.

A private evaluator found the student qualified for special education with a hearing impairment. A hearing officer found for the board, as did a federal court. Appeal reached the U.S. Court of Appeals, Eleventh Circuit, which held a proper evaluation would have uncovered the cause of the student's hearing deficits. **Although the parent agreed to forgo a reevaluation due to fears that the student would test out of eligibility, the board was not excused from conducting future reevaluations.** The parent told the IEP team about her child's hearing loss and need for a hearing aid. The board had a continuing obligation to evaluate the student based on suspicion of a disability. Failure of a parent to request an evaluation did not absolve the board of its independent responsibility to evaluate a child suspected of having a disability. *Phyllene W. v. Huntsville City Board of Educ.*, 630 Fed.Appx. 917 (11th Cir. 2015).

♦　An Idaho school district reevaluated an eighth-grader and found him ineligible for special education. His parents obtained a private evaluation that diagnosed him with a high-functioning form of autism. They sought a new evaluation, but the district refused. During ninth grade, the student was arrested and placed in a juvenile detention center. The school district in which the detention center was located evaluated him for special education but found no evidence of any adverse effect of disabilities on his educational performance. Noting the other district's evaluation was limited because of his confinement, the parents asked their home district for a reevaluation. But the home district declined to perform its own evaluation. When the student returned home, the parents requested additional assessments and an IEP. The district refused and found him ineligible for special education. By this time, the student was in grade 11. His parents requested an IEE, which the home district denied. In a due process proceeding, a hearing officer held the home district failed to conduct an appropriate evaluation. A federal court then issued a preliminary order preventing the district from graduating the student. It held the parents were entitled to an IEE at the district's expense, plus an award of attorneys' fees. A district reevaluation then found the student ineligible for special education.

After a second round of hearings, the finding of ineligibility was confirmed. The parents appealed to a federal court, which held the student was not IDEA-eligible. Appeal reached the U.S. Court of Appeals, Ninth Circuit, which held the parents were entitled to an IEE at public expense. **The conditions for evaluation at a juvenile center were very different from the home setting and evidence indicated the home district relied too heavily on the student's grades in its assessments.** Since he was ineligible for IDEA services, the parents did not meet the IDEA definition of "parent of a child with a disability" and were ineligible for IDEA attorneys' fees. The court found the order to prevent the school district from graduating the student was questionable, since he was not receiving special education. It appeared that since he met graduation criteria, he likely received all the benefits that the district's general education program offered. It had been three years since the preliminary order was issued. As any benefit resulting from the order was now exhausted, the court vacated it. *Meridian Joint School Dist. No. 2 v. D.A.*, 792 F.3d 1054 (9th Cir. 2015).

♦   The parents of a nonverbal and self-abusive Georgia child with autism and brain injuries were unable to agree on the terms of a triennial evaluation of the child. At another IEP meeting, they submitted an extensive addendum that imposed strict conditions on any reevaluation, including the particular expert who would conduct it. The district rejected the addendum, and the parents sought due process. They sought an independent evaluation at public expense as well as a private residential placement. **A hearing officer found their conditions to be essentially a refusal to consent to a reevaluation such that they were not entitled to public funding.** The Eleventh Circuit upheld that decision. *G.J. v. Muscogee County School Dist.*, 668 F.3d 1258 (11th Cir. 2012).

♦   After Texas parents refused to allow their school district to reevaluate their child, the district filed for due process, seeking to override their decision. **A hearing officer authorized the district to conduct the evaluation without the parents' consent.** After that evaluation, the district revised the IEP over the parents' disagreement. The parents then filed for due process, and the district filed an administrative complaint against the parents. When the parents dropped their case, the district sought attorneys' fees. A federal court denied them, but the Fifth Circuit ruled that the district could pursue its attorneys' fees even though it was the party that initiated the action. *Alief Independent School Dist. v. C.C.*, 655 F.3d 412 (5th Cir. 2011).

♦   The parents of a New Jersey student with autism and other disorders placed him in a private school for grade five after becoming dissatisfied with his IEP. The district denied tuition reimbursement. The following year, the parents sought an evaluation and IEP meeting, but the district claimed that the student had to re-enroll in the district to be served by it. The parents kept the student in the private school and filed for due process, seeking tuition reimbursement. An administrative law judge and a federal court ruled that the district had offered a FAPE for the first year the student attended the private school. However, **the court rejected the district's claim that it did not have to reevaluate the student or offer an IEP because he wasn't enrolled in a district school**. The parents were entitled to tuition reimbursement for the time period after the district failed to reevaluate the student. *Moorestown Township Board of Educ. v. S.D.*, 811 F.Supp.2d 1057 (D.N.J. 2011).

G. Response to Intervention

An October 23, 2015 "Dear Colleague" letter by the U.S. Office of Special Education and Rehabilitation Services (OSERS) clarifies that the IDEA does not prohibit the terms dyslexia, dyscalculia and dysgraphia in evaluations, eligibility determinations or IEPs. Dyslexia is a "specific learning disability" under the IDEA and its regulations. Students needing additional academic and behavioral support in general education environments may be served with a multi-tiered system of supports (MTSS) such as response to intervention (RTI) or positive behavioral intervention. MTSS may also be used to identify children suspected of having a specific learning disability.

*Children whose response to intervention is minimal or who do not respond must be referred for an IDEA eligibility evaluation. Parents may request an initial special education evaluation at any time. The OSERS letter explained that the **use of MTSS, including RTI, cannot be used to delay or deny a full and individual IDEA evaluation if a child is suspected of having a disability.** U.S. Office of Special Education and Rehabilitation Services, Letter of October 23, 2015. https://www2.ed.gov/policy/speced/guid/idea/memosdcltrs/guidance-on-dyslexia-10-2015.pdf.*

♦ In 2005, a California school district began to implement a Response to Intervention (RTI) approach to assist struggling learners in general education environments as an intermediate step before special education referrals. Student RTI assessment results were not shared with parents. Via RTI, a kindergartner was found in need of reading intervention and given additional instruction. The next school year, the parents requested an evaluation of their child for learning disabilities. After two student study team (SST) meetings, the school district referred him for a special education evaluation. The student's RTI graphs were not reviewed in the SST meetings and were not shared with the parents. In late April of the student's first-grade year, an IEP team found he had a phonological processing disorder and declared him eligible for special education. But the parties continued to disagree about evaluations, and the parents eventually withdrew the child from his ISP and enrolled him in an intense private reading and comprehension program. They filed a due process complaint with a state agency, asserting 16 claims against the district regarding the child's eligibility.

An administrative law judge (ALJ) held for the district, and the parents filed three federal court cases that were eventually consolidated. When the case reached the U.S. Court of Appeals, Ninth Circuit, it found the school district had incorporated RTI data into the child's initial evaluation and had used a variety of assessment tools (including the RTI data) during the child's initial evaluation. **While the court upheld the evaluation, it held the team violated the IDEA by failing to ensure RTI data was documented and carefully considered by the parents.** The school was required to furnish data to the parents to allow them to give their informed consent for the initial evaluation and the services he was to receive. Even if the district never proposed to use the RTI assessments to determine eligibility, **the IDEA required notice to parents regarding the tests it intended to conduct on a child. The parents had to be informed of those test results.** Without the benefit of the RTI data, the parents were unaware of the discrepancy in reported scores and were unable to meaningfully participate in the IEP process. Finding a denial of FAPE, the court returned the case to the lower court for it to reconsider the parents' claim for reimbursement for private assessments. The lower court was also to reconsider their claim for attorneys' fees and a retaliation claim under Section 504. *M.M. v. Lafayette School Dist.*, 767 F.3d 842 (9th Cir. 2014).

♦   An Illinois student had behavioral problems in kindergarten that prompted a school counselor to refer him to counseling. During the student's first- and second-grade years, his disruptive behavior continued. The school provided him with academic and behavioral support in the context of response to intervention (RTI). During second grade, the student was admitted to a hospital psychiatric facility and diagnosed with intermitted explosive disorder. His mother requested a due process hearing, asserting the school district violated its IDEA child find duty and failed to respond to her request for a full and individual evaluation (FIE). She also challenged the adequacy of the IEP and related services.

A hearing officer found for the school district on the child find and timeliness issues, and a claim for compensatory education was denied. On appeal, a federal court observed that schools are not required to formally evaluate all struggling students. The standard for whether a school failed to identify a student with a disability was whether it overlooked "clear signs of a disability" and was "negligent in failing to order testing," or there was no rational justification for deciding not to evaluate. Under this standard, the court held the hearing officer did not commit an error. As the hearing officer found, **the district could have rationally believed that the interventions provided under RTI might ameliorate the student's behavior up to the time of his hospitalization**. The parent challenged the hearing officer's refusal to credit her primary witness, who said there should have been an FIE at the time the school counselor referred the student for counseling. The hearing officer properly rejected the expert testimony bearing on the timing of an FIE. As there had been no child find obligation, the court held it had been appropriate for the hearing officer to deny compensatory education. *Demarcus L. v. Board of Educ. of City of Chicago, Dist. 299*, No. 13 C 5331, 2014 WL 948883 (N.D. Ill. 3/11/14).

♦   A Hawaii student with ADHD received accommodations and achieved average scores on standardized tests. An eligibility team found the student ineligible for special education. The parents requested an independent education evaluator, who recommended a functional behavioral assessment. The team rejected that recommendation. A hearing officer found that the student's accommodations did not provide him with access to the general education curriculum, and a federal court agreed that the student's ADHD adversely affected his educational performance. He made no progress in science or social studies, and he failed spelling. **The standardized test results did not address the student's ability to perform in a regular classroom setting.** The student was entitled to compensatory education. *State of Hawaii, Dep't of Educ. v. Zachary B.*, No. 08-00499 JMS/LEK, 2009 WL 1585816 (D. Haw. 6/5/09).

III. INDEPENDENT EVALUATIONS

Phillip C. v. Jefferson County Board of Educ., *this chapter, involved a challenge to federal regulations allowing parental reimbursement for the cost of independent educational evaluations (IEEs). If parents disagree with the school district's assessment, they may request an IEE at public expense. If such a request is made, a school must elect to defend its evaluation or provide the IEE.*

♦ A Georgia school district evaluated a second-grader and found him eligible for special education in its autism and speech impairment programs. Using the same evaluation, a school IEP team met with the parents and prepared an IEP for the next school year. The parents did not object to the eligibility findings or the proposed IEP and also raised no objection to the evaluation or the child's IEP at the next year's IEP meeting. But about two months into the school year, the parents claimed the initial evaluation — now over two years old — was improper. They asked the school district to pay for an IEE. The district denied the request as untimely, relying on a two-year IDEA limitations provision for due process hearing requests. The district then asked the parents for permission to conduct a triennial reevaluation of the child, even though it was not yet due.

But the parents declined to consent to a district reevaluation. Both parties then requested due process hearings. An administrative law judge (ALJ) heard the cases and issued separate orders in the district's favor. On appeal, a federal court agreed with the ALJ. The parents appealed to the U.S. Court of Appeals, Eleventh Circuit, which found the parents had abandoned some of their arguments on appeal. They did not support their claim for reimbursement or explain how a psychological assessment of the child qualified as an IEE. There was no evidence that they even paid for a psychological assessment. Any claim for an IEE at public expense was limited to two years, and the issue was moot. In this case, the initial evaluation was not current because more than three years had passed. Regardless of the merits of the case, the court held any order for an IEE at public expense would be futile. **There was no right to a publicly funded IEE until the parents disagreed with a school reevaluation.** Because a reevaluation of the child was due, the relief sought by the parents would no longer remedy any injury they alleged. Since the case was moot it had to be dismissed. *T.P. v. Bryan County School Dist.*, 792 F.3d 1284 (11th Cir. 2015).

♦ A Pennsylvania student was reevaluated in grade eight to update his IEP. This led to a determination that he no longer required special education under the IDEA. After his parent objected, the school district requested a hearing. A hearing officer ordered the district to update a reevaluation report to include classroom observations and input from teachers and the parent. But she held the district did not have to pay for an independent educational evaluation (IEE). A federal court held the hearing officer committed an error by declining to order the district to fund an IEE despite finding the district's report was inappropriate.

Appeal reached the Third Circuit, which observed that **school districts must reevaluate students with disabilities at least once every three years unless the parents and the district agree otherwise**. If a parent disagrees with a district reevaluation report, the district must fund an IEE unless it shows its evaluation was appropriate in a due process proceeding. In this case, the court found it was clear that the tools and strategies of the district evaluation were not sufficiently comprehensive and did not satisfy federal requirements to "provide relevant information that directly assists persons in determining the educational needs of the child are provided." The district had relied on anecdotal and non-specific data when assessing the student's progress. There was also evidence that the assessment tools did not provide relevant information to make a prospective determination of the student's eligibility for future services in light of his transition to high school. Once the hearing officer found the district's reevaluation inappropriate, the student's parent was entitled to an IEE at public expense. *M.Z. v. Bethlehem Area School Dist.*, 521 Fed.Appx. 74 (3d Cir. 2013).

◆   Alabama parents disagreed with a reevaluation of their child and obtained an independent educational evaluation (IEE) at a private facility. Despite state and federal regulations requiring schools to reimburse parents in such situations, the school board refused to reimburse the parents for the cost of the IEE. It asserted that the regulations were invalid. In response, the parents filed a due process hearing request. After a hearing, a state-appointed hearing officer found that the board was required to reimburse the parents for the costs of obtaining the private IEE. **The board appealed to the Eleventh Circuit, which upheld the regulations requiring reimbursement.** *Phillip C. v. Jefferson County Board of Educ.*, 701 F.3d 691 (11th Cir. 2012).

◆   A Pennsylvania school psychologist conducted a comprehensive psychoeducational evaluation of a student and found that he was not entitled to special education. His father was dissatisfied with that decision and obtained an independent educational evaluation, which found that the student had a possible specific learning disability in reading comprehension. He then sought reimbursement for the evaluation. However, the Third Circuit ruled against him, finding that **he was not entitled to reimbursement because the district's evaluation was "appropriate."** *Council Rock School Dist. v. Bolick, II,* 462 Fed.Appx. 212 (3d Cir. 2012).

◆   The mother of a New Jersey student with disabilities agreed to an IEP with the district, but she later objected to the IEP and repeated her earlier request for an independent psychological evaluation and a functional behavioral assessment. The district and an administrative law judge denied her request, but a federal court held that she was entitled to the independent evaluation. **She did not need to disagree with the IEP or the eligibility determination to invoke the right to an independent evaluation.** She only needed to disagree with the district's assessment. *K.B. v. Haledon Board of Educ.*, No. 08-4647 (JLL), 2010 WL 2079713 (D.N.J. 5/24/10).

CHAPTER THREE

Individualized Education Programs

I. PROCEDURAL MATTERS

A. Generally

An individualized education program (IEP) is a written statement for each student with a disability that describes the student's present levels of educational performance, progress in the general curriculum, services to be provided, annual goals and many other statutory requirements.

Specific IEP requirements are found at 20 U.S.C. § 1414(d). Many of the issues in this chapter of the book involve claims that IDEA procedures were violated. The general rule is that only those procedural inadequacies that result in the loss of educational opportunity or seriously infringe upon parental participation in the IEP formulation process result in denial of a free appropriate public education (FAPE). A procedural violation of the IDEA that does not cause some actual harm in the form of lost educational opportunities or denial of parental participation rights will be considered harmless error.

♦   The District of Columbia Public Schools (DCPS) paid for a student's private special education costs. After some time, DCPS representatives found he was ready to attend a general education school with support. A few weeks into the school year, the parents expressed concerns to the DCPS that the student was missing assignments and needed attendance monitoring. After a meeting with the DCPS special education coordinator to address attendance, the student apparently attempted suicide. Near this time, the parents notified the DCPS they had returned the student to the private school and would seek public funding for this. Despite their communication with the DCPS that they would attend an IEP meeting, the special education coordinator advised them that there would be no meeting. The parents filed a due process hearing complaint.

A hearing officer held for the DCPS, finding no denial of a free appropriate public education (FAPE) and excusing an IEP meeting. No meeting was found necessary because the parents had already decided on a placement of their choice. On appeal, a federal court faulted the hearing officer's "shocking proposition" that the DCPS had no obligation to conduct an IEP meeting and prepare an IEP for a student whose parents had unilaterally withdrawn him from district schools. This ruling conflicted with applicable case law. Next, the court disagreed with the hearing officer's finding that by privately placing their child, the parents waived the DCPS' offer to provide a FAPE. Instead, the court held parental action did not relieve DCPS of its obligation to offer a FAPE. **Even when a student is parentally placed in a private school, the district in which the child resides must continue to periodically evaluate his or her special education needs.** A student's return to a private school was of no consequence to the DCPS' ongoing duty to offer him a FAPE. The case was returned to a hearing officer for consideration of whether the parents would be entitled to reimbursement for their private school tuition and other costs. *Lague v. District of Columbia*, 130 F.Supp.3d 305 (D.D.C. 2015).

♦   A California student's behavior included pulling out her eyelashes, toenails and fingernails and screaming profanities. Due to her maladaptive behaviors, the student was often removed from classes. Her parents felt her program was too difficult and that bad behavior by classmates was harming her. The school district denied their request for a private placement, and they notified the district they intended to place her in a private school at public expense. The district requested an IEP meeting, but the parents responded that none of the suggested dates were acceptable. Although they expressly stated that they did not consent to an IEP meeting in their absence, the district held a meeting without them.

Later, the meeting was rescheduled without any notice. The parents initiated a due process hearing. An ALJ held for the district, and the parents appealed to a federal court. The court found no merit to the district's argument that ongoing daily informal observations as part of the child's support services amounted to an assessment. No formal tests had been administered, and the district did not assess the student's behavior despite many parental requests and ample evidence that she was becoming more aggressive. The court held the district's failure to assess the student's behavior and anxiety deprived her of educational benefits and denied her a FAPE. In addition, the district deprived the parents of their procedural rights by holding an IEP meeting in their absence. **The district was required to keep records of its calls, correspondence and home visits to document efforts to obtain parental attendance at IEP meetings.** Since the district did not try to notify the parents of the date of the IEP meeting, the court found an IDEA violation. They were due reimbursement for their private tuition costs, plus the costs of an independent educational evaluation. *M.S. v. Lake Elsinore Unified School Dist.*, No. 13-CV-01484-CAS (SPx), 2015 WL 4511947 (C.D. Cal. 7/24/15).

♦   After a dispute over the IEP of a student with learning and developmental disabilities and behavior problems, California parents requested a due process hearing. Appeal reached the Ninth Circuit, where the parents claimed the district denied their child a FAPE due to procedural flaws in the IEP process. According to the court, **a procedural violation of the IDEA must affect the substantive rights of the parents or child in order to have legal significance**. The parents did not show the absence of a general education teacher from an IEP meeting was a denial of FAPE.

Even though the teacher's absence violated the IDEA, the court held it was a harmless procedural error. According to the parents, the district denied their child a FAPE by failing to conduct a functional analysis assessment and by not providing a behavior intervention plan. The court disagreed, finding California regulations governing functional analysis assessment and behavior intervention plans apply only to students with severe behavior problems. As the student did not seriously damage property or pose a threat to himself or others, the court found he had no serious behavior problem. In addition, the student's IEPs were effective because he was making progress. The court disagreed with the parents' claim that the IEP did not provide measureable goals because the district did not identify a measureable baseline of his abilities. While the IDEA requires a statement of a student's measureable annual goals, the court found it does not require "a statement of quantifiable baselines." *A.G. v. Paso Robles Unified School Dist.*, 561 Fed.Appx. 642 (9th Cir. 2014).

B. IEP Meeting and Attendance Issues

The makeup of an IEP team is described at 20 U.S.C. § 1414(d)(1)(B). IEP teams include the parents, at least one of the student's regular education teachers, at least one special education teacher of the student, and a local educational agency (LEA) representative qualified to provide (or supervise the provision of) specially designed instruction to meet the student's unique needs and who is knowledgeable about the general curriculum and LEA's resources.

An IDEA regulation (34 C.F.R. Part 300.322) explains the steps necessary to ensure that parents are present at an IEP meeting. This section requires ample notice to parents and the scheduling of a mutually agreed-upon time and place. The same regulation (34 C.F.R. Part 300.322) states that if a parent cannot attend an IEP meeting, a school must offer alternatives. A meeting can be conducted without a parent only if the district cannot convince the parent to attend.

In A.G. v. Placentia-Yorba Linda Unified School Dist., 320 Fed.Appx. 519 (9th Cir. 2009), the Ninth Circuit held the IDEA does not require the child's most current teacher to attend an IEP meeting. It requires a special education teacher or provider who has actually taught the student. The court also held not all a student's special education teachers need to attend an IEP meeting.

Although it would be preferable to have a staff member with extensive experience in a child's particular disability, a federal court in Kansas held the IDEA does not require this. Huffman v. North Lyon County School Dist., No. 08-2083-KGS, 2009 WL 3185239 (D. Kan. 9/30/09).

♦   The parents of a California student rejected an IEP offered by his school district. After a hearing officer upheld the district's IEP, a federal court upheld the administrative decision. Among the court's findings was that the district satisfied IDEA requirements by ensuring the IEP team included all required members. At issue was the attendance of a particular regular education teacher. In the court's view, this teacher satisfied 34 C.F.R. Part 300.321(a) as a teacher "who is, or may be, responsible for implementing a portion of the IEP." Next, the court upheld four challenged IEP goals regarding the child's need for reciprocal communication. It found the supportive services were listed in the IEP. Last, the court upheld the student's placement in a general education setting. On appeal, the U.S. Court of Appeals, Ninth Circuit, held the district complied with IDEA procedures. **The general education teacher's presence at IEP meetings met an IDEA requirement that "not less than 1 regular education teacher" of the child be in attendance.** Even if there was procedural error, the court found it was harmless. There had been no deprivation of educational opportunities or infringement on the parent's participatory rights.

The IEP adequately addressed the student's demonstrated needs. There was also no error in placing the student in a general education setting, as the IEP satisfied the IDEA's statutory preference for placing students with disabilities with their non-disabled peers. Since there were no errors in the decisions of the lower court or the hearing officer, the court held for the school district. *Z.R. v. Oak Park Unified School Dist.*, 622 Fed.Appx. 630 (9th Cir. 2015).

♦   Hawaii parents wanted to discuss their child's inappropriate behaviors at an IEP revision meeting. But they were told these had to be discussed at a "team meeting," not at an "IEP meeting." The parents wrote letters to the principal, who responded that "IEP meetings are meant to address Student's program and placement. Strategies, interventions and methodologies, however, are not IEP issues." After providing notice to the school, the parents enrolled their child in a private school. They filed a hearing request for reimbursement for their tuition and tutoring costs. A hearing officer held that by not discussing the student's needs at the IEP meeting, the school impeded his right to a FAPE. As a result, the school department was ordered to reimburse the parents for their private school tuition and related costs. The court explained that 20 U.S.C. § 1414(c)(1) requires an IEP team to review existing evaluation data at an IEP revision meeting. Further, **the IDEA imposes "the duty to conduct a meaningful meeting with the appropriate parties."**

The court held the school impeded the parents' opportunity to participate in the decision-making process by preventing them from discussing the students' needs. In reevaluating the student, the IEP team had a duty to review existing data, including parent-provided information. The court held the school had a duty to allow their meaningful participation. As there was insufficient evidence to support a finding that the private school was appropriate, the reimbursement issue was returned to the hearing officer. *Dep't of Educ., State of Hawaii v. Z.Y.*, No. 13-00322 LEK-RLP, 2013 WL 6210637 (D. Haw. 11/27/13).

♦ A New York student with pervasive developmental disorder - not otherwise specified (PDD-NOS) attended a general education preschool class. As the student neared age five, the department of education formed a CSE to prepare an IEP. Although the CSE included a school psychologist, special education teacher and the student's parent, no general education teacher participated in the meeting. The school psychologist did not provide reports and observations of the child to other CSE members. She prepared a draft IEP but did not give copies to others. At the meeting, the psychologist recommended a special education classroom with a teacher, paraprofessional and six or 12 students (6:1:1 and 12:1:1 placements, respectively). Both the mother and the special education teacher disagreed with the recommendation and told the psychologist of the PDD-NOS diagnosis. Based on the psychologist's input alone, a 12:1:1 special education classroom was recommended. The parents re-enrolled their child in the private school and requested a hearing. An IHO held the department of education did not properly constitute the CSE and did not fully evaluate the child's needs. Lack of a full evaluation was significant, as it led to the 12:1:1 placement. A federal court held the CSE meeting was defective and that the procedural violations were legally significant. An IEP team (called a CSE in New York) must include at least one of the student's regular education teachers.

A regular education teacher serving as a team member should be one who is (or may be) responsible for implementing the IEP. The absence of a general education teacher from the CSE raised important concerns. The court found the school psychologist ignored the opinions of other CSE members and attempts to discuss a general education placement. She also did not provide reports to other CSE members. Since there was no evidence that the CSE had considered a general education placement, the court held for the parents. It returned the matter to the CSE for a properly constituted meeting. Meanwhile, the district was liable for funding under the IDEA's stay-put provision. *R.G. and C.G. v. New York City Dep't of Educ.*, 980 F.Supp.2d 345 (E.D.N.Y. 2013).

♦ A New York school CSE staffed an IEP meeting with a special education teacher who was not the student's current teacher. Team members recommended a 12-month ESY program, but the parent rejected the placement without visiting the school site. She enrolled her child in a private school and filed a due process complaint. An impartial hearing officer held for the school department on most claims, but agreed with the parent on the issue of least restrictive environment regarding the ESY placement. Appeal later reached a federal court. It found that while the teacher who had attended the CSE meeting was not the "special education teacher of the child," there was no showing that this harmed the student. **The teacher's presence at the meeting did not harm the student, and the parent participated extensively in the CSE meeting.**

Participation by the private school's staff and the parent enabled the team to obtain specific information about the child. In the court's view, "all that is required is a parent's participation, not that the parent have the final word." Although the parent made many other arguments, the court rejected each of them. It found no evidence that the IEP had been pre-determined or not properly based on relevant evaluations, reports and medical history. While the parent claimed the CSE placed her child improperly and deprived her of a safe learning environment, the court found this speculative. *A.M. v. New York City Dep't of Educ.*, 964 F.Supp.2d 270 (S.D.N.Y. 2013).

◆   A New Jersey student with cerebral palsy attended grades 11 and 12 in a mainstream setting with various accommodations. After she left school, her father sought two years of compensatory education, asserting that she had been denied a FAPE through both grades and citing various IDEA violations. A federal court and the Third Circuit ruled against him, noting that **the IEP team did not have to include an expert on cerebral palsy**. Further, even though her IEPs lacked objectively measurable goals, that procedural error did not affect her substantive rights. Also, the student was not deprived of any educational opportunity by the inadequate description of transition services to post-school activities in her IEPs. She performed well at a private school after her senior year. *Rodrigues v. Fort Lee Board of Educ.*, 458 Fed.Appx. 124 (3d Cir. 2011).

◆   The parents of a California student with speech and language impairments claimed that their district violated the IDEA by not having the student's current special education teacher attend IEP meetings. Instead, the district had a teacher who had provided speech and language services to the student three years earlier attend the IEP meetings. The case reached the Ninth Circuit, which held **the IDEA does not require the participation of a student's current special education teacher**. Federal guidance calls for at least one special education teacher who has actually taught the student. *Mahone v. Carlsbad Unified School Dist.*, 430 Fed.Appx. 562 (9th Cir. 2011).

◆   The parents of a New York student who had problems in large group settings attended committee on special education (CSE) meetings at which the student's IEP was changed from a classroom of 24 students to a 12:1:1 setting. The parents rejected the proposed IEP and placed the student in a private school, then sought tuition reimbursement. A federal court found the IEP procedurally deficient because the student's special education teacher did not attend the CSE meetings. However, the Second Circuit reversed, noting that **the IEP coordinator at the student's school had attended the CSE meetings along with the student's general education teacher**, and that the IEP was reasonably calculated to provide educational benefits. No tuition was awarded. *A.H. v. Dep't of Educ. of City of New York*, 394 Fed.Appx. 718 (2d Cir. 2010).

◆   The parents of a Vermont student with a disability asserted that their school district violated the IDEA because the student's applied media instructor (regular education teacher) missed some IEP meetings. They claimed his increased presence might have led to a different placement. When they initiated due process proceedings, the case reached the Second Circuit, which ruled against them. The court of appeals noted that **the mere absence of a regular**

educator at any given IEP meeting is not necessarily a procedural violation of the IDEA. Here, the instructor's participation was appropriate under the circumstances. He attended some meetings, and the parents decided to enroll their child in a particular applied media course without regard to the instructor's opinion. Thus, they suffered no harm. *K.L.A. v. Windham Southeast Supervisory Union*, 371 Fed.Appx. 151 (2d Cir. 2010).

C. Parental Participation

In Doe v. East Lyme Board of Educ., *790 F.3d 440 (2d Cir. 2015), the court held parental participation rights do not include "a right to be physically present throughout the agency's own decisional process." Relying on an IDEA regulation at 34 C.F.R. Part 300.501(b)(3), the court found parental participation does not require parental presence at informal or unscheduled conversations by school staff. So long as a parent has a meaningful opportunity to offer input, be part of an IEP team and participate in any group decision about the educational placement of the child, the parent's IDEA rights are respected.*
In K.A. v. Fulton County School Dist., *this chapter, the Eleventh Circuit found no IDEA provision requiring parental consent to amend an IEP at a team meeting. The court agreed with cases such as* Hjortness v. Neenah Joint School Dist., *507 F.3d 1060 (7th Cir. 2007), which have held that "parents do not have a veto" power over IEP team meetings. In* Drobnicki v. Poway Unified School Dist., *358 Fed.Appx. 788 (9th Cir. 2009), the Ninth Circuit disapproved of a California school district's decision to schedule an IEP meeting without first checking on the parents' availability, even though the parents had a history of not attending meetings and did not return a signed copy of a meeting notice.*

♦   Following a dispute with their school district about their child's placement, California parents pursued their IDEA remedies. After they placed the child in a private school, the school excluded them from an IEP meeting. The dispute reached a federal court, which held the parents were entitled to their private school tuition costs for a full school year. The school district appealed. In a brief memorandum, the U.S. Court of Appeals, Ninth Circuit, held the lower court had properly found the exclusion of the parents from the IEP meeting was an IDEA procedural violation. **IDEA regulations require that parents participate in meetings concerning the formulation of an IEP and the educational placement of a child.** According to the court, an educational agency can make an educational decision without the parents "only if it is unable to obtain their participation, which was not the case here." Proceeding without the parents could not be justified by the scheduling needs of school employees. The attendance of parents at IEP meetings took priority over the attendance of other members. The school district was not faced with a decision about whether to comply with conflicting procedural requirements. In fact, even if the parents had already decided to enroll their child at a private school, their exclusion from the meeting was impermissible. As a result, the court held the parents were entitled to tuition reimbursement. *D.B. v. Santa Monica-Malibu Unified School Dist.*, 606 Fed.Appx. 359 (9th Cir. 2015).

♦   After a student was diagnosed with an autism spectrum disorder, the New York City Department of Education (DOE) agreed to fund his placement at a private center for students with special needs. He made progress there, but the DOE recommended a public school placement for his fourth-grade school year. No representative of the private center attended his committee on special education (CSE) meeting, but a center report was discussed. CSE members discussed the related services indicated on the prior year IEP and no one objected to continuing them. During the meeting, the parent was consulted on a range of topics. The CSE recommended placing the child in a community school classroom with 12 students, a special education teacher and a paraprofessional. A final notice of recommendation indicated he would receive occupational therapy, speech and counseling. But it did not detail the frequency, duration or group size for these services. When the parent toured the school where the IEP was to be implemented, she rejected it as too noisy. Noting the IEP did not include specific recommendations for related services, she re-enrolled her child in the center. In a due process proceeding against the DOE, an impartial hearing officer found the DOE excluded related services recommendations from the IEP. The services were offered without consideration for the child's levels of performance and sufficient parental input.

A federal court later held that **while the absence of any representative from the private center from the CSE meeting was an IDEA violation, it did not impede the parent's participation**. The center's 20-page progress report was considered at the meeting. The parent attended with her attorney and actively participated in the CSE's discussion. **The inadvertent omission of a related services program from the IEP was not as significant as the parent argued.** She was informed of the particular services at the team meeting, and the team relied upon the prior year's related services program as described by the progress report. The court held failure to include the related services in the properly designated space did not render the IEP inadequate, since it was discussed in other areas of the IEP. The parent did not show the DOE's recommended placement was inappropriate. Her single visit to the school site did not prove it was a noisy environment or otherwise inappropriate. Rejecting all of the parent's arguments, the court held for the DOE. *C.K. v. New York City Dep't of Educ.*, No. 14-cv-836 (RJS), 2015 WL 1808602 (S.D.N.Y. 4/9/15).

♦   Parents of a Georgia student with Down syndrome agreed with the IEP devised for her for grade one. An IEP meeting was held to discuss concerns by teachers that the student was being disruptive and having trouble keeping up with the first-grade curriculum. The parties were unable to agree on a proposal to change her program and reassign her to a different school. Over the parents' objection, the school district decided to implement changes to the IEP. The parents requested a hearing to challenge the proposal. They claimed they were not provided prior written notice of their IDEA rights. A hearing officer dismissed the case, and a federal court affirmed the decision.

On appeal, the Eleventh Circuit Court of Appeals found that although parental participation is required by the IDEA, **the IDEA does not explain whether IEP teams have to "act by consensus, majority vote, or otherwise."** In this case, any failure by the school district to provide prior written notice before the team meeting was harmless. As the parents participated in two meetings to discuss the IEP proposal and observed the new school proposed for their child, the court held they fully and effectively participated in the IEP process. Agreeing with the school district, **the court held an IEP team can amend the IEP even if the parents do not consent to the proposal**. IDEA provisions addressing IEP amendment procedures allow a school district to amend an IEP at a team meeting without parental consent. *K.A. v. Fulton County School Dist.*, 741 F.3d 1195 (11th Cir. 2013).

♦   A Virginia student attended a public school autism inclusion program with access to the general curriculum. During her transition to middle school, she was assisted by a 1:1 paraprofessional. But the student had many difficulties during middle school and she had a number of outbursts. At an IEP meeting, the parents and IEP team agreed to a more restrictive setting in an autism spectrum program operated by a public school cooperative education program (CEP). Team members and the parents later agreed that the IEP was not working and that the student should remain in a restricted learning lab until her annual IEP review. But the parents once again declined permission for further observations to facilitate a CEP placement. When the school district filed a notice of proposed action placing the student in a more restrictive CEP setting, the parents rejected it. The district then requested a due process hearing. At the hearing, the parents stated the IEP could not be implemented because it did not identify a specific CEP classroom. A hearing officer upheld the district's IEP.

Later, a federal magistrate judge found the IEP would have provided educational benefits to the student. In fact, the parents' refusal to permit a placement observation prevented the identification of a classroom. **While Congress intended parents to be actively involved in placement decisions, the magistrate noted that "this involvement does not rise to the level of a parental veto."** In this case, the school district had offered the student a free appropriate public education. There was no dispute that the CEP had suitable services and could deliver them in small classes with limited transitions. The parents based their objections to the CEP on the father's belief that it "has the reputation for being a dumping ground." There was "overwhelming and uncontradicted" evidence that the CEP autism spectrum program could meet the student's needs. As the parents were not denied an opportunity to participate in the IEP formulation, and the CEP setting was appropriate, the court adopted the magistrate's recommendation to rule for the school district. *Bobby v. School Board of City of Norfolk*, No. 2:13cv714, 2014 WL 3101927 (E.D. Va. 7/7/14).

♦   A Hawaii student with autism attended a private special education school at the expense of the state education department. After he had been at the school six years, his parent said he was unavailable for an IEP meeting. Another date for a meeting was chosen, but the parent reported he was ill on the day of the meeting. A special education coordinator proposed two other IEP meeting dates. While the parent stated that he might be able to participate, he said he was sick and could not guarantee his attendance. The coordinator said he could participate in an IEP meeting by phone or online, but the parent said he was too sick. As an annual IEP review deadline was nearing, the coordinator decided to proceed with the meeting. Although the parent was absent and no private school representative attended, the IEP team changed the student's placement to a public school workplace readiness program. At a follow-up meeting, the parent rejected the IEP. When no changes were made to the IEP, he requested a due process hearing. A hearing officer held for the education department, as did a federal district court. Appeal then went to the U.S. Court of Appeals, Ninth Circuit. It held **the IDEA required parental participation to assure quality education for disabled students**. Parents represented the best interests of their children and had information that was unavailable from any other source.

School districts have to document their attempts to include parents in IEP meetings. **Parents have to be involved in the IEP process unless they affirmatively refused.** In this case, the parent did not affirmatively refuse to attend a meeting. While the department was frustrated with his unavailability, the court held this did not excuse its obligation to include him in a meeting when he expressed a willingness to participate. A school district cannot avoid its affirmative IDEA duties by blaming parents. There was no merit to the department's claim that it could not accommodate the parent due to the approach of an annual IEP deadline. In ruling for the parent, the court held his attendance took priority over that of other team members. There was no merit to the department's claim that it had to cease providing services to a student whose annual IEP review was overdue. A school faced with conflicting IDEA duties has to decide a reasonable course that promotes IDEA purposes. As the coordinator had improperly prioritized staff schedules, the court held for the parent. *Doug C. v. Hawaii Dep't of Educ.*, 720 F.3d 1038 (9th Cir. 2013).

♦   The parents of a Pennsylvania student became increasingly dissatisfied with his IEP. They removed him from his public school and placed him in a private learning center for children with autism. The student flourished at the center, but midway through the school year the family's home burned down. Two days later, the father died. The mother claimed that the student could not transition back to the public school after the tragedy, and she sought tuition reimbursement. A federal court ruled against her, noting that **the district was not required to devise a new IEP for the student mid-year**. Further, the original IEP offered a free appropriate public education. Thus, the district did not have to pay for the private school placement. On appeal, the Third Circuit held the district had no duty to update the student's IEP after his parents placed him in a private school without notice of intent to re-enroll him in public schools. *D.P. v. Council Rock School Dist.*, 482 Fed.Appx. 669 (3d Cir. 2012).

♦   California parents claimed their district's special education director spoke with a third-party speech provider after an IEP meeting at which no agreement had been reached. They asserted that this was a procedural and substantive violation of the IDEA. The Ninth Circuit disagreed. The conversation did not significantly deprive the parents of meaningful participation in the IEP process. Rather, **it sought a clarification of information about a speech goal on which there had been discussion**. *J.W. v. Governing Board of East Whittier City School Dist.*, 473 Fed.Appx. 531 (9th Cir. 2012).

♦   The parents of an Alaska student with autism challenged his grade-three IEP. The district postponed efforts to update the second-grade IEP until after a final administrative decision was released. Because of the continuing impasse over the IEP, staff relied on the second-grade IEP but provided third-grade materials and lessons. A hearing officer found that the student had regressed in reading, math and several behavioral areas. She awarded the parents tutoring costs for a year. A federal court reversed, noting that the failure to update the IEP was mostly due to the parents' litigious approach. However, the Ninth Circuit reversed the lower court, holding that **the district could not abdicate its responsibilities by blaming the parents**. *Anchorage School Dist. v. M.P.*, 689 F.3d 1047 (9th Cir. 2012).

♦   Two New York students with autism spectrum disorders sought private school tuition. Both students progressed in preschool in 1:1 settings, and both districts offered only 6:1:1 settings once they reached school age. As a result, the parents placed them in the same private school, which offered a 1:1 setting. However, only one student was entitled to tuition reimbursement. That student's IEP was deficient because its annual goals and objectives were based on expected grade level rather than his actual needs and abilities, **whereas with the second student, his parents had been involved in the IEP process and his IEP had been updated annually**. *M.H. v. New York City Dep't of Educ.*, 685 F.3d 217 (2d Cir. 2012).

D. Specific IEP Elements

In Sytsema v. Academy School Dist. No. 20, *558 F.3d 1306 (10th Cir. 2008), the Tenth Circuit Court of Appeals explained that the failure to provide a student his final IEP did not cause substantive harm. It held procedural violations of the IDEA are not by themselves sufficient to prove an IDEA violation. The violation must also result in some lost educational opportunity.*

♦   An Alabama student struggled in elementary school and had to repeat a grade. He was placed in special education in middle school and passed only two classes in grade nine. But the IEP team agreed to his mother's request to place him on a regular diploma track and let him "double up" on his grade nine and 10 classes so he could remain with his peers. Asserting that the school board denied her child a FAPE, the mother filed a due process hearing request. A hearing officer held the school district provided the student a FAPE.

When the case reached the U.S. Court of Appeals, Eleventh Circuit, it found the student's IEP reading goals were not adapted to address his individual needs. His reading skills were assessed at a first-grade level, but the reading goal for the IEP was derived from the state standard for ninth-graders. Moreover, the student's IEP goals remained largely the same from year to year. **The school used "boilerplate IEPs" with goals that did not provide him educational benefits.** The court found another child's name had been printed on a form describing IEP narratives for the student's reading, math and personal management areas. The other name was crossed out and replaced by the student's name three times on the IEP. Postsecondary goals and transition services stated in the IEPs did not meet relevant standards. Finding a lack of individualized planning and a program that denied the student a FAPE, the court held for the parent. *Jefferson County Board of Educ. v. Lolita S.*, 581 Fed.Appx. 760 (11th Cir. 2014).

♦   The parents of a Delaware student with Down syndrome and a severe mental impairment sought compensatory education and private school tuition, asserting that the district did not formulate or implement appropriate IEPs for the student's sixth- and seventh-grade years. An administrative hearing panel agreed that the district denied the student a FAPE, and it awarded compensatory education. The district appealed to a federal court, which reversed. It noted that the **IEP was not defective because of the absence of historical baseline data and stated that there was no strict requirement that an IEP include such data**. The IEP was created with considerable baseline information. *Red Clay Consolidated School Dist. v. T.S.*, 893 F.Supp.2d 643 (D. Del. 2012).

♦   A Texas student had a 142 IQ and above-average math and social studies abilities, but he had poor writing, handwriting and spelling skills. In his senior year, his parents became convinced he could not perform college work. To delay his graduation and preserve his eligibility for school, the student dropped an economics class required for graduation. His parents had him reevaluated and began looking into a Massachusetts private school. Although the school district urged the student to graduate and obtain a waiver of the exit exam if necessary, the student enrolled in the Massachusetts school. A hearing officer held the IEPs had insufficient transitional planning for entry into college and did not address the student's learning disability. A federal court agreed, and the case reached the U.S. Court of Appeals, Fifth Circuit. It held a student's "whole educational experience, and its adaptation to confer 'benefits' on the child, is the ultimate statutory goal" under the IDEA. Using this "holistic perspective," the court held **the school district had customized the student's IEP on the basis of his assessments and his performance**. *Klein Independent School Dist. v. Hovem*, 690 F.3d 390 (5th Cir. 2012).

♦   New Jersey school district officials planned for a disabled student's transition to high school. He had pervasive developmental disorder, ADD and sensory integration difficulty. He was also short in stature. The child study team proposed a mainstream setting with an aide and a "replacement English" class. His parents disagreed with the IEP. In fact, they contracted with a private school before the IEP was even issued. The child study team rejected the private school sought by the parents, and a lawsuit resulted. The Third Circuit ultimately ruled that **the IEP was proper. The student could succeed at the public school with accommodations and modifications** similar to those he received in his prior successful placement. *G.S. v. Cranbury Township Board of Educ.*, 450 Fed.Appx. 197 (3d Cir. 2011).

♦   The parents of a Missouri student with autism challenged two IEPs used during his fourth- and fifth-grade years after becoming dissatisfied with his progress. They sought a private school placement, which the district rejected. A state hearing panel determined that the IEPs were deficient because they lacked baseline data, but a federal court and the Eighth Circuit ruled that **the IDEA does not explicitly require recitation of baseline data**. It only commands that each IEP include a statement of the "present levels of educational performance," which the IEPs in this case included. Also, the IEPs did not have to include specific behavior goals. It was enough that they described the student's disruptive behaviors and included strategies to address them. *Lathrop R-II School Dist. v. Gray*, 611 F.3d 419 (8th Cir. 2010).

E. Predetermination

The IDEA requires placement decisions to take place at IEP meetings. But an IDEA regulation at 34 C.F.R. Part 300.501(b)(3) contemplates that school staff members will conduct "preparatory activities" to develop IEP proposals for eventual discussion at an IEP meeting with the parents.

In Nack v. Orange City School Dist., *454 F.3d 604 (6th Cir. 2006). the Sixth Circuit Court of Appeals held predetermination is not the same as preparation. IEP team members may prepare reports and come to meetings with pre-formed opinions about the best course of action for a student. In* H.B. v. Las Virgenes Unified School Dist., *239 Fed.Appx. 342 (9th Cir. 2007), the Ninth Circuit Court of Appeals stated that "although an educational agency is not required to accede to parents' desired placement, it must remain open about placement decisions and be willing to consider a placement proposed by the parents."*

◆ A New York child attended a public school integrated co-teaching (ICT) kindergarten class. Her parents felt she struggled in kindergarten, and her report card indicated her reading was below grade-level. She returned to an ICT class for grade one. Due to continuing concerns about the child's development and below-grade-level performance, the parents obtained an evaluation from a private learning center, found a private school, and signed an enrollment contract for the next school year. They requested a CSE meeting to consider a full-time special education placement. Relying on the private reports, the parents urged the CSE to approve the private placement they had already made.

After conducting an updated psychological evaluation of the child, the CSE met three times with the parents to consider an IEP for the next school year. At each meeting, the parents urged the CSE to approve the private placement they selected. Although CSE members attended the meetings with a draft IEP, they agreed to some suggestions of the private reports. But the team rejected a private placement. The team then offered a special education class placement. The parents visited the school where the IEP would be implemented and rejected it. After a third CSE meeting, the parents rejected the IEP and requested a hearing. An impartial hearing officer awarded them $46,000 in private school tuition. **A federal court found the parents had attended the CSE meetings and had "ample opportunity to participate in the decision-making process." Disagreement with staff IEP recommendations did not amount to denial of meaningful participation in the decision-making process.** In fact, the IEP cited the private report and incorporated aspects of it. The IDEA allows staff members to prepare for a meeting by developing a proposal. While the parents may have wanted a private education for their child, the court held there was no IDEA entitlement to one. *P.G. v. City School Dist. of New York*, No. 14 Civ. 1207 (KPF), 2015 WL 787008 (S.D.N.Y. 2/25/15).

♦   A Hawaii child attended a private school to address his central processing disorder, anxiety, depression and speech/language issues. The state Department of Education (DOE) paid his tuition for some time, but at the start of the 2010-11 school year he remained at the private school without DOE approval. No placement was agreed upon, and the DOE did not propose a specific placement until January 14, 2011. As late as April 20, 2011, the DOE wrote to the parents that the January placement offer was "the final IEP." The parents kept their child in the private school and requested a due process hearing. A hearing officer found the DOE had predetermined its placement offer. In addition to finding the parents were deprived of meaningful participation in the IEP process, the hearing officer found the placement "ill advised, inappropriate, and potentially disastrous to the student." But tuition reimbursement was denied under a state 180-day limitation period. On appeal, a federal court held the hearing officer's decision was an "agreement" between the DOE and the family that rendered the private school placement "bilateral," and not unilateral. It found the decision to re-enroll the student at the private school was the continuation of a bilateral placement. When the case reached the U.S. Court of Appeals, Ninth Circuit, the DOE conceded that it had violated the IDEA by predetermining the placement.

By waiting so far into the school year to propose a placement, the court found the DOE tacitly consented to enrollment of the student at the private school. The DOE knew he was going to enroll there, and it offered him no other alternative. Had the DOE offered a placement, the court found it might have maintained the position that reimbursement was now time-barred. But the court held the placement was not unilateral, and the 180-day limit did not apply. In addition to affirming the tuition reimbursement award, the court affirmed an award of attorneys' fees to the parents of over $77,000. *Sam K. v. State of Hawaii Dep't of Educ.*, 788 F.3d 1033 (9th Cir. 2015).

♦   A federal court found New Jersey parents who accused their child's IEP team of predetermining his placement did not keep open minds about placing him. An ALJ found the district had predetermined the placement in violation of the IDEA. The school district appealed to a federal court, which found nothing indicated the district had predetermined a placement or denied the parents participation opportunities. It appeared instead that the parents had been inflexible. According to the court, the IEP adequately explained why the student could not be educated in his current setting.

Moreover, the IEP team stated that the student needed a placement where a school-wide behavioral plan could be implemented. The court found the IEP detailed the special education services and supplementary aids that the out-of-district placement would provide him. It found no evidence that the team had impeded the parents' rights or failed to discuss prospective placements. **To the contrary, the evidence showed the school team believed it could not provide a meaningful education for the student and considered several out-of-district alternatives.** But the parents refused to visit any of these programs or discuss an out-of-district setting. The court rejected the parents' remaining arguments and returned the case to the ALJ to reconsider the IEP. *Alloway Township Board of Educ. v. C.Q.*, Civil No. 12-6812 (RMB/AMD), 2014 WL 1050754 (D.N.J. 3/14/14).

◆   A Hawaii student had attended a small private school for students with autism since grade one. Although the private school provided individualized instruction, it did not offer community-based instruction, and it was a segregated setting. The state department of education (DOE) had been paying the student's tuition at the private school since he was a second-grader. Near the midpoint of a school year, the DOE sought to transition the student to a public school. An IEP team proposed changing the placement to his home school. The parents broke off the transition discussions and requested a due process hearing.

A hearings officer held the IEP proposal did not deny the student a FAPE, and the parents appealed to a federal court. On appeal, the parents urged the court to find the IEP had been predetermined. The court rejected the parents' procedural claims, including an assertion that the IEP did not list specific behaviors of concern. Overall, the court found the IEP addressed the student's performance, needs and strengths. The goals and benchmarks were specific, capable of measurement and directly related to his focus areas. In response to concerns that the DOE did not properly consider relevant factors when seeking to change their child's placement, the court found the IEP team had discussed the continuum of available placements. The team was aware of the family's desire for the student to earn a high school diploma, and it sought to keep him on course. **There was no merit to the parents' claim of predetermination, as they had opportunities to address their concerns.** Rejecting their other arguments, the court held for the DOE. *Matthew O. v. Dep't of Educ., State of Hawaii*, Civil No. 12-00612 DKW-RLP, 2014 WL 467288 (D. Haw. 2/5/14).

◆   A Texas student had autism and a mental disability, and she was essentially non-verbal. She used communication methods such as sign language, picture cards and voice communication devices. Her parents disagreed with her ARD committee about assistive technology assessments and methodology. She began borrowing a "DynaVox" voice output device and made significant progress. The parents filed a due process hearing request, and the dispute reached the U.S. Court of Appeals, Fifth Circuit. It found no significant IDEA procedural violations. According to the parents, the principal prematurely ended some ARD meetings, used an improper "voting method" instead of seeking team consensus, and failed to meaningfully consider their input. Although the lower court identified a history of tension between the parents and school staff, the court found the parties had usually worked together cooperatively. The court held the district did not deny FAPE when the meetings occasionally ended early because it promptly scheduled follow-up meetings.

No evidence indicated voting by district staff rather than attempts to reach consensus. As for the argument that staff members made decisions outside the ARD meetings, the court noted that **IDEA regulations contemplate that school staff members will conduct "preparatory activities" to develop IEP proposals for eventual discussion at an IEP meeting**. Numerous ARD meetings were held for the student at which the parents had a chance to contribute. Some of their proposals were incorporated into the IEP. Although the district failed to complete a required evaluation in time for the student's third-grade year, this did not result in a denial of a FAPE. While the IEP may not have maximized the student's potential, there was no IDEA violation. *R.P. v. Alamo Heights Independent School Dist.*, 703 F.3d 801 (5th Cir. 2012).

◆   In the midst of discussions to revise a California student's IEP, the school district notified his parents that a new service provider would replace the one that had served him for four years. In an IDEA proceeding, the parents claimed the district predetermined their child's transition between service providers without their input. An ALJ held the termination of the provider's contract did not constitute predetermination of the IEP. On appeal, a federal court found the parents never explained how the district's action denied their child a FAPE. And **the school district correctly argued that it had the authority to select a service provider.** A recent Ninth Circuit case held moving a student from a private to a public school was not by itself an IDEA violation. **"Predetermination" occurs when a school district makes a decision prior to an IEP meeting and is unwilling to consider other alternatives.** There was no denial of FAPE, as the district action did not indicate it was unwilling to consider parental input. *Z.F. v. Ripon Unified School Dist.*, No. 2:11-CV-02741-KJM-GGH, 2013 WL 127662 (E.D. Cal. 1/9/13).

◆   An Ohio student received Lindamood-Bell reading services in a private learning acceleration center for three years. When the district sought to return him to his home school, his parents requested a hearing. An impasse was reached over his placement and goals for grade seven. In the parents' opinion, IEP team members came to the meeting with a predetermined plan to return the student to his home school. They refused to consent to the placement but agreed to the rest of the IEP. The school district requested a hearing, seeking approval of its IEP. An impartial hearing officer agreed with the district, as did a state review officer. In addition to asserting the team had predetermined a change in reading programs, the parents claimed the district did not identify a specific program to be implemented at the home school. **The court found evidence that school team members did not come to the IEP meeting with open minds.** "Preplanning notes" by staff members indicated an IEP placing the student in his home school would be recommended. A staff member testified that the team was prepared to force the parents into pursuing a hearing. As the court found the district did not engage in a good-faith process to determine a placement in the student's best interest, the IDEA was violated. *P.C. v. Milford Exempted Village Schools*, No. 11-CV-398, 2013 WL 209478 (S.D. Ohio 1/17/13).

◆   Arizona parents rejected a public school IEP offer for their child and placed her in the private school she had attended the previous summer. After a hearing, an ALJ rejected a claim by the parents that the school district had impermissibly predetermined the public school placement. On appeal, a federal court held **placement decisions must be based on an IEP, and parents must be provided with the opportunity to participate in IEP meetings.** In this case, the court held the ALJ's findings supported a conclusion that the parents meaningfully participated in the development of their child's IEP. Since the school staff "maintained an open mind at the IEP meeting and discussed all available programs," the court rejected the predetermination claim. *S.P. v. Scottsdale Unified School Dist. No. 48*, No. 2:12-cv-01193 JWS, 2013 WL 5655527 (D. Ariz. 9/16/13).

◆ For three years, the parents of an autistic student objected to the full-time autistic program placement the district wanted. The district refused to consider a placement with typically developing peers on the grounds that it had already been determined not to be an appropriate program. When the parents sued, claiming the district had predetermined their son's placement, **the district asserted that the mere presence of the parents at IEP meetings was sufficient to avoid a ruling of predetermination**. However, a federal court disagreed. It ordered the district to create a new IEP with the parents' input, but it refused to award monetary damages. On appeal, the Third Circuit found clear evidence that the placement had been predetermined without parental participation or input. It affirmed the decision for the parents. *D.B. and L.B. v. Gloucester Township School Dist.*, 489 Fed.Appx. 564 (3d Cir. 2012).

II. APPROPRIATENESS OF IEP

A. Methodology Questions

In W.R. and K.R. v. Union Beach Board of Educ., *this chapter, the Third Circuit Court of Appeals held parents cannot dictate what methodology will be used for their children. Many courts have refused to intervene in questions of educational methodology, finding this area is best left for educators. But in* Deal v. Hamilton County Dep't of Educ., *258 Fed. Appx. 863 (6th Cir. 2008), the Sixth Circuit held the differences between two methodologies may be so great that the provision of a lesser program amounts to a denial of FAPE.*

◆ A New Jersey child had childhood apraxia of speech and dyspraxia. For over a year, his parents disagreed with the school district's child study team (CST) about his test results, IEP and placement. They said the CST severely underestimated his abilities. A hospital evaluation team recommended placing him in a full day pre-school disabled (PSD) room. The school district suggested a classroom utilizing applied behavioral analysis (ABA). A short-term IEP was agreed upon that allowed the child to attend a PSD classroom for 45 minutes each day. Over the next few months, the parents continued to seek more PSD class time. They said their child was not progressing in the ABA program.

After the school again proposed a full-time ABA program with only 45 minutes in a PSD classroom per day, the parents placed their child in a private school and requested funding for it. An administrative law judge (ALJ) held the district relied too heavily on one assessment, did not tailor a program for the child's disabilities and did not carefully consider recommendations by the parents and their experts. After finding the district did not offer the child an appropriate program, the ALJ approved the school selected by the parents and held they should be reimbursed for their tuition costs. When the case reached a federal court, it found **the ABA classroom limited peer interactions and was not an appropriate setting**. The parents repeatedly told the district that their child was regressing in the ABA class and functioned much better in the PSD class. There was evidence that the IEP was not tailored to meet the child's needs and that the district gave only token consideration to the views of the parents. As a result, the court held for the parents. *T.O. & K.O. v. Summit City Board of Educ.*, Nos. Civ. 2:12-5350, 2:12-6089, 2015 WL 4548780 (D.N.J. 7/27/15).

◆   A New York student did not progress in a private school program and was enrolled in a public school collaborative team teaching (CTT) setting. A committee on special education (CSE) met and proposed changing his program to a 6:1:1 classroom (six students, one teacher and one aide) using TEACCH methodology. This was described as a group teaching method similar to CTT.

The parents rejected the proposal and notified the New York City Department of Education (DOE) that they were making a private placement. An impartial hearing officer held for the parents, and the case eventually reached the U.S. Court of Appeals, Second Circuit. On appeal, the parents mainly argued that both the CTT and TEACCH methodology had been inappropriate and that their child required Applied Behavior Analysis (ABA). But the court held neither the procedural nor the substantive violations claimed by the parents were sufficient to deprive the child of a free appropriate public education. The court noted the DOE witnesses had testified that TEACCH was appropriate for the student. **The court was required to give particular deference to the DOE, as it involved a question of methodology.** There was not enough merit to the parents' other claims to warrant discussion. Since the evidence did not indicate that the student could progress only in a program of ABA, the court held for the DOE. *A.S. v. New York City Dep't of Educ.*, 573 Fed.Appx. 63 (2d Cir. 2014).

◆   A New York student with autism attended a private school for students with neuro-developmental delays. Pursuant to a 2010 impartial hearing decision, the New York City Department of Education (DOE) paid his tuition for the 2009-10 school year. A committee on special education (CSE) then proposed an IEP for 2010-11 that placed the student in a public school classroom of six students, one special education teacher and a paraprofessional (a 6:1:1 classroom). A 1:1 paraprofessional was to be assigned to the student for three months to ease his transition to a public school. The parent rejected the IEP because she felt the proposed TEACCH methodology would be inappropriate. After enrolling the student at the private school, she requested a hearing. An impartial hearing officer (IHO) held the DOE had denied the student a FAPE. But a state review officer held for the DOE, crediting testimony that 1:1 transitional services might be provided beyond the three months specified in the IEP. A federal court upheld the review officer and appeal went before the U.S. Court of Appeals, Second Circuit. According to the court, both the review officer and the district court had improperly relied upon retrospective testimony. At the time of the IEP offer, the parent could not know whether the DOE would provide 1:1 paraprofessional services for more than the three months stated in the IEP.

The court held the DOE could not simply declare that it would reevaluate the student after three months. **This would undermine a core purpose of the IDEA to ensure orderly annual review of each child's needs and to create a comprehensive IEP.** Refusing to take into account the possibility of mid-year amendments to the student's IEP, the court held the IHO's decision was entitled to deference. She issued a well-reasoned opinion in finding the student needed a 1:1 paraprofessional for longer than three months. Since the IEP constituted a denial of FAPE, the court returned the case to the lower court for more review. *Reyes v. New York City Dep't of Educ.*, 760 F.3d 211 (2d Cir. 2014).

♦ New Jersey parents enrolled their two-year-old child in a private autism center where he received 20 hours of weekly ABA therapy. They rejected an IEP offer by his school district. When a similar IEP was offered to the child before the next school year, the parents rejected it and requested a due process hearing. An ALJ held the IEPs for both school years would have offered the child a FAPE. He found the absence of goals and objectives for the initial IEP did not deny him FAPE. The ALJ found the district had offered the child a full-day program based on ABA principles, with additional programs and on-site speech therapy. It was not significant to the ALJ that there was no specification of ABA hours, as this depended on the child's progress. And the district's IEP proposals used various methodologies that were not limited to ABA therapy.

When the case reached a federal court, it noted the child was progressing at the private center with only 17.5 hours of weekly ABA instruction and no home instruction. Like the ALJ, **the court rejected testimony suggesting that any program not devoted to ABA instruction would have been a waste of time.** Evidence indicated the child would have benefitted under the IEP proposals. Although the lack of goals and objectives in the first IEP was an IDEA procedural violation, the court held this defect did not impact substantive rights. A good-faith effort was made to complete an IEP based on his most recent evaluations. Rejecting all the parents' arguments, the court held for the school district. *P.C. v. Harding Township Board of Educ.*, Civ. No. 2:11-06443, 2013 WL 3938969 (D.N.J. 7/31/13).

♦ A Pennsylvania student with a malformation of the brain had learning disabilities, speech impairments and sensory impairments. Her district partially funded a private placement for her in first grade. It then pulled its funding and offered a regular education setting with seven students, two aides and a teacher, along with part-time life skills education. The parents wanted a more rigorous program. When the dispute reached a federal court, it noted that the IEP was reasonably calculated to provide meaningful educational benefits. Further, **the public school IEP was very similar to the one used by the private school.**

The parents appealed to the U.S. Court of Appeals, Third Circuit, arguing the lower court had improperly analyzed the IEP issue by undermining the child's potential. Instead, the court found there had been a proper review of the administrative proceedings. Next, the court held additional evidence which the parents had sought to introduce in trial court proceedings had been properly found irrelevant to determining whether the IEP was adequate. This evidence was cumulative, since it covered what was already presented to the hearing officer during the due process proceeding. No other argument was offered by the parents, and the court held they were only trying to re-litigate issues that had been thoroughly covered by the lower court decision. Last, the court held the discrimination claims were indistinguishable from IDEA claims that had already been dismissed. For this reason, the court affirmed the judgment for the school district. *R.G. v. Downingtown Area School Dist.*, 528 Fed.Appx. 153 (3d Cir. 2013).

♦   A New York City student with autism attended school in a classroom with a ratio of eight students to one teacher and three aides (an 8:1:3 ratio). School officials proposed an IEP with a 6:1:1 student-teacher-aide ratio for the next year. His parents objected and requested a hearing. An impartial hearing officer held for the parents, but a state review officer disagreed. On appeal, a federal court held the IEP did not provide FAPE. The department appealed to the U.S. Court of Appeals, Second Circuit, which held **the IEP was inadequate because it failed to provide the student sufficient 1:1 instruction**. Also of concern was a limitation of speech and language therapy to weekly group sessions, which violated the state regulation in place at the relevant time. There was evidence that the student required just the type of therapy that the IEP excluded. She benefitted from repetition, visual cues and verbal prompts for her speech and language development. As the child study team had access to this information but decided to place the student in group setting, the court held FAPE had been denied. And since the placement found by the parents was appropriate, the court held they were entitled to the full amount of tuition reimbursement they sought. *P.K. and T.K. v. New York City Dep't of Educ.*, 526 Fed.Appx. 135 (2d Cir. 2013).

♦   The mother of a California student rejected an initial IEP that would have placed her daughter in a district school. The parties agreed on a private preschool. Negotiations over an IEP for the next year broke down, and an administrative law judge determined that the district did not predetermine a placement for the student. However, the IEP improperly called for moving the student from special day classes to general education classes in a manner that created too many transitions. The judge awarded $6,100 for the cost of the private preschool. A federal court upheld the award as well as the finding that the district did not predetermine the child's placement. It also ruled that **the mother was not entitled to be paid for personally providing supplemental ABA therapy services to her daughter at home**. On appeal, the Ninth Circuit affirmed the judgment for the parents. Here, the IEP called for a half-day in the large general education classroom. This overly inclusive placement was inappropriate for the student. *Ka.D. v. Nest*, 475 Fed.Appx. 658 (9th Cir. 2012).

♦   A Pennsylvania student had health-related problems. She struggled at the start of her kindergarten year, but a special education evaluation found that she was not eligible because her cognitive ability and academic achievement levels were in the average range. Some time during first grade, an IEP was recommended for her because of learning disabilities, fine motor delays and a language disability. Her parents first rejected but later accepted the district's IEP proposal. However, after researching the district's "Project Read" program, they withdrew her from school and placed her in a private setting. When a lawsuit ensued, the Third Circuit ruled against the parents, finding no denial of FAPE. **The "Project Read" program was research-based, and the parents couldn't decide the educational methodology to be used.** *Ridley School Dist. v. M.R.,* 680 F.3d 260 (3d Cir. 2012).

♦ The parents of a Washington student claimed that their district denied their son a FAPE by allowing a pair of students who had been harassing their son to transfer with him to a different school. They also claimed that his program was improperly changed and that aversive interventions were used in violation of his IEP and state law. However, a federal court and the Ninth Circuit ruled that **district officials were entitled to select the method for implementing his IEP.** And they did not deny the student a FAPE. *B.D. v. Puyallup School Dist.,* 456 Fed.Appx. 644 (9th Cir. 2011).

♦ New Jersey parents challenged their son's IEPs in two consecutive years, claiming that the district deprived them of meaningfully participating in the IEP process by failing to identify the specific reading methodology that would be used. The case reached the Third Circuit, which held **the district had informed the parents of the methodology it would employ, stating in the IEP that it intended to use a multi-sensory reading program,** including Wilson Reading. This was sufficient under the IDEA. Parents cannot dictate the methodology to be used, and the district here engaged in numerous acts of communication with the parents, who maintained significant involvement in the IEP process. *W.R. and K.R. v. Union Beach Board of Educ.,* 414 Fed.Appx. 499 (3d Cir. 2011).

B. Student Progress

The special education process is not guaranteed to produce any particular outcome. Under Board of Educ. v. Rowley, *458 U.S. 176 (1982), an IEP need not assure academic success, but must be reasonably calculated to lead to a meaningful educational benefit. Courts and hearing officers are to evaluate IEPs as of the time they are developed, and not judge them on later progress.*

♦ A parent asked her child's IEP team to refer him to the California School for the Deaf in Riverside (CSDR). Because no representative at the meeting knew about available district resources for the child's needs, a CSDR placement was not discussed. Two "addendum meetings" were held. Although the mother sought more intensive services for her child, the school district offered only to maintain the current placement for grade seven. A school psychologist assessed the child's articulation skills in the 4-7-year-old range. The mother filed a due process action, seeking an order for a CSDR referral. At a meeting to discuss the student's grade-eight IEP, the parent again asked about a CSDR referral. But the team refused to discuss placement because of the pending due process proceeding. An ALJ issued a decision for the school district, and the mother appealed. A federal court found that the student could not read many first-grade words and had progressed less than a year in reading in the past three years. The absence of key school personnel from IEP meetings was a significant IDEA violation, hampering discussion of a CSDR placement.

The court held it was a violation of the mother's rights to tell her that a CSDR placement would be discussed at a later date. **Failure to properly staff IEP meetings violated the IDEA, as did the team's refusal to discuss placement because of a due process request.** The IDEA stay-put provision does not excuse a district from the duty to have a valid IEP in place at the start of each school year. Finding the proposed IEP did not meet the student's needs, the court held the district denied him a free appropriate public education. As a remedy, the district was ordered to refer him to the CSDR. Any placement decision had to be made by a full IEP team. *J.G. v. Baldwin Park Unified School Dist.*, 78 F.Supp.3d 1268 (C.D. Cal. 2015).

◆   A Pennsylvania student with a specific learning disability was at a 3.5 grade level in reading in grade five. An assessment noted his anxiety and depression, and at school he sometimes seemed lonely and sad. When the student was in grade eight, he was involved in a series of incidents at school and on his school bus. His mother said he endured constant bullying and was threatened on the bus. Although school staff did not observe any bullying or difficult peer interactions, the mother removed him from school for homebound instruction.

Soon, the parents notified the district that they were seeking a private placement at district expense. They requested a due process hearing. Prior to the start of the next school year, the district issued a reevaluation report identifying the student as having general anxiety and a disability in mathematics. An IEP team drafted a behavioral intervention plan and an IEP addressing his social-emotional needs. A hearing officer denied any relief to the parents. On appeal, a federal magistrate judge found the student was making progress in reading and receiving a meaningful educational benefit. His teachers had credibly testified about his progress in reading, and changes to his IEP reading goals from year to year bore this out. Although his writing progress was mixed, the magistrate judge found **"mixed results do not equate to a lack of progress."** The parents did not show the student's emotional needs or social issues were not being served. Staff had testified credibly that they saw no bullying or other difficulties when the student interacted with peers. Finding the student was receiving a free appropriate public education, the magistrate recommended judgment for the district. A federal court adopted the recommendation. *N.M. v. Cent. Bucks School Dist.*, 992 F.Supp.2d 452 (E.D. Pa. 2014).

◆   A New York preschool child with autism had delays in social attention, speech and language, motor skills, chewing and eating. An IEP was drafted that placed him in a children's readiness center operated by a board of cooperative education services (BOCES). As the school year progressed, the mother grew concerned about the student's feeding program and began coming to school early to remove him from the school for feeding. The parents eventually advised the BOCES of their intent to place the child in a private school and to seek tuition reimbursement. At the student's annual IEP review, **the team reported that he had progressed on many of his goals, including following his class routines and increasing his time on task**. The BOCES found the student was independently putting a spoon in his mouth 88% of the time and was no longer crying during feedings. After rejecting placement offers by the district, the parents placed their child in a private school and sought reimbursement.

Appeal reached a federal court, which found the child was putting food in his mouth 88% of the time, swallowing his food and staying in his seat 100% of the time at lunch. A home food therapist found he was making progress in using proper bite and chew patterns, and he appeared to be gaining weight. The court held for the BOCES, finding it had offered the child a FAPE. *L.M. v. East Meadow School Dist.*, 11 F.Supp.3d 306 (E.D.N.Y. 2014).

♦ Parents of a New York student with hearing and language disabilities said her school district offered her an IEP using the same "failed programs from previous years." Asserting the IEP did not address their child's individualized special education needs and did not offer her assistive technology allowing her to hear, the parents unilaterally placed her in a private school and filed a due process hearing request. An impartial hearing officer agreed with the parents that the IEP was inadequate. But a state review officer held for the district, as did a federal district court. On appeal, the U.S. Court of Appeals, Second Circuit, found the IEP was reasonably calculated to enable the child to make progress. In doing so, **the court recited longstanding Second Circuit precedent holding that a child's progress is to be viewed in light of the limitations of his or her disability**. While the IEP resembled those from prior years, the court found it enabled her to receive meaningful educational benefits. In addition, the district did not fail to provide the child a FAPE by identifying a different assistive technology model than the one preferred by the parents and their audiologist. As many courts have held, an IEP need not maximize a child's potential. As a result, the court held for the district. *H.C. v. Katonah-Lewisboro Union Free School Dist.*, 528 Fed.Appx. 64 (2d Cir. 2013).

♦ The parents of a New York student became dissatisfied with the education the public school was providing. They placed him in a private school and sought tuition reimbursement. The case reached the Second Circuit, which noted that the student had made progress at the private school but that the district failed to take note of that when it created the IEP for the following year. Because of that, the court ordered the school district to pay private school tuition for the second year. The **failure to consider the student's progress made it likely that the second-year IEP would cause regression or allow only trivial progress**. The parents were also entitled to attorneys' fees and costs. *E.S. and M.S. v. Katonah-Lewisboro School Dist.*, 487 Fed.Appx. 619 (2d Cir. 2012).

♦ A New Hampshire student had a seizure disorder as well as speech and language impairments. Her parents rejected an IEP and enrolled her in a private learning skills academy. They requested a due process hearing. A hearing officer found the parents did not disagree with the stated IEP goals or objectives. He held courts in the First Circuit used a "some educational benefit" standard from cases such as *Lessard v. Wilton Lyndeborough Coop. School Dist.*, this chapter. The hearing officer held "the fact that the student is capable of doing better work, or making more meaningful progress at a private unilateral placement is not something I can consider." On appeal to a federal court, the parents argued the hearing officer had used the wrong standard to assess their claims. But the court found this argument flawed, as they only addressed their child's progress during prior years and said nearly nothing about the IEP. Without addressing the IEP at issue, the parents claimed the case hinged on the hearing officer's erroneous legal analysis. **The court held the parents had to show the IEP proposed for the student would have violated the IDEA by denying her a free appropriate education.** As they did not claim the IEP was not reasonably calculated to enable the child to benefit from her education, the court found no basis for an IDEA violation. *Richards v. Hudson School Dist.*, No. 12-cv-041-LM, 2013 WL 992756 (D.N.H. 3/12/13).

♦   The mother of a New York student rejected an IEP proposal, claiming that it lacked the support and services her child needed. The committee on special education proposed another IEP in the same school the mother had already rejected. At due process, the mother argued that the district violated the IDEA by leaving the "Methods of Measurement" sections of the IEP blank. The school district maintained that the IEP had evaluative mechanisms in place to assess the student, measure his progress and alter his goals and objectives if needed. A federal court issued a decision for the school district. **Each of the 35 short-term objectives in the IEP described a required skill for the student to meet his goals, and 26 of them specified a percentage of required accuracy to meet the goal.** The court noted that the Methods of Measurement sections of the IEP were left blank deliberately to allow for flexibility. *J.A. and S.A. v. New York City Dep't of Educ.*, No. 10 Civ. 9056(DAB), 2012 WL 1075843 (S.D.N.Y. 3/28/12).

♦   The parents of a California student with autism claimed that their child was capable of making more progress than she would make under the IEPs proposed by her school district. They asserted that the district merely recycled her IEP goals from year to year, and they sought 30 hours of weekly intensive applied behavioral analysis (ABA) therapy. The case reached the Ninth Circuit Court of Appeals, which held that **the school district's eclectic educational approach met the IDEA's substantive requirements**. It did not have to provide the intensive ABA therapy the parents preferred. Also, the IEPs themselves demonstrated that the district did not simply recycle her IEP goals. Not every IEP goal has to be achieved every year. The student obtained a meaningful educational benefit from her IEPs. *K.S. v. Fremont Unified School Dist.*, 426 Fed.Appx. 536 (9th Cir. 2011).

♦   A Hawaii student with ADHD attended a private school under a settlement with the state education department. At an IEP meeting for the following year, prior levels of educational placement were updated to include standardized test scores, observations and parent concerns. At the end of the meeting, the student's mother handed the department's care coordinator a copy of the previous year's progress report from the private school. The care coordinator didn't circulate that report among other team members. After placing the student in the private school and rejecting the IEP, the parents sought state funding for the placement, which a federal court awarded. Here, **the failure to include and consider the progress report, which was provided at the very end of the IEP meeting, violated the IDEA**. *Marc M. v. Dep't of Educ.*, 762 F.Supp.2d 1235 (D. Haw. 2011).

◆   A student moved to Texas and was found eligible for special education due to ADHD and a speech impairment, but not for dyslexia. Later, the district agreed that he had dyslexia and provided a reading attainment program. It discontinued that program after one semester and offered the parents two other options. The district then reduced the student's speech therapy based on his speech therapist's recommendation. The parents placed the student in a private school and sought tuition reimbursement, which a federal court denied. It noted that **the procedural violations cited by the parents did not impede any substantive rights under the IDEA** and that the student's academic performance had improved based on standardized tests. *C.H. v. Northwest Independent School Dist.*, 815 F.Supp.2d 977 (E.D. Tex. 2011).

C. Maximizing Potential

Courts have long held the IDEA does not require schools to maximize student potential or offer the best education available. A school district must instead consider a student's potential and educational needs when creating an IEP that is appropriately individualized for the student.

◆   A Maryland child with Down syndrome had a low full-scale IQ. His parents asked the school IEP team to place him at a private school with an Orthodox Jewish curriculum. Instead, the team proposed a public school placement. In response, the parents requested a due process hearing, seeking a placement at their school of choice plus tuition costs. They argued their child could not generalize between his home and school environments. The parents sought an IEP including Hebrew literacy, identification of Kosher symbols and other bicultural and bilingual measures. After four IEP meetings over a seven-month period, a proposal was completed. But the parents rejected it. When the case came before a federal court, it held that before any private school tuition claim could be considered, the parents had to show the school system deprived their child of a free appropriate public education. The court rejected their claim that the school had denied the child an appropriate IEP by not allowing him to access the curriculum while remaining a part of his religious community.

According to the court, the parents did not identify any faults in the IEP or in the ALJ's decision. In the court's view, **an IEP that did not account for a student's "individual religious and cultural needs" could still be appropriate**. There was no IDEA requirement for a personalized curriculum based on a child's cultural and religious needs or the parents' beliefs. Since the failure of the school district to address the child's religious and cultural needs and to place him in an Orthodox school did not deny him a free appropriate public education, the court upheld the decision for the school district. *M.L. v. Starr*, 121 F.Supp.3d 466 (D. Md. 2015).

◆   Within three years of moving into a California school district, parents of a
student with disabilities disputed his IEP. When the case reached the U.S. Court
of Appeals, Ninth Circuit, it explained that an IDEA procedural violation may
deprive a student of a FAPE if it results in loss of educational opportunity,
seriously infringes upon parental participation opportunities or deprives the
student of educational benefits. In this case, the IEP included baseline goals and
sufficient information to measure progress. In the court's view, lack of
specificity in the baselines did not deny the student a FAPE. Moreover, the lack
of a specific IEP section listing accommodations did not result in loss of
educational opportunity. Instead, the IEP team discussed the appropriate
accommodations, as evidenced by meeting notes. Any inadequacy in transition
services did not deny the child a FAPE. Team members listened to service
providers and collaborated with the parents in developing IDEA goals.

The court found the team had an open mind about placement and offered to
place the student in the least restrictive environment in which she could receive
a FAPE. **The district only had to show the IEP offered some educational
benefit; it did not have to maximize benefits to the student.** Noting she had
been in the district less than three years and there had been only one opportunity
to observe her before the IEP meeting, the court held for the district. *C.B. v.
Garden Grove Unified School Dist.*, 575 Fed.Appx. 796 (9th Cir. 2014).

◆   Throughout elementary school, a Rhode Island student continued to
progress in all IEP areas and attained some but not all of his IEP goals. At an
IEP meeting before the start of his seventh-grade year, his mother informed the
team that she was rejecting the IEP and placing him in a private school. She
later sought tuition reimbursement, which a federal court denied. It rejected her
argument that the district had recycled her son's IEP goals. They changed, at
least in part, from year to year. Also, **although the student struggled with
some subjects, he performed well in others**. The IEP did not have to provide
an optimal or ideal level of educational benefit. *James S. v. Town of Lincoln*, No.
CA 11–236 ML, 2012 WL 3645339 (D.R.I. 8/23/12).

◆   A Texas student with emotional disturbance was placed in a behavioral
services class for 25 hours a week. Her mother became dissatisfied with the
placement and challenged it. Appeal reached the Fifth Circuit, which upheld the
placement as appropriate. It held **the IEP was individualized, and was
administered in the least restrictive environment in a coordinated and
collaborative manner by the key "stakeholders." Finally, positive academic
and non-academic benefits were demonstrated.** *Ruffin v. Houston
Independent School Dist.*, 459 Fed.Appx. 358 (5th Cir. 2012).

◆   The parents of a New Jersey preschool student with autism rejected the IEP
offered by their district. The IEP called for a public school ABA program four
and a-half days a week as well as speech therapy, and staff and parent training
sessions. The IEP could be further molded to fit the student's specific needs
upon his enrollment. But the parents placed their son in a private school and
sought tuition reimbursement. A federal court ruled against them. The IDEA
does not require a school district to maximize a student's potential or provide

the best education possible, and **the district properly considered the student's potential and educational needs**. The district's program was extremely flexible in adapting programs for preschool students who were receiving their first educational services. *G.B. v. Bridgewater-Raritan Regional Board of Educ.*, No. 07-4300 (JJH), 2009 WL 512122 (D.N.J. 2/27/09).

D. Transfer Students

In a California case, the Ninth Circuit recognized that school districts need not replicate a program created by a previous district for a transfer student. An interim placement created by a student's current school district was her stay-put placement and did not have to be identical to the IEP drafted by her former school district. Termine ex rel. Termine v. William S. Hart Union High School Dist., *90 Fed.Appx. 200 (9th Cir. 2004).*

◆   A Maryland child with autism was placed in a multiple intensive needs classroom. An IEP team proposed another school believed to be similar to his present setting. But the transfer school did not have a 12-month session, and the parents objected to it. A school district autism specialist said the transfer school could provide a "bridging" period of five weeks for the summer. The parents filed a due process hearing request. After a hearing, an administrative law judge (ALJ) held for the school district. The parents then appealed to a federal court, which noted the transfer school had an 11-month program with five weeks of summer services. Moreover, the district's autism specialist had said that all the IEP components were in place at the transfer school, including staff training in autism methodology. One of the parents' witnesses had only observed the child for an hour and could not testify about the ability of the school to implement his IEP. Another had been found to lack necessary experience and firsthand knowledge of the child's unique circumstances. By contrast, school witnesses had worked with the child and were able to testify about the school's ability to implement his IEP. Moreover, **the ALJ found the transfer school could equal the program at the student's current school through "bridging services."**
    In the court's opinion, the ALJ had carefully weighed the credibility and persuasiveness of all the witnesses. She had found them more credible because of their testimony and not "simply because of who they were." Although the parents complained that the ALJ had improperly relied on retrospective testimony about the IEP, the court held the testimony was relevant regarding whether the district could sufficiently implement the IEP. This was not improper "retrospective testimony." Rejecting the parents' other arguments, the court affirmed the judgment for the school district. *S.T. v. Howard County Public School System*, Civ. No. JFM-14-00701, 2015 WL 72233 (D. Md. 1/5/15).

◆   A California student had high grades and participated in the Model United Nations and a forensics class at Antioch High School. After experiencing cold-like symptoms, she was hospitalized and later diagnosed with multiple sclerosis. After missing over two months of school, the student returned but had difficulty due to fatigue, pain, and decreased strength, stamina and stability. She was provided a Section 504 plan with accommodations but had to drop out of

Model United Nations and forensics. Her grade average dropped. The student withdrew from school and later enrolled in the Pittsburg School District. She and her mother met with Pittsburg staff members to discuss a Section 504 plan and possible IDEA eligibility. A school counselor said the student was not IEP-eligible and explained that her Section 504 plan would stay in place. The student missed 58 days of school for the year and had to be hospitalized twice. Her parent filed a due process hearing request against both the Antioch and Pittsburg School Districts for failing to find her IDEA eligible. An administrative law judge (ALJ) held for the school districts. On appeal, a federal court agreed with the ALJ that the Antioch School District did not violate its child find duty. But it held the Pittsburg School District should have treated the mother's initial question regarding eligibility for an IEP as a request for an IDEA assessment. In the court's view, Pittsburg should also have noted the student's long "downward slide" in academic performance, despite having a Section 504 plan.

Pittsburg's failure to conduct an IDEA assessment significantly impeded the parent's participation in the decision-making process and deprived the student of educational benefits. **A school district is not permitted to delay an assessment of a student with a suspected disability because it is using a general education intervention.** Finding Section 504 accommodations were not enough to meet the student's needs, the court held Pittsburg violated its child find duty under the IDEA. *Simmons v. Pittsburg Unified School Dist.*, No. 4:13-cv-04446-KAW, 2014 WL 2738214 (N.D. Cal. 6/11/14).

◆   A New Jersey student attended a charter school for seven years. The school was responsible for creating his IEP, while his district of residence bore the financial duty to implement it. When the student reached sixth grade, the charter school advised his parent that it could no longer meet his needs. The school then developed an IEP that proposed a private school for students with disabilities located outside his school district of residence. As the district would have had the duty to fund such a placement, it challenged the IEP under New Jersey law.

A state ALJ held the school district's IEP proposal was appropriate and that the private school suggested by the charter school was overly restrictive. In appealing the adverse result, the parent was joined by the charter school. A federal court found no conflict between the IDEA and a state law. Appeal reached the U.S. Court of Appeals, Third Circuit. It agreed with the district that IDEA procedural safeguards were not implicated in the case. Instead, the case involved a resident school district that was not responsible for developing a child's IEP. Agreeing with the district, **the court held the IEP would provide the student FAPE in the least restrictive setting.** *L.Y. v. Bayonne Board of Educ.*, 542 Fed.Appx. 139 (3d Cir. 2013).

◆   A student with multiple disabilities was home-educated through the California Virtual Academy under an IEP that the parents agreed to for one year. However, they rejected the IEP for the following year and eventually agreed to an IEP that would place the student in a third-grade classroom with appropriate supports. Since the academy had no general education classrooms, the student was enrolled in a district school, but the district failed to implement the IEP within 30 days because of insufficient time to evaluate the student. IEP meetings were then scheduled and rescheduled, and the parents sued the district. Their son died during the case, but the Ninth Circuit held **the IDEA does not require a district to implement a transfer student's IEP within 30 days** if the IEP was never implemented by the sending district. *A.M. v. Monrovia Unified School Dist.*, 627 F.3d 773 (9th Cir. 2010).

♦ A family moved to Montana from New Jersey after a doctor determined that the son's performance had an autistic component, and after an IEP was crafted providing the student with speech/language therapy. **The IEP team at his new school refused to consider the New Jersey doctor's evaluation** and reduced the student's speech/language therapy. After two months, the IEP team referred the student to a child development center for free autism testing. Five months later, a report came back confirming that his behavior was consistent with autism spectrum disorder. By that time the school year was almost over. The IEP team met to develop an IEP for the next year and determined that the student did not need extended school year services. The parents brought a challenge that reached the Ninth Circuit. The court of appeals held that the referral of the student to the child development center did not comply with the IDEA. The district failed to meet its obligation to evaluate the student. *N.B. and C.B. v. Hellgate Elementary School Dist.*, 541 F.3d 1202 (9th Cir. 2008).

♦ An Alabama student with diabetes and ADHD had an unacceptable attendance level at school. He sought to transfer to another school, but his request was denied. His parents then sued under the ADA and Section 504, seeking a preliminary order that would permit him to transfer to the new school. A federal court refused to grant the order, and the Eleventh Circuit affirmed. Here, **the student failed to show that he would be irreparably harmed by not being allowed to immediately transfer to the new school**. He would continue to receive educational services at his neighborhood school while the case was pending. *C.B. v. Board of School Commissioners of Mobile County, Alabama*, 261 Fed.Appx. 192 (11th Cir. 2008).

E. Particular Schools

In J.W. and L.W. v. New York City Dep't of Educ., *No. 13-CV-6905 (JPO), 2015 WL 1399842 (S.D.N.Y. 3/27/15), a federal court held New York parents were not entitled to reject a placement without "engaging in a conversation" with school officials about the school where their child's IEP was to be implemented. The court found the parents' action in rejecting the IEP with no discussion suggested they sought a "veto" over school choice, rather than "input." As the Second Circuit held in* T.Y. v. New York City Dep't of Educ., *584 F.3d 412 (2d Cir. 2009), the IDEA does not provide for parental veto power.*

♦ A New York student attended a private school in a classroom with eight students, one teacher and three paraprofessionals (known as an 8:1:3 setting). At an IEP meeting, the child's committee on special education proposed a 6:1:1 setting made up of six students, one teacher and a paraprofessional. The parents objected, noting this would reduce the overall student-to-adult ratio. In response, the IEP was amended to provide a full-time paraprofessional to help the student's transition to a public school. This maintained the 2:1 student-to-adult ratio sought by the parents. They filed a due process challenge against the New York City Department of Education (DOE). After appearing before two levels of administrative review and a trial court, the case reached the U.S. Court of Appeals, Second Circuit. According to the parents, school officials denied them meaningful participation in selecting the site where the IEP would be implemented. And they said the IEP lacked provisions for parent counseling.

The court recited federal court authority declaring that schools need only provide a basic floor of opportunity for each child with a disability. Any flaws in the IEP process did not impede the child's right to a free appropriate public education or deprive him of educational benefits. Nor was there a significant infringement upon the parents' participation. **The court held parents were not assured a role in selecting the "bricks and mortar of the specific school."** While the IEP did not specify parent counseling and training, the court held they were assured of receiving it by virtue of a state regulation. In addition, the DOE offered to maintain the 2:1 student-to-adult classroom ratio the parents sought. **The court held it was only speculation that the school to which the child was assigned could not have implemented the IEP.** Since speculation was not an appropriate basis for a parental challenge, the court held for the DOE. *R.B. v. New York City Dep't of Educ.*, 603 Fed.Appx. 36 (2d Cir. 2015).

♦ New York parents challenged the school selected for their child by the New York City Department of Education (DOE). Without designating a school site, the DOE proposed a 12-month program for the child in a 6:1:1 classroom (six students, a teacher and a paraprofessional). Later, the DOE identified a public school assignment for the student. After visiting the school proposed by the DOE, the parents decided it would not meet their son's needs. They advised the DOE that their child would attend a private school, then requested a hearing.

An impartial hearing officer (IHO) held for the DOE. A state review officer upheld the IHO's decision, and the parents appealed. A federal court held the review officer's decision reflected a comprehensive review of the record. Although the parents said no IEP was provided to them until two weeks before the school year, the court held they timely received a copy of the IEP. **State and federal regulations only required that "an IEP must be in effect for the student at the beginning of the school year."** The court found the parents attended the relevant CSE meeting. It appeared to the court that any procedural violation did not harm the child. Evidence indicated the IEP appropriately described his present levels of performance and that they had been discussed at the CSE meeting. Finally, the court held the IHO and review officer had appropriately declined to consider the challenge to the DOE's selection of a school. As the hearing and review officers reached correct results, the court held for the DOE. *B.P. v. New York City Dep't of Educ.*, No. 14 Civ. 1822 (LGS), 2014 WL 6808130 (S.D.N.Y. 12/3/14).

♦ A New York student with autism attended public school special education programs from kindergarten through junior high school. His parent enrolled him in a private school, which the city school department funded for two school years. A committee on special education (CSE) proposed a public school IEP for the student but did not identify the school he would attend. A final notice of recommendation (FNR) from the CSE called for a 12-month program in a specialized school with counseling and weekly therapy sessions. The IEP called for placing the student in a 12:1:1 classroom (a setting with a ratio of 12 students to one teacher and a paraprofessional). By the time a FNR was sent to the parent, she had already signed an enrollment contract with a private school.

The parent tried to visit the school designated in the FNR three times. On the third visit to the school, the assistant principal said the student would attend a 6:1:1 classroom. As no 12:1:1 placement was available at the school, the parent sought a hearing. An impartial hearing officer agreed with the parent that the DOE had denied the student a FAPE. A state review officer reversed the decision, and the parent appealed. A federal court held the CSE had based the IEP on sufficient evaluative data. But the court held the DOE's failure to offer a 12:1:1 classroom and the school's inability to provide adequate speech instruction services violated the IDEA. The DOE repeatedly failed to respond to the parent's concerns, and the court held the student was entitled to tuition reimbursement. **As the parent was never shown a 12:1:1 classroom, the court held the DOE did not show it could implement the IEP.** *Scott v. New York City Dep't of Educ.*, 6 F.Supp.3d 424 (S.D.N.Y. 2014).

♦ An Arizona student had Autism Spectrum Disorder and had high to average cognitive abilities and language skills. At an IEP meeting, team members found the student needed "a special school level of services." But no location for IEP services was stated at the meeting. Without the parent's knowledge and with no discussion at the IEP meeting, a district management team selected a school for the student. After learning of this, the parent requested a hearing and notified the school district of her intent to place her child in a private school.

An ALJ held the school selected by the district did not meet the child's needs. It was also found the district violated IDEA procedures by placing him through a management team and without including either the parent or the IEP team in the decision. As the private school selected by the parent was appropriate, the district was ordered to reimburse her for her tuition costs. On appeal, a federal court agreed with the ALJ that the school district's plan to place the student with lower-functioning children would not benefit him. But unlike the ALJ, the court found the selection of a school site was an "administrative decision." It found **"educational placement" refers to classes and services, not a specific building. In fact, the IDEA does not require that the IEP specify a school location**. Since the parent had fully participated in the IEP process, the court found the district had authority to choose a school site without her participation. But the court held the school district had committed a substantive IDEA violation by attempting to place the child with lower-functioning students. It upheld the award of tuition reimbursement. *Deer Valley Unified School Dist. v. L.P.*, 942 F.Supp.2d 880 (D. Ariz. 2013).

♦ A New York student had motor apraxia and other disabilities. When he was 12, his CSE recommended placing him in a class of six students with a teacher and paraprofessional, and a one-on-one crisis management paraprofessional for transitions. After receiving the district's final recommendation, the parents unilaterally enrolled their child in a private school. They requested an impartial hearing and sought tuition reimbursement. Among the claims was the determination that the size of the school would overwhelm the child. The parents further claimed there was no music teacher or therapist at the school and that paraprofessional support was insufficient. An IHO and a state review officer held for the school system. A federal court found the parents had fully participated in the IEP process. Contrary to their claims, the district's evaluations were sufficient for the CSE to develop an appropriate IEP.

The parents did not identify any procedural violations that caused harm. Moreover, the substantive provisions of the IEP were found appropriate. There was no merit to a claim that the classroom proposed for the child lacked appropriate staff to offer differentiated instruction. **The appropriate inquiry was into the nature of the program offered in the IEP.** Students in the class received 1:1 attention about 50% of the time, and the student would have had a 1:1 paraprofessional. **"Placement" refers only to the general type of program and not to a specific location or classroom.** *N.K. v. New York City Dep't of Educ.*, 961 F.Supp.2d 577 (S.D.N.Y. 2013).

♦   Chicago parents signed an IEP calling for a half-day preschool placement for their daughter. The IEP did not identify a particular school for her to attend. The parents then challenged the placement, asserting that the IEP should have included the location of a particular school and that it should have called for a full-day placement. A federal court held **the failure to identify a particular school in the IEP did not violate the IDEA**. As the parents never challenged the half-day placement at IEP meetings, they could not now do so. *Brad K. v. Board of Educ. of City of Chicago*, 787 F.Supp.2d 734 (N.D. Ill. 2011).

III. IMPLEMENTATION OF IEPS

A. Generally

In D.D. v. New York City Board of Educ., *465 F.3d 503 (2d Cir. 2006), the Second Circuit Court of Appeals held IEPs must be implemented as soon as possible after being developed. The IDEA does not require immediate implementation. But IDEA regulations specify that there can be no undue delay.*

Many courts have refused to hold school districts to a standard of perfection when assessing the implementation of an IEP. Courts have rejected parental demands to assign particular staff members to work with students.

♦   Through his sophomore year in high school, an Illinois student earned As and Bs in honors classes with accommodations. He said some teachers stopped giving him study guides and extra time, claiming it was wrong to provide such assistance in advanced classes. Teachers also said extra time hurt him, and they pressured him to drop advanced placement and honors classes, claiming they would be too difficult for him. The student said that without accommodations, he started to fail advanced placement and honors classes. He refused to drop them and said teachers did not record his good grades, lowered some scores and ignored his questions about assignments. During the student's junior year, his parents withheld their consent for a mandatory triennial evaluation. The school district filed a due process complaint to overrule the need for parental consent.

Later, the student responded with a complaint alleging denial of educational services, discrimination and retaliation. By the time a hearing officer dismissed the complaint, the student was 19 years old and in college. A federal court held the parents lacked standing to file suit. After the lower court closed the case, the U.S. Court of Appeals, Seventh Circuit, found enough detail in the complaint to put the district on notice of a claim based on denial of a free appropriate public education. The student asserted his high school had denied him study guides and extra time to complete tests and homework as required in his IEP. The court reversed the dismissal of the student's IDEA-based educational claim. It was error for the lower court to dismiss federal disability discrimination claims. **The student said teachers tried to push him out of classes, refused to comply with his IEP and required him to work on group projects despite a disability that prevented him from working with peers.** While he did not allege a valid claim for retaliation, the court found the parents could proceed with theirs. Since the IDEA guarantees certain rights to parents that were implicated here, the court held they could proceed with claims under the IDEA, ADA and Section 504. In future activity before the lower court, the court held the parents might be able to seek recourse under 42 U.S.C. § 1983. The case was returned to the lower court for further activity. *Stanek v. St. Charles Community Unit School Dist. #303,* 783 F.3d 634 (7th Cir. 2015).

♦   A Second Circuit decision denied a claim by New York parents for private school tuition reimbursement based on the school site selected for their child by the New York City Department of Education (DOE). The court found it was speculative to find a school with the capacity to implement an IEP would simply fail to adhere to the IEP. On the other hand, it would not be speculative to find an IEP could not be implemented at a school lacking appropriate services required by the IEP. In this case, the court held the parents were not challenging the proposed school site, but were attacking the IEP itself. For example, they said the school and teacher-student ratio were too large, and that the school's language-based program was inappropriate. The mother had based her arguments on speculation that her child would simply "shut down" at the proposed school site. **The court held the DOE was not required to provide evidence regarding the school site's adequacy.** Like a lower court and state review officer, the court denied the request for tuition reimbursement. *M.O. and G.O. v. New York City Dep't of Educ.,* 793 F.3d 236 (2d Cir. 2015).

♦   A Hawaii student received special education as a child with an other health disability. He had stomach issues, allergies, asthma, febrile seizures, arthritis and behavior problems. Until the student reached grade four, he was homeschooled. During that school year, the parents briefly placed him in a charter school. After the student attended a public elementary school for grade five, the parents placed him in a new charter school that was in the process of "getting organized." Significantly, the school did not obtain a copy of the student's IEP until a week or two into the school year. Near this time, the parents became convinced that the charter school could not serve their child. They briefly enrolled him in a private school before returning him to a homeschool program. When the Hawaii Department of Education (DOE) denied the parents' request for private school tuition reimbursement, they filed an IDEA proceeding. A hearing officer held the DOE did not fail to implement the IEP and did not deny the child a free appropriate public education (FAPE).

Before a federal court, the parents argued the DOE should have classified their child as having autism. But the court noted the DOE was unaware of any autism diagnosis when the IEP team met. In any event, the court found no evidence that the child's IEP would have been different had he qualified under the category of autism. There was no evidence that a difference in category would have yielded different programs or services in the IEP. **Ninth Circuit cases held any claim based on failure to implement an IEP must show a "material failure to implement an IEP" to prove an IDEA violation.** In this case, the court held any failure to implement the IEP was not "material" and therefore did not implicate a possible denial of FAPE. Although the parents made much of the failure of the charter school to have an IEP by their child's first day of school, the court found this fact alone did not prove a denial of FAPE. Evidence indicated the school had a copy of the IEP by the second week of the school year and that the staff members were familiar with it. The court found the DOE was not in violation of the IDEA for failing to implement the IEP. Evidence showed the school promptly responded to the mother's bullying concerns. Rejecting the remaining arguments of the parents, the court affirmed the hearing officer's decision for the DOE. *Tyler J. v. Dep't of Educ., State of Hawaii*, Civ. No. 14-00121 DKW-KSC, 2015 WL 793013 (D. Haw. 2/24/15).

In *Z.R. v. Oak Park Unified School Dist.*, 622 Fed.Appx. 630 (9th Cir. 2015), this chapter, the Ninth Circuit found California school administrators credibly testified that the high school in which a student's IEP would be implemented had the resources to provide the program described in his IEP. **Arguments by the family that the school district could not have implemented the IEP at the designated school were premature and unsupported.** There was also no error in placing the student in a general education setting, which complied with the IDEA's statutory preference for placing students with disabilities with their non-disabled peers.

♦ A California student exhibited autism-like behaviors and attended a special day class. Before a meeting to discuss an IEP for the next year, the parents sent the district a set of proposed goals for their child along with an independent assessment. Although the district distributed the proposed IEP goals to the team, it did not circulate the assessment. The omission was discovered during the meeting and briefly discussed. But no placement offer was made prior to adjournment. Believing the failure to consider the assessment showed "the district was not interested in parental input," the father requested a due process hearing. He took the position that the IDEA's stay-put provision prevented further consideration of the IEP offer. Six weeks later, the district finalized an IEP for the next school year. It did not convene an IEP meeting, instead sending the parents a letter that it had finalized the IEP. In the following weeks, the child had seizures and the family obtained a doctor's letter. The parties agreed to an "amended IEP" that increased the level of services for the child. But the district had difficulty implementing the amended IEP, due to staff scheduling conflicts.

After a due process hearing, an ALJ found the district predetermined parts of the IEP and did not materially implement it. She awarded the child more than 500 hours of compensatory education services. On appeal, a federal court held the IEP was not predetermined. The IEP offer showed the district was willing to consider parental input and hold another meeting. The team reviewed the child's private assessment. If parents refused to attend a meeting or were unresponsive, the school district had a duty to move forward with the IEP process. Nothing compelled a district to conduct a follow-up IEP meeting if it knew parents would not attend. The court found the parents stopped cooperating after being offered a revised IEP. **But the court agreed with the parents that the finalized IEP was not implemented in large part due to the scheduling conflicts of district staff.** As the ALJ found, the school district failed to implement the IEP. Further proceedings were needed to determine an appropriate remedy for failure to provide IEP services. *Cupertino Union School Dist. v. K.A.*, No. 13-cv-04659-BLF, 2014 WL 6790182 (N.D. Cal. 12/2/14).

♦   A Wisconsin student with a moderate cognitive disability attended multi-categorical classes with students who had various types of disabilities. A district IEP team noted she performed at a first-grade level in math and a second-grade level in reading and language arts. An IEP drafted for the student's ninth-grade year sought to decrease her inappropriate behaviors from 60% of the time to 40%. Based on her eighth-grade record, the team doubted she would succeed in a grade-nine multi-categorical classroom. Despite these findings, team members acquiesced to a strong parental preference to keep the child in multi-categorical classes where she would stay on a diploma track. But in grade nine, the student had poor grades and often refused to participate in class. Her IEP team prepared a behavioral intervention plan (BIP) to address her lack of participation. Despite the modifications, the student's performance did not improve. When the IEP team proposed a self-contained class for students with cognitive disabilities, the parents requested a due process hearing. They charged the district with improperly implementing the IEP. An ALJ found the parents did not show the IEP was inappropriate or had been improperly implemented.

Appeal reached the U.S. Court of Appeals, Seventh Circuit, which found the IDEA has no substantive requirements for BIPs. The parents identified only poor grades as evidence that teachers did not properly implement the IEP. **Poor grades did not show teachers had failed to make a good-faith effort to help the student meet her IEP goals.** The court held the record did not show better work by teachers would have led to higher grades. Rejecting the parents' other arguments, the court held for the district. *D.W. v. Milwaukee Public Schools*, 526 Fed.Appx. 672 (Table) (7th Cir. 2013).

♦   A South Carolina student with moderate to severe autism was nonverbal and very sensitive to noise. His IEP called for 15 weekly hours of ABA therapy, but the district provided only 7.5 to 10 hours a week. His parents briefly removed him from school. When he returned, his new lead teacher was not trained in ABA therapy, though she had experience and a child of her own with autism. Eventually the parents hired an experienced ABA therapist to provide services in the home. They sought reimbursement, which the district fought. The case reached the Fourth Circuit, which ruled for the parents. **The evidence indicated the lead teacher and her aides didn't understand or use ABA techniques,** and the district failed to provide the 15 hours called for by the IEP. *Sumter County School Dist. 17 v. Heffernan,* 642 F.3d 478 (4th Cir. 2011).

♦   A Pennsylvania student with speech and language impairments progressed through her fifth-grade year with the district offering articulation therapy, but she had problems in sixth grade meeting her IEP goals. Her parents placed her in a private residential school for grades seven and eight and then sought tuition reimbursement. A hearing officer upheld the IEP offered to the student for grade eight and dismissed the IEP challenge for seventh grade as untimely. A panel then found that the IEP, though far from optimal, was not fatally inadequate. A federal court and the Third Circuit agreed. **The parents failed to show that more testing was needed prior to drafting the eighth-grade IEP.** *R.R. v. Manheim Township School Dist.,* 412 Fed.Appx. 544 (3d Cir. 2011).

♦   The parents of a Texas student with autism claimed their school district did not properly implement the IEP or offer him the least restrictive environment. A hearing officer agreed with them, noting that not all the minutes of general and special education were always provided – nor was paraprofessional support always provided. The district appealed, and a federal court held that it did not violate the IDEA by having the student leave special education classes 10 to 15 minutes before they ended. Also, he was rarely without the assistance of a paraprofessional, and the IEP did not require that the district provide one at lunch, during recess or on the bus. **The small deviations from the IEP did not violate the IDEA.** *Corpus Christi Independent School Dist. v. C.C.,* Civil Case No. 2:11–cv–00224, 2012 WL 2064846 (S.D. Tex. 6/7/12).

♦   After a due process hearing, an IEP was created for an Illinois student authorizing a summer program and therapeutic day school placement as well as compensatory education services. Within weeks, the parents filed a new due process request, asserting the district had failed to implement the IEP within 10 days as specified by Illinois regulations. A hearing officer ruled for the parents. A federal court affirmed the judgment, finding no distinction between compensatory services and other services. **The law required implementing an IEP within 10 days of notice.** *Board of Educ. of City of Chicago v. Illinois State Board of Educ.,* 741 F.Supp.2d 920 (N.D. Ill. 2010).

♦   The parents of a Massachusetts student missed five IEP meetings scheduled by the district. They instead sought to hold two "emergency" IEP meetings, to which the district refused to agree. After placing their son in a private school, the parents requested due process, asserting that the district had failed to have an IEP in place at the start of the school year. A hearing officer and a federal court noted that **the delay was due primarily to the parents' failure to attend**

scheduled IEP meetings. While there were some recordkeeping lapses by the district, the student continued to receive an adequate IEP while in the district. The court denied tuition reimbursement to the parents. *Doe v. Hampden-Wilbraham Regional School Dist.*, 715 F.Supp.2d 185 (D. Mass. 2010).

♦ The mother of a Maine student challenged her daughter's 2007-08 placement decision after previously filing a complaint about the 2006-07 school year. A hearing officer ruled that the 2007-08 placement was appropriate even though the district did not have an IEP in place at the start of the year. The hearing officer then ruled that the 2006-07 placement denied the student a free appropriate public education. On appeal, a federal court held that the 2007-08 placement violated the IDEA because **the district failed to have an IEP in place at the start of the year**. The court also stated that the hearing officer had the power to expand the hearing to include the 2006-07 school year. However, the hearing officer had improperly held that the 2006-07 placement violated the IDEA. *Millay v. Surry School Dep't*, 707 F.Supp.2d 56 (D. Me. 2010).

♦ A New York school department's committee on special education developed an IEP for a student with autism. The IEP stated that the student would attend school in District 75 (a group of schools for students with disabilities) but did not specify which school he would attend. Instead, a citywide placement officer would make that determination. The student's parents objected to the school that was eventually proposed, but rather than visit a second school, they enrolled their son in a private school. When they sought tuition reimbursement, a federal court and the Second Circuit ruled against them. **The IDEA does not require a school district to name the particular location for receiving special education services.** *T.Y. v. New York City Dep't of Educ.*, 584 F.3d 412 (2d Cir. 2009).

B. Bullying and FAPE

The U.S. Department of Education has explained that a school district has an obligation to address serious student-on-student bullying and respond to reasonable requests by parents about student special education programs. An August 20, 2013 "Dear Colleague" letter by the Department's Office of Special Education and Rehabilitative Services (OSERS) has an overview of school responsibilities under the IDEA to address bullying of disabled students.

The letter states that the bullying of disabled students may signal the need for an IEP meeting, and may implicate the IDEA child find duty. See http://www2.ed.gov/policy/speced/guid/idea/memosdcltrs/index.html. Also at this address is "Effective Evidence-based Practices for Preventing and Addressing Bullying." An October 21, 2014 "Letter to Colleague" from the U.S. Department of Education's Office for Civil Rights (OCR) declares that bullying of students with disabilities may result in a finding of disability-based harassment or a denial of a free appropriate public education under Section 504. See http://www2.ed.gov/about/offices/list/ocr/letters/colleague-bullying-201410.pdf. The letter documents a growing number of bullying complaints by students with disabilities, which now makes up over half of the OCR's caseload.

In Shore Regional High School Board of Educ. v. P.S., *381 F.3d 194 (3d Cir. 2004), the court held a New Jersey school denied a FAPE to a student by failing to offer an environment sufficiently free from harassment. The court upheld a hearing officer's decision to reimburse the parents for tuition costs.*

◆   New York parents said their third-grade daughter was subjected to bullying almost every day and that staff members did not confront bullies. Classmates pushed and tripped her, laughed at her and called her "ugly," "stupid" and "fat." When the parents sought to raise the issue of bullying with the IEP team (called a committee on special education or CSE in New York), they said the principal "flatly refused to discuss the issue with them." The parents said team members told them bullying was "an inappropriate topic to consider" during an IEP meeting. They located a private school for students with learning disabilities and placed her there. The parents then filed a due process action against the department to obtain private school tuition reimbursement. An impartial hearing officer (IHO) held for the department and a review officer affirmed the decision.

A federal court held for the parents, finding that significant, unremedied bullying may deny a free appropriate public education (FAPE). After the case was returned to administrative levels, the IHO and review officer again held for the DOE. The trial court again held for the parents, and the case later reached the Second Circuit. On appeal, the court found the DOE denied the student a FAPE by refusing to discuss bullying with her parents, despite their reasonable concerns. Three staff members confirmed that the student was constantly teased, excluded from groups and subjected to a hostile environment. **Since the DOE's persistent refusal to discuss bullying at important times in the IEP process significantly impeded the parents' participation rights, the court found a procedural denial of FAPE.** While the DOE raised several objections to the private school selected by the parents, the court found it appropriate for the student. She was making progress "across the board" there, both academically and behaviorally. Finding the balance of equities favored the parents, the court upheld the award of private school tuition reimbursement. *T.K. and S.K. v. New York City Dep't of Educ.*, 810 F.3d 869 (2d Cir. 2016).

◆   The mother of a Pennsylvania student with a specific learning disability said he was enduring constant bullying at school and on the bus. Although school staff did not observe bullying or difficult peer interactions, she removed him from school and began homebound instruction. Soon, the parents notified the district that they were seeking a private placement for their son at the district's expense. They requested a due process hearing. A hearing officer then denied the parents' request for compensatory education and tuition reimbursement. The parents appealed to a federal district court. The case was assigned to a magistrate judge, who found evidence that the student was progressing in reading. Although his writing progress was mixed, the magistrate judge found "mixed results do not equate to a lack of progress." The parents failed to show the student's emotional needs or social issues were not being served. **School staff had testified credibly that they saw no bullying or other difficulties when the student interacted with peers.** Evidence indicated the district was trying to create an atmosphere in which the student could learn.

Finding he was receiving a free appropriate public education, the magistrate recommended judgment for the school district. The court then adopted and approved the recommendation. *N.M. v. Cent. Bucks School Dist.*, Civ. No. 11-3272, 2014 WL 185219 (E.D. Pa. 1/16/14).

IV. BEHAVIOR INTERVENTION

A. Behavior Intervention Plans

The IDEA does not specify substantive requirements for a behavioral intervention plan (BIP). Instead, schools must consider positive behavioral interventions and supports, and other strategies when behavior impedes a child's learning. In D.W. v. Milwaukee Public Schools, *526 Fed.Appx. 672 (7th Cir. 2013), this chapter, the U.S. Court of Appeals, Seventh Circuit, found the IDEA has no substantive requirements for BIPs. In* School Board of Independent School Dist. No. 11 v. Renollett, *440 F.3d 1007 (8th Cir. 2006), the Eighth Circuit Court of Appeals held federal law did not require a written BIP in a student's IEP. Since a school responded to a student's behavioral incidents using set procedures, it found no substantive or procedural IDEA violation.*

♦   The New York City Department of Education paid the private school tuition costs of a child with autism. The private school used a methodology called "DIR/Floortime." For the next school year, the department offered the child an IEP and a behavior intervention plan (BIP) that would have placed him in a public school classroom for year-round services and other support. Many of the goals for this IEP came from a report created by the private school. The parents rejected the IEP and filed a due process complaint against the department. An impartial hearing officer ordered the school department to pay for the private school tuition. When the case reached the U.S. Court of Appeals, Second Circuit, it rejected the parents' claim that the BIP was inadequate. It disagreed that the department's failure to conduct a functional behavioral assessment denied the child an appropriate IEP. This was true despite the fact that state law at the time required each school district to conduct a full functional behavioral assessment for any child who exhibited behavior that impeded learning.

The court found the department evaluated the child's psychological reports and his progress at the private school. It also contacted teachers and asked the parent for her input. This process adequately identified the child's behavioral impediments. In addition, **the BIP accurately characterized the child's behavior problems, which included spitting and biting**. As a result, the court upheld the BIP. But the court held more consideration was required for a claim that the IEP should have included DIR/Floortime methodology. *E.H. o./b./o. M.K. v. New York City Dep't of Educ.*, 611 Fed.Appx. 728 (2d Cir. 2015).

♦   A New York student attended a private school for persons with autism spectrum disorder. His committee on special education (CSE) proposed placing him in a class of six children, a teacher, and a behavior management aide (a 6:1:1 class). The IEP noted the student's need for a highly structured, predictable setting due to his tantrums. It included a behavior intervention plan (BIP) but not a functional behavioral assessment (FBA). The parents returned their child to the private school and filed a due process complaint. An impartial hearing officer (IHO) found FAPE had been denied based on failure to consider the child's social, emotional and behavioral needs and self-injurious behavior.

The IHO found the CSE did not consider the use of appropriate methodology and denied the parents meaningful participation in the CSE meeting. On appeal, a state review officer found no denial of FAPE. New York law does not require a CSE to state the type of methodology in an IEP, and it was not shown that the child could benefit only through ABA therapy. When the case reached a federal court, it held the failure to conduct an FBA did not deny the child a FAPE. **The IDEA only requires a school to consider the use of positive behavior interventions and supports and other strategies when a child's behavior impedes learning.** The BIP addressed the student's behaviors and had strategies to address them. The IEP incorporated supports, including a 1:1 behavior management professional. It was not a substantive IDEA violation to place the child in a 6:1:1 program or to fail to specify ABA methodology in the IEP. Parents were not entitled to select a preferred methodology. Rejecting the parents' arguments, the court held for the DOE. *P.S. v. New York City Dep't of Educ.*, No. 13 Civ. 04772 (LGS), 2014 WL 3673603 (S.D.N.Y. 7/24/14).

♦   A New York student with a severe form of autism had cognitive delays, oral motor/articulation difficulties, language deficits and socialization weaknesses. A school team recommended placing her in a special education class with a 6:1:1 student-teacher-paraprofessional ratio. Although the IEP proposed by the school department included a behavioral intervention plan (BIP), it did not have a functional behavior assessment (FBA). Some issues addressed by the BIP were the student's chewing and shredding of clothes, and hitting and kicking others. After rejecting the IEP, the parents placed their child in a private school and filed a due process challenge. An impartial hearing officer awarded them compensation, and appeal eventually reached the U.S. Court of Appeals, Second Circuit. **It found evidence that the 1:1 paraprofessional support described in the IEP would allow the student to receive educational benefits.** A suitable BIP addressed her behavioral issues. Despite a violation of state law regulations requiring parent counseling and training for the parents of a child with autism, the court found no denial of FAPE. Rejecting the parents' claim that the proposed school site was inadequate and unsafe, the court held for the school department. *K.L. v. New York City Dep't of Educ.*, 530 Fed.Appx. 81 (2d Cir. 2013).

♦   A Pennsylvania student with behavioral problems caused by a disability began to have new and more severe problems during his sixth-grade year. Although he was placed in small, socially controlled classes with other special needs students, he continued displaying new and severe behavior problems. His district's **proposed IEP for the next year did not address his socialization outside his self-contained class or provide a behavior plan**. Instead, it called for some social support. His parents placed him in a private school, and a federal court awarded them part of their tuition costs. It penalized the parents for failing to share relevant information with the school, but it also noted that the school failed to address known behavior problems. *Council Rock School Dist. v. M.W.*, No. 11–4824, 2012 WL 3055686 (E.D. Pa. 7/26/12).

♦ Kansas parents of an autistic child became dissatisfied with his IEP and his behavior intervention plan (BIP). They believed the district needed to consult an autism expert and consider an out-of-district placement. The district agreed to hire an autism consultant, but the parents hired an expert on their own anyway and then challenged the new IEP and BIP. A hearing officer and a federal court found that the district had offered the student a FAPE. The court noted that neither of the parents' experts was a teacher and that the IEP team responded appropriately to their concerns. **The district did not need to follow the parents' preferred methods for instructing their child.** And the child made more than minimal educational progress. *J.W. v. Unified School Dist. No. 231, Johnson County*, No. 09–2357–CM–DJW, 2012 WL 628181 (D. Kan. 2/27/12).

♦ A Missouri student with ADHD and a seizure disorder exhibited extreme behavior problems, including spitting, hitting and kicking, refusing to follow directions and trying to destroy school property. His district eventually transferred him to a separate public day facility based on safety concerns for him and his classmates. His mother objected to him being isolated in a small, padded observation room as an intervention technique. Eventually a federal court held that the segregated placement was proper. **The district considered a variety of strategies and interventions to allow for his academic progress.** His behavior improved following the use of the rooms, and he needed them less frequently. *Clark v. Special School Dist. of St. Louis County*, No. 4:10CV2128SNLJ, 2012 WL 592423 (E.D. Mo. 2/23/12).

♦ A Missouri student had impaired speech articulation, behavioral problems and severe delays in reading achievement by second grade. His parents brought a host of claims over the years, asserting that the district's delay in identifying their son's disability and creating a behavior intervention plan amounted to an IDEA violation. However, a federal court disagreed. It noted that **the parents never timely complained to the district about the generality of the behavior plan in place**. And since the student had moved to a private placement at district expense, that issue was moot. *Weston v. Kansas City, Missouri School Dist.*, No. 07-0239-CV-W-HFS, 2011 WL 5513207 (W.D. Mo. 11/10/11).

♦ A Connecticut student with Down syndrome had serious behavioral issues. Her parents were critical of the proposed behavior intervention plan and asked the district to hire a behavior specialist. After the district adopted an IEP that incorporated the specialist's plan (which avoided aversive, negative or punishing interventions), the student shoved and punched her tutor and then threatened to poke a teacher in the eye with a hanger. The district suspended the student for 10 days and placed her in an interim homebound program, assuming her behavior was a manifestation of her disability. The district then sought an out-of-district placement. The parents sued, alleging that the behavior plan the district had implemented was a failure. A federal court found that the district had offered the student an appropriate behavior plan. Indeed, it was the parents' plan. **The fact that the student could not be educated in district schools did not mean that the district had violated the IDEA.** *L. v. North Haven Board of Educ.*, 624 F.Supp.2d 163 (D. Conn. 2009).

♦   The mother of a Hawaii student with behavioral problems unilaterally placed him in a private school because she thought the public school wasn't adequately addressing his behavior problems. When she sought approval for the private placement, the Hawaii Court of Appeals ruled against her, noting that her son was receiving an educational benefit in school, earning passing grades and advancing from grade to grade. It seemed that **his behavioral problems largely occurred at home**. His IEP addressed his emotional and self-esteem and confidence issues. And even if the private school improved his behavior, the state did not have an obligation to maximize the student's potential. *State of Hawaii Dep't of Educ. v. M.S. and J.S.*, 243 P.3d 1054 (Haw. Ct. App. 2010).

♦   The parents of a New York student with autism had a number of concerns about their school district's IEPs and began to homeschool their son. For the student's third-grade year, the IEP team specified a 12:1:2 placement, a behavior intervention plan and a transition plan for bringing the child back to school. Before that transition occurred, the parents became upset at the quality of home instruction their son was receiving and challenged the IEPs for the previous few years. The case reached a federal court, which held that the lack of a behavior intervention plan in earlier IEPs was not an IDEA violation. The court also upheld the IEP with respect to the transition plan and the other challenged elements. The Second Circuit affirmed the ruling for the district, finding that **the absence of a behavior intervention plan did not violate the IDEA because his IEPs addressed his needs**. *E.H. and K.H. v. Board of Educ. of Shenendehowa Cent. School Dist.*, 361 Fed.Appx. 156 (2d Cir. 2009).

♦   A New Hampshire student with multiple disabilities attended a day school program for special needs students. When she reached age 18, her mother met with the school IEP team on at least four occasions to discuss her IEP, but no agreement was reached. She refused to sign the district's proposed IEP – which contained a transition plan but no behavior plan – but she did not communicate any specific objections to it. Several months later, the district presented her with a new IEP, which contained a behavior plan and a full-blown transition plan. The mother again refused to sign it, so the district filed a due process hearing request. A hearing officer upheld the IEP plan, and the mother appealed. A federal court, and later the U.S. Court of Appeals, First Circuit, agreed that the IEP should be put into effect. The First Circuit noted that the IDEA does not require transition plans to be articulated as a separate component of an IEP. Nor were behavior plans necessary unless certain disciplinary actions had been taken. **The first IEP, which discussed a behavior plan without specifically including it, did not violate the IDEA.** And the lateness of the second IEP was caused by the mother's conduct. *Lessard v. Wilton-Lyndeborough Cooperative School Dist.*, 518 F.3d 18 (1st Cir. 2008).

B. Functional Behavioral Assessment

While failure to conduct an FBA is a "serious procedural violation," it will not deny a free and appropriate public education "if the IEP adequately identifies problem behavior and prescribes ways to manage it." See R.E. v. New York City Dep't of Educ., *694 F.3d 167 (2d Cir. 2012);* A.C. and M.C. v. Board of Educ. of Chappaqua Cent. School Dist., *553 F.3d 165 (2d Cir. 2009). The IDEA does not specify the substantive requirements for behavior intervention plans. In* M.W. v. New York City Dep't of Educ., *725 F.3d 131 (2d Cir. 2013), this chapter, the court held the absence of a functional behavioral assessment did not violate the IDEA, so long as the IEP adequately identified a student's behavioral impediments and implemented strategies to address that behavior.*

◆ A Colorado child with autism had significant behavior problems. Near the end of his fourth-grade school year, his behavior worsened and a new behavior intervention plan (BIP) was included in his IEP. But the parents withdrew him from the district and enrolled him in a private school. An ALJ denied their request for tuition reimbursement, and a federal court later affirmed the decision. The parents appealed to the Tenth Circuit, which held they did not show a failure to adequately report their child's progress denied them meaningful participation in his education. While his progress reports "could have been more robust," the court found evidence that they knew about his progress and were active participants in his education. When developing an IEP for a child whose behavior impedes his or her own learning or that of others, **the IDEA requires a school to "consider the use of positive behavioral interventions and supports and other strategies to address that behavior."** The school district was working to address the student's behavior at the time the parents rejected the IEP and privately placed him. The district satisfied its IDEA duty to consider the use of behavioral interventions. In fact, the IDEA only requires a BIP or a functional behavioral assessment if there is a disciplinary change in placement, which was not the case here. *Endrew F. v. Douglas County School Dist. RE 1*, 798 F.3d 1329 (10th Cir. 2015).

◆ The parents of a child with autism filed a challenge to IEPs proposed for the child by the New York City Department of Education (DOE). When the case reached the U.S. Court of Appeals, Second Circuit, it found the IEP proposed a full-time behavior management program with a paraprofessional assigned to the child. **In its previous cases, the court held that a failure to conduct a functional behavioral assessment is a serious IDEA procedural violation. But it is not legally actionable if the IEP adequately identified the problem behavior, addressed it and prescribed ways to manage it.** In this case, the court found the DOE gave extensive consideration to behavioral concerns at a meeting attended by the parents. At the meeting, committee members were guided by recommendations of staff at the child's school. With this input, the committee developed a behavioral intervention plan that the court found was reasonably calculated to address his behaviors. This included predictable routines, visual support, repetition, positive reinforcement, and a full-time 1:1 behavioral management paraprofessional. The committee's failure to conduct its own functional behavioral analysis did not deny the student a FAPE. As there was no merit to the parents' other arguments, the court held for the DOE. *F.L. v. New York City Dep't of Educ.*, 553 Fed.Appx. 2 (2d Cir. 2014).

♦   A New York child with autism and other disabilities had behavioral and social-emotional problems which led him to under-perform academically. Early in his elementary school career, his parents rejected an IEP offer and placed him in a private school where he continued to have behavioral issues. Prior to the next school year, the New York City school department recommended placing the child in a general education room with integrated co-teaching services.

As the child's behavior seriously interfered with his instruction, the IEP included a behavioral intervention plan (BIP). But the BIP was not based on a functional behavioral assessment (FBA). The parents rejected the IEP and again placed their child in a private school. Seeking reimbursement for their private school tuition, they filed a due process hearing request. When the case reached the U.S. Court of Appeals, Second Circuit, it found the lack of an FBA did not make the IEP inadequate. State regulations did not deem an IEP without an FBA improper. **The IDEA required consideration for positive behavioral interventions and supports, and other strategies, when behavior impeded learning.** The court held the lack of an FBA did not render an IEP inadequate, if the IEP identified a student's behavioral impediments and implemented strategies to address them. In this case, the BIP described the child's meltdowns and other problems. Strategies were identified to manage those problems, and a collaborative intervention plan was offered to address them. The court held the BIP described the student's behavior problems and provided a broad, collaborative approach to implement specific strategies to modify his behavior. *M.W. v. New York City Dep't of Educ.*, 725 F.3d 131 (2d Cir. 2013).

♦   A Nebraska child with autism experienced behavior problems. By second grade, he became aggressive, and the school had to use calming strategies. When the student reached grade-three, he began to harm school staff members. Before the end of his third-grade year, his parents took him to a rehabilitation facility for a functional behavioral assessment. A behavior analyst found the calming room increased his aggressive behavior. A three-level behavior plan was devised to eliminate use of a calming room. The first level of intervention was a 30-second baskethold. When the parents presented these findings to the school district, a behavior specialist found it conflicted with her understanding of appropriate responses to aggressive behavior by autistic children and would allow the student to hit others or act aggressively before being removed from class. The district devised a behavior intervention plan that replicated parts of the rehabilitation facility plan, but it continued to rely on the calming room.

The parents objected, placed their child in a private setting and requested a hearing. When the case reached the U.S. Court of Appeals, Eighth Circuit, it found the student was progressing and the school district was addressing his behavior. A detailed behavior intervention plan was attached to the IEP with the approach devised by the rehabilitation facility. The court found it "largely irrelevant if the school district could have employed more positive behavior interventions as long as it made a good-faith effort to help the student achieve the educational goals outlined in his IEP." **An IEP team does not have to adopt all the parents' recommendations, and does not have to change methodologies based on parental preferences.** Since there was evidence supporting continued use of a calming room, the court held for the district. *M.M. v. Dist. 0001 Lancaster County School*, 702 F.3d 479 (8th Cir. 2012).

C. Restraint and Seclusion

In Miller v. Monroe School Dist., *this chapter, the court addressed a Washington parent's concern for restraint and isolation of her child at school by noting any future use of restraint or isolation would be limited by a state law cited as RCW 28A.600.485(3)(b). Under this provision, "restraint or isolation of any student is permitted only when reasonably necessary to control spontaneous behavior that poses an imminent likelihood of serious harm."*

♦   A 13-year-old New Mexico student with Down syndrome became involved in an altercation with school employees. According to the school district, its employees "physically managed" him under a district policy statement and a best practices manual. The student's parent claimed the district applied a discriminatory restraint policy only to students with disabilities. In her lawsuit against the school district, a federal court found a district "Staff Conduct with Students" policy allowed physical management of students to quell a threat to serious, imminent bodily harm. A provision of the Staff Conduct with Students policy applied to use of restraints on students who received special education. It stated that any use of restraints beyond the policy had to be identified in a student's IEP as part of his or her behavior plan. A second district policy called "Best Practices for Use of Physical Management for Students with Disabilities" supplemented the general policy by stating that physical management is always a last resort after less restrictive interventions have been exhausted or ruled out.

The court found the district required the provision of additional procedures and documentation whenever a disabled student was restrained. In the court's view, the Best Practices memo only amounted to guidelines. It found the parameters for physical intervention were drawn from the "Staff Conduct with Students" policy, which applied to all students. **The policy did not rely on stereotypes about disabled persons, as the parent argued. In any event, the court held the school was justified in its conduct.** Finding the Best Practices document required employees to be more conscientious in physical interventions with disabled students by demanding certain procedures and documentation, the court held for the school district. *Hernandez v. Board of Educ. of Albuquerque Public Schools*, 124 F.Supp.3d 1181 (D. N.M. 2015).

♦   A Washington parent said her child's school district committed multiple IEP violations and did not inform her when he was being isolated. In response, she filed a due process hearing request. The school district asked for many continuances and an ALJ did not issue a decision for 217 days after the parent's request. She petitioned a federal court for an order requiring the district to pay for a private placement. In considering the request, the court held the child had been denied a free appropriate public education during the 142-day period between the date a due process decision was due and the date it was actually issued. In the court's opinion, the failure to comply with this crucial procedural requirement negated the stay-put requirement of the IDEA for 142 days. Although the parent claimed the district did not use the isolation safeguards in her child's IEP, the court found staff members were in the quiet room with the student. Since he was not alone at these times, the court held they could not be considered "isolation" and there was no IDEA violation.

Next, the court held the parent did not show the district failed to document or inform her about restraints. She had not been denied meaningful participation in the creation of the current IEP. The draft IEP included an amended aversive intervention plan and a behavior intervention plan permitting isolation when needed. The district let the parent review its draft IEP before the meeting, and she had ample time to present her concerns at the meeting. In the court's view, **the district was justified in preserving some ability to restrain the child, given his physical reactions and prior record of harming educators**. The parent was granted partial reimbursement for her costs arising from the 142-day period during which a hearing was delayed, but she was otherwise denied relief. *Miller v. Monroe School Dist.*, 131 F.Supp.3d 1107 (W.D. Wash. 2015).

♦   An Iowa seventh-grade student's IEP called for a 1:1 aide and a quiet place to go if he became overstimulated. A behavior intervention plan (BIP) described how staff was to intervene if he acted out. On a day when the student was having problems, he tried to go to his quiet room. While on the way to the room, he pushed a classmate. The student's teacher and the school principal approached him in the quiet room. The student tried to run away, pushing another student. According to the student, the teacher restrained him, causing injury. His parents then filed a lawsuit against the school district and teacher in a federal court. The family's complaint asserted the teacher did not follow the IEP or BIP. The court held the student was not seeking relief that could have been included in an IEP. Instead, the claims asserted teachers did not provide an environment free from fear, did not follow the BIP or IEP, allowed teachers to use illegal physical restraints, failed to train teachers and did not assign qualified aides. **Claims based on alleged assault by the teacher appeared far removed from the IDEA** at this early stage of the case. Since the court found no reason to believe an IDEA claim could include the kind of harm described in the complaint, IDEA administrative exhaustion was not required. *A.P. v. St. Johnson*, No. 14-CV-4022-DEO, 2015 WL 1297534 (N.D. Iowa 3/23/15).

CHAPTER FOUR

Placement

I. PLACEMENT IN SPECIAL EDUCATION PROGRAMS

A. Educational Benefit Generally

In R.E. v. New York City Dep't of Educ., *694 F.3d 167 (2d Cir. 2012), the U.S. Court of Appeals, Second Circuit, explained that "educational placement" of a child with a disability "refers only to the general type of educational program in which the child is placed." Placement "does not refer to a specific location or program." For this reason, a school district did not have to specify the school or classroom where a disabled student's IEP would be implemented.*

♦   The Los Angeles Unified School District (LAUSD) delayed requesting a due process hearing when the parent of a child with autistic-like behaviors refused to consent to a placement. When the case reached the U.S. Court of Appeals, Ninth Circuit, it rejected a lower court's finding that the IDEA foreclosed the LAUSD from initiating a due process hearing as required by state law. In ruling for the LAUSD, the lower court relied on an IDEA provision (20 U.S.C. § 1414(a)(1)(D)(ii)(II)), which states that a school district must obtain parental consent before providing special education. A federal regulation forecloses a district's ability to file a due process complaint if the parent fails to respond to a request for (or refuses to consent to) the initial provision of special education.

In this case, the parent had consented to the provision of special education. As a result, the lower court committed an error in finding the LAUSD was not free to initiate a due process hearing to address the parent's refusal of the placement. State law required the school district to request a due process hearing in this case. The court held the district could not continue to hold more IEP meetings in lieu of a hearing. While a district was entitled to some flexibility in deciding when to request a hearing, the court held the **LAUSD did not act reasonably in keeping the child in a general education placement for almost two years when it had decided he should be in special education classes**. A delay of over a year in requesting a due process hearing was held unreasonable. Finding the LAUSD had concluded that the child was not receiving a FAPE in her current placement, **the court found the child lost educational opportunities and was deprived of educational benefits**. The case was returned to the lower court for determination of an appropriate remedy for denying FAPE for an unreasonable time. *I.R. v. Los Angeles Unified School Dist.*, 805 F.3d 1164 (9th Cir. 2015).

♦   A New Jersey student with specific learning disabilities attended language-based learning disabilities classes at his middle school. His mother said he was subjected to bullying, and he began to fall behind. Asserting her son was not making progress and that his school was not addressing bullies, she requested an alternative placement. When the school district declined this, the parent placed her son in a private school and requested a hearing. After a nine-day due process hearing, an administrative law judge (ALJ) upheld the student's seventh-grade IEP. The parent's request for private school tuition reimbursement was denied. She appealed to a federal court, arguing the IEP was inappropriate as it "provided more and more bypass strategies, coached as accommodations, which kept him more dependent on other people, and did not give him the ability to see himself making meaningful educational progress." Although expressing concern with the ALJ's uniform approval of school witnesses, the court noted the parent did not raise specific objections to their testimony.

The ALJ had found the student was making "more than trivial progress, albeit slowly," and was receiving a free appropriate public education. As the parent's arguments lacked support, the court refused to depart from the ALJ's finding. **It held the relevant inquiry was not a comparison between the public and private school, but whether the student was receiving meaningful educational benefits.** The court rejected the parent's remaining arguments and held for the school district. *C.P v. Fair Lawn Board of Educ.*, Civil No. 12-cv-05694 (SDW) (MCA), 2014 WL 1716453 (D.N.J. 5/1/14).

♦   A New York City child with a physical disability and autism attended a preschool classroom with a 10:1:2 student-teacher-paraprofessional ratio. His student-teacher-paraprofessional classroom ratio went from 10:1:2 to 12:1:4 for kindergarten, and his parents believed this setting was too distracting. After a lengthy search for an appropriate school, the City Department of Education (DOE) agreed to a private school placement found by the parents. The DOE paid the school's $63,000 tuition. When a CSE considered a new IEP, school members classified him as having multiple disabilities and renewed the proposal for a 12:1:4 setting. The parents rejected the IEP and informed the DOE they would seek reimbursement for the private school. They sought $92,100 in tuition reimbursement. An IHO found the DOE did not offer the student a FAPE, but a state review officer (SRO) reversed the decision.

Appeal reached a federal court, which explained that **an IEP is to be evaluated as of the time it was created**. The court held the SRO had failed to address testimony by the student's physician, who had stated that autism was his most pressing educational need. He also said that **children with autism benefit the most from programs specifically targeted to address their autism**. The court found the SRO had failed to consider testimony from experts with significant knowledge of the child. There was evidence that a 12:1:4 setting was designed primarily for students with a physical disability. By contrast, there was support for the IHO's findings that the IEP proposal did not provide a program targeted toward autism. The court held the proposal for a 12:1:4 setting would be inappropriate. As the private school was found appropriate, the court held the parents were entitled to reimbursement. *F.O. and E.O. v. New York City Dep't of Educ.*, 976 F.Supp.2d 499 (S.D.N.Y. 2013).

◆   A Minnesota student had an IEP integrating her with non-disabled peers for over 70% of the school day. When she entered middle school, her parents proposed full integration while the district proposed a segregated, center-based program for special education students that focused on structured teaching strategies for 30% of the day. A hearing officer and a federal court determined that the district's proposed placement was appropriate. Because the student was still not reading, **a mix of programs would provide her with the structured environment she needed while also allowing social interaction** in her mainstream classes. The district did not violate the IDEA by failing to classify the student as deaf/hard of hearing because the parents could not show that she lost any educational benefits as a result. The parents appealed to the Eighth Circuit Court of Appeals, which held the least restrictive environment requirement does not apply where a student cannot progress in a mainstream environment. *Pachl v. Seagren*, 453 F.3d 1064 (8th Cir. 2006).

B. Neighborhood Schools

According to the Third Circuit Court of Appeals, no federal appeals court has recognized a right to a neighborhood school assignment under the IDEA. In J.T. v. Dumont Public Schools, *533 Fed.Appx. 44 (3d Cir. 2013), the Third Circuit explained that while a school district must take into account the proximity of a placement to a student's home, it is not obligated to place students in their neighborhood schools. Since the IDEA's key requirement is providing a free appropriate public education to students with special needs, the court found students are to be educated in the schools they would attend if not for a disability, unless their IEPs require placement elsewhere.*

◆   Kentucky parents insisted that their diabetic child attend his neighborhood school. But their school district refused because no school nurse worked at the site. Although full-time nurses worked at two other district schools, the parents rejected both sites. School nurses believed he needed assistance from a nurse and that his insulin injections were a nursing function. The district again denied enrollment at the neighborhood school, and the child began attending a district school that was staffed by a nurse. His parents sued the school board in a federal court for violations of the Americans with Disabilities Act (ADA), Section 504 and the Kentucky Civil Rights Act. In ruling for the board and superintendent, **the court found the student had no right under Section 504 to attend a neighborhood school**. In 2012, the U.S. Court of Appeals, Sixth Circuit, returned the case to the trial court for further proceedings. The court again held for the board of education, and the case returned to the Sixth Circuit in 2016.

According to the court, a recent change to Kentucky law barred a school from excluding students on the sole basis that it does not have a full-time nurse. Since state law forbade the actions which the student sought to enjoin, the court found his request was now moot. It found the board had not singled him out for different treatment on the basis of his diabetes for years. Next, the court considered the student's claims for damages under the ADA, Section 504 and state law. It found no evidence that the board of education knew it would likely violate the student's rights by assigning him to a school with a full-time nurse. As a result, the federal claims failed. Kentucky Civil Right Act claims are treated like federal claims, so the state law claim failed. *R.K. v. Board of Educ. of Scott County, Kentucky*, 637 Fed.Appx. 922 (6th Cir. 2016).

♦   A New Jersey student with autism attended an inclusion preschool class in his neighborhood school for half days. For kindergarten, the school district proposed an inclusion class that was not in his neighborhood school. His parent objected and filed a federal class action suit against the school district for systemic IDEA violations and discrimination. The court dismissed the case for failure to exhaust administrative remedies. Since the federal court had declined to consider the state law claims, the parent filed a new state court case against the district for discrimination under the state Law Against Discrimination (LAD). She sought an order requiring neighborhood school placements whenever possible. The court found the child thrived in his kindergarten class.

Since nobody in the proposed class was harmed by not attending a neighborhood school or by being bused, the case was dismissed. On appeal, a state appellate court found the federal claims had already been resolved against the student by the Third Circuit. The state court rejected the parent's claim that attending a neighborhood school was a benefit protected by the LAD. It rejected an argument that disabled children were stigmatized by having to take smaller school buses. **Federal courts have held that if a disabled child is not entitled to a neighborhood placement under the IDEA, there is no entitlement under Section 504 of the Rehabilitation Act.** There was no evidence that the student or any class member had been denied a free appropriate public education. Since there is no entitlement to a neighborhood school placement, the court dismissed the case. *J.T. v. Dumont Public Schools*, 438 N.J.Super. 241, 103 A.3d 269 (N.J. Super. Ct. 2014).

♦   Parents of a Massachusetts student with pervasive developmental disorder obtained a private psychologist's recommendation that their child attend school in an enclosed classroom. Since all first-grade classrooms at his neighborhood school were open, the parents sought to place him in a school with enclosed rooms. They signed an intra-district request form in which they agreed to provide transportation for their child. Later, the parents filed an IDEA due process request, asserting procedural violations by the IEP team and stating the team coerced them into signing the transportation form in order to secure their preferred placement. A hearing officer held for the school committee, but a federal court returned the case to the hearing officer for additional proceedings.

Before the hearing, the parents declined an offer by the school committee to reimburse them for their transportation costs. A hearing officer then found no coercion in their signing of an intra-district placement form and no procedural violations of legal significance. When the case returned to the court, it held the parents were not deprived of participation opportunities. A FAPE had not been denied, nor had there been a deprivation of educational benefits. The student remained at the school chosen by his parents, and there was insufficient evidence that he would not have received a FAPE at the school recommended for him. **The fact that the parents had chosen to voluntarily incur transportation costs did not deny their son a FAPE.** As there had been no coercion, the school committee prevailed. *Doe v. Attleboro Public Schools*, 960 F.Supp.2d 286 (D. Mass. 2013).

◆   An Illinois school district placed a student with severe developmental dyslexia and a learning disorder in a neighborhood school, offering her special education services for about half of her school day. Her parents declined extended school year services. They became frustrated by her lack of progress and placed her in a private school, then requested due process. A hearing officer and a federal court held the student was properly placed in the neighborhood school and that the parents were not entitled to tuition reimbursement. The IEPs created by the district stated broad annual goals and listed short-term objectives that showed the district had offered an appropriate education. And **the student made some academic progress at the neighborhood school**. *James D. v. Board of Educ. of Aptakisic-Tripp Community Consolidated School Dist. No. 102*, 642 F.Supp.2d 804 (N.D. Ill. 2009).

◆   The mother of a Kansas student with Down syndrome challenged the IEP proposed for his entry into high school, as it would require a long bus ride to a high school in another town. She sought to place him in the high school in their town. An educational cooperative serving eight school districts ran a "level program" (also known as a cluster system) that used a functional educational approach. A hearing officer and a federal court found that **the Level IV program at the distant high school was the least restrictive placement** and that the neighborhood school had no teachers qualified to teach the student. The student's inability to focus in regular classrooms was documented, and the Level IV program provided a continuum of placements and support services. Although neighborhood placements are preferred under the IDEA, they are not an enforceable right. *M.M. v. Unified School Dist. No. 368*, No. 07-2291-JTM, 2008 WL 4950987 (D. Kan. 11/18/08).

◆   A nine-year-old Mississippi student functioned at a four-month cognitive level and a nine-month linguistic level. Her school district proposed a placement in a program offered by another district under an inter-agency agreement. Her parents objected, asserting that this wasn't the least restrictive environment, and that the district had come up with this option after the IEP meeting ended. A federal court disagreed. The parents produced no evidence that the IEP was cobbled together after they left the meeting. Also, **the student could obtain more sophisticated resources at the program in the other district**. And the district had the discretion to determine the geographic location of the educational placement. *Russell v. Water Valley School Dist.*, No. 3:06-CV-101-SAA, 2008 WL 723842 (N.D. Miss. 3/17/08).

C. Extended School Year Services

Extended school year (ESY) services must be provided where necessary to provide students with a free appropriate public education. ESY services are typically required if a student with disabilities would otherwise experience significant regression because of an interruption in the instructional program.

◆ A New York student with autism attended private preschools, and his district provided special education through private providers. When he turned five, the district's committee on special education (CSE) decided he needed a 12-month educational program to prevent substantial regression. The parties reached an agreement for the student to attend a regular classroom with special education services from the same providers that he had worked with previously. Although the CSE offered to place the child in one of two summer programs, the parents rejected them as overly restrictive. The school district did not offer any summer program for general education students, and it did not offer to place the student in any public or private general education program for the summer months.

The parents filed a due process complaint and invoked their rights under the IDEA's stay-put provision. After the case went through the administrative process, it reached the U.S. Court of Appeals, Second Circuit. The court held the district's offer to place the student in special education classrooms for the summer violated the IDEA's least restrictive environment (LRE) requirement. **The court held that if a child needed extended school year services to prevent substantial regression, they had to be an integral part of the child's 12-month program.** Here, the district failed to offer the student a FAPE in the LRE for the summer months. As a result, the court returned the case to the lower court for it to consider whether tuition reimbursement was required. But the school district correctly argued that it had been improperly ordered to continue reimbursing the parents for pendency services they were obtaining from private providers. It was up to the district to decide how to offer such services. *T.M. v. Cornwall Cent. School Dist.*, 752 F.3d 145 (2d Cir. 2014).

◆ A 10-year-old Ohio student was nonverbal due to autism, Down syndrome, speech apraxia, sensory integration and cognitive impairments. For two years, the district provided him ESY services including therapy and 1:1 services from a paraprofessional. According to the student's mother, the student could not participate in many of the ESY activities. At an IEP meeting, team members presented the parents with two options. One was a four-week classroom program, and the other was based in a recreation center. After rejecting both proposals, the parents expressed interest in ESY programs at an autism center. The member of the IEP team met again. At this subsequent meeting of the IEP team, the team found the student was eligible for ESY services in reading, math and communication. The offer for a classroom or recreation center ESY program was renewed. The parents continued to press their claims for an autism program setting. Just a short time before school ended, the parents sought federal court relief.

The federal court that considered the parent's case determined that in order **to support a claim for ESY services, parents must show, in a manner specific to a child, that "an ESY [program] is necessary to avoid something more than adequately recoupable regression."** The court held that in this particular case the parents did not show the student would suffer irreparable harm without court intervention. The parents did not present any expert testimony supporting the claim for an ESY autism center program. In addition, there was no evidence indicating that the student would suffer irremediable regression. The district did not reject ESY services wholesale, the court was careful to point out in its decision. By contrast, the parents had demanded a private autism program and did not truly engage in a constructive dialogue with the school district. A number of district proposals remained available. In addition, mediation and the administrative hearing process remained available as well. As a result, the court dismissed the case. *T.H. v. Cincinnati Public School Dist. Board of Educ.*, No. 1:14-cv-516, 2014 WL 2931426 (S.D. Ohio 6/27/14).

◆   The parents of a California student with autism placed the child in a private preschool setting. At some point in time, the student's Part C eligibility expired. After the student's Part C eligibility expired, the school district proceeded to take steps to hold an IEP meeting. Though it held the meeting, it did a poor job of communicating with the student's parents. In addition, the school district declined to offer a special education placement for the student. The parents proceeded to file a due process request. A hearing officer made a determination that procedural violations had occurred. As a result, the hearing officer ordered the school district to pay for the private program until the school district could offer the student a free appropriate public education. The hearing officer also ordered the provision of ESY services and a transition plan to a district program. As part of the school district's offer, the student would stay in his ESY program and would then transition to public school in the fall. However, the parents disliked the IEP and sought tuition reimbursement for the private school, asserting that it was the student's stay-put placement. A federal court disagreed with the position of the parents. **The ESY services could not support a request for a stay-put order at the private school.** *Huerta v. San Francisco Unified School Dist.*, No. C 11–04817 CRB, 2011 WL 5521742 (N.D. Cal. 11/14/11).

◆   A student who received ESY services when he lived in California did not receive them after he and his family moved to Washington. His new district, after a disciplinary incident, agreed to place him in a private school, but justified the refusal to offer ESY services on the lack of data needed from the private school. The case reached the Court of Appeals of Washington, which noted that **the district could not shift the duty for collecting student data to the private school**. It should have conducted tests, evaluations or assessments on its own rather than wait for the information to be provided by the private school. The district had to provide the student with the number of hours of counseling or instruction he would have received had he attended an ESY program. *A.D. v. Sumner School Dist.*, 166 P.3d 837 (Wash. Ct. App. 2007).

♦   A Colorado school district found an autistic student eligible for ESY services, which would help him maintain learned skills over the summer. **His parents instead wanted the district to focus on developing skills identified in his IEPs for the prior and upcoming years.** They obtained private ESY services and requested due process. A hearing officer found that the state ESY guidelines did not violate the IDEA. But before the hearing officer ruled on whether the district denied the student a FAPE, the parents appealed to a federal court. The case reached the Tenth Circuit, which dismissed the case. It held the parents should have first exhausted their administrative remedies. *McQueen v. Colorado Springs School Dist. No. 11*, 488 F.3d 868 (10th Cir. 2007).

♦   A Hawaii student with specific learning disabilities was unilaterally placed in a private school, then sent to an Illinois residential school. Her parents sought to return her to a Hawaii school, but rejected the IEP placing her in a public school. They believed she needed extended school year services and that the district/state predetermined her public school placement. A hearing officer rejected their claims, and a federal court agreed. **The lack of ESY services did not amount to a denial of a free appropriate public education.** Also, the lack of a specific transition plan did not mean that the district/state had predetermined where the student should attend school. Since she was only a sophomore, the transition plan did not yet need to be specific. However, there was a question as to whether the district/state had conducted IEP meetings or evaluations while the student was in the private schools. And the parents might be entitled to some tuition reimbursement. The case was remanded to the hearing officer for further action. *Virginia S. v. Dep't of Educ., State of Hawaii*, No. 06-00128 JMS/LEK, 2007 WL 80814 (D. Haw. 1/8/07).

♦   The parent of a disabled Minnesota student rejected the district's IEP, and a due process hearing was conducted on, among other issues, whether the district had failed to develop a timely extended school year (ESY) program. The hearing officer held that the district had always intended to offer ESY services and that the parent had not cooperated in discussing ESY issues. The Eighth Circuit agreed, ruling the student was not entitled to compensatory education for the delay, and that **IDEA regulations do not prescribe the time in which an ESY proposal must be made**. *Reinholdson v. School Board of Independent School Dist. No. 11*, 187 Fed.Appx. 672 (8th Cir. 2006).

♦   A student who received extended school year services turned 21 on August 21, 2006 and his ESY services ended. He claimed he was entitled to receive funding for his residential placement through the end of the 2006-07 school year. The school district disagreed, and a lawsuit resulted. A New Jersey federal court held that the student was entitled to educational benefits through the end of the 2006-07 school year (the school year during which he turned 21). **The date the ESY program ended was not the time frame to be used for determining the student's school-year eligibility.** ESY programs are not considered extensions of a school year, but are additional special education services outside the normal educational program. *C.T. v. Verona Board of Educ.*, 464 F.Supp.2d 383 (D.N.J. 2006).

II. LEAST RESTRICTIVE ENVIRONMENT

The IDEA, at 20 U.S.C. § 1412(a)(5)(A), requires that schools provide a free appropriate public education in a disabled student's "least restrictive environment" or LRE. A student's LRE is the one that, to the greatest extent possible, satisfactorily educates the student together with non-disabled peers. Ideally, this would be in the same school the disabled student would attend if he or she were not disabled, but courts have held such placements are only appropriate to the extent that the student with a disability is properly served.

In T.M. v. Cornwall Cent. School Dist., *752 F.3d 145 (2d Cir. 2014), this chapter, the Second Circuit Court of Appeals held the IDEA's least restrictive environment requirement applies to extended school year placements the same as it does to school-year placements. The court held a New York school district could not avoid the LRE requirement by simply deciding not to operate certain types of educational programs during the summer months.*

A. Appropriateness

In B.E.L. v. State of Hawaii, *this chapter, a federal court relied on a test from* Sacramento City Unified School Dist. v. Rachel H., *14 F.3d 1398 (9th Cir. 1994), to evaluate a parent's claim that his child's placement was overly restrictive. In* Rachel H., *the court recited four factors to assess whether a placement was in the least restrictive environment: 1) the educational benefits of placement of the student in full-time regular classes; 2) the non-academic benefits of such a placement; 3) the effect the disabled student has on the teacher and other children in a regular class; and 4) costs of mainstreaming.*

♦ A Pennsylvania child had learning disabilities in reading and written language. Her parents rejected her IEP and placed her in a private school with a curriculum based on creative thinking and "strong experiences that stir the emotions." The school district paid for the private school for a year. But prior to the next school year, the parents rejected an IEP that would have placed their child in a public school. They filed a due process challenge to the IEP. A hearing officer agreed with the parents that the school district did not seriously consider supplementary aids and services that might have kept their child in regular classes. He held the district did not place her in a setting that offered a free appropriate public education (FAPE) in her least restrictive environment (LRE).

A federal court held the private school was not appropriate. On appeal, the

U.S. Court of Appeals, Third Circuit, found the district did not adequately consider greater inclusion opportunities. Schools are to offer a continuum of placements to meet the needs of a disabled child. Applying *Oberti v. Board of Educ. of Borough of Clementon School Dist.*, 995 F.3d 1204 (3d Cir. 1993), the court held a school was required to give serious consideration to including a child in a regular classroom with supplementary aids and services and to modify the regular curriculum. In this case, the court held the IEP and the notice of recommended educational placement provided no insight into the options considered by the school district before it recommended pull-out language arts instruction. Under the circumstances, the court found it impossible to assess whether the student could have learned in a regular education setting with assistance. Before the lower court, the school district did not show what steps it took toward full inclusion. For this reason, the court upheld the findings that the district did not show it considered the whole range or continuum of possible placements as required by the IDEA. The court held the failure to implement the IEP in the child's LRE was a substantive shortcoming and an IDEA violation. But it held the parents would have to show the private school was a proper placement in order to recover tuition reimbursement. The private school was not licensed as either a private academic school or a school for students with disabilities. Since the parents did not show it was an appropriate placement, their request for private school tuition reimbursement was denied. *H.L. v. Downingtown Area School Dist.*, 624 Fed.Appx. 64 (3d Cir. 2015).

♦   A Hawaii first-grade student struggled with directions, had trouble with the alphabet and could not stay focused. His teacher tried minor modifications such as preferential seating, a behavior chart, extra time on assignments and tutoring. She later stated she could do no more for him without teaching below grade level. Late in the year, the student was tested and found eligible for special education. An IEP was devised calling for special education in language arts and math in segregated classes. For other subjects and activities, the student would attend general education classes with preferential seating and repeated instructions. Although the parent did not initially object to the special education classrooms, he changed his mind after learning that special education could be provided in general education settings. During grade two, the student continued to study language arts and math in a special education setting. His teacher felt he was still about one year behind in math. After an IEP meeting, the student's father accused the school of not discussing alternative placements. He started homeschooling the child and advised the department of education he would make a private school placement. The father requested a due process hearing.

A hearing officer held for the education department, and the father appealed to a federal court. After reciting that the IDEA requires the education of students in the least restrictive environment, the court noted that **teachers found the student was unlikely to receive educational benefits from a full-time general education placement**, even with modifications. In contrast, the parent did not offer expert opinions or evidence that a full-time general education placement would have been beneficial. Rejecting the parent's other arguments, the court held for the department. *B.E.L. v. State of Hawaii*, Civ. No. 14-00066 SOM/BMK, 2014 WL 5431186 (D. Haw. 10/24/14).

♦ The New Jersey Department of Education (DOE) determined the Learning Center for Exceptional Children (LCEC) was mainstreaming certain students in violation of its authorization as a private school for students with disabilities. Later, a child's school district drafted an IEP placing her at the LCEC. Her IEP called for integrating her with regular education students in a small classroom at a private regular education school in the LCEC's building. Nearly two years later, the county school superintendent wrote to the LCEC for assurances that students in this classroom did not attend school with LCEC public school students. When the DOE required the LCEC to assure that it would not implement any part of a child's IEP specifying academic mainstreaming, the LCEC complied. Near this time, the child's parents sued the DOE and two officials in a federal court, asserting violations of the IDEA, Section 504 of the Rehabilitation Act and the Americans with Disabilities Act.

Although the court found the case did not involve a typical IDEA dispute between a school district and the parents of a disabled child over placement, it involved a child's IEP. It was immaterial that the DOE was the defendant, since the state was ultimately charged with the duty to implement the IDEA. **As the parents argued, the child required mainstreaming, and the court held she was entitled to continue receiving this under the stay-put provision.** The court held the stay-put provision would preserve her placement at the LCEC under her IEP for as long as the litigation went on. *D.M.; L.M. on behalf of E.M. v. New Jersey Dep't of Educ.,* Civ. No. 14-4620 (ES), 2014 WL 4271646 (D.N.J. 8/28/14).

♦ A New Jersey child study team prepared an IEP for a child with autism, but it made no provision for interaction with non-disabled children. After about three months, her parents requested consideration for alternatives that would allow her to interact with typically developing peers – and they sought a particular inclusive preschool. The CST rejected the proposal on the grounds that she would not benefit from an inclusive setting. After the parents transferred their daughter to the school, they sought tuition reimbursement. The Third Circuit denied their request. **Ample evidence showed that the student needed a highly structured environment and that she lacked the skills to participate in a less restrictive setting.** *L.G. v. Fair Lawn Board of Educ.,* 486 Fed.Appx. 967 (3d Cir. 2012).

♦ A New York student attended public schools through grade six. She had a history of developmental problems and was classified as learning disabled. The student's parents enrolled her in a summer program at a Massachusetts school for students with language-based learning disabilities at the school district's expense. When the parents unilaterally decided to keep her at the private school for the next school year, the district rejected their request for tuition costs and recommended that she return to a public school in the district. The parents rejected the recommendations and filed an IDEA due process hearing request.

An IHO found the school district had offered the student a FAPE. Appeal reached the Second Circuit, where the parents asserted that the hearing officer failed to address the totality of the circumstances and had placed too much emphasis on the restrictiveness of the Massachusetts facility. Citing *Florence County School Dist. Four v. Carter*, 510 U.S. 7 (1993), **the court held parental placements are not subject to the exacting standards as placements made by school districts**. But the restrictiveness of a school remains a consideration in parental placement cases. Although the parents claimed the student had made academic progress at the Massachusetts facility, the court found no evidence "that this extremely restrictive residential immersion was appropriate" for the student. Since the parents did not show the totality of the circumstances justified tuition reimbursement, the court held for the school district. *D. D–S v. Southold Union Free School Dist.*, 506 Fed.Appx. 80 (2d Cir. 2012).

♦   A New York school district prepared an IEP for an autistic student that placed her in a class made up entirely of students with severe disabilities. It did so despite earlier IEPs that rejected segregated placements as overly restrictive, and it rejected the parents' request for a fully integrated setting. The parents located a private placement in an integrated setting and challenged the IEP in a due process proceeding. A federal court and the Second Circuit ultimately ruled for the parents, finding that **the district's IEP was inappropriate and the private school placement was appropriate**. The parents received tuition reimbursement of $71,041. *G.B. v. Tuxedo Union Free School Dist.*, 486 Fed.Appx. 954 (2d Cir. 2012).

♦   A Texas school district removed a 14-year-old disabled student from general education classes after he became overwhelmed and began to engage in problem behaviors due to frustration. His parents challenged the action, but a hearing officer found that the special education placements were appropriate. A federal court and the Fifth Circuit agreed with that assessment. **The student had received no academic benefit from mainstream social studies and science classes.** He could continue to take two other general education classes, where he was having some success. *J.H. v. Fort Bend Independent School Dist.*, 482 Fed.Appx. 915 (5th Cir. 2012).

♦   An Indiana student with autism and other disabilities had no verbal communication skills. The district agreed to fund one year at a private school with ABA therapy, after which a psychologist recommended he continue there. Instead, the district proposed a public school placement with 6.5 hours per day in the same comprehensive improvement program he had previously attended (and with 20 hours of one-to-one instruction, and five hours of small group interaction each week). The **IEP incorporated ABA strategies** but did not contain specifics, nor did it include a functional behavioral assessment. The parents challenged this placement, and a federal court ultimately held that the IEP was appropriate. *A.B. v. Franklin Township Community School Corp.*, 898 F.Supp.2d 1067 (S.D. Ind. 2012).

♦   The parents of a seven-year-old Hawaii child who was terrified of going to school took him out of public school and put him in a private school. A new IEP was proposed for the following year, but the parents rejected it because it didn't address the child's terror at returning to the public school. When they sought public financing for that placement, a hearing officer ruled against them, but **a federal court reversed the hearing officer, noting that the child was so afraid of going to the public school that his rights under the IDEA were implicated**. Therefore, the child may have been denied a free appropriate public education. However, the rest of the IEP complied with the IDEA. *Nalu Y. v. Dep't of Educ., State of Hawaii,* 858 F.Supp.2d 1127 (D. Haw. 2012).

♦ An 18-year-old Pennsylvania student with multiple disabilities was non-verbal and not toilet trained. Her district proposed placing her in a full-time life skills support class. Her parents filed a due process hearing request, asserting that the placement would deny her a FAPE because it was too restrictive. A hearing officer agreed with them and ordered compensatory education, but an appeals panel held that the student required mainstreaming only for lunch, recess, physical education, homeroom, music, art and a single academic class. The award of compensatory education was reversed. The Third Circuit upheld the decision, noting **the student was making progress in her life skills class and her frequent loud vocalizations had a negative effect on other students**. *A.G. v. Wissahickon School Dist.,* 374 Fed.Appx. 330 (3d Cir. 2010).

B. Services and Aids

In Beth B. v. Van Clay, *282 F.3d 493 (7th Cir. 2002), the U.S. Court of Appeals, Seventh Circuit, held **the IDEA's strong preference for placing disabled children in the least restrictive environment does not suggest a regular classroom placement that would provide an unsatisfactory education**.*

♦ A Pennsylvania IEP proposed an IEP for a student with increasing behavior problems that revised his goals and behavior plan. It would move him from a program of itinerant learning support services to a full-time emotional support program at another school. His parents objected to the IEP, wanting more learning support than emotional support, but they later agreed to IEP revisions that included daily 30-minute meetings with a special education teacher. When the parents challenged the IEP, a federal court ruled against them. **Placement in an emotional support program was necessary** to meet the student's needs. The IEP offered the student the least restrictive environment. *H.D. v. Cent. Bucks School Dist.,* 902 F.Supp.2d 614 (E.D. Pa. 2012).

♦ The parents of an autistic student in North Carolina sought the opinion of an independent specialist as part of the IEP process when their school district wanted to transfer the student to a new setting. The specialist recommended a minimum of 25 hours of 1:1 ABA therapy a week and suggested that a "shadow aide" accompany the student. The district refused to consider the shadow aide, but it discussed the issue of staffing at an IEP meeting, noting that more staffing would be provided, if needed. The parents rejected the IEP. A federal court ruled that although the district committed a procedural violation of the IDEA by refusing to consider the shadow aide, **it did not commit a substantive violation because it discussed staffing issues and provided a FAPE**. It did not have to develop a utopian program for the student. *B.W. v. Durham Public Schools,* No. 1:09CV00970, 2012 WL 2344396 (M.D.N.C. 6/20/12).

♦ A New Jersey student with reading and writing disorders received pull-out resource room instruction until sixth grade, when her parents became concerned about low self-esteem and sought to have her mainstreamed full time, with homework accommodations and supplemental multi-sensory reading instruction. School team members prepared two draft IEPs, one calling for continued pull-out instruction and the other calling for mainstream instruction but without the homework accommodations and reading supplements that the parents wanted. The parents rejected the IEPs and placed the student in a private school. When they sued for tuition reimbursement, they lost at the district court level. On appeal, the Third Circuit held **the final, mainstream IEP offered to the student would have offered a free appropriate public education in the least restrictive environment**. The lack of the homework accommodations and reading supplements did not render the IEP ineffective. *G.N. and S.N. v. Board of Educ. of Township of Livingston*, 309 Fed.Appx. 542 (3d Cir. 2009).

♦ A Connecticut school district behavioral consultant notified the parents of a student with Down syndrome and other impairments that because of his behavior problems it was becoming more difficult to keep the student in a regular classroom. A performance and planning team drafted an IEP that called for only 60% regular classroom placement instead of the 80% urged by the parents. The district hired a consultant who recommended gradually increasing the student's time, and the district agreed to increase it to 74%. However, the parents were determined to achieve 80% time in regular classrooms. A federal court and the Second Circuit eventually upheld the IEP, noting that while mainstreaming is an important objective, it has to be weighed against the need for appropriate education. **Mandating a percentage of time in regular classes would be inconsistent with the individualized approach of the IDEA.** *P. v. Newington Board of Educ.*, 546 F.3d 111 (2d Cir. 2008).

C. Homebound Instruction

In R.L. v. Miami-Dade County School Board, *757 F.3d 1173 (11th Cir. 2014), the court rejected a Florida school board's argument that no IDEA provision authorizes reimbursement for 1:1 home programs. Instead, the court held the IDEA definition of "special education" includes home instruction.*

In School Dist. of Wisconsin Dells v. Z.S., *295 F.3d 671 (7th Cir. 2002), the court upheld the assignment of a student with autism to a temporary homebound placement. He had a "disastrous history" in regular placements and failed to function well in any setting except a residential facility.*

♦ A Pennsylvania high school student attended a rigorous, advanced program for gifted students. In her junior year, she was diagnosed with gastroparesis and was intermittently hospitalized. She received weekly homebound instruction, which her parents supplemented with private tutoring. Although she returned to school for her senior year, she had a relapse and remained at home. The school found the student eligible for a Section 504 service plan allowing her to attend school when her health allowed. Near this time, she was diagnosed with an anxiety disorder. Her parents questioned the effectiveness of homebound instruction, noting a school district instructor was unable to provide substantive guidance in advanced placement courses such as Japanese and Chinese. The student dropped some courses and completed others with tutoring. Although the district sought permission to evaluate the student for eligibility under the IDEA, the parents declined. A Section 504 plan was offered to her with "significantly more permissive accommodations" such as a lack of attendance penalties for medical absences and permission to enter and exit the school as needed. But the student soon fell behind in her classes and began taking refuge in the library.

After finishing the school year at home with the help of private tutoring, the student graduated 21st in her class of 336. But she had to withdraw from college in her second year. Her parents sued the school district, claiming it did not properly implement the Section 504 plan. A federal court held for the district, and the parents appealed. The U.S. Court of Appeals, Third Circuit, rejected the argument that state law entitled the student to accommodations that maximized her potential. **Homebound services were never intended to be a substitute for in-class learning.** As a result, the court found no discrimination. *K.K. v. Pittsburgh Public Schools*, 590 Fed.Appx. 148 (3d Cir. 2014).

◆   A Georgia student with disabilities was placed on a strict diet and began taking nutritional supplements every 45 minutes. Based on the need to follow her regimen in a low-stress setting, her parents requested home-based services for the last three months of the school year. After first offering to provide the student her diet in school, the district agreed to provide in-home services until the end of the school year. It also suggested in-home extended school year services and a return to school in a classroom for students with severe autism.

The parents rejected the placement and filed a due process complaint, urging in-home services to maintain their child's diet. An administrative law judge dismissed the case, and a federal court upheld the decision. On appeal, the U.S. Court of Appeals, Eleventh Circuit, held the parents' demand for an in-home placement conflicted with the IDEA's preference for educating students with disabilities with their non-disabled peers. **Separate education or other removal of a child from regular educational settings was to take place only when the nature or severity of the disability prevented education with non-disabled peers.** In the court's view, the evidence did not justify in-home education. The student did not have a life-threatening condition, and her strict diet was not prescribed by a doctor. Evidence indicated she would best be served by reintegrating into school. The court affirmed the judgment. *A.K. v. Gwinnett County School Dist.*, 556 Fed.Appx. 790 (11th Cir. 2014).

◆   An Idaho student with autism and anxiety disorder had significant cognitive and developmental deficits and had behavior problems such as hitting, kicking and exposing himself. Prior to his entry into junior high school, his school prepared a functional behavioral assessment (FBA) and behavioral intervention plan. After his teacher reported he had stabbed her in the arm with a pencil and hit her in the face, the parents began keeping him at home. They refused to attend an IEP meeting but asked the school to conduct a new FBA and to update his IEP. The parents later rejected proposals for a new IEP. The district claimed the student could return to school any time and did not formally assess a homebound placement. Near the end of the school year, the district agreed to his gradual return to school. A federal court found there was no disciplinary exclusion. Although the district did not deny the student a free appropriate public education before his prolonged absence, it did not adequately evaluate his need for homebound services. **The court held it was improper to reject a request for homebound services without evaluating the student's need for an alternative placement and reintegration plan.** The court held the district had a continuing duty to provide him a FAPE during the protracted dispute and found a denial of FAPE. *Rodriguez v. Independent School Dist. of Boise City No. 1*, No. 1:12-cv-00390-CWD, 2014 WL 1317697 (D. Idaho 3/28/14).

♦   A Hawaii student with autism attended a small private school for students with autism from grades one through seven. Near the midpoint of a school year, the IEP team proposed changing the placement to his home school. To do so, the team devised a transition plan they described as "slow, methodical and appropriate" to address his anxiety at school. The parents broke off the transition discussions and requested a hearing. A hearings officer held the IEP did not deny the student a FAPE, and the parents appealed to a federal court.

While the parents claimed the IEP's present levels of educational performance (PLEPS) were insufficient, the court held they were developed with the most current information available and were thorough and accurate. It rejected the claim that the IEP did not list specific behaviors of concern, including bedwetting and clingy behavior. The PLEPS delineated reading strengths, and his correlating annual goals were listed in the IEP. Overall, the court found the IEP addressed the student's performance, needs and strengths. The goals and benchmarks were specific, capable of measurement and directly related to the student's focus areas. And the IEP had discussed the continuum of available placements. The IEP team was aware of the family's desire for the student to earn a diploma, and it sought to keep him on course. **In the court's view, the placement "was not immutable." It could be revised based on the student's performance in home school.** *Matthew O. v. Dep't of Educ., State of Hawaii*, Civil No. 12-00612 DKW-RLP, 2014 WL 467288 (D. Haw. 2/5/14).

♦   The Georgia parents of students with a nonspecific immune deficiency believed that their children should be educated at home, but an administrative law judge ruled that the public schools could provide an adequate education in the least restrictive environment. The parents appealed to a federal court and then the Eleventh Circuit, which ruled against them. **A physician said the children's medical condition did not require preventative treatment, and their immune systems were improving.** If one of them became ill, he or she could get intermittent homebound instruction. *Stamps v. Gwinnett County School Dist.*, 481 Fed.Appx. 470 (11th Cir. 2012).

♦   A New Hampshire student with mental retardation, orthopedic impairment and other disabilities attended a rehabilitation day center for four years under an IEP. However, when she was 19 and the IEP team recommended a continued placement there, her parents refused to consent to the IEP and withdrew her from school. They sought a home- and community-based program to help her with basic life skills and community interaction. The case reached the First Circuit, which ruled for the school district. The student's behavior appeared to be improving, and **the day center was a less restrictive placement than the home service setting the parents wanted**. Further, the court found the district's IEP proposal called for a significant increase in services in the area of pre-vocational skills. *Lessard v. Lyndeborough Cooperative School Dist.*, 592 F.3d 267 (1st Cir. 2010).

III. PRIVATE SCHOOL PLACEMENT

An IDEA provision allows school districts to place children with disabilities in private schools and facilities in accordance with their IEPs as one means of carrying out their duty to provide special education and related services. See Woods v. Northport Public School, *487 Fed.Appx. 968 (6th Cir. 2012). In* Blount County Board of Educ. v. Bowens, *the Eleventh Circuit held a board's failure to offer an adequate program to a preschool child with autism resulted in consent to a private placement made by the parents. For more cases involving private school tuition payment disputes, see Chapter Seven.*

◆ New York parents found a private school for their child and signed an enrollment contract for the next school year. Relying on private reports, the parents urged the committee on special education (CSE) to approve the private placement they had already made for the child. Team members met three times with the parents to consider an IEP for the next school year. Although CSE members attended the meetings with a draft IEP, they agreed to some of the suggestions from the private reports. But the team rejected the parents' request for a private school placement. At one meeting, the team offered a special education class placement in a room with 12 students, a special education teacher and paraprofessional. Despite a suggestion by a team member that a smaller class would be too restrictive, the parents rejected the IEP and requested a hearing. An impartial hearing officer (IHO) awarded them the $46,000 they had paid for tuition. Later, a state review officer reversed the IHO's decision.

On appeal, a federal court found the parents had "ample opportunity to participate in the decision-making process." Changes had been made to the IEPs in response to their concerns. **Disagreement with staff IEP recommendations was not a denial of meaningful participation in the decision-making process.** In fact, the IEP cited the private report and incorporated aspects of it. The IDEA allows staff members to prepare for a meeting by developing a proposal. The court held the IEP was reasonably calculated to confer educational benefits on the child and provide her with a free appropriate public education. While her parents may have wanted a private education for her, the court held there was no IDEA entitlement to one. *P.G. v. City School Dist. of New York*, No. 14 Civ. 1207 (KPF), 2015 WL 787008 (S.D.N.Y. 2/25/15).

◆ A federal court held **New York City's Department of Education could not be ordered to place a child in a school that was not approved by the state**. Case law authorizing parents to place children in non-approved facilities did not apply to a public agency's placement. *Florence School Dist. 4 v. Carter*, 510 U.S. 7 (1993), distinguished parental placements from district placements. *Z.H. v. New York City Dep't of Educ.*, 107 F.Supp.3d 369 (S.D.N.Y. 2015).

♦ The parents of an Alabama preschool child with autism attended IEP team meetings where a speech and language pathologist represented the board of education. Although the speech and language pathologist offered three placement options for the child, none of them met the child's needs. The parents felt a private school for children with autism could best serve their child. At one of the meetings, the speech and language pathologist agreed with them that the private school was "an excellent placement option." But the meeting closed with no offer of placement. As a new school year approached, the parents asked for private school tuition reimbursement. The board offered another program, which they declined. At a due process hearing, the parents said the speech and language pathologist seemed to be unaware of relevant services in the county.

A hearing officer held for the parents, finding the board did not offer any appropriate services or facilities. Moreover, as the board's representative, the speech and language pathologist had acquiesced to the parental placement. A federal court affirmed the decision, and the board appealed. The U.S. Court of Appeals, Eleventh Circuit, held the parental action was not unilateral. **The speech and language pathologist (and by extension, the board) had agreed to the school located by the parents.** Since the board had agreed to the private placement, the court held the parents had no duty to notify the board they were seeking reimbursement. The board had a duty to offer the child an appropriate education and could not wait and see if they would seek reimbursement. The court held for the parents, finding the board had presented them with inadequate placement options and now sought to wash its hands of its IDEA obligations. *Blount County Board of Educ. v. Bowens*, 762 F.3 1242 (11th Cir. 2014).

♦ A Massachusetts middle school student with autism was not progressing in his public school setting. In a mediation process to resolve a placement dispute, his parents agreed to visit some private schools. Only one school accepted the student, but the parents rejected it. The student finished grade eight at his public school, and the parents obtained a new functional behavioral assessment (FBA) from a board-certified behavioral analyst. In the analyst's view, the student could function in a public school with clear goals, consistent structure and support. The IEP team adopted some of the analyst's suggestions but suggested the private school, which the parents had already rejected. They requested a due process hearing. A hearing officer found the student would not receive an appropriate education at either of the schools urged by the parties. The district was ordered to hold another IEP meeting and to find or create an appropriate placement. On appeal, a federal court found evidence that the student was not likely to benefit from a regular education setting. Evidence showed he had emotional, social and behavioral impairments that inhibited his development.

A therapeutic program had been suggested as the proper setting for the student to develop trust of both his educators and peers. A public high school was unable to provide the structure and consistency he needed. **The court found no reason to disturb a finding that the private school was not an**

appropriate setting for the student. He had to be placed in a program for highly intelligent students with Asperger's Syndrome and similar disorders. *Andover School Committee v. Bureau of Special Educ. Appeals*, Nos. 12-12288-DPW, 13-10184-DPW, 2013 WL 6147139 (D. Mass. 11/21/13).

♦ A Connecticut student with emotional disturbance attended a district school under an IEP, but he regressed in his placement. A psychiatrist evaluated him and cautioned against using restraints and seclusion when responding to his problem behaviors. However, the district sometimes used "level III" therapeutic holds and closed-door timeouts. Eventually he was placed in an intensive education academy that did not use physical restraints, but after striking two staff members he was suspended and discharged. His mother placed him in a private residential facility and sought reimbursement. The district sought to have him evaluated, but she refused to consent. It then argued before a federal court that it had the right to require her consent to an evaluation. The court disagreed. Further, **the district's failure to provide an appropriate education required it to pay the private school tuition**. *Plainville Board of Educ. v. R.N.*, No. 3:09–CV–241, (RNC), 2012 WL 1094640 (D. Conn. 3/31/12).

♦ The New York City Department of Education agreed to fund a student's private school placement for kindergarten. But before the next school year began, the department sought to place her in a public school. A few days after reserving a private school spot for her child, the parent received the department's offer for a public school placement. She visited the school and learned the 1:1 occupational therapy required in the IEP was unavailable there.

After writing to reject the public school placement, the mother requested a hearing. An IHO found the school department failed to show it offered the student a FAPE. A state review officer reversed the decision. On appeal, a federal court found the department failed to show the private placement would have provided the student the out-of-classroom, 1:1 occupational therapy specified in her IEP. Among the IHO's findings was that the student's severe disability required 1:1 therapy for her to make progress. There was evidence that the school's therapist no longer worked for the department, and that the department intended to offer related service authorization "vouchers" for services. The court explained that the department could not rehabilitate this IEP deficiency after the fact. Instead, the relevant focus was whether the department had offered an adequate placement when the parent was evaluating the school. **As the department did not show it could provide the student 1:1 occupational therapy outside her classroom, the court held the public school placement was inappropriate.** And because the private school setting was found appropriate, the department was liable for her tuition there. *B.R. v. New York City Dep't of Educ.*, 910 F.Supp.2d 670 (S.D.N.Y. 2012).

♦ An Indiana student with hearing problems struggled in school. His parents requested a reevaluation, believing he had attention problems. His IEP indicated no behavior problems. The parents obtained a private evaluation that diagnosed dyslexia and recommended a transfer to a highly structured environment in a private day school. After discussion, the district rejected that idea because the private school wasn't the least restrictive environment. In the lawsuit that followed, a federal court ruled for the district. **The student was progressing under his IEPs, and his teachers were providing the highly structured multisensory education called for in the private evaluation.** Even though the student was held back in grade four, his academic deficiencies didn't define his educational experience. *J.D. v. Crown Point School Corp.*, No. 2:10–CV–508–TLS, 2012 WL 639922 (N.D. Ind. 2/24/12).

♦   A Minnesota student made little progress in public schools, slipping behind his peers each year and never progressing beyond a first-grade reading level. After fourth grade, the district offered a placement in a Coordinated Learning for Academic and Social Success (CLASS) program, but the parents rejected it and instead placed him in a private school for students with IEPs and other learning or attention issues. When they sought tuition reimbursement, a hearing officer ruled in their favor. A federal court reversed. On appeal, the Eighth Circuit reversed the district court. Here, **the IEP team knew that the student was losing ground to his peers every year, and his IEPs were not reasonably calculated to assist him in making reading progress** during grades four and five. *C.B. v. Special School Dist. No. 1*, 636 F.3d 981 (8th Cir. 2011).

♦   A New York school district failed to have an IEP in place for a learning disabled student until some 10 days after the start of the school year. Near the end of the year, the district convened a committee on special education meeting but failed to have a speech therapist in attendance. During the summer, the district proposed a public school placement for the following year. The parents instead chose a private school and then sought tuition reimbursement. The Second Circuit held that **while the school district violated the IDEA's procedures so as to deny the student educational benefits, the private school placement was not appropriate**. The private school's multisensory methods were not specially designed for the student and did not address areas of need identified by the student's evaluator. No tuition reimbursement was due. *Davis v. Wappingers Cent. School Dist.*, 431 Fed.Appx. 12 (2d Cir. 2011).

♦   A New York student attended a private school under an IDEA due process order. The next year, the school district offered to place him in a class for severely disabled students in a public school. The student's mother rejected the offering. She signed a contract to put the student in a private school with a 2:1 student/adult ratio and filed a request for due process. A federal court later held **the student should attend the private school because he needed constant adult supervision**. Also, the signing of the contract with the private school was simply the mother's way of keeping her options open and not evidence that she wasn't cooperating with the district. *New York City Dep't of Educ. v. V.S.*, No. 10-CV-05120(JG)(JO), 2011 WL 3273922 (E.D.N.Y. 7/29/11).

♦   An Indiana student was identified as having an emotional disability. He engaged in disruptive behavior at school, which adversely affected his academic progress. His grandmother became dissatisfied with his public school IEP and placed him in a private school. When she sought tuition reimbursement, a federal court ruled against her. The only evidence presented about the adequacy of the private school was the grandmother's testimony that he earned better grades there than in the public schools. The record showed that **the student was not receiving any special education at the private school. Thus, there was no basis for upholding a placement there** under the IDEA. *Indianapolis Public Schools v. M.B.*, 771 F.Supp.2d 928 (S.D. Ind. 2011).

◆ A learning disabled student in Massachusetts attended a private school. A new IEP recommended a public school placement and would have put the student in general education science and social studies classes. The mother rejected the IEP and placed him again at the private school. When she sought tuition reimbursement, a federal court held she was entitled to it. Her experts convincingly concluded that the student should attend a classroom with six to eight students at his developmental level. Further, the **school staff didn't fully understand the student's multiple deficits, so it could not tailor an adequate program for him**. *Sudbury Public Schools v. Massachusetts Dep't of Elementary and Secondary Educ.*, 726 F.Supp.2d 254 (D. Mass. 2010).

◆ A Texas school district determined that a child with autism should receive weekly speech therapy and attend an early childhood public school classroom with both special education students and typically developing students. His parents agreed to the placement, but when his behavior regressed, they asked for a summer school placement. When the district didn't respond, they placed him in his old private school and sought tuition reimbursement. When the case reached the Fifth Circuit, it held for the school district. The child had been placed in the least restrictive environment and **made enough progress in the public school setting to demonstrate that his IEP was providing him a FAPE**. *R.H. v. Plano Independent School Dist.*, 607 F.3d 1003 (5th Cir. 2010).

◆ A 14-year-old Arizona student suffered a traumatic brain injury that confined him to a wheelchair and made him dependent on caregivers for daily activities. His IEP team determined that he had a better chance of achieving his IEP goals if he were placed at a particular private day school 35 miles away. A hearing officer found that the student failed to respond despite the district's best efforts and that the private day placement was better for him. The Arizona Court of Appeals agreed. **The student's severe disability made continued mainstreaming inappropriate.** *Stallings v. Gilbert Unified School Dist. No. 41*, No. 1 CA-CV 08-0625, 2009 WL 3165452 (Ariz. Ct. App. 10/1/09).

IV. RESIDENTIAL SCHOOL PLACEMENT

A. Appropriateness

School districts are not financially responsible for placing students in residential facilities for 24-hour supervision based on medical, social or emotional reasons if they receive only incidental educational benefit from the placement. In Richardson Independent School Dist. v. Michael Z., *580 F.3d 286*

(5th Cir. 2009), the Fifth Circuit denied a request for a residential placement. It held the parents did not show the placement was necessary for educational (rather than medical or behavioral) reasons. A parental placement must be made for educational reasons to qualify for reimbursement by a school district.

♦ A Texas student had a drug habit and attempted suicide. He had attention deficit hyperactivity disorder, emotional deficits, anxiety and depression. But the student's academic achievement was found average or above in every tested area. An admission, review and dismissal (ARD) committee met and offered him an IEP with in-class support and meetings with a school psychologist. After entering high school, the student refused to do his schoolwork and told teachers he intended to sell marijuana. Although the ARD committee met to discuss his progress, his IEP remained unchanged. Early in the student's ninth-grade year, his parents placed him in a Utah wilderness camp. The school district declined their request for reimbursement for the camp, and they placed him in a Missouri mental health facility where he was diagnosed with reactive attachment disorder (RAD). The parents sought tuition reimbursement for both placements. A hearing officer found the district denied the student a free appropriate public education and ordered reimbursement for the Missouri residential placement.

The Utah facility was held ineligible for IDEA reimbursement. A federal court agreed with the parents and ordered the district to reimburse them at a rate of $7,000 per month for the Missouri placement. An award of transportation costs and $90,000 in attorneys' fees was also entered in the parents' favor. The school district appealed to the U.S. Court of Appeals, Fifth Circuit, which held the parents did not show the Missouri placement was appropriate. The student's progress at the facility was to be primarily judged by educational achievement. By relying on evidence that the Missouri school would focus on the root cause of his RAD, the lower court committed an error. The court held the benefits to the child were irrelevant if they were only incidental to the parents' reasons for making the placement. **The court found the parents made the Missouri placement over concerns that their son would again attempt suicide and because of his continuing drug problem.** As no educational reason was given for the placement, the court held for the school district. *Fort Bend Independent School Dist. v. Douglas A.,* 601 Fed.Appx. 250 (5th Cir. 2015).

♦ A New York student with a learning disability was placed in a residential facility for more than four years under an agreement between her parents and her school district. She earned mostly As and Bs but had oppositional behavior, poor social skills, verbal aggression, tantrums and social problems. In her last year at the facility, the student earned some Cs and Ds but made academic and behavioral progress. Her mother had concerns about the school's administration of asthma medication and the program's restrictiveness. She obtained a private evaluation of the child, removed her from the facility and sought home tutoring.

A school committee on special education (CSE) recommended a state-approved residential placement. The parent enrolled the student in a private academy and filed an impartial hearing request. An impartial hearing officer found the school district did not offer the student a FAPE for part of the school year. A state review officer found no denial of FAPE during the year of the unilateral private placement. It was also found that the private academy was not an appropriate placement, so reimbursement was denied. On appeal, a federal court affirmed the review officer's decision, and the parent appealed to the U.S. Court of Appeals, Second Circuit. It found **the facility had a specialized curriculum that enabled the student to achieve academic success and improve her behavior**. As the review officer had conducted a thorough review of the record, the court upheld the decision. And since the lower court had correctly found the private academy inappropriate, the court held for the school district. *Ward v. Board of Educ. of Enlarged City School Dist. of Middletown, New York*, 568 Fed.Appx. 18 (2d Cir. 2014).

◆   After a Pennsylvania student made multiple suicide attempts, his parents placed him in a New Hampshire therapeutic residential center. Upon review of an analysis by the center, the student's school district accepted a diagnosis of emotional disturbance and offered him an IEP. Although the IEP incorporated most of the center's recommendations, the parents rejected it because it did not offer the student small classes or the kind of counseling he had been receiving at the center. For the next school year, the parents located a private residential school in Pennsylvania that offered small classes and a supportive environment.

When the dispute reached the Third Circuit, it held **a school district was only liable for a residential placement that was "necessary" to provide a student with special education and related services**. No reimbursement was required if a parental placement was a response to medical, social or emotional problems that were segregable from the learning process. Further, there had to be some "link" between the private services and the child's educational needs. The court held the student was placed in the New Hampshire facility to address his mental health. Any educational benefit he received there was incidental. As the school district's IEP offer had complied with the IDEA, the court held for the district. *Munir v. Pottsville Area School Dist.*, 723 F.3d 423 (3d Cir. 2013).

◆   Parents of a 20-year-old Massachusetts student with disabilities questioned why he was unable to replicate at home the progress he was making at school. They sought a year-round residential placement and rejected a series of IEP proposals that offered alternative accommodations and more emphasis on daily living skills. After placing their son in the residential facility, they sought tuition. A hearing officer heard testimony from school district professionals who had worked with the student over the years as well as a neuropsychologist and an educational consultant, who spoke for the parents. The hearing officer ordered the district to provide limited compensatory services, and the First Circuit eventually upheld that order. The parents failed to show that the residential placement was appropriate, and **the district's multiple witnesses validated the ruling that the district had complied with the IDEA**. *Sebastian M. v. King Philip Regional School Dist.*, 685 F.3d 79 (1st Cir. 2012).

◆   Since birth, a Rhode Island student struggled with attentional, emotional and behavioral disabilities. His parents became upset that his sixth-grade IEP did not include goals or objectives relating to his social, emotional or behavioral functioning. They placed him in a residential school and sought to keep him there. A hearing officer agreed that a residential placement was necessary, and a federal court upheld that determination. The court noted that **a residential placement is necessary when consistent instructional and therapeutic interventions are needed throughout the day for the student to make meaningful educational progress**. The district's IEP denied the student a FAPE by failing to address his behavior. *Coventry Public Schools v. Rachel J.*, 893 F.Supp.2d 322 (D.R.I. 2012).

♦   The parents of a Massachusetts student with a cortical visual impairment, sought to place him at a school for the blind located 78 miles from their home. Eventually the district agreed to the placement. However, the parents refused to let the student stay there overnight more than a few times. Instead, they drove him there and back. Because of the distance involved, the parents were unable to get him to school every day, making only 48 of 70 days during the first term. They asked for transportation from the district, which refused to provide it on a daily basis. In the lawsuit that followed, **a federal court ruled for the district, holding that the placement should be residential**. *I.M. v. Northampton Public Schools*, 869 F.Supp.2d 174 (D. Mass. 2012).

♦   A California special education student had significant behavioral problems in the classroom and left the school building at least five times. The district rejected the parents' request to place him in a Tennessee religious school with his older brother and also refused to return him to a county program where he had fewer issues. Rather than address his runaway issues, it proposed removing him from a general education writing class. The parents placed him in the Tennessee school and then sought tuition reimbursement, which a federal court rejected. **Although the district denied the student a FAPE for more than a year, the parents' placement at the religious school had nothing to do with his special needs**, and his behavior problems continued there. *Covington v. Yuba City Unified School Dist.*, 780 F.Supp.2d 1014 (E.D. Cal. 2011).

♦   A New York student with ADHD attended a private school at his district's expense for several years. For grade 10, his parents placed him in a Massachusetts residential facility for students with language-based disabilities, and the district partially reimbursed them under a settlement agreement. At the end of the year, the district conducted an IEP meeting that the student's mother didn't attend. The IEP team declassified the student because he was functioning at, or close to, grade level. The mother missed another IEP meeting and placed her son at the residential facility for grade eleven. When she sought reimbursement, a federal court denied it. **Although the district had denied the student an appropriate placement for grade eleven, the residential school was also inappropriate because it was overly restrictive**. *S.H. v. New York City Dep't of Educ.*, No. 09-CV-6072(PGG), 2011 WL 609885 (S.D.N.Y. 2/18/11).

♦   An autistic student with aggressive behavior was placed in a psychiatric hospital and attended an Oahu academy under an IEP. His IEP team sought to transfer him to another location, and his parents challenged that decision. Under the stay-put rule, he remained at the academy. The parties reached a settlement on the issue of placement and left him at the academy. He was then discharged from the psychiatric hospital and placed in child protective services at an Oahu residential facility. When his parents sought to have the state pay for his residential costs there, the state refused. Eventually, the Ninth Circuit ruled that **the state did not have to pay the residential costs because the placement in that facility was outside the scope of the student's educational needs**. *Dep't of Educ., State of Hawaii v. Karen I.*, 435 Fed.Appx. 670 (9th Cir. 2011).

♦   A Colorado student with emotional issues attended a private school under a settlement agreement. Two years later, her parents placed her in a psychiatric hospital in Utah to evaluate her condition. A month after that, the district notified the parents that it would no longer fund the student's placement because she was no longer a district student. The parents then informed the district that they were placing the student in an Idaho residential treatment center and that they wanted tuition reimbursement. The district instead offered to place her in a public school. Eventually, a federal court ruled that **the district had to reimburse the parents because the placement in the Idaho center was for educational purposes**, and several experts at the due process hearing had testified that a residential placement was appropriate. *Jefferson County School Dist. R-1 v. Elizabeth E.*, 798 F.Supp.2d 1177 (D. Colo. 2011).

♦   A New York mother claimed that her son was improperly restrained at the Massachusetts school to which she had agreed to send him. She sued in both states. A New York appellate court held that she could not sue her school district because she had consented to the Massachusetts placement, and the Massachusetts court had found the use of the restraints reasonable. Further, the district had contracted out the duty to supervise the use of restraints to the Massachusetts school with her consent. *Nicholson v. Freeport Union Free School Dist.*, 74 A.D.3d 926, 902 N.Y.S.2d 192 (N.Y. App. Div. 2010).

♦   A California student who weighed 250 pounds was unpredictably violent. His district offered to place him in a special education school for autistic and emotionally disturbed children, but his mother rejected the placement. An administrative law judge (ALJ) found the district's placement appropriate. Four months later, the student's doctor diagnosed him with an emotional disturbance, and the mother requested a residential placement. The district denied the placement, and an ALJ upheld that action. A federal court agreed, but on further appeal, the Ninth Circuit Court of Appeals held that **the student's right to request a residential placement arose only when his doctor diagnosed him with emotional disturbance**. The court returned the case to the lower court with orders for it to determine if a residential placement was required. *T.G. v. Baldwin Park Unified School Dist.*, 443 Fed.Appx. 273 (9th Cir. 2011).

♦   An Oregon student with ADHD and depression made progress in school but engaged in defiant and risky behavior at home. Her parents sought a more restrictive placement for her, but the school district ruled it out because she was earning good grades when she did her work. Her parents unilaterally placed her in a residential facility, but she was expelled for having sex with another student. Her parents then placed her in an out-of-state facility and sought tuition reimbursement, which the Ninth Circuit denied. **The student did not require residential placement for any educational reason.** She was not disruptive in class and was well-regarded by teachers. *Ashland School Dist. v. Parents of Student R.J.*, 588 F.3d 1004 (9th Cir. 2009).

◆   An Oregon student began having emotional problems in school, but performed well academically. He was later hospitalized for migraines and attempted suicide. His doctors recommended a residential placement. His parents sought his placement in an alternative school, but the district refused because it couldn't monitor him properly there. The parents then placed him in a residential school without giving proper notice to the district. When they sued for tuition reimbursement, a federal district court ruled against them, and they appealed to the U.S. Court of Appeals, Ninth Circuit. It held **ample evidence indicated that the placement had been made for medical reasons** and that the parents did not provide proper notice to the school district. *Ashland School Dist. v. Parents of Student E.H.*, 587 F.3d 1175 (9th Cir. 2009).

◆   The parents of a Maine student placed her in a private residential facility before the district could evaluate her. They then demanded a due process hearing and met with the district to consider her eligibility for IDEA services. The hearing was delayed while an independent evaluation was conducted. At an IEP meeting, the parents insisted on a therapeutic residential placement while the district asserted that a non-residential public school setting would be appropriate. The parents challenged the district's placement, claiming it failed to offer a finalized IEP. A federal court and the First Circuit ruled for the district, noting that **the IEP was never finalized because the parents disrupted the IEP process. Their fixation on a residential placement at district expense caused the breakdown of the IEP process.** *C.G. and B.S. v. Five Town Community School Dist.*, 513 F.3d 279 (1st Cir. 2008).

◆   A Colorado student with autism and mental retardation had numerous behavioral problems (including crying, screaming, tantrums and other resistance) at school. He was even worse at home. His school behavior incidents lasted up to 40 minutes a day. His parents sought a residential placement and requested tuition reimbursement. A federal court held the district failed to offer an appropriate placement option, and the student was not receiving educational benefit because of his behavior problems. But the Tenth Circuit held the parents were not entitled to reimbursement. **Every evaluation of the student while he was in public schools determined that he was making some progress.** It was only away from school that his behavior was "unmanageable." And even though generalization of learned skills to home and other locations was critical for self-sufficiency and independence, the school district was not required to assure this goal. *Thompson R2-J School Dist. v. Luke P.*, 540 F.3d 1143 (10th Cir. 2008).

◆   The parents of a New York student with disabilities sought to place her in a private treatment facility. The school district declined, asserting that the private therapeutic high school day placement in which she was enrolled satisfied the

IDEA. The parents placed her in the residential facility and sought tuition reimbursement, but a due process hearing officer ruled for the district. A court reversed, finding the day program inadequate, but the Second Circuit reversed the lower court, noting that **generally, students must be regressing in day placements to be eligible for a residential placement.** *M.H. v. Monroe-Woodbury Cent. School Dist.*, 296 Fed.Appx. 126 (2d Cir. 2008).

B. Behavioral/Emotional Problems

In assessing claims for residential placements based on behavioral or emotional problems, courts focus on whether the student's behavior problems may be separated from the learning process. In Independent School Dist. No. 284 v. A.C., *258 F.3d 769 (8th Cir. 2001), the Eighth Circuit upheld a residential placement, finding a student would not receive educational benefit until her behavior was addressed in a residential setting. It held that if she could not reasonably be expected to benefit from instruction in a less restrictive setting, residential placement would be found educationally necessary.*

By contrast, in State of Wisconsin v. Randall H., *257 Wis.2d 57, 653 N.W.2d 503 (Wis. 2002), the Wisconsin Supreme Court held that a child was placed in a residential facility under a child-protection order for reasons separate from his educational needs. An IEP prepared after his residential placement did not demonstrate that the placement was necessary to meet his educational needs.*

◆   An Iowa student with Asperger's syndrome and obsessive-compulsive, mood and adjustment disorders was gifted academically. She ranked high in her class and participated in show choir, a school musical and volleyball. Her IEP specified a program for high-functioning students with autism spectrum disorder. During a family vacation, the student was raped by two men. Mental health providers recommended she return to a routine as quickly as possible. An interim IEP was offered to maintain her IEP and ease her transition back to school. Due to the circumstances, both parents waived any objection to an IEP meeting in their absence. Finding it would be best to delay a comprehensive IEP review until fall, the rest of the team decided to retain the current IEP. When she returned to school, the student began to have social problems with peers. She falsely accused a male show choir member of holding a knife to her throat, slapped another member of the school musical and used foul language. After an audition near the end of the school year, the student was not selected for show choir. Her parent filed a civil rights action in a federal court, seeking an order to require the school district to place her child in the upper-tier show choir.

A judge denied the request for relief. No evidence showed the show choir selection process had anything to do with a disability. At an IEP meeting held just before the onset of a new school year, the parent pushed for placing her child in the upper-tier choir. Staff meeting notes indicated she repeatedly conditioned her child's return to school on upper-tier choir participation. In her action, the parent sought tuition reimbursement for placing her child at a special school in Connecticut. An administrative law judge (ALJ) held for the district, as did a federal court. On appeal, the U.S. Court of Appeals, Eighth Circuit, found the parent had consented to an IEP meeting in her absence. It found the school district responded to the student's changed circumstances. While she suffered setbacks due to the rape, she made significant progress at school until being excluded from the show choir. Her progress continued at summer volleyball workouts, where she was getting along with her peers. **Although the parent claimed the student's emotional changes after the rape required more than minor changes to the IEP, the school did not find her behaviors were new.** In sum, the court held the district provided the student appropriate educational opportunities and did not deny her a free appropriate public education. *Sneitzer v. Iowa Dep't of Educ.*, 796 F.3d 942 (8th Cir. 2015).

♦   After a New York child attended a private school for grades one and two, a committee on special education (CSE) proposed a public school placement for a 12-month school year with various forms of therapy. His behavior did not seriously interfere with his instruction, but the CSE included a behavioral intervention plan (BIP) in his IEP. After visiting the site where the child was assigned, his parents rejected the placement for numerous reasons and filed an impartial hearing request. Meanwhile, they reenrolled him in the same private school. An impartial hearing officer (IHO) held the CSE offered the child a free appropriate public education (FAPE). A state review officer upheld the IHO's decision, and the parents appealed. A federal court rejected their claim that a functional behavioral analysis (FBA) of the child was improper and inadequate.

The CSE considered a sufficiently broad and appropriate range of sources in devising the FBA. With one exception, the CSE relied on the sources identified in state regulations. **In fact, the court held even a complete failure to conduct an FBA would not deny FAPE if the IEP identified problem behavior and ways to manage it.** The BIP addressed the child's interfering behaviors and provided goals and strategies for improvement and supports to help him change his behaviors. As a result, the court upheld the administrative findings that the FBA and BIP did not cause substantive harm to the child or amount to a denial of FAPE. As for the substantive challenge to the IEP, the court upheld the CSE's decisions. The IEP identified the child's present levels of performance and his health and physical development factors. As for the IEP goals, the court found they were achievable and measurable. In sum, the court found the IEP was more likely to produce progress than regression. The court rejected a claim by the parents based on the lack of an IEP provision for 1:1 support. It held for the school district, finding a district was not required to provide every special service to maximize a child's potential. *M.L. v. New York City Dep't of Educ.*, No. 13-CV-2314, 2015 WL 1439698 (E.D.N.Y. 3/27/15).

♦   A New York child with an emotional disturbance had some oppositional issues but made progress in regular education classes. During her ninth-grade year, her academic performance began to decline, and her behavior became more problematic. After she was diagnosed with bipolar disorder and put on medication, she was arrested for shoplifting and placed in a diversion program that required her to receive mental health counseling. By the end of the student's ninth-grade year, she was failing most of her classes and had been disciplined 25 times. The student had to repeat grade nine and was ordered by a family court to undergo a 30-day psychiatric evaluation and a 10-day hospitalization.

Soon after returning to her high school, the student tried to commit suicide. This led to another hospitalization and diagnosis of an unspecified mood disorder. The district and parents then agreed to place the student in a program in which she received daily tutoring. A school psychologist evaluated her and found that "outside mental health factors appeared to be causing significant disruption" in her life. The school district held a CSE meeting but did not create an IEP. The parents said the student then collapsed into depression. They placed her in a therapeutic boarding school that used a 12-step program. While at the boarding school, the student met with a counselor and her grades improved. The parents kept her there for another year before seeking tuition assistance. The district denied their request, and the parents asked for a hearing. The IHO found the district had denied the student a free appropriate public education for two school years. But a review officer found little objective evidence to support this. When the case reached the U.S. Court of Appeals, Second Circuit, **it found the review officer had reasonably found there was insufficient evidence about the boarding school's instruction to support the parents' claim for tuition reimbursement**. As a result, the court held for the school district. *Hardison v. Board of Educ. of Oneonta City School Dist.*, 773 F.3d 372 (2d Cir. 2014).

♦ A Pennsylvania student functioned well academically but had many home behavior problems. She attended religious schools before making an apparent suicide attempt. After the student was hospitalized, her mother put her in a public school homebound instruction program. Meanwhile, she received outpatient therapy, drug/alcohol counseling and family services. A school psychologist evaluated her and found her eligible for special education with an "other health impairment." After another suicide attempt, the student was placed in an inpatient substance abuse rehabilitation center. Although the school district offered to place the student in a public school with full-time emotional support, the parent rejected the offer. The parent filed a due process complaint, placed her child in a residential 12-step treatment facility and sought tuition reimbursement. A hearing officer held for the school district, and the case reached a federal court. It noted the IEP contained goals in areas related to the student's disability and set organizational/behavioral goals related to her needs.

The hearing officer had found the case "was really about the Parent's desire for a residential setting to address [the student's] drug addiction and out-of-control home behaviors." As the IEP called for specially designed instruction and services through a positive behavior support plan, full-time emotional support, counseling and social skills instruction, the court found it appropriate. **Although the parent's choice was a rational response to her child's drug addiction, the court found it did not address her disability.** As the district was not responsible for treating drug addiction, family problems and delinquency, the court held for the district. *EK v. Warwick School Dist.*, Civil No. 09-4205, 2014 WL 737328 (E.D. Pa. 2/26/14).

♦ An 18-year-old Indiana student had significant behavioral issues relating to his autism. A hearing officer ruled that he was entitled to a residential placement. The district appealed, but a federal court ruled against it. Although the district claimed that the parents did not allow the IEPs to be fully implemented, **it did not provide essential IEP services**. A homebound placement offered by the district wasn't reasonably calculated to provide educational benefits. *Mt. Vernon School Corp. v. A.M.*, No. 1:11–cv–00637– TWP–TAB, 2012 WL 3764019 (S.D. Ind. 8/29/12).

♦   An adopted child in Maryland was found eligible for special education in eighth grade because of emotional problems. His grades slipped the next year, and his parents enrolled him in a hospital outpatient program, where he received counseling for substance abuse. His tenth-grade IEP called for a private school placement and when he attended class he received As and Bs. But he often violated school rules and eventually ran away from home to resume using drugs and alcohol. His parents claimed he required a residential placement, but the district disagreed. A federal court held for the district, noting that **the student's emotional problems could be segregated from the learning process**. Thus, he did not require a residential placement. *Y.B. v. Board of Educ. of Prince George's County*, 895 F.Supp.2d 689 (D. Md. 2012).

♦   An adopted student in Maryland with learning disabilities and emotional disturbance exhibited suicidal tendencies and clinical depression. Her IEP team placed her in a private special education day school. She later self-mutilated and attempted suicide. Her parents placed her in a residential school even though a school psychologist found that she should be placed in a therapeutic school for students with serious emotional issues. When the parents sought reimbursement, a federal court and the Fourth Circuit ruled against them, noting that **the placement was based on the parents' desire to ensure that she did not harm herself**. It was not made for educational reasons and was not the least restrictive environment. She made progress in the day school when her mental health issues stabilized. *Shaw v. Weast*, 364 Fed.Appx. 47 (4th Cir. 2010).

CHAPTER FIVE

Changes in Placement and Student Discipline

I. CHANGES IN PLACEMENT

A. Generally

The IDEA requires a school district to provide parents prior written notice whenever it "(A) proposes to initiate or change; or (B) refuses to initiate or change, the identification, evaluation, or educational placement of the child, or the provision of a free appropriate public education to the child." See 20 U.S.C. § 1415(b)(3). This notice requirement also applies when a school district proposes graduating a student with a disability and awarding the student a regular education diploma. See 34 C.F.R. Part 300.122(a)(3)(iii). A hearing must be granted to parents wishing to contest a change in placement.

♦ A Kentucky child had autism and apraxia. A school admissions and release committee (ARC) placed him in a private school for one year. But the parents grew unhappy with the program and placed him at another private school. When the ARC reconvened, the parties could not agree on a placement. After going through mediation, the school district agreed to pay part of the parents' tuition and transportation costs. They agreed to discuss a transition plan for the child to return to a district school for the next year but then requested a due process hearing. In challenging the district's IEP proposal, the parents asked the hearing officer to deem the private school they had selected as their child's stay-put placement pending the outcome of the case. A hearing officer held the IEP would have denied the child a FAPE and the school selected by the parents would be the child's stay-put placement throughout the proceeding. As a result, the district was ordered to reimburse the parents for their private school costs.

A federal court held the child's operative placement was the parentally selected private school, and it ordered the district to reimburse the parents for it. On appeal, the U.S. Court of Appeals, Sixth Circuit, held **a school district is not required to pay for private education costs unless a court or hearing officer finds that a FAPE was denied**. An IDEA regulation at 34 C.F.R. Part 300.116 indicates that **a school district must approve of a placement decision in some manner to be subject to reimbursement**. Parents could not unilaterally decide which school was the child's stay-put placement. In this case, the last "agreed-upon" placement was the school from which the parents had removed the child before the mediated settlement. Since none of the parents' stay-put arguments had merit, the court denied reimbursement. *N.W. v. Boone County Board of Educ.*, 763 F.3d 611 (6th Cir. 2014).

◆   The Texas Education Agency conducted a hearing to discuss suspending school operations at a charter school that served special education students. After the agency voted to suspend school operations, notices were sent to parents advising them of the closure and providing lists of other schools. The parents of 14 students sued the agency, alleging a violation of the IDEA because closing the school amounted to a change in placement. The agency countered that **any transfer of students was only a change in location**, and a federal court agreed that closing the charter school was not grounds for a temporary order preventing the action. The parents failed to identify any specific elements that would be modified or eliminated from their children's IEPs as a result of the school's closure. On appeal, the U.S. Court of Appeals, Fifth Circuit, rejected an effort by the parents to pursue their invalid IDEA claims by casting them as violations of federal law under 42 U.S.C. § 1983. In addition, the court held a lower court could not consider constitutional claims brought by charter school teachers against the school. It found their employment contracts designated them as at-will employees who had no property interest in continued employment there. *Comb v. Rowell*, 538 Fed.Appx. 371 (5th Cir. 2013).

◆   A Pennsylvania student had a specific learning disability. His parents and the school district disagreed on a placement after his third-grade year. Over the next two years, his third-grade IEP became his stay-put placement under the IDEA. The district proposed providing itinerant learning support primarily in a regular classroom, instead of the daily hour of resource room support specified in the third-grade IEP. The parents rejected that proposal, arguing that it amounted to a change in placement. In the lawsuit that followed, the Third Circuit held that the district provided the same services to the student in the inclusive setting, on a daily basis and with the same special education teacher.

Thus, **providing the itinerant learning support was not a change in placement so as to violate the IDEA's stay-put provision**. *In re Educ. Assignment of Joseph R.*, 318 Fed.Appx. 113 (3d Cir. 2009).

♦ A Hawaii student with mental retardation and a heart condition reported feeling unsafe while at his home school. The state Department of Education (DOE) held an IEP meeting to discuss a placement for the 2004-05 school year at a location where the student would feel safe. The DOE offered to place him at a large public school building, but the parents rejected the placement as being intimidating to the student. They placed the student in a home program and a private academy, then sought reimbursement. A hearing officer ruled against them, but a federal court reversed. **Although a change in schools is not necessarily a change in placement, it was a change in placement here.** Placing him in the larger school could be emotionally, educationally and psychologically detrimental. No one at the IEP meeting, apart from the parents, had information about the student. It was apparent that the DOE had pre-determined the physical location of the student's placement and thus violated the IDEA. The parents were entitled to reimbursement. *Melodee H. v. Dep't of Educ., State of Hawaii*, No. 07-000256 HG-LEK, 2008 WL 2051757 (D. Haw. 5/13/08).

♦ An Ohio school district made addendums to a student's IEP in three consecutive months during his sixth-grade year. The third addendum sought to phase out a point reward system used to reinforce his behavior. The addendum also stated if the target behavior was not maintained, the original IEP would be reinstated. The parents did not agree to the third addendum at an IEP meeting. They did not learn that the addendum was being implemented until the district sent them a certified letter several days after the meeting. The parents challenged the addendum to the IEP, asserting that it fundamentally changed their child's placement. The case reached the Ohio Court of Appeals, which noted that the addendum was neither a fundamental change in nor an elimination of a basic element of the IEP. The original IEP called for a behavior plan that would eventually thin the reinforcers. **Not every change to an IEP constitutes a change in placement.** *Stancourt v. Worthington City School Dist.*, No. 07AP-835, 2008 WL 4151623 (Ohio Ct. App. 9/9/08).

B. Notice and Hearing

♦ A New Jersey school district placed a child with autism in a private school offering an intensive program of ABA therapy. After three years, the district sought to move him to a public school. The private school's director said the child was progressing, no longer needed intensive private school services and would benefit from a less restrictive setting. Based on the director's comments, the district recommended an in-district, special class for students with autism. This recommendation was incorporated into the IEP, but no school site was indicated. The parents filed a due process petition. After the parents visited their child's school assignment, they sought a stay-put order to preserve his private placement. An ALJ credited the private school director's testimony and held the IEP proposal would not deny the child a free appropriate public education

(FAPE). In a federal district court action, the parents said the private school retaliated against them because they had invoked their stay-put rights to preserve his current placement. But the court held for the district. On appeal, the U.S. Court of Appeals, Third Circuit, held the school district provided the parents adequate written notice of the proposal to change the IEP.

Although the classroom was not identified in the district's notice, the IDEA only required a description of the general type of educational program, such as the type of classes, individualized attention and services to be provided. The court held the notice did not have to describe the "bricks and mortar" of a school. Next, the court held the IEP proposal offered the child a FAPE. A school district does not have to incorporate every program requested by the parents and does not have to describe the particular methodology in the IEP. As the IEP was reasonably calculated to provide the child with educational benefits, the court held for the school board. *M.A. v. Jersey City Board of Educ.*, 592 Fed. Appx. 124 (3d Cir. 2014).

◆   An Arkansas student with severe autism had low verbal and cognitive skills and great difficulty with personal interactions. He was often violent at school, and his IEPs called for self-contained special education classes with constant monitoring by staff. When he was 11, he punched a paraprofessional aide, causing her to lose consciousness and go to the hospital. After suspending the student for four days, the school moved up a scheduled IEP meeting five days. At the meeting, team members urged the parents to accept a homebound setting for the child. Instead, they withdrew him from school, requested a due process hearing and sought reimbursement for a private placement. A hearing officer found the school district provided inadequate notice of a change in placement, but denied reimbursement. A federal court held the change in agenda converted the meeting into a manifestation determination review without adequate and proper notice. But the parents had sufficient information to actively participate.

As the student was progressing, the court held the parents were not entitled to private school tuition reimbursement. On appeal, the U.S. Court of Appeals, Eighth Circuit, found the failure to provide proper notice of the meeting was a procedural error. But it found the error was mitigated, because the parents knew before the meeting that their child's behavior and the safety of staff would be discussed. The team did not make a placement decision before the meeting. And the parents had many chances to meet with staff to agree on a placement. Eighth Circuit cases held **neither the IDEA nor its regulations prohibit schools from coming to IEP meetings with tentative recommendations prepared in a parent's absence.** The court denied the parents' request for reimbursement. *W.K. v. Harrison School Dist.*, 509 Fed.Appx. 565 (8th Cir. 2013).

◆   The parents of Philadelphia students with autism claimed that their school district "automatically" transferred autistic students from one school to another after they completed a certain grade, while non-disabled students enjoyed continued, uninterrupted attendance in their schools. They asserted that this policy violated the IDEA, the ADA, the Rehabilitation Act and state law. **A hearing officer held that the district violated the students' rights by reassigning them without proper IDEA notices.** When the parents brought a class action lawsuit against the district, the district asked for dismissal, but a federal court denied the request. *P.V. v. School Dist. of Philadelphia*, No. 2:11-CV-04027, 2011 WL 5127850 (E.D. Pa. 10/31/11).

II. STAY-PUT PROVISION

A. Generally

The IDEA's stay-put provision, found at 20 U.S.C. Section 1415(j), was included in the IDEA to protect eligible children and their parents during due process proceedings. The stay-put provision states in relevant part: "during the pendency of any proceedings conducted pursuant to this section, unless the State or local educational agency and the parents otherwise agree, the child shall remain in the then-current educational placement of the child." A state hearing officer's decision is considered an "agreement" that binds the parties.

A child's "then-current educational placement" is "the operative placement actually functioning at the time the dispute first arises." If an IEP has been implemented, the placement specified in the IEP will be the one subject to the stay-put provision. But where the dispute arises before any IEP has been implemented, the "current educational placement" will be the operative placement under which the child is actually receiving instruction at the time the dispute arises. In A.D. v. State of Hawaii Dep't of Educ., *727 F.3d 911 (9th Cir. 2013), the Ninth Circuit held students have "an automatic right" to stay put. A stay-put placement remains the student's current educational placement from the time a due process complaint is filed until the case is resolved.*

♦ A Connecticut child attended a private school at his school district's expense. His parent later grew dissatisfied with his progress and placed him in a private religious school outside the district that provided no special education. The parent paid the school's tuition while the district paid for related services. School officials discontinued the agreement at the end of the year and suggested placement in a public school in the district. But the parent rejected this and filed a due process complaint. A hearing officer held for the school board, finding the IEP offered a free appropriate public education (FAPE). The private school was found an inappropriate setting as it provided the child no special education. The parent appealed to a federal court, which held the IEP offered the child a FAPE.

But the court held the board violated the stay-put provision by refusing to fund the related services described in the IEP. Appeal reached the U.S. Court of Appeals, Second Circuit. After rejecting the parent's claim that the IEP denied her child a FAPE, the court found her participation rights had not been violated. Throughout the dispute, the student was a resident of the district and the board violated the IDEA by not offering him an IEP. **There was no merit to the board's argument that once a child was enrolled at a school outside the district, any IDEA obligations were terminated.** But the court refused to reverse the findings that the private religious school was an inappropriate placement. It offered no special education and did not modify its curriculum to accommodate the student. In the court's opinion, **the board violated the stay-**

put provision by discontinuing the provision of related services at the private school. It held the stay-put provision applies to related services. As the parent argued, she was entitled to the full value of services which the board was required to fund from the time of the due process request until the end of the proceeding. *Doe v. East Lyme Board of Educ.*, 790 F.3d 440 (2d Cir. 2015).

♦   A Maryland student with Down syndrome completed eighth grade at a charter school. Her IEP team prepared a plan for her entry into high school. Although school district officials were invited into the IEP process, no representative from the district attended. As a result, the IEP was crafted by charter school staff members and the parents. Later, the school district rejected a private placement recommended by the team. The parents disagreed with the district's proposal and placed their child in a private school. After mediation, the parties agreed that the child would attend the private school for the rest of the year at the district's expense. Near the end of the school year, the school district determined the child should be removed from the diploma track and placed in a certificate program. The parents requested a due process hearing.

An ALJ found the child was entitled to remain at the private school pending resolution of the case. But the district refused to pay her tuition. In response, the parents filed a federal case. The court granted their request for a preliminary order. While an appeal to the Fourth Circuit was pending, the ALJ held the parents did not prove the IEP was inadequate. A school district official wrote to the parents that the child would be reassigned. Days later, a bus was sent to take the child to a district school. According to the parents, the district approved an IEP on the same day. They asked the court for an order to maintain the private placement. In addition to asserting IDEA violations, they included Rehabilitation Act and Americans with Disabilities Act (ADA) claims. The court held the parents could pursue their discrimination claims against the district based on "blatant disregard" of the stay-put order. **Since the ALJ found the private school was the child's stay-put placement, the school district had to fund the placement for the duration of the case.** There is no personal liability under Section 504 or the ADA, so claims against the staff members were dismissed. *A.B. v. Baltimore City Board of School Commissioners*, Civ. No. WMN-14-3851, 2015 WL 4875998 (D. Md. 8/13/15).

♦ ` Pennsylvania parents withdrew their child from her public school and placed her in a private setting. A hearing officer held the school district denied the child a FAPE. Compensatory education was awarded to the parents for part of their child's first-grade year and all of grade two. The district was ordered to reimburse some of their tuition and transportation costs. A federal court reversed the hearing officer's decision. It held the district's IEP proposal would have offered a FAPE. Later, the U.S. Court of Appeals, Third Circuit, affirmed the court's judgment in *Ridley School Dist. v. M.R.*, 680 F.3d 260 (3d Cir. 2012).

The parents sought reimbursement for their costs for parts of grade one and grade two under the stay-put provision. After the district denied the request, they filed a new federal case, claiming rights to funding of the private placement until the conclusion of all appeals in the prior lawsuit. The court agreed and awarded them $57,658. On appeal, the Third Circuit explained that **the stay-put** provision acts as an automatic preliminary injunction, fixing a child's "then-current educational placement" as the status quo for the duration of an IDEA proceeding. When a hearing officer holds for parents, a school district has to fund the private stay-put placement. Despite the district's success on appeal, the private school remained the child's stay-put placement for the duration of the dispute. The stay-put provision intends to ensure educational stability until a placement dispute is resolved regardless of the merits of a claim. *M.R. v. Ridley School Dist.*, 744 F.3d 112 (3d Cir. 2014).

♦   The U.S. Court of Appeals, Ninth Circuit, upheld a decision by Hawaii school officials to move a child from a private facility for children with autism to a public school. Although the parents claimed the public school was "one of the worst performing schools in all of Hawaii," the court held they did not show it was an inappropriate school setting under the IDEA. Among other things, the court held **the state's decision to stop paying private tuition was not a unilateral change in placement under the circumstances of the case.** Stay-put funding was resumed after a court issued a preliminary order for the parents. *F.K. v. State of Hawaii, Dep't of Educ.*, 585 Fed.Appx. 710 (9th Cir. 2014).

♦   A Pennsylvania child with Down syndrome, sleep apnea and a heart condition was often late to school and sometimes missed school entire days. A charter school became responsible for implementing her IEP after taking over the management of her public school. For about two years, the school never recorded the child's attendance and did not enforce its truancy policies against her. But the relationship between the school and her parent deteriorated, and the parent disrupted a faculty meeting on a day when she was unable to find her child's classroom. The school began to mark the child's absences and eventually dropped her from its attendance roll. This was done to comply with a state law mandating the disenrollment of students after 10 consecutive school absences.

   In the parent's due process complaint against the charter school and the School District of Philadelphia, a state hearing officer denied her request to preserve the charter school placement. He found the child had no operative placement at the time the dispute arose. On appeal, a federal court held the school's unilateral act of disenrolling the student was a change in placement that violated the stay-put provision. Appeal reached the U.S. Court of Appeals, Third Circuit. It held that if a child's IEP had been implemented, the "then-current educational placement" was determined by the IEP. In this case, the student's current IEP unequivocally provided that the charter school was her local education agency and that her IEP would be implemented there. **As the IEP designated the charter school as her education agency, unilaterally removing her from school by disenrolling her violated the stay-put provision.** The court rejected the claim that disenrolling a student was not an IDEA "proceeding." The status quo was determined by the existing IEP, and the placement had to be maintained throughout the dispute. Finally, the court held it was not error for the lower court to find the stay-put provision preempted state law requirements related to mandatory attendance. As a result, the court held for the child. *R.B. v. Mastery Charter School*, 532 Fed.Appx. 136 (3d Cir. 2013).

B. Settlements and Administrative Cases

IDEA stay-put language at 20 U.S.C. Section 1415(j) declares that a child is to remain in the "then-current educational placement" during the pendency of any IDEA proceeding, unless the parents and educational agency otherwise agree. A state hearing officer's decision changing a placement is deemed an "agreement" of the parties under the stay-put provision. When a hearing officer holds for the parents, a school district must fund the private stay-put placement.

As the Supreme Court held in Honig v. Doe, *this chapter, the stay-put provision was intended to strip schools of any unilateral power to exclude disabled students from school. The stay-put provision reflects a Congressional policy choice that all students with disabilities are to remain in their placements during IDEA disputes, regardless of the merits of their cases.*

♦   A Rhode Island parent requested a due process hearing in an effort to obtain a private school placement for her disabled son. She also sought eight new evaluations of him. In return for dismissal of the action, the school committee agreed to pay for private school tuition and to perform four evaluations. The settlement recited that the parent relinquished any right to the other evaluations.

After the parties reached the agreement, the school committee conducted the required evaluations. But a month after the student enrolled at the private school, the parent requested 10 more evaluations. The school committee filed a new request for a hearing. A hearing officer found some of the evaluations done by the school committee were inappropriate. The school committee was ordered to pay for an occupational therapy evaluation and a psychoeducational evaluation. In response, the committee filed a federal court action. After review, the court held the settlement agreement released the committee from the claim to a new psychoeducational evaluation. On appeal, the U.S. Court of Appeals, First Circuit, found evidence that some of the assessments were adequate. The school committee did not agree to a psychoeducational evaluation. Moreover, **the parent had given up her right to seek evaluations beyond the four specified in the agreement**. Although a change in circumstances would have allowed her to obtain a new evaluation, she did not argue there had been any changed conditions. But the school committee did not even challenge a finding by the hearing officer that the educational evaluation had been inappropriate. *South Kingstown School Committee v. Joanna S.*, 773 F.3d 344 (1st Cir. 2014).

♦   A Colorado student with learning disabilities, anxiety and attention deficit hyperactivity disorder had trouble with class sizes and the pace of instruction as she transitioned to middle school. In grade seven, she failed her classes and was bullied and teased by classmates. Her parents placed her in a private academy for students with learning difficulties. They reached a settlement agreement with the school district by assuming "full responsibility for her education." In return, the district paid the parents $16,681 and required them to notify the district whether or not they intended to return their child to a public school for the 2012-13 school year. If they did so, the parties agreed to develop an IEP.

The parents further agreed that the private school would not be deemed the student's stay-put placement in the event of an IEP dispute. Near the end of the school year, the parents asked to renew the settlement for the 2012-13 school year. The district refused and proposed an IEP for a public high school. After rejecting the IEP, the parents returned the child to the private academy. An ALJ held for the parents, finding the district did not assess the student in all areas of suspected disability and denied her a free appropriate public education. They then asked a federal court to order the district to pay their private placement costs from the date of the ALJ's decision. The court held the ALJ's decision shifted the stay-put placement to the private academy. Under 34 C.F.R. Part 300.518(d), **an administrative decision is an "agreement" between the parties to change a student's placement**. The court rejected a claim that the agreement governed a stay-put placement even after the ALJ's decision. *Taylor F. v. Arapahoe County School Dist. 5*, 954 F.Supp.2d 1197 (D. Colo. 2013).

◆   The mother of a Hawaii student with autism placed him in a private school for one year under a settlement agreement with the department of education, agreeing to allow the department to observe him at the private school and to transition him to public school the following year, "if appropriate." She placed limitations on observation and did not attend an IEP meeting, so the department finalized an IEP without her that placed the student in a public school. She kept her son in the private school for several years and then sued for tuition reimbursement, claiming that it was the stay-put placement under the IDEA. A federal court and the Ninth Circuit disagreed. **The settlement agreement was only for the one school year, and the IEPs offered by the department were valid.** *K.D. v. Dep't of Educ., State of Hawaii*, 665 F.3d 1110 (9th Cir. 2011).

◆   A New Jersey student with autism endured bullying and ridicule until a new IEP allowed his placement in an accredited K-12 Christian School. However, after he entered high school, a state official notified the district and his parents that his placement violated the state's Naples Act because they did not get approval from the state education department and the school was not nonsectarian. The district later proposed a public school placement. The parents appealed, seeking to keep their son at the Christian school under the stay-put placement. A federal court allowed the student to stay at the school during the litigation. **Even though the placement had been mistakenly made, it was the student's stay-put placement under the IDEA.** *R.S. v. Somerville Board of Educ.*, No. 10-4215 (MLC), 2011 WL 32521 (D.N.J. 1/5/11).

◆   After a Minnesota student spent time in detention facilities, his mother claimed IDEA violations and requested a due process hearing. She reached a settlement with the school district, agreeing on a level of services that did not continue the provisions of his stay-put IEP and releasing any claims arising out of his education at the time of the agreement. Before being transferred to a state prison, the student complained that his district failed to provide a FAPE during his incarceration. A federal court eventually held **the settlement agreement superseded the stay-put IEP** and that the student's mother's waiver was valid under the IDEA. *D.B.A. v. Special School Dist. No. 1, Minneapolis, Minnesota*, No. 10-1045 (PAM/FLN), 2010 WL 5300946 (D. Minn. 12/20/10).

C. Transfers and Grade Transitions

An IDEA provision at 20 U.S.C. § 1414(d)(2)(C)(i)(l) governs cases where a child with a disability transfers between school districts during the same school year. If a child transfers into a new school district with an IEP from another school district, the receiving district is required to provide the child a free appropriate public education. This includes "services comparable to those described in the previously held IEP, in consultation with the parents until such time as the [district] adopts the previously held IEP or develops, adopts and implements a new IEP that is consistent with Federal and State Law."

♦   The parents of a New Jersey student with learning disabilities agreed with Westwood Regional School District on an IEP placing him in a private school. But before the school year, the parents moved into the Byram School District. Byram officials reviewed the IEP and decided the student's program could be implemented within the district. After mediation failed, the parents initiated an IDEA due process proceeding. An administrative law judge (ALJ) denied their request to approve the private placement under the IDEA stay-put provision.

A federal court agreed with the ALJ. On appeal, the U.S. Court of Appeals, Third Circuit, found **the stay-put provision preserves the educational status quo during the pendency of an IDEA proceeding**. Unless agreed otherwise, a child must remain in his "then-current educational placement" for the duration of a due process proceeding. In the court's view, the case did not implicate the stay-put provision, because the parents had acted unilaterally. If a child transfers to a new school district with an IEP from a different school district, the receiving district is required to provide the child a free appropriate public education. In *Michael C. v. Radnor Township School Dist.*, 202 F.3d 642 (3d Cir. 2002), the court held that in the context of interstate transfers, unilateral family relocations can override the stay-put provision. Stay-put protections are "inoperative" until a new placement is agreed upon. In this case, the court held the parent's choice to move to Byram made the stay-put provision inoperative. Byram could meet its IDEA obligations by complying with 20 U.S.C. § 1414(d)(2)(C)(i)(l), which governs cases where a child transfers during a school year. Byram offered services comparable to those stated in the Westwood IEP, complying with the IDEA. Both the ALJ and the lower court noted the parents' refusal to cooperate with Byram over any placement beside the private school described in the Westwood IEP. As a result, the court held for Byram. *J.F. v. Byram Township Board of Educ.*, 629 Fed.Appx. 235 (3d Cir. 2015).

♦   Taking advantage of the Colorado school choice law, the parents of a child with autism spectrum disorder removed him from a school in their residence district and placed him at a charter school in another school district. Later, the child was denied enrollment at the charter school for the next school year. The parents filed a due process complaint against the school district in which the school was located, asserting IDEA procedural violations. An administrative law judge (ALJ) denied their request to preserve the placement via the stay-put provision. A federal court held the charter school was the child's "then current" placement under the stay-put provision. It found a child's current educational placement could be found by examining the IEP in place when the stay-put provision was invoked along with other relevant factors. **While the stay-put provision did not require that a child remain in the exact physical location, schools were not permitted to make changes that might significantly effect a child's learning experience.** The court found the charter school district incorrectly argued that it was not required to enroll the child because he could return to his district of residence. The School Choice law did not change this outcome. A state law did not allow the district to avoid its IDEA obligations.

Finding the charter school was the child's current educational placement, the court held he was entitled to a stay-put order preserving his placement there pending the outcome of the dispute. *Smith v. Cheyenne Mountain School Dist. 12*, No. 14-cv-02651-PAB-CBS, 2015 WL 4979771 (D. Colo. 8/20/15).

♦ Hawaii education department officials proposed moving a student with autism to a public school after he had attended a private school for 10 years with state funding. It was recommended that he prepare for post-high school goals and obtain a diploma. The parents disagreed with the IEP and refused to participate in transfer meetings to discuss a move to a public school setting.

The dispute came before a hearings officer who found the IEP did not deny the student an appropriate education as it had accurate goals, objectives and baseline data. The parents appealed to a federal court, which held they did not show the IEP lacked baseline information or had goals that were insufficient. The hearings officer had correctly found the IEP goals and objectives were measureable. **While placements must be in the least restrictive setting, this must also "be the least restrictive environment which also meets the child's IEP goals."** The court found no evidence of predetermination. It instead found the department had investigated and addressed the concerns of the parents. It was appropriate to await the development of a transition plan until after the IEP meeting took place and the IEP was completed. As a result, the court held for the department of education. *Anthony C. v. Dep't of Educ., State of Hawaii*, No. 12-00698 DKW-BMK, 2014 WL 587848 (D. Haw. 2/14/14).

♦ A Wisconsin ninth-grader attended a multi-categorical classroom in which she studied a core academic curriculum with modifications. Late in the school year, the district determined it could not meet her special education needs in a multi-categorical setting. It proposed a self-contained classroom aligned to extended grade-band standards at a different school. Because of the functional and non-grade-level standards associated with the self-contained classroom, most of the classes in the setting were ineligible for credit toward graduation.

The parents requested a due process hearing and obtained a stay-put order pending review. An administrative law judge (ALJ) held for the school district, and the student remained in her school pending appeal to a federal court. Over a year later, the court upheld the decision to place the student in self-contained classes at the transfer high school. A federal court lifted the stay-put order and the U.S. Court of Appeals, Seventh Circuit, affirmed the decision. But on the first day of the next school year, the parents returned their child to the school at which she attended multi-categorical classes. After a few weeks, she began to attend the transfer high school. Her parents sought a new order, arguing they were not informed about the transfer to the new school. The ALJ held they had been informed of the transfer, and the case returned to federal court. This time, the parents argued their child was placed in an unsafe classroom made up of boys with behavioral disabilities. **The court upheld the ALJ's decision for the school district, finding a placement with students who had minor behavioral problems could still be found adequate.** *Williams v. Milwaukee Public Schools*, No. 13-C-207, 2014 WL 7156830 (E.D. Wis. 12/12/14).

♦   An 18-year-old District of Columbia student missed 95 school days and failed grade nine. He tried to repeat grade nine in an extended school day program for at-risk students. Despite discussions about changing his program, no formal IEP meeting was held, and no assignment was made. When he tried to attend classes at the school, he was not allowed into the building.

After being excluded on later occasions, the student filed a federal district court action, seeking an order to allow his return to the school. In the court's view, he was entitled to stay-put relief. It found any district reassignment proposal was "amorphous at best." The district did not assure there would be no fundamental change in his program. While the district had excluded the student from his neighborhood school, it conceded it would be possible to implement his IEP there. **Since the district made a "vague and belated" proposal for alternative services at a distant location, the court granted the request for stay-put relief.** *Douglas v. Dist. of Columbia*, 4 F.Supp.3d 1 (D.D.C. 2013).

♦   A group of parents of students with autism attending Philadelphia schools claimed the district's transfer policy for students with autism violated IDEA notice requirements and denied parents their IDEA participation rights. The district placed its 1,684 students with autism in grades K-8 in one of three types of autistic support classrooms based on their grade level. Students were divided into groups including grades K-2, grades 3-5 and grades 6-8. Some schools only offered one grade level of autism support. Many students in need of support who completed the highest grade provided for in a current school were subject to transfer to a different school where those services were provided. This was referred to as "upper-leveling." A federal court held the students could represent a class of students who claimed to be harmed by upper-leveling. Agreeing with the parents, the court found the relief they were seeking could not be obtained through IDEA due process proceedings. Locations at which a child's services were offered did not determine "educational placement."

The Third Circuit has recognized that the distance between a student's classes, available facilities, and the student's history at a particular school were all relevant factors. Upper-leveling did not involve a move to a new classroom but the relocation of a child to an entirely new school. Since transition was likely to have a significant impact on the learning of the autistic students in this case, the court held the upper-leveling of students was a "change of placement" under the IDEA. **The district's upper-leveling process violated IDEA procedural safeguards for proper notice and parental participation, and the court ordered the school district to alter its process.** *P.V. v. School Dist. of Philadelphia*, Civ. No. 2:11-cv-04027, 2013 WL 618540 (E.D. Pa. 2/19/13).

D. Individual Family Service Plans

In Johnson v. Special Educ. Hearing Office, *287 F.3d 1176 (9th Cir. 2002), the Ninth Circuit stated the change in responsibility for an autistic student's education from an individualized family service plan (IFSP) to an IEP necessarily changed the status quo of a student placement.* **When a student transfers from one public agency to another, the receiving agency is required only to provide a program that conforms to the last agreed-upon placement.**

◆   A New Jersey student diagnosed with autism at the age of two attended a special nursery school and received applied behavioral analysis (ABA) services under an individualized family service plan. The school district proposed an IEP for preschool that included ABA services different than what the student had previously received. His parents challenged the IEP, and a federal court held that **they did not have to place their son in the class before challenging the IEP**. They could seek reimbursement for private services despite language in the IDEA stating that reimbursement was available only where a student has been denied FAPE and "previously received special education and related services from a public agency." *D.L. and K.L. v. Springfield Board of Educ.*, 536 F.Supp.2d 534 (D.N.J. 2008).

◆   Florida triplets with autism aged out of Part C eligibility under the IDEA when they reached three years old. They then became eligible for services under IDEA Part B. However, their parents rejected the temporary IEPs offered by their school district and sought to continue the individualized family service plans (IFSPs) the triplets had received until they aged out of Part C. The parents claimed that the IFSPs were the triplets' stay-put placement under the IDEA. The school district disagreed, and the Eleventh Circuit sided with the school district. **IFSPs don't necessarily focus on educational needs as IEPs do.** Therefore, the IFSPs were not the triplets' stay-put placement. The stay-put placement does not apply to an initial public school application. *D.P. v. School Board of Broward County*, 483 F.3d 725 (11th Cir. 2007).

◆   When a Pennsylvania preschooler with cerebral palsy approached age three, the intermediate unit responsible for her education conducted a reevaluation so as to transition her from the individual family service plan (IFSP) to an IEP. Her parents rejected the IEP because it did not include conductive education, which she had been receiving. They then sued to require the continuation of conductive education through the stay-put provision. The court ruled that the stay-put provision did not apply because **the IFSP was not a "current educational placement"** under Section 1415(j). Even though the intermediate unit was offering them the IEP on a "take it or leave it" basis, it did not have to replicate the child's IFSP services. Under 34 C.F.R. § 300.514, if a dispute arises about a child's initial placement in public schools, the IDEA stay-put placement is the public school IEP. The Third Circuit reversed, holding that **Congress did not intend to use a prospective IEP as a student's stay-put placement**. The "then current educational placement" referred to by the IDEA connotes the operative placement actually functioning at the time the dispute arises. The school district had to continue providing conductive education to the student until the question of whether it should be in her IEP was resolved. *Pardini v. Allegheny Intermediate Unit*, 420 F.3d 181 (3d Cir. 2005).

E. Other Stay-Put Issues

When a hearing officer issues a decision approving of a private parental placement, the private school becomes the "stay-put" placement by an "agreement" of the parties. In such cases, the school district is required to fund the private stay-put placement through the duration of the proceeding. The stay-put provision intends to ensure educational stability until a placement dispute is resolved, regardless of the merits of a claim.

♦   The parent of a District of Columbia student who had never attended public schools and had no IEP filed a due process case against the District of Columbia Public Schools (DCPS). After a hearing, a hearing officer found the DCPS had denied the student a free appropriate public education by refusing to provide an IEP despite finding her eligible for special education. The hearing officer also found the private school placement made by the parent was proper. As a result, the DCPS was ordered to "place and fund the Student" at the private school for the rest of the 2012-13 school year. In response, the DCPS filed a federal court challenge. Although the DCPS funded the placement for the rest of the 2012-13 school year, it refused to develop an IEP. The parent asked the court for a preliminary order to retroactively fund the private placement for the school year, and to continue the placement until the completion of the proceeding. As the student showed an IDEA proceeding was pending, the court held the stay-put rule applied. Next, the court rejected the DCPS's assertion that in the absence of an IEP, the student had "no educational placement to be maintained."

Nothing in the IDEA indicates an "educational placement" is limited to the placement identified in an IEP. Instead, the court held the provision expressed the intent to preserve the status quo existing at the time a dispute first arises. Where no IEP had been prepared or implemented, the court found a child's current educational placement was the place where the child was actually receiving instruction when the dispute arose. There had been an administrative finding that the student's placement was the private school, and the court found refusal to pay for the 2013-14 tuition was a unilateral change in placement. Failure to maintain the placement by denying funds was grounds for stay-put relief. *District of Columbia v. Oliver*, 991 F.Supp.2d 209 (D.D.C. 2013).

♦   In 2010, Hawaii enacted Act 163, which declared that no person who had reached age 20 or older on the first day of a school year was eligible for public school. A severely disabled Hawaii student turned 20, and the state Department of Education notified him that his special education eligibility would end on the last day of the school year. He challenged the termination of his services in a due process hearing. Although representatives for the student asked to preserve his placement pending the outcome of the action under the IDEA stay-put provision, a state hearing officer dismissed the proceeding. Appeal reached the U.S. Court of Appeals, Ninth Circuit. According to the court, **the stay-put**

provision functions as an automatic preliminary order by prohibiting changes to a child's educational placement pending resolution of a case. At the time the case was initiated, the student was still eligible for public education under state law. Hawaii students remained eligible for the full school year if they reached 20 after the first instructional day of the school year. As the student was eligible for services when the case was commenced, he was entitled to a stay-put order. According to the court, the IDEA stay-put provision preserved a student's eligibility until the resolution of the dispute. *A.D. v. State of Hawaii, Dep't of Educ.*, 727 F.3d 911 (9th Cir. 2013).

♦   A Florida student with autism and a speech-language impairment received special education services in a mostly general education setting. He disliked school and was suspended three times for conduct that included assaults. His mother then educated him at home and requested due process, claiming that the school failed to properly implement the IEP. Later she returned him to public schools, where he was again suspended. **A question arose regarding the stay-put provision, and a federal court held that the standard should be more flexible than the hearing officer had ruled, particularly where a child is transitioning from one educational setting to another.** The parties would have to address that flexibility in further arguments. *L.J. v. School Board of Broward County*, 850 F.Supp.2d 1315 (S.D. Fla. 2012).

♦   A Pennsylvania school district funded a private placement as part of a resolution to due process proceedings. Eight years later, the parents placed the student in a private prep school without the district's consent. A hearing officer later found the district's private school IEP inappropriate and the prep school appropriate. The following year, the district sought to place the student in a public school autism support class. The parents rejected the placement, and **a federal court ordered the district to continue paying the prep school costs under the stay-put provision**. On further appeal, the Third Circuit affirmed. The district had to pay the prep school costs during IDEA proceedings. *J.E. v. Boyertown Area School Dist.*, 452 Fed.Appx. 172 (3d Cir. 2011).

♦   A Washington school district determined that a child did not have a disability but that he was entitled to a variety of accommodations. It allowed him to be homeschooled under a collaborative program called H.O.M.E. His parents, believing he was IDEA-qualified, filed a due process request and then sued the district. When the district tried to remove the student from the H.O.M.E. program, the parents asserted that **their child's placement was protected by the stay-put provision even though he had not been ruled IDEA eligible**. A federal court agreed. The IDEA used the language "current educational placement" and not "IEP." *Mangum v. Renton School Dist.*, No. C10-907RAJ, 2011 WL 307376 (W.D. Wash. 1/27/11).

♦   A disabled New Jersey student attended a charter school. His parents and the charter school agreed on an IEP that called for an out-of-district private placement for the next year. The district challenged the IEP, and the parents asserted that the private school was his stay-put placement. A federal court held the charter school should be the stay-put placement. The case reached the Third Circuit Court of Appeals, which noted that **the private school could not be his stay-put placement because he had not yet received any services under the new IEP**. Further, the district had the right to object to the placement. It continued to maintain that it could provide a FAPE in the least restrictive environment. *L.Y. v. Bayonne Board of Educ.*, 384 Fed.Appx. 58 (3d Cir. 2010).

III. STUDENT DISCIPLINE

A. Generally

If a school seeks a change in placement that would exceed 10 school days and the behavior that gave rise to the violation is determined not to be a manifestation of the child's disability, the disciplinary procedures applicable to children without disabilities may be applied to the child in the same manner and for the same duration in which the procedures would be applied to children without disabilities, so long as this does not deny the student a free appropriate public education. Children with disabilities who are removed from their placements for disciplinary reasons must continue to receive educational services to enable their participation in the general education curriculum, although in another setting, and to progress toward meeting their IEP goals. Such students must receive appropriate functional behavioral assessments, behavioral intervention services and modifications to address the violation.

An IDEA provision found at 20 U.S.C. Section 1415(k) allows schools to consider any unique circumstances on a case-by-case basis when determining whether to change the placement of a child with a disability who violates a code of student conduct. Schools may place a child with a disability who violates a code of student conduct in an appropriate interim alternative educational setting, another setting, or suspension, for not more than 10 school days, if such alternatives apply to children without disabilities. Schools may remove a student to an interim educational setting for up to 45 days if a child carries or possesses a weapon at school, knowingly possesses or uses illegal drugs (or sells or solicits the sale of a controlled substance) at school, or inflicts serious bodily injury upon another person while at school.

♦   *Honig v. Doe* is a U.S. Supreme Court case interpreting IDEA disciplinary procedures. The case involved two emotionally disturbed children in California who were given five-day suspensions from school for misbehavior that included destroying school property and assaulting other students. Pursuant to state law, the suspensions were continued indefinitely during expulsion proceedings. The students argued that the suspensions violated the stay-put provision, which provides that students must be kept in the "then current" educational placement during proceedings to change placement. The case reached the U.S. Supreme Court, which declared that the purpose of the stay-put provision is to prevent schools from changing a child's educational placement over a parent's objection until all review proceedings are complete. While the IDEA provided for interim placements where parents and school officials were able to agree on one, no emergency exception existed for dangerous students. However, **where a disabled student poses an immediate threat to the safety of others, school officials may temporarily suspend him or her for up to 10 school days**. This ensures that school officials can protect others by removing dangerous students, seek a review of the student's placement and try to persuade the student's parents to agree to an interim placement, and seek court rulings to exclude students whose parents adamantly refuse to permit any change in placement.

Schools may seek a court order without exhausting IDEA administrative remedies "only by showing that maintaining the child in his or her current placement is substantially likely to result in injury either to himself or herself, or to others." Indefinite suspensions violated the stay-put provision. Suspensions up to 10 days do not constitute a change in placement. In addition, **a school may use "its normal procedures for dealing with children who are endangering themselves or others," such as "timeouts, detention, the restriction of privileges," or suspension**. And states could be required to provide services directly to disabled students where a school district failed to do so. *Honig v. Doe*, 484 U.S. 305, 108 S.Ct. 592, 98 L.Ed.2d 686 (1988).

♦   A Janesville (Wisconsin) student was expelled after a hearing. His mother unsuccessfully tried to enroll him in the Oregon School District. Oregon relied on a state law permitting a school district to deny enrollment to a student who is subject to expulsion by another district. Later, the student's mother sued the Oregon School District, asserting the violation of her son's state constitutional right to public education. She also claimed Oregon violated his right to due process by failing to offer notice or a hearing prior to the decision denying his enrollment application. Oregon began providing the student special education services. The court then held for the district, and the parent appealed to the state court of appeals. While the parent argued the student was entitled to a hearing before being denied enrollment, the court noted she was not challenging the expulsion by Janesville. For this reason, any claim to a hearing was forfeited.

The student had received notification of his possible expulsion and a hearing by Janesville. At the time he sought enrollment in Oregon, he was subject to a pending expulsion order by Janesville. A district could undisputedly expel a student for violating rules. The parent claimed "expulsion" meant the "exclusion of a student from a physical school while still being required to provide alternative educational services." But the court found the parent's argument had been foreclosed by a 2011 Wisconsin Supreme Court case in which the court noted the state department of public instruction has long held **a school district had no responsibility for providing an education to an expelled student**. There was no state law responsibility to provide services in expulsion cases, and no requirement for a separate notice and hearing. As state law did not require a district to enroll an expelled student while an order of expulsion was in effect in another district, the court held for Oregon. *Patricia L. v. Oregon School Dist.*, 354 Wis.2d 323 (Table) (Wis. Ct. App. 2014).

♦   A California charter school student with ADHD was dismissed for threatening others with a knife. The charter school board notified him of its decision in a one-sentence letter that did not explain its reasons. The student asked a state court for a special order to set aside the action for failing to provide a hearing. He also said he had no "knife" as defined by the state education code. The court denied the petition. On appeal, the Court of Appeal of California noted the student took a knife out during class and called a classmate a "stupid Asian bitch." He admitted saying "When I turn 21, I'm going to get a gun and shoot you." The school had suspended the student for five days and called the police. In addition, the school prepared a letter for his mother to explain the suspension and held a manifestation determination review meeting. The review found his bringing of a knife to school was not a manifestation of his ADHD.

Charter schools are generally exempt from laws governing school districts, so the court held the hearing requirements of education code Section 48918 were inapplicable. **A charter school is a "school of choice," so the dismissal did not implicate the same concerns or protections as an expulsion**. While an expelled student must serve an expulsion before being admitted to another school, a dismissed student may enroll in another school immediately. As the student was not entitled to a hearing and his dismissal was justified, the court affirmed the judgment. *Scott B. v. Board of Trustees of Orange County High School of Arts*, 217 Cal.App.4th 117, 158 Cal.Rptr.3d 173 (Cal. Ct. App. 2013).

♦   Due to violent rages, a Missouri student was suspended on two occasions. His mother then educated him at home for two months. After he returned to school, the IEP team decided he should attend school for half days only. Later, he was suspended for violent behavior again. His mother withdrew her consent for special education, and he was then suspended for five days for assaulting a student. After returning to school as a special education student, he was reassigned to an alternative program. His parents claimed that there had been a change in placement because of all the missed school. The case reached a Missouri federal court, which disagreed. **Although the total days of suspension exceeded 14, many came after the mother withdrew her consent for special education.** And both the half-days and the reassignment were for non-disciplinary reasons. *M.N. v. Rolla Public School Dist. 31*, No. 2:11–cv–04173–NKL, 2012 WL 2049818 (W.D. Mo. 6/6/12).

♦   A Michigan school district suspended a disabled ninth-grader for 180 days after he threatened and assaulted another student. A school investigation determined that the student's actions were not a manifestation of his disability. Before the school board, the student claimed that the student handbook specified a suspension of only 5 to 10 days and possible referral for expulsion. After the board upheld the discipline, the family appealed. The case reached the Court of Appeals of Michigan, which described the lavatory assault as an "extreme bullying incident." **School officials have wide latitude and discretion in creating rules to maintain order and discipline.** The court affirmed the discipline. *Stansky v. Gwinn Area Community Schools*, No. 305287, 2012 WL 5290301 (Mich. Ct. App. 10/25/12).

♦   A New Jersey freshman twice tested positive for marijuana. He was suspended for 10 days after the first incident and expelled after the second because of his **failure to enroll in an intensive drug program recommended**

by professional drug counselors after the first positive test. The student abandoned the administrative appeal of the expulsion and then sued the district for damages in a state court. However, the court dismissed the lawsuit because of the student's failure to exhaust his administrative remedies. A state appellate division court affirmed the decision. *Gutin v. Washington Township Board of Educ.*, No. L-1124-08, 2011 WL 650379 (N.J. Super. Ct. App. Div. 2/24/11).

♦ Four Michigan teachers and their union sued, claiming that students assaulted the teachers and yet were not expelled from school as required by law. A state court dismissed their action, holding that the school board retained the discretion to determine whether there had been a physical assault under the law (intentionally causing or attempting to cause physical harm through violence). The court of appeals affirmed, but the Supreme Court of Michigan held that they had standing to sue. On remand, the court of appeals held that **the school board had already determined that the conduct of the students did not constitute physical assault**. Thus, it properly exercised its discretion not to expel the students. *Lansing Schools Educ. Ass'n, MEA/NEA v. Lansing Board of Educ.*, 810 N.W.2d 95 (Mich. Ct. App. 2011).

♦ The father of a Maryland student with ADHD got into a conflict with an assistant coach of the football team on which his son was a member. A few days later, the student was suspended for five days for allegedly being intoxicated at school. Eight days later, the student was assigned in-school detention for unexcused absences earlier in the year. His father, claiming this was retaliation for the conflict with the coach, sued. A federal court ruled against him, noting that suspensions of less than 10 days do not result in the denial of FAPE. **Short-term and in-school suspensions don't implicate due process rights.** *Mason v. Board of Educ., Howard County Public School System*, No. WMN-10-3143, 2011 WL 89998 (D. Md. 1/11/11).

♦ A South Dakota learning disabled student got into a fight after bringing a knife to school. The assistant principal suspended him and, at a manifestation determination meeting, school officials determined that his misconduct was not a manifestation of his disability. After missing four days of school, he was placed in an alternative educational setting. His grandmother asked for a school board hearing but was informed that was not possible because the student was no longer suspended. In his alternative placement, the student received two hours of instruction four days a week instead of his usual 30 hours per week – a 73% reduction. When a lawsuit arose over the district's actions, a federal court found that the alternative placement amounted to a long-term suspension that exceeded 10 days. However, the Eighth Circuit reversed, noting that **the student had only been suspended for four days** and that the student's grandmother had agreed to the alternative placement. *Doe v. Todd County School Dist.*, 625 F.3d 459 (8th Cir. 2010).

♦ The divorced, noncustodial mother of a New Hampshire student with a disability sought to be notified whenever he was suspended for fighting or dismissed for illness. However, a federal court ruled that **she had received due** process in the custody proceedings and was not now entitled to notice before her son was released to his father. *Vendouri v. Gaylord*, No. 10-CV-277-SM, 2010 WL 4236856 (D.N.H. 2010).

♦ A Michigan student with Tourette's Disorder and related disabilities received special education services and had a behavioral plan. After his school district suspended him for 10 days in successive years, it petitioned a state court to find him guilty of school incorrigibility because of his repeated rules violations. The court found the student guilty, and the state court of appeals affirmed the decision. **The filing of a juvenile petition was not a change in placement under the IDEA.** Since the student was never suspended for more than 10 days, he was not entitled to a manifestation determination hearing. *In re Nicholas Papadelis*, No. 291536, 2010 WL 3447892 (Mich. Ct. App. 9/2/10).

B. Manifestation Determinations

The IDEA manifestation determination requirement, found at 20 U.S.C. Section 1415(k)(E), states that within 10 school days of any decision to change an eligible student's placement based on discipline, the educational agency, parent and relevant members of the IEP team (as determined by the parent and educational agency) must review all relevant information in the student's file, including the IEP, teacher observations, and any relevant information provided by the parents to determine if the conduct in question was caused by or had a direct, substantial relationship to the child's disability or was the direct result of the agency's failure to implement the IEP. If the local educational agency, the parent, and relevant members of the IEP team determine that either the conduct in question was caused by or had a direct, substantial relationship to the child's disability, or was the direct result of the agency's failure to implement the IEP, the conduct will be determined to be a manifestation of the child's disability.

If a child's conduct was a manifestation of a disability, the IEP team must conduct a functional behavioral assessment and implement a behavioral intervention plan. If the child already had a behavioral intervention plan, the team is to review and modify it, as necessary, to address the behavior. In the absence of special circumstances, the student must then return to the placement from which he or she was removed, unless the parent and the local educational agency agree as part of the modification of the behavioral intervention plan.

♦ A New Jersey student was sent home early for inappropriately touching a teacher during horseplay. He was suspended for 10 school days. In a state court, he sued the school board for violating state and federal anti-discrimination laws and his state constitutional right to free, appropriate public education. He sought monetary damages, maintaining he had been denied a manifestation determination hearing to review whether his misconduct related to a disability.

The court dismissed the claims as capable of being redressed by the IDEA. It found no merit to the claim for a manifestation hearing, since the student was not suspended for over 10 days. On appeal, a New Jersey Appellate Division Court explained that before the filing of a civil action seeking relief that is available under the IDEA, there must be an exhaustion of IDEA administrative remedies. The student's claims could be addressed in an IDEA proceeding, since they all sought services and identification of his needs. The case should have been dismissed on the ground that the student waited two years to file it. **The court held the manifestation hearing requirement was not triggered, since the student was not suspended for over 10 days. Sending him home early on the day of the incident was not "an additional day in which he was removed" from his educational placement.** *L.W. v. Egg Harbor Township Board of Educ.*, 2015 WL 1013164 (N.J. Super. Ct. App. Div. 3/10/15).

♦ A day after a note was found stating a bomb would go off at an Illinois high school, police took custody of a student and interviewed him for four hours. Despite the extensive questioning, the police did not call the student's parents. He was arrested on suspicion of making the bomb threat. The school then held an IDEA manifestation determination hearing, at which it was determined that his actions were a manifestation of his autism and/or other impairments.

A disorderly conduct charge was filed against the student in juvenile court. His parents sued school officials in a federal court, charging them with violating the IDEA, the U.S. Constitution and the Illinois school code. They asserted false imprisonment, slander, assault, battery and infliction of emotional distress. In pretrial activity, the court explained that administrative exhaustion applies not only to IDEA claims but to any claim seeking relief that is also available under the IDEA. The relevant question was not the form of relief preferred by the parent, but whether the claimed injuries "could be redressed to some degree by the IDEA's administrative procedures." In this case, the actions were said to have deprived the student of access to an education under the IDEA. Since this is what the IDEA administrative process is designed to redress, the court held the exhaustion rule was not excused. **After holding the federal claims had to be dismissed for failure to exhaust administrative remedies, the court held the state claims could be refiled in the state court system.** *Watson v. St. Rich Cent. High School, Board of Educ., Rich Township High School Dist. 227*, No. 14 C 7530, 2015 WL 1137658 (N.D. Ill. 3/10/15).

♦ A Tennessee student was disciplined 55 times from kindergarten through grade three. Early in his third-grade school year, he was found eligible for special education based on ADHD and an adjustment disorder. In his third-grade school year, the student hit four first-graders on their heads while passing them in the hallway. As a result, the school suspended the student and notified his mother of its intent to expel him for a calendar year for "willful/persistent violation of school rules," "other conduct prejudicial to good order," and bullying. At a manifestation determination meeting, the parent agreed to sign a form reciting that her son's ADHD diagnosis did not "cause a substantial impact on his consistent willful disobedience with all adults making requests." While she agreed with the manifestation determination, she appealed further. The parent rejected an offer to place her son in an alternative learning center, and he finished his third-grade year in homebound education. When the dispute reached a Tennessee chancery court, it found the evidence supported discipline.

On appeal, the Court of Appeals of Tennessee held substantial evidence supported the discipline. There was evidence that the student was disciplined 55 times during his elementary school career. According to the parent, her child's behavior issues were linked to his disability. But the court held **the IDEA did not eliminate a school's ability to discipline a disabled student for misbehavior**. A manifestation review is required to determine whether the conduct was caused by (or had a direct and substantial relationship to) a disability. It must also be determined if the conduct in question was the direct result of a school's failure to implement the IEP. In this case, the parent had agreed that neither her son's diagnosis nor any failure to implement his IEP were direct causes of his misbehavior. She also refused an alternative placement for him. As the evidence supported the disciplinary decision, the court held for the board. *Link v. Metropolitan Nashville Board of Public Educ.*, No. M2013-00422-COA-R3-CV, 2013 WL 6762393 (Tenn. Ct. App. 12/19/13).

◆   A New York high school student told some classmates and a teacher that he was "going to just blow this place up" and warned them not to come to school on a Friday. School administrators called the student's parents and the police. The student was immediately suspended and charged with insubordinate, disorderly, violent, disruptive conduct and violation of the code of conduct. A manifestation determination was held, at which no connection was found between the student's behavior and his disability. The school board held a disciplinary hearing, found the student guilty of the charges and recommended suspension for an additional 25 days. The student appealed, but the New York Supreme Court, Appellate Division, upheld the discipline, finding **a substantial disruption was reasonably foreseeable and his First Amendment rights were not violated**. *Saad-El-Din v. Steiner*, 953 N.Y.S.2d 326 (N.Y. App. Div. 2012). The state's highest court refused to hear the student's appeal in 2013.

◆   During his high school career, a disabled Maryland student was charged three different times with violating school rules. The incidents involved fighting and assault, and two resulted in criminal charges. **Manifestation meetings after the latter two incidents found no relationship between the disability and the misconduct.** Prior to his expulsion, his mother enrolled him in another district school. In a lawsuit alleging discrimination, a federal court found none under either the ADA or Section 504. *N.T. v. Baltimore City School Commissioners*, No. JKB–11–356, 2012 WL 3028371 (D. Md. 7/24/12).

◆   An Ohio student with ADD received interventions in grades one and two but was determined not to need an IEP. In third grade, she became physically aggressive and was referred to a mental health agency. Later, she was suspended for threatening behavior. Her mother requested a manifestation determination review (MDR) and an evaluation, which found her eligible for special education. Her mother then sought due process for various IDEA violations, and a hearing officer awarded compensatory education for the delay in identifying the student as IDEA-eligible. A federal court agreed that **the district should have conducted an MDR before suspending the student**. It also ordered the discipline wiped from her record. *Jackson v. Northwest Local School Dist.*, No. 1-09-CV-300, 2010 WL 3452333 (S.D. Ohio 8/3/10).

◆   A Pennsylvania student who caused a bomb scare at his school was eligible for a Section 504 plan but ineligible for special education under the IDEA. The school district refused his parents' request for a manifestation determination hearing and ultimately expelled him. A federal court held that **a manifestation determination is required only under the IDEA, not Section 504**. *Centennial School Dist. v. Phil L.*, 559 F.Supp.2d 634 (E.D. Pa. 2008).

C. Interim Placements

"Special circumstances" permit school personnel to remove a student to an interim alternative educational setting for not more than 45 school days without regard to whether the behavior is determined to be a manifestation of the child's disability. This authority exists only if the child: (1) carries a weapon or possesses a weapon at school, on school premises or school functions; (2) knowingly possesses or uses illegal drugs, or sells or solicits the sale of a controlled substance, while at school, on school premises, or at a school function; or (3) has inflicted serious bodily injury upon another person while at school, on school premises, or at a school function. In those cases, the child remains in the interim alternative educational setting. See 34 C.F.R. Parts 300.530 and 300.533.

A parent who disagrees with a placement decision or a manifestation determination may request a hearing. Likewise, if a local educational agency believes that maintaining the current placement of the child is substantially likely to result in injury to the child or to others, it may request a hearing.

◆   A Texas student with severe ADHD photographed another student while he was using a toilet. A school administrator found this justified a suspension. The student's parents claimed the administrator then encouraged the parent of the student who was photographed to file a criminal charge. A manifestation determination review (MDR) committee found the incident did not result from the student's ADHD, and he was placed in a disciplinary alternative educational placement (DAEP) setting for 60 days. After the criminal charges were dismissed, the MDR did not revoke the DAEP. After a hearing officer upheld the discipline, the parents appealed to a federal court, where they added claims under Section 504 of the Rehabilitation Act and constitutional theories.

Appeal reached the U.S. Court of Appeals, Fifth Circuit, which found **the complaint was conclusory and did not show discrimination under federal law**. Instead, the parents charged school officials with a conspiracy based on their child's disability. The parents did not attribute any misconduct to the school district that was based on the student's disability. In fact, the student was not placed in a DAEP until after the MDR determination found his behavior was not the result of a disability. Since the parents did not sufficiently plead that any of the school's actions were taken on the basis of a disability, the Section 504 claim was properly dismissed. *C.C. v. Hurst-Euless-Bedford Independent School Dist.*, No. 15-10098, 2016 WL 909418 (5th Cir. 3/9/16).

◆   During a Michigan student's sixth-grade school year, seven IEP meetings and 12 behavior planning sessions were held to address his disruptive and dangerous behavior. The school evacuated classrooms eight times in response to incidents, and emergency responders were called five times before his parents agreed to a home program. An IEP was finalized for the student's transition to middle school proposing to divide his school days between general education classes and a classroom for students with autism spectrum disorder (ASD). The student's grade seven IEP discontinued reliance on a 1:1 aide, which was felt to trigger his aggressive behavior. On the fourth day of seventh grade, the student cursed and threatened others, threw chairs, bit a support staff member (drawing blood) and ran away. The school sought to impose long-term discipline and held a meeting to determine whether his conduct was a manifestation of a disability.

The district urged a 45-day interim alternative setting for the student, but the parents did not agree to the center-based program selected by the IEP team. They resumed a home program for him and requested a due process hearing. An administrative law judge (ALJ) held the district did not properly implement the student's seventh grade IEP. It was found that staff lacked proper training and the IEP was inappropriate. As a result, the ALJ ordered a placement with a 1:1 ASD trained psychologist. The school district appealed to a federal court, which found the district committed many IDEA procedural errors. Significant changes were made to the student's placement without a meeting or changes to the IEP. No formal notice was sent to the parents of a suspension, and his status was unclear to them for several weeks. Supports were not in place for the student at the time of a significant behavior episode. The parents felt the alternative placement was predetermined and that their child was regressing. Based on the district's many procedural errors, the court held the IDEA had been violated. Last, the court denied the district's request for an order excluding the student from school. **Evidence indicated he could be educated in general education classes with the right support and an appropriate IEP.** *Troy School Dist. v. K.M.*, No. 12-CV-15413, 2015 WL 1495334 (E.D. Mich. 3/31/15).

♦   A District of Columbia student eligible for special education taunted a substitute teacher and refused to follow several instructions. Because he had two prior infractions in the same school year, he was suspended for 54 days and placed in an alternative educational setting as a result of this Level II infraction. A team found his behavior was not a manifestation of his disability. After a hearing officer reduced the suspension to 10 days, an assistant district superintendent raised it to 45 days. **Another hearing officer found that the alternative placement was not appropriate under the IDEA and reduced the suspension to 11 days.** When the district challenged that decision, the D.C. Circuit upheld it because the alternative placement denied the student a FAPE. The hearing officer did not exceed his authority in modifying the suspension. *District of Columbia v. Doe*, 611 F.3d 888 (D.C. Cir. 2010).

♦   A disabled New Jersey student was caught smoking marijuana after she had previously been suspended for refusing a drug test. She again refused to take a drug test and was suspended for 20 days. She requested an expedited due process hearing, which was adjourned because her mother refused to participate. An administrative law judge then ordered the student returned to class because the school had improperly suspended her for over 10 days without a manifestation hearing. A federal court reversed that ruling. Under the IDEA,

a student can be suspended for up to 45 days, without a manifestation determination, for drug or weapon possession. *A.P. v. Pemberton Township Board of Educ.*, No. 05-3780 (RBK), 2006 WL 1344788 (D.N.J. 5/15/06).

D. Regular Education Students

Section 1415(k)(5)(B) of the IDEA addresses the issue of regular education students seeking IDEA protections in disciplinary cases. A student who has not been found eligible under the IDEA may assert the act's procedural protections if the school has knowledge that the student was a child with a disability prior to the misconduct giving rise to discipline. A school may be deemed to have knowledge that a child has a disability if (i) before the behavior leading to discipline, the child's parent "has expressed concern in writing" to a teacher or to supervisory or administrative personnel that the child is in need of special education or related services; (ii) the child's parent has requested an individual initial evaluation to determine if the child has a disability; or (iii) the child's teacher, or other school personnel, "has expressed specific concerns about a pattern of behavior demonstrated by the child, directly to the director of special education of such agency or to other supervisory personnel of the agency."

A 2015 Illinois law limits the number and duration of expulsions and out-of-school student suspensions to the greatest extent practicable. Out-of-school suspensions of over three days, expulsions and alternative school removals may only be used if other appropriate, available interventions have been exhausted, and the student's continuing presence in school is a threat to others or would substantially disrupt, impede or interfere with school operations. Non-exclusionary discipline must be considered first. Unless required by state or federal law, school boards cannot institute zero-tolerance policies against students for particular behaviors. School officials are required to make all reasonable efforts to resolve threats, address disruptions and minimize the length of exclusions. Ninety-Ninth Illinois General Assembly, P.A. 99-456, S.B. 100. Illinois School Code §§ 10-20.14, 10-22.6, 27A-5, 34-19.

♦ A Texas student wrote a "shooting list" in his English journal, identifying classmates he wanted to harm. The principal found the list violated the student conduct code and assigned the student to a disciplinary alternative placement for 35 days. Within days, a team met for a manifestation determination review (MDR). At the meeting, the parents presented a report diagnosing their son with an autism spectrum disorder. Although the ARD committee offered to evaluate the student for autism, the parents withdrew from the MDR proceedings. After a second MDR meeting, the team found the shooting list incident was not a manifestation of an other health impairment or an emotional disturbance.

Instead of reporting to the disciplinary alternative school, the student stayed at home for the last three weeks of the school year. His parents filed a due process request. A hearing officer found the school district failed to diagnose him with autism two years prior to the shooting list incident. A federal court held the parents could not now challenge an evaluation that took place over two years prior to the lawsuit. In any event, the court found it irrelevant that the student was later diagnosed with autism. For most of two years before the shooting list incident, he made academic and non-academic progress. **As the hearing officer applied an incorrect standard in reversing the manifestation findings,** the court held for the school district. *Z.H. v. Lewisville Independent School Dist.*, No. 4:12cv775, 2015 WL 1384442 (E.D. Tex. 3/24/15).

♦   An Oregon student was charged with bullying two disabled students after school as they left campus. A school instructional aide intervened. After investigating, school administrators concluded that the student had engaged the disabled students in a conversation about sexual topics and innuendo. During the investigation, the student admitted making inappropriate comments. After he was suspended for two days, his parents sued the school district for speech and due process violations. A federal court held the student was trying to second-guess the school's investigation. While labeling his claim as one for free speech, the court held he was really seeking a new review of what had occurred.

Schools may suspend students in response to an identifiable threat of school violence, even if it occurs off campus. Students may also be suspended for off-campus, sexually explicit and degrading comments about females. Schools need not wait until an actual disruption occurs and may rely on a reasonable forecast of disruption. In this case, the district reasonably believed bullying and harassment could lead to substantial disruption. It was reasonable to forecast that failure to discipline the harassment could lead to more of it. Rejecting the student's "tortured argument that he engaged in no harassment," the court found no speech rights violation. A due process claim failed, despite his argument that he was not notified of the sexual harassment charge. Finding the student's retaliation claim was based on an "absurd" argument, the court dismissed it. While he advanced claims for defamation and negligence, the court refused to entertain them and dismissed the case. *C.R. v. Eugene School Dist. 4J*, No. 6:12-cv-1042-TC, 2013 WL 5102848 (D. Or. 9/12/13).

IV. GRADUATION

An IDEA regulation (34 C.F.R. Part 300.122) declares that the obligation to make a free appropriate public education (FAPE) available to all children with disabilities does not apply to those who have graduated from high school with a regular high school diploma. This exception does not apply to students who have graduated but have not been awarded a regular high school diploma.

Graduation with a regular diploma constitutes a change in placement, requiring written prior notice to the parents and a student who has reached age 18. In Cobb County School Dist. v. A.V., *this chapter, a Georgia school denied a student with disabilities a FAPE by changing his diploma track from general education to special education just before his fourth year of high school.*

A. FAPE Issues

An Idaho school district reevaluated an eighth-grader and found him ineligible for special education. His parents obtained a private evaluation which diagnosed him with a high-functioning form of autism. They sought a new evaluation, but the district refused. During ninth grade, the student was arrested and placed in a juvenile detention center. The school district in which the detention center was located evaluated him for special education but found no evidence of any adverse effect of disabilities on his educational performance.

Since the other district's evaluation was limited because of his confinement, the parents asked their home district for a reevaluation. But the home district declined to perform its own evaluation. When the student returned home, the parents requested additional assessments and an IEP. The district refused and found him ineligible for special education. By this time, the student was in grade 11. His parents requested an IEE, which the home district denied. In a due process proceeding, a hearing officer held the home district failed to conduct an appropriate evaluation. A federal court issued a preliminary order preventing the district from graduating the student. It held the parents were entitled to an IEE at the district's expense, plus attorney's fees. After a second round of hearings, a finding of ineligibility was confirmed. The parents appealed to a federal court, which held the student was not IDEA-eligible. On appeal, the U.S. Court of Appeals, Ninth Circuit, held the parents were entitled to an IEE at public expense. Since the student was ineligible for IDEA services, the parents did not meet the IDEA definition of "parent of a child with a disability" and were ineligible for IDEA attorneys' fees. **The court found the order to prevent the school district from graduating the student was questionable, since he was not receiving special education.** It appeared that since he met graduation criteria, he likely received all the benefits that the district's general education program offered. It had been three years since the preliminary order was issued. As any benefit from the order was now exhausted, the court vacated it. *Meridian Joint School Dist. No. 2 v. D.A.*, 792 F.3d 1054 (9th Cir. 2015).

♦ Georgia parents wanted their son to graduate with a college preparatory diploma despite his apraxia, language impairments, and reading and executive functioning deficits. Just before his fourth year of high school, school members of his IEP team sought to change his diploma track because they felt he would not be able to pass the state-required high school exit examination. The student had failed a practice test and was currently failing U.S. history a second time. To graduate with an employment-preparatory diploma, he would not have to pass U.S. history and only had to master related IEP goals and objectives. He needed only four courses, including U.S. history, to obtain a college preparatory diploma. The student's mother refused to participate in a second IEP meeting, as she had already rejected the proposed IEP. She notified the district that she would make a private placement and would seek reimbursement for it.

The second IEP meeting went forth without the mother. The team found the student could not achieve satisfactorily in a regular education setting, even with supplementary aids and services. An ALJ held he could have been educated in regular classes with supplemental aids and services. But she held he would not receive FAPE in the self-contained classes stated in the IEP. Although the ALJ found the private school selected by the parents was appropriate, she awarded them only half the tuition because they had refused to attend the second IEP meeting. When the case reached a federal court, it held the student could have remained in the regular classes he had attended before the change proposed by the IEP team. He was passing his classes with appropriate aids and services, and **it appeared that "the IEP team just wanted A.V. to graduate in the next year, and the fastest way to do this was to place him in access classes for his core classes."** As the ALJ's decision was supported by evidence, the court held the district denied the student a FAPE by changing his classes and diploma track. In addition, the court found the private school selected by the parent was appropriate. As the ALJ had found, there was fault on both sides of the dispute. A 50% reduction in reimbursement was held appropriate. *Cobb County School Dist. v. A.V.*, 961 F.Supp.2d 1252 (N.D. Ga. 2013).

♦   A Rhode Island student with Asperger's syndrome, ADHD and severe social anxiety was working toward a high school diploma. She received notice that her right to a FAPE would terminate upon her 21st birthday. Based on this notice, the parent brought an action on her behalf in federal court against the state department of elementary and secondary education. In reviewing the IDEA, the court noted the act requires states to make a FAPE available to resident students with disabilities between the ages of 3 and 21, inclusive. But another section of the act makes the obligation to offer a FAPE inapplicable to those aged 18-21 – if this would not be consistent with the state's law or practice regarding the provision of public education to general education students in the same age range. A Rhode Island special education regulation provides that FAPE must be available to eligible children between the ages of 3-21, inclusive, but only until the child's 21st birthday or the receipt of a regular high school diploma.

According to the court, the state regulation would terminate the eligibility to receive a FAPE on a student's 21st birthday. While the department said the mother lacked standing to pursue the case, the court found this could be easily cured. It allowed the student 30 days to file an amended complaint in her own right. **As she had stated a desire to add a person to represent a class of students in her age range she could also add a class representative.** Since the case involved only legal questions, the court excused the student from exhausting her administrative remedies. It denied the department's dismissal motion. *K.S. v. Rhode Island Board of Educ.*, 44 F.Supp.3d 193 (D.R.I. 2014).

♦   Hawaii's Act 163 of 2010 barred any student from attending public school after the last day of the school year in which the student turned age 20. Soon after the act became law, four disabled Hawaii students and their parents filed a class action lawsuit in a federal court against the state Department of Education (DOE). Asserting disability discrimination and violation of the IDEA, the families claimed Act 163 violated federal law by denying public education to students with special needs ages 20 to 21. After certifying a class, the court held for the DOE. Appeal then went before the Ninth Circuit, which noted that Act 163 had exempted from its coverage a network of adult education schools called Community Schools for Adults (CSA). The DOE described the CSA program as "Adult Secondary Education" in the form of tuition-free opportunities to earn a high school diploma. CSA offered a GED program and a "competency-based program" featuring life skills. Since neither program offered IDEA services, the court found students who required special education could not participate in them after aging out as declared in Hawaii Act 163.

IDEA language specified that each state provide a FAPE to each student with a disability between the ages of 3 and 21. States could elect against providing special education to students ages 3-5 or 18-21, but only if they elected not to provide "free public education to nondisabled students. For this reason, the court found the case depended on an interpretation of "free public education," and not the more familiar IDEA term "FAPE." The court found the CSA programs provided secondary school education, but not beyond grade 12 and only to students who never graduated. **Since the state offered a "free public education" to non-disabled students ages 18-21, the court held Act 163 violated the IDEA.** States could elect against providing special education to students ages 3-5 or 18-21, but only if they elected not to provide "free public education" to non-disabled students. The students' disability discrimination claim failed because they did not show a reasonable accommodation was available. *E.R.K. v. Hawaii Dep't of Educ.*, 728 F.3d 982 (9th Cir. 2013).

♦   A Texas student had a 142 IQ and above-average math and social studies abilities, but he had poor writing, handwriting and spelling skills. In his senior year, his parents became convinced he could not perform college work. To delay his graduation and preserve his eligibility for school, the student dropped an economics class required for graduation. His parents had him reevaluated and began looking into a Massachusetts private school. Although the school district urged the student to graduate and obtain a waiver of the exit exam if necessary, the student enrolled in the Massachusetts school. A hearing officer held the district IEPs had insufficient transitional planning for entry into college and did not address the student's learning disability. A federal court agreed, and the case reached the U.S. Court of Appeals, Fifth Circuit. It held a student's "whole educational experience, and its adaptation to confer 'benefits' on the child, is the ultimate statutory goal" under the IDEA. Using this "holistic perspective," the court held the school district had customized the student's IEP on the basis of his assessments and his performance. The student's IEPs were reasonably calculated to enable him to earn passing marks and advance in grade. **His IEPs specified graduation with a regular diploma as a goal, but the parents did not use available college application resources.** *Klein Independent School Dist. v. Hovem*, 690 F.3d 390 (5th Cir. 2012), cert. denied 3/18/13.

♦   A Massachusetts student with disabilities made progress toward all his IEP goals in grade eleven. His mother agreed to his grade-twelve IEP, which stated that he was working toward graduation. As graduation neared, however, his mother asserted that he needed to attend a residential program. She placed him there after graduation and claimed the proctor had changed her son's answers on the standardized test. A hearing officer found the student had unmet deficits in emotional control and navigating social situations, among other things. The case reached a federal court, which ruled that no private tuition was required. **The student had been properly graduated despite failing to meet two IEP goals.** The student's emotional and social deficits would follow him all his life and could not be eliminated with additional services. *Doe v. Marlborough Public Schools*, No. 09-11118-WGY, 2010 WL 2682433 (D. Mass. 6/30/10).

B. Academic Requirements

♦   The parents of a New York special education student placed him in a private school, and their district paid part of the cost. They later notified the district that they intended to place him in a Connecticut residential school. The district sought his transcripts to determine how close he was to graduation, but the parents refused to cooperate. When they sought tuition reimbursement, a federal court ruled that **they were not entitled to it because the student had earned enough credits at the private school to earn a Regents diploma**. His graduation made him ineligible for further tuition reimbursement; also, the parents' actions weighed against any tuition award. *T.M. v. Kingston City School Dist.*, 891 F.Supp.2d 289 (N.D.N.Y. 2012).

♦   The mother of a California student with autism learned in May of her son's senior year that district staff did not intend to award him a diploma. She pulled him from school, after which the district offered an IEP that would return him to school the next year or have him attend a transition program. She challenged the education he'd been given, and an administrative law judge found in her favor on three of the 15 claims she raised. A federal court then held **the district had been properly ordered to devise a placement that would allow the student to work toward a diploma**. The mother was also a prevailing party because she received significant relief that materially altered the relationship of the parties. However, she was not entitled to reimbursement for the private school where she placed her son. *Struble v. Fallbrook Union High School Dist.*, No. 07CV2328-LAB (CAB), 2011 WL 291217 (S.D. Cal. 1/27/11).

♦   An Indiana school district offered special education to a learning disabled student until his parents decided to homeschool him. Later, they sought to reintegrate him into public schools and obtained private evaluations showing he had autism. The district did not identify an autism spectrum disorder until he was 17. When he was 19, the district awarded him a diploma. His parents challenged the graduation, asserting that the student should continue to receive special education. Using the stay-put provisions of the IDEA, federal court ordered the district to continue educating the student in a college preparatory program. **The parents' challenge to the validity and good faith of the decision to graduate their son warranted a stay-put placement.** *Tindell v. Evansville-Vanderburgh School Corp.*, No. 309-CV-00159-SEB-WGH, 2010 WL 557058 (S.D. Ind. 2/10/10).

♦   A New York student with ADHD and bipolar disorder was suspended from school numerous times for cutting classes and insubordinate behavior. Among other things, the student cursed at members of the school's staff. **After the student graduated from school, he sought to obtain a copy of his transcript. He claimed that the transcript wrongly lowered his grades.** However, the school district asserted that it properly lowered the grades due to the suspensions caused by his behavior problems. The student then claimed that the district interfered with his second SAT exam because he was not given accommodations for the test. When he sued, he lost. A federal court noted that the grades were accurately recorded. He did not receive accommodations for his second SAT because he did not take the test at the scheduled time, and the approved accommodations had expired by the time he took the test. *Rafano v. Patchogue-Medford School Dist.*, No. 06-CV-5367 (JFB) (ARL), 2009 WL 789440 (E.D.N.Y. 3/20/09).

♦   A 19-year-old special education student in Florida became incarcerated. He completed the math part of his studies while in prison and obtained his general equivalency diploma (GED). He then claimed that the state Department of Corrections and the Department of Education violated the IDEA by granting him his GED. A federal court held that the adult educational program at the correctional facility was not contrary to the state's FAPE obligation under the IDEA. **By acquiring his GED, the student essentially graduated.** He was not entitled to special education services. *MP v. Florida Dep't of Corrections*, No. 4:06CV52-SPM/WCS, 2008 WL 4525134 (N.D. Fla. 9/30/08).

♦   A Florida high school notified the parents of a nonverbal student with autism that the student would graduate if he received all of his academic credits. The parents requested a new IEP meeting or mediation and new evaluations. Less than two weeks before graduation, the board advised the parents it would hold an IEP meeting to discuss a diploma and review the IEP the day after the graduation ceremony. Although the student graduated with a 3.09 grade average and passed the Florida Comprehensive Assessment Test, the parents asked for an emergency order to preserve his placement. The Eleventh Circuit held **his placement could not be preserved under the IDEA stay-put provision, since the parents did not request a due process hearing until after he graduated**. *Sammons v. Polk County School Board*, 165 Fed.Appx. 750 (11th Cir. 2006).

The district court then held the student was not entitled to stay-put protection or compensatory education. As a 22-year-old, the student was no longer entitled to injunctive relief for any continuing violation of the stay-put provision. The student was not entitled to injunctive relief regarding the stay-put provision, nor was he entitled to compensatory education. The clerk of the court was directed to close the case. *Sammons v. Polk County School Board*, No. 8:04-CV-2657-T-24 EAJ, 2007 WL 4358266 (M.D. Fla. 12/10/07).

C. Graduation Ceremonies

♦   An Alabama student with a specific learning disability under the IDEA was removed from school after he was found with a handgun that had the serial number filed off. After a manifestation determination hearing, he was expelled for one year. He received education services at a private school for a year and a half. His mother sought to have him graduate with his former classmates at the public school, but the district denied the request. When a lawsuit resulted, a federal court held that **the student did not have the right to walk with his former classmates at the graduation ceremony**. The court found nothing to indicate that a graduation ceremony was part of the IDEA's FAPE guarantee. *Jefferson County Board of Educ. v. S.B.*, 788 F.Supp.2d 1347 (N.D. Ala. 2011).

♦ A Washington student with a genito-urinary defect and self-esteem issues, eligible for a Section 504 plan, moved to a new school district, which **failed to follow the Section 504 plan because the family did not disclose the nature of the student's condition**. The student began failing classes, and his family finally disclosed the nature of his disability. He was promoted to grade nine but was not allowed to walk in graduation ceremonies with his class. His parents sued for discrimination because of the district's failure to follow the Section 504 plan, but a federal court ruled against them. They had not informed the district of their son's condition in a timely manner. *S.L.-M. v. Dieringer School Dist. No. 343*, 614 F.Supp.2d 1152 (W.D. Wash. 2008).

♦ A Louisiana student with spondylolisthesis **missed a mandatory practice session for commencement exercises because she slept through her alarm after taking a painkiller**. She was barred from the graduation ceremony as a result, though she did receive her diploma. When she sued for discrimination, a federal court ruled against her. It noted her back condition did not substantially limit her ability to perform major life activities. *Soirez v. Vermilion Parish School Board*, No. 6:04 CV 00959, 2005 WL 2286951 (W.D. La. 9/16/05).

♦ A high school senior in Washington became pregnant and failed a quiz near the end of the year. Hours before the graduation ceremony, she and her mother were told that her grade could not be raised under the class grading policy. As a result, she could not participate in the ceremony. Later, the district superintendent met with the family and suggested that a Section 504 plan could be used to increase the student's point total for the failed course. This resulted in an increase in points earned, allowing the student to graduate. She then sued the district for refusing to allow her to participate in the graduation ceremony. A jury awarded her damages, but the Washington Court of Appeals reversed. **She had no constitutional right to attend her graduation ceremony**, and no state law granted her that right either. *Nieshe v. Concrete School Dist.*, 128 Wash.App. 1029 (Wash. Ct. App. 2005).

CHAPTER SIX

IDEA Procedural Safeguards

I. DUE PROCESS HEARINGS

The procedural safeguards of the IDEA provide the means for students with disabilities and their parents to enforce their rights under the act. The safeguards include an "impartial due process hearing" under 20 U.S.C. § 1415(f) when parents or guardians are dissatisfied with any matter relating to the identification, evaluation, or educational placement of the child, or the provision of a free appropriate public education to the child.

Many states provide for a single due process hearing opportunity, but New York and North Carolina retain two-tier systems. In E.L. v. Chapel Hill-Carrboro Board of Educ., this chapter, the Fourth Circuit Court of Appeals upheld a challenge to North Carolina's two-tier administrative review scheme.

In two-tier systems, the state or local educational agency conducts a hearing with the assistance of an impartial hearing officer. An initial due process hearing may be provided at the state or local educational agency level. If held at the local level, either party may appeal to the state educational agency, which shall conduct an impartial review of the hearing. See 20 U.S.C. § 1415(g). Unless appealed, the initial hearing officer's decision becomes final. Likewise, the state officer's decision becomes final unless a party brings a challenge in a state or federal court. See 20 U.S.C. § 1415(i)(2).

A. Generally

♦   In separate cases, parents filed complaint resolution proceedings with the California Department of Education (CDE). They charged their school districts with failing to provide disabled children with appropriate educational services. After both parents prevailed in their state complaint resolution proceedings, the districts sued the state in a federal court, asserting the CDE routinely violated IDEA procedures in special education disputes. The districts sought a court order declaring certain CDE practices unlawful. They objected to the CDE's frequent reconsideration of its "final" decisions. In one case, the CDE first held for the parents and then held for the school district. Upon reconsideration, the CDE reversed itself and held for the parents. According to the school districts, the CDE considered conduct outside a relevant one-year statute of limitations from a federal regulation published under the IDEA (at 34 CFR Part 300.153(c)). And the districts claimed the CDE improperly imposed the burden of proof on the districts when it should have instead burdened the parents. After the cases were dismissed, the districts appealed to the U.S. Court of Appeals, Ninth Circuit. In the court's view, the only IDEA provision that could conceivably allow the districts to sue the CDE was 20 U.S.C. § 1415(i)(2)(A). This IDEA provision describes the appeal process from a due process hearing case.

In advancing their argument, the districts acknowledged the lack of express language allowing them to sue the state. But they argued Section 1415 gave them an implied right to sue. The court noted prior cases rejecting an implied right in cases where the underlying dispute involved a due process proceeding. In *Lake Washington School Dist. No. 414 v. Office of Superintendent of Public Instruction*, 634 F.3d 1065 (9th Cir. 2011), the court found school districts may only litigate IDEA issues raised by parents in a due process complaint. **IDEA procedures are "intended to safeguard the rights of disabled children and their parents,"** not the rights of school districts. Since the lower court had correctly dismissed the cases, the court held for the CDE. *Fairfield-Suisun Unified School Dist. v. California Dep't of Educ.*, 780 F.3d 968 (9th Cir. 2015).

♦   The guardian of a Missouri student with disabilities was denied further review of a decision by the state court of appeals, which held she could not pursue a due process complaint against the student's former school district. The court held any claims based on denial of a free appropriate public education (FAPE) were barred because of the student's withdrawal from the district. Applying federal Eighth Circuit precedent, **the court held the failure to file a due process complaint before the child left district schools barred any claim based on the provision of a FAPE**. *A.H. v. Independence School Dist.*, 466 S.W.3d 17 (Mo. Ct. App. 2015). (Rehearing and/or transfer denied, 6/2/15).

♦   A North Carolina parent became involved in a special education dispute with her child's school district. After prevailing on only one of the disputed issues, she appealed to a federal court. There, she argued the state's two-tiered due process procedure violated the IDEA. The court held the IDEA only requires that a state educational agency conduct an administrative review immediately before any action in a court. Whether this was the first or second tier of administrative review was irrelevant. Hearings before ALJs satisfy the "due process hearing" requirement of the IDEA. And SRO hearings satisfy the "appeal" aspect of the IDEA. **Since North Carolina's two-tiered review process was authorized by the IDEA, the court rejected the parent's IDEA violation claim.** It agreed with the board that as she did not appeal the adverse ALJ rulings, she did not exhaust her administrative remedies under the IDEA. Regarding the merits of the parent's speech language service claim, the court noted that the IEP did not specify that such services must be 1:1. It required that the student receive a specific number of sessions and that they would be offered Since an embedded model meant therapy would be provided in the classroom, the court found no merit to the parent's claim to one-on-one services. *E.L. v. Chapel Hill-Carrboro Board of Educ.*, 975 F.Supp.2d 528 (M.D.N.C. 2013).

On appeal, **the U.S. Court of Appeals, Fourth Circuit, held North Carolina satisfied an IDEA requirement for administrative review to "immediately" precede any civil action**. It held the state's decision to add a level of review enhanced protections for disabled students. The student's IEP for the relevant school year called for daily sessions of speech therapy in the "total school environment," as part of the "embedded, inclusive model" of instruction. The court found the evidence did not show the child had been denied appropriate therapy by the school district. Since the child received the speech therapy specified in her IEP, the court held for the board of education. *E.L. v. Chapel Hill-Carrboro Board of Educ.*, 773 F.3d 509 (4th Cir. 2014).

♦   A Minnesota student did not meet the criteria for a learning disability, but a school team found her eligible for a Section 504 plan. She had a 3.0 grade average in her first year of high school. But she was removed from school by her parent without notice. The parent enrolled her child in a hospital adolescent day treatment program that provided intensive therapeutic services and filed a formal complaint with the Minnesota Department of Education (MDE), asserting the district failed to evaluate her child for special education. The MDE found the child should be evaluated for special education but did not award private school tuition. While the child was still in the treatment program, the parent filed a due process hearing complaint. Although the child returned to the school district, the parties were unable to agree upon an IEP. At an IEP meeting, the district offered to conduct a comprehensive evaluation of the child, create an interim IEP and update her Section 504 plan. But the parent rejected the proposal, stating she wanted her child to be identified for special education.

One day after the IEP meeting, and only seven days after returning her child to the district, the parent filed a second due process complaint. An administrative law judge (ALJ) dismissed the second case, finding the parent had withdrawn her child from the district before it could deliver any services. In addition, the ALJ found no showing of harm to the child in the seven days between the IEP meeting and her departure. The parent appealed both decisions to a federal court. It held the first case had been properly dismissed as the student was not enrolled in the school at the time of the hearing request. **Eighth Circuit cases stated that if a student changed districts and did not request a hearing, his or her right to challenge prior educational decisions was not preserved.** Case law supported the ALJ's decision to dismiss the second due process matter. If a school district was denied an opportunity to formulate a plan, it could not be shown that the IEP was inadequate. In this case, the parent had removed her child from school before the school district could develop an appropriate IEP. There was no showing that the child had lost any educational benefits, and the court held for the school district. *I.E.C. v. Minneapolis Public Schools, Special School Dist. No. 1*, 34 F.Supp.3d 1006 (D. Minn. 2014).

♦   A Kentucky school district knew that the parents of a student who had sometimes been eligible for special education were unhappy with his fifth-grade IEP, and a school employee even assisted the parents in the preparation and filing of a due process request. However, **the due process complaint did not specifically state that the fifth-grade IEP was being challenged**. The school district argued that it did not receive proper notice that a hearing officer was going to consider that IEP. The Sixth Circuit disagreed. Potential relief for the student would have to be reconsidered by the lower court. *Adam Wayne D. v. Beechwood Independent School Dist.*, 482 Fed.Appx. 52 (6th Cir. 2012).

♦   A school board sought to join the state of North Carolina as a party to a due process proceeding in which it had been found to deny a student FAPE. A federal court denied this request, as the state knew of the case but never sought to join it. In the court's view, the state either saw its interests were not at stake or that one party was representing its position. Under the IDEA, **if a state allows local agencies to hold due process hearings, a state-level appeal has to be offered**. If due process hearings are held by the state, no appeal is required. North Carolina is one of a few states with a "modified two-tier system," in which both hearings are held at the state level. The court held the IDEA did not prohibit the state from this arrangement. Because of the way the parties argued the case, the court found no way to assess the record. It declined to dismiss the board's counterclaim related to a procedural issue of appeal, finding further proceedings were necessary to review the timeliness of the district's notices. *O.M. v. Orange County (North Carolina) Board of Educ.*, Civ. No. 1:09CV692, 2013 WL 664900 (M.D.N.C. 2/22/13).

♦   A Pennsylvania student with ADHD took medication for his condition. His district found him ineligible for special education under both the IDEA and Section 504. After he scrawled a bomb threat on a school lavatory wall, his parents sought a manifestation determination, which request was denied. A hearing officer found him eligible under Section 504 but also found no due process violation. The case reached a federal court, which stated that **Section 504 students do not have the same protections as IDEA students**. The student was not denied due process. However, the hearing officer should have considered the effect of the medication on the student's condition before determining that he was eligible under Section 504. *Centennial School Dist. v. Phil L.*, No. 08-982, 2010 WL 1174206 (E.D. Pa. 3/26/10).

♦   New Jersey students with disabilities left their public school to enroll in charter schools, which then transferred them to private schools. The charter schools sought tuition reimbursement from the school district under the IDEA provision of the Charter School Act. The district paid the tuition, even though it was not consulted about the placements, but objected to the transfers and complained to the state department of education. It requested that school districts have input into private school placements by charter schools. When the department did not provide relief, the district sued the charter schools and the department in a federal court, arguing the department's application of the Charter School Act was preempted by the IDEA mainstreaming requirement. The court ruled against the district, finding that it had **no private right of action to dispute the placement of students by charter schools** without first requesting a due process hearing. This, it failed to do. *Asbury Park Board of Educ. v. Hope Academy Charter School*, 278 F.Supp.2d 417 (D.N.J. 2003).

♦   A hearing-impaired student and his family moved from Michigan to Indiana. His parents sought compensatory education from their old school district, asserting that the district failed to provide their son with a properly endorsed teacher, necessary speech/language services and an interpreter. The state education department determined that the student was entitled to compensatory speech/language services, but otherwise exonerated the district. The parents requested due process, but a hearing officer dismissed the case because the student had moved from the district. A state review officer reversed. A federal court then held the school district had properly asserted that it had no obligation to provide services to a student residing outside its boundaries. But **the district could not deny the student a hearing just because the due process request came after he moved out of the district**. *Lewis Cass Intermediate School Dist. v. M.K.*, 290 F.Supp.2d 832 (W.D. Mich. 2003).

♦   A student with disabilities attended a Catholic elementary school in New Hampshire but received special education services from a public school district. He was transported to a speech/language program at a public school for one hour a week, then returned to the private school. His parents sought compensatory education from the district after it failed to provide him with services for parts of two school years and caused him to miss speech/language sessions because of unreliable transportation. They requested a due process hearing, which was refused because of their voluntary placement of their son in a private school. A federal court agreed that they were not entitled to a due process hearing. Laws that set conditions on the ability to receive government benefits are not invalid. And **private school students do not have individually enforceable rights under the IDEA**. *Andrew S. v. Manchester School Dist.*, 241 F.Supp.2d 111 (D.N.H. 2003).

♦   A Virginia student with autistic spectrum disorder attended public schools in a class-based, noncategorical program. His father sought intensive one-to-one Applied Behavioral Analysis training, which the school district refused to provide. The father rejected the proposed IEP, and the district responded with an explanation of its reasoning. It also notified him of his right to a due process hearing or administrative review. The father enrolled his son in a private school and, more than 29 months later, filed a due process hearing request. A hearing officer held that he had waited too long, but a federal court ruled that the district should have given him notice of Virginia's two-year statute of limitations. The Fourth Circuit reversed, noting that **nothing in the IDEA requires school districts to provide parents with notice of appropriate limitations periods**. *R.R. v. Fairfax County School Board,* 338 F.3d 325 (4th Cir. 2003).

◆   A Utah student was removed from school when his parents felt his school district was unwilling to provide an appropriate IEP. The parents placed him in a private school and commenced due process proceedings. The parties initially agreed upon a hearing officer, but the district withdrew its consent and the selected officer recused himself. A state special education compliance officer appointed a replacement. At the hearing, the compliance officer appeared as an expert witness on behalf of the school district. The hearing officer then denied relief to the parents. They sought review by a state special education appeals panel, but the parties were unable to agree on the composition of the panel. The state superintendent of public instruction appointed a three-member panel, which affirmed the hearing officer's decision. The parents then sued state and local education officials and entities, asserting that the hearing process violated the IDEA. The court held that **under the IDEA, procedural due process is afforded where a party has legal representation and the opportunity to cross-examine witnesses. The parents received these rights**, and the officials and agencies were entitled to pretrial judgment. Also, state officials had not acted improperly and with bias for the district, since the parents did not allege specific factual determinations demonstrating bias. *L.C. v. Utah State Board of Educ.*, 188 F.Supp.2d 1330 (D. Utah 2002).

B. Evidence

In B.S. v. Anoka Hennepin Public Schools ISD No. 11, *this chapter, Minnesota parents did not convince the Eighth Circuit Court of Appeals that a pre-hearing agreement limiting the time for the parties to present their cases to an administrative law judge violated their child's due process rights.*

◆   Unable to reach an agreement with their child's school district over his program, Minnesota parents requested a due process hearing. During a pretrial conference, an administrative law judge (ALJ) asked counsel how long they needed to present their cases. The parents' counsel said one and a half days. The school district's attorney asked for one day. On the first day of the hearing, the parents' attorney questioned a special education administrator for five hours. The school's attorney objected, noting the parents' attorney had used almost half of her time. When the parents' time expired the next day, the ALJ offered to let their attorney formally introduce evidence through additional witnesses. But she instead chose to make an informal offer of proof of additional evidence she had hoped to present. Later, the ALJ issued a decision for the school district.

After a federal court held for the school district, the U.S. Court of Appeals, Eighth Circuit, found **the IDEA requires open hearings, the creation of a hearing record, the right to be advised by counsel, the right to present evidence and confront witnesses, and rights to access hearing transcripts, findings of fact and decisions**. Beyond these minimums, the states may devise their own special education hearing procedures. At the time of the hearing, Minnesota law required ALJs to set hearing times to allow the parties to present their cases. State regulations added that the amount of time each party had to present its case was determined by balancing the due process rights of the parties with the need for administrative efficiency. Given these state law requirements, the court found the ALJ committed no abuse of discretion. In the court's view, there was no due process violation in this case. *B.S. v. Anoka Hennepin Public Schools ISD No. 11*, 799 F.3d 1217 (8th Cir. 2015).

♦   New Jersey parents requested a hearing to seek applied behavior analysis (ABA) and applied verbal behavior (AVB) for their three-year-old autistic child. In settlement of the matter, the parties agreed to provide the child 20 hours of weekly ABA/AVB direct 1:1 instruction from a private service provider. After a reevaluation of the child and observation of the private clinic, a child study team proposed a full-time placement in a preschool class for the rest of the school year. A kindergarten placement in a class for children with autism was offered for the next school year. The parents responded by filing a second due process petition. In an attempt to gain evidence that the child was being denied a free appropriate public education (FAPE) for preschool and kindergarten, the parent requested that an expert be permitted to observe the child's classroom.

The district denied the request, and a hearing followed. An ALJ then found the IEPs for both preschool and kindergarten would have provided the child a FAPE. The parents appealed to a federal court, which held for the school district. On appeal to the Third Circuit Court of Appeals, they said the district violated IDEA procedural protections by denying them access to the expert's report. The parents cited 20 U.S.C. § 1415(b)(1), an IDEA section which mandates that parents have an opportunity to examine all records relating to their child. But the court found no evidence that the report related to the child in any way, as it only addressed the district's AVB program generally. A team's failure to adopt the suggestions of parents does not mean there was a denial of meaningful participation in the decision-making process. Next, the court held the parents' rights were not violated when the district refused to allow their expert observe the child. **Although they sought permission to supplement the administrative record before the lower court, the court found no abuse in denying the request.** It held for the district. *R.K. and D.K. v. Clifton Board of Educ.*, 587 Fed.Appx. 17 (3d Cir. 2014).

♦   A New York CSE recommended that an autistic child attend a specialized class in a public community school. After the DOE sent the parent a final notice of recommendation, she rejected it and notified the department of education (DOE) of her intent to re-enroll her child in the private school. In a due process action, the parent sought tuition reimbursement. The hearing officer found she had been denied a meaningful opportunity to participate in the CSE meeting.

A state review officer held the parent's objection to the composition of the CSE could not be considered because it had not been included in her due process complaint. The review officer held the CSE had based the proposed IEP on sufficient evidence. On appeal, a federal court found it inappropriate for the review officer to rely on testimony that the DOE would have provided a 1:1

transitional paraprofessional for over four months if the child needed this. Cases by the U.S. Court of Appeals, Second Circuit, have held **school officials may not present evidence that they would have provided any services not specified in an IEP in seeking to justify an IEP proposal. This is called "retrospective testimony."** Instead, the Second Circuit has held an IEP must be evaluated "prospectively as of the time of its drafting." In this case, the court found no support for administrative findings regarding whether a 1:1 paraprofessional would have been provided if appropriate for the student. As the review officer improperly relied on retrospective evidence in ruling for the DOE, the court returned the case to her for further proceedings. *M.T. v. New York City Dep't of Educ.*, 47 F.Supp.3d 197 (S.D.N.Y. 2014).

♦   When a Maryland private school student with learning, language and other health impairments did not succeed despite the school's small size, significant accommodations and his receipt of additional services, his parents contacted a school district and sought special education. The district found the student eligible and proposed a draft IEP calling for the student's placement in a public middle school. The parents requested a due process hearing and enrolled the student in a different private school. The administrative law judge (ALJ) assigned the burden of proof to the parents. Since they could not meet this burden, the district prevailed. On appeal, a federal court held that the hearing officer had erroneously allocated the burden of proof to the parents. The Fourth Circuit vacated and remanded the case, and the ALJ held for the parents, finding that the IEP offered by the district was inadequate.

A federal court agreed with the ALJ's conclusion that the district did not provide the student with a FAPE during the year it first proposed an IEP. It awarded the parents full reimbursement for the costs of private school during the first year. Because the parents did not exhaust their administrative remedies concerning the two subsequent years of private school tuition, the court denied those claims. The Fourth Circuit reversed the district court, and the case reached the U.S. Supreme Court, which agreed with the court of appeals that **parents who challenge IEPs have the burden of proving that the IEPs are not appropriate**. To do otherwise would force courts to assume that every IEP is invalid until the school district demonstrates that it is not. *Schaffer v. Weast*, 546 U.S. 49, 126 S.Ct. 528, 163 L.Ed.2d 387 (2005).

On remand, the parents challenged the student's eighth-grade IEP by presenting evidence of the changes made to his tenth-grade IEP. The school district countered with evidence that the student had graduated with a 3.4 grade point average. A Maryland federal court ruled for the district, and the Fourth Circuit affirmed. Using the tenth-grade IEP to challenge the eighth-grade IEP would promote a hindsight-based review that conflicted with the IDEA's structure and purpose. *Schaffer v. Weast*, 554 F.3d 470 (4th Cir. 2009).

♦   The parents of a Virginia student with autism became dissatisfied with his public school education and requested due process. The hearing officer determined that he could not resolve the case on the basis of the credibility of the witnesses because they were all credible. Nevertheless, he ruled for the school district, finding that it offered the student a FAPE by providing a self-contained special education classroom, a full-time instructional aide and opportunities for ABA. A federal court reversed the hearing officer's award, making its own findings of fact and determining that the private school placement sought by the parents was appropriate. The Fourth Circuit then vacated the lower court's ruling, noting that **the district court should not have questioned the hearing officer's findings**. The IDEA did not require the hearing officer to offer a more detailed explanation of credibility assessments. *Peterson v. County School Board of Hanover County, Virginia*, 516 F.3d 254 (4th Cir. 2008).

◆   When the parents of a learning-disabled Missouri student challenged his IEP, a special education panel found that the district denied the student a free appropriate public education (FAPE), after putting the burden of proving compliance with the IDEA on the district. A federal court largely upheld that decision. The Eighth Circuit reversed, noting that **the burden of proof was on the parents**, as the parties challenging the IEP, to show noncompliance with the IDEA. Since this was a close case, putting the burden on the parents might result in a decision for the district. *West Platte R-II School Dist. v. Wilson*, 439 F.3d 782 (8th Cir. 2006).

C. Hearing Officer Bias and Authority

◆   **A federal appeals court dismissed a case by a Texas parent who claimed her son's school district violated the IDEA and that a state hearing officer failed to provide her a fair hearing.** According to the parent, her son's school did not provide appropriate counseling and accommodations to her son and did not communicate with her about his progress at school. A hearing officer disagreed with the parent and held for the school district. A federal court held for the district and held the parent could not act as her child's attorney for non-IDEA claims. As she included claims that went beyond the scope of the due process hearing, they were dismissed. In a brief memorandum opinion, the U.S. Court of Appeals, Fifth Circuit, held the parent failed to address the lower court's reasoning. Her papers were a "disorganized and incoherent repetition of arguments made and rejected below," requiring dismissal of the lawsuit. *K.F. v. Houston Independent School Dist.*, 548 Fed. Appx. 964 (5th Cir. 2013).

◆   The parents of a Maine student requested a due process hearing, seeking tuition reimbursement. After the hearing officer ruled against them, they challenged her decision on the grounds that she was **not an impartial hearing officer because she had also served as a complaint investigator** for the state. A federal court disagreed with them. Hearing officers enjoy a presumption of honesty and integrity. Further, the parents did not timely object to the hearing officer or exhaust their administrative remedies. *Mr. and Mrs. V. v. York School Dist.*, 434 F.Supp.2d 5 (D. Me. 2006).

◆   The parents of a 12-year-old gifted high school student with Asperger's syndrome and significant difficulties in writing and interpersonal skills filed a complaint with the Maine education department. A complaint investigator concluded that the district had failed to implement some of the student's IEP goals, objectives and modifications, failed to provide the parents with certain notices, and did not address the extent to which the student would participate with non-disabled students. At a pre-hearing due process conference, the hearing officer commented that the investigator's findings were not binding on him. After he issued a ruling for the school district, the parents appealed.

A magistrate judge found nothing improper in the conduct of the hearing by the hearing officer. Other than the issue of the appropriateness of the IEP and the existence of a behavior plan, he had confined the issues to those identified in the pre-conference hearing. The parents themselves had acquiesced to the addition of the "IEP/modification or implementation" issue. They had brought up the issue of the lack of behavior intervention plan in the first place and could not now argue that the issue was improperly before the hearing officer. **The hearing officer had the power and responsibility to make independent determinations of law and was not bound by the factual findings of the complaint investigator.** *Donlan v. Wells Ogunquit Community School Dist.,* 226 F.Supp.2d 261 (D. Me. 2002).

♦   When a school district and the parents of a gifted student were unable to agree on his IEP for the 2000-2001 school year, a hearing officer ordered the parties to develop a new IEP and required the district to give the student certain credits toward graduation. At the resulting IEP meeting, the district proposed an IEP calling for the student's graduation in 2002, with an agreement that if he completed the 28.5 credits he needed for graduation, he would graduate a semester early. The parents challenged the 2002 graduation decision. A hearing officer upheld the district's IEP and the 2002 graduation date. A due process appeals panel reversed, finding that the IEP contained both substantive and procedural errors. The panel ordered the student classified as a member of the 2000-2001 class, provided he completed the required number of credits. The school district was ordered to provide certain personnel involved in the student's education with 10 hours of special education in-service education, and to hire an outside expert to help develop an appropriate IEP.

The Pennsylvania Commonwealth Court noted that **although appeals panels have the authority to order remedies such as compensatory education, the appeals panel was not authorized under Pennsylvania law to order the special education in-service it ordered in this case.** Since the panel lacked the authority to order district personnel to participate in an in-service session, this part of the panel's decision was reversed. Under Pennsylvania special education regulations, the composition of the IEP team is the school district's responsibility. Because the inclusion of an outside expert was not a statutory requirement for the composition of an IEP team, the panel lacked the authority to order the inclusion of an outside expert on the student's IEP team. Also, the district could not be forced to graduate the student before he earned the statutorily established minimum number of credits toward graduation. The student had to earn 28.5 credits, since this was the graduation requirement when he started high school. The court reversed the appeals panel's order. *Saucon Valley School Dist. v. Robert O.,* 785 A.2d 1069 (Pa. Commw. Ct. 2001).

♦   A Maine school committee and the parents of a student with disabilities went to due process over the parents' decision to unilaterally place the student in a private school. The hearing officer ordered the school committee to reimburse the parents for their tuition. Shortly after the hearing concluded, the committee learned the hearing officer had a disabled student who attended private school. When the committee requested a new hearing to consider the family's failure to cooperate with requested evaluations of the student, the same hearing officer was appointed. The committee requested she recuse herself. She declined to do so, and the school committee appealed her original decision on the grounds that she had a disqualifying personal interest and was biased. The court observed that Maine special education regulations permit the challenge of a hearing officer only on the grounds of conflict of interest or bias. The appearance of impartiality alone was insufficient to disqualify a hearing officer. **The fact that the hearing officer had a child with moderate hearing loss in private schools did not indicate any conflict of interest, bias, hostility or prejudgment** against the school committee. The alleged conversations with the parents had been about the hearing officer's son, not the student whose case was being considered. The court disallowed the committee's request for further fact finding. *Falmouth School Committee v. B.*, 106 F.Supp.2d 69 (D. Me. 2000).

II. EXHAUSTION OF ADMINISTRATIVE REMEDIES

Before a party may file a lawsuit under the IDEA (or seeking relief which may be available under the IDEA), the party must exhaust IDEA administrative remedies by going through IDEA due process procedures. The exhaustion of remedies doctrine provides that "no one is entitled to judicial relief for a supposed or threatened injury until the prescribed administrative remedy has been exhausted." Myers v. Bethlehem Shipbuilding Corp., 303 U.S. 41 (1938).

The U.S. Supreme Court, in McKart v. U.S., 395 U.S. 185 (1968), *explained that the doctrine allows for the development of an accurate factual record, thereby allowing more informed judicial review, encouraging "expeditious decision making," and taking advantage of agency expertise.*

A. Operation of the Exhaustion Doctrine

♦   Pennsylvania parents said their children's school placed their daughter in the same classroom with a boy who had sexually assaulted their older daughter. They claimed the boy and his brother subjected the younger daughter to verbal and psychological harassment while at school. Eventually, they transferred her to a homebound education program to avoid contact with the boys. When the parents sued the school district in a federal court, they asserted claims under Section 504 and the Americans with Disabilities Act. They charged the district with failing to accommodate their child's disabilities and retaliation for asserting her protected rights. During pretrial activity, the court dismissed the case for failure to exhaust IDEA administrative remedies before filing the case.

On appeal, the U.S. Court of Appeals, Third Circuit, explained that **the IDEA's administrative process applies not only in actions filed under the**

IDEA but also in non-IDEA cases where relief may be obtained under the IDEA. Parents cannot circumvent the IDEA exhaustion requirement by taking claims that could have been brought under the IDEA and "repackaging them as claims under some other statute." A non-IDEA claim is subject to the exhaustion requirement if it relates to the identification, evaluation or educational placement of a child, or the provision of a free appropriate public education. In this case, all the claims related to placement and could have been remedied through an IDEA due process proceeding. As a result, the court held the case was properly dismissed due to failure to exhaust IDEA remedies. *M.S. v. Marple Newtown School Dist.*, 635 Fed.Appx. 69 (3d Cir. 2015).

♦   A Michigan child with spastic quadriplegic cerebral palsy wished to bring her service dog to school. The school refused the request, as her IEP already included a 1:1 aide to support her at school. A trial period for the dog to accompany the child was allowed, but the dog was not with her at all times and did not perform some functions for which it was trained. The parents began homeschooling their child and filed a complaint with the U.S. Department of Education's Office for Civil Rights (OCR). The OCR found the school district violated Rehabilitation Act Section 504 and the Americans with Disabilities Act (ADA). Although the district allowed the student to return to school with the service dog, the parents enrolled her in a different school system where they encountered no opposition to use of the dog. In a federal court, the family sued the school district for disability discrimination under Section 504 and the ADA.

The court dismissed the case, finding the IDEA administrative exhaustion rule applied. It noted the use of the service dog implicated issues relating to the child's IEP. When the case reached the U.S. Court of Appeals, Sixth Circuit, it explained that IDEA procedures must be exhausted before filing a case under the ADA, Section 504 or other federal laws protecting children with disabilities, if relief is also available under the IDEA. **The court held the exhaustion requirement applied in this case, since the action turned on the same questions that would have been considered had IDEA procedures been followed.** Affirming the lower court's judgment, the court held the family should have pursued IDEA procedures before filing the action. *Fry v. Napoleon Community Schools*, 788 F.3d 622 (6th Cir. 2015).

♦   A nonverbal five-year-old child with Down syndrome who communicated through sound imitation and signs had an IEP with a behavior intervention plan (BIP) allowing her to work in a distraction-free setting. The BIP noted her need for occasional breaks in a quiet place. When the parents toured their child's school during teacher conferences, they learned that the quiet room was a small, dirty, unvented, unheated, windowless room lined with filing cabinets. They expressed concerns to the school district and removed their child from school until the principal promised not to use the room. In a federal court, the parents sought orders requiring the district to discontinue the use of the quiet room.

After a hearing to consider an application for temporary and preliminary relief, the court noted the school district had already agreed to stop using the room. After denying relief for a temporary order on grounds that the family had already obtained the relief being sought, the court held the IDEA administrative exhaustion rule applies to any party seeking relief available under the IDEA. In this case, the claims were "not wholly unrelated to the IEP process." Although the parents claimed disability discrimination had occurred, **the court held the use of the quiet room was based on provisions in the IEP and BIP**. Since the claims were all related to the IEP process, the court held administrative exhaustion was required under the IDEA. *J.A. v. Moorhead Public Schools, ISD No. 152*, Civ. No. 14-4639 ADM/LIB), 2015 WL 756885 (D. Minn. 2/23/15).

♦   The parent of a Pennsylvania high school student with ADHD believed the school principal was hostile and offensive. When testing revealed the student had a math disability, an IEP meeting was held and the school district developed an IEP for the student. The school offered to provide him compensatory education services in return for a waiver of his claims. But the parent said the district did not reimburse her for tutoring costs specified in the agreement, and she filed a breach of contract action against the district. The next school year, the parent alleged a series of retaliatory actions by the school, including the replacement of a math tutor by a teacher she considered to be a bully. She said the student was wrongly disciplined and humiliated. According to the parent, the district failed to implement either the agreement or her son's IEP during his senior year. She withdrew him from school and sued the school district. Noting the absence of a due process hearing request, the court dismissed the case. On appeal, the Third Circuit Court of Appeals held **IDEA administrative processes must be exhausted in non-IDEA cases, if a party seeks relief that can be obtained under the IDEA**. While the parent asserted retaliation under three federal laws, the court found all the claims related to the provision of a FAPE and were properly dismissed under the administrative exhaustion rule. *Batchelor v. Rose Tree Media School Dist.*, 759 F.3d 266 (3d Cir. 2014).

♦   During an administrative challenge against the New York City Department of Education (DOE), the parents of a child with autism sought 690 hours of compensatory education services. At the close of the hearing, the parents for the first time complained that their child's teacher was not certified to teach special education. They argued that this was a failure to implement the IEP as it was written. An impartial hearing officer found an award of corrective services was not warranted. Many inconsistencies were found in the parents' request for such services. A review officer affirmed the decision, as did a federal court. On appeal, **the U.S. Court of Appeals, Second Circuit, held the failure to properly raise the issue of special education certification was a failure to exhaust administrative remedies**. Next, the court dismissed the procedural challenges, finding no reason to depart from findings that they had already been resolved. The parents had only sought corrective services, and the IHO had found no such entitlement. As a result, the judgment for the DOE was affirmed. *B.M. v. New York City Dep't of Educ.*, 569 Fed.Appx. 57 (2d Cir. 2014).

♦   The parents of four New York children with disabilities charged a school district with violating their rights. One parent said the district prevented a student from using a power wheelchair based on safety grounds. Another said the district imposed toileting requirements upon a child who was incorrectly claimed to be incontinent. One of the parents said a school employee called child protective services after a home visit during which the parent shouted at district representatives. Finally, the parents said school employees made several adverse decisions against them in retaliation for their advocacy for reasonable accommodations for their children. Instead of requesting impartial hearings under the IDEA, the families sued the school district and several officials in a federal court for disability discrimination and retaliation. Finding they were required to exhaust their remedies under the IDEA, the court dismissed the case.

On appeal, the U.S. Court of Appeals, Second Circuit, held **the IDEA requires an aggrieved party to exhaust all administrative remedies before bringing a civil action in court**. This rule applies even if the claims are brought under a statute other than the IDEA. In the court's view, most of the grievances here related to the education of disabled children and were subject to exhaustion. It held the lower court had properly dismissed the claims based on wheelchair use, toileting and the provision of specific services. On the other hand, **claims that the school district failed to implement specific aspects of an IEP were not subject to administrative exhaustion**. The court reversed this aspect of the decision. It also held the implementation claims that were not time-barred deserved further consideration by the lower court. *Stropkay v. Garden City Union Free School Dist.*, 593 Fed.Appx. 37 (2d Cir. 2014).

◆   Families of two Missouri special education students had ongoing disputes with their school district about IEP implementation. They filed a complaint with the U.S. Department of Education's Office for Civil Rights (OCR). After an investigation, the OCR found the district's process regarding IEP complaints was adequate. But it found the district process for disability discrimination was inadequate. Instead of requesting due process hearings, the families filed a joint action against the school district in a federal court. They sought compensatory education, compensatory damages and attorneys' fees. The court dismissed the case for failure to exhaust IDEA administrative remedies, and the families appealed to the U.S. Court of Appeals, Eighth Circuit. After consolidating the cases, the court noted all the claims related to the implementation of IEPs.

Before a party may file a lawsuit seeking relief, which may also be available under the IDEA, the party must exhaust IDEA administrative remedies. Although the parents claimed their action was based on the district's failure to have an adequate disability discrimination grievance process, they had also alleged the district failed to adequately implement the IEPs. As the parents were seeking educational costs, they were asking for relief that was available under the IDEA. It would not have been futile for them to request an IDEA due process hearing. The OCR case did not show the resolution process was inadequate to resolve IEP-related claims. Since the families were seeking relief that was also available under the IDEA, they had to exhaust their administrative remedies. *J.B. v. Avilla R-XIII School Dist.*, 721 F.3d 588 (8th Cir. 2013).

◆   A special education dispute between a Florida school district and parents became complicated by the filing of three due process hearing requests. The parents requested a due process hearing after a November 2010 IEP meeting. As a result, a June 2010 IEP became the student's "stay-put" IEP. Numerous hearings followed. While they were ongoing, the parents filed a second due process challenge in April 2012. The second due process request asserted denial of a free appropriate public education. A final order for the second due process matter was issued in June 2012. But a new dispute arose in July 2012 regarding several IEP issues and the parents' request to record IEP meetings. The school district filed a third due process hearing request to review these issues.

Meanwhile, the parents appealed from the hearing officer's decision in the second due process case. The court noted that no decision had yet been issued in the first and third administrative hearings. Since all three due process matters involved the same questions, the case was dismissed for failure to exhaust administrative remedies. On appeal, the U.S. Court of Appeals, Eleventh Circuit, found the claims in all three cases were substantially similar. **There had been a failure to exhaust administrative remedies, since no final decision had been issued for two cases when the federal action was filed.** The second case (the subject of this appeal) had been filed before a final ruling in the other two. Since it raised similar claims as the first two cases, there had been a failure to exhaust administrative remedies regarding the second case. *A.L. v. Jackson County School Board*, 543 Fed.Appx. 1002 (11th Cir. 2013).

◆ The parents of a New York student with a speech impairment grew dissatisfied with his education in their district school. However, rather than file a request for an administrative hearing, they sued the district for discrimination under Section 504 and the ADA. They claimed that the district sought to classify him as emotionally disturbed so it could place him in a segregated setting. A federal court and the Second Circuit ruled that **they could not bypass the requirement that they exhaust their administrative remedies by suing under discrimination laws**. *Baldessarre v. Monroe-Woodbury Cent. School Dist.*, 496 Fed.Appx. 131 (2d Cir. 2012).

◆ The parents of an autistic student sued their district, claiming that a bully had attacked their son on numerous occasions despite their reporting of the problem to the school. **They claimed their son was taken off the "graduation" track and was not afforded an opportunity to pursue an education in the least restrictive environment.** However, a Maryland federal court dismissed their lawsuit because they failed to exhaust their administrative remedies. *Wright v. Carroll County Board of Educ.*, No. 11–cv–3103, 2012 WL 1901380 (D. Md. 5/24/12).

◆ An Alabama mother challenged her preschool son's academic program under Section 504 and the ADA. She made no claim of an IDEA violation. Instead, she complained that he was unable to participate in the Preschoolers Acquiring Learning Strategies (PALS) program to the same extent as students without disabilities. A hearing officer found no issues under the IDEA and ruled that he had no authority under Section 504 or the ADA. A federal **court held that the mother should have claimed an IDEA violation and that the matter had to be returned to the administrative level for resolution.** *Jennifer B. v. Chilton County Board of Educ.*, 891 F.Supp.2d 1313 (M.D. Ala. 2012).

♦   According to the mother of an Oklahoma student with disabilities, school staff repeatedly and forcibly placed her son in a time-out room and kept him there for periods spanning more than 15 minutes. When she complained, school staff allegedly lied to her and failed to conduct an investigation. Without first requesting a due process hearing, she sued the school district. However, a federal court dismissed her lawsuit because she had failed to exhaust her administrative remedies. Further, **even if she had exhausted her administrative remedies, she could not show that the use of the time-out room implicated any constitutionally protected property or liberty interest**. *Ashford v. Edmond Public School Dist.*, 822 F.Supp.2d 1189 (E.D. Okla. 2011).

♦   The father of two disabled New Hampshire students claimed that his daughter was sexually abused by another disabled student and that his son was left without adult supervision. He sued the district for discrimination. A federal court dismissed the action on the grounds that he failed to exhaust his administrative remedies. **He should have filed a due process request because his discrimination claim was based on an IDEA violation.** *Hatch v. Milford School Dist.*, No. 10-CV-263-JD, 2010 WL 3489037 (D.N.H. 9/2/10).

♦   The Ninth Circuit held that a California student's non-IDEA claims had to be addressed by a hearing officer before a lawsuit could be filed. **Exhaustion was required even though the district had found the student ineligible for special education.** The student was pursuing identification, evaluation and placement claims, as well as a Section 504 claim. *Huson v. Simi Valley Unified School Dist.*, 346 Fed.Appx. 150 (9th Cir. 2009).

B. Exceptions to the Exhaustion Doctrine

The administrative exhaustion doctrine does not apply when it would be futile or cause irreparable harm. Delay by an agency in making a decision, or the fact that the agency may not be empowered to grant relief, may excuse the exhaustion requirement. The unavailability of a state or local remedy or a predetermined result by an agency may also excuse the requirement.

♦   A New Jersey student was sent home early for inappropriately touching a teacher during horseplay. He was suspended for 10 school days. In a state court, he sued the school board for violating state and federal anti-discrimination laws and his state constitutional right to a free appropriate public education. He sought monetary damages, maintaining he had been denied a manifestation determination hearing to review whether his misconduct related to a disability.

The court dismissed the claims as capable of being redressed by the IDEA. It found no merit to the claim for a manifestation hearing, since the student was not suspended for over 10 days. On appeal, a New Jersey Appellate Division Court explained that before the filing of a civil action seeking relief that is available under the IDEA, there must be an exhaustion of IDEA administrative remedies. **When a party seeks relief that is available under the IDEA, the exhaustion rule applies, even where the claims have been "repackaged" under other laws, including the state laws in this case.** The student's claims could be addressed in an IDEA proceeding, since they all sought services and identification of his needs. The case should have been dismissed on the related ground that the student waited two years to file it. In the court's view, he could not skip his administrative remedies and argue the passage of time rendered this remedy "futile." *L.W. v. Egg Harbor Township Board of Educ.*, 2015 WL 1013164 (N.J. Super. Ct. App. Div. 3/10/15).

♦   When an Iowa student was in grade seven, his IEP called for a 1:1 aide and a quiet place to go if he became overstimulated. A behavior intervention plan (BIP) described how staff was to intervene if he acted out. On a day when the student was having problems, he tried to go to his quiet room. While on the way to the room, he pushed a classmate. His teacher and the school principal approached him in the quiet room. The student tried to run away, pushing another student. According to the student, the teacher restrained and injured him. His parents then filed a lawsuit against the school district and teacher in a federal court. The family's complaint asserted the teacher did not follow the IEP or BIP. In response, the district argued the family had to request an IDEA administrative hearing. In explaining the IDEA's administrative exhaustion rule, the court found the rule applies whenever a claim relates to the IEP process, individual identification, evaluation, educational placement or the provision of a free appropriate public education to a disabled child. Only when the relief being sought is wholly unrelated to the IDEA will the exhaustion rule not apply.

In this case, **the court held the student was not seeking relief that could have been included in an IEP**. Instead, the claims asserted teachers did not provide an environment free from fear, did not follow the BIP or IEP, allowed teachers to use illegal physical restraints, failed to train teachers and did not assign qualified aides. Claims based on alleged assault by the teacher appeared far removed from the IDEA, at least at this early stage of the lawsuit. Since the court found no reason to believe an IDEA claim could include the kind of harm described in the complaint, exhaustion was not required at the present time. *A.P. v. St. Johnson*, No. 14-CV-4022-DEO, 2015 WL 1297534 (N.D. Iowa 3/23/15).

♦   A New York student's grandmother regularly picked him up after his off-campus special education program. Although his IEP included multiple special education programs and services, it did not specify the after-school program. A reference to the after-school program was included as a special alert in the student information summary section of the IEP to alert the student's teacher he would receive school transportation to the after-school program two days per week. After the grandmother passed away, the student's parent said he could not pick up his son from the after-school program. He said that without appropriate transportation home, the student would "eventually run away." But the district rejected the parent's request for transportation to and from classes or programs at other sites, as this was not a part of the IEP. Without requesting an impartial hearing, the parent sued the school district. A federal court explained that administrative exhaustion is required not only when an IDEA claim is filed, but whenever a claim is asserted for relief that is also available under the IDEA.

The court held all of the claims were subject to the IDEA's exhaustion requirement. While the parent said it would have been futile to go through the hearing process, the court disagreed. It also rejected the argument that the district had committed systemic violations that could be remedied administratively. Finally, the court rejected the parent's claim that a court order was necessary to remedy an emergency. The district never failed to provide the student with necessary transportation home when he did not attend the after-school program. **As it was not shown that the administrative process would not have provided relief, the case was dismissed.** *Licata v. Salmon*, No. 14-CV-2637, 2015 WL 153843 (E.D.N.Y. 1/12/15).

♦   West Virginia parents brought a due process complaint against their child's board of education. A hearing officer ordered the board to contract with an educational service provider within five days and to train the child, his parents and school staff to use his speech-generating device. The board also had to develop and implement an applied behavior analysis program. Over a month later, the parents informed the board it was violating the order by failing to contract with the provider. They advised the board they would transport their child to receive the services ordered by the hearing officer, even though the board had not contracted with the provider. The board filed an action to appeal the hearing officer's decision. The parents responded and added counterclaims under the Rehabilitation Act, the Americans with Disabilities Act and the IDEA. A federal court denied the board's request to stay (temporarily block) implementation of the administrative order. It held the IDEA's stay-put provision has been interpreted as making a school system financially responsible for the cost of a placement during the pendency of an IDEA dispute.

Since the board's request to stay the administrative order ran afoul of the stay-put provision, the court held for the parents. It rejected a claim that the parents failed to exhaust their administrative remedies. It appeared that the parties had fully run the IDEA administrative process. A second round of administrative proceedings did not have to be brought before the parents could raise counterclaims for money damages. **The court held the case should not be dismissed as it was an original civil action, not an IDEA appeal.** *Board of Educ. of County of Boone, West Virginia v. K.M.*, Civ. No. 2:14-cv-10563, 2015 WL 1481775 (S.D. W.Va. 3/31/15).

♦   California parents said their school district tried to remove their child from general education classrooms so he could be "warehoused" with severely disabled children. Eventually, the school district filed a due process hearing request regarding FAPE and assessment issues. While the case was pending, the parents filed five state complaint resolution proceeding (CRP) complaints against the school district, asserting non-compliance with state and federal law.

After the student was removed from the school district, the district dismissed the due process case. For this reason, there was no final administrative ruling in that matter. The parents filed a federal lawsuit against the school district and the state education department. The court held the IDEA administrative exhaustion requirement applies when a party "seeks a remedy under the IDEA or its functional equivalent." It applies when a party seeks relief to alter an IEP or the placement of a student with a disability, or makes a claim involving a FAPE. Ninth Circuit authority clarified that the exhaustion rule was a "claims processing provision" that could be excused if administrative remedies would be futile or if a government agency acted contrary to law. In this case, the parents said the education department did not monitor, investigate and enforce the IDEA. The court held it could not determine yet whether the department failed to investigate the claims or otherwise stymied attempts to obtain district compliance. **Prior Ninth Circuit cases held CRPs can suffice for exhaustion purposes and had found the CRP and due process hearing procedures to be simply alternative means of addressing an IDEA complaint.** It would have been futile for the parents to file a due process complaint, as they alleged noncompliance with a final order. They also alleged systemic violations of the state administrative complaint process. As a result, the parents could pursue their IDEA and Rehabilitation Act claims. *Everett H v. Dry Creek Joint Elementary School Dist.*, 5 F.Supp.3d 1184 (E.D. Cal. 2014).

♦   A New Jersey student with autism had inclusive placements and the help of an aide. When he entered middle school, the district placed him in more restrictive settings with 10 hours of weekly home instruction. But the parent claimed the district only provided him two to four hours of weekly instruction and removed him from school. She claimed the district then considered truancy charges, and she filed a due process petition in which she sought an emergency order to obtain the district's funding to place him in another school district.

Although the parent claimed an emergency existed, an ALJ held a full hearing was necessary. Dissatisfied, the parent petitioned a federal court for the same emergency relief that had been denied by the ALJ. **According to the parent, the urgency of the situation excused her from the IDEA's administrative exhaustion requirement.** The court denied her request, finding nothing to indicate the child would otherwise face irreversible damage. The sole emergency relief she sought was an order directing the district to pay the costs for her child to attend school in another school district. This and other federal law claims brought by the parent were deemed premature. In the court's opinion, the current, undeveloped record had to go before an ALJ at a due process hearing for resolution. There was no reason to excuse the administrative exhaustion requirement based on a parent's claim that an IEP was inadequate. **Since the parent's disagreement with the ALJ's order did not excuse administrative exhaustion, the court dismissed the case** in view of pending activity before the ALJ. *L.V. v. Montgomery Township School Dist. Board of Educ.*, No. 132595, 2013 WL 2455967 (D.N.J. 6/5/13).

♦   A Texas teacher with a provisional license taught special education students despite the district's assurances to parents that a fully licensed teacher would be in charge. He yelled at and shook students, as well as making them kneel for extended periods, and he grabbed one student by the neck and slammed his head onto a desk. He later pled guilty to criminal charges of causing injury to a child. The parents of the student sued the district and the teacher. When the teacher sought to have the case dismissed, a federal court refused to do so. The **parents did not have to exhaust their administrative remedies before suing**. *Tristan v. Socorro Independent School Dist.*, 902 F.Supp.2d 870 (W.D. Tex. 2012).

♦   The parents of a California student with severe disabilities sued the school district under Section 504, alleging deliberate indifference to her needs and rights. She also claimed that for several years, the district virtually ignored her, leaving them to create an educational program for her. The district sought to have the lawsuit dismissed on the grounds that the parents failed to exhaust their administrative remedies, but a federal court allowed it to proceed. **The parents were excused from exhaustion because such action would have been futile. California administrative law judges had refused to consider Section 504 claims in prior cases.** *Cayla R. v. Morgan Hill Unified School Dist.*, No. 5:10–CV–04312 EJD, 2012 WL 1038664 (N.D. Cal. 3/27/12).

♦   A Washington student attended a contained classroom in a public school. His teacher used a small "time out" room for overly stimulated students. When the student was placed in the "time out" room, he sometimes took off his clothes and urinated or defecated on himself. His mother complained about the use of the "time out" room and eventually removed him from school. She sued the district for constitutional violations, seeking relief under 42 U.S.C. § 1983. A federal court dismissed the case, finding that she should have exhausted her administrative remedies, but the Ninth Circuit held **the constitutional claims should not be dismissed if the mother could show a violation of laws other than the IDEA** and point to an authorized remedy that would be unavailable under the IDEA. *Payne v. Peninsula School Dist.*, 653 F.3d 863 (9th Cir. 2011).

♦   A former student claimed that a New York school district discriminated against him on the basis of his learning disability. He brought an IDEA action and also sued under Section 504. The district asserted that he was required to exhaust his administrative remedies by appealing the due process determination, but an appellate court disagreed. **The student did not have to exhaust administrative remedies because his IDEA claims had been fully reviewed at the administrative level.** *Calhoun v. Ilion Cent. School Dist.*, 90 A.D.3d 1686, 936 N.Y.S.2d 438 (N.Y. App. Div. 2011).

♦   A group of 10 special education students and their parents sued their Washington school district for negligence and discrimination, claiming that staff members physically, verbally and psychologically abused the students. The school sought to have the lawsuit dismissed on the grounds that the families failed to file an IDEA due process request first. The case reached the Supreme Court of Washington, which ruled that **nothing in the IDEA restricts a person's right to sue under the ADA or the Rehabilitation Act.** Further, state tort laws are also not subject to the IDEA exhaustion requirement. The lawsuit was allowed to continue. *Dowler v. Clover Park School Dist. No. 400*, 258 P.3d 676 (Wash. 2011).

♦   Parents of two autistic students in Arizona claimed that their school district had no autism program and no qualified teachers. Instead of requesting a due process hearing, they sued the school district in a federal court. After the case was dismissed, the Ninth Circuit affirmed the judgment. It ruled that the parents had failed to exhaust their administrative remedies under the IDEA. **They failed**

to show that the district had admitted it could not serve their children and that any administrative due process hearing would be futile. *Wiatt v. Prescott Unified School Dist.*, 357 Fed.Appx. 28 (9th Cir. 2009).

C. Regular Education Students

♦   An Oregon student with ADHD had a Section 504 plan. He got suspended for accessing a school database to change his grades. A hearing was conducted to consider expulsion, but the student's father claimed he received improper notice and thought the meeting was just for fact-finding. The district agreed to further investigate, and the family filed a Section 504 complaint, challenging the suspension and seeking restoration of class credit. A hearing officer ordered the school district to give the student the opportunity to recover lost credits. The student graduated with a regular diploma but sued the district under Section 504 and the IDEA, seeking to modify his final grades and also asking for money damages. A federal court dismissed the case, holding that **even though he had graduated, he should still have pursued administrative remedies** before suing. *Ruecker v. Sommer*, 567 F.Supp.2d 1276 (D. Or. 2008).

♦   A Massachusetts student with Crohn's disease and depression attended the Boston Latin School, a competitive public school that relies on an entrance test and grade point average for admission. He was unable to complete his studies for ninth grade, and he applied for a third year in grade nine. The school denied him admission until it was ordered to admit him by a special education hearing officer, who found a Section 504 violation. The city appealed the finding of a Section 504 violation, and the parents counterclaimed for money damages. The court held that the parents' claims were barred by their failure to exhaust their administrative remedies. **Even though their son had been given a general education placement, he met the definition of a "child with a disability" under the IDEA. Thus, administrative exhaustion was required.** *City of Boston v. Bureau of Special Educ. Appeals*, No. 06-11703-RWZ, 2008 WL 2066989 (D. Mass. 4/30/08).

♦   A regular education student failed one high school math course, and on seven occasions failed the math portion of the Texas Assessment of Academic Skills (TAAS). After modifications, she was able to pass the TAAS and graduate. She then sued the district for failing to refer her for special education. A federal court held **she was required to exhaust her administrative remedies even though she had graduated**. The student's mother never made a written request for school assistance, so the IDEA's child find duty was never triggered. And since compensatory education could be awarded after graduation, pursuing administrative remedies would not be futile. *Oliver v. Dallas Independent School Dist.*, No. Civ.A. 3:01-CV-2627, 2004 WL 1800878 (N.D. Tex. 8/11/04).

♦   The Tenth Circuit Court of Appeals upheld pretrial judgment against an Oklahoma student who alleged race and disability discrimination by his school district and unlawful disclosure of private information by a former teacher. There was no evidence of discriminatory intent, and **even though the student**

was never identified as a student with disabilities, he had to exhaust available administrative procedures under the IDEA prior to filing a lawsuit. Applying a recent U.S. Supreme Court decision, the court also found that his privacy claim failed. The dispute between the parents and the district arose partially from the parents' refusal to approve the home-bound teacher the district assigned. As a result, the student did not have a teacher for a year. The family's Section 504 claims had to be dismissed because of the family's failure to follow procedures under the IDEA. Even though the student had never been identified as a student with disabilities under the IDEA, a student with a disability who brings a claim alleging educational deficiencies must exhaust IDEA administrative remedies before filing suit. The student's condition would have qualified him as eligible for services under the IDEA. *Cudjoe v. Independent School Dist. No. 12*, 297 F.3d 1058 (10th Cir. 2002).

D. Claims for Money Damages

In J.B. v. Avilla R-XIII School Dist., *721 F.3d 588 (8th Cir. 2013), this chapter, the Eighth Circuit dismissed a case in which Missouri parents were seeking to recover their educational costs without first requesting a hearing. The court found they were asking for relief that was available under the IDEA, and it would not have been futile to request an IDEA due process hearing.*

♦   An Alabama grandparent who failed to mention a Section 504 claim in an IDEA appeal notice regarding her grandchild could not pursue any Section 504 claim at the hearing. When the case reached the Eleventh Circuit Court of Appeals, it noted the grandparent's notice did not mention Section 504 other than to say that the child had once been found eligible for Section 504 services. **For any claim seeking relief available under the IDEA, the act's due process procedures must be used.** The rule applies to Section 504, Americans with Disabilities Act and constitutional claims. Since the grandparent did not seek a due process hearing for her Section 504 claims, she could not now pursue them. Because she did not exhaust her administrative remedies and did not show it would have been futile to do so, the case was properly dismissed. *Laura A. v. Limestone County Board of Educ.*, 610 Fed.Appx. 836 (11th Cir. 2015).

♦   During a home economics class, a Michigan student stopped working on a project. He said this caused his teacher to become enraged and yell "why don't you just go kill yourself" to the class. According to the student, the teacher then ripped his project from his hands and threatened to lock him in a room. In a state court, the student sued the teacher and school district for intentional infliction of emotional distress. Finding reasonable minds could differ regarding whether the teacher's conduct was "extreme and outrageous," the court held it had been error for the trial court to dismiss the case during pretrial activity. As an alternative argument, the teacher said that the case could not go forward due to the family's failure to first exhaust available IDEA administrative remedies. Other courts had applied the exhaustion doctrine to actions filed under federal laws seeking relief that was available under the IDEA. **But the court found no authority declaring that the IDEA administrative requirement applied to a**

tort case. As there was no requirement to exhaust IDEA remedies in a tort case, the court reversed the judgment and returned the case to the trial court. *Melson v. Botas*, No. 315014, 2014 WL 2867197 (Mich. Ct. App. 6/19/14).

♦ The parents of an Arizona student with autism became frustrated with her school situation and moved out of the district. They claimed that the district failed to implement an IEP and used a makeshift system of security guards and student aides to guide their daughter between classes rather than facilitated socialization and mobility navigation assistance. Seeking only money damages, they sued the district. The Court of Appeals of Arizona held **the parents had to exhaust their administrative remedies despite their assertion that their claims arose under tort (personal injury) law**. Regardless of the language in their lawsuit, the parents were alleging a breach of duties that arose under the IEP. *Hance v. Fountain Hills Unified School Dist.*, No. 1 CA-CV 09-0281, 2010 WL 2773545 (Ariz. Ct. App. 7/13/10).

♦ The mother of Pennsylvania students with disabilities alleged that their school district retaliated against her for contesting her children's IEP and writing an article about the school board for the local newspaper. She and her husband sued the district in a federal court, but the court held that they should have pursued a due process action first. **They were not seeking purely money damages but also declaratory relief, and they made no persuasive argument for not filing a due process request.** *Hesling v. Avon Grove School Dist.*, No. 02-8565, 2010 WL 2649909 (E.D. Pa. 6/30/10).

♦ The parents of a California student waited until after he graduated to challenge his education, bringing a Section 504 claim against the school district. A federal court dismissed the case, and the U.S. Court of Appeals for the Ninth Circuit affirmed that decision. Although Section 504 imposes slightly different obligations than those set by the IDEA, **parties seeking Section 504 relief that is also available under the IDEA must exhaust their administrative remedies** to the same extent as they would for IDEA claims. *Fraser v. Tamalpais Union High School Dist.*, 281 Fed.Appx. 746 (9th Cir. 2008).

♦ A West Virginia student with ADHD, a depressive disorder and a low-average IQ graduated from high school and then had trouble finding a job. The Social Security Administration found him functionally illiterate, unable to perform activities within a schedule, and unable to maintain regular attendance. He was therefore declared eligible for Social Security Income benefits. When he later sued the school district for providing a defective education, the Supreme Court of Appeals of West Virginia upheld lower court decisions to dismiss the lawsuit for failing to exhaust his administrative remedies. *Sturm v. Board of Educ. of Kanawha County*, 672 S.E.2d 606 (W.Va. 2008).

♦ The family of a California student with disabilities had a history of disagreeing with their school district. After the district proposed a placement in a class with disabled students regardless of age, grade or specific disability, the family rejected the placement, removed the student from school and sued for discrimination, seeking money damages. A federal court and the Ninth Circuit dismissed the lawsuit because the family should have requested a due process hearing first. **The issues raised by the lawsuit were educational in nature** and should have been considered by a due process hearing officer. *Kutasi v. Las Virgenes Unified School Dist.*, 494 F.3d 1162 (9th Cir. 2007).

♦ The mother of a Washington student represented her son at a due process hearing, where it was determined that the district did not properly implement his IEP. Compensatory education was ordered. Over the next two years, the mother filed four additional due process hearing requests, seeking to implement and modify the IEP. She then sued the district for money damages, claiming she lost income and suffered emotional distress during the IDEA challenge. After the Ninth Circuit held that she did not have to exhaust her administrative remedies before suing, the case reached the Ninth Circuit again. This time, it held that **she could not recover lost wages or pain and suffering under the IDEA on her own behalf**. Nor could she sue under 42 U.S.C. Section 1983. *Blanchard v. Morton School Dist.*, 504 F.3d 771 (9th Cir. 2007).

♦ The parents of a Rhode Island student filed a due process hearing request, but the hearing was postponed and rescheduled several times. The parents agreed to the first delay; the others resulted from problems within the school district. **The parents then refused to participate any further and sued the district for money damages.** The case reached the Supreme Court of Rhode Island, which held that they should have exhausted their administrative remedies. The 45-day period for resolving complaints was not as strict as the parents had argued and could be extended by continuances and postponements. They failed to show that exhausting their administrative remedies would be futile. *Doe v. East Greenwich School Dep't*, 899 A.2d 1258 (R.I. 2006).

III. LIMITATION OF ACTIONS

An IDEA provision states that a parent or educational agency must request an impartial due process hearing within two years of the date the parent or agency knew (or should have known) about the facts forming the basis of the complaint. But if the state has an explicit time limitation for requesting such a hearing, the state time period applies. The IDEA's two-year limitation period does not apply if the parent was prevented from requesting a hearing because the local educational agency made specific misrepresentations, or if the local educational agency has withheld information from the parent.

In W.H. v. Schuylkill Valley School Dist., *954 F.Supp.2d 315 (E.D. Pa. 2013), a federal court found no state or federal law deadline for evaluating a child who is suspected of having a qualifying disability.*

♦ Parents of a New Jersey child with severe asthma and a congenital disorder said state and local agencies did not contact them about early intervention services. After the child was placed in a school for special needs children, the parents claimed an aide's disregard for their instructions caused a hysterical reaction by their son. As a result, they immediately withdrew him from school. Home instruction was provided to the student for brief periods, but he largely went without services for three years. A New Jersey Division of Family and Youth Services (DFYS) learned the student had almost no formal education. The district then created an IEP for him. The parents sued state agencies, including the DFYS and the school district in a federal court under laws including Section 504 of the Rehabilitation Act and the Americans with Disabilities Act (ADA). Noting the claims charged officials with intentional discrimination and sought monetary damages, the court held the administrative exhaustion rule applied. But the court found no factual support for the claims against the state. Moreover, the claims against the state related to the provision of EIS, which had taken place some 10 years prior to the filing of this lawsuit.

It appeared to the court that a two-year state limitations period might apply to the ADA and Section 504 claims and possibly defeat state liability. While the vast majority of the claims were likely time-barred, the court held that refiled claims on behalf of the student might survive. This was because the limitations period in personal injury cases did not run until a minor reached age 18 or was emancipated. As for the claims filed on behalf of the parents, the court found they had asserted a "continuing violation" as part of an ongoing practice or pattern of discrimination. To succeed under that theory, the court held they would have to refile their claims and assert additional facts showing ongoing intentional discrimination. *S.B. v. Trenton School Dist.*, No. 13-949 (FLW)(LHG), 2013 WL 6162814 (D.N.J. 11/25/13).

◆ An Idaho charter school enrolled a seventh-grader whose parents provided his IEP and an expired eligibility report from his previous school. Although the charter school considered the student disabled, it did not evaluate him or hold an IEP meeting. His teacher provided him extra time for assignments and tests. Despite several inquiries by the parents, the school did not assess the student for special education needs. In the second half of the year, his attendance became sporadic and he was placed on a homebound program. Near the end of the next school year, an interim school administrator notified the parents that the student was "administratively withdrawn" from school, and he was then "disenrolled."

The parents complained to the state education department. But the department considered it an IDEA claim and found the complaint untimely under a one-year limitation period. In a federal court, the parents filed Section 504 claims against the school. It held a claim is subject to IDEA administrative exhaustion if the complaint seeks relief that is also available under the IDEA. Applying a Ninth Circuit test, the court noted the parents were seeking some $276,810 in damages. As they sought relief that was clearly available in a due process proceeding, they were required to exhaust their administrative remedies by filing a due process request. A formal complaint with the state education department did not satisfy the exhaustion requirement. Although the court dismissed the case, it noted the parents could still file a due process complaint. A one-year limitation period applied to state agency complaints, and a two-year period applied to due process hearing requests. The charter school had never provided the parents appropriate IDEA notices, and they did not know of

their IDEA rights until learning about them from the education department. As this had been less than two years earlier, they could still pursue a due process action. *Kelly O. v. Taylor's Crossing Public Charter School*, No. 4:12-cv-00193-CWD, 2013 WL 4505579 (D. Idaho 8/21/13).

♦   The parents of a Washington student sought due process over their son's educational program. Their lawyer asked for a continuance at a pre-conference hearing, but the district objected. It cited an IDEA provision requiring an administrative decision within 45 days of expiration of the 30-day resolution period for IDEA disputes. After the continuance was granted, the district appealed, but the Ninth Circuit ultimately ruled that **the district had no standing to contest the state education agency's policy of granting time extensions beyond the 45-day timeline**. *Lake Washington School Dist. No. 414 v. Office of Superintendent of Public Instruction*, 634 F.3d 1065 (9th Cir. 2011).

♦   A Texas hearing officer ruled that a school district denied a student a FAPE. Ninety days later, the parents filed a federal court action to obtain attorneys' fees and costs. Twenty-eight days after that, the district filed a counterclaim against the parents. The parents claimed that the district filed too late, saying it should have sued in the 90 days following the hearing officer's decision. But the Fifth Circuit ruled for the district, **noting that the 90-day period did not apply to counterclaims but rather to the party bringing the action**. *Ruben A. v. El Paso Independent School Dist.*, 414 Fed.Appx. 704 (5th Cir. 2011).

♦   Parents of a Pennsylvania student with a learning disability appealed an administrative ruling to a federal court on the 90th day after the ruling – the last day allowed by the IDEA. The school district filed a counterclaim 70 days later, and the parents claimed it was untimely. They asserted the district should have filed the counterclaim on the same day they filed their appeal. The Third Circuit ruled for the district, noting that **since the counterclaim was "reactive" rather than the bringing of an action, the district was not bound by the 90-day limit**. *Jonathan H. v. Souderton Area School Dist.*, 562 F.3d 527 (3d Cir. 2009).

IV. OTHER IDEA PROCEEDINGS

A. Class Actions

♦   A group of Compton Unified School District (CUSD) students convinced a federal court that their claims to disability law protection based on their traumatic circumstances have merit. (A summary of the case appears in Chapter Two, Section II.B. of this volume.) However, the court issued separate orders denying the students' requests for preliminary relief and certification of the case as a class action. The court found the disability issues were novel, and the evidence supporting the claim of trauma-induced disability was too unclear to justify preliminary relief. In a separate order, the court denied the student's request to certify a class action. It found **the students could not currently estimate the size of a proposed class of present and future CUSD students**

with trauma-induced disabilities. The students' estimate of the proposed class required more than a good-faith guess. Even if the court accepted the student's methodology and found their expert testimony persuasive, it found questions remained that prevented class certification at this time. But the court left open the possibility that the requirements for class certification could be met based on a fuller record. *P.P. v. Compton Unified School Dist.*, No. CV 15-3726-MWF (PLAx), 2015 WL 5752770 (C.D. Cal. 9/29/15).

♦ In 1992, a group representing disabled students in Chicago Public Schools (CPS) filed a class action against the Illinois State Board of Education (ISBE) and CPS to challenge the placement of students by disability category alone. Of over 500,000 students enrolled in CPS schools, at least 10% were classified as disabled. A federal court certified a class representing certain disabled students in CPS schools. In 1998, the CPS agreed to a consent decree, which committed it to a series of reforms to bring the system into compliance with the IDEA. The ISBE went to trial, which resulted in a finding that it had violated the IDEA.

The ISBE was ordered to submit to a compliance plan, then entered into a consent decree with the students outlining its duties. In 2005, a court-appointed monitor set a formula for a district-wide maximum by which the percentage of students with disabilities in any CPS school could not exceed 20% of the school's total student population. Although CPS could seek waivers from the 20% cap, it failed to do so until the consent decree expired in 2006. CPS then sought waivers for 96 schools. The court complied with the monitor's request to extend the term of the decree for four years and to keep a 20% ceiling. When appeal of the enrollment cap issue reached the U.S. Court of Appeals, Seventh Circuit, it found the challenge premature. The case returned to the district court, which set dates for termination of the consent decrees. While the CPS consent decree had terminated in 2012, CPS moved to decertify the class and vacate the original 1998 consent decree. The court denied the motion, and CPS appealed to the Seventh Circuit. It found the only remaining aspect of the case was the filing of a report by the monitor. Since there was no longer a consent decree, **the court found no live controversy remaining between the parties and it held the case was moot**. Although the CPS suggested that information from the monitor's pending report might provide the grounds for future lawsuits, the court found this did not create a live controversy. It dismissed the CPS motion. *Corey H. v. Chicago Board of Educ.*, 528 Fed.Appx. 666 (7th Cir. 2013).

♦ A New Jersey preschool student divided time between an inclusion class at his neighborhood school and an out-of-district, self-contained classroom. His child study team recommended a kindergarten inclusion class with a transition back to the neighborhood school for grade one. The parent claimed an inclusion class was not a general education setting and objected because it was not at the child's neighborhood school. In a due process petition to contest the placement, the parent claimed the school district had a general rule that no special education students would be placed at their neighborhood schools.

Before an administrative ruling was issued, the parent withdrew her petition and filed a class action complaint against the district in a federal court. She sought an order requiring school officials to consider placing each special needs kindergartener in regular classrooms. Agreeing with the district, the court held the parent had no standing and did not exhaust her administrative remedies. The case reached the U.S. Court of Appeals, Third Circuit, which held that to establish standing, a party must assert an "injury in fact" that is traceable to the challenged action. Any injury must be capable of being redressed by a favorable order. **Affirming a rule stated by many other courts, the Third Circuit found special education services may be provided in a centralized location.** Since the family had not alleged any individual harm and a procedural violation alone did not justify a court order, the court held the parent lacked standing. Although she had attached a discrimination claim under Section 504, this claim was based on the theory that the busing of her child and his placement in an inclusion class "involuntarily marked" him as a disabled child. There was no support for the theory that being identified as disabled against one's will could be considered an injury. There was also no reason to entertain the case as a class action. *J.T. v. Dumont Public Schools*, 533 Fed.Appx. 44 (Table) (3d Cir. 2013).

◆   Seven students with disabilities sued the Milwaukee Public Schools for widespread violations of the IDEA. They sought to represent a class of all school-age Milwaukee students with disabilities. A federal court certified a narrower class and then determined that the schools had committed systemic violations of the IDEA. Appeal reached the U.S. Court of Appeals, Seventh Circuit, which vacated the class certification order. It held the IDEA claims were highly individualized and vastly diverse, making the case unsuitable for class action treatment. The court held the class itself was "fatally indefinite," as it was not possible to order final injunctive or declaratory relief on a class-wide basis. Because the class should not have been certified, liability and remedial orders were vacated as well. A settlement agreement with the class required more of the school district than the students had statutory authority to demand, so an order approving the parties' settlement was also vacated. *Jamie S. v. Milwaukee Public Schools*, 668 F.3d 481 (7th Cir. 2012).

◆   Several parents of autistic students in Pennsylvania filed a lawsuit against their school district, seeking class action status. They asserted that the district denied their children a free appropriate public education and that it misrepresented the educational progress of autistic children. A federal court dismissed the lawsuit, noting that **the parents should have exhausted their administrative remedies before suing. It did not matter that they were seeking relief on behalf of a class.** *N.A v. Gateway School Dist.*, 820 F.Supp.2d 649 (W.D. Pa. 2011).

◆   A group of 350 parents and children sued 60 people and entities in Utah, accusing them of fraudulently offering students sham services such as sending them to schools and centers for troubled youth. They asserted that the entities convinced desperate parents of troubled youths to send their children to what were represented to be educational facilities specializing in improving the students' behavior. **According to the plaintiffs, the services were a sham and students were subjected to horrific treatment that was covered up.** A federal court dismissed the lawsuit, finding no RICO violations. The plaintiffs failed to show any prohibited use or investment of racketeering income that caused them harm. *Wood v. World Wide Ass'n of Specialty Programs and Schools, Inc.*, No. 2:06-CV-708 CW, 2011 WL 3328931 (D. Utah 8/2/11).

B. Expert Witness Fees

◆   After the parents of a special education student obtained reimbursement for tuition at a private school, they sought reimbursement for the cost of an educational consultant they used during the course of litigation. A New York federal court awarded them $8,650 of the $29,350 in fees they claimed, reducing the award because the consultant did not keep contemporaneous time records. The Second Circuit upheld the award, noting that the IDEA permits the recovery of fees and costs for individuals with "special knowledge." On further appeal, the U.S. Supreme Court held **the IDEA does not authorize prevailing parents to recover expert fees**. The Court noted that the IDEA was enacted under the Spending Clause, and that it does not even hint that the acceptance of IDEA funds makes a state responsible for reimbursing prevailing parents for the services of experts. The statute simply adds reasonable attorneys' fees to the list of recoverable costs. Further, the expert witness fees could not be deemed costs so as to be reimbursable. *Arlington Cent. School Dist. Board of Educ. v. Murphy*, 548 U.S. 291, 126 S.Ct. 2455, 165 L.Ed.2d 526 (2006).

◆   The District of Columbia had a policy authorizing the payment of expert witness fees in due process hearings. However, in 2006, the U.S. Supreme Court held that expert fees could not be recovered by prevailing parties in IDEA cases. When the parents of a disabled student sought to recover their expert fees as prevailing parties, the U.S. Court of Appeals, D.C. Circuit, held that they could not do so. **Even though they had sought their expert fees prior to the Supreme Court's decision, that ruling took precedence.** *Fisher v. District of Columbia*, 517 F.3d 570 (D.C. Cir. 2008).

◆   After prevailing in IDEA due process hearings, the families of five students with disabilities sought to recover their expert witness fees. A federal court denied the fees, and the U.S. Court of Appeals, D.C. Circuit, affirmed. **There is no language in the IDEA allowing expert witness fees to prevailing parties.** Only "reasonable attorneys' fees" are provided for by Section 1415. *Goldring v. District of Columbia*, 416 F.3d 70 (D.C. Cir. 2005).

◆   The parents of a disabled New York student prevailed in an IDEA hearing, then filed an action seeking $84,000 in attorneys' fees and $5,375 for an independent evaluator. The court reduced their attorneys' fees to $52,500 and denied the evaluator's fee, stating that the IDEA provides no explicit authorization for the reimbursement of an expert witness. The Supreme Court, Appellate Division, noted that **the parents' claim failed to explain the evaluator's role or significance**. Nor did they explain why an evaluation at public expense would have been insufficient. *Pawling Cent. School Dist. v. Munoz*, 788 N.Y.S.2d 267 (N.Y. App. Div. 2005).

C. Parent Actions and Representation

A general rule is that non-attorneys are not competent to represent the legal rights of others. For this reason, non-attorney parents may not advance claims on behalf of their children. In Winkelman v. Parma City School Dist.*, this chapter, the Supreme Court held parents have enforceable IDEA rights that are independent of their children's rights. As a result, the Court held Ohio parents could pursue an IDEA claim on their own behalf against a school district.*

♦   A Chicago parent sought to have her child's open-enrollment charter school perform an evaluation to assess her for special education eligibility. According to the parent, the child began receiving services under Section 504 of the Rehabilitation Act but an IEP meeting and case study were delayed. When an IEP meeting was finally held, the parent declared it a sham and filed an IDEA due process hearing request. The hearing officer found the school had ample evidence that the child needed special education and ordered the school to pay for 25 sessions with a pathologist, plus an award of compensatory education. The parent appealed the hearing officer's decision to a federal court.

The court held the parent could not represent her child since she was not a lawyer. While she had enforceable IDEA rights of her own, it held she was not "aggrieved" by the hearing officer's decision. Claims for reimbursement for the cost of her child's sessions with a speech and language pathologist were not before the hearing officer, and since the parent was not awarded any other relief, she had no valid IDEA claim. On appeal, the U.S. Court of Appeals, Seventh Circuit, clarified that parents of a child with a disability have their own enforceable rights under the IDEA. But the court rejected the parent's argument that she could represent her child in an IDEA action without a lawyer. **Seventh Circuit authority prohibits nonlawyers from representing others in court.** But the court held the parent's own claims should not have been dismissed. It held she stated sufficient facts that her parental rights were violated under the IDEA. These claims deserved further consideration by the lower court. *Foster v. Board of Educ. of City of Chicago*, 611 Fed.Appx. 874 (7th Cir. 2015).

♦   A Vermont grandparent said a teacher assaulted her learning disabled grandson. When she learned the teacher had also been involved in an argument with a parent, she claimed the teacher received lighter punishment by the school for his misconduct based on the grandchild's African-American race. After police involvement regarding the student's home placement, the grandparent claimed police and child protection authorities did not handle his case properly. She said he had emotional detachment disorder, oppositional defiant order and attention deficit hyperactivity disorder. In a federal court, the grandparent sued state, local and school authorities. She claimed some of the student's conduct was not his fault but was attributable to his disabilities. She sought damages because she claimed he had been a discrimination victim and had been suicidal.

The court explained that a non-lawyer may not represent another person or entity in a federal court. As the student was 18 years old at the time the case was filed, the court held his grandparent's appearance on his behalf was improper. Despite the grandparent's claim to have been given a power of attorney for his affairs, the court held she could not provide him with representation. The court held it could not rule on the case unless the student himself appeared on his own behalf or through counsel. He was given 30 days to appear on his own behalf (or with counsel), or to amend his complaint. Some of the claims would still be dismissed as untimely or barred by a $10,000 settlement agreement signed by the grandparent in return for the release of her claims against the district. *Miller v. Town of Morrisville*, No. 2:14-cv-5, 2015 WL 1648996 (D. Vt. 4/14/15).

♦   A Florida court adjudicated a parent to be the permanent legal guardian of his children. He was given express rights to make all educational decisions on their behalf. The children's non-custodial parent filed a federal court action to challenge their educational programs. The court dismissed the case because she was a non-custodial parent with no authority to make educational decisions for the children. On appeal, the U.S. Court of Appeals, Eleventh Circuit, noted that **IDEA language specifies the "parent of a child with a disability" is authorized to request an IDEA hearing**. An IDEA regulation defined "parent" as a "guardian generally authorized to act as the child's parent, or authorized to make educational decisions for the child." If a judicial order identified a specific person to act as the child's parent, or to make the child's educational decisions, such a person was to be deemed the child's "parent."

Under Florida law, the term "parent" excluded a person whose parental rights had been transferred or terminated. A permanent guardianship of a child indicated a transfer of decision-making rights. In any event, federal courts have held parents who are not represented by counsel may not bring actions on behalf of a child who was denied relief in an IDEA due process hearing. Since the parent did not have the authority to make educational decisions on behalf of her children at the time she filed suit, the court held she could not proceed. *Driessen v. Lockman*, 518 Fed.Appx. 809 (Table) (11th Cir. 2013).

♦   A dispute arose regarding services for a California student with disabilities. The parties reached a two-year agreement that applied unless the family moved outside the district. The parent released her right to claims under the IDEA, Rehabilitation Act and California law. A few months after the agreement was reached, the parent filed a complaint with the state department of education, asserting the district was out of compliance. The department ordered corrective action. Near the start of the next school year, the district claimed the parent no longer lived in its boundaries and that the agreement was no longer valid. After the parent received notice that her child's services were terminated, she sued the district in the state court system for breach of contract and other claims.

Although the court allowed the parent to pursue claims for a five month time period, it held she could not challenge the district's termination of services based on residency. It dismissed her other claims. On appeal to the Court of Appeal of California, the parent argued the lower court had arbitrarily limited her claims. But the court found the agreement was not related to that IEP. The district did not revoke the student's enrollment until October 12, 2010. So the lower court had erroneously limited the contract claims to the period ending August 2010. That holding was reversed and returned to the superior court. On the other hand, the court held the residency issue had been properly dismissed. It held exhaustion requirements applied to internal grievance procedures established by public and private entities. The residency issue did not involve any programmatic changes to the IEP. **Once the parent learned the district intended to end her child's enrollment, she had to use district procedures to challenge the residency issue.** Only the breach of contract claim would go forward when the case returned to the superior court. *T.L. v. Brentwood Union School Dist.*, No. A133428, 2013 WL 1209040 (Cal. Ct. App. 3/26/13).

♦   The parents of a Texas student with severe autism placed him in a private learning center for applied behavioral analysis and brought him to the public school three days a week instead of the five specified in the IEP. When they later sought tuition reimbursement, the Fifth Circuit noted that the student was dually enrolled in public and private schools, so the parents had a limited ability to raise challenges under Texas law. Reimbursement can be denied due to parental actions that frustrate a school's efforts. However, the parents here were entitled to $14,625 for the first three weeks of school because **the failure to provide a representative from the private school resulted in a procedural violation of the IDEA. The deficiencies in the IEP would have been cleared up sooner if the representative had attended the IEP meeting.** *S.H. v. Plano Independent School Dist.*, 487 Fed.Appx. 850 (5th Cir. 2012).

♦   The disabled mother of a disabled Massachusetts student had ongoing issues with his IEP and eventually challenged it before a hearing officer. However, because of her disabilities, she failed to appear at a hearing dismissing her retroactive claims. Subsequently, a hearing officer and a federal court ruled for the district on her current claims. The current IEP was appropriate. But **the court allowed her to pursue her retroactive claims against the district in front of a hearing officer because of her disabilities**. *Nickerson-Reti v. Lexington Public Schools*, 893 F.Supp.2d 276 (D. Mass. 2012).

♦   The parents of a disabled New York child divorced, with the mother taking custody of the child. The father later challenged the special education services the student was receiving, and the question of a non-custodial parent's rights to direct the child's education came before the state's highest court. The New York Court of Appeals held that **although a non-custodial parent has the right to participate in a child's education, that parent does not have the right to "control educational decisions"** absent an express provision in the custody agreement. Thus, the father could not challenge the educational services.

Later, the father contended that the state's implementation of the IDEA violated his due process and equal protection rights. A federal court disagreed. If non-custodial parents had the rights asserted here, school officials would have to navigate potential disputes between divorced parents. *Fuentes v. New York City Dep't of Educ.*, 2012 WL 1078779 (E.D.N.Y. 3/30/12).

♦   The mother of a North Carolina student reached a settlement with the school district over her son's special education. A state department of public instruction investigation revealed that the district was not in compliance with the agreement. She sued the district on her son's behalf, alleging constitutional violations, but a federal court ruled against her. Also, **as a non-attorney, she could not pursue an action on her's behalf**. *R.W. v. Wake County Public Schools*, No. 5:07-CV-136-F3, 2010 WL 3452376 (E.D.N.C. 9/1/10).

◆   An Oklahoma parent sued school officials on his child's behalf, asserting that the school used physical force to restrain the student in violation of the IEP. However, the court dismissed his lawsuit, noting that **non-attorney parents can't represent their children in court**. And the parent failed to exhaust his administrative remedies for any violation on his own behalf. As a result, the child would have to pursue any claims regarding the improper restraints via due process. *M.D.F. v. Independent School Dist. No. 50 of Osage County*, No. 09-CV-548-GKF-PJC, 2010 WL 2326260 (N.D. Okla. 6/3/10).

◆   The parents of an Ohio special education student had a contentious relationship with their school district, filing numerous administrative complaints. They sought to tape record IEP meetings without prior consent from the school district, and they objected to the presence of the school district's attorney at the meetings. As a result of the disputes, the parties were unable to negotiate an IEP. The district filed a due process request, and the case reached a federal court, which held that the district's attorney could be present at the IEP meetings. Further, the court held that **canceling IEP meetings because of the conditions the parents imposed did not deprive them of any due process rights**. *Horen v. Board of Educ. of Toledo City School Dist.*, 594 F.Supp.2d 833 (N.D. Ohio 2009).

◆   The mother of an Indiana student with a disability complained that a teacher harassed her daughter and allowed other students to do the same. However, when she sued the school district without an attorney, a federal court dismissed the lawsuit, noting that **non-lawyer parents cannot represent their children in federal court**. Further, the mother failed to exhaust her administrative due process remedies. *Lenker v. Gray*, No. 2:07-CV-274-PRC, 2008 WL 4613534 (N.D. Ind. 10/10/08).

◆   Ohio parents disagreed with the IEP prepared for their autistic son and placed him in a private school. They filed a due process hearing request, but lost at two administrative levels. Without the assistance of an attorney, the parents appealed to a federal court. The court held for the school district, and the U.S. Court of Appeals, Sixth Circuit, then held that they could not pursue the case unless they hired an attorney. The U.S. Supreme Court agreed to review the parents' appeal and held that **the IDEA accorded the parents independent enforceable rights**. It would be inconsistent with the statutory scheme to bar the parents from continuing to assert these rights in federal court. Because the IDEA did not differentiate between the rights of disabled children and their parents, the Court reversed the judgment, permitting the parents to pursue their case. *Winkelman v. Parma City School Dist.*, 550 U.S. 516, 127 S.Ct. 1994, 167 L.Ed.2d 904 (2007).

♦   The parents of an Illinois student with disabilities claimed that their district denied their son a free appropriate public education under the IDEA by ignoring or flouting many provisions of his IEP. During administrative proceedings, the student died and a hearing officer dismissed the case. The parents continued the action in a federal court, which also dismissed the case. Without an attorney, the parents appealed to the Seventh Circuit Court of Appeals, which ruled **that they could not represent their son's estate without a lawyer**. They were given 60 days to find an attorney. *Malone v. Nielson*, 474 F.3d 934 (7th Cir. 2007).

♦   The mother of a Florida autistic student pursued at least six due process complaints against the school district, appealing to a federal court after a hearing officer ruled in favor of the district. The court first noted that the mother failed to exhaust her administrative remedies with respect to her claim that the district retaliated against her for vigorous advocacy of her son's rights. Next, the court stated that **although the Supreme Court had recognized parental rights under the IDEA, the mother could not pursue her discrimination claims without the assistance of legal counsel**. *N.N.J. v. Broward County School Board*, No. 06-61282-CIV, 2007 WL 3120299 (S.D. Fla. 10/23/07).

♦   Under a settlement agreement, a New Jersey parent agreed to apply to a private day school for her son if the district would provide a number of independent evaluations. She balked at sending her son to the private school until the evaluations were completed, and the district sued to enforce the settlement agreement by requiring the parent to send her son to the school. She did not hire a lawyer to represent her son. A federal court issued a preliminary order requiring the parent to send her son to the private school, and she appealed. The Third Circuit held that **she was entitled to a rehearing because she should not have been allowed to represent her son**. The case was returned to the lower court. *Montclair Board of Educ. v. M.W.D.*, 182 Fed.Appx. 136 (3d Cir. 2006).

♦   In an effort to obtain private school tuition reimbursement, the mother of a Connecticut student sued the school board without the assistance of an attorney. A federal court ruled that she could not represent her son in an IDEA action. Eight days before the student turned 18, his mother sought to include him as a party. The court refused to let her. However, the Second Circuit held that the son should have been allowed to join the lawsuit. **Once he became 18, he could represent himself without a lawyer.** *Cortese v. New Fairfield Board of Educ.*, 210 Fed.Appx. 83 (2d Cir. 2006).

♦   The attorney-father of a New York student with health and learning impairments challenged a change to the student's IEP and represented her at the due process hearing. He later sued to recover his attorneys' fees, and the case reached the Second Circuit. The court of appeals agreed with the Third and Fourth Circuits that **parent attorneys cannot recover fees in IDEA cases in which they represent their own children**. *S.N. v. Pittsford Cent. School Dist.*, 448 F.3d 601 (2d Cir. 2006).

◆   The U.S. Court of Appeals, Second Circuit, held that a Vermont parent who was not an attorney could not bring an appeal in federal court on behalf of her son after an adverse due process decision unless she obtained the assistance of counsel. *Tindall v. Poultney High School Dist.*, 414 F.3d 281 (2d Cir. 2005).

◆   The parents of a California student with autism sought reimbursement from their school district for educational services they paid for during a school year and an extended school year. They requested a due process hearing that resulted in a decision for the district. They appealed to a federal court without an attorney. The district claimed they could not represent their child without an attorney, but the court ruled that **they had substantive rights of their own that were enforceable** even though they were not the intended recipients of the education. The court refused to dismiss the case. *D.K. v. Huntington Beach Union High School Dist.*, 482 F.Supp.2d 1088 (C.D. Cal. 2006).

D. Settlement

◆   A New Mexico parent charged her dyslexic child's school district with failing to address her needs and requested a hearing. Before the hearing, she sought mediation. After the mediation, the parties reached a settlement and the parent asked the state administrative agency to dismiss her IDEA claims. She then sued the district in a federal court for discrimination under Section 504 of the Rehabilitation Act. Finding the parent did not exhaust her administrative remedies, the court dismissed the case. On appeal, the U.S. Court of Appeals, Tenth Circuit, found the parent's complaint from the administrative action and her current federal complaint were nearly identical in scope. In order to bring a lawsuit under any federal law that seeks relief that is also available under the IDEA, the procedures of the IDEA found at 20 U.S.C. § 1415 subsections (f) and (g) must first be exhausted. In prior decisions, the Tenth Circuit has held a party must file an IDEA administrative complaint if the party has alleged injuries that could be redressed to any degree by the IDEA's administrative procedures and remedies. Moreover, the party must be "aggrieved" by a decision in the administrative proceeding. In this case, the parent admitted she was seeking relief that was available under the IDEA. And the court held she was not "aggrieved" by any IDEA proceeding. According to the parent, her pursuit of mediation satisfied the requirement of administrative exhaustion.
　　But the court disagreed, ruling that by choosing to settle her IDEA claims and dismiss the administrative complaint, the parent had barred the present case. In affirming the judgment for the school district, the court pointed out that the parent was not aggrieved by the findings and decision of a hearing officer. **Since mediation did not count as exhaustion, the court held for the school district**. *A.F. v. Espanola Public Schools*, 801 F.3d 1245 (10th Cir. 2015).

◆   The mother of a 20-year-old former student with cerebral palsy and other disabilities claimed staff members of a Tennessee school district often left him unattended in school lavatories. She said her son had a seizure in one case and was returned to class with bloody underwear in another. In addition to stating that aides regularly failed to help her son clean himself, the parent said an aide sexually abused him. After the parties attended a resolution session under the IDEA, they agreed to a settlement by which the parent dropped her IDEA and state law claims. It was recited in the agreement that the settlement did not cover any claims arising after the date of the agreement and that the agreement was made in a resolution session and could be enforced in a state or federal court. The parent then sued the school district in a federal court for breach of the settlement agreement and violations of the U.S. Constitution, Rehabilitation Act Section 504 and the Americans with Disabilities Act. The court held for the school district, finding the claims were subject to administrative exhaustion.

On appeal, the U.S. Court of Appeals, Sixth Circuit, held the student alleged non-educational injuries that had no IDEA remedy. **Since the constitutional claims did not "arise under the IDEA," the court held they were not released by the settlement agreement.** Moreover, the court rejected the district's argument that the claims concerned a free appropriate public education. The settlement was reached at an IDEA resolution session and was, by its terms, enforceable in a court. As a result, the court held the breach of contract claim was not subject to the IDEA administrative exhaustion rule. *F.H. v. Memphis City Schools,* 764 F.3d 638 (6th Cir. 2014).

♦   A Pennsylvania parent removed her child from a school in her school district, then filed a due process hearing complaint against the district. Prior to a hearing, the parties and their attorneys reached a basic settlement. Almost three months after the cancelled hearing, the parent promised to release her claims in return for funds to homeschool the child. Later in the school year, the district grew concerned that she never filed a homeschool plan and did not re-enroll her child in school. The school district commenced a federal court action against the parent, claiming her inaction imperiled its funding for noncompliance with educational programs. The court held that it was equitable to enforce the promise against the parent. Enforcement of her promise would ensure that she would receive funds to provide for her son's education while avoiding a substantial injustice to the school district due to her change of heart.

The parent appealed to the U.S. Court of Appeals, Third Circuit. It noted the parties had never actually reduced their agreement to a valid writing. Under Pennsylvania law, where a party makes a promise that can reasonably be expected to induce action (or forbearance) by the other party, and the other party acts (or refrains from acting) in reliance on the promise, the promise may be enforced by a court – if injustice may be avoided only by enforcing the promise. Like the lower court, **the Third Circuit held the mother's promises caused the school district to refrain from initiating truancy proceedings**. Finding injustice could only be avoided by enforcing the mother's promises to the school district, the court held the district was entitled to enforce them. *I.K. v. Haverford School Dist.,* 567 Fed.Appx. 135 (3d Cir. 2014).

♦   A California student with severe autism was placed in a different school than the one his siblings attended, which prompted a due process complaint from his family. After the case was settled, the family brought another complaint alleging that the district had violated the settlement agreement. A hearing officer ruled for the district, and the family then sued, adding other claims against the district. A federal court held **the family failed to exhaust its administrative remedies** on those other claims. *Andrew W. v. Menlo Park City School Dist.*, No. C-10-0292 MMC, 2010 WL 3001216 (N.D. Cal. 7/29/10).

◆ The guardian of a California student with mental health problems entered into a settlement whereby the student was placed in a Colorado residential treatment facility. After she turned 18, she sued state officials, challenging California's failure to make in-state residential services available to emotionally disturbed students over age 18 who had not graduated and would not do so by age 19. A federal court ruled that she had to exhaust her administrative remedies first. **The settlement agreement did not satisfy the exhaustion requirement.** *Washington v. California Dep't of Educ.*, No. 2:10-CV-0186 FCD KJM, 2010 WL 4157139 (E.D. Cal. 10/19/10).

◆ The parents of a disabled student believed their district was denying their son special education. They requested an IDEA due process hearing. Before the hearing, the district allegedly agreed to a settlement with the parents. It sought to have the settlement enforced, but a hearing panel ruled that it did not have the authority to do so. The district appealed to the Missouri Court of Appeals, which ruled that **the hearing panel in fact had the authority to determine the settlement's enforceability**. Disputes over settlements relate to the provision of FAPE. *State of Missouri v. Missouri Dep't of Elementary and Secondary Educ.*, 307 S.W.3d 209 (Mo. Ct. App. 2010).

◆ A private school contracted with a Virginia school district to provide educational services for an autistic student. The contract allowed either party to terminate the agreement upon 30 days' notice. The school could also terminate the contract if the student committed a serious incident. When the school sought to discharge the student over safety concerns, his parents objected and requested a due process hearing. A hearing officer ordered the school to comply with the stay-put provision, finding the contract with the district required it to comply with the IDEA. The private school sued to challenge the stay-put order, then reached a settlement with the district releasing it from the contract. The federal court then refused to intervene in the dispute, leaving the due process hearing (over the decision to expel the student) to the hearing officer. *Virginia Institute of Autism v. Virginia Dep't of Educ.*, 537 F.Supp.2d 817 (E.D. Va. 2008).

◆ The mother of a Pennsylvania student with Down syndrome rejected an IEP offer to place her daughter in a life skills support class for most of each school day. She believed a largely mainstream setting was appropriate and requested a due process hearing. A hearing officer ruled in her favor, but an appeals panel reversed that decision. She appealed to a federal court but settled on the morning of the trial. She then changed her mind and sought to revoke the settlement, claiming duress and lack of effective counsel. The court rejected her request, and the Third Circuit affirmed. Here, **any pressure of time constraints did not amount to duress** that would justify revoking the settlement. *Ballard v. Philadelphia School Dist.*, 273 Fed.Appx. 184 (3d Cir. 2008).

♦ The mother of a Pennsylvania student with autism challenged his educational program and eventually entered into a settlement agreement with the district, returning her son to his neighborhood school. However, she and the district deadlocked on one issue, and she then sought to withdraw her consent from the entire settlement agreement. A federal court and the Third Circuit ruled that **she could not withdraw her consent just because she had later found it inadequate**. There was no change in circumstances that would make enforcement of the agreement improper. *Muse B. v. Upper Darby School Dist.*, 282 Fed.Appx. 986 (3d Cir. 2008).

♦ The parents of an Illinois student sued their school district over her education, then reached a settlement agreement and signed a release of all claims against the district. Later, the student reached the age of majority and sued the district on her own for discriminating against her. The Seventh Circuit dismissed her claims, noting that even though she was asserting different legal theories, **her claims were based on the same set of events as had defined the earlier settlement**. It did not matter that her parents had brought the earlier lawsuit. The parties were still the same. *Ross v. Board of Educ. of Township High School Dist. No. 211*, 486 F.3d 279 (7th Cir. 2007).

E. Other Proceedings

♦ A California mother sued her school district five times. The district sought to have the most current case dismissed, and the mother declared a "vexatious litigant" based on her history of suing it. A federal court agreed that the case was barred and that the mother was a vexatious litigant. It imposed a pre-filing order upon her, but the **Ninth Circuit found insufficient evidence to determine that the mother was a vexatious litigant**. It remanded the case for further fact-finding. *Stewart v. California Dep't of Educ.*, 493 Fed.Appx. 889 (9th Cir. 2012).

♦ A California family complained that a county agency failed to provide their child with directions in American Sign Language during testing required by the state. They asked the state department of education for a compliance investigation, which resulted in a report by the department that the county was out of compliance with state and federal law. The county appealed. On reconsideration, the department found the student received accommodations during the testing, but it refused to change its conclusion that the county was noncompliant. The county sued the department, but a court held **it had no right to sue under the IDEA**. *Yolo County Office of Educ. v. California Dep't of Educ.*, No. 2:11–cv–03224–MCE–JFM, 2012 WL 3143904 (E.D. Cal. 8/1/12).

♦ The mother of a California student with autism believed her daughter was not ready for middle school, but the district's IEP called for a seventh-grade placement with reduced speech therapy and no vision therapy. The mother received documents that led her to believe her daughter would remain in grade six the following year, but when she took her daughter to school the next fall, **the district allegedly told her she had until 5:00 p.m. that day to sign a settlement offer agreeing to the district's IEP** and waiving her rights under the IDEA if she wanted the child in sixth grade. Later, she challenged the IEP in a federal court, which ruled that the agreement was likely unenforceable as unconscionable. Her claims could proceed. *Y.G. v. Riverside Unified School Dist.*, 774 F.Supp.2d 1055 (C.D. Cal. 2011).

♦ A Massachusetts family asserted that their child's IEP was inappropriate. They placed him in a private Connecticut school and requested due process. An appeals board found the district's proposed placement inappropriate, but it ordered consideration of other nearby public schools. The family later moved to Connecticut for financial reasons, and a federal court held that their move rendered their IDEA claims moot. However, the First Circuit held that the move to Connecticut did not moot the case. **The family was seeking compensation for an obligation that was incurred before the move and not for obligations that arose afterward.** *E.D. v. Newburyport Public Schools*, 654 F.3d 140 (1st Cir. 2011).

♦ Michigan school districts attempted to pursue an IDEA action against the state department of education, asserting that it had unlawfully exercised its power over an administrative appeal involving a student with autism. However, since the student had settled with the districts, the Sixth Circuit held that the districts could no longer sue the state. **School districts are not "aggrieved parties" under the IDEA**, and the statute does not give districts the right to sue state agencies. *Traverse Bay Area Intermediate School Dist. v. Michigan Dep't of Educ.*, 615 F.3d 622 (6th Cir. 2010).

♦ The mother of a Pennsylvania student with disabilities sought a Mandarin Chinese translation of the transcript from due process proceedings. When the school district refused to provide such a transcript, she sued. The Pennsylvania Commonwealth Court held that she was not entitled to a translated transcript. **Although due process may require a translator during administrative proceedings, that right does not extend to the provision of a transcript in any language.** *Bethlehem Area School Dist. v. Zhou*, 976 A.2d 1284 (Pa. Commw. Ct. 2009).

♦ Florida parents of two students with disabilities claimed the students were improperly sent to a new school, where they were bullied and subjected to unfair punishment by teachers. They requested private school placements, which were denied. When they sought due process, a hearing officer dismissed their cases as moot because the school year had ended. They appealed to a federal court, which held that **their lawsuit could proceed even though the hearing officer had failed to compile an administrative record on their IDEA claims**. *Lewellyn v. Sarasota County School Board*, No. 8:07-CV-1712-T-33TGW, 2009 WL 1515737 (M.D. Fla. 6/1/09).

♦ The mother of a New Jersey special education student sent him to live with his aunt in another district, which approved the student's attendance as a resident. Later the mother again took custody of the student, claiming that she now lived in the district and producing a lease agreement, a copy of her driver's license and a sworn statement of residency. The school district nevertheless rejected her claim of residency. It asserted that the lease agreement was fraudulent and relied on investigative evidence showing the student and parent leaving from a non-district residence four days in a row. Before an administrative law judge, the mother again produced her documentation, while the district's attorney argued that the documentation was worthless. The ALJ ruled for the district, but a New Jersey appellate court ruled that a new hearing was required. **The district could not simply rely on its attorney's arguments to prove nonresidency.** *Y.E. ex rel. E.E. v. State-Operated School Dist. of City of Newark*, 2008 WL 2492258 (N.J. Super. Ct. App. Div. 6/24/08).

♦   The parents of two disabled New Jersey students filed an administrative complaint against their school board rather than seek due process. They alleged violations of the IDEA, and they brought the complaint under the dispute resolution procedure described in federal regulations at 34 C.F.R. Part 300.661. The state education department's Office of Special Education Programs resolved the complaint in their favor, and the school board sought review. The Superior Court of New Jersey, Appellate Division, ruled that OSEP's final decision was not reviewable in the courts. **The complaint resolution procedure described in the regulations was designed to be a low-cost alternative to due process actions.** *Board of Educ. of Lenape Regional HS Dist. v. New Jersey State DOE, OSEP*, 945 A.2d 125 (N.J. Super. Ct. App. Div. 2008).

♦   Two Kansas students with disabilities received special education services from a school district. When the district learned that their mother and her boyfriend might be living outside the district's boundaries, an investigator confirmed that suspicion. The district sued the mother and boyfriend in a state court seeking nonresident tuition and an order prohibiting the children from attending district schools. The mother, boyfriend and children then brought a lawsuit against the district in federal court. The court ruled against them, and the Tenth Circuit affirmed. **The federal court could not grant any relief against the district without first determining whether the children were entitled to be educated in the district** – which was the very subject of the state court lawsuit. Also, the boyfriend had no standing to sue. *D.L. v. Unified School Dist. No. 497*, 392 F.3d 1223 (10th Cir. 2004).

CHAPTER SEVEN

Private School Tuition

I. TUITION REIMBURSEMENT

A. Unilateral Placement by Parents

1. Generally

An IDEA section – 20 U.S.C. § 1415(i)(2)(C) – authorizes a court to "grant such relief as [it] determines is appropriate" when reviewing a due process challenge to the provision of a free appropriate public education (FAPE). Many courts have held this authorizes private school tuition reimbursement where a school district fails to offer an IEP that would provide a FAPE.

In C.L. v. Scarsdale Union Free School Dist., *this chapter, the Second Circuit recited the test for reimbursement of private school tuition from* School Committee of the Town of Burlington, Massachusetts v. Dep't of Educ. of Massachusetts, *471 U.S. 359 (1985) and* Florence County School Dist. Four v. Carter, *510 U.S. 7 (1993). First, the child must be denied a free appropriate public education. Next, the private placement selected by parents must be held appropriate. Third, the equities must favor an award of tuition reimbursement.*

♦ A District of Columbia parent placed her child in a private residential school with a $58,000 annual tuition rate because no IEP was in place when the school year began. Although the student had been identified as having above-average intelligence, she failed most of her classes and threatened suicide. In the student's junior year, the parent twice requested evaluations. When the

District of Columbia Public Schools (DCPS) recommended that she obtain a private evaluation instead, she filed a due process complaint that eventually reached the U.S. Court of Appeals, District of Columbia Circuit. It held nothing in the IDEA required an objecting parent to wait until the first day of school to pull her child out of a school system. In addition, the court found the residential school selected by the parent was appropriate. The parental placement was primarily educational and not a response to medical, social or emotional problems that could be segregated from the learning process.

Moreover, the court found **the residential school was the only placement on record that could have provided the child with an education meeting her identified needs**. In further proceedings, the DCPS could challenge aspects of the residential placement it opposed, such as its horseback riding and other extracurricular programs. The case would return to the lower court for it to determine whether the IEP that the DCPS finally produced was adequate and whether reimbursement for the residential placement should be reduced in part. *Leggett v. District of Columbia*, 793 F.3d 59 (D.C. Cir. 2015).

♦   A Pennsylvania student had behavioral issues such as spitting, poking and hitting. A school evaluation in his kindergarten year did not find him eligible for special education. During grade one, he continued engaging in disruptive behavior at school and was often sent to a timeout room. As he was not meeting expectations, the parents placed him in a private school where his lead teacher was not state-certified. During second and third grades, the student still had significant behavior problems. His parents kept him in the private school when the school district informed them the child could not attend a multi-age class.

An independent educational evaluation found the child eligible for special education based on a learning disability. The school district evaluated him and also found him IDEA-eligible. It proposed dividing his school days equally between regular and special classrooms. The parents rejected the IEP due to concerns about the support available in a regular classroom. A hearing officer found the school district denied the child a free appropriate public education. But since the private school was inappropriate for their child, reimbursement was denied. A federal court held the district improperly failed to identify the student as eligible for special education. But the private school was not an appropriate setting for him. It lacked any detailed or coherent plan for addressing his significant academic and behavioral needs. **Overwhelming evidence indicated the child made no academic and little behavioral progress at the private school.** As a result, parental requests to be reimbursed for costs of the IEE, tuition and transportation were all denied. *Matthew D. v. Avon Grove School Dist.*, No. 12-0777, 2015 WL 4243471 (E.D. Pa. 7/13/15).

♦   A severely autistic New York child who was nonverbal and prone to self-injurious behavior attended a private preschool for applied behavioral analysis therapy. A CSE proposed an IEP for a 6:1:1 placement (six students, a teacher and a paraprofessional) for her kindergarten year. After evaluating the public school classroom recommended for her child, the parent found it was not appropriate. She notified the city Department of Education (DOE) that she was returning her child to the private center and signed an enrollment contract with the center. The parent then filed a due process case against the DOE. An IHO found she had no standing to pursue the case because she had paid nothing to the center. A state review officer held the parent lacked standing to pursue the action and that a 6:1:1 setting was appropriate. On appeal, a federal court held the parent had standing to bring the lawsuit even if she did not pay the tuition.

But like the review officer, the court held the 6:1:1 setting was appropriate. Appeal then reached the U.S. Court of Appeals, Second Circuit. It held the parent stated an "injury in fact" by asserting the denial of a FAPE to her child. In addition to having accepted a legally enforceable obligation to pay the tuition, **the court held the parent showed she incurred the obligation as a result of the DOE's alleged failure to provide the child a FAPE**. Next, the court found the lower court had improperly credited the DOE's evidence that 1:1 services would be provided. The IEP specified a 6:1:1 program. The court returned the case to the lower court for further proceedings to determine whether the IEP was appropriate. *E.M. v. New York City Dep't of Educ.*, 758 F.3d 442 (2d Cir. 2014).

◆   In *School Committee of the Town of Burlington, Massachusetts v. Dep't of Educ. of Massachusetts,* the U.S. Supreme Court held that parents who unilaterally place children in private schools may nevertheless receive tuition reimbursement from the school district if the IEP proposed by the school is later found to be inappropriate. Parents who place a disabled child in a private educational facility are entitled to reimbursement for the child's tuition and living expenses if a court later determines that the school district proposed an inappropriate IEP. Conversely, reimbursement could not be ordered if the school district's proposed IEP was appropriate. The Court observed that to bar reimbursement claims under all circumstances would violate the IDEA, which requires appropriate interim placement for children with disabilities. **Parents who unilaterally change the placement of a child during the pendency of IDEA proceedings do so at their own financial risk.** If the courts ultimately determine that a proposed IEP is appropriate, the parents are barred from obtaining reimbursement for an unauthorized private school placement. *School Committee of the Town of Burlington, Massachusetts v. Dep't of Educ. of Massachusetts,* 471 U.S. 359, 105 S.Ct. 1996, 85 L.Ed.2d 385 (1985).

2. Behavioral Challenges

In Jenna R.P. v. City of Chicago School Dist. No. 229, *this chapter, the Illinois Appellate Court explained that for parents to qualify for tuition reimbursement for a unilateral private placement, the school they select must be consistent with IDEA purposes. In addition, the court found a private placement must offer the student at least some element of special education services in which the public school placement was deficient.*

◆   The U.S. Court of Appeals, Fifth Circuit, reversed a lower court decision awarding Texas parents tuition reimbursement for a Missouri residential school placement. The court held the placement was made over concerns that the student would attempt suicide and because of his continuing drug problem. **The**

parents made the placement for noneducational reasons, and no educational reason was given for it. Evidence did not show the student's progress at the facility was judged primarily by educational achievement. Instead, the goal had been to treat his reactive attachment disorder. Since the lower court committed error, the court held for the school district. *Fort Bend Independent School Dist. v. Douglas A.*, 601 Fed.Appx. 250 (5th Cir. 2015).

♦ A 14-year-old New York student had autism and a neurological condition that impaired his speaking and caused him to act aggressively. He attended a private school approved by the New York City Department of Education (DOE), where he received special education in small group settings until it was determined he could not function academically in groups. A CSE recommended using a 1:1 instruction program of ABA therapy. Eight years after being placed in the private school, the DOE convened meetings to devise a new IEP. Private school representatives urged continued 1:1 instruction. But the DOE instead adopted the recommendation of a school psychologist who had observed the student for only 75 minutes. He suggested a 6:1:1 setting. The parents rejected the IEP and re-enrolled their child in the private school. A federal court held the DOE did not show a 6:1:1 setting enabled the student to learn new material and receive educational benefits. Despite a wealth of testimony in support of a 1:1 program, the review officer had relied on contrary testimony by the DOE psychologist.

A 75-minute observation gave the psychologist no basis for concluding that the student could learn in a group. **Since the IEP was inappropriate, and the private school was appropriate, the court held the parents were entitled to tuition reimbursement.** On appeal, the Second Circuit affirmed the judgment, finding the DOE had denied the child a free appropriate public education. *C.L. v. New York City Dep't of Educ.*, 552 Fed.Appx. 81 (2d Cir. 2014).

♦ The parents of a child with autism asked the New York City Department of Education (DOE) to continue a program of ABA he had received at a private school. They said he needed a 1:1 setting to address his behavior problems. But a CSE proposed a class with a 6:1:1 student-teacher-paraprofessional ratio. The IEP did not have a functional behavioral assessment (FBA), but it included a behavior intervention plan (BIP). The parents rejected the IEP and returned their child to the private school. An impartial hearing officer held reimbursement was proper, finding the DOE failed to create an individualized program and FBA, and did not offer parent training or counseling.

Appeal reached the U.S. Court of Appeals, Second Circuit. It explained that schools must conduct an FBA where necessary to identify student behaviors and how they related to the environment. **If a student's behaviors impeded learning despite consistent interventions, a school was required to consider a BIP based on the FBA.** The court found the DOE did not develop an FBA or an adequate BIP for the student. Nor did the DOE provide for parent counseling and training as required by state regulations. As the parents argued, the DOE ignored the recommendations for a 1:1 placement. They had been excluded from the site selection decision. While the lack of an FBA was not an automatic IDEA violation, the DOE did not create and implement behavioral strategies in the BIP. It did not match strategies to specific behaviors, instead simply listing behaviors and strategies. In addition, the court agreed with the parents that the IEP was substantively deficient and denied the student a FAPE. In sum, the court found the private placement was appropriate and the equities favored the parents. *C.F. v. New York City Dep't of Educ.*, 746 F.3d 68 (2d Cir. 2014).

♦   An Illinois student went missing for more than a month. She later admitted engaging in high-risk activities such as living with a prostitute and pimp, smoking crack cocaine and having an abortion. Hospital staff found the student severely depressed, oppositional and defiant, and made a recommendation for long-term residential care. Her father placed her in a Utah wilderness program. The father sent the school district a 10-day notice of his intent to place the student in a Maine residential school. Although the district advised the father it could not fund the Maine placement and would not call an IEP meeting, he went forward with the placement. The student made the honor roll and earned a high school diploma from the state of Maine. Just before her graduation, an IEP team met and rejected the Maine placement. The father requested a hearing, where he said that when the student returned to Chicago, her high-risk behavior resumed.

A hearing officer found the district had denied the student a free appropriate public education (FAPE). An Illinois circuit court agreed but found the Maine placement was made primarily due to safety and security concerns. On appeal, the Appellate Court of Illinois agreed with the father that he was left with little choice at the time of the Maine placement. He had tried to meet with the IEP team but was told the team could not meet near the end of the school year. **The court stated that if a school district defaults on its IDEA obligations, a private school placement by parents may be approved if it is found to be reasonably calculated to confer educational benefits upon the child.** Parents need to show only a denial of FAPE by a school district and that the selected private school provided specially designed instruction to meet the unique needs of the child. Since the father's placement choice resulted from the district's refusal to hold an IEP meeting, the court returned the case to a hearing officer to calculate an award of tuition reimbursement. *Jenna R.P. v. City of Chicago School Dist. No. 229*, 3 N.E.3d 927 (Ill. App. Ct. 2013).

♦   A New York student with severe emotional and behavioral problems had trouble with organizational skills, executive functioning and fine motor skills. His parents disputed the IEP prepared by their school district and placed him in a private setting. In a due process proceeding, they sought to be reimbursed for the private placement. A hearing officer agreed with the parents, but a state review officer (SRO) found the private school inappropriate because it did not develop an IEP or provide the student with support to address his organization, executive functioning, and fine motor skills. In addition, the school's behavioral program relied on inappropriate use of time-outs and other sanctions.

A federal court affirmed the decision, and the parents appealed to the U.S. Court of Appeals, Second Circuit. It found **the dispute involved the types of decisions involving educational methodology that should be afforded deference by a reviewing court**. Among the administrative findings was that the parents did not provide sufficient evidence for a hearing officer to determine whether counseling sessions at the private school were appropriate for the student. There was support for this finding in the record, and the lower court gave appropriate weight to the SRO's opinion. While the evidence indicated the student made some academic and behavioral progress in the private setting, this by itself did not demonstrate that a private placement was appropriate. Since the court held the parents did not show the school they selected was an appropriate placement for their child, the judgment for the school district was affirmed. *M.B. v. Minisink Valley Cent. School Dist.*, 523 Fed.Appx. 76 (2d Cir. 2013).

3.   Preferred Placement or Methodology

In W.D. v. Watchung Hills Regional High School Board of Educ., *this chapter, a federal appeals court found the IDEA does not require an IEP to describe instructional methodologies. In fact, the U.S. Department of Education has a longstanding position that the instructional methodologies in an IEP are left up to the IEP team. Nothing in the IDEA requires a school to provide parents information about the qualifications of teachers or service providers.*

Other courts have held questions of educational methodology are best left to educators and are generally not for court review. The Ninth Circuit held in B.D. v. Puyallup School Dist., *456 Fed.Appx. 644 (9th Cir. 2011), that school officials may select the method for implementing an IEP. In* W.R. and K.R. v. Union Beach Board of Educ., *414 Fed.Appx. 499 (3d Cir. 2011), the Third Circuit held parents cannot dictate what methodology to use for their children.*

But in Deal v. Hamilton County Dep't of Educ., *258 Fed. Appx. 863 (6th Cir. 2008), the Sixth Circuit held the differences between two methodologies may be so great that the provision of a lesser program amounts to a denial of FAPE.*

♦   A New York parent claimed a program of applied behavioral analysis (ABA) therapy suggested by a committee was inappropriate for her autistic child. She sought to place him in a private school that used Developmental Individual-Difference Relationship-based Model (floortime) methodology. An impartial hearing officer held for the parent, but the decision was reversed by a state review officer. A federal court noted the parent did not challenge the appropriateness of the IEP, which did not specify a particular methodology. In the court's view, the parent could not show the public school would not properly implement her son's IEP. She relied on statements by a parent coordinator and speculation that ABA methodology would be used by the public school teacher. As the Second Circuit has often held, a school district was not required to designate a school site in an IEP. **Speculation that a school would not comply with an IEP was not an appropriate basis for a unilateral parental placement.** As the IEP did not specify any particular teaching methodology and the parents relied on pure speculation that the school would use only ABA therapy, the court held for the New York City Department of Education. *J.W. and L.W. v. New York City Dep't of Educ.*, 95 F.Supp.3d 592 (S.D.N.Y. 2015).

♦   A New York student with a learning disability also had an anxiety disorder, attention deficit hyperactivity disorder and problems with sensory processing, motor skills, writing, and reading social cues. Prior to his second-grade year, his parent researched several private schools. She rejected an IEP that would have placed him in an integrated, co-teaching public school classroom with monthly individual and group counseling services and 1:1 occupational therapy. Instead, the parent signed an enrollment agreement with the Kildonan School, which provides Orton-Gillingham instruction but did not offer the student counseling. An impartial hearing officer held Orton-Gillingham instruction at Kildonen was appropriate, and the parent was awarded tuition reimbursement. A state review officer reversed the judgment, and the parent appealed to a federal court.

In the court's opinion, the parent did not specifically address or challenge the SRO's decision. She simply sought to convince the court that the impartial hearing officer's findings were correct. **A court should not disturb a hearing officer's denial of tuition reimbursement if the benefits of a chosen private school were simply the kinds of advantages that might be preferred by any parent.** Deference to the SRO decision was found appropriate, as it appeared he had thoroughly reviewed the entire record. Evidence supported the SRO's findings that the school did not offer him any formal occupational or physical therapy. Since the parent did not identify an error by the SRO requiring reversal, the court affirmed the judgment for the school district. *L.K. v. Northeast School Dist.*, 932 F.Supp.2d 467 (S.D.N.Y. 2013).

♦   A New York learning disabled student with other disorders began to have significant academic and emotional difficulties during grades four and five. In grade five, the school provided Wilson reading instruction and his behavior intervention plan was revised. His parents obtained a private evaluation, which recommended a placement in a special school such as Kildonan. When the student's behavior deteriorated further, the committee on special education looked into a therapeutic program for the next year. However, his parents signed him up for Kildonan. After the public school created an IEP for the next year, the parents challenged it, asserting that it did not contain a specific reading program. They kept him at Kildonan for three years and asked for tuition reimbursement, but a federal court denied their request. **The IEP specifically listed reading goals and did not have to specify a particular reading program.** *M.C. v. Katonah/Lewisboro Union Free School Dist.*, No. 10 CV 6268(VB), 2012 WL 834350 (S.D.N.Y. 3/5/12).

♦   A Massachusetts student with significant developmental delays received occupational, physical and speech therapy in his preschool years. A kindergarten evaluation indicated that his focus and communications skills had improved. He received therapy in the summer and returned to kindergarten the next year. The next summer, his parents enrolled him in the Lindamood-Bell Learning Center. In grade one, he did a little better, but a speech pathologist noted that he was a good candidate for multi-sensory structured learning like in Lindamood-Bell. The parties failed to agree on an IEP for the next year, and the parents placed him in the Lindamood-Bell school. In the lawsuit that followed, a federal court and **the First Circuit held that the student had received some meaningful educational benefit.** Thus, the parents were not entitled to tuition reimbursement. *D.B. v. Esposito*, 675 F.3d 26 (1st Cir. 2012).

♦   The parents of a New Jersey student became dissatisfied with his placement during second grade. Near the end of that year, his classification was changed to autistic. They rejected two IEP proposals for third grade. One would have placed him in a self-contained language learning disability class for academics; the other would have put him in a regular class with an aide and pullout instruction in a resource center for math, reading and language arts. Instead, they "shopped around" for an out-of-district placement and put him in a private school. When they sought tuition reimbursement, a federal court ruled against them. Here, **the IEPs were appropriate and would have conferred a meaningful educational benefit**. *L.W. v. Norwood Board of Educ.*, No. 11–2246 (SRC), 2012 WL 529582 (D.N.J. 2/17/12).

♦   A Pennsylvania student attended private schools through grade nine, when she withdrew due to problems with ADHD. She switched to a public school and, after an evaluation, the district issued an IEP that proposed a public school placement. Her parents rejected the IEP and placed her in a different private school. They requested due process, but the district did not process the request for more than a year. A hearing officer eventually found that the IEP would have provided the student with a free appropriate public education. The parents appealed, arguing that the delay required awarding them tuition reimbursement, but the Third Circuit disagreed. **The IEP offered an appropriate education, and the parents didn't dispute that.** *C.W. v. The Rose Tree Media School Dist.*, 395 Fed.Appx. 824 (3d Cir. 2010).

4. Regular Education Students

♦   A New York high school student began having problems related to her anxiety and depression. She twice tried to commit suicide, and her parent placed her in a private Utah boarding school for teenage girls with histories of eating disorders, substance abuse or behavioral issues. At the school, the student earned good grades. The student's grandmother paid the boarding school's $9,950 monthly tuition, and her mother signed a loan document agreeing to repay her. Later, a CSE found the student had no qualifying disability since her psychiatric issues did not affect her strong academic performance. An impartial hearing officer (IHO) found the student had a disability that required special education and held the department had denied her a free appropriate public education (FAPE). But due to the grandmother's payment, the IHO denied the request for reimbursement. It was found that the loan document was not legally binding. A state review officer found the student did not have a disability and that her education was not affected by her emotional disturbance.

The parent appealed to a federal court, which held the review officer had improperly found the student had no disability. The review officer had dwelt on the student's grades without considering the question of whether she could attend school at all. Since the review officer ignored this key factor, the court reinstated the IHO's decision regarding disability status. Finding the student was disabled, the court also held the IHO had properly found she was denied a FAPE. Next, the court found ample evidence that the Utah placement was appropriate for her. It had small classes and provided therapeutic interventions.

Second Circuit cases have held parents are not obligated to make a placement in the least restrictive setting after a public school system has denied a FAPE to a child. Since the school department denied the student a FAPE, and the Utah placement was found appropriate for her, the parent was entitled to tuition reimbursement. Unlike the IHO, the court held the equities favored reimbursing the parent. It ordered the department to reimburse the parent for her costs, with instructions that she repay the loan to the grandparent. *M.M. v. New York City Dep't of Educ.*, 26 F.Supp.3d 249 (S.D.N.Y. 2014).

♦   A Chicago student generally earned As until entering high school. After his grades plummeted, his parents obtained private psychological services and counseling for him. The school district did not evaluate him for eligibility, despite a psychologist's recommendation for achievement testing. A private neuropsychologist identified the student as likely having depression and ADHD. But the district still delayed special education testing. As the school year reached a conclusion, the student was suspended twice, including a 10-day suspension for smoking marijuana at school. The parents placed him in a month long wilderness program for troubled adolescents. Near this time, they requested a hearing and placed him in a Montana residential school. The district conducted a formal evaluation and found the student IDEA-eligible. Although the district drafted an IEP for him, the parents placed him in a Utah private school, where he eventually graduated. They requested a due process hearing.

A hearing officer held the school district failed to provide the student a free appropriate public education. It was ordered to reimburse the parents for the academic portion of the Montana placement, the full cost of the Utah placement, and fees paid for expert testimony. When the case reached a federal court, it agreed with the board of education that the parents were not entitled to their expert witness fees. But it held they were entitled to reimbursement for their private school tuition costs. The board had admitted failing to provide them with a copy of their notice of procedural safeguards until months after their unilateral action to remove the child from district schools. Moreover, the court rejected the board's argument that the Montana and Utah schools were not proper placements. **Both schools were certified by their respective states, and both were good academic fits for the student.** He had earned As and Bs from the Utah school, and he graduated. Agreeing with the hearing officer's finding that the board had denied the student a free appropriate public education, the court upheld the award of over $152,270 in tuition and transportation costs. *Board of Educ. of City of Chicago v. Illinois State Board of Educ.*, No. 13 C 2783, 2013 WL 5477596 (N.D. Ill. 10/1/13).

♦   A student attended Oregon public schools through grade eleven. He had problems paying attention and finishing work, but he was able to pass his classes with help from family members at home. The school district evaluated him but found him ineligible for special education and related services. After he exhibited multiple behavioral problems, a psychologist determined that he had ADHD, depression and other issues. His parents enrolled him in a three-week wilderness program, then a private residential school. They then sought due process. A hearing officer found the student disabled and eligible for IDEA services but held that the district only had to pay for the residential placement, not the wilderness program or the evaluation. The district appealed, and the Ninth Circuit held that **the fact that the student had never received special education from the district was not a categorical bar to reimbursement**.

On further appeal, the U.S. Supreme Court noted that the district's failure to provide an IEP was at least as serious a violation of its responsibilities under the IDEA as a failure to provide an adequate IEP. It rejected the district's argument that the student first had to receive special education and related services from the district to advance any claim for tuition reimbursement. The 1997 amendments did not mandate a different result from *Burlington. Forest Grove School Dist. v. T.A.*, 129 S.Ct. 2484, 174 L.Ed.2d 168 (U.S. 2009).

When the case returned to a federal district court, it held that the school district did not have to pay the student's tuition because the parents failed to notify the school district of their private school selection until well after making it, and because the parents seemed to choose the private school because of the student's drug use and behavioral problems. On appeal, the U.S. Court of Appeals, Ninth Circuit, affirmed the decision for the school district. *Forest Grove School Dist. v. T.A.*, 628 F.3d 1234 (9th Cir. 2011).

5. Failure to Cooperate

In Rohn v. Palm Beach County School Board, *below, a federal court held the parents of Florida twins were not entitled to private school tuition after they removed the children from school based on their lack of trust of school officials.*

◆   An 18-year-old Hawaii private school student read at a grade 3-6 level. But his parent said he could do high school level math and had taken a pre-algebra class at a community college. An IEP proposed for the student stated that he would not participate with non-disabled peers but would attend a workplace readiness program in a self-contained classroom for students on track for a certificate of completion. He was to "participate with non-disabled peers in activities of his own choosing." At IEP meetings, the parent told other team members that he wanted his child to remain at the private school. But he did not voice any specific concerns about the IEP and did not seek a general education setting. Two months later, the parent filed a due process hearing request. An impartial hearing officer found the IEP team did not consider general education classes and did not consider whether the student's goals and objectives could be implemented in general education classes. In addition, the hearing officer found the IEP was not properly individualized in that it allowed the student to select his own participation opportunities with non-disabled peers. Since the private school was found appropriate for the student, the hearing officer awarded the parent the cost of tuition and related services there for a full year. A federal court then considered the department's claim that the IEP was appropriate.

According to the department, the parent had withheld his complaints about the IEP offer until the hearing. Although previous IEPs had contained similar provisions, the court found student needs changed from year to year. It held the department had failed to even consider placing the student in general education classes for math. Since the school district failed to place the student in the least restrictive environment, the court affirmed that aspect of the decision. Like the hearing officer, the court found the IEP provision allowing the student to select his own nonacademic peer participation opportunities was not specific enough to address his socialization needs. **In the court's opinion, the "parent's conduct was unreasonable and tainted what should be a collaborative IEP process."** He failed to express relevant concerns and withheld opinions until the time of the administrative hearing, and the court found his sole concern was to obtain the private school placement. It appeared to the court that the department had made a good-faith effort to provide an IEP. As a result, the court reduced the tuition reimbursement by half, based on the parent's unreasonable conduct. *Dep't of Educ., State of Hawaii v. S.C.*, 938 F.Supp.2d 1023 (D. Haw. 2013).

♦ After a school IEP team offered to place a disabled preschool child in a two-day per week placement with same-age peers in a typical setting, the parents believed she was being dismissed from her school. They removed the child and her twin sister from the school system, enrolled them in a private pre-kindergarten and requested a due process hearing. After the hearing officer held for the school district, the dispute came before a federal court. It found the district had timely evaluated the twins. **The district's decisions to reduce services resulted from a reasonable evaluation of their current performance.** Nothing indicated that a change in placement was incorrect. Changing the classification of one twin from the "developmental delay" category to "other health impaired" was not improper. Finally, the removal of the students from their public school program after only two days based on lack of trust did not support reimbursement for private school tuition. Since the hearing officer did not commit error by ruling for the school board, the decision was affirmed. *Rohn v. Palm Beach County School Board*, No. 11-81408-CIV, 2013 WL 6479294 (S.D. Fla. 12/10/13).

♦ The parents of a disabled New York student agreed to a recommended preschool program but then asked that transition services be advanced by three months. After agreeing to a public placement, the father asked the district to adopt a 6:1+3 staff ratio. The district agreed to do so. Later, the father asked for a 1:1 paraprofessional and sought a meeting on the matter. The district agreed to the meeting and granted his request for a 1:1 paraprofessional. However, **the father stated that he'd already paid $20,000 to a private school and he rejected a public school placement**. When he sought tuition reimbursement, a federal court ruled against him. He had no intention of placing the student in the public school system, and the IEP offered by the district was adequate. *L.K. v. Dep't of Educ. of City of New York*, No. 09-CV-2266 (RMM)(LB), 2011 WL 127063 (E.D.N.Y. 1/13/11).

♦ Missouri twins with autism spent 15 days in a public early education program before their parents withdrew them and sought due process. To resolve the dispute, the district agreed to pay for private school tuition the rest of the year. IEPs prepared for the next year had substantial parental input, but the parents nonetheless filed more due process requests, keeping the twins in a private school under the stay-put provision. Eventually, the Eighth Circuit ruled that **the parents had frustrated the district's attempts to create IEPs by filing a series of due process requests to keep their children in the private school**. Although the district's IEPs didn't maximize the students' potential, they provided some educational benefit. Thus, tuition reimbursement was denied. *Park Hill School Dist. v. Dass*, 655 F.3d 762 (8th Cir. 2011).

♦   The mother of a Delaware student with disabilities placed him in a private school after a dispute about his IEP. The district agreed to fund the placement for one year and began the formal IEP process for the next year. However, the mother failed to return the form requesting permission to evaluate her son until midway through the summer. She also claimed she could not attend an IEP meeting because of scheduling conflicts. She then returned her son to the private school and refused to participate in the IEP process any more, asserting that FAPE was denied because the IEP was not in place at the start of the school year. A federal court ultimately ruled against her when she sued for tuition reimbursement, noting that **the delays were at least partly her fault and did not deny her son FAPE**. On further appeal, the Third Circuit affirmed, noting that not all procedural violations of the IDEA result in a denial of FAPE. Here, the parents' non-cooperation caused the delay. *C.H. v. Cape Henlopen School Dist.*, 606 F.3d 59 (3d Cir. 2010).

♦   The parents of a New York student with dyslexia lost faith in their district's ability to teach him and placed him in a private residential school. They later sought tuition reimbursement, but a federal court denied it. The court stated that the district provided adequate IEPs and that it used multisensory instruction, even though it didn't provide the Orton-Gillingham multisensory methodology preferred by the parents. Further, the self-contained program in the private school was too restrictive. The parents were not entitled to tuition reimbursement just because **the education they sought was perhaps superior to the appropriate education available** in the district. *D.G. v. Cooperstown Cent. School Dist.*, 746 F.Supp.2d 435 (N.D.N.Y. 2010).

♦   The parents of an Indiana student with a traumatic brain injury sought placement for him in a full-day kindergarten program. The district did not offer such a program, so attending both sessions would be duplicative and would not constitute special education. They eventually stopped communicating with the district and enrolled their son in a private Lindamood Bell program. When they sought reimbursement for their costs, they lost. A federal district court noted that **they had stopped participating in conferences** and that the student had been progressing in his placement. Thus, they were not entitled to reimbursement. *M.B. v. Hamilton Southeastern Schools*, No. 1:09-CV-0304-TWP-TAB, 2010 WL 3168666 (S.D. Ind. 8/10/10).

♦   The parents of a California student with autism placed their child in a private Lovaas program after obtaining an independent educational evaluation. **They never gave the district an opportunity to make a formal placement offer.** When they sought tuition reimbursement, a federal court and the Ninth Circuit ruled against them. The courts noted that the student had never received special education and related services from a public agency. Therefore, reimbursement was unauthorized by IDEA Section 1412(a)(10)(C). *C.S. v. Governing Board of Riverside Unified School Dist.*, 321 Fed.Appx. 630 (9th Cir. 2009).

6. Least Restrictive Environment

In C.L. v. Scarsdale Union Free School Dist., below, the Second Circuit Court of Appeals held New York parents should not be denied tuition reimbursement on the sole ground that the private school they selected for their child was not his least restrictive environment (LRE). Parents are not held to the same standard as school districts when making private placements.

◆ A Pennsylvania student had specific learning disabilities in reading and written language. Her parents rejected her IEP and placed her in a private school with a curriculum based on creative thinking and "strong experiences that stir the emotions." The parties reached a settlement under which the school district paid the student's tuition at the private school for a school year. But prior to the next school year, the parents rejected an IEP that would have placed their child in a public school. A hearing officer agreed with the parents that the school district did not seriously consider supplementary aids and services that might have kept her in regular classes. The district did not place her in the least restrictive setting. The case reached the U.S. Court of Appeals, Third Circuit.

On appeal, the court held the district did not counter evidence that it did not adequately consider greater opportunities for inclusion. A school district must comply with the least restrictive environment requirement by considering whether education can take place in regular classes, with supplementary aids and services. Schools must offer a continuum of placements to meet the needs of a disabled child. They must seriously consider including a child in a regular classroom with supplementary aids and services and to modify the regular curriculum. The district did not show what steps it took toward full inclusion, and the court upheld findings that the district did not show it considered the whole range or continuum of possible placements as required by the IDEA. **But because the parents did not show the private school they selected for their child was appropriate, their request for tuition reimbursement was denied.** *H.L. v. Downingtown Area School Dist.*, 624 Fed.Appx. 64 (3d Cir. 2015).

◆ A New York student had a Section 504 plan to assist him with problems arising from ADHD, anxiety, stuttering, motor development and coordination. As he prepared for grade four, his parents asked the school district to determine if he was entitled to an IEP. But the district found him ineligible for special education. Instead of accepting another Section 504 plan, the parents enrolled the student in a private Connecticut special education school. They then filed a due process hearing request, seeking reimbursement for their private school tuition costs. An impartial hearing officer (IHO) agreed with the parents that the district had denied their child a free appropriate public education (FAPE). As the IHO found the private school was appropriate, the district had to reimburse the parents for their tuition costs. A state review officer found that the private school selected by the parents was not the student's least restrictive environment under the IDEA. For this reason, reimbursement was denied. A federal court affirmed the review officer's decision and rejected a discrimination claim that the parents had attached to their IDEA appeal. The parents appealed to the U.S. Court of Appeals, Second Circuit. It held **parents are not barred from obtaining private school tuition reimbursement when the school selected does not meet the IDEA definition of a FAPE**. Parents whose children are denied a FAPE by their school districts are often forced to turn to private placements that are "necessarily restrictive." As a result, the court found that when a public school system denies a child FAPE, the restrictiveness of a private placement cannot be measured against that of a public school option.

In this case, the review officer should not have solely relied on the restrictiveness of the private school placement. It appeared to the court that the parents cooperated with the school district in its efforts to meet its duties under the IDEA. So the court found it was reasonable for them to turn to a private placement. Agreeing with the IHO's decision, the court held reimbursement for the private placement was proper. But the court found that since the parents had presented no evidence of bad faith or gross misjudgment by the school district, their disability discrimination claim failed. *C.L. v. Scarsdale Union Free School Dist.*, 744 F.3d 826 (2d Cir. 2014).

♦   The mother of a Hawaii student with autism placed him in a private school that used verbal behavior science and applied behavioral analysis methods. She then sought tuition reimbursement. A hearing officer noted the state's failure to address the student's transition needs but also noted the student's lack of progress in many areas and the mother's failure to cooperate with the department of education. A federal court agreed with the hearing officer that the mother was not entitled to tuition reimbursement. It held the private school was inappropriate for the student, not only because of his lack of progress there, but also because it was found to be an overly restrictive setting. On appeal, the U.S. Court of Appeals, Ninth Circuit, affirmed the judgment denying reimbursement for the cost of the private school. School officials acknowledged that the IEP proposal for a public school violated the IDEA, but **the Ninth Circuit found the private school offered only "meager" educational benefits**. In support of these findings, the court found the student made no progress at all in a "host of essential areas" despite spending more than a year in a private setting. In addition, the court found both the private school and the parents hindered the development of the child's IEP through their uncooperativeness. As a result, the court held for the public school officials. *M.N. v. State of Hawaii, Dep't of Educ.*, 509 Fed.Appx. 640 (9th Cir. 2013).

♦   A South Carolina student with anxiety and depression often "shut down" at school and eventually refused to attend altogether. He was enrolled in a new district, which did not include attendance issues in his IEP, even though it knew about his prior attendance problems. Counseling was discontinued because the new district found that it didn't solve his attendance issues. After the student again refused to go to school and became unresponsive to the district-provided homebound teacher, his mother placed him in a private residential facility in

Michigan. The student made significant progress there. The next year, **the district offered counseling and virtual classes in its IEP**, but the mother rejected it. In the eventual lawsuit for tuition reimbursement, a federal court held that the mother was entitled to reimbursement for the first year at the Michigan facility, but not for the later years when the district offered counseling and virtual classes. *Lexington County School Dist. One v. Frazier ex rel. D.T.*, No. 3:10-01808-MBS, 2011 WL 4435690 (D.S.C. 9/22/11).

◆   A Pennsylvania student with a specific learning disability needed social modeling and did not meaningfully interact with his peers. His parents placed him in a private school and rejected the district's IEP proposal, claiming that it did not meet their child's need for intensive and rigorous instruction. They sought tuition reimbursement, which a hearing officer and a federal court denied. Here, the IEP would offer the student a meaningful educational benefit. The district's teachers were well trained in the Orton-Gillingham method, and **the public school setting was the least restrictive environment**. As the private school was not an appropriate setting, the parents were not entitled to tuition reimbursement. On appeal, the Third Circuit affirmed, noting that the IEP called for social interaction with non-disabled peers and that it was reasonably calculated to provide meaningful educational benefits. *N.M. v. School Dist. of Philadelphia*, 394 Fed.Appx. 920 (3d Cir. 2010).

7. Other Issues

In R.L. v. Miami-Dade County School Board, *below, the Eleventh Circuit authorized a request to reimburse parents for 1:1 home programs they provided their child. The court held the IDEA definition of "special education" included home instruction. In A.C. v. Maple Heights City School Dist. Board of Educ., this chapter, a federal court held Ohio law precluded a claim by the parents of a child with a disability that her IEP did not do enough to address her attendance issues. In fact, the court found no support for the argument that schools, not parents, are responsible for getting children to class on time.*

◆   A Florida student had autism and other conditions that caused anxiety, obsessive-compulsive behavior and sensory processing problems. By grade seven, his parents removed him from school because he was becoming violent. While the student was out of school, the school district provided him 1:1 home instruction, which the parents supplemented at their own expense. A private treatment team found the student was regressing from the sensory overload of a large school environment. At a pair of IEP meetings, the parents urged a high school placement in a small magnet school. Over their objection, the IEP team placed the student in a large high school. His symptoms worsened, and his home behavior became almost uncontrollable. The parents withdrew their child from school and designed a home 1:1 program for speech and occupational therapy. The board then requested a due process hearing. When the case reached the U.S. Court of Appeals, Eleventh Circuit, it stated that if parents reject an IEP and make an alternative placement, they may claim reimbursement only if the IEP did not provide a FAPE. A court must also find the parents' alternative was appropriate. Like the ALJ, the court found the school's IEP offer was so deficient that it would not matter where it was implemented. So the parents were entitled to reject the IEP and seek reimbursement. Since the 1:1 program created by the parents was reasonably calculated to confer some educational benefit upon the student, the court held they were entitled to reimbursement. **Rejecting the board's argument that no IDEA provision authorized reimbursement for 1:1 home programs, the court found the IDEA definition of "special education" included home instruction.** *R.L. v. Miami-Dade County School Board*, 757 F.3d 1173 (11th Cir. 2014).

♦   An Ohio student with behavior problems was disciplined numerous times after being moved to a public school from a day treatment center. Her parents claimed the misconduct related to her disabilities, and they argued the school district intentionally discriminated against her. A hearing officer held the student's actions were the result of her disabilities. Although it was found that the district denied her a free appropriate public education (FAPE), the hearing officer held she could return to a public school. Finally, the hearing officer awarded the student 234 hours of one-on-one compensatory education. In a federal court, the parents sought an order to return their child to the day treatment center. The court explained that as the hearing officer did not find the district was incapable of providing FAPE to the student, there was no ground for the parents' request to fund the out-of-district placement. **Sixth Circuit cases hold that a school district need not pay for private education when there is no evidence that the district is incapable of providing FAPE.**

The court held the parents' IEP challenge lacked specificity. It also took issue with their references to the child's tardiness, finding no support for a claim that schools, rather than parents, are responsible for getting their children to class on time. In a footnote, the court noted that Ohio statutes imposed criminal liability upon parents for failure to cure their children's tardiness. Although the parents challenged the behavior plans, the court found the parties had never discussed them. Rejecting the parents' arguments, the court denied their request to return the child to a day treatment center. *A.C. v. Maple Heights City School Dist. Board of Educ.*, No. 1:13CV2710, 2014 WL 953387 (N.D. Ohio 3/11/14).

♦   The Second Circuit Court of Appeals consolidated three cases involving tuition reimbursement. In each case a state review officer had relied on testimony from school department staff about the services that would have been provided if the students attended the public school placements described in their IEPs. The parents sought a rule banning administrative officers from hearing any testimony about services beyond what is written in an IEP. However, the court of appeals held that **testimony about services may be used to explain or justify what is written in the IEP.** Such testimony could not be used to alter the terms of a deficient IEP, however. *R.E. v. New York City Dep't of Educ.*, 694 F.3d 167 (2d Cir. 2012).

♦   A Missouri school district refused to reimburse the parents of an autistic student for a life skills program. The parents had challenged the district's special education program more than once and had unilaterally removed their son from school. When they sought reimbursement, a federal court and the Eighth Circuit ruled against them. The **court of appeals stated that the home-based program focused on tasks like brushing teeth, keeping a clean home, budgeting and choosing clothes**. Any math or other educational services in the program were incorporated into the life skills lessons. *T.B. v. St. Joseph School Dist.*, 677 F.3d 844 (8th Cir. 2012).

♦   The guardian of a California student rejected his IEP as inadequate and placed him in a private agency's program. The private program was certified by the state to provide only language-based services; it was unable to provide the math instruction the student needed. Nevertheless, the guardian sought tuition reimbursement as well as transportation costs. A federal court granted reimbursement, and the Ninth Circuit affirmed. The IEP violated the IDEA, and **the private program, though it didn't meet all the student's educational needs, did meet many of them**, allowing the student to make significant progress. *C.B. v. Garden Grove Unified School Dist.*, 635 F.3d 1155 (9th Cir. 2011).

♦   A New Jersey school district proposed a kindergarten placement with services and therapies, but the parents thought their son should stay in preschool another year. They filed for due process and placed their son as a regular preschool student in a county special services program. They agreed on an education plan with the county program. In the lawsuit that resulted, the district claimed that the parents should be denied reimbursement because of their unilateral placement decision. A federal court agreed, but the Third Circuit reversed, noting that **the lower court should have considered whether the placement was appropriate. Also, the parents did not fail to cooperate.** They merely disagreed with the district's decision to place their son in kindergarten. *Upper Freehold Regional Board of Educ. v. T.M.*, 496 Fed.Appx. 238 (3d Cir. 2012).

♦   The parents of a New York student rejected his IEP, which called for occupational therapy three times a week and one-to-one speech therapy twice a week. It also included a behavior intervention plan, but it incorrectly identified the school he would be attending. The parents instead placed the student in a private school and sought tuition reimbursement. The case reached a federal court, which ruled against them. First, the IEP was not deficient because of the incorrect identification of the school. Second, **the private school was similar to the one recommended by the city's department of education**. *S.H. and B.P. v. New York City Dep't of Educ.*, No. 10 Civ. 1041(PKC), 2011 WL 666098 (S.D.N.Y. 2/15/11).

♦   A New York fifth-grader's IEP stated that his homework assignments would be broken down into manageable parts. However, in sixth grade, his parents requested that accommodation be discontinued. He struggled in grade six, and his parents sought tuition reimbursement for a private school placement. A hearing officer found that the discontinuation of the homework modifications played a part in the student's lack of progress in sixth grade, along with a lack of daily multi-sensory reading classes. The parties agreed that the student needed daily reading instruction, and the hearing officer ruled that no tuition reimbursement was necessary. A federal court reversed, but the Second Circuit reversed the lower court, finding **the hearing officer's refusal to grant reimbursement supported by the evidence**. *Bougades v. Pine Plains Cent. School Dist.*, 376 Fed.Appx. 95 (2d Cir. 2010).

♦   The parents of a Maine student sought tuition reimbursement from a school district, which sought coverage under an educator's liability policy. The insurer denied coverage on the grounds that "reimbursement" was not covered by the policy. When the district sued the insurer, the case reached the First Circuit, which held that **the underlying claim for reimbursement under the IDEA was covered by the policy because it was a claim for "money damages,"** which included equitable monetary relief under Maine law. *School Union No. 37 v. United National Insurance Co.*, 617 F.3d 554 (1st Cir. 2010).

♦   An Illinois student with Type 1 diabetes and a social anxiety disorder began missing classes and instead enrolled at a community college. She sought reimbursement for her tuition there, but a federal court and the Seventh Circuit ruled against her. She had a Section 504 plan in place for her diabetes and was not IDEA eligible. Also, **there was no medical evidence that she stopped attending high school because her anxiety had worsened**. There was no medical basis for her better performance at the community college. *Loch v. Edwardsville School Dist. No. 7*, 327 Fed.Appx. 647 (7th Cir. 2009).

♦   A Pennsylvania student with learning disabilities received special education in reading, math and writing. In the sixth grade, his parents placed him in a private school and sought tuition reimbursement as well as compensatory education for the prior two years. After **a federal court upheld the student's-sixth grade IEP**, the Third Circuit agreed that it addressed his deficiencies. And the lack of occupational therapy in the student's seventh-grade IEP was attributable to the delay by the parents in providing an OT evaluation. Once they did so, a revised IEP provided for reevaluation for potential OT needs within 30 days of his return to a district school. *Souderton Area School Dist. v. J.H.*, 351 Fed.Appx. 755 (3d Cir. 2009).

♦   The mother of a New Hampshire wheelchair-bound student claimed that the district failed to follow his IEP and erroneously decertified him from eligibility for special education. She filed a complaint with the state department of education. After an administrative ruling against her, she placed her son in a private school outside the district. When she sued under the IDEA and Section 504, a federal court held that **most of her claims failed because the private school was outside the district and she did not intend to return her son to district schools**. The court then determined that tuition reimbursement was not in order because the student's classroom performance demonstrated that he was no longer qualified as a child with a disability under the IDEA. *J.P.E.H. v. Hooksett School Dist.*, No. 07-CV-276-SM, 2009 WL 1883885 (D.N.H. 6/30/09).

B. Placement in Unapproved Schools

In Florence County School Dist. Four v. Carter, *below, the Supreme Court held parents who placed their children in unapproved private schools could claim tuition reimbursement despite the lack of state approval. The Court focused on the appropriateness of the placement selected by the parents and the inability of a local school district to provide an appropriate alternative.*

♦   A New York child with autism had many behavior problems, including severe tantrums. She once jumped from a first-floor window and later jumped from a school bus. After the child attended a public school from grades three through six, her parent concluded her behavior was not improving and that she was not being challenged academically. She was withdrawn from school in favor of home instruction. But the child's negative behaviors continued, and her home instructor struggled with them. Soon after the child returned to a public school, she had a bus altercation that led to her handcuffing. Her parent rejected a private school placement located by the school staff. She then filed a due process hearing request. Following a hearing, an impartial hearing officer (IHO) held the child should be referred to the Central Based Support Team for consideration of all placement options. The IHO agreed with the parent that any school search should include private schools that were not approved by the state of New York. The New York City Department of Education (DOE) appealed to a state review officer, who held the DOE could only contract with approved schools. Appeal reached a federal court, where the parent cited a line of federal court authority governing reimbursement to parents who unilaterally place children in an unapproved school. This included *Florence School Dist. 4 v. Carter,* 510 U.S. 7 (1993). But the court found *Carter* involved a parent's right to independently place a child in a private school over a district's objection.

Moreover, the Second Circuit had held in 1988 that **school districts must satisfy state approval requirements when placing a child with a disability in a private school**. Since *Carter* did not rule that a school district could be ordered to place a child in an unapproved private school, the court held the review officer correctly rejected the parent's arguments and held for the DOE. *Z.H. v. New York City Dep't of Educ.,* 107 F.Supp.3d 1369 (S.D.N.Y. 2015).

♦   The parents of a South Carolina ninth-grader with a learning disability disagreed with the IEP proposed by their school district. The IEP called for mainstreaming in most subjects, with individual instruction three periods a week, and specific goals of increasing the student's reading and mathematics levels by four months for the entire school year. The parents requested due process and unilaterally placed their daughter in a private school that specialized in teaching students with disabilities. A hearing officer held that the IEP was adequate. After the student raised her reading comprehension three full grades in one year at the private school, the parents sued the school district for tuition reimbursement. A federal court found that the educational program and achievement goals of the proposed IEP were "wholly inadequate" under the IDEA. Even though the private school did not comply with all IDEA procedures – by employing noncertified staff members, for example – it provided the student with an excellent education that complied with IDEA substantive requirements. The court awarded tuition reimbursement, a result upheld by the Fourth Circuit. The school district appealed to the U.S. Supreme Court.

The Court expanded upon its decision in *School Committee of the Town of Burlington, Massachusetts v. Dep't of Educ. of Massachusetts,* Section I, where it held that parents had the right to unilaterally change their children's placement at their own financial risk. To recover private school tuition costs, parents must show that the placement proposed by the school district violates the IDEA and that the private school placement is appropriate under the act. Here, **the failure by the school district to provide an appropriate placement entitled the parents to an award of tuition reimbursement, even though the private school was not approved by the state**, because the education provided at the private school had been determined by the district court to be appropriate. The decisions in favor of the parents were upheld. *Florence County School Dist. Four v. Carter,* 510 U.S. 7, 114 S.Ct. 361, 126 L.Ed.2d 284 (1993).

◆   After being bullied, a New York student began to experience anxiety about school. He was diagnosed with severe anxiety and depression, and the committee on special education found him eligible under the IDEA with emotional disturbance. The district developed an IEP specifying individualized counseling, resource room services and test modifications. The parents later withdrew their consent for the IEP and sought home tutoring. The district then recommended several alternative high school placements. **The parents unilaterally placed their son in an unapproved private school without informing the district, then rejected the district's recommendations.** When they sought tuition reimbursement, the Second Circuit ruled against them. The private school lacked a therapeutic setting and was inappropriate. *Gagliardo v. Arlington Cent. School Dist.,* 489 F.3d 105 (2d Cir. 2007).

C. Notice

The IDEA contains provisions requiring notice when parents decide to unilaterally enroll their children in a private school. These provisions are listed at 20 U.S.C. § 1412(a)(10)(C)(iii). Before reimbursement can be limited under this section, the school district must have previously provided the parents with all applicable IDEA notices. Parents seeking private school tuition are required to notify the district, in writing, of their objections to the district's program and their intent to enroll the child in a private program before actually doing so. Failure to do so may result in denial or reduction of a reimbursement claim.

◆   A New Jersey parent signed an enrollment agreement and paid tuition to a private school. He then attended an IEP meeting, where staff members proposed a developmental reading program for his child. The parent requested more specific information about the reading program, but IEP team members only responded that the program would be research-based and focused on phonic skills and comprehension. They also stated it would be instructed by a certified teacher. The parent later claimed his son was denied a free appropriate public education (FAPE) because the team had failed to share basic information about the reading program. An administrative law judge (ALJ) dismissed his claim for tuition reimbursement, finding his notice letter to the district was untimely.

A federal court held for the school district, and the parent appealed to the U.S. Court of Appeals, Third Circuit. The court explained that **an IDEA provision permits a court or hearing officer to reduce or deny a private school tuition reimbursement claim where parents fail to provide timely written notice of their intention to make a private placement and seek reimbursement for it**. Such notice must be made at least 10 business days prior to a parental removal. In addition, a court may deny reimbursement if it finds parental actions were unreasonable and reimbursement is inequitable. As the lower court and ALJ had found, the parent did not follow IDEA statutory notice requirements. He did not advise the district of his intent to remove the child from district schools at least 10 days prior to placing his child at the private school. The court held the parent did not provide adequate notice to the district when making a private placement. Next, the court upheld the finding that no IDEA procedural violation took place when the school district declined to elaborate on inquiries about methodology to be used in the developmental reading program it had proposed. As the lower court had correctly found the parent was not denied a meaningful opportunity to participate in the IEP process, the judgment for the board was affirmed. *W.D. v. Watchung Hills Regional High School Board of Educ.*, 602 Fed.Appx. 563 (3d Cir. 2015).

♦   A Hawaii parent said school officials did not provide her with a prior notice of placement offer for her autistic child. She challenged an offer for a community-based instruction (CBI) program at a Maui public school. Instead of sending her child to the school, the parent sent him off-island to a residential school and requested an IDEA hearing. A hearing officer denied reimbursement for the off-island placement, finding the state department of education (DOE) made appropriate placement offers for two relevant school years. A federal court affirmed the decision regarding the FAPE issue. The parent then appealed to the U.S. Court of Appeals, Ninth Circuit, where she sought reimbursement for housing expenses and for her visitation costs under the stay-put provision.

The court found no error in the hearing officer's decision to deny the notice claim. **Even if there was a procedural error by the DOE, it did not significantly restrict the parent from participation in the IEP process.** The hearing officer had credited DOE witnesses who were involved with the CBI program. There was no error in the finding that a FAPE was offered to the child. Evidence indicated the DOE paid for weekend visitation expenses for the family and provided weekend support. But the hearing officer had improperly failed to consider a claim to reimbursement for housing expenses as a related service while the student was at the off-island school. Further administrative proceedings were needed to resolve the housing reimbursement issue. *Marcus I. v. Dep't of Educ., State of Hawaii*, 583 Fed.Appx. 753 (9th Cir. 2014).

♦   A New Jersey student performed well through eighth grade in general education classes with some accommodations. Since he was much smaller than his peers, his parents decided to place him in a private school rather than the public high school. They then challenged the district's proposed placement and sought tuition reimbursement. A federal court ruled against them, noting that the student had succeeded in public school with accommodations and modifications. Further, **the parents had made up their minds about the private school placement in advance and had failed to notify the district of their intentions**. *G.S. v. Cranbury Township Board of Educ.*, No. 10-774 (FLW), 2011 WL 1584321 (D.N.J. 4/26/11).

◆   A New Jersey student with a specific learning disability made tremendous progress in a mainstream setting with resource support. The following year, his child-study team ruled him ineligible for special education. Several years later, he was suspended after a positive marijuana test. His parents placed him in an outback treatment center in Utah without notifying the district and then placed him in an adolescent treatment center, where he earned his diploma. Two years later, they filed a due process action, seeking tuition reimbursement. A hearing officer and a New Jersey federal district court ruled against them, noting that **they had waited too long to challenge the declassification and had failed to give timely notice of their private placement**. *Mittman v. Livingston Township Board of Educ.*, No. 09-4754 (DRD), 2010 WL 3947548 (D.N.J. 10/7/10).

◆   After an Illinois student was hospitalized, her parents placed her in a private residential facility. Three days later, they notified the district of their intent to seek their costs. The district agreed to pay the educational and therapeutic costs but not the residential costs. A hearing officer found the parents did not provide prior written notice and so were not entitled to reimbursement for the eight months prior to obtaining state approval for the placement. A federal court held relief still could be awarded under the IDEA. The court explained that **under 20 U.S.C. § 1412(a)(1)(C)(ii), private school reimbursement "may" be reduced or denied by a court if the parents fail to provide the school at least 10 days written notice. But the statute does not say reimbursement "shall" be denied**, so reimbursement might still be appropriate. *Erin K. v. Naperville School Dist. No. 203*, No. 08 C 6997, 2009 WL 3271954 (N.D. Ill. 10/6/09).

◆   The mother of a Maine student with disabilities placed the student in public schools for five years, then homeschooled him for a while before placing him in a series of out-of-state private schools. She never objected to the IEPs prepared for him while he was in public schools. And she received tuition for the placements, supplemented by an amount for special education services, under the state's "local choice" option. After the student reached age 19, his mother sought reimbursement for room, board, transportation and related expenses. A hearing officer awarded her $52,000, but a federal court held that she waited too long to seek reimbursement. The First Circuit agreed with the lower court that **her delay in seeking reimbursement prejudiced the school district's ability to defend the IEPs it had offered**. *School Union No. 37 v. Ms. C.*, 518 F.3d 31 (1st Cir. 2008).

◆   The parents of a Maryland student with ADHD placed him in a private school after he began suffering academic and emotional problems. Their district agreed to fund the placement through 2001-02. When they sought to continue the placement through 2002-03, the district notified them that the school had not yet been approved as a fundable special education school for that year. The district recommended another private school, but the parents kept their son where he was. The school was approved as a fundable special education school for the 2003-04 year, and the parents then sought tuition reimbursement for the 2002-03 year. The case reached the Fourth Circuit, which denied reimbursement because **the district had offered a free appropriate public education at the other private school, and the parents did not properly notify the district of their intent to reject the IEP.** *Z.W. v. Smith*, 210 Fed.Appx. 282 (4th Cir. 2006).

♦   The parents of a New Jersey student with disabilities rejected their school board's proposed IEP advancing their son to first grade. They placed him in a private school, then wrote a series of letters to school officials, informing them that the student would be placed in the private school the next year and asking what services the board might provide. The board did not hold a child-study team meeting or prepare an IEP for the next year. When the parents sought tuition reimbursement for the two years, a hearing officer and a federal court determined that they were entitled to reimbursement for the second year because **they had given proper notice and the board had failed to have an IEP ready at the start of the year.** However, they were not entitled to tuition reimbursement for the first year of attendance at the private school, because they did not properly notify the board of their intent with respect to that year. *A.Z. v. Mahwah Township Board of Educ.*, No. Civ. A. 04-4003(KSH), 2006 WL 827791 (D.N.J. 3/30/06).

II. VOUCHER PROGRAMS AND RELIGIOUS SCHOOLS

A. Vouchers and Public Assistance

Arizona, Florida, Georgia, Louisiana, North Carolina, Oklahoma and Utah are among the states with special education voucher programs. Such programs typically require the parents of students wishing to attend a private school through a voucher or scholarship to waive their child's right to a free appropriate public education. In 2015, the Supreme Court of Oklahoma rejected a challenge to the state's voucher program for disabled students.

♦   In 2010, Oklahoma legislators enacted the Lindsey Nicole Henry Scholarships for Students with Disabilities Act to provide money for eligible students with disabilities to offset their tuition costs at participating private schools. Under the program, families decide whether to participate and determine which schools their children will attend. A group of taxpayers filed a state court action, seeking a permanent order to prohibit state officials from using program funds for sectarian schools. They asserted claims under several articles of the Oklahoma Constitution. When the case reached the Supreme Court of Oklahoma, the court found the program is voluntary. **Parents decide which school offers the best learning environment for their children, so** that **"the circuit between government and religion is broken."** Persuaded by the fact that program funds are paid to parents and not private schools, the court found no violation of the "no aid clause" of the state constitution. It upheld the program. *Oliver v. Hofmeister*, 368 P.3d 1270 (Okla. 2016).

◆   Taking advantage of the Colorado school choice law, the parents of a child with autism spectrum disorder removed him from a school in their residence district and placed him at a charter school in another district. After the child had attended the charter school for a year, his IEP was revised to state that he would attend the charter school. But shortly after the IEP was written, he was denied enrollment at the charter school for the next school year. The parents filed a due process complaint against the school district in which the charter school was located. An ALJ denied their request to preserve the placement via the IDEA stay-put rule. The parents appealed to a federal court.

The court held the charter school was the child's "then current" placement under the stay-put provision. It denied the parents' request to provide a private school placement and related services pending the outcome of the case. While the stay-put provision did not require that a child remain in the exact physical location, schools were not permitted to make changes that might significantly effect a child's learning experience. The court found it was pure speculation that the residence district could have provided the child a free appropriate public education. **The school choice law did not change the outcome of the case.** A state law could not allow a district to avoid its IDEA obligations. Finding sufficient evidence that the charter school was the child's current educational placement, the court held he was entitled to a stay-put order preserving his placement there under the stay-put rule. *Smith v. Cheyenne Mountain School Dist. 12*, No. 14-cv-02651-PAB-CBS, 2015 WL 4979771 (D. Colo. 8/20/15).

◆   Arizona parents disputed their child's placement and requested a due process hearing. This led to a decision approving a private academy placement they sought for the child. The parents received Arizona Empowerment Scholarships Account (ESA) funds while the case was pending, and they enrolled their child in their school of choice. The school district appealed to a federal court, which found the hearing officer had relied on testimony by an advocate who lacked relevant experience and training. By contrast, school witnesses reliably testified that the center would have provided the student with a support system to overcome transition problems through skill development.

Rejecting all the parents' arguments, the court held for the school district. The school district asked the ALJ to consider the impact of the parents' decision to apply for ESA funds. Although the district argued the receipt of ESA funds relieved it of its duty to provide a FAPE to the child, the court found **the ESA program temporarily released the district from its duty to educate the child. But the court held this duty would resume if the family stopped receiving ESA funds.** On appeal, the Ninth Circuit Court of Appeals reversed the lower court's decision. It held the placement proposed by the district called for excessive transitions and jeopardized the child's safety. Evidence indicated the child would have been placed with older students and exposed to a student population with more severe behavioral issues. Testimony established that students at the setting proposed by the district were grouped according to ability, not age. Since the administrative findings were supported by the evidence, the case was returned to a lower court for further proceedings. *Pointe Educational Services v. A.T.*, 610 Fed.Appx. 702 (9th Cir. 2015).

♦   Florida students with disabilities may receive John M. McKay scholarships under a program that provides public funding for private school education. When parents select a private school for an eligible child, the school district must evaluate the child's matrix of services level. The matrix of services information is provided to the state department of education, which notifies the private school of the scholarship amount. For each student, the nature and intensity of the services indicated in the matrix is to be consistent with his or her IEP. The parents of a deaf student claimed their school district understated their child's matrix of services score to reduce the available McKay Scholarship funds he would receive. In a state court, the parents claimed their son's school deliberately miscalculated his matrix score and misled them about services in violation of the Florida Deceptive and Unfair Trade Practices Act (FDUTPA).

The court dismissed the case, and the parents appealed. A state district court of appeal noted the parents had failed to file an administrative complaint objecting to their child's IEP. In the court's view, the parents were not excused from the administrative process. As for the FDUTPA claim, the court held **the scoring of a matrix under the McKay program was a ministerial act for the department of education to use in allocating state funds for exceptional students**. Scoring was not a "thing of value" under the FDUTPA. As the scoring of a McKay program matrix of services was not "engaging in trade or commerce" as defined by the FDUTPA, the case was properly dismissed. *Montero v. Duval County School Board*, 153 So.3. 407 (Fla. Dist. Ct. App. 2014).

♦   Arizona legislators enacted a voucher program that allowed public school students with disabilities to attend a private school or a public school outside their own districts. They also enacted a program that permitted children in foster care to attend private schools. Opponents of the programs sued, claiming violations of the state constitution. The case reached the state supreme court, which agreed that **the programs violated the Arizona Constitution's "Aid Clause," which prohibited the payment of any public funds to a private school**. *Cain v. Horne*, 202 P.3d 1178 (Ariz. 2009).

♦   The Ohio General Assembly adopted the Ohio Pilot Scholarship Program in 1995 in response to a federal court order to remedy problems in the Cleveland School District. The program made vouchers of up to $2,500 available for Cleveland students to attend public or private schools, including schools with religious affiliations. The state supreme court struck down the program on state constitutional grounds in 1999. Legislators cured these deficiencies and reauthorized the program for 1999-2000. A new lawsuit was filed in a federal court, which permanently enjoined the state from administering the program.

The case reached the U.S. Supreme Court, which held the program allowed government aid to reach religious institutions only because of the deliberate choices of the individual recipients. Any incidental advancement of religion, or perceived endorsement of a religious message, was attributable to the individual recipients, not to the government. The New York program struck down in *Committee for Public Educ. and Religious Liberty v. Nyquist*, 413 U.S. 756 (1973), gave benefits exclusively to private schools and the parents of private school enrollees. **Ohio's program offered aid directly to a broad class of individual recipients defined without regard to religion.** Where government aid is religiously neutral and provides direct assistance to a broad class of citizens that in turn directs funds to religious schools through genuine and independent private choices, the program is not readily subject to an Establishment Clause challenge. *Zelman v. Simmons-Harris*, 536 U.S. 639, 122 S.Ct. 2460, 153 L.Ed.2d 604 (2002).

B. Religious Schools

Public aid to students who attend private religious schools implicates the Establishment Clause of the First Amendment. Public school funding for students with disabilities for private religious school education and related services has been held constitutionally permissible, as the benefit to the private school has been characterized as only "attenuated."

◆   A Maryland child with Down syndrome and related disabilities had a full-scale IQ in the first percentile. His parents asked the school IEP team to place him at a private school with an Orthodox Jewish curriculum. Instead, the team proposed a public school placement. In response, the parents requested a due process hearing, at which they sought a placement at the school of their choice along with their tuition costs. At the hearing, the parents argued the child could not generalize what he learned at home to the school environment and vice versa. They urged that his IEP should include Hebrew literacy, identification of Kosher symbols and other bicultural and bilingual measures. After four IEP meetings over a seven-month period, a proposal was completed. But the parents rejected it because it did not provide instruction in preparing the child for life in his Orthodox Jewish community. When the case came before a federal court, it held that before any private school tuition claim could be considered, the parents had to show the school system deprived their child of a free appropriate public education. The court rejected the parents' claim that the school had denied the child an appropriate IEP by not allowing him to access the curriculum "whilst still remaining a part of his community." It found they did not identify any faults in the IEP or the ALJ's decision.

An IEP that did not account for a student's "individual religious and cultural needs" could be appropriate. In the court's view, nothing requires a school district to expand IDEA requirements for an IEP by tailoring it to a child's religious and cultural enclave. And there was no IDEA requirement for a personalized curriculum based on a child's cultural and religious needs or the beliefs of the parents. Since the failure of the school district to address the child's religious and cultural needs and to place him in an Orthodox school did not deny him a free appropriate public education, the court upheld the decision for the school officials. *M.L. v. Starr*, 121 F.Supp.3d 466 (D. Md. 2015).

♦ A California student attended public school kindergarten. Her parent became dissatisfied with her progress and placed her in a parochial school. In a due process proceeding, the parent sought an order that the school district violated her child's right to a free appropriate public education over four school years. The parties reached a settlement agreement by which the district agreed to pay the parent $18,000. It further agreed to provide the student a private intensive reading program, as well as speech and language services. The parent agreed to make her child available to the district for assessments at reasonable times and to sign necessary releases so the district could obtain relevant data.

The parties then disputed the terms of an assessment, leading the district to write to the parent of its belief that she did not intend to comply with the agreement. In response, the parent requested a due process hearing. She said the district denied her child a FAPE by failing to hold an IEP meeting at her request. In addition, the parent claimed the district failed to conduct the agreed-upon assessments. An administrative law judge (ALJ) held for the district on the issue of denial of the parent's request to hold an IEP meeting. But the ALJ held the parent prevailed on the assessment issue, finding the district did not abide by the settlement. Despite finding the parent did not cooperate with the district regarding the assessments, the ALJ held she was entitled to some reimbursement. Although the parochial school was held inappropriate for the student, the ALJ found she received educational benefits from her instructional aides at the school. The district was ordered to pay her $6,999.25 for their cost. A federal court upheld the ALJ's decision, and appeal reached the U.S. Court of Appeals, Ninth Circuit. It noted the school district did not appeal from the finding that FAPE had been denied during the relevant school year. **Parents were not required to show a private placement furnished every special service needed to maximize a child's potential.** The court held the school provided the child with instructional materials, a curriculum, structure, support and socialization. It also provided her with accommodations under a Section 504 plan. Significantly, the school allowed the student to have 1:1 aides in class, something the school district never indicated it would provide. The court held the parent should be reimbursed for $4,010 in tuition costs. It also approved $6,999.25 for the cost of the aides, $2,693 for transportation costs and almost $35,000 of the over $92,000 in attorneys' fees she claimed. *S.L. v. Upland Unified School Dist.*, 747 F.3d 1155 (9th Cir. 2014).

♦ A Maryland religious school student had attention deficit hyperactivity disorder and anxiety. Although he was IDEA-ineligible, his residence school district declared him eligible under Rehabilitation Act Section 504. But the district advised the parents that it could not provide Section 504 services unless he enrolled in a public school. Maryland law did not permit simultaneous dual enrollment in a public and private school. A hearing examiner found the district was not required to provide the student with special education services at his private school. An appeal went to a federal court, which upheld the district's decision. The case then came before the U.S. Court of Appeals, Fourth Circuit.

The court found support for the district's arguments in guidance from the U.S. Department of Education's Office for Civil Rights (OCR). A 1993 OCR letter stated that **a school district was not responsible under Section 504 for**

the provision of educational services to students not enrolled in a public school based on the choice of the parents. The court held a requirement that would extend to private school students would conflict with limitations Congress placed on school district responsibilities. A 1997 IDEA amendment clarified that the states only had to allocate a proportionate amount of their federal funds to eligible private school students. The parents' argument would allow all IDEA-eligible students in private schools to claim full services under Section 504. But the court found this interpretation "would create an individual right to special education and related services where none exists." Since the school district had provided the student with access to a free appropriate public education on equal terms with all other eligible students in the district, the court held it had satisfied its Section 504 obligations. Based on the OCR guidance, statutory purposes, case law and policy considerations, the court held for the school district. *D.L. v. Baltimore City Board of School Commissioners*, 706 F.3d 256 (4th Cir. 2013).

◆   A 2011 Arizona law established the Empowerment Scholarship Accounts (ESA) to provide scholarships to students with disabilities. A group of challengers filed a state court action to block implementation of the program. Grounds for the challenge included violations of the Aid and Religion Clauses of the Arizona Constitution. After the court held for the state superintendent of public instruction, the challengers appealed to the Court of Appeals of Arizona. It held the Religion Clause forbade appropriating public money for any religious worship, exercise or instruction, or the support of any religious establishment. Parents of disabled children who received an ESA voucher had a duty to provide education in reading, grammar, math, social studies and science. Whether this was done at a secular or religious school was a matter of parental choice and did not violate the Religion Clause. The clause is not a blanket prohibition against sending public funds to a religious organization.

The court explained that the Aid Clause of the state constitution prohibited an appropriation of public funds to aid any church, private or sectarian school. In this case, the court found no violation of the Aid Clause, as the "specified object" of the appropriation was the beneficiary families, not schools. Parents could use ESA funds to "customize an education" that met their children's unique educational needs. Since the beneficiary families had discretion about how to spend ESA funds, no program funds were "preordained for a particular destination." **The court held this distinguished the ESA program from other voucher programs that did not meet constitutional requirements.** As the ESA program was religiously neutral, the court held for the superintendent. *Niehaus v. Huppenthal*, 223 Ariz. 195, 310 P.3d 983 (Ariz. Ct. App. 2013).

◆   An Arizona student attended a school for the deaf from grades one through five and then transferred to a public school for grades six through eight. During his public school attendance, the school district furnished him with a sign-language interpreter. His parents enrolled him in a parochial high school for ninth grade and asked the district to continue providing a sign-language interpreter. The district refused, and the student's parents sued. The court ruled for the school district. The Ninth Circuit affirmed, determining that the furnishing of a sign-language interpreter to a parochial school student had the primary effect of advancing religion in violation of the Establishment Clause of the U.S. Constitution. The placement of a public school employee in a parochial school would create the appearance that the government was a joint sponsor of the private school's activities. The U.S. Supreme Court granted the parents' petition for review. On appeal, the school district cited 34 C.F.R. § 76.532(a)(1), an IDEA regulation, as authority for the prohibition against using federal funds for private school sign-language interpreters.

The Court stated that the Establishment Clause did not completely prohibit religious institutions from participating in publicly sponsored benefits. If this were the case, religious groups would not even enjoy police and fire protection or have use of public roads and sidewalks. Government programs that neutrally provide benefits to broad classes of citizens are not subject to Establishment Clause prohibition simply because some religiously affiliated institutions receive "an attenuated financial benefit." Providing a sign-language interpreter under the IDEA was part of a general program for distribution of benefits in a neutral manner to qualified students. The provision of the interpreter provided only an indirect economic benefit to the parochial school and was a neutral service that was part of a general program not "skewed" toward religion. A sign-language interpreter, unlike an instructor or counselor, was ethically bound to transmit everything said in exactly the same way as it was intended. Because **the Establishment Clause did not prevent the district from providing the student with a sign-language interpreter under the IDEA**, the Court reversed the court of appeals' decision. *Zobrest v. Catalina Foothills School Dist.*, 509 U.S. 1, 113 S.Ct. 2462, 125 L.Ed.2d 1 (1993).

♦   The New York City Board of Education attempted to implement Title I programs at parochial schools by allowing public employees to instruct students on private school grounds during school hours. In 1985, the U.S. Supreme Court agreed with a group of taxpayers that this violated the Establishment Clause in *Aguilar v. Felton*, 473 U.S. 402, 105 S.Ct. 3232, 87 L.Ed.2d 290 (1985). On remand, a federal court ordered the city board to refrain from using Title I funds for any plan or program under which public school teachers and counselors furnished services on sectarian school grounds. In response to *Aguilar*, local education boards modified Title I programs by moving classes to remote sites, including mobile instructional units parked near sectarian schools. A new group of parents and parochial school students filed motions seeking relief from the permanent order.

The court denied the motions, and the Second Circuit affirmed. On further appeal, the U.S. Supreme Court agreed with the city board and students that recent Supreme Court decisions required a new ruling on the question of government aid to religious schools. For example, the provision of a sign-language interpreter by a school district at a private school was upheld in *Zobrest v. Catalina Foothills School Dist.,* above. The Court held that it would no longer presume that the presence of a public school teacher on parochial school grounds creates a symbolic union between church and state. The provision of Title I services at parochial schools resembled the provision of a sign-language interpreter under the IDEA. **New York City's Title I program**

was constitutionally permissible because it did not result in government indoctrination, define funding recipients by reference to religion or create excessive entanglement between education officials and religious schools. The Court reversed the lower court judgments. In the process, the Court substantially overruled *Aguilar* and its companion case, *School Dist. of City of Grand Rapids v. Ball,* 473 U.S. 373, 105 S.Ct. 3216, 87 L.Ed.2d 267 (1985). *Agostini v. Felton,* 521 U.S. 203, 117 S.Ct. 1997, 138 L.Ed.2d 391 (1997).

◆   A blind person sought vocational rehabilitative services from the state of Washington's Commission for the Blind pursuant to a state law, which provided that visually disabled persons were eligible for educational assistance to enable them to "overcome vocational handicaps and to obtain the maximum degree of self-support and self-care." However, because the plaintiff was a private school student intending to pursue a career of service in the church, the Commission for the Blind denied his request for assistance. The Washington Supreme Court upheld this decision on the ground that the First Amendment prohibited state funding of a student's education at a religious college. The U.S. Supreme Court reversed, finding that Washington's program was such that the commission paid money directly to the student, who would then attend the school of his or her choice. **The fact that the student in this case chose to attend a religious college did not constitute state support of religion** because the individual, not the state, made the decision to support religious education. The First Amendment was therefore not offended. The case was returned to the Washington Supreme Court. *Witters v. Washington Dep't of Services for the Blind,* 474 U.S. 481, 106 S.Ct. 748, 88 L.Ed.2d 846 (1986).

On remand, the Washington Supreme Court reconsidered the matter under the Washington Constitution, which more strictly limits expenditures of public funds for religious instruction than the U.S. Constitution. **The disbursement of vocational assistance funds for the student's religious education violated the state constitution** because it would result in the expenditure of public money for religious instruction. The court rejected the student's argument that the restriction on public expenditures would violate his right to free exercise of religion. Also, denial of funds to the student did not violate the Fourteenth Amendment's Equal Protection Clause because the commission had a policy of denying any student's religious vocational funding. The classification was directly related to the state's interest in ensuring the separation between church and state. The court reaffirmed its previous order disallowing financial assistance. *Witters v. State Comm'n for the Blind,* 771 P.2d 1119 (Wash. 1989).

CHAPTER EIGHT

Transition Services and Related Services

I. TRANSITION SERVICES

Beginning not later than the first IEP to be in effect when a child with a disability is age 16 (and updated annually thereafter), an IEP must include appropriate measurable postsecondary goals based upon age-appropriate transition assessments related to training, education, employment, and (where appropriate) independent living skills. A student's IEP must state the transition services (including courses of study) needed to assist the child in reaching those goals. Beginning not later than one year before the child reaches the age of majority under state law, the IEP must include a statement that the child has been informed of his or her rights. See 20 U.S.C. § 1414(d)(1)(A)(i)(VII).

Federal courts in New York have clarified that transition plans are required for the transition to post-school activities, rather than school transfers. *See E.Z. -L. ex. rel. R.L. v. New York City Dep't of Educ., 763 F.Supp.2d 584 (S.D.N.Y. 2011) and M.L. v. New York City Dep't of Educ., this chapter. The IDEA requires "transition services" not when a child transfers between schools, but when a child transitions from school to post-school activities. In A.L. v. New York City Dep't of Educ., 812 F.Supp.2d 492 (S.D.N.Y. 2011), the court held "there is no requirement that an IEP specify a transition plan for a student attending a new school placement."*

An Alaska state law clarifies that a school district's primary objective and preferred outcome when offering transition services to students over 15 years of age is to help them become gainfully employed in an integrated workplace. An integrated workplace is where individuals with disabilities work with and alongside of individuals without disabilities, or become enrolled in postsecondary education. Twenty-Eighth Alaska Legislature, Second Regular Session, Ch. 19, H.B. 21. Alaska Statutes Section 14.03078.

♦   A federal court rejected a claim for private school tuition reimbursement by New York parents. It found the IEP proposed for their child was more likely to produce progress than regression. As the parents pointed out, the IEP did not provide for parent counseling and training, nor was it discussed at the IEP meeting. But the court found this violation was not serious and did not justify reimbursement. This omission could be rectified at a later date. Last, the court rejected a claim based on failure to provide the child a transition plan for his planned move to a new school. A prior New York federal court decision noted there is no IDEA requirement for a transition plan for students who will be attending a new school. **The court explained that the IDEA requires transition services for the transition from school to post-school activities, not for school transfers.** A state requirement to provide transitional support services for students with autism did not apply, as the child was being placed into a setting with other children who had autism diagnoses. The court rejected a claim by the parents based on the lack of an IEP provision for 1:1 support. It held for the school district, finding it was not required to provide every special service to maximize a child's potential. *M.L. v. New York City Dep't of Educ.*, No. 13-CV-2314, 2015 WL 1439698 (E.D.N.Y. 3/27/15).

♦   An Ohio student with a seizure disorder and other disabilities had severe difficulty with transitions, and her conduct included hitting and scratching. She typically wore a helmet in public settings for safety in case of a seizure, and she was always accompanied by an adult. Even after the student turned 16, she was excluded from IEP meetings where transition services were discussed. It was believed that the meetings would frighten her because they were long and adversarial. The parents filed a due process complaint against the school district just before the student's nineteenth birthday. They claimed the district denied her a free appropriate public education (FAPE) due to the lack of transition services. An independent hearing officer held for the family on some of the issues, and the dispute later reached a federal court. In the court's view, the school district violated the IDEA by failing to provide the student with adequate transition services. **State and federal regulations require schools to invite students to IEP team meetings to discuss their postsecondary goals.** It was clear to the court that the district had violated this mandate and that its informal steps were not enough. In addition, the district did not offer the student age-appropriate assessments for postsecondary goals. After finding the district's conduct resulted in a denial of FAPE, the court held a conference with the parties to reach an agreement on an appropriate remedy. The parties were unable to agree, and the court provided an opportunity to propose remedies.

In reviewing Sixth Circuit authority, the court noted reservations about basing compensatory education awards on "rote hour-by-hour" calculations. While such awards are not per se inappropriate, the Sixth Circuit has warned against awards that appear punitive. Even though the student had reached age 22, the parties agreed that the court was authorized to order compensatory services. In the court's view, neither of the parties had proposed an appropriate remedy. It held **the student was entitled to transition services regardless of whether she was likely to attain competitive employment or achieve a high level of independence**. The remedy proposed by the parents' expert appeared likely to provide her more than the district could have provided her during her high school career. As a result, the court adopted an employment goal recommended by the expert and an assessment by Goodwill Industries. The student would have some 600 hours of compensatory services. *Gibson v. Forest Hills School Dist.*, No. 1:11-cv-329, 2014 WL 533392 (S.D. Ohio 2/11/14).

♦ In 2003, New York parents of a student with disabilities filed a due process hearing request for relief including a psychiatric evaluation and transition services to prepare him for graduation. Meanwhile, the school district graduated the student, who was then 19. He was directed to the state's office of Vocational and Educational Services for Individuals with Disabilities (VESID) for services. Nine months after the request for a hearing, and over six months after the student's graduation, the case came before an IHO. An order was issued in October 2004, some 16 months after his graduation. Among the IHO's findings was that the district did not provide psychological and vocational counseling, psychiatric evaluations or transitional services. The IHO ordered the district's CSE to "immediately reconvene" and create a transition plan. When the CSE met six months later, it discussed transitional services and prepared an IEP noting that services were available for the student through VESID. According to the student, he went to VESID but was informed that he did not qualify for services because his parents were over the relevant income limits. But he did not contact the school district about this. Claiming the school district did not comply with the IHO's order, the parents requested review by a new IHO. In 2006, another IHO agreed to review the 2004 order but held he lacked authority to issue relief. A state review officer (SRO) denied the family's appeal.

A federal court found the IHO's 2004 order was the result of numerous time extensions with the consent of the parties. Many of the claims, including those asserting due process violations, arose before October 2004 and were untimely. There was no evidence that the delay in holding the CSE meeting deprived the student of due process. The CSE had met to discuss transition services. It had recommended psychiatric and vocational evaluations and directed him to VESID. **Nothing convinced the court that the student was denied transition services due to a disability.** Nor was there "deliberate or reckless indifference" or "gross misconduct." An improper decision about an IEP did not indicate bad faith or gross misjudgment. *Pape v. Board of Educ. of Wappingers Cent. School Dist.*, No. 07 Civ. 8828(ER), 2013 WL 3929630 (S.D.N.Y. 7/30/13).

♦ A student with speech apraxia was placed in the West Virginia Schools for the Deaf and Blind. After three years, the state ordered the exit of all students who did not meet state eligibility criteria for hearing or visual impairments. Because she did not have significant hearing loss, she was going to be transferred. Her parents objected, and a federal court ruled in their favor. **The county system to which she would be transferred couldn't provide the total communication environment she required.** Further, the transition IEP lacked a statement of her present levels of performance as well as annual goals and objectives in a total communication setting. *West Virginia Schools for the Deaf and Blind v. A.V.*, No. 3:11–CV–38, 2012 WL 1677939 (N.D. W.Va. 5/14/12).

♦   The mother of a Pennsylvania student with disabilities rejected 12 placement options suggested by the district before agreeing to math tutoring. The student accepted a volunteer position to work on employment skills and worked with a job coach to prepare for employment. But he often didn't go to class and was placed in juvenile detention twice during high school. Later, a hearing officer ordered the district to provide him with 349.5 hours of compensatory education. His mother eventually sued, claiming that the district denied him a FAPE, but a federal court rejected her claim. **The district provided transition services, and its IEPs contained clear objectives and detailed annual goals.** *Dudley v. Lower Merion School Dist.*, No. 10–2749, 2011 WL 5942120 (E.D. Pa. 11/29/11).

♦   A Hawaii student who received Part C services through an Individualized Family Support Plan was supposed to receive Part B services under an IEP, but because of a dispute over which school he would be attending, the department of education offered him no services for about a month. A lawsuit erupted, and a federal court held that **the failure of the department to transition the student to an IEP violated the IDEA.** This failure resulted in lost educational opportunities that required a hearing officer to consider an appropriate placement and compensatory education. *Shaun M. v. Hamamoto*, No. 09-00075 DAE/BMK, 2009 WL 3415308 (D. Haw. 10/22/09).

II. RELATED SERVICES

Related services are defined by the IDEA, at 20 U.S.C. § 1401(26), to include transportation, speech pathology, psychological services, physical and occupational therapy, recreation and medical services that are necessary for the student to receive an educational benefit. Since school obligations under the IDEA are well-defined, an increasing number of related services disputes reach the courts as discrimination claims under Section 504 of the Rehabilitation Act and the Americans with Disabilities Act (ADA).

A. Communication Services

Prior to K.M. v. Tustin Unified School Dist., 725 F.3d 1088 (9th Cir. 2013), this chapter, most courts did not emphasize the distinctions among the IDEA, Rehabilitation Act Section 504, and Title II of the Americans with Disabilities Act (ADA). In K.M., the court held a valid IEP did not necessarily satisfy ADA Title II communication requirements. The court held that in some cases, the ADA might require schools to provide different services than under the IDEA.

A 2015 Louisiana law requires public schools to include communication plans in the IEPs of students who are deaf, hard of hearing, or deaf-blind, where appropriate. Public schools must provide individual considerations for free appropriate education across a full spectrum of educational programs and support services from qualified professionals in educational settings. Louisiana 2015 Regular Session, Act 250. Louisiana R.S. §§ 17:1960, 17:3996(B)(39).

♦ A California student with profound hearing loss was able to attend general education classes. She had cochlear implants, but an audiologist concluded she heard only about 52% of what was said. At an IEP meeting to discuss the transition from middle to high school, her parents requested Communication Access Real-Time Translation (CART) transcription services. Although the school district offered the student a number of accommodations, it refused to provide her CART services. In response, she requested a hearing, asserting she had to concentrate intently to understand, leading to fatigue and headaches after her school day. An administrative law judge ordered the school district to provide the student CART services in four classes. When the case reached a federal court, it declined to rule on it until the Ninth Circuit issued an opinion in *K.M. v. Tustin Unified School Dist.*, this chapter. By the time the court was ready to rule on the IDEA claim, the student had graduated from high school.

While the court dismissed the IDEA claim and held the student was no longer entitled to injunctive or declaratory relief, it held the case was not moot because she sought monetary damages. According to the student, the district did not ensure effective communications and did not provide her auxiliary aids that would allow her an equal opportunity to participate in school programs, activities or benefits. The court found **ADA regulations require a school to furnish appropriate auxiliary aids and services where necessary to afford individuals with disabilities an equal opportunity to participate in and enjoy the benefits of a service, program or activity of the public entity.** An ADA regulation required schools to ensure that communications with students with disabilities were as effective as with others. By contrast, a public entity was not required to take any action that would result in a fundamental alteration in a service, program or activity, or to undergo an undue burden. Noting a factual dispute, the court held it could not award judgment on the ADA or state law claims without further consideration. *Poway Unified School Dist. v. K.C.*, No. 10CV897-GPC (DHU), 2014 WL 129086 (S.D. Cal. 1/14/14).

♦ Two California students with hearing impairments sought word-for-word transcription services. In separate cases, administrative law judges rejected their claim that decisions by their school districts to deny Communication Access Real-Time Translation (CART) services violated the IDEA. On appeal, a federal court affirmed the decisions, also ruling for the districts on discrimination claims under Section 504 of the Rehabilitation Act and Title II of the ADA. When the case reached the U.S. Court of Appeals, Ninth Circuit, it stated that a federal ADA Title II regulation, found at 28 C.F.R. Part 35.160, required public entities to furnish appropriate services where necessary to provide equal opportunities for individuals with disabilities to participate in services and benefits. The regulation required public entities providing auxiliary aids and services to give primary consideration to the requests of disabled individuals. The Ninth Circuit found this did not necessarily mean that a valid IEP also satisfied ADA Title II. **Title II regulations established independent obligations on the part of public schools.**

According to the court, the IDEA's FAPE requirement was significantly different from Title II communication requirements. In some situations, the court held, **the ADA might require schools to provide different services to**

hearing-impaired students than what they had to provide under the IDEA. As a result, the court returned the case to the district court for it to determine whether the school districts had violated ADA Title II. Both districts would have the opportunity to use Title II defenses such as undue burden and fundamental alteration of their educational programs. *K.M. v. Tustin Unified School Dist.*, 725 F.3d 1088 (9th Cir. 2013).

♦ A Texas student had autism, a mental disability and speech impairments. She was essentially nonverbal and used communication methods such as sign language, picture cards and voice communication devices. For some time, her parents disagreed with her ARD committee about assistive technology assessments and methodology. She began borrowing a "DynaVox" voice output device and made significant progress with it. The parents filed a due process hearing request, and the dispute reached the U.S. Court of Appeals, Fifth Circuit. It recited the general rule that the IDEA does not assure an IEP that is "the best possible" or designed to maximize potential. An IEP must be designed to meet a child's unique needs and be calculated to confer educational benefits. On the other hand, an IEP must be likely to produce progress, not regression or only trivial advancement. In this case, the court found no significant IDEA procedural violations. According to the parents, the principal prematurely ended some ARD meetings, used an improper "voting method" instead of seeking team consensus, and failed to meaningfully consider their input.

Although the lower court had identified a history of tension between the parents and school staff, the court found the parties had usually worked together cooperatively. The court held the district did not deny FAPE when the meetings occasionally ended early. In each case, the district had promptly scheduled follow-up meetings. No evidence indicated voting by district staff rather than attempts to reach consensus. As for the argument that staff made decisions outside the ARD meetings, the court noted that 34 C.F.R. Part 300.501(b)(3) contemplates that school staff members will conduct "preparatory activities" to develop IEP proposals for eventual discussion at an IEP meeting with the parents. Numerous ARD meetings were held for the student, at which the parents had a chance to contribute. Some of their proposals were incorporated into the student's IEP. **Even though the IEP may not have maximized the student's potential, the court found there was no denial of FAPE.** *R.P. v. Alamo Heights Independent School Dist.*, 703 F.3d 801 (5th Cir. 2012).

♦ An Ohio school district provided a student several different augmentative and alternative communication (AAC) devices to address her communication and developmental delays. She had little success with the devices. When the student was in seventh grade, her teachers noticed the quality of her school work was poor, but the work she did at home was "perfect or near perfect." Staff grew concerned that the parents' use of a physical support technique was in fact "facilitated communication" and was the cause of this discrepancy. A dispute arose about the student's grade-nine IEP. According to the district, the student had a full scale IQ score of 33. It was estimated that her reading level was near grade one, and testing indicated she had significant adaptive behavior delays. A math achievement test indicated a performance level of about five years old.

Disagreeing with the district evaluations, the parents requested a hearing. An impartial hearing officer (IHO) found the IEP proposed by the district was designed to offer a FAPE. She reached the contradictory finding that the IEP "does not provide a FAPE to the extent that it does not sufficiently address behavioral and communication goals." According to the IHO, the student was receiving little or no educational benefit in a regular education setting, and her IEP needed to be modified. She held the district had to provide an AAC device along with intensive training to allow her to independently communicate. The case reached a federal court, which noted the IHO had relied on the opinions of two experts hired by the parents to support their argument that the child could perform grade-level work with physical support. It was improper for the IHO to rely on parentally obtained evaluations completed months after the IEP was proposed. There was evidence that the evaluations were unreliable. One of the parents' evaluators improperly allowed the use of physical support that was considered a form of "facilitated communication." This rendered the tests nonstandard. **The student could not effectively communicate the extent of her cognitive abilities**, and her parents had already rejected the AAC devices. Since the district's evaluation was valid and the IEP provided the child a FAPE, the court held for the district. *T.J. v. Winton Woods City School Dist.*, No. 1:10-cv-847, 2013 WL 1090465 (S.D. Ohio 3/15/13).

♦ Parents of students with cochlear implants sued the Department of Education in a District of Columbia federal court, seeking a declaration that cochlear implant mapping should be a related service under the IDEA. The department had issued **a regulation excluding cochlear implant mapping as a related service** because cochlear implants are surgical implants. The department's interpretation of the law was entitled to deference, and the regulation was upheld. On further appeal, the D.C. Circuit Court upheld the lower court's decision. Although cochlear implants are surgically implanted, they have both internal and external components, and mapping was not a routine service such that staff members could perform it without a substantial burden. *Petit v. U.S. Dep't of Educ.*, 675 F.3d 769 (D.C. Cir. 2012).

♦ A Connecticut student with deafness and a specific language learning disability was not fluent in sign language. As a result, his IEP called for captioning to be provided for all classes, group meetings and assemblies. However, the school planning and placement team "tabled" the discussion of how to accommodate him with respect to the daily morning news broadcasts. After three years of no action on the issue, he sued the state and the school district to force the district to caption the broadcasts. A federal district court held that the state could not be sued. It also ruled that **the news broadcasts were not a limited public forum but rather a closed forum, justifying the school district's decision not to caption them**. *Quatroche v. East Lyme Board of Educ.*, 604 F.Supp.2d 403 (D. Conn. 2009).

♦ An Arizona school district furnished a sign-language interpreter to a student with hearing impairments who attended public schools. When the student's parents enrolled him in a parochial school, they requested that the school district continue providing the sign-language interpreter. The district refused to provide this service on Establishment Clause grounds, and the parents sued. Appeal reached the U.S. Supreme Court, which held that **the provision of a sign-language interpreter is a religiously neutral distribution of IDEA benefits that provides only an indirect financial benefit to a parochial school**. The Court held that the Establishment Clause did not prohibit the school district from sending the sign-language interpreter to the parochial school for the student's benefit. *Zobrest v. Catalina Foothills School Dist.,* 509 U.S. 1, 113 S.Ct. 2462, 125 L.Ed.2d 1 (1993).

B. Voluntarily Enrolled Private School Students

In Jasa v. Millard Public School Dist. No. 17, *206 F.3d 813 (8th Cir. 2000), the court held local education agencies are not required to pay the cost of a private school education if they have offered a FAPE to the student and the parents nonetheless make a voluntary private school placement.*

◆   A Connecticut child attended a private school at his school district's expense. His parent later grew dissatisfied with his progress and placed him in a private religious school outside the district that provided no special education. The parent paid the school's tuition while the district paid for related services. School officials discontinued the agreement at the end of the year and suggested placement in a public school in the district. But the parent rejected this and filed a due process complaint. A hearing officer held for the school board, finding the IEP offered a free appropriate public education (FAPE). The private school was found an inappropriate setting as it provided the child no special education. The parent appealed to a federal court, which held the IEP offered the child a FAPE.

But the court held the board violated the stay-put provision by refusing to fund the related services described in the IEP. Appeal reached the U.S. Court of Appeals, Second Circuit. After rejecting the parent's claim that the IEP denied her child a FAPE, the court found her participation rights had not been violated. Throughout the dispute, the student was a resident of the district and the board violated the IDEA by not offering him an IEP. **There was no merit to the board's argument that once a child was enrolled at a school outside the district, any IDEA obligations ended.** But the court held the religious school was an inappropriate placement. It offered no special education and did not modify its curriculum to accommodate the student. In the court's view, the board violated the stay-put provision by discontinuing related services at the private school, because **the stay-put provision applies to related services.** As the parent argued, she was entitled to the full value of services which the board was required to fund from the time of the due process request until the end of the proceeding. *Doe v. East Lyme Board of Educ.,* 790 F.3d 440 (2d Cir. 2015).

◆   After a student was diagnosed with an autism spectrum disorder, the New York City Department of Education (DOE) agreed to fund his placement at a private center for students with special needs. He made progress there, but the DOE recommended a public school placement for his fourth grade school year. At his committee on special education (CSE) meeting, a center report was discussed. CSE members discussed the related services from a prior IEP and no one objected to this. At the meeting, the parent was consulted on many topics and the CSE recommended a community school placement. A final notice of recommendation described occupational therapy, speech and counseling, but did not detail the frequency, duration or group size for these services. When the parent toured the school where the IEP was to be implemented, she rejected it as too noisy. Noting the IEP did not include specific recommendations for related services, she re-enrolled her child in the center. In a due process proceeding, an impartial hearing officer found the DOE excluded related services recommendations from the IEP. The services were offered without consideration for the child's levels of performance and sufficient parental input.

A federal court later held that while the absence of any representative from the private center from the CSE meeting was an IDEA violation, it did not impede the parent's participation. The center's progress report was considered at the meeting. The parent actively participated in the CSE's discussion. The inadvertent omission of a related services program from the IEP was not as significant as the parent argued. The court held a failure to include the related services in a properly designated space did not make the IEP inadequate, since it was discussed in other areas of the IEP. The parent did not show the DOE's placement was inappropriate. Rejecting all of the parent's arguments, the court held for the DOE. *C.K. v. New York City Dep't of Educ.*, No. 14-cv-836 (RJS), 2015 WL 1808602 (S.D.N.Y. 4/9/15).

♦ A New York first-grader with ADHD sought a 1:1 aide at his private school, and administrative rulings agreed that the aide would be sent to the private school. The district then sought a court ruling that the aide should be provided only at the public school. The Supreme Court, Appellate Division, held that state law permitted a school district to provide services at a private school. It ruled that the decision must be made on a case-by-case basis, with the student's needs in the least restrictive environment serving as a guide. The New York Court of Appeals affirmed, noting that **the state's dual enrollment statute was intended to offer private school students with disabilities "equal access** to the full array of specialized public school programs." *Board of Educ. of Bay Shore Union Free School Dist. v. Thomas K.*, 14 N.Y.3d 289 (N.Y. 2010).

♦ The parents of a New Hampshire student with disabilities placed him in a Catholic school and then met with a school district team to develop an IEP. The IEP called for transportation to and from a public school speech/language program for one hour per week. Later, the parents challenged the IEP, asserting that some services were not provided and that the district had furnished unreliable transportation. A hearing officer held that they were not entitled to a due process hearing because they had voluntarily placed their son at the religious school. The First Circuit Court of Appeals agreed. By placing their son in the private school, the parents had to accept the disadvantages as well as the benefits. And **Congress had chosen not to provide the same benefits to private school students** as it did to public school students. *Gary S. v. Manchester School Dist.*, 374 F.3d 15 (1st Cir. 2004).

♦   A disabled student attending a parochial school in Rhode Island received resource services at her school because it was within "walking distance" of a public school. When she began attending a religious school in another town, the school committee stopped providing services on site. Her parents later sought to have the services provided at the private school. They claimed that the unwritten "walking distance" rule was unfair to their daughter. A due process hearing officer agreed with the parents, stating that because the school committee provided resource services to other parochial school students in the district (who were within walking distance of a public school), it had to provide them to the student here. A federal court overturned the hearing officer's decision. **The IDEA regulation that permits on-site services could not be used to require on-site services.** The hearing officer's decision resulted from her "sense of arm-chair equity" and was improper. *Bristol Warren Regional School Committee v. Rhode Island Dep't of Educ.*, 253 F.Supp.2d 236 (D.R.I. 2003).

C. Occupational Therapy and Rehabilitation Services

♦   A Pennsylvania school district determined that a student was not IDEA-eligible, but that he was eligible for occupational therapy under Section 504. The student's parents enrolled him in a private school, but also dually enrolled him in public schools so that he would be able to get occupational therapy at a public school. The district refused to provide the services, but a court ordered it to do so. Here, the student was not seeking tuition reimbursement or even related services at a private school. He was merely seeking Section 504 services at a public facility and he was "enrolled" in the district. He did not have to actually attend classes to be eligible for occupational therapy. The Supreme Court of Pennsylvania then ruled that the student was entitled to Section 504 services. **Federal regulations didn't require the student to attend classes in the district to qualify for Section 504 services.** Further, Section 504 required schools to seek out eligible beneficiaries based on residency, not school attendance. *Lower Merion School Dist. v. Doe*, 931 A.2d 640 (Pa. 2007).

♦   A New Jersey student with developmental delays due to complications from his premature birth received occupational therapy (OT) as part of his pre-school IEP. The IEP specified that he receive 30 minutes of OT per week. His mother sought an independent evaluation, which recommended 60 minutes of OT per week. She asked the school district for more OT and requested that it pay for the increased OT she was providing. **The child study team sought to conduct a reevaluation of the child,** but his mother removed him from school and placed him in a private school, where he received OT six times a week. She then sought tuition reimbursement, which a federal court denied. Not only did she fail to cooperate with the school district, but the district also provided a free appropriate public education for her son. *M.S. and D.S. v. Mullica Township Board of Educ.*, 485 F.Supp.2d 555 (D.N.J. 2007).

♦   A Hawaii student with multiple disabilities received one hour a week of occupational therapy (OT) and one hour a week of speech/language therapy. Her 2004-05 IEP stated that extended school year (ESY) services were appropriate for the summer of 2005, but it did not specify how much therapy the student should receive during the summer. She nevertheless received one hour per week of OT and speech/language therapy. The following year, settlement of an earlier dispute raised the student's OT and speech/language therapy levels to two hours per week of each. However, the IEP team decided to reduce to 90 minutes per week the OT and speech/language therapy the student would receive during the 2006 ESY. The parents challenged that decision, and a federal court ruled in their favor. **By challenging the ESY IEP, the parents effectively invoked the stay-put provision, requiring the school to provide two hours a week of both OT and speech/language therapy.** *Dep't of Educ., State of Hawaii v. A.F.*, No. 06-00488 SOM/BMK, 2007 WL 1080085 (D. Haw. 4/9/07).

◆   An Illinois student with Down syndrome was entitled to occupational therapy under his IEP. His district provided the therapy, but its **occupational therapist was unlicensed** and could only work in the district with more supervision than she actually received. After his parents rejected his IEP, a hearing officer found that the hiring of the therapist was a violation of the IDEA. She awarded the student 60 minutes of weekly direct occupational therapy services. A federal court then ruled that the student was entitled to a year of compensatory education, reimbursement for the independent evaluation and attorneys' fees. On appeal, the Seventh Circuit reversed the order to reimburse for the independent evaluation, but otherwise affirmed. Noncompliance with the state licensure requirements was not a minor procedural violation of the IDEA. *Evanston Community Consolidated School Dist. No. 65 v. Michael M.*, 356 F.3d 798 (7th Cir. 2004).

D. Other Services

A 2015 Maryland law requires orientation and mobility instruction in the IEPs of blind or visually impaired children, unless the IEP team determines it is inappropriate for the child. A child may not be denied orientation and mobility instruction solely because he or she has some remaining vision. If an IEP team determines orientation and mobility instruction is inappropriate for a child, the team must order an orientation and mobility assessment by a qualified individual in accordance with state regulations. Within 30 days after receiving an orientation and mobility assessment, the IEP team is to meet to determine whether orientation and mobility instruction is appropriate for the child. Maryland General Assembly, 2015 Regular Session Chapter 430, H.B. No. 535. Education Article Section 8-408.

◆   Due to autism and complex motor and speech disabilities, a North Carolina student had developmental delays. Her parents became disenchanted with her IEP and requested a due process hearing. An administrative law judge (ALJ) agreed with the school board on every issue in dispute. But the ALJ held the school did not provide the child necessary speech therapy for several months. The school board was ordered to reimburse the parents for 64 hours of speech therapy and their related transportation expenses. The board appealed to a review officer, who reversed the speech therapy ruling. The parents never appealed the ALJ's adverse rulings to the review officer. But they sued the school board in a federal court. The parents claimed the board should have provided their child direct, intensive, one-on-one applied behavior analysis. The court held for the school board, ruling that the parents did not exhaust their administrative remedies. As for the speech therapy question, the court held for the board. In addition, the court rejected the parents' claim that North Carolina's two-tier due process procedure violated the IDEA. The parents appealed to the U.S. Court of Appeals, Fourth Circuit, which held the state satisfied an IDEA requirement for administrative review to immediately precede any civil action.

The student's IEP called for daily sessions of speech therapy in the "total school environment," as part of the "embedded, inclusive model" of instruction. According to this model, therapists worked with students directly in their regular classrooms when other instruction was taking place. This differed from models such as pulling out students from classrooms. It appeared that the ALJ had ruled against the board primarily on the basis of the speech therapist's decision to shred her personal therapy notes for the relevant times. **The court found the evidence did not show the school district denied the child appropriate therapy.** Her IEP specified a total school environment, not isolated, one-on-one instruction. Since the court found the child received the speech therapy specified in her IEP, it held for the board of education. *E.L. v. Chapel Hill-Carrboro Board of Educ.*, 773 F.3d 509 (4th Cir. 2014).

♦ A California student with severe autism was nonverbal and functioned at a low cognitive level. He received a service dog that his parents sought to have accompany him in school. However, school officials refused to allow the dog on the premises, determining that it was only for the student's comfort and not really a service dog. The parents sued, and a federal court granted a temporary injunction allowing the student to bring the dog to school. **The school failed to show that the presence of the dog would fundamentally alter the nature of the school's services, programs or activities.** *C.C. v. Cypress School Dist.*, No. SACV 11-352 AG (MLGx) (C.D. Cal. 6/13/11).

♦ A disabled North Carolina student engaged in aggressive, self-injurious behavior and was hyperactive. A service dog was trained to help him redirect some of his problem behaviors. The dog was able to provide deep pressure therapy through physical contact with the student, as well as other techniques for redirecting him. But **school officials rejected the parents' request to permit the student's full-time use of the dog at school** and also questioned whether the dog was a service animal. The IEP team found the dog was not necessary. Instead of challenging that determination, the parents sued for discrimination. A federal court dismissed the case, holding that the parents should have exhausted their administrative remedies before suing. *A.S. v. Catawba County Board of Educ.*, No. 5:11CV27-RLV, 2011 WL 3438881 (W.D.N.C. 8/5/11).

♦ An Illinois autistic student had daily tantrums, an eating disorder and episodes of running on impulse. A doctor prescribed a service dog, which the family obtained two years later. This calmed the student greatly. However, at a preschool IEP meeting, district officials told the mother the service dog could not accompany him to school because even though the dog was hypoallergenic, another student was highly allergic to dogs. The family then sought an order defining the dog as a "service animal" that would allow it to accompany the student to school. The Appellate Court of Illinois found that **the dog met the state's definition of a "service animal"** even though the commands to assist the student came from staff members and not the student himself. The student could bring the dog to school. *K.D. v. Villa Grove Community Unit School Dist. No. 302*, 936 N.E.2d 690 (Ill. App. Ct. 2010).

◆   A New York student with autism received related services in addition to what he received in a special education classroom. He later won a lottery to attend an autism charter school, which used an ABA model and lowered his student-teacher-aide ratio from 8:1:2 to 4:1:3. His parents nevertheless asserted that he should continue to receive related services even though they were embedded within the charter school's curriculum. A due process hearing officer disagreed with them, and a federal court affirmed that decision. The student's IEP addressed his individual needs, and **he was making educational progress with the embedded related services in the school's curriculum**. *M.N. v. New York City Dep't of Educ.*, 700 F.Supp.2d 356 (S.D.N.Y. 2010).

◆   The parents of a Minnesota child sought to have accommodations provided for extracurricular activities in which she might wish to engage. However, they didn't identify any specific activity at that time. The student later identified volleyball and after-school clubs as activities she was interested in. Her parents also sought accommodations so that she could attend an off-campus fifth-grade graduation party. The district refused to provide accommodations to the party because it was a private event sponsored by the parent-teacher organization. In the lawsuit that followed, the Minnesota Court of Appeals held that **the district did not have to accommodate the child's attendance at the PTA-sponsored, fifth-grade graduation party**. However, it did have to provide accommodations for volleyball and after-school clubs, the specific activities she had identified. The Minnesota Supreme Court affirmed in part. The student didn't have to prove that she would receive educational benefits from extracurricular and nonacademic activities in order to qualify for supplemental aides and services. But the IEP team had to consider whether the extracurricular and nonacademic activities were appropriate. *Independent School Dist. No. 12, Centennial v. Minnesota Dep't of Educ.*, 788 N.W.2d 907 (Minn. 2010).

◆   A California student with multiple disabilities could not swallow food. Instead, he received nutrition through a surgical opening into his stomach called a gastrostomy tube or "G-tube." His mother claimed he developed a severe reflux disorder from liquids, necessitating that he be fed only pureed foods. She used a syringe plunger even though standard medical practice called for using a gravity methodology. A dispute arose over the method of feeding her son, and she kept him at home for a time and then sought compensatory education. A federal court ultimately ruled that **the mother could not dictate the method to be used to feed her son**. The doctor's prescription did not specify the plunge method, and the mother never provided the IEP team with evidence that the gravity method would not work. No compensatory education was due. *C.N. v. Los Angeles Unified School Dist.*, No. CV 07-03642 MMM (SSx), 2008 WL 4552951 (C.D. Cal. 10/9/08).

♦ A Missouri student with multiple disabilities attended a state school for severely disabled persons for 12 years. His parent challenged his educational program, alleging that staff failed to engage him in stretching exercises and that as a result his body began to conform to his wheelchair shape, and his motor skills regressed. The parent sought audiovisual surveillance as part of the relief, and a federal court ruled that **audiovisual surveillance could be a related service under the IDEA**. It therefore denied the motion to dismiss that part of the lawsuit. The court also allowed the claim for compensatory education to proceed. *J.T. v. Missouri State Board of Educ.*, No. 4:08CV1431RWS, 2009 WL 262094 (E.D. Mo. 2/4/09).

♦ A New Jersey student's IEP called for a personal aide for the full school day as well as 10 hours of at-home tutoring a week at district expense. Aides were to be Lovaas trained. **When the district could not find a Lovaas-trained aide, the student's mother did so, and the district hired him.** The aide later resigned. It took the district a while to replace him, during which time the mother kept her son at home and hired another Lovaas-trained aide, whom the district also hired. She made extra payments to the aides the district provided, then sought reimbursement for those payments, but a federal court and the Third Circuit ruled against her. Here, the school board had no idea she was making the payments. Further, the delay in finding a replacement aide did not amount to a denial of a free appropriate public education. *Fisher v. Stafford Township Board of Educ.*, 289 Fed.Appx. 520 (3d Cir. 2008).

♦ A Pennsylvania school district offered an incoming kindergartner with autism an IEP that included ABA therapy and verbal behavior (VB) services in an autistic support class, but reduced the student's ABA therapy from his early intervention IEP and also reduced his occupational therapy. His parents challenged the IEP and reached a settlement in which the student was to receive two hours of ABA and VB therapy a day. The district then provided three hours a day, exceeding the interim IEP requirements. Later, the district proposed reducing the ABA/VB therapy for the rest of the school year and for the ESY program in the summer. Again the parents objected. The case reached a federal court, which ruled for the district. **The district could provide less than three hours of ABA therapy a day**, and it did not have to provide more than 1.5 hours a day during the summer. It had already provided more ABA therapy than the interim IEP required. *Travis G. v. New Hope-Solebury School Dist.*, 544 F.Supp.2d 435 (E.D. Pa. 2008).

♦ A Minnesota school district provided developmental adapted physical education (DAPE) swimming to special education students. It later conducted a study that resulted in a recommendation to discontinue the program. The district's board informed parents that the DAPE program was under review, but it did not notify parents when it finally canceled the program. Instead, parents were notified during IEP meetings. After a parent complained, the state education department found that **the district violated the IDEA by canceling the DAPE program without proper notice** to the parents. It ordered the district to restore DAPE swimming services at the beginning of the next school year and to provide a year of compensatory DAPE swimming for the year in which such services ended. The Minnesota Court of Appeals affirmed that decision. *Independent School Dist. No. 281 v. Minnesota Dep't of Educ.*, No. A06-1617, 2007 WL 2774337 (Minn. Ct. App. 9/25/07).

♦ A Tennessee student with profound bilateral hearing loss received a cochlear implant at the age of 14 months. Her school district later developed an IEP for her, offering to place her in a new collaborative program that was being developed with Head Start, and which served low-income students, many of whom did not have disabilities. The district also proposed to discontinue the mapping service (optimization of the implant) it had been providing for the student. When the parents objected, a hearing officer held that the district's placement met IDEA requirements, but that it had to continue the mapping services. A federal court then held that **the 2004 IDEA Amendments excluded the mapping of a cochlear implant as a related service** under the IDEA. *A.U. v. Roane County Board of Educ.*, 501 F.Supp.2d 1134 (E.D. Tenn. 2007).

♦ A California student's IEP did not include extended school year (ESY) services. Her parents unilaterally placed her in "Camp Kodiak," then sought placement in a Utah residential treatment facility called the "Alpine Academy." They asserted that the district had failed to provide counseling sessions required by the IEP. A hearing officer agreed that the parents should be compensated for the counseling sessions but held that the ESY services and the residential placement were not necessary. A federal court agreed. Although **the failure to provide all the counseling sessions specified in the IEP was a denial of a free appropriate public education**, it did not justify the residential placement or ESY services. *Roxanne J. v. Nevada County Human Services Agency*, No. Cir. 5-05-2602 KJM, 2006 WL 3437494 (E.D. Cal. 11/28/06).

♦ After a dispute with their district over placement, the parents of a Pennsylvania student with deaf-blindness finally agreed on an IEP. However, they then withdrew their son from school and sued the district, alleging that it failed to comply with the requirements of the IEP. A federal court held that the district had largely complied. It had assigned its Supervisor of Hearing and Vision Support Programs to serve as the student's deaf-blind coordinator. However, the district had not properly given the certified "intervener" one-on-one training. **The district had to provide further training to the intervener,** but it did not have to replace her based on the parents' preferences. *Derrick F. v. Red Lion Area School Dist.*, Civil No. 1:06-CV-1463, 2006 WL 2547050 (M.D. Pa. 9/1/06).

♦ A Georgia student with a disability complained that words became fuzzy or three dimensional when he tried to read. A behavioral optometrist diagnosed accommodative and convergence disorder, and recommended visual therapy to reduce vision loss. The district refused to pay for such therapy on the grounds that the student was receiving a free appropriate public education. The parents paid for the therapy, then sought due process. An administrative hearing officer and a federal court found that the parents were entitled to reimbursement for the therapy as a related service. The Eleventh Circuit agreed. **Although the student's condition had not yet caused poor academic performance, it did prevent him from receiving a FAPE.** *DeKalb County School Dist. v. M.T.V.,* 164 Fed.Appx. 900 (11th Cir. 2006).

III. MEDICAL SERVICES

The IDEA specifically excludes medical services from its definition of related services, unless provided for diagnostic or evaluative purposes. In determining whether a service is an excluded medical service, courts tend to focus on who has to provide the service and the nature of the service being provided to determine whether it is part of the school district's obligation.

◆   A private Pennsylvania school provided medical services to children through the partial hospitalization program (PHP). The PHP is federally subsidized under the Medicaid Act. PHP medical services were integrated into the school's academic program throughout the school day. To settle a dispute, a school district paid some of the costs of educational and medical services for children attending the school. After voluntarily extending the agreement for four years, the district then stopped paying tuition subsidies for PHP services.

In a federal court, the private school sued the school district. It claimed to represent students at the school who were enrolled by parents for the purpose of receiving medical services in the PHP. A federal magistrate judge recommended dismissing the case, and the court accepted his report. It found the school and parents lacked standing under the Medicaid Act. Alternatively, the school did not state a valid claim. The court denied a request to amend the complaint and appeal reached the U.S. Court of Appeals, Third Circuit. It agreed with the lower court that the parents lacked standing. It noted that the parents were still able to select the school as the provider for their children and were not denied services or required to withdraw their children. Since the parents were able to select the school as a provider of partial hospitalization medical services, the court found they did not assert any injury. Their lack of standing was held fatal to the school's claim of representational standing. **No federal law required a school district to subsidize private education provided in conjunction with a medical program at the school.** An equal protection claim on behalf of the students was not timely raised, and the court of appeals affirmed the judgment for the school district. *Community Country Day School v. Erie School Dist.,* 618 Fed.Appx. 89 (3d Cir. 2015).

◆   Nursing organizations challenged a California Education Department advisory on students with diabetes in public schools. The advisory authorized student insulin administrations in schools by several groups of persons, including school employees who were adequately trained to administer insulin (pursuant to a treating physician's orders) under a Section 504 plan or IEP. According to the nurses, the advisory condoned the unauthorized practice of nursing. The case reached the Supreme Court of California, which found a long-term shortage of school nurses had led to a previous federal court class action suit. A settlement ended the class action, which led to the advisory at issue. Under it, trained school staff who were not licensed healthcare providers could administer insulin under medical orders, where no nurse was available.

Public school students with diabetes who could not self-administer insulin were entitled to no-cost administration under the IDEA, Section 504 and other federal laws. But the court found some school nurses refused to train unlicensed staff members to administer insulin out of concern for discipline by the nursing board. The advisory concluded it was unlawful for a school district to have a general practice asserting it need not comply with student IDEA or Section 504 rights to have insulin administered at school in the absence of a licensed professional. State Education Code Section 49423 declared that any student required to take prescribed medication during the school day may be assisted by the school nurse or other designated school personnel. **The court rejected the claims and held Section 49423 permitted unlicensed school personnel to administer prescription medications.** *American Nurses Ass'n v. Torlakson*, 57 Cal.4th 570, 304 P.3d 1038 (Cal. 2013).

♦ In 1984, the U.S. Supreme Court ruled that clean intermittent catheterization (CIC) is a related service not subject to the "medical service" exclusion of the IDEA. The parents of an eight-year-old girl born with spina bifida brought suit against a local Texas school district after the district refused to provide catheterization for the child while she attended school. The parents pursued administrative and judicial avenues to force the district to train staff to perform the simple procedure. After a federal court held against the parents, they appealed to the Fifth Circuit, which reversed. The district then appealed to the U.S. Supreme Court, which affirmed that portion of the court of appeals decision that held CIC is a "supportive service," not a "medical service," within the meaning of the IDEA. CIC may be administered by a nurse or trained layperson. The Court listed four criteria to determine a school's obligation to provide services that relate to both the health and education of a child.

First, to be entitled to related services, a child must be disabled so as to require special education. Second, **only those services necessary to aid a child with disabilities to benefit from special education must be provided**, regardless of how easily a school nurse or layperson could furnish them. Third, IDEA regulations state that school nursing services must be performed by a nurse or other qualified person, not by a physician. Fourth, the child's parents in this case were seeking only the services of a qualified person at the school; they were not asking the school to provide equipment. *Irving Independent School Dist. v. Tatro*, 468 U.S. 883, 104 S.Ct. 3371, 82 L.Ed.2d 664 (1984).

♦ In 1999, the Supreme Court decided another case involving the extent of a school district's obligation to provide medical services, adopting a bright-line, physician/non-physician test to determine whether a requested service is a related service or a medical service. An Iowa student suffered a spinal cord injury that left him quadriplegic and ventilator dependent. For several years, his family provided him with personal attendant services at school. When the student entered grade five, his mother asserted that the district should provide him with continuous one-on-one nursing services. The district refused. A due process hearing officer determined that the school district had to reimburse the family for nursing costs in the current school year and provide the services in the future. A federal court ruled for the family, and the U.S. Court of Appeals, Eighth Circuit, found the services were related services as defined by the IDEA that were necessary to enable him to benefit from special education.

The court rejected the district's argument that the services were medical services excluded under the IDEA and state law. On appeal, the U.S. Supreme Court held the requested services were not medical services. The Court based its decision on the IDEA definition of related services, the *Tatro* decision, and the purpose of the IDEA to make special education available to all disabled students. **Adopting a bright-line, physician/non-physician standard, the court held that since the disputed services could be performed by someone other than a physician, the district had to provide them.** The district's assertion that a multi-factor standard that includes cost as a consideration was appropriate was rejected. *Cedar Rapids Community School Dist. v. Garret F.,* 526 U.S. 66, 119 S.Ct. 992, 143 L.Ed.2d 154 (1999).

♦   California parents were unable to agree on an IEP for their son. They objected to the district's offer of eight hours of nurse services for the year and also to its refusal to designate a specific individual to perform g-tube feedings. Eventually a federal court ruled that the district had violated state law by failing to designate a person to perform g-tube feedings. The parents then sued the district, asserting that staff implemented the IEPs in a way that discriminated against their son. A federal court ruled against them, finding no evidence of discrimination. **The district reasonably interpreted the hearing officer's earlier order as requiring a nurse to supervise a staff member until that individual was adequately trained.** *T.B. v. San Diego Unified School Dist.,* No. 08CV28–MMA (WMc), 2012 WL 1611021 (S.D. Cal. 5/8/12).

♦   A Michigan school district's insurer sued the district to enforce its rights under state law with respect to the provision of nursing services to a student. It sought reimbursement for services it believed the district was providing and it was paying for. However, when the case reached the court of appeals, it noted that the student's IEPs did not specify the services in dispute and that **the services being provided by the district were not being paid for by the insurer**. Further, the insurer had no right to try to determine, through a lawsuit, whether the district should be providing nursing services to the student. *Progressive Michigan Insurance Co. v. Calhoun Intermediate School Dist.,* No. 290564, 2010 WL 2680112 (Mich. Ct. App. 7/6/10).

♦   A West Virginia student with medical problems suffered abuse and neglect at the hands of his parents. He was placed in foster care. Thirteen years later, a state court conducted a review of his pending abuse and neglect petition and **ordered the school board to provide and pay for a full-time nurse even**

though the board received no notice or opportunity to appear at the review hearing. The Supreme Court of Appeal of West Virginia then issued an order in favor of the board, finding that it should have been given notice and an opportunity to be heard so that it could have helped shed light on the best interests of the student. For example, its records showed that the student hadn't suffered a seizure in two years and that he hadn't had a full-time nurse assigned to him for four of his 11 years in the school system. *State of West Virginia v. Beane*, 680 S.E.2d 46 (W. Va. 2009).

♦   A Maryland student with disabilities received two types of medication from the school nurse under an agreement signed by her treating/prescribing psychiatrist. When teachers and other staff members observed that the student was lethargic and drowsy, the psychiatrist prescribed another medication. However, the student's fatigue continued. The nurse sought clarification from the doctor on giving the student medication when symptoms contraindicated further drug administration. The parents told the doctor not to provide further information to the nurse or other district employees regarding the student's medical condition and treatment. The district then refused to continue medicating the student. When the parents challenged that decision, they lost. The Court of Appeals of Maryland held that the dispute was about medical treatment and not special education. **The nurse could not be forced to medicate the student without free communication with the doctor.** *John A. v. Board of Educ. for Howard County*, 929 A.2d 136 (Md. 2007).

♦   **A Virginia school board did not have to reimburse a disabled student for hospitalization costs** that were paid years earlier by his father's group health insurance, even though the payments counted against the lifetime medical benefits limit of the policy. The father made several requests to recover the $200,000 cost of the hospitalization from the board but did not request a due process hearing for almost 10 years. The hearing officer held the action was barred by a one-year Virginia statute of limitations. A federal district court affirmed. The Fourth Circuit agreed that the action was untimely. Also, the student was now an adult and was no longer covered by his father's insurance policy. He had his own Medicaid coverage, and this insurance was not affected by the decrease in lifetime medical benefits to his father's plan. *Emery v. Roanoke City School Board*, 432 F.3d 294 (4th Cir. 2005).

♦   A student had over 150 absences and numerous behavioral referrals during her sophomore year of high school. She also exhibited signs of drug use. She was absent from school 79 times and had many behavior referrals her junior year. A school support team began an initial evaluation for special education, and a social worker urged her parents to have her tested for drug use late in her junior year. Two days later, the mother confronted the student about drug use, and the student threatened to kill her mother. The student was hospitalized and tested positive for marijuana. She underwent a special education evaluation that resulted in her classification as emotionally impaired. She completed a residential program at another hospital during the summer. She received tutoring and graduated the following spring. Her parents filed an administrative action against state education officials seeking reimbursement for the hospitalization costs, characterizing them as IDEA-related services. A hearing officer concluded that the costs were reimbursable and awarded the parents $7,713.

The Hawaii education department appealed to a federal court, which noted that the state violated the IDEA child find provisions by failing to evaluate the student earlier. The court rejected the state's argument that the student's graduation under the IEP it eventually developed satisfied its obligation to provide a FAPE. The student's receipt of some educational benefit was not determinative, because instruction was not provided under an appropriate IEP, despite numerous warning signs, before the end of her junior year. **The services provided at the hospital were diagnostic and for evaluation.** While they had been precipitated by a crisis, the student's disability might never have been addressed, and she might not have ever received IDEA services if not for her hospitalization. The parents were entitled to reimbursement for the hospitalization costs. *Dep't of Educ., State of Hawaii v. Cari Rae S.*, 158 F.Supp.2d 1190 (D. Haw. 2001).

♦ After an Indiana student was released from a medical center, her parents contacted local school officials, seeking a residential placement. The parties met at an IEP conference and agreed on the need for a residential placement. While the student awaited the outcome of the administrative process, she was placed in a psychiatric hospital for over sixth months, incurring significant costs for psychiatric counseling, medication and therapy. Her parents then sought to have her involuntarily committed. The court found that the student was mentally ill and required long-term education in a residential placement. She remained in the hospital for an additional five months, since the least restrictive appropriate facility had no available space. The hospital notified the court that she was no longer a threat to herself or others and recommended termination of her civil commitment. In a separate action, a class of Indiana students with disabilities and their parents sued the Indiana Department of Education, alleging that the department's long delays in residential placement matters violated the IDEA.

The lawsuit settled under an order that provided for recovery of certain educational and related services costs from the state where there was a delay between the date of the IEP and the date of placement. The student and her parents joined the action and sought reimbursement for the services she received while hospitalized. The case reached the Seventh Circuit, which held that the hospitalization charges incurred by the student resulted from "special circumstances" as described in the settlement order; therefore, the delay in placing her in a residential facility, as called for in her IEP, did not violate the terms of the settlement agreement. Her IEP was designed for homebound services and contemplated a residential placement for her educational needs, not a placement based on medical treatment. **The hospital placement was for medical reasons related to the student's psychiatric crisis; therefore, reimbursement was not warranted.** The student's IEP team had unanimously concluded that she did not require hospitalization, and her parents had failed to challenge the adequacy of the IEP. The hospital was not equipped to serve as an educational provider. *Butler v. Evans*, 225 F.3d 887 (7th Cir. 2000).

♦   The mother of a Rhode Island student who was profoundly retarded, paraplegic and required a ventilator challenged the student's IEP. The city school department prevailed in administrative proceedings, and the mother appealed. However, she voluntarily dismissed the action. At that time, an IEP team meeting was already one month overdue under state law. A state education department compliance officer requested an IEP review meeting. The state education department then initiated compliance proceedings against the city school department for failure to conduct an annual IEP review. After a hearing, the education department authorized the compliance officer to take necessary action to develop a revised IEP. At a final hearing in the compliance action, the officer testified that nursing services were appropriate in order to provide the student with a safe environment in which to receive a FAPE. The city later refused to pay for a full-time nurse to assist the student, and the commissioner deducted almost $55,000 from the city's operation aid to pay for services.

The case then came before the Rhode Island Superior Court, which found that the state's general laws authorized the commissioner to deduct funds from a city's operation aid for a violation or neglect of law, or for a municipality's violation or neglect of rules and regulations. Here, the city had violated state special education law by failing to timely arrange for an IEP meeting. Withholding of funds had therefore been appropriate. Also, **full-time nursing services were necessary for the student to maintain her health and safety while she received education**. *City of Warwick v. Rhode Island Dep't of Educ.*, No. PC 98-3189, 2000 WL 1879897 (R.I. Super. 12/5/00).

IV. TRANSPORTATION

The IDEA requires school districts to provide students with disabilities necessary transportation as a related service. School districts must also furnish transportation to disabled students attending private schools, if this is necessary for the student to receive a FAPE. Transportation includes travel to and from school and between schools, as well as travel in and around school buildings. It also includes any specialized equipment that might be needed.

A 2015 New Hampshire law clarifies that pupils with disabilities may be transported to or from school activities in mixed use school buses unless the pupil's individualized education program or Section 504 accommodation plan states that such a vehicle shall not be used. "School activities" include sporting and intramural events, events associated with student clubs or organizations, job training programs, field trips, and special education transition services. "School activities" do not include transportation between home and school. New Hampshire 2015 Regular Session, Ch. 100, H.B. 604. New Hampshire Revised Statutes Annotated Section 198:6-c.

♦   A Georgia parent said her child was entitled to an aide to administer seizure medication called Diastat on his bus to and from school. But the school denied her request and after efforts to resolve the dispute, the parent filed a due process request. An administrative law judge (ALJ) held the district violated the IDEA by failing to staff an IEP meeting with a person having authority to commit district resources or someone who had knowledge of the district's transportation and emergency response capabilities. The ALJ found the administration of Diastat in the event of a prolonged seizure was necessary to enable the child to receive a free appropriate public education. As a remedy, she ordered the school district to reimburse the parent for her driving expenses from the date of the due process request until the district provided a Diastat-trained aide for the child's daily bus ride. But the ALJ found the parties had both acted unreasonably.

The parent was denied 50% of her daily driving costs because she denied the district access to medical information. The IEP was to be amended to provide for a Diastat-trained aide on the bus. When the case reached a federal court, it held the child was denied a FAPE because his IEP did not include adequate health services on the school bus. The ALJ's remedy required a trained aide on the bus who would be ready to administer Diastat if the bus did not reach the child's home or school within five minutes of a seizure. Should the parent decide she wanted the child to receive Diastat without having the bus try to reach home or school, she would have to sign the doctor release form. If the bus could not reach home or school within five minutes, a trained aide could prevent an unreasonable risk to the child. Since the parties shared the blame for derailing the collaborative IEP process, the court found the ALJ was justified in ordering an amended Diastat procedure and reducing the reimbursement of transportation costs. *Oconee County School Dist.v. A.B.*, No. 3:14-CV-72, 2015 WL 4041297 (M.D. Ga. 7/1/15), 11th Cir. appeal dismissed 8/31/15.

◆   An Alabama child had a seizure disorder and other serious disabilities. Her school district had no nurse to accompany her on the school bus, so her parent transported her to and from school each day. When the family moved to California, a school district there devised an IEP addressing her transportation needs. Days before the start of the school year, the family returned to Alabama. After the parent reenrolled the child in the school she previously attended, the principal asked the parent to temporarily provide transportation. Since the child was deemed an out-of-state transfer, an IEP meeting was not held immediately.

Transportation became burdensome to the parent, and she declined the school district's demand for a transportation reimbursement contract. She claimed she should be paid hourly wages in addition to reimbursement. The district then hired a nurse to accompany the child on her bus and drafted a new IEP to specify bus transportation with medical support. But the parent requested a due process hearing, seeking compensatory education, hourly wages and reimbursement for her costs. A hearing officer denied all relief, and the parent appealed to a federal court. The court held the school district satisfied the IDEA by offering services in accordance with the California IEP. It found the district never refused to provide transportation and offered an interim arrangement that replicated the terms of the California IEP. **A school receiving a transfer student from another state generally must provide services in a preexisting IEP until an evaluation can be held.** The parent was entitled to reimbursement for her costs, but not for hourly wages. Last, the court held for the board on a Section 504 claim, finding no discrimination. *Ruby J. v. Jefferson County Board of Educ.*, 122 F.Supp.3d 1288 (N.D. Ala. 2015).

♦   A New York student's grandmother regularly picked him up after his off-campus special education program. Although his IEP included multiple special education programs and services, it did not specify the after-school program. A reference to the after-school program was included as a special alert in the student information summary section of the IEP to alert the student's teacher he would be receiving school transportation to the after-school program twice per week. After the grandmother passed away, the student's parent said he could not pick up his son from the after-school program. He said that without appropriate transportation home, the student would "eventually run away." But the district rejected the parent's request. Without seeking an impartial hearing, the parent sued the school district in a federal court. It held all of the claims were subject to the IDEA's administrative exhaustion requirement. While the parent said it would have been futile to go through the hearing process, the court disagreed. It rejected his argument that the district committed systemic IDEA violations.

Finally, the court rejected the parent's claim that a court order was necessary to remedy an emergency. **The district never failed to provide the student with necessary transportation home when he did not attend the after-school program.** As it was not shown that transportation from the after-school program to the child's home was a school district obligation or that the administrative process would not have provided relief, the case was dismissed. *Licata v. Salmon*, No. 14-CV-2637, 2015 WL 153843 (E.D.N.Y. 1/12/15).

♦   The parents of a disabled child in Hawaii sued after the state failed to reimburse them for **mileage incurred in transporting the child to school**. The case reached the Ninth Circuit, which held that the state rightly withheld reimbursement. The parents failed to provide proof of insurance and did not submit reimbursement forms as required. *Russell v. Dep't of Educ.*, 377 Fed.Appx. 595 (9th Cir. 2010).

♦   A California parent **sought a temporary order for transportation costs for her son's attendance at a charter school that was outside their district** of residence. She claimed that district officials retaliated against her for her efforts to provide a FAPE for her son and that the state department of education failed to ensure that the district would comply with its obligations under the IDEA. A federal court refused to grant the temporary relief, holding that she was not alleging irreparable harm. If she prevailed in later proceedings, she could be reimbursed for her transportation costs. *Stassart v. Lakeside School Dist.*, No. C 09-1131 JF (HRL), 2009 WL 2566717 (N.D. Cal. 8/18/09).

♦   A Maine student with cerebral palsy, visual impairments, a seizure disorder, and mental retardation received in-home services after school from a developmental disabilities provider. However, the provider could not always be at the bus stop when the student was dropped off, nor could his mother. His IEP described an informal protocol that applied when no adult was there to meet him at the bus stop. The bus driver violated the protocol on two occasions by dropping him off when no adult was there to meet him. The district offered to let him ride a special education bus, but his mother rejected that offer because it would result in increased time on the bus. A hearing officer found that the school district did not violate the IDEA, and a federal court agreed. **The student's mother here was seeking assistance related to childcare**, not special education. The district had mainstreamed the student to the maximum extent appropriate under the IDEA. *Ms. S. v. Scarborough School Committee*, 366 F.Supp.2d 98 (D. Me. 2005).

◆   The grandparents of an Ohio student with Asperger's Syndrome requested two due process hearings over two school years – once to deal with extended school year issues, and once to resolve issues relating to her return to school after worsening behavior kept her at home. Both times the grandparents reached mediated settlement agreements stating that all educational issues in dispute were resolved. However, after the tutor, provided for by the second agreement, had to stop transporting the student because he lacked the proper certification, the grandparents sued. A federal court and the Sixth Circuit ruled against them. The mediated agreements prevented court review, and **the tutor remained available except for his inability to transport the student**, so there was no breach of contract by the district. *Amy S. v. Danbury Local School Dist.*, 174 Fed.Appx. 896 (6th Cir. 2006).

◆   A South Dakota student who suffered epileptic seizures was provided transportation both to and from school by her district as a related service under the IDEA. She was accompanied by a nurse during the ride. Although parents could designate different pick-up and drop-off sites within a specific boundary, students were not transported outside the boundary unless it was necessary to obtain an educational benefit under an IEP. When the student's mother asked the district to drop off her daughter at a daycare center outside the boundary, it refused to do so. The state Office of Special Education ordered the district to pay for transportation to the daycare center, but a hearing examiner ruled that was not necessary. A federal court and the Eighth Circuit agreed that **the district did not have to provide transportation to the daycare center**. Here, the request was for the mother's own convenience and was not necessary to provide the student with educational benefit. *Fick v. Sioux Falls School Dist. 49-5*, 337 F.3d 968 (8th Cir. 2003).

CHAPTER NINE

School Liability

I. LIABILITY FOR NEGLIGENCE

Negligence is the failure to use reasonable or ordinary care under the circumstances. In order for a school district to be held liable for negligence, it must have a duty to the person claiming negligence. If a reasonably prudent person cannot foresee any danger of direct injury, there is no duty, and thus no negligence. A school district may be held liable for the acts or omissions of a negligent employee. A pattern of negligence showing a conscious disregard for safety may be "willful or wanton misconduct"– a form of intentional conduct.

The elements of a negligence claim are: 1) the existence of a legal duty to conform one's conduct to the relevant standard of care established by law,

2) a breach of that duty of care that is 3) the direct cause of the injury, and 4) damages or injury. Foreseeability of harm is also a prerequisite to liability in negligence cases. In A.W. v. Lancaster County School Dist. 0001, *784 N.W.2d 907 (Neb. 2010), the Supreme Court of Nebraska held that foreseeability questions are generally for juries, not judges, to determine.*

A. Compliance with IEP Provisions

♦   An Alabama student with cognitive and physical disabilities used a walker or wheelchair. An aide assigned to help him at school began taking him to the weight room to do his classwork. At least two other staff members saw the student and aide there at various times. A classmate reported to a parent that the aide kicked the student's wheelchair and failed to pick up a pencil he had dropped and could not retrieve. When the student's parents learned of this, they put a recording device in his wheelchair. After listening to the recordings, the parents felt they had proof that the aide and a teacher yelled at their child. They reported their suspicions, and both employees were placed on leave. The aide resigned, and the teacher's contract was not renewed. The parents sued the board in a federal court. After some of the issues were settled, the court dismissed the claims under Section 504 and ADA due to failure to administratively exhaust them. The parents filed a due process action, which was resolved. The ADA and Section 504 claims were then refiled. After discussing the parents' federal anti-discrimination claims, the court held they could not show school officials had actual knowledge of any verbal or physical abuse by the aide or the teacher.

There was no evidence of any abusive behavior toward other students by the employees. The court disagreed that taking the child to the weight room in violation of his IEP was disability discrimination. **More than noncompliance with the child's IEP had to be shown to create liability under federal law.** Last, the court held the family could not state a claim against the board based on any failure to maintain certain policies and educate students about their rights. As the family did not show that a departure from the IEP amounted to gross misjudgment, and there was no showing of intentional discrimination under the ADA or Section 504, the court held for the board of education. *J.S. v. Houston County Board of Educ.*, 120 F.Supp.3d 1287 (M.D. Ala. 2015).

♦   A New York sixth-grader crossed a busy highway to try to catch her school bus after the driver forgot to stop at her house. She was struck by a vehicle and seriously injured. A state court negligence action was filed on the student's behalf and eventually reached the New York Court of Appeals. It held a school district breaches a duty of care if it releases a child without further supervision into "a foreseeably hazardous setting it had a hand in creating." But the court rejected all three of the parent's theories of district liability. It held the injury did not take place "during the act of busing." Evidence showed the student walked onto the highway and there was also no merit to a claim that the district created a hazard. The student was not in the school district's physical custody at the time of the injury. Her mother was at home when the accident occurred.

Finally, the court found **no special duty was owed to the student by virtue of her IEP**. In fact, the IEP only directed the school district to transport her to and from school, providing her the same busing services required for all K-8 students living more than two miles from their schools. Rejecting the parent's other arguments, the court held for the school district. *Williams v. Weatherstone*, 23 N.Y. 384, 15 N.E.3d 792 (N.Y. 2014).

♦   A severely disabled Indiana student did not always chew her food and had a safety plan and a dining plan. Although the dining plan stated that the child's food had to be cut up, a paraprofessional who was assigned to her was unaware of the safety and dining plans. She did not cut up the food, and the child choked. Nobody attempted the Heimlich maneuver or tried to administer CPR. The school nurse was called, but since nobody told her the child was choking, it took her 10 minutes to arrive. Emergency responders arrived in a few minutes and restored the student's airway before taking her to a hospital. Later, school administrators visited the hospital. The student's mother said she asked the assistant principal how long the child had been without oxygen and that he responded "it was a very short period of time." The child died three days after the incident. About nine months later, a school cafeteria worker contacted the parents and said "things were not done properly." The parents filed a notice of tort claim and sued the school district in a state court for negligence, wrongful death and civil rights violations. During the pretrial fact-finding process known as discovery, the parents sought an order preserving video evidence of the incident. The court held for the district and its insurer.

Appeal reached the Supreme Court of Indiana. It found enough evidence of possible fraudulent concealment to allow the tort claims against the district to proceed. While the parents said the assistant principal told them the child was without oxygen for "a very short period of time," there was evidence she may have been without oxygen for as long as 20 minutes. In addition, school officials did not preserve video records from the day of the incident. There was evidence that the cafeteria worker who contacted the parents was threatened with retaliation. **Since a jury might find fraudulent concealment, the parents could pursue their state tort claims.** But the court dismissed their federal civil rights claims. It returned the case to the trial court with instructions for the jury. *Lyons v. Richmond Community School Corp.*, 19 N.E.3d 254 (Ind. 2014).

♦   A 15-year-old Louisiana student was hearing impaired, nonverbal and visually impaired. Because he ate too fast and often did not chew his food, his IEP required staff members to closely supervise him as he ate. While eating his breakfast at school, the student choked. A substitute teacher and an aide tried to assist him, and the school's adaptive physical education teacher also tried to help. Paramedics were unable to intubate the student because of large amounts of food in his airway. They took him to a hospital, where he later died.

In a state court, the student's estate sued the school board for negligent supervision. The court found the board negligent and awarded the estate more than $330,000 in damages. On appeal, the state court of appeal found that **a school board may be held liable for failing to adequately supervise students if there is proof of negligence**. In this case, the student's IEP said he had to be monitored to prevent him from eating too fast and swallowing food without chewing. His food was to be cut up into bite-size pieces. In the court's view, the testimony supported the estate's version of the facts. A paramedic stated that a great deal of unchewed food had been suctioned from the student's airway. **The evidence regarding the death implicated exactly what the IEP sought to prevent.** Evidence indicated the student was eating too fast and not chewing, and that food was not cut up. As a result, the court affirmed the judgment that school staff members did not adequately supervise and monitor the student according to the IEP. *Robertson v. East Baton Rouge Parish School Board*, No. 2012 CA 2039, 2013 WL 3947124 (La. Ct. App. 7/29/13).

The state's highest court later refused to review the decision. *Robertson v. East Baton Rouge Parish School Board*, 126 So.2d 472 (La. 2013).

♦   An Iowa student with a walker fell while trying to negotiate a curb outside his school. He lost four teeth and needed surgery on a broken bone. His IEP called for adult supervision at all times, but his teacher was about six feet away and his private nurse was 20 feet away when he fell. He and his mother sued the school district and various employees for negligence, but a jury determined that the defendants weren't at fault. The Iowa Court of Appeals upheld that determination. **Nothing in the IEP required a school district employee to have constant physical contact with the student's walker**, and the IEP stated that the student was independent with his walker. *Carter v. Davenport Community School Dist.*, 801 N.W.2d 628 (Iowa Ct. App. 2011).

♦   A Michigan student with brittle bone disease used a motorized wheelchair controlled by a joystick. His IEP specified that he was to receive four to six hours of paraprofessional support per day. He was injured when a fellow student accidentally hit the joystick, causing his wheelchair to run into a table, which then fell on him. His parents sued the district and three employees for negligence, asserting that the IEP wasn't followed because the students had been allowed in the computer lab without supervision. The employees sought immunity, which the Michigan Court of Appeals granted. It noted that **the IEP didn't require constant supervision by a paraprofessional**, and it held that the employees' conduct was, at worst, negligence, for which they would still be entitled to immunity. *Parent v. Lapeer Community Schools*, No. 297656, 2011 WL 2555719 (Mich. Ct. App. 6/28/11).

♦   A vulnerable high school student in Washington attended school under an IEP that placed her in a self-contained classroom and called for no contact with other students (to prevent inappropriate conduct). School staff escorted her to classes and to the bus at the end of the day. However, despite the IEP, a teacher let her use a lavatory next to her classroom unsupervised. When the student's mother learned that the student had sex with another developmentally disabled student in the lavatory, she sued the teacher for violating the student's due process rights. A federal court and the Ninth Circuit held that **there was no special relationship between the teacher and student so as to create a higher duty of care**. While the teacher may have been negligent, there was no deliberate indifference and no constitutional liability. *Patel v. Kent School Dist.*, 648 F.3d 965 (9th Cir. 2011).

B. Student Injuries

In Doe v. New Haven Board of Educ., *this chapter, the court held that for a negligence case to survive dismissal, there must be evidence that a legal duty exists which was breached. Next, the injured party must have suffered an injury that was caused by the allegedly negligent party. If a duty exists, the injured party must show the other party did not exercise reasonable care under the circumstances. It must further be shown that in the absence of the negligence, the injury would not have occurred and that the defending party's conduct was more likely than not the cause of the injury. A threshold inquiry is whether the specific harm alleged by the injured party was foreseeable. Negligence is established if a reasonable person would foresee that injuries of the same general kind would be likely to happen in the absence of adequate safeguards.*

In M.P. v. Chico Unified School Dist., *No. CO5770 (Cal. App. Ct. 2/2/09), the court clarified that students are not at risk because they are at school, and schools, including restrooms, are not dangerous places per se.*

♦ Connecticut parents sued their school district in the state court system, claiming his teacher repeatedly chose a certain classmate to accompany their child during lavatory breaks. They claimed the classmate sexually assaulted their child on more than one occasion and charged the school district with negligence. According to the parents, allowing special education students to leave a classroom unattended was unsafe and the teacher ignored their child's request that the classmate not go with him during lavatory visits. After three years of pretrial activity, the school officials sought a judgment in the case.

Finding reasonable minds could find the harm in this case was foreseeable to the school officials, the court denied pretrial judgment on the foreseeability question. Although the teacher claimed state law immunity on the theory that her decisions involved discretion and judgment, the court found the evidence was disputed. It was possible that she would not have immunity for her actions, which could be deemed "ministerial" and not protected by immunity. While the duty to supervise students or provide adequate security to protect students from classmates has generally been considered a discretionary government activity in Connecticut, exceptions apply. **Testimony by the school principal indicated she was not aware of any lavatory policy in the building and she stated there was no mandated or prescribed manner for teachers to supervise and monitor students.** As a fact issue existed regarding whether there was a school policy or directive in place creating a ministerial duty, the court denied the officials' claim to immunity. *Doe v. New Haven Board of Educ.*, No. NNHCV 1050 33148S, 2015 WL 6144099 (Conn. Super. Ct. 9/18/15).

♦ Due to pulmonary and respiratory problems, a Florida student needed medication and a breathing machine. Her medication caused significant weight gain, and she had lung disease and emphysema. The student hurt her foot while walking from lunch to a class. She reported that her teacher mocked her instead of calling the school nurse or trying to help. The student claimed he then sent her to a P.E. class, where the P.E. teacher did not inspect her foot and required her to participate in the class despite her complaints about pain. The student said she was written up for discipline and denied permission to see the nurse. She collapsed in a school hallway due to excruciating pain in her foot.

After her parent took her to an emergency room, the student was diagnosed with a metatarsal bone fracture. She returned to school in a cast and on crutches, and said the school insisted she could not use crutches without a doctor's note. Asserting constitutional rights violations and state law claims, the student's parent sued the school board in a federal court. It held an affirmative act by the state had to be "conscious shocking" in order to impose constitutional liability. In fact, very few cases had met the Eleventh Circuit's constitutional liability standard. Those cases involved extreme instances of excessive corporal punishment and student injuries. **Since no physical contact was alleged by the staff members in this case, the court held their conduct did not meet the standard for intentional and excessive corporal punishment.** Since the federal claims were dismissed, the court refused to hear the state law claims. *K.W. v. Lee County School Board*, 67 F.Supp.3d 1330 (M.D. Fla. 2014).

♦   A federal court dismissed claims filed by a 21-year-old former Texas student-athlete who said school staff members overlooked his numerous sports injuries, including concussions and dehydration. The court held Section 504 of the Rehabilitation Act "does not create general tort liability for educational malpractice." Despite voluminous evidence presented by the student, the court found nothing indicating any bad faith or gross professional misjudgment by the school district. His doctors annually cleared him to play football without imposing restrictions. There was evidence that coaches never sent the student back onto the field during a game when he suffered an injury. The only time he actually told the staff about a concussion, he avoided treatment in an attempt to stay competitive for a college football scholarship. **As there was no evidence of intentional discrimination, bad faith or gross professional misjudgment by the school district, the Section 504 claims were dismissed.** *Ripple v. Marble Falls Independent School Dist.*, 99 F.Supp.3d 662 (W.D. Tex. 2015).

♦   A Utah student who was pushed down twice by peers before transferring out of a school system was unable to show negligence by her former school district. In a federal court, she brought claims under various legal theories, asserting she was forced to leave her school system after twice being pushed down. She said that the school district failed to reasonably accommodate her health problems resulting from the incidents. Moreover, the student said at least three school employees made degrading remarks about her, including calling her "cripple" and saying she appeared to be drunk. After she withdrew from the school system, she sued the school district, asserting theories of negligence and infliction of emotional distress. She also alleged violations of the Constitution, the Americans with Disabilities Act and Rehabilitation Act Section 504.

Initially, the court rejected the student's claim that the school district violated her due process rights. It held **inaction by school officials is not enough to trigger liability for a constitutional violation.** Next, the court dismissed disability-related claims under Section 504 and the ADA. These claims asserted the school district failed to accommodate the student' disability or offer her a specialized educational program. Finding the claims were education-related, the court held she had to exhaust her administrative remedies under the IDEA before filing them in court. Since the court dismissed all of the federal claims, it declined to consider the negligence and emotional distress claims, which could go before a state court for resolution. *Harper v. Carbon County School Dist.*, 105 F.Supp.3d 1317 (D. Utah 2015).

♦ The Ohio Court of Appeals affirmed the dismissal of a case against a private school accused of feeding a student dairy products and peanuts, despite being told of his dietary restrictions. According to a parent, the student vomited on himself and the school staff refused to help him clean up. She stated that the school then made a false report to a truancy officer and also made a false report of abuse to county family authorities. Based on statements by school staff, a trial court dismissed the case. **The court of appeals disagreed with the parent's claim that the lower court had disregarded her testimony and evidence.** *Morrow v. Sacred Heart School*, No. 2015CA0004, 2015 -Ohio- 5321 (Ohio Ct. App. 12/18/15).

♦ Because of a rare, progressive neurological condition, a New Mexico student was unable to walk, talk or take care of himself. He also had severe osteoporosis. On a morning at his elementary school, the student began crying and his aide removed him from class. She later stated that his leg was "swollen like a balloon." At a medical center, it was determined that the student had a spiral fracture of the femur. He died nine months after breaking his leg.

The student's parents sued the school system in a state court for negligence. The court found the school system owed the student a duty of care to handle him in a way that minimized the stress upon his bones. But due to his weak bones, the student was subject to a fracture (including a spiral fracture) from virtually any routine and non-negligent handling. Finding the school did not breach its duty to the student, the court held for the school system. The parents appealed to the Supreme Court of New Mexico. It noted expert testimony indicated the injury could have resulted from a minimal force. Even the parents' expert had stated a fracture could be the result of any care maneuver, such as putting on clothes, turning over in bed or bathing. Her statements supported a finding that the student could have suffered a fracture from virtually any non-negligent handling. **As the trial court had found, due to the very weak state of his bones the injury could have been caused either by negligent or non-negligent handling.** Since the parents did not show their child's injury could not have occurred in the absence of a negligent act by the school, the court affirmed the judgment for the school system. *Nez v. Gallup-McKinley Public Schools*, No. 31,728, 2014 WL 1314937 (N.M. 2/17/14).

♦ A Colorado student had blindness, cerebral palsy and cognitive delays. Her school invited students to a ski trip hosted by an education center. Among the documents sent to parents before the trip was a waiver and release form. By signing the form, students acknowledged that they shared the responsibility for safety during all activities. The form recited that outdoor programs created unknown and not reasonably foreseeable risks. Parents assumed all the risks and responsibility for damages, injury, disability or death, and the form released the education center and its employees from all claims. Both the student and her parent signed the release. On her first day of skiing, the student was injured while on a bi-ski with her instructor. In the family's lawsuit against the center based on negligence and gross negligence, a federal magistrate judge held the waiver form barred the negligence claim. Pretrial judgment was denied regarding the gross negligence claim, but a jury later found no liability.

On appeal, the U.S. Court of Appeals, Tenth Circuit, found the release was a clear and unambiguous waiver of liability. The parent claimed she was not notified of specific risks relating to bi-skis. But the court found Colorado law did not require waivers to specify the at-risk activity. A cover letter from the school referred to "your ski lesson" and identified bi-skis as among the adaptive ski methods to be used. The waiver form explained the impossibility of guaranteeing absolute safety and noted the possibility of unknown risks. **Although the parent may not have expected the precise incident that led to injury in this case, this did not invalidate the waiver.** There was no merit to the parent's claim that she was fraudulently induced to sign the waiver. As a result, the court affirmed the judgment for the education center. *Squires v. Breckenridge Outdoor Educ. Center*, 715 F.3d 867 (10th Cir. 2013).

♦ In the hallway of his high school, a Washington student was fatally shot by a student with disabilities. In a state court, the student's family said the disabled student's behavior and medical records indicated he was at risk for harming others. Evidence was produced that the disabled student was diagnosed with paranoid schizophrenia after attempting suicide two years earlier. After being hospitalized, he underwent 11 months of outpatient care and was prescribed anti-psychotic medication. There was evidence that the disabled student had transferred often and attended at least four different high schools. But there was no evidence he had committed any assaults. During the year of his suicide attempt, the disabled student was categorized as emotionally behaviorally disabled. In pretrial activity, the court rejected the estate's theories of liability.

The case went before the Court of Appeals of Washington. It held school districts must exercise reasonable care when supervising students. But the duty to exercise reasonable care extends only to foreseeable risks of harm. Although the court agreed with the estate that foreseeability is normally a jury question, it pointed out that a trial judge has authority to make the decision if "reasonable minds cannot differ." **As nothing in school or medical records indicated the disabled student presented a risk of harm to anyone at school, the court found the shooting was not foreseeable.** The court found the estate's arguments ignored state and federal antidiscrimination laws and obligations requiring schools to provide appropriate educational opportunities to students with disabilities. As it was not foreseeable to the school district that the student would act violently, the court affirmed the judgment for the district. *Kok v. Tacoma School Dist. No. 10*, 177 Wash.App. 1016 (Wash. Ct. App. 2013). (Wash. review denied), 180 Wash.2d 1016, 327 P.3d 55 (Wash. 2014).

♦ The parents of five nonverbal children with autism sued a Nevada school district for civil rights violations and negligence, alleging that a teacher who had been fired had abused their children, grabbing them by the neck and forcibly moving them. The district sought pretrial judgment, arguing that it conducted a background check on the teacher and required her to take autism-specific training before working in district classrooms despite her 10 years of autism classroom experience. Thus, it could not be liable for negligent hiring, training or supervision. A federal court allowed the case to proceed. **There was an issue of fact as to whether the district had acted appropriately.** *Ferguson v. Clark County School Dist.*, No. 2:08–CV–31 JCM (GWF), 2012 WL 1963607 (D. Nev. 5/31/12).

◆ An Alabama student with ADHD went to the lavatory with two classmates and injured herself trying to climb over a jammed stall door. Her family sued the teacher and the school board, claiming that she shouldn't have been allowed to visit the lavatory without teacher supervision even though she was not assigned to a special education program. The Alabama Supreme Court disagreed, finding the board and teacher entitled to immunity. **No school rule or policy required teachers to go with students to the restroom, and the student had done so unsupervised in the past without incident.** *Ex Parte Montgomery County Board of Educ.*, 88 So.3d 837 (Ala. 2012).

◆ A Kentucky student with severe visual impairments fell from improperly retracted bleachers at a pre-school program and was badly hurt. His family sued a number of school officials, alleging that the school failed to provide a safe environment and that he was unsupervised at the time of the fall. The school officials asked for immunity, but the Kentucky Court of Appeals held that not all of them were entitled to it. **Only those officials not on school grounds and not responsible for student safety were entitled to immunity.** The other officials would have to defend their actions at trial. *Marson v. Thomason*, No. 2010–CA–002319–MR, 2012 WL 876754 (Ky. Ct. App. 3/16/12).

◆ An Ohio student with a cognitive disability often acted inappropriately in class. He was also involved in a number of incidents outside of class, some of which he initiated. His parents complained that he was being bullied. After his nose was broken in a fight, his parents hired an attorney and the school devised a safety plan, which the parents approved. However, they asserted that the bullying continued, and they sued. A federal court ruled against them, finding no evidence to suggest that school officials increased the student's exposure to teasing or bullying. Also, **the school took action to protect him whenever it learned of bullying incidents**. And most of the incidents occurred outside of class. *Doe v. Big Walnut Local School Dist. Board of Educ.*, No. 2:09-CV-0367, 2011 WL 3204686 (S.D. Ohio 7/27/11).

◆ A Michigan student suffered from cerebral palsy and epileptic seizures. One day, her paraprofessional either hit her or shoved her to the ground, and she suffered a seizure. She went home early but returned to school the next day. However, she died in a hospital a few days later. After the paraprofessional was fired, the student's estate sued the principal and paraprofessional. A federal court dismissed the constitutional claims against the principal but allowed the claims against the paraprofessional to proceed. **The most that was alleged**

against the principal was negligent training and supervision, which wasn't enough to amount to a constitutional violation. *Shinn v. Detroit Public Schools*, No. 09-13799, 2011 WL 346482 (E.D. Mich. 2/2/11).

C. Allergies, Asthma and Other Medical Conditions

♦   A sixth-grade Philadelphia student died from an asthma attack. According to a complaint against her school district, her teacher, principal and other staff knew of her chronic asthma. On the morning of the student's death, she told her teacher she was having trouble breathing. The teacher responded that no nurse was on duty and that she "should be calm." Although her condition worsened, the complaint alleged that nobody contacted emergency medical aid or took her to the hospital. Instead, it was asserted that she was kept at school despite having reported that she could not breathe. Later in the day, the student was driven home and then immediately taken to a hospital. On the way, she suffered a respiratory arrest. Emergency workers and hospital staff were unable to revive the student. Later, a medical examiner declared her cause of death to be acute exacerbation of asthma. In pretrial activity, the court refused to dismiss claims against the school district. **There was evidence that the student was kept at school and denied medical care or permission to take asthma medication.**

As an intentional violation of rights was asserted, the court denied the school district's request for a pretrial ruling. A claim for deprivation of life and liberty was also not dismissed at the present time, as facts were alleged to support a state-created danger claim. Since willful misconduct was alleged, the court denied the district's request for immunity under state law. *Estate of Massey v. City of Philadelphia*, 118 F.Supp.3d 679 (E.D. Pa. 2015).

♦   A Washington student with diabetes and hearing loss had to undergo blood sugar testing every two or three hours. Her mother and grandmother came to school to monitor her blood sugar levels throughout the school day. Later, the mother said the district failed to develop a plan for diabetic care. She demanded that the school district provide her child blood sugar monitoring throughout the day by a licensed health care provider. In response, the district stated that within a few days, the child would be transferred to another school. The parent objected, finding the abrupt transition would jeopardize her child's education.

Near this time, the parent said the voice amplification systems provided to her child did not work. In response, the school seated a paraeducator next to the student to help with class instructions. But the parent believed this contravened provisions of the IEP which required the student to become more independent. By mid-year, the parent withdrew her child from school and requested a due process hearing. An administrative law judge found the district failed to provide the student a free appropriate public education and awarded her 520 hours of private tutoring. **A federal court held a reasonable jury could find the offer to transfer the child on only two days' notice amounted to deliberate indifference to her known disabilities.** This led the court to deny the school district's request for pretrial judgment. Given the child's IEP goal of increasing her independent development, the court found the parent raised a valid issue regarding accommodations for her hearing loss. Since the parent's arguments under state law resembled her successful federal claims, the court held those claims should also proceed. *Snell v. North Thurston School Dist.*, No. C13-5786 RBL, 2015 WL 6396092 (W.D. Wash. 10/21/15).

♦   A Colorado student with hypoglycemia, asthma and a muscular/skeletal weakness claimed her charter school required her to participate in a "human pyramid" and delayed providing necessary nutrition. She said she became dizzy and fell while standing on the backs of two classmates and was injured because no mat or other protection was there. According to the student, classmates verbally and physically harassed her over several months. She said she reported this, but school officials took no action. Largely due to bullying, the student withdrew from the school. In a federal court, the student's parent sued the charter school and the school district in which it was located for negligence, disability discrimination and constitutional rights violations.

The court dismissed the claims against the charter school, finding it could not be sued as an entity separate from the school district. The court then granted the school district immunity from any liability for the human pyramid incident under the state Governmental Immunity Act. It found the exception to state law immunity sought by the student applies only to injuries arising from dangerous conditions in public buildings. But the court held the disability discrimination claims failed because **the student did not allege that the bullying was based solely upon a disability**. It was not alleged that the human pyramid and snack deprivation incidents related to a disability. In the court's view, the conduct was not shocking to the conscience and no "state-created danger" existed. *Dorsey v. Pueblo School Dist. 60*, 140 F.Supp.3d 1102 (D. Colo. 2015).

♦   A Pennsylvania student with a severe nut allergy was deemed at risk of life-threatening allergic reactions. Although at least four meetings were held to develop a Section 504 accommodation plan, no agreement was reached. Although the district offered new Section 504 plan proposals, the parents rejected each of them – even one that had been approved by the student's doctor.

A hearing officer found the district did not discriminate against the student or deny him a free appropriate public education. Appeal reached the U.S. Court of Appeals, Third Circuit. It found a Section 504 plan relating to food allergies had to be accessible and understandable to staff in the event of an emergency. District teachers and staff were trained to identify symptoms of anaphylaxis and to administer epinephrine. The court held the failure to include each requested accommodation and detail requested by the parents was not a Section 504 violation. **There was evidence that the district worked diligently with the parents to ensure their child participated in school activities and had access to educational benefits.** Since the parents did not show their child was denied program benefits or subjected to discrimination, the court held for the school district. *T.F. v. Fox Chapel Area School Dist.*, 589 Fed.Appx. 594 (3d Cir. 2014).

♦   A Washington child had asthma and life-threatening allergies. After arriving at school, she had trouble breathing. Staff members felt she was having an asthma attack. They did not consider that she might be having an allergic reaction and did not use epinephrine. A call was made to 911, but no one used

CPR or followed an emergency healthcare plan prepared by the school nurse. By the time emergency responders arrived, the child had stopped breathing and lost consciousness. The child died while being transported to a hospital. In a state court, her parents sued the school district, health clerk and school nurse for negligence. A medical examiner attributed the child's death to asthma. By contrast, the family's expert stated she had more likely died of anaphylaxia. After a long and contentious trial, jurors found the district, clerk and nurse negligent, but found any negligence did not cause the death.

A series of post-trial motions seeking a new trial was rejected, and the family appealed to the state court of appeals. A primary theory by the parents was that the jury made inconsistent findings. In the court's view, there was no inconsistency in the jury verdict with regard to causation of death. **It was not inconsistent to find staff negligence did not cause death, if there was evidence that death would have occurred without regard to staff members' actions.** The jury could have found that even if staff errors amounted to negligence, the student still would have died because of her emergency. The same was true of a negligent supervision claim, since the jury found better supervision would not have helped her. Since the jury findings were not clearly contradictory and substantial evidence supported them, the court found no error. As the parents' arguments lacked merit, it held for the district, nurse and clerk. *Mears v. Bethel School Dist. No. 403*, 332 P.3d 1077 (Wash. Ct. App. 2014).

◆   The New York City Department of Education (DOE) placed a child with autism, asthma and a wide range of food and substance allergies in a New Jersey private school. A registered nurse accompanied him throughout each school day, and at least one epi-pen had to be at hand at all times. But no IEP provision required that a nurse sit next to him. A teacher noticed the student was red in the face and seemed agitated after he had attended a lesson about blueberries. He was seated at least five feet away from a basket of blueberries, and nobody saw him touching the berries. At the end of his lunch period, the student reported trouble breathing, and he asked for his asthma medication. His breathing did not improve, and he became agitated. The nurse administered epi-pens. An ambulance was called about 10 minutes after symptoms were first noticed, but it did not arrive for 20 minutes. The student was taken to a hospital, where he died two days later. The parent sued the DOE and the private school. She added claims against the nurse for malpractice and negligence.

Although the court awarded judgment to the DOE, the court denied it to the private school and nurse. Appeal reached the New York Supreme Court, Appellate Division, which held **the DOE's obligation to provide the student a free appropriate public education did not impose a duty to supervise the student while he was in the private school's custody**. The court rejected the parent's theory that the nurse was a school employee. It held the school adequately supervised the classroom. No IEP provision required a nurse to stay by the student's side at all times. It appeared that the school took reasonable steps to protect the student by alerting teachers and staff about his allergies and taking adequate precautions. School personnel called 911 within minutes after the student began showing signs of distress. **While the mother theorized that blueberries may have been the triggering substance, the student had never**

been tested for a reaction to blueberries. She admitted that she had never actually learned what triggered her son's reaction. The court rejected her other arguments and held for the DOE, private school and the nurse. *Begley v. City of New York*, 111 A.D.3d 5, 972 N.Y.S.2d 48 (N.Y. App. Div. 2013).

◆ To help manage their child's Type 1 diabetes, Tennessee parents used equipment that recorded her blood glucose levels and communicated with a pump to supply insulin as needed. For some three years, the parents and school administrators and staff could not agree upon accommodations for the child. The parents insisted on testing her glucose levels manually four times per day in the classroom. The school offered to conduct the testing in its clinic. Two school nurses quit based on their belief that they were exposed to liability, and a third nurse threatened to quit. The principal initially rejected a teacher's wish to file an abuse report on the parents with the state Department of Children's Services (DCS). By the next school year, the parties' relationship deteriorated further and school officials discussed placing the child on homebound services.
 Tensions increased over the issue of in-class blood glucose testing. The principal called the DCS after a school nurse found the child's glucose levels were high. Near this time, the principal reported that a teacher had suffered an "anxiety attack" due to "constant harassment" by the parents. She said they failed to monitor the child at home and claimed to have "documentation on this neglect." After a few weeks, the DCS closed the case as unfounded. In a federal court, the parents claimed the DCS reports were retaliatory. When the case reached the U.S. Court of Appeals, Sixth Circuit, it found evidence that the DCS reports were retaliatory. People with Type 1 diabetes may have sweets so long as sugar is measured and compensated for with insulin. **Extensive records showed the parents were taking necessary precautions, and the principal knew Type 1 diabetes "had nothing to do with lifestyle choices."** Since the DCS reports were "arguably false and suspiciously timed," the case would proceed. *A.C. v. Shelby County Board of Educ.*, 711 F.3d 687 (6th Cir. 2013).

◆ Due to a Michigan student's severe, life-threatening allergy to nuts, his school district made his school nut free. The parent of another child attending the school claimed the schoolwide ban on nuts infringed upon their rights. She sued the school district in a state court, seeking to overcome the school ban on nuts. When the case reached the Court of Appeals of Michigan, it held that neither the challenging parent nor her daughter had been parties to the Section 504 plan created for the allergic student. For this reason, neither of them had standing to challenge the allergic student's 504 plan. **The court held the district had authority to adopt a schoolwide ban on nuts**, given the finding that a ban was necessary for the allergic student's safety. As there was no merit to any of the parent's claims, the court held for the district. *Liebau v. Romeo Community Schools*, No. 306979, 2013 WL 3942392 (Mich. Ct. App. 7/30/13).

◆ The parents of a California student with a nut allergy were told by the principal that there would no longer be a nut-free table in the cafeteria, but that their son could eat lunch in the office. At a school playground event, the student was given a cookie with peanut butter, and he required medical treatment. The parents reported the incident to the state board of education, and the principal then made statements to doctors that resulted in the filing of a child protective services report. **The parents sued the school, claiming that the principal violated their constitutional rights by making false statements.** The district sought to have the case dismissed, but a federal court refused to do so. The lawsuit alleged that special needs students were denied accommodations and were subsequently removed from their families without probable cause based on reports by the principal. *McCue v. South Fork Union Elementary School*, No. 1:10-CV-00233-OWW-MJS, 2011 WL 2118572 (E.D. Cal. 5/24/11).

D. Injuries to Nonstudents

♦   **A North Carolina court held a school board had immunity in a case filed by a wheelchair-bound school visitor who claimed she was injured due to a fall caused by unsafe conditions.** The Court of Appeals of North Carolina held a recent state supreme court decision clarified that immunity applies to acts performed pursuant to a "governmental" function. State law vests school boards with ownership and control of school property. Since the conduct was "governmental" in nature, the board had immunity from any liability. *Bellows v. Asheville City Board of Educ.*, 777 S.E.2d 522 (N.C. Ct. App. 2015).

♦   A New York nurse slipped and fell on urine in a lavatory while assisting a student who had a seizure. She sued the district for negligence. A state court held for the school district, but an appellate court reversed, finding **issues of fact as to whether the district had notice of the hazardous condition** and sufficient time to clean up the floor. *Goodyear v. Putnam/Norther Westchester Board of Cooperative Educ. Services*, 927 N.Y.S.2d 373 (N.Y. App. Div. 2011).

♦   A New York child with severe autism hit and kicked an occupational therapist, who then sued the child's parents and the district for negligence. An appellate court upheld a ruling against the therapist because the parents had no ability to control their child in school. They had **no duty to warn the therapist because the therapist knew of the student's condition**, and it could also be readily observed. *Johnson v. Cantie*, 905 N.Y.S.2d 384 (N.Y. App. Div. 2010).

♦   A New York City special education teacher initiated a Type Three referral to remove an aggressive student from her class and contemplated quitting because of his behavior. Her supervisors told her to "hang in there" because a Type Three referral could take up to 60 days. Forty-one days after the referral was initiated, the student attacked another child, and the teacher intervened. She was hurt while attempting to protect the other child from the aggressor. She then sued the city for negligence, alleging that a "special relationship" supported her claim. A jury awarded her more than $512,000, but the New York Court of Appeals struck down the award. It noted that **the teacher had no rational basis for relying on the assurances of the board of education**. Thus, she was not lulled into a false sense of security that justified a finding of liability against the board. *DiNardo v. City of New York*, 921 N.E. 2d 585 (N.Y. 2009).

♦ An Ohio school aide supervised an autistic student who had previously injured fellow students on the bus. The aide rode with the student on the bus, and was hit and bitten by the student on one occasion. Later, the aide accompanied the student on a field trip to a bowling alley, where the aide intervened to protect another student from the autistic student's attack. The aide sued the school board for negligence and civil rights violations, asserting a "state-created danger" theory. A federal court and the Sixth Circuit ruled in favor of the school board, noting that **the state did not create the danger or increase the risk to the aide**. The board was attempting to discharge its duties under the IDEA at the time of the injury. *Hunt v. Sycamore Community School Dist. Board of Educ.*, 542 F.3d 529 (6th Cir. 2008).

E. Suicide

Suicide has historically been viewed by the courts as an intervening event that breaks the chain of legal causation and precludes tort liability. In addition, many court decisions have found a student suicide could not have been foreseen by school officials.

♦ A 10-year-old Illinois student was found hanging by his shirt collar on the back of a school restroom stall door. He died the next day. A medical examiner ruled his death a suicide. In a state court, the student's mother sued the school district for negligence and willful and wanton conduct. The court dismissed the case, finding the district was entitled to immunity. But the mother was given permission to file a new complaint. After the court dismissed the case, she was allowed to file a third complaint. Unlike the first two complaints, the mother now claimed students at the school played a "hanging game" in the lavatory. She said police investigators found evidence that the game was being played in the stall where her son had been found hanging. The court held the mother again failed to show any evidence that the death was foreseeable to the school district.

Regardless of whether the death was caused by suicide or a hanging game, the parent did not show any connection between the death and actions by the school district. On appeal, the Appellate Court of Illinois held no facts showed any special duty to the student or negligence in failing to alert teachers about his mental health history. No negligence regarding a hanging game had been asserted and the claim relating to it had been properly dismissed. **Under Illinois law, a party may not recover in a tort case for suicide, because the act of suicide is an intervening event that is not foreseeable.** No facts were asserted to show the student was depressed or having suicidal ideas. The mother failed to show staff members should be aware of any particular danger or acted in a willful and wanton manner. Even if the court had found the claims were sufficient to proceed, the school district would be entitled to immunity under the Illinois Tort Immunity Act. *Marshall v. Evanston Skokie School Dist. 65*, No. 1-13-1654, 2015 IL App (1st) 131654-U (Ill. Ct. App. 3/27/15).

♦ Due to Tourette's syndrome, ADHD and another condition, a New York student received special education. According to a federal court complaint filed after his suicide death, he was subjected to teasing, taunting, bullying, name-calling, violence, offensive touching, hitting and other misconduct by peers. But the estate claimed this conduct was minimized, dismissed and ignored by the school district. In pretrial activity, the court found the only specific facts in the estate's papers pertained to isolated events taking place some seven months prior to the suicide. The court explained that the Due Process Clause of the Fourteenth Amendment is a limit on state power, not a guarantee of safety and security. There was no special relationship or state-created danger in this case.

The court found no individual school employee was liable for a due process violation. While the estate claimed there had been an equal protection violation, the court held it was not shown that the student was treated differently from his peers. Retaliation claims under the First Amendment and Section 504 also failed. State and federal constitutional claims against the board of education failed because there was no showing of a district-wide policy or custom of due process violations. While the estate argued the district violated the Americans with Disabilities Act and Section 504, the court held the "brief references to Gregory exhibiting 'disability related tics' fails to describe the impairment of a major life activity." **According to the court, the fact that the student received special education did not automatically qualify him for protection under Section 504 and the ADA.** As the federal claims all failed, the court dismissed them. The estate could pursue the state law claims in a state court. *Spring v. Allegany-Limestone Cent. School Dist.*, 138 F.Supp.3d 282 (W.D.N.Y. 2015).

♦　Alabama parents of a 15-year-old student with disabilities who committed suicide sought to impose federal law liability on school officials. They claimed the officials knew about peer harassment and bullying but failed to address it. A federal court rejected the parents' theory that any school employee named in the lawsuit had authority to take corrective action to end peer harassment. While the bullying alleged in this case was severe, the court rejected the family's claim that the bullying was so open and obvious that anyone at the school would know it was taking place. **Only actual knowledge of peer harassment could trigger school liability under Title IX of the 1972 Education Amendments.** Of the three identified school employees who might have some knowledge of misconduct, only the assistant principal had the ability to take corrective measures in response to bullying complaints. But the parents did not prove he knew of the bullying or had even heard about it. Since the parents could not show an "appropriate person" with the authority to act to end the bullying had actual knowledge of any misconduct, the court held for the board of education. *Moore v. Chilton County Board of Educ.*, 1 F.Supp.3d 1281 (M.D. Ala. 2014).

♦　A Delaware teacher told an intervention specialist who contracted with her school district that a student was contemplating suicide. The specialist met with the student for four hours, decided he was feeling better and sent him back to class. Although the specialist emailed the student's teacher, an administrator and school counselors about the meeting, she did not advise the student's grandmother, who was his guardian. That evening, the student hanged himself at home. In a state court, his estate sued the school district under the state wrongful death statute. The court held for the district. On appeal, the Supreme Court of Delaware held the lower court had properly held for the school district on the wrongful death statute claim, as the district had no duty of care to prevent a suicide. No Delaware case suggested there could be liability for an injury to a high school student based on failure to alert medical professionals or parents.

Moreover, the suicide took place while he was at home and out of the school's custody. But the district maintained guidelines for handling suicidal ideation, and school counselors, nurses and psychologists had to follow them. The court found that the school protocol was created to comply with a state regulation requiring emergency preparedness guidelines for each school. The regulation called for schools to immediately contact the parents or guardians of a child who was clearly dangerous to himself or others. In the court's view, **failure to follow the mandated procedures of the protocol amounted to negligence per se**. District procedures directed a school counselor to stay with a student, assess the student, contact parents, get help, document the case and follow up. As the specialist's failure to contact the family was negligence per se, the court reversed the judgment and returned the case to the lower court. *Rogers v. Christina School Dist.*, 73 A.3d 1 (Del. 2013).

II. LIABILITY FOR INTENTIONAL CONDUCT

Parties injured as the result of intentional conduct often seek to hold school districts and their officials liable for constitutional rights violations. Defamation, assault, battery and false imprisonment are some of the intentional tort theories of liability advanced in court actions against school districts and their employees. Courts have rejected constitutional claims for school liability based on intentional conduct except where a "special relationship" exists between the victim and district and there is proof of an official policy of deliberate indifference to the victim's clearly established constitutional rights.

A. School Employees

◆ New York parents said a school bus monitor physically and mentally abused their severely disabled child on a school bus. Asserting the school district knew of the monitor's propensity for misconduct, the parents sued her and the school district in a state court for negligence, assault and battery. After the court held for the bus monitor and the district, the parents appealed. A New York Appellate Division Court recited the general rule that **schools have a duty to adequately supervise students in their care and may be held liable for foreseeable injuries related to the absence of adequate supervision**. In this case, there was evidence that the school received prior complaints of the bus driver's misbehavior toward children on the school bus. As a result, the court reversed the judgment on the claim for negligent supervision of the child.

Similarly, the court held the claims for negligent supervision and training of the monitor should not have been dismissed. It held the parents had to show the district knew (or should have known) of the monitor's propensity for the conduct causing injury. Since the school district failed to prove it had no specific knowledge of the monitor's propensity to engage in misconduct, the negligent supervision and training claim would also return to the trial court. As the parents had established a preliminary case for assault, the case was returned to the lower court for reconsideration. *Timothy Mc. v. Beacon City School Dist.*, 127 A.D.3d 826, 7 N.Y.S.3d 348 (N.Y. App. Div. 2015).

♦   A Washington grandparent said she heard a teacher yelling at her special needs granddaughter before she arrived at the classroom to observe him. She said that when she entered the room, the teacher had the child "pinned against the wall" and that the child's face was covered with spit as the result of the teacher's continuing tirade against her. In a state court, the grandparent sued the school district and teacher and raised a variety of claims. Eventually, the claims were narrowed to assault, battery and outrage. During pretrial activity, the school district sought to dismiss the case, presenting the court with a radically different explanation of the incident than that of the grandmother. In addition, the district said her account of the incident "became progressively worse over time."

Noting the grandparent did not present evidence that the teacher acted intentionally, the court awarded pretrial judgment to the school district. Appeal then went before the Court of Appeals of Washington. It held the grandparent had presented enough evidence to create a jury question on the assault and battery claims. It was not appropriate for a judge to resolve inconsistencies in the grandparent's account. **While the school district complained that the grandparent's statements were self-serving, the court noted she was an eyewitness whose statements were based on personal observations.** Inconsistencies in her testimony would have to be resolved by a jury. The appeals court returned the assault and battery claims to the lower court. *Sutton v. Tacoma School Dist. No. 10*, 324 P.3d 763 (Wash. Ct. App. 2014).

♦   Due to a neuromascular disorder, a Florida student had difficulty holding her head up and had to be positioned in her wheelchair. Her parents often noted concerns that staff members did not properly secure her wheelchair and did not properly position her in her chair. Midway through the school year, the mother received a call from a bus attendant, asking her to come to the bus as the child was unable to breathe. When she arrived, she found her child "unresponsive, blue, and not breathing." She tried to resuscitate her child, then called 911.

Although the child was airlifted to a hospital, she died the next day. In a federal court action against the school board and district, the mother charged school staff with taking no action to resuscitate her child or call 911. She stated that the child had been improperly positioned and secured on the bus. In seeking to hold the board and district liable for her child's death, the mother asserted claims under Section 504, the Americans with Disabilities Act and 42 U.S.C. § 1983. **According to the parents, the school staff had a poor record of complying with their instructions to keep their child's head upright.** They recited events during the past 14 years, which they claimed established a pattern of deliberate indifference to the well-being and safety of exceptional students. While the board argued the complaint did not meet the relevant "deliberate indifference" standard, the court found the parents stated sufficient facts to avoid pretrial dismissal of the case. *Herrera v. Hillsborough County School Board*, No. 8:12-cv-2484-T-30EAJ, 2013 WL 3063721 (M.D. Fla. 6/18/13).

♦ Due to her child's asthma, a Missouri mother did not authorize the H1-N1 vaccination on a school consent form. Although the student told the nurse his mother did not consent to the vaccination, the nurse administered the vaccine anyway. His mother sued the school board for negligence and constitutional rights violations under 42 U.S.C. § 1983. A federal court dismissed the claims, and the Eighth Circuit affirmed. **Any substantive due process claim required proof of "conscience-shocking behavior," and that did not happen here.** Also, the Fourth Amendment claim for unlawful search and seizure failed because the student himself had not "refused to consent to this minimally invasive procedure." Instead, he only informed the nurse of his mother's refusal to consent to the vaccination. *B.A.B. v. Board of Educ. of City of St. Louis*, 698 F.3d 1037 (8th Cir. 2012).

♦ The mother of a New York student who had Asperger's syndrome claimed that their school district retaliated against her for complaining about her child's education. She asserted that the district falsely reported her to child protection services. However, a federal court ruled for the district. It noted that **she never lost custody of her son, so even though the district's call to child protection services may have been infuriating, she could not show a due process violation**. *McCaul v. Ardsley Union Free School Dist.*, No. 11 CV 5586(VB), 2012 WL 1898897 (S.D.N.Y. 5/3/12).

♦ An Illinois teacher had to deal with a violent autistic student whose parents refused to move him into an alternative setting. His violent outbursts became so common that teachers stopped documenting each occurrence. When he reached grade three, the teacher said she could no longer deal with him, but the principal declined her request for reassignment. Eventually, the student attacked the teacher with a chair. She suffered injuries and, after collecting workers' compensation benefits, sued the district for constitutional violations. A federal court and the Seventh Circuit held that **while the principal's actions may have been negligent, there was no constitutional rights violation**. *Jackson v. Indian Prairie School Dist. 204*, 653 F.3d 647 (7th Cir. 2011).

♦ A Florida teacher tried to break up a fight between two disabled students instead of calling the trained first responders she was supposed to call and simply using verbal commands to try to stop the fighting. She fell on her knee during the action and sustained injuries. Later, she sued the school board, asserting intentional conduct that qualified for an exception to the exclusivity of workers' compensation. However, the court of appeal ruled against her, noting that she was only entitled to collect workers' compensation for her injuries. She **failed to follow the school policy** requiring her to give only verbal instructions to the fighters until trained staff could arrive. *Patrick v. Palm Beach County School Board*, 50 So.3d 1161 (Fla. Dist. Ct. App. 2010).

♦ A South Carolina special education teacher formed a close bond with a student and let him use her car. She also gave him school computer passwords and wrote him excuses from his classes. The principal, after learning of her activity, fired her. She was also arrested and charged with contributing to the delinquency of a minor, but the charges were dropped. Later, the principal told a staff member that she had "cleaned [them] out," referring to the fact that when she left, she took a great deal of equipment that she had purchased. She sued the principal for defamation, among other claims, and the state court of appeals held that **she could pursue the defamation claim against the principal** because she was accused of a crime involving moral turpitude. *McBride v. School Dist. of Greenville County*, 698 S.E.2d 845 (S.C. Ct. App. 2010).

B. Abuse and Sexual Abuse Reporting

In Walker v. State of Maryland, *this chapter, Maryland's highest court held that intimate, though not sexually explicit letters from a paraeducator to an eight-year-old student with disabilities supported a sexual abuse conviction.*

♦   An Ohio preschool teacher noticed a three-year-old child had a bloodshot eye. When she asked what happened, he gave conflicting answers. The teacher brought the child under the light and noticed red marks on his face. She told the lead teacher, who lifted the child's shirt and noticed more injuries. After some prodding, the child identified his mother's boyfriend as the perpetrator. One of the teachers called a child protection hotline to report suspected abuse. When the boyfriend arrived at school to pick up the child, he denied responsibility for the injuries and quickly left with the child. The next day, a social worker took the child and his 18-month old sister from their grandparent's home. A doctor discovered injuries suggesting child abuse. The child had a black eye, belt marks and bruises. His sister had black eyes, a swollen hand, a large burn, and two of her pigtails had been ripped out at the roots. At the boyfriend's criminal trial, the court allowed the child's statements to his teachers to come into evidence. In doing so, the court denied the boyfriend's attempt to exclude the statements from evidence under the Confrontation Clause of the Constitution.

A jury found the boyfriend guilty on all but one of the counts, and he was sentenced to 28 years in prison. But he obtained reversal by higher courts in the Ohio court system, which held the child's statements were "testimonial" and geared toward gathering evidence, not in response to an emergency. On appeal, the U.S. Supreme Court noted the state court's view that the teachers acted as state agents under a mandatory reporting law, implicating the Confrontation Clause of the Sixth Amendment to the U.S. Constitution. In general, the Sixth Amendment prohibits testimonial statements of witnesses who do not testify at trial. In the Court's view, **the child's statements took place in the context of an ongoing emergency involving suspected child abuse and were not made with the primary purpose of creating evidence** for the prosecution. Use of his statements did not violate the Confrontation Clause. When teachers noticed the injuries, they "rightly became worried" that the child was a victim of serious violence. They needed to know whether it was safe to release him to his guardian and to find the source of his injuries. The teachers were not sure who had abused the child and how to secure his safety. Since the teachers' questioning was primarily aimed at identifying and ending the threat of harm to the child, the Court held for the state. *Ohio v. Clark*, 135 S.Ct. 2173 (U.S. 2015).

◆   An Ohio school administrator told teachers to document comments by a 17-year-old student. One of the teachers noted that during a classroom discussion about menstruation and hygiene, the student said her "dad puts her tampons in her and it really hurts her." The teacher also noted the student said "sometimes she and her dad lick each other on the faces and necks" and "her whole family hangs around the house naked sometimes." In addition, the teacher wrote the child told her "her Dad put her cream on her vagina for her." Despite knowledge of these and other strange comments, the administrator told the teachers not to report them. When the administrator finally made a report to child protection authorities, she added irrelevant information about the father, describing him as "unkempt," "creepy" and obsessed about a boyfriend for his daughter.

A criminal investigation of the father was dropped, and he sued the director and other officials in a federal court. When the case reached the U.S. Court of Appeals, Sixth Circuit, it agreed with the parent that the administrator's report was motivated at least in part by his protected conduct. **A child abuse report that was made for a partly retaliatory motive could be grounds for liability,** even if there was some evidence of a reasonable basis to suspect child abuse or neglect. Since the court found a reasonable official in the administrator's position would have understood that she violated the parent's right to be free from retaliation for exercising his constitutional rights, the court held she would have no immunity in the case. *Wenk v. O'Reilly*, 783 F.3d 585 (6th Cir. 2015).

◆   A Florida parent said her disabled child was sexually assaulted at school. In a federal court action against the school board, she advanced claims based on the Equal Protection Clause and Americans with Disabilities Act. She added state law claims for infliction of emotional distress. The court dismissed the case but allowed the parent to file an amended complaint. She did so, asserting that after she reported the assault, her child was transferred to a different and even more hostile school environment where she was again sexually assaulted.

The court found the complaint was essentially identical to the one it had already held insufficient. Appeal then went before the U.S. Court of Appeals, Eleventh Circuit. It explained that a complaint may be amended in light of newly discovered evidence. **In this case, the parent did not include anything new in her complaint.** Instead, she submitted an undated letter to the court to which she had attached three police reports. The court found nothing to indicate this information was unavailable to the parent at the time of her original filing. Since her complaint did not correct the deficiencies identified by the lower court and she did not include any newly discovered evidence, the court found no reason to disturb the judgment for the school board. *M.G. v. St. Lucie County School Board*, 741 F.3d 1260 (11th Cir. 2014).

◆   Georgia parents of a child with severe disabilities claimed her teacher was abusive to the special needs students in her classroom. They sued the teacher, principal and school district in a federal court. In response, the principal filed a counterclaim against the student and crossclaims against the school district and several members of the board of education. She argued the district had to provide her legal defense. The court noted that after an investigation into the charges, the principal and district had entered into a settlement agreement.

Although the principal argued the agreement bound the district to provide her defense, the court found the agreement provided the board with discretion on the issue. Georgia law provided school boards with discretion to pay such expenses in a civil case against an employee for their acts or omissions. In sum, **the court found the district and board were not obligated to provide the principal a legal defense in the abuse case**. Provision of liability insurance was itself contingent upon any limits the board found appropriate. Since no mandatory language required the board to provide the principal with the defense she sought, her breach of contract claims failed. For similar reasons, a claim based on denial of her due process rights failed. Rejecting the principal's other arguments, the court held for the school district and board members. *Persadi v. Fulton County School Dist.*, 24 F.Supp.3d 1249 (N.D. Ga. 2014).

♦ A Michigan student communicated through facilitated communication (FC). After a few months of working with the student, a paraprofessional reported that the student communicated to her through FC that her father had sexually abused her. The teacher facilitated similar statements with the student, and a report was made to the state children's protective services agency. Family members tried to tell a state agency social worker about proper FC protocols for authenticating abuse allegations through the use of a "naive" facilitator (one who was unaware of the allegations or could not hear the questions to assure that the facilitator was not "authoring" the answers). But the social worker did not return the family's calls, explore the use of naive facilitators, or assure that authentication protocols were being used. Based only on statements obtained through FC, prosecutors charged the father with child abuse, took both children into protective custody and jailed both parents. Early in the prosecution, the court found the student "mostly typed gibberish" and could not answer questions without facilitators. Prosecutors soon dropped the case because she could not testify. The father was released from jail, and the children were returned home.

The family sued law enforcement officers, child protection and social workers, prosecutors, school personnel and agencies involved in the investigation and prosecution. When the case reached **the Sixth Circuit, it held it had to be determined whether there had been "gross negligence." Such conduct would be unprotected by immunity.** Evidence indicated the coordinator disregarded her supervisor's instructions to obtain naive facilitators during interviews. The social worker and special services coordinator were not entitled to immunity. As for the prosecutors, the court found they should have immunity from the constitutional claims and from claims arising from their interviews of the student to prepare for the prosecution. Claims against the state department of human services remained viable. The social worker, teacher and paraprofessional had no immunity from tort claims based on evidence that they "cleaned up" some of the FC interviews. *Wendrow v. Michigan Dep't of Human Services*, 534 Fed.Appx. 516 (6th Cir. 2013).

♦ A Maryland paraeducator wrote love notes to an eight-year-old student. He was convicted of sexual abuse and appealed to the Court of Appeals of Maryland. The court held there was sexual abuse despite the lack of actual sexual contact. **Child sexual abuse included failure to act to prevent molestation or exploitation when it was reasonably possible to do so.**

Another Maryland case had found exploitation when a person in custody of a child took advantage of the child or unjustly used the child for his own benefit. Based on the letters and evidence that the two had hugged and held hands, the court found the child was exploited under the Maryland Child Sexual Abuse Statute. In affirming his prison sentence of 13 years, the court rejected numerous arguments by the paraeducator and found sufficient evidence to support the conviction. It held "sexual abuse" was not limited to specified acts of incest, rape, sexual offense, sodomy and other practices listed in the statute.

The court found the statute was not impermissibly vague and held the broad statutory language struck a careful compromise between the need for specificity and the desire of legislators to craft a law to "target the ever-shifting manner in which some people will target and abuse children." *Walker v. State of Maryland*, 432 Md. 587, 69 A.3d 1066 (Md. 2013).

C. Parents and Other Third Parties

♦ A Louisiana second-grader was hospitalized and diagnosed with bipolar disorder. Upon returning to school, he told a teacher "he could kill her because he knew jujitsu." The student hit and threatened others, including his teacher. An assistant principal urged the principal to remove the student from school. But the principal said he should remain because there were no alternative school options for him. In November of his second-grade year, the student pushed his teacher against a locker. The assistant principal escorted him to the office. En route, he tripped and injured her. Later, the assistant principal sued the student's divorced parents, the principal and the school board in a state court. In pretrial activity, the court held the father, who was the custodial parent, could not be held liable because the student was under the school's supervision and control at the time of the incident. It also found the mother was not liable as she only had visitation rights. On appeal, **the Court of Appeal of Louisiana found a basis for parental liability in Louisiana Civil Code Article 2318**.

Article 2318 made parents responsible for damages caused by a minor child who resides with a parent or who has been placed in the care of others. While the assistant principal looked out for the student, the court found she was not his "caretaker" under Article 2318. So she was not barred from pursuing claims against the father. Public policy militated against imposing liability on the school board. The assistant principal said she urged the principal to remove the child from school, but was told this was not an option. She denied being told of the student's diagnosis. The extent, if any, of her knowledge and acceptance of risk would be subject to a comparative fault analysis when the case returned to the lower court for a trial. Assumption of risk would not bar the assistant principal's claims. *Penton v. Castellano*, 127 So.3d 944 (La. Ct. App. 2013).

The state supreme court decided not to review the decision. *Penton v. Castellano*, 131 So.3d 867, 131 So.3d 869 (La. writ denied, 2014).

♦ A Minnesota teacher was threatened by a parent who demanded speech therapy for her son. The teacher obtained a state court harassment restraining order against the parent. The order did not prevent the parent from coming to school, but it did prevent her from coming near the teacher's second-floor classroom. On two later occasions, the teacher saw the parent at school. The first time, she called 911 and left early. The second time, she told the principal to take her students to the bus and also left early. After the school admonished her, she sued it for negligence. The Minnesota Court of Appeals agreed with the school that it was entitled to immunity. **The district's anti-harassment policy did not apply to parents**, and school officials did not commit any willful or malicious wrong. *Ellison-Harpole v. Special School Dist. No. 1*, No. A07-1070, 2008 WL 933537 (Minn. Ct. App. 4/8/08).

D.   Corporal Punishment

♦   A Pennsylvania teacher's aide knocked a student's feet from his chair. Although the conduct was later found inappropriate and unnecessary, it did not result in injury and was not reported to school administrators. Two months later, the aide grabbed the student by the arm, shook him and yelled at him. This incident was promptly reported to the district special education director. A few days later, the aide again yelled at the student, shook him and hit him in the head. The aide was transferred and had no further contact with the student. A seven-count lawsuit was filed against the school district and aide, including charges of constitutional rights and IDEA violations, assault and battery.

A federal court dismissed the case, finding no evidence of intentional discrimination. Appeal reached the U.S. Court of Appeals, Third Circuit. It held that **to obtain compensatory damages under Section 504, a party must show intentional discrimination. This requires proof that a school was deliberately indifferent to a violation of rights.** Deliberate indifference, in turn, requires that the party show knowledge that a federally protected right is substantially likely to be violated and failure to act despite that knowledge. In this case, the court found the first of the three incidents of inappropriate conduct was not reported to the school administration. And when the second incident was reported, a meeting was promptly called to discuss it. Upon reporting of the third incident, the school district immediately transferred the aide to prevent her from having any further contact with the student. Since this did not show deliberate indifference, the court upheld the judgment for the district. *Shadie v. Hazelton Area School Dist.*, 580 Fed.Appx. 67 (3d Cir. 2014).

♦   An Ohio intervention specialist hit a wheelchair-bound student because he was blocking the way of another child. After the incident was reported to the principal, the specialist was charged with fourth-degree assault. Prior to her trial, she objected to the introduction of surveillance video as evidence. The court denied her objection. A jury found the specialist guilty of felony assault. On appeal, the Ohio Court of Appeals held a jury could have reasonably found the testimony of other staff members more credible than that of the specialist. Two employees who were present at the time heard the noise of the impact.

The court found the surveillance video was properly introduced as evidence. Another specialist who witnessed the events testified that the video accurately depicted the incident. The court rejected a claim that the state should not have been allowed to refer to the Licensure Code of Professional Conduct for Ohio Educators during the trial. **The code was used to determine whether**

the specialist had a duty of care and protection regarding the student, not whether she committed conduct unbecoming a teacher. Even though the student was not on the specialist's roster, her duties included provision of services to students with disabilities in various groups or settings. As none of her arguments had merit, the court held for the state. *State of Ohio v. Cox*, 12 N.E.3d 46 (Ohio Ct. App. 2014), (Appeal denied, Ohio 2014).

♦   Oklahoma parents of a student with autism said a teacher's aide told them the child had been physically punished. They also claimed the child was placed in a dark closet as punishment. In a federal court, they sued the school district, their child's teacher, the district special services director, the district school security chief, the principal and others. In pretrial activity, the court held the parents did not show the director and chief acted with willful and wanton negligence. In addition, they did not assert these officials were acting outside the scope of their employment. Since the parents offered only conclusory statements about the officials, the court dismissed their negligence claims.

The court held a civil conspiracy claim could not be based on violation of the state child abuse reporting statute. As a result, the court dismissed all the claims against the special education director and security chief. Next, the court considered a motion by the district to dismiss the claims brought against it. It was said the teacher threatened to have aides fired if they told the parents about the punishment. But the court held it could not find for the parents where they asserted facts that only raised a possibility of misconduct. **They did not assert any district policy or custom was the moving force behind a constitutional rights violation and did not cite facts indicating school district involvement.** The court found no merit to the negligence, battery, assault, infliction of emotional distress and conspiracy claims against the teacher. But the parents could amend the assault, battery and emotional distress claims. *AKC v. Lawton Independent School Dist. No. 8*, 9 F.Supp.3d 1240 (W.D. Okla. 2014).

♦   Parents of a Florida student claimed she was bruised after a male classroom aide "slammed" her into a chair. While the student was in the chair, the aide shoved her against a table, causing her to cry. Two staff members left the room and reported the incident to the school's vice principal. Police were called, and the male aide was charged with abuse. Later, the charge was dropped. The parents sued the school board for due process violations and negligence. After the male aide and the school principal were dismissed from the case, the court considered the board's motion for pretrial judgment. As many courts have held, **governmental action must shock the conscience to open the door for constitutional liability**. In this case, the court found the male aide's use of force could be construed as serving an educational purpose. The student had refused to move from the floor and go to the table as instructed. She had also broken a pipe supporting a screen, so the court found it was reasonable to intervene to prevent her from harming herself or causing further disruption to the classroom.

In the court's opinion, the use of physical force to put the student in her chair could be construed as an attempt to restore order, maintain discipline or protect the student from self-injurious behavior. While the aide had likely used more force than necessary when pinning her at the table, the court held it was not conscience-shocking. As the aide had the prerogative to intervene when the student disobeyed his directions, the court held his possibly "ill-considered" response did not violate the Constitution. *Smith v. School Board of Brevard County*, No. 6:12-cv-931-Orl-37TBS, 2013 WL 3773245 (M.D. Fla. 7/17/13).

♦   School employees made a six-year-old Florida charter school student with non-verbal autism crawl through a fabric tunnel even though she screamed and cried. The employees then dragged her over to a trampoline and made her jump up and down on it as she continued to have a tantrum. Several weeks later, she was forcibly restrained in a chair while watching a movie with her classmates. She sued under the Fourteenth Amendment, claiming she had suffered severe psychological trauma. A federal court held that the "tunnel incident" did not constitute corporal punishment and was not shocking to the conscience. While the "chair incident" was corporal punishment, it was also necessary, since the student was being disruptive and disobedient at the time. **The psychological injury did not meet the high threshold of liability in 42 U.S.C. § 1983 cases.** The court dismissed her constitutional rights claim and refused to consider her state law claims. *S.S. v. Princeton House Charter School*, No. 6:11-cv-1145, 2012 WL 5562762 (M.D. Fla. 11/15/12).

♦   Tennessee parents of five special education students sued their district, asserting that their children had been physically abused by their teacher. They claimed that she used excessive force on the students and that the district failed to properly supervise her. **A federal court and the Sixth Circuit held that while the evidence was troubling, it did not add up to a substantive due process violation.** Further, the parents' filings contained many errors and did not adequately allege specific facts that would allow for a finding of liability. Instead, they merely alleged a pattern of abuse. Their case was dismissed, and the district could pursue attorneys' fees against them. *Sagan v. Sumner County Board of Educ.*, 501 Fed.Appx. 537 (6th Cir. 2012).

♦   The parents of New York students with long histories of aggressive, self-injurious, destructive and non-compliant behavior wanted aversive interventions for their children. They sued the state education department seeking to disallow regulations that prohibited the use of aversive interventions they wanted for their children. The case reached the Second Circuit, which held that the regulation did not violate the IDEA. **It still allowed for a wide range of treatments and individualized assessments and conformed to the IDEA's clear preference for positive behavioral interventions.** *Bryant v. New York State Educ. Dep't*, 692 F.3d 202 (2d Cir. 2012).

♦   A Florida student with autism sued his former teacher and school board based on five incidents of corporal punishment. He claimed that she violated his due process rights and also violated the Rehabilitation Act by abusing him in class, and pointed to her suspension and later conviction on one count of child abuse. He lost, as four incidents he cited were related to his refusal to go to the cool-down room or his calling the teacher names or threatening her. The fifth incident involved her tripping him, which was not corporal punishment. And **in**

each case of corporal punishment, the teacher used restraint on the student only until he calmed down or agreed to comply with her instructions. *T.W. v. School Board of Seminole County, Florida*, 610 F.3d 588 (11th Cir. 2010).

♦ An Alabama teacher administered corporal punishment to a student who had been held behind in school. She claimed that she struck him once, but he asserted that she repeatedly struck him, injuring his legs and one of his arms. He enrolled in another school and sued her and the school board for negligence. The teacher argued that she should be entitled to immunity without a trial, but the Supreme Court of Alabama ruled against her. **She violated the education board's own policy, which required her to have a witness present whenever corporal punishment was being administered.** Despite her and her supervisors' assertion that she couldn't leave the other students alone to go find a witness, a further inquiry into the matter was necessary. *Ex Parte Monroe County Board of Educ.*, 48 So.3d 621 (Ala. 2010).

E. Restraint and Seclusion

♦ A Colorado student with Down syndrome and other disabilities, who had been born addicted to cocaine, was sometimes placed in a wrap-around desk at her school that prevented her from pushing the chair out. She could escape by sliding under the restraining bar or crawling over the table. Her mother, concerned about her lack of progress and the belief that the school district was using the wrap-around desk more than for disciplinary reasons, revoked her consent for use of the desk. School staff continued using the desk until the student went home with a broken arm one day. Although the Tenth Circuit Court of Appeals rejected the student's constitutional claims in 2012, it held her federal disability discrimination claims should proceed to a trial. In 2013, the U.S. Supreme Court refused to consider the case, and the dispute later came before a jury. After the jury reached a verdict for the student, **the trial court entered a final judgment in her favor for $2.2 million plus post-judgment interest**. The trial court later granted the school district's motion to stay execution of the judgment pending appeal. *Ebonie S. v. Pueblo School Dist. 60*, Civ. No. 09-cv-00858-WJM-MEH, 2015 WL 4245831 (D. Colo. 7/14/15).

In a later order, the court approved an award of $977,900 in attorneys' fees plus additional expenses of $123,460.22. *Ebonie S. v. Pueblo School Dist. 60*, Civ. No. 09-cv-00858-WJM-MEH, 2016 WL 1110442 (D. Colo. 3/22/16).

♦ The mother of a New Jersey student filed a due process challenge to their school district's failure to provide an aide. She claimed her son was disciplined for behavior that was a manifestation of his disabilities. She became frustrated with the district's use of restraints and kept him home for the last six weeks of the school year. The parties were unable to agree on a placement, and the family later moved to Georgia. The mother sought compensatory education for the improper restraints, and the district claimed that the action was mooted by the move out of the district. The Third Circuit Court of Appeals ultimately ruled that **the claim for compensatory education was not mooted by the family's move**. Otherwise, school districts could simply stop providing services until a family gave up and moved away. The lawsuit could proceed. *D.F. v. Collingswood Borough Board of Educ.*, 694 F.3d 488 (3d Cir. 2012).

When the case returned to the district court, it found no merit to the parent's argument that the administrative decision disrupted the child's stay-put placement and denied him a free appropriate public education. As for the claim that the child had been improperly restrained, the court found the complaint did not state any relevant facts. **There were no descriptions of any incidents, no dates for any incidents, and no names were given to indicate who allegedly performed the restraints.** Since the hearing officer had correctly held the parent did not put the school district on sufficient notice of the nature of the problem, the district was entitled to judgment. *D.F. v. Collingswood Public Schools*, No. 10-594 (JEI/JS), 2013 WL 103589 (D.N.J. 1/8/13).

In 2015, the parent appealed again to the Third Circuit, which found her arguments were without merit. In the court's view, **the lower court's opinion clearly and convincingly showed the improper restraint claim was deficient**. Next, the court held the claim for compensatory education had been properly resolved. As a result, it held for the board of education. *D.F. v. Collingswood Borough Board of Educ.*, 595 Fed.Appx. 49 (3d Cir. 2015).

♦   An Oklahoma student with disabilities claimed that a teacher, an aide and a principal confined and restrained him in a dark room and that he was slapped and held down for long time periods. He sued the school district and officials for negligent supervision, assault, battery, false imprisonment and due process violations. A federal court dismissed most of the claims, but not a claim for infliction of emotional distress and constitutional claims against the teacher and two others. It also allowed claims against the school system for battery, assault, false imprisonment, negligent supervision and negligent hiring to proceed.

On appeal, the U.S. Court of Appeals, Tenth Circuit, likened the restraint allegation to a state law tort claim. It found no authority showing Congress meant to funnel tort claims into the IDEA administrative regime. Although the use of restraints was typically treated in a student's IEP and would usually require IDEA administrative exhaustion, the court found the family was no longer contesting an IEP. Significantly, the family had used administrative channels to try to prevent use of the time-out rooms. As for the substance of the claims, the court found that **to hold school officials liable for a substantive due process violation, there must be some abuse of power that shocks the conscience**. None of the incidents asserted by the family met this standard. There had been "a rather mild slap" of the student and restraint incidents that were found only careless or unwise. Use of the time-out rooms, which had been limited to four minutes per incident, did not shock the conscience. There could be no liability for the principal or the district based on a constitutional theory. As a result, the judgment for the school district and officials was affirmed. *Muskrat v. Deer Creek Public Schools*, 715 F.3d 775 (10th Cir. 2013).

♦   A Tennessee student with autism repeatedly violated a school policy against cell phone use. Her teacher took the phone and put it in a desk. When the student tried to recover it, the teacher brought it to the office. The student followed the teacher to the office, where the principal told her the phone could only be released to her parents. When the student's sister came to take her home, she refused to leave without the phone. A municipal police officer arrived and struggled to remove the student from the office. In the process, the officer handcuffed the student. He brought her to a juvenile detention center, where she was charged with disorderly conduct. After the charges were dropped, the student's parents sued the school district, police officer, teacher and principal.

A federal court held for the school district and officials, and appeal reached the U.S. Court of Appeals, Sixth Circuit. It considered the parents' claims that the summoning of the police without describing the child's autistic condition created and increased the danger to her under the "state-created danger doctrine." Like the lower court, **the Sixth Circuit found no other case holding that failure to communicate information about a person's disability to an arresting officer could be a constitutional violation**. Although the Fourteenth Amendment's Due Process Clause prevents certain arbitrary and wrongful acts by the states, it does not affirmatively require a state to protect citizens from the actions of private actors. Conduct attributed to the teacher and principal did not deprive the student of a liberty interest in bodily security. Since the parents could not show an affirmative act by the teacher or principal created or increased a risk to the student, there was no constitutional violation. *Chigano v. City of Knoxville*, 529 Fed.Appx. 753 (6th Cir. 2013).

♦ A Florida student had disabilities affecting his communications, as well as social anxiety, motor and vocal tics, and gastrointestinal reflux. By grade six, he experienced significant incidents of self-injurious behavior and was aggressive toward others. According to claims brought by the student's parents in a federal court, the school district subjected him to years of excessive and improper restraints in his public middle school. They claimed he suffered psychological trauma from the restraints that required placement in a residential treatment facility. In pretrial activity, the court considered school logs kept to document restraints imposed on the student. It found these **records showed restraint was necessary to avoid injury to himself or to others**. Each time he was restrained, it was due to a perceived crisis. Physical assistance logs indicated that all the restraint incidents consisted of a staff member holding the student's hands or feet. No mechanical restraint was ever used. Although the school should have reviewed and updated a functional behavioral assessment (FBA) after three restraints, the court found the staff knew what worked for the student and what did not. The parents claimed the restraints amounted to disability discrimination under Section 504 and the Americans with Disabilities Act.

But the court found no evidence supported the claim that teachers or staff who restrained the child intended to discriminate against him on the basis of disability. There was also no showing that it was substantially likely that a violation of his federally protected rights would occur. In the court's view, there was not enough evidence to avoid pretrial dismissal of the case. It held the board was entitled to judgment on the remaining federal claims. If the family wished to pursue their state law claims, they could do so in a state court. *J.P.M. v. Palm Beach County School Board*, 916 F.Supp.2d 1314 (S.D. Fla. 2013).

♦ A Wisconsin teacher worked with cognitively disabled children for a school district for over 26 years. Paraprofessional aides grew concerned about her use of force. After an aide made a report, officials investigated and learned the teacher used physical force against students and had body-slammed a student onto a table. She was placed on leave and eventually discharged. A report was made to child protective services, and the police investigated. Several other incidents were identified in the investigation which involved grabbing a child by the arm and/or neck and force-feeding. A state court charged the teacher with felony child abuse and strangulation. She pleaded no contest to a battery charge and received probation. In a separate federal court proceeding, the families of six cognitively disabled children sued the teacher, district and school officials for constitutional rights violations. In pretrial proceedings, the court noted that before the aide's report, nobody had voiced any concerns about the teacher.

The other aide had worked with her for 17 years and never reported any misconduct. According to the court, **second-guessing school disciplinary action would "federalize the state tort law of battery," as limited by a privilege of reasonable discipline**. The court found no children suffered observable or medically determined injuries. Most of the teacher's actions came in response to failure to follow her instructions. While the court held she acted inappropriately, no constitutional violations occurred. Since the claims against the teacher failed, the court held the claims against other school officials and the school district necessarily failed. *B.B. v. Appleton Area School Dist.*, No. 12-C-115, 2013 WL 3972250 (E.D. Wis. 7/31/13).

♦ A California student with autism had a tendency to run away from school. In a federal court case, he said school staff members placed him in dangerous and harmful basket holds and other restraints. The student claimed an aide caused deep scratches on his neck and that the aide and the school psychologist dragged him to the school office and pulled him in different directions at least one other time. During the relevant time period, the student ran away from school 29 times. He was typically restrained by school staff and returned to school. After the parents and the district agreed to a private placement, the parents sued the school district and school officials in a federal court. In pretrial activity, the court found some of the claims were superficially plausible and deserving of further consideration. This included a Section 504 claim that indicated the school did not investigate or prevent harm to the student.

But the court held the discrimination claims against the school district failed because no district policy was implicated. In the court's view, **the family provided enough facts to avoid pretrial dismissal of Fourth Amendment claims based on the scratching, dragging and other restraints**. While the claims against staff members deserved further consideration, the court held their supervisors could not be held liable since they were not personally involved in any incident. An equal protection claim could not proceed, as the court found the student did not compare his treatment to that of any similarly situated group. But his claims against staff members for assault, battery and infliction of emotional distress would not now be dismissed. *E.H. v. Brentwood Union School Dist.*, No. C13-3243 TEH, 2013 WL 5978008 (N.D. Cal. 11/4/13).

♦   A Connecticut parent claimed school staff members improperly restrained her developmentally disabled child in a time-out room. She said staff members hit the student so hard that he was knocked unconscious and that part of his right ear was severed. The student was then brought to a medical center, where his ear was reattached. In pretrial activity, the court dismissed nine of the 14 claims. But it refused to dismiss claims for infliction of emotional distress and assault and battery. In the court's view, the parent did not state sufficient facts to pursue infliction of emotional distress claims on her own behalf. She was not present at the relevant time and so failed to meet one of the key requirements for an emotional distress claim. A breach of contract claim failed because the parent did not assert enough facts to support an implied or express agreement by the parties to provide the child with a safe school environment.

In addition, the court found no facts supported the student's discrimination claims. An IDEA claim only stated a legal conclusion that the student's education program was inappropriate and had to be dismissed. **But the court held the assault and battery claim as well as a claim for infliction of emotional distress on behalf of the student were legally sufficient at this stage of the case.** *Vargas v. Specialized Educ. Services*, No. HHD CV 126028454, 2013 WL 6671230 (Conn. Super. Ct. 11/19/13).

♦   While on the playground at his school, a New York student with disabilities began to throw rocks. He became agitated and defiant when told to stop by a teacher's assistant. School security guards were unable to control the student, who thrashed around and tried to bang his head. A municipal officer arrived and placed him in handcuffs. Later, the student's parent sued the school district, principal, security guards and other staff. When the case reached the U.S. Court of Appeals, Second Circuit, it held **the use of force to seize the student "for his safety and the safety of those around him" was reasonable under the circumstances.** *E.C. v. County of Suffolk*, 514 Fed.Appx. 28 (2d Cir. 2012).

III. AWARDS AND DAMAGES

A. Attorneys' Fees

The IDEA allows parents to recover their attorneys' fees where they prevail in "any action or proceeding" under the IDEA. Many courts have held that prevailing party status requires a change in the legal relationship of the parties due to a judgment on the merits of the case or a court-ordered consent decree. School districts may seek their attorneys' fees from parents, or the attorneys of parents, if a due process action or court case is found frivolous, unreasonable or without foundation, or if the parents filed a case for an improper purpose.

♦   A California school district conducted a triennial assessment of a child with multiple disabilities. An occupational therapist conducted the assessment and issued a report that did not indicate whether the child needed occupational therapy (OT). The parent objected to an IEP without OT that only provided for discussions between a teacher and OT therapist. She requested an independent educational evaluation (IEE), but the school district denied payment for it. An administrative law judge (ALJ) upheld the OT assessment. The parent's attorney wrote a letter to the school district offering a settlement. The district's attorney charged the parent with a pattern of litigating and threats to litigate nonexistent claims. The school attorney threatened to seek sanctions against the parent and her attorney should there be any further appeal. The parent appealed the ALJ's decision to a federal court, adding retaliation and discrimination claims. The court affirmed the ALJ's decision and awarded the school district $94,602.34 in attorneys' fees and costs. It found the parents' claims were frivolous, unreasonable, without foundation and brought for improper purposes.

On appeal, the U.S. Court of Appeals, Ninth Circuit, explained that **school districts may recover fees from parents and their attorneys "when a complaint is found frivolous, unreasonable or without foundation, or when a claim is filed for an improper purpose."** While the parent did not prevail on her IDEA claims, the court held they were not frivolous and she did not improperly continue to litigate the case. But the court agreed with the school district that three retaliation-based claims were frivolous, as were claims for monetary damages and injunctive relief. In the court's view, the letter from the parent's attorney was not an attempt to improperly "extort funds" from the district. The court returned the case to the lower court with instructions to determine which fees were attributable solely to litigating the frivolous claims. The school district would only be entitled to attorneys' fees for those claims. *C.W. v. Capistrano Unified School Dist.*, 784 F.3d 1237 (9th Cir. 2015).

1.   Administrative Proceedings

♦   California parents asked their child's school district to provide her with Communication Access Realtime Translation services beginning in grade nine. The district refused, instead offering an alternative transcription technology called TypeWell. A hearing officer held a seven-day hearing before finding the district complied with its IDEA obligations. A federal court upheld the ALJ's decision, and the U.S. Court of Appeals, Ninth Circuit, issued a decision for the parents on their Americans with Disabilities Act (ADA) claim. The parties then reached a settlement by which the district paid the parents $197,500. The parents petitioned the court for over $458,000 in attorneys' fees and costs. It found a "prevailing party" in an IDEA action is one who effects a material alteration of the parties' legal relationship though an enforceable judgment, a consent decree or settlement. The court explained that while the parents did not prevail on their IDEA claim, the IDEA and ADA claims were intertwined.

Litigating the IDEA claim at all levels was necessary for the development and success of their ADA claim. Courts consider many factors in awarding attorneys' fees. **The court held the most critical factor is the degree of success obtained.** Even if a specific claim failed, the time spent on it might still be compensable, if it contributed to success on other claims. The court held the parents were entitled to 50% of the fees they claimed at the administrative level. For the proceedings before the district court, they were entitled to 75% of their claimed attorneys' fees. As the parents prevailed on their Ninth Circuit appeal, they were entitled to 100% of the fees for the district's appeal and subsequent proceedings. In all, the court approved an award of attorneys' fees and costs of almost $385,000. *K.M. v. Tustin Unified School Dist.*, No. SA CV 10-1011-DOC (MLGx), 2015 WL 3465757 (C.D. Cal. 6/1/15).

◆ A federal district court held a school board was not entitled to the $661,000 in attorneys' fees it claimed from the parents of a child with a disability who filed an unsuccessful administrative action against the board. After an administrative law judge issued a 191-page opinion in the board's favor, it sought fees under the IDEA and other federal laws. The court explained that **the IDEA allows a local educational agency to recover attorneys' fees from parents who file a claim for an improper purpose**. The IDEA also permits a local educational agency to recover fees from the attorney of a parent who has filed a claim that is found frivolous or unreasonable. The court held the board did not support its claim that the parents' attorney had made a frivolous claim or that the parents filed the action for an improper purpose. *A.L. v. Jackson County School Board*, No. 13-15071, 2015 WL 74999 (N.D. Fla. 1/6/15).

◆ Ohio parents filed an administrative complaint against their child's district, asserting denial of a free appropriate public education (FAPE) for three years. An independent hearing officer (IHO) held a 20-day hearing and then held the district had denied the student a FAPE for two years. The district was ordered to provide him 240 hours of compensatory education in both reading and math. Finding the parents bore at least some of the responsibility for the difficulties in creating an IEP and providing services, the IHO denied the parents prevailing party status, which would defeat any claim for attorneys' fees under the IDEA.

Appeal went before a state review officer, who affirmed some parts of the IHO's decision, including the decision to award compensatory education. Meanwhile, the school district filed a separate suit, which claimed the review officer committed error on the question of the compensatory education awards in reading and math. The court dismissed the district's claim because the district had not appealed the compensatory education issue to the review officer. Turning to the parents' appeal, the court affirmed the review officer's decision for the most part but held the district violated the IDEA by not providing adequate transition services. The court then considered the parents' claim for more than $800,000 in attorneys' fees. It held the hourly rates sought by the parents' attorneys were reasonable. In the court's view, the district did not show the parents had overstaffed the case. But it held **an across-the-board reduction in fees was appropriate due to the parents' limited success on the merits of the claim. Equitable reasons supported a fee reduction.** The student had ultimately won 240 hours of both reading and math instruction as well as about 500 hours of transition services. As a result, the court held the parents should receive attorneys' fees of $300,000. *Gibson v. Forrest Hills School Dist.*, No. 1:11-cv-320, 2014 WL 3530708 (S.D. Ohio 7/15/14).

◆ During elementary school, the parent of a Connecticut student claimed he had to miss significant school time due to respiratory issues. Before the student advanced to grade six, the mother asked the school district to declare him eligible for special education under the other health impairment (OHI) category due to his asthma and allergies. The district only offered to place him in another district school. The mother instead placed him in a private school that lacked a state-approved special education program for grade six. In a due process proceeding, the parent claimed the district failed to identify the student as requiring special education and related services under the OHI category for four years. A hearing officer generally held for the school district, finding that the case involved only a child find issue. The parent then sued the school district in a federal court, which found the district did not abide by its responsibility to hold planning and placement team (PPT) meetings and develop IEPs after the parents made a private placement. On the other hand, the court found the student did not need special education during the years at issue. As he was not IDEA-eligible, the court found no merit to the claims for tuition reimbursement.

Finally, the court considered the parent's claim to more than $176,000 in attorneys' fees. It explained that **a party will be deemed to "prevail" if he changes the legal relationship of the parties through a judgment or a legally enforceable settlement**. In this case, the court held the family did not ultimately prevail on the goal of receiving four years of private school tuition reimbursement. But the court agreed with the family that the student was denied the process to reach a determination of special education eligibility. The court held the family succeeded on a significant issue in the case when the hearing officer ordered the district to hold a PPT meeting. Under these unique circumstances, the court held the parent was entitled to $55,950 in attorneys' fees. *M.A. v. Torrington Board of Educ.*, 980 F.Supp.2d 279 (D. Conn. 2014).

◆   New York parents claimed a school district denied their child a free appropriate public education and requested a hearing. Before the case went before an impartial hearing officer (IHO), the school district offered a proposed agreement to the parents. But the parents rejected the offer, and the case went before the IHO. Finding the district failed to take certain remedial steps for the child, the IHO held for the parents. This decision was substantially affirmed by a review officer. A federal court then found the parents were entitled to attorneys' fees for work done prior to the settlement offer and for the actual claim for fees. In view of the similarity between the IHO's award and the offer by the district, the court reduced the claimed attorneys' fees by 80%, for a total of $16,830. Appeal then went before the U.S. Court of Appeals, Second Circuit.

The court held **a court may award attorneys' fees in an IDEA case to parents who prevail by achieving a judicially sanctioned change in the legal relationship of the parties**. There must be a judgment on the merits of the case or a court-ordered consent decree. In this case, the court found the parents were awarded a compensatory counseling fee that was not part of the district's prior settlement offer. Since the counseling was not previously offered by the district, the court held an IDEA section limiting attorneys' fees did not apply. In calculating fees, the district court had correctly multiplied the number of hours expended on the case by a reasonable hourly rate in the community. It then adjusted the fee downward by 80% after comparing the relief awarded to the settlement offer. As this was not error, the court affirmed the award of $16,830. *C.G. v. Ithaca City School Dist.*, 531 Fed.Appx. 86 (2d Cir. 2013).

♦   The parents of an autistic New York student rejected a school district IEP proposal and made a private placement in a Connecticut development center. An impartial hearing officer (IHO) agreed that the school district had denied the child a free appropriate public education. A court held that the parents were prevailing parties and thus eligible for attorneys' fees. It computed a reasonable rate for attorneys in the area and awarded the parents over $103,000 in fees and costs. On appeal, the Second Circuit noted that the IEP for the school year in question was inadequate and the Connecticut center was an appropriate placement. As a result, **the parents were eligible for their attorneys' fees and costs under the IDEA**. The court affirmed the judgment. *J.S. v. Carmel Central School Dist.*, 501 Fed.Appx. 95 (2d Cir. 2012).

♦   The father of a Texas student who was supposed to receive 60 minutes of speech therapy a week contacted the district with concerns about the failure to provide all required therapy. The district conducted an admission, review and dismissal committee meeting and, within a week, admitted that it had failed to provide the full amount of therapy required by the IEP. It offered 56.5 hours of compensatory therapy, but it made no mention of attorneys' fees.

However, the student's father, whose attorney had logged 13.8 hours by that point, rejected the settlement offer. Subsequently, a Texas hearing officer ordered an award of 19.55 hours of compensatory therapy because the claims for earlier years were untimely. In the resulting lawsuit over attorneys' fees, the case eventually reached the Fifth Circuit. It ruled that the father's attorney was entitled to be paid for only the 13.8 hours he worked prior to the rejection of the settlement offer. As a result, he was entitled to $3,243. *Gary G. v. El Paso Independent School Dist.*, 632 F.3d 201 (5th Cir. 2011).

2. Court Proceedings

♦   An Ohio charter school attorney obtained the reversal of a federal court order that awarded the parent of a disabled child her attorney's fees as a sanction for filing frivolous or harassing actions. After a lower court found the charter school's attorney made a frivolous argument and filed confidential documents as exhibits, it awarded the parent $7,500 from the attorney. When the case reached the U.S. Court of Appeals, Sixth Circuit, it held **the case had "needlessly devolved" into a dispute over fees and unjustified sanctions**. The court found none of the attorney's actions were unreasonable and it reversed the lower court's order. *Oakstone Community School v. Williams*, 615 Fed,Appx. 284 (6th Cir. 2015).

♦   A federal court allowed a Michigan school district to pursue claims against the parents of a child with a disability and an attorney based on the argument that their conduct needlessly prolonged litigation. In a case that reached the U.S. Court of Appeals, Sixth Circuit, the student obtained 768 hours of 1:1 compensatory education by a teacher certified to teach students with autism. Later, the parents claimed district evaluations of their child were inappropriate and that they were entitled to reimbursement for the cost of an independent educational evaluation (IEE). The district filed a federal case against the parents and their attorney, seeking attorneys' fees and costs for prolonging the litigation and pursuing claims for improper purposes. In addition, the school district sought an order allowing the release of documents that the administrative law judge (ALJ) had reviewed in private during the IEE hearing.

The school district claimed these documents would show "active collusion and planning" by the parents and attorney to needlessly delay and prolong the IEP process and administrative hearing. At the hearing, the ALJ had denied the district's request to access these documents. The court agreed with the parents' attorney that as the administrative action was over, the IEE issue was moot. The school district was the prevailing party in the action, and **the district stated a plausible claim for attorneys' fees against the parents and their attorney**. The district asserted the parents had continued to pursue a complaint that was "patently frivolous, unreasonable, or without foundation." As the court found enough facts were stated to give rise to plausible support for the claim for fees against the parents and their attorney, it denied their motions for dismissal. *Northport Public School v. Woods*, No. 1:11-cv-982, 2014 WL 1920429 (W.D. Mich. 5/14/14).

♦   Illinois parents filed a due process request, charging their child's school district with providing an IEP that was lacking in research-based instructional programs and occupational therapy. They claimed the district did not fully implement the IEP by neglecting to record lectures and let the child access computers. The parents sought compensatory education in the form of speech and occupational therapy, the cost of independent educational evaluations, and at least $10,000 worth of assistive technology devices. A hearing officer found the school "largely succeeded" in providing the student with a free appropriate public education. But the hearing officer held the school did not set appropriate goals for reading and writing, and did not administer an appropriate vocational evaluation. The hearing officer ordered the school district to provide the student with three additional hours per week of reading and writing instruction and a vocational evaluation. In a federal court, the parents asked for attorneys' fees.

The court upheld the administrative decision. While acknowledging the parents were "technically prevailing parties" due to the relief granted, the court declined to award them attorneys' fees as their success was minimal. On appeal, the U.S. Court of Appeals, Seventh Circuit, held **the amount of an award of attorneys' fees correlates to the degree of success obtained**. For minor success, the appropriate award is zero. In this case, the school district had "largely succeeded" in providing the child with a free appropriate public education. As the lower court decision was correct, the court rejected the parents' additional claims and held for the school district. *Giosta v. Midland School Dist. 7*, 542 Fed.Appx. 523 (7th Cir. 2013).

♦   Texas parents asserted multiple IDEA violations by their child's school district. But after the district requested a hearing, they decided to voluntarily dismiss the complaint. The district proceeded to the hearing and "presented unopposed evidence demonstrating its compliance with the IDEA." A hearing officer held for the district, and school officials filed a federal action for attorneys' fees. According to the school district, the parents filed their complaint for an improper purpose. The court refused to award fees to the district, and the parents then filed an attorneys' fee claim of their own. They argued that by defeating the school district's claim for fees, they had become the prevailing party. After the court denied the parents' petition, they appealed.

On appeal, the U.S. Court of Appeals, Fifth Circuit, held that **to qualify for prevailing party status under the IDEA, a lawsuit must materially alter the parties' legal relationship**. But the parents in this case had only "prevailed in a very narrow and hollow sense." The court held their successful defense of the school district's attempt to hold them liable for attorneys' fees was only a "technical victory" that did not render them "prevailing parties." Since case law convinced the court that the parents did not qualify as prevailing parties in an IDEA action, the court held for the school district. *Alief Independent School Dist. v. C.C.*, 713 F.3d 268 (5th Cir. 2013).

♦   The foster parents of a Colorado student with disabilities placed her in a residential treatment facility after a dispute with the school district. They reached a settlement allowing the placement. Later, the parents had to hospitalize her in a Utah institute because of deteriorating behavior. Their district then informed them that it was withdrawing the child from her Colorado placement and that it had no responsibility to evaluate her, hold IEP meetings or serve her under the IDEA. The parents placed her in an Idaho facility and sought tuition reimbursement. **A federal court held that the district failed to offer a free appropriate public education.** It later awarded attorneys' fees of $141,000 – finding the parents were prevailing parties. *Jefferson County School Dist. R-I v. Elizabeth E.*, 862 F.Supp.2d 1138 (D. Colo. 2012).

♦   A New York court issued a final judgment for a school district, denying the parents' claims of procedural violations, an inadequate IEP, and other items. While it held that the district didn't mainstream the student to the maximum extent appropriate, **the parents also didn't select an appropriate unilateral private school placement**. Both parties then sought their attorneys' fees, but the court refused both parties' requests. The parents didn't prevail on any disputed issue, but their lawsuit also wasn't frivolous. *J.G. v. Kiryas Joel Union Free School Dist.*, 843 F.Supp.2d 394 (S.D.N.Y. 2012).

♦   A three-year-old Hawaii student was denied special education for a 26-day period during the transition from IDEA Part C to Part B. The delay was largely due to a dispute between the parents and educator over the school he would attend. After a court ruled that the failure to implement the IEP was material and significant, the parents sought their attorneys' fees. **The court awarded the parents over $48,000 even though school officials were still appealing the earlier ruling.** *Shaun M. v. Hamamoto*, No. 09-00075 DAE, 2010 WL 346451 (D. Haw. 1/27/10).

♦   An attorney in New Jersey represented a student with autism, winning a new IEP for the student. When he sought attorneys' fees of $400 per hour, he submitted statements by an environmental law attorney who charged $575 an hour and a veteran Philadelphia special education attorney who charged $375 an hour. The court awarded him only $250 per hour and reduced the hours chargeable from 236 to 177. He appealed, but the Third Circuit ruled against him. It noted his **"unprofessional and contentious" performance in the litigation** and also found that lawyers in his community with similar experience were paid much less than he claimed. *L.J. v. Audubon Board of Educ.*, 373 Fed.Appx. 294 (3d Cir. 2010).

◆   A dispute arose between a New Jersey school district and the parents of a student with disabilities over extended school year (ESY) services and transportation. A federal court ruled for the district on the ESY and transportation claims but awarded 17 days of compensatory education due to the district's failure to serve the student for the same number of days at the start of his fifth-grade year. The family then sought costs and attorneys' fees of $118,787. The court modified the award but still granted them all their costs and $71,850 in attorneys' fees because **even though they were successful on only one claim, their claims were all related**. *L.T. v. Mansfield Township School Dist.*, No. 04-1381 (NLH), 2009 WL 1971329 (D.N.J. 7/1/09).

◆   The mother of a Pennsylvania student sued to challenge an adverse administrative decision, and a court agreed that **the student's IEP had not been properly implemented for part of the year**. When she then sought attorneys' fees, the Third Circuit ruled that she was entitled to more than $104,000. *Damian J. v. School Dist. of Philadelphia*, 358 Fed.Appx. 333 (3d Cir. 2009).

3.   Settlement

◆   A California student's parents disputed gastrostomy tube feeding services provided to their son at school. They removed him from district schools for significant time periods for home instruction. They rejected a school district offer to pay them $75,000 annually for a home program and rejected a counter offer of $150,000 per year. The parents said their annual home school costs were $157,000. When the district rejected a parental demand of $250,000 per year for the home program, the parties requested due process hearings. An administrative law judge (ALJ) consolidated the cases and held for the district on 12 of 15 claims, including those involving the provision of a free appropriate public education. But the court refused to dismiss claims under the Americans with Disabilities Act (ADA) and Section 504. The parents sought almost $1.4 million in attorneys' fees and costs, but the court instead awarded them about $55,000. On appeal, the U.S. Court of Appeals, Ninth Circuit, held gastrostomy tube feeding is a specialized physical health care service that must be described in an IEP. State law went beyond the federal minimum by defining a required accommodation, and this accommodation was enforceable in court.

In the court's opinion, the school district failed to provide a required accommodation by not identifying the category of employee who would assist the child with gastrostomy tube feedings. But since the evidence did not show the district was deliberately indifferent to the student's rights under the ADA and Rehabilitation, the court found no liability on these claims. The family was entitled to reconsideration of a claim that the district did not comply with an

administrative ruling requiring that a school nurse personally assist the student
with tube feedings. The court found the school district's offer to pay the parents
$150,000 per year for their educational costs was not more favorable than the
decision issued by the ALJ. This award was less than the $157,000 in annual
costs they claimed for the home program. The Ninth Circuit ordered the lower
court to reconsider the claim based on compliance with the ALJ's order that a
school nurse personally assist the child with gastrostomy tube feedings. It also
returned the claim for attorneys' fees to the lower court. Later, the U.S. Supreme
Court denied the school district's appeal. *San Diego Unified School Dist. v. T.B.*,
No. 15-1059, 136 S.Ct. 1679 (U.S. cert. denied, 4/18/16).

♦   A Pennsylvania parent removed her child from school and filed a due
process hearing complaint against the school district. Prior to a hearing, the
parties and their attorneys reached a settlement and then asked the hearing
officer to cancel the hearing. For several months, the parties' attorneys
exchanged draft documents outlining a plan for homeschooling of the child and
related financial and waiver/release terms. Almost three months after the
cancelled hearing, the parent again promised to release her claims in return for
funds to homeschool the child. Later in the school year, the district grew
concerned that she never filed a homeschool plan and did not re-enroll her child
in school. The school district sued the parent in a federal court, stating her
inaction imperiled its funding for noncompliance with educational programs.

The court held it was equitable to enforce the promise against the parent,
and she appealed to the U.S. Court of Appeals, Third Circuit. It noted the parties
had never reduced their agreement to a valid writing. Where a party makes a
promise that can reasonably be expected to induce action (or forbearance) by
the other party, and the other party acts (or refrains from acting) in reliance on
the promise, the promise may be enforced by a court if injustice may be avoided
only by enforcing the promise. **Like the lower court, the Third Circuit held
the mother's promises caused the school district to refrain from initiating
truancy proceedings.** Finding injustice could be avoided only by enforcing the
mother's promises to the district, the court held the district could enforce them.
I.K. v. Haverford School Dist., 567 Fed.Appx. 135 (3d Cir. 2014).

♦   A federal lawsuit led to an agreement by Connecticut officials in 2002 to
increase the participation rate of students with intellectual disabilities in general
education classes and take measures to reduce the discriminatory identification
of such students. The agreement stated five goals to encourage compliance with
the IDEA, including an increase in the percent of students with intellectual
disabilities in regular classes, a reduction in discriminatory identification of
such students, and an increase in the share of the school day students would
spend with their non-disabled peers. The agreement sought to increase the
placement of students with intellectual disabilities in neighborhood schools,
and to increase their extra-curricular participation rates. In 2009, representatives
of the students asserted the state was out of compliance with the agreement.

After the court refused to find state officials frustrated the essential
purposes of the agreement, appeal reached the U.S. Court of Appeals, Second
Circuit. In the court's view, the agreement operated as a consent decree, which

gave the lower court continuing authority to supervise it. There was no showing of "substantial noncompliance" with the agreement. The essential purposes of the agreement were limited to five identified areas. Its goals addressed numerical improvements in the integration and classification of students with intellectual disabilities. The court found nothing in the agreement covered the quality of education. **Evidence indicated students made significant progress toward the goals of the agreement, including a reduction in the discriminatory identification of students.** It appeared to the court that the state was trying to implement the agreement even after it was no longer bound to do so. As it was not shown that the state failed to comply with the agreement, the court held for the state. *P.J. v. Connecticut Board of Educ.*, 550 Fed.Appx. 20 (2d Cir. 2013).

◆   Pennsylvania parents prepared to file a due process action against a school district. Attorneys for the parties negotiated an agreement to resolve their complaint. About three weeks later, the parents reviewed an agreement reducing the terms to writing. They changed some of the terms and sent the agreement to their lawyer, who made the changes and returned a draft to them. The draft contained terms that were explicitly rejected by the school district during the settlement negotiations. Without notifying their own attorney, the parents signed the draft document and hand-delivered it to the school district's office.

School officials did not closely review the draft and forwarded it to the superintendent. Unaware of any revisions, the school board voted to approve the draft agreement without any discussion. Later, the parents submitted costs to the district for educational services. The district denied payment, noting that it had rejected responsibility for the service during settlement talks. School officials then realized they had approved the parents' draft rather than the agreement their attorneys created. The district rescinded the agreement and filed a due process complaint with the state office of dispute resolution. A hearing officer found neither the district's original document nor the parents' draft was valid. The parents appealed to the Commonwealth Court of Pennsylvania, which held the hearing officer had ignored the fact that the agreement was signed by both parties and ratified by the board. **Failure by the school district to read or have the agreement reviewed by its attorneys was no defense.** As a result, the court held the draft was valid. A party wishing to invalidate a contract must show fraud or mutual mistake. Here, there was only a unilateral mistake by the district. As there was no basis for rescission and any failure to read the contract before signing it was no defense, the court held for the parents. *A.S. and R.S. v. Office for Dispute Resolution*, 88 A.3d 256 (Pa. Commw. Ct. 2014).

◆   In an IDEA action, the parent of a Washington, D.C. charter school student claimed the school denied her a free appropriate public education. Among other things, the parent claimed the school did not identify her daughter as eligible for IDEA services, did not fully or comprehensively evaluate her in all areas of disability and did not develop an appropriate IEP for her for two school years.

After the parent requested a due process hearing, the parties reached an agreement. In it, the school agreed to pay for 80 hours of tutoring and enroll the student in a special camp. A provision of the agreement bound the school to pay "reasonable and documented attorney fees and related costs." In response, the parent withdrew the due process complaint and the hearing officer dismissed the case. The parent's attorneys sent the school an invoice for more than $17,000 in attorneys' fees and costs. The school paid only $6,416, asserting that the fees were unreasonable. The parent sued the school in a federal court, which cited a **general rule that parties who settle IDEA cases before an administrative ruling cannot claim "prevailing party" status**. While the agreement provided for attorneys' fees, it was a private agreement that was unenforceable under the IDEA. As the administrative order simply noted the parent had voluntarily withdrawn the complaint pursuant to a settlement agreement, the court found she was not a prevailing party in an IDEA action. *Smith v. Imagine Hope Community Public Charter School*, 934 F.Supp.2d 132 (D.D.C. 2013).

◆   New York parents rejected a 12:1:1 IEP placement for their autistic son and placed him in a private therapeutic setting. A hearing officer found the IEP inadequate, and a new IEP called for a 6:1:1 placement with a behavior intervention plan. The parents rejected that IEP too. Later, the school department agreed to pay for private services. The parents nevertheless sued, but a federal court ruled against them, noting that **the lawsuit appeared to be nothing more than an attempt to recover attorneys' fees**. Since the parents had already received full compensation for their private expenditures, they were not entitled to relief. *M.S. v. New York City Dep't of Educ.*, 734 F.Supp.2d 271 (E.D.N.Y. 2010).

◆   West Virginia parents entered into mediation with their school board over the education of their autistic son. Eventually they rejected the board's settlement offer. A hearing officer then ruled for the parents on four of five issues but found that the board had offered an appropriate IEP. The parents appealed the IEP issue and sought attorneys' fees of $112,292. A federal court upheld the IEP decision and ruled that the board could not assert that its settlement offer was better than what the parents received from the hearing officer because mediation discussions are confidential and the parties had signed an agreement prohibiting releasing that information to anyone, including a judge. **The court reduced the attorneys' fee award to $34,072 to reflect the failure to prevail on the IEP issue.** *J.D. v. Kanawha County Board of Educ.*, 571 F.3d 381 (4th Cir. 2009).

◆   New York parents reached a favorable agreement with a school district over eligibility for one student and evaluation and additional services for another student receiving special education. However, the district refused to pay their attorneys' fees. The parents requested a due process hearing and, just before the hearing, they agreed to a consent decree that included a provision for attorneys' fees. The hearing officer signed the consent decrees, and the parents then sought to be paid attorneys' fees. The case reached the Second Circuit, which held that **the parents became prevailing parties in an IDEA action when the hearing officer signed the consent decrees**. *V.G. v. Auburn Enlarged Cent. School Dist.*, 349 Fed.Appx. 582 (2d Cir. 2009).

♦   After a Texas student failed the state's standardized test three years in a row, his father requested a special education evaluation. The district instead set up a committee to evaluate the student's placement and found it appropriate. The student failed the test again, and his father requested due process. At a pre-hearing resolution meeting, the district offered the father all the relief he sought, including $3,000 in reasonable attorneys' fees. He rejected the offer and sued, obtaining the same relief as well as $45,000 in attorneys' fees. However, the Fifth Circuit reversed the award of attorneys' fees, noting that **rejecting the settlement offer protracted the proceedings**. He got no greater relief after the settlement offer. *El Paso Independent School Dist. v. Richard R.*, 591 F.3d 417 (5th Cir. 2009).

♦   Wisconsin parents became upset when their school district didn't evaluate their son for special education. They placed him in a private school, then requested tuition reimbursement of $15,638. **The district voluntarily paid the amount sought**, but the parents continued with their due process hearing, seeking attorneys' fees. The case reached the Seventh Circuit Court of Appeals, which held that they were not entitled to them because of the district's voluntary payment. However, the district might be entitled to attorneys' fees for defending the action. *Bingham v. New Berlin School Dist.*, 550 F.3d 601 (7th Cir. 2008).

4. Other Proceedings and Issues

♦   A service provider contracted with Minnesota school districts to provide a site-based structured program of group psychotherapy and other therapeutic services. The provider was not subject to state education department oversight. When the provider began employing its own teachers, the districts grew concerned about the appropriateness of its programs and compliance issues. After the districts determined they could each begin to directly provide the services to their students, they informed the provider that they would no longer reimburse it for services or sign new tuition agreements for students to attend its treatment program. Although the provider received written notices from each of the districts to sever their relationships with it, it continued to serve program attendees and billed the districts. One district sent a school bus to the provider's campus to remove its students and bring them to another site. But the provider prevented students from boarding. In a state court action against the districts, the provider advanced claims for breach of contract. It added claims for violation of a state deceptive trade practices law and false advertising. A state district court dismissed the case, and appeal reached the state court of appeals.

The court held a state district court lacks authority to consider municipal decision-making, as this would violate the constitutional separation of powers. But **some of the claims in this case were garden-variety breach of contract claims**. As they did not involve municipal decision-making, the lower court incorrectly dismissed them. Aspects of the case that only challenged failure to perform on the contracts were returned to the district court. But decisions about how to educate students were beyond the scope of the district court's review. As for the claims filed under deceptive trade practices and false advertising laws, the court held these laws regulate commerce and not public schools. The court returned to the district court the provider's breach of contract claims involving failure to pay for services prior to the end of contract termination dates. The other claims were dismissed. *Lifespan of Minnesota v. Minneapolis Public Schools, Independent School Dist. #1*, 841 N.W.2d 656 (Minn. Ct. App. 2014).

♦   The parents of a disabled child in Indiana threatened costly litigation in an attempt to get their own way. After a due process complaint was filed, the parents made many redundant filings and records requests. Eventually the district sought its attorneys' fees, claiming the attorney/mother of the student engaged in frivolous and unreasonable behavior. She sought to have that issue dismissed, but a federal court disagreed. **The district had presented more than six pages of specific, detailed factual claims.** *I.S. v. School Town of Munster*, No. 2:11–CV–160 JD, 2012 WL 928880 (N.D. Ind. 3/19/12).

♦   The parents of an autistic child in Arizona believed that he was not getting a proper education. They filed a due process action against the district, but they lost. When they appealed to a federal court, the court ruled that their complaint was frivolous and awarded attorneys' fees of $140,000 to the district. However, the Ninth Circuit reversed in part, finding the award of attorneys' fees was improper. **The parents' lawsuit, though properly dismissed, was not frivolous.** *R.P. v. Prescott Unified School Dist.*, 631 F.3d 1117 (9th Cir. 2011).

♦   A Texas student entitled to speech therapy missed some sessions because of a shortage of qualified therapists. The school offered a settlement of one hour of compensatory services for each hour missed by the student, plus attorneys' fees. The parent rejected the offer and eventually sued. A court found that **the parent's attorney "stonewalled" attempts to resolve disputes with the district**, including refusing to allow a reevaluation and not participating in the review committee process. It ordered the parent's attorney to pay $10,000 in attorneys' fees to the school district, and the Fifth Circuit affirmed that decision. *El Paso Independent School Dist. v. Berry*, 400 Fed.Appx. 947 (5th Cir. 2010).

♦   A private school in Ohio provided special education services to a student but later expelled him over a dispute concerning the IEP. His parents sued the private school and the school district. After the private school was dismissed from the case, it sought its attorneys' fees from the parents, but the Sixth Circuit ruled that it was not entitled to them. The IDEA only allows for attorneys' fees to be paid to prevailing parents or to state and local educational agencies. The private school was neither. *Children's Center for Developmental Enrichment v. Machle*, 612 F.3d 518 (6th Cir. 2010).

♦   A Texas third-grader with ADHD was found ineligible for special education but was provided accommodations under Section 504. In sixth grade, he was progressively disciplined for misconduct and was reassigned to a special school. His parents challenged the reassignment, claiming that he should have been declared eligible for special education. A hearing officer ordered the district to reconsider his eligibility. A federal court awarded attorneys' fees to the student, but the Fifth Circuit held **a student who is not deemed a "child**

with a disability" under the IDEA cannot obtain attorneys' fees. If he was later ruled IDEA-eligible, he could seek attorneys' fees at that time. *T.B. v. Bryan Independent School Dist.*, 628 F.3d 240 (5th Cir. 2010).

◆   The mother of a D.C. student with disabilities filed a due process complaint against a charter school, asserting various IEP failures. However, when school officials met with her during a resolution meeting, she refused to cooperate, claiming that only a "full time out of district placement" would do, and that the school she'd selected was appropriate. A hearing officer later determined that her claims were frivolous because the IEPs were developed with the mother's full participation. The school then sought its attorneys' fees as a prevailing party, and a federal court held that it could sue to recover the fees. **The mother's lawsuit lacked any factual or legal basis,** and the school she had selected did not even offer the kind of placement she insisted was necessary. *Bridges Public Charter School v. Barrie*, 709 F.Supp.2d 94 (D.D.C. 2010).

◆   The parents of a Georgia student with autism settled their dispute with their school district. The district agreed to provide a functional behavior analysis at a clinic. Six months later, the district determined that the student should return to his local high school placement. The parents disagreed and requested due process, seeking to keep the student in his placement. An administrative law judge agreed with them, and they then pursued a claim for attorneys' fees. However, the Eleventh Circuit ruled against them, noting that **a stay-put placement victory is not the same thing as prevailing on the merits.** *Robert K. v. Cobb County School Dist.*, 279 Fed.Appx. 798 (11th Cir. 2008).

◆   A New Jersey student who molested two younger siblings was placed in a public high school and underwent several independent evaluations. After the district's child study team met several times and determined that the student was not eligible for special education and related services, his parents sought due process. A state administrative law judge denied the parents' request for relief. They appealed to a state court, which ordered the student placed in a treatment facility, with the school district paying for the educational component. The district again found the student ineligible for special education. When the parents then sued for attorneys' fees, a federal court and the Third Circuit ruled against them. **Because the student was never identified as a student in need of special education, attorneys' fees were unavailable.** It did not matter that the parents obtained some relief in getting their child committed. *D.S. v. Neptune Township Board of Educ.*, 264 Fed.Appx. 186 (3d Cir. 2008).

◆   The mother of a multiply-disabled Ohio student sought door-to-door transportation for him. After she and the district agreed to delay the due process hearing, the district offered to reimburse her for the $368 she had spent on transportation to that point, as well as $1,000 for her attorneys' fees. It also offered to have an aide escort her son from her apartment to the bus stop. She rejected the offer and sued the district, receiving essentially the same relief the district had offered, as well as $57,000 in attorneys' fees. The Ohio Court of Appeals reversed the award of attorneys' fees, finding that she failed to exhaust her administrative remedies prior to suing the district and that **she received substantially what the district had offered**. *Olivas v. Cincinnati Public Schools*, 872 N.E.2d 962 (Ohio Ct. App. 2007).

B. Compensatory Education

Compensatory education is a judge-made remedy calling for the belated provision of necessary educational services by a school district to a student with a disability. It is intended to provide a child with the educational benefits that likely would have accrued from services that should have been provided, but were not. Courts award compensatory education even after a student has reached age 21 to remedy the denial of FAPE during time periods when the student was still IDEA-eligible. In M.W. v. New York City Dep't of Educ., a federal court explained that compensatory education may be available to students over age 21, based on "gross procedural violations."

1. Generally

♦   A District of Columbia student had behavioral problems early in his school career and was evaluated for attention deficit disorder and similar disabilities. Before anything came of the evaluation, the parent filed an administrative complaint against the school district, asserting failure to comply with the IDEA's child find obligation despite its knowledge that her child had a suspected disability. A hearing officer ruled against the parent, finding the child's performance and behavior had improved and he was able to keep up with his classmates. No compensatory education was awarded. Noting that the hearing officer did not address the child's future special education needs, the parent made a formal request for a special education evaluation. When the district did not act, she asked for relief from a federal court. There, she raised the issue of a retrospective award of compensatory education as well as the prospective issue of the district's failure to offer an IEP. Before the court issued a ruling, the school district completed a comprehensive evaluation of the child.

Based on the evaluation, the child was found eligible for IDEA services, and an IEP was developed for him. There was no provision in the IEP for compensatory education for his K-1 school years. After the court held the school district's IEP offer made the case moot, the parent appealed. The U.S. Court of Appeals, District of Columbia Circuit, found the parent was now demanding compensatory education, not just a special education evaluation. **The district's decision to provide an IEP for the child did not moot the parent's request for compensatory education.** Since the action was not moot, the case would return to the trial court for consideration of a compensatory education award. *Boose v. District of Columbia*, 786 F.3d 1054 (D.C. Cir. 2015).

♦   California parents said their school district tried to remove their child from general education classes so he could be "warehoused" with severely disabled children. The school district filed a due process hearing request, but while the case was pending the parents filed five state complaint resolution proceeding (CRP) complaints against the district. They asserted non-compliance with state and federal law. After the student was removed from school, the district dismissed the due process case. For this reason, there was no final administrative ruling in that matter. The parents sued the school district and the state education department, seeking compensatory education and damages.

A federal court held the IDEA administrative exhaustion requirement applies when a party "seeks a remedy under the IDEA or its functional equivalent." This includes a party seeking to alter an IEP or a child's placement, or a claim for denial of a FAPE. Ninth Circuit authority clarified that the exhaustion rule is a "claims processing provision" that can be excused if administrative remedies would be futile or if a government agency acts contrary to law. In this case, the parents said the education department did not monitor, investigate and enforce the IDEA. The court held it could not yet determine whether the department failed to investigate the claims or otherwise stymie attempts to obtain district compliance. **Prior Ninth Circuit cases held CRPs can suffice for exhaustion purposes and had found the CRP and due process hearing procedures to be simply alternative means of addressing an IDEA complaint.** As a result, the parents could pursue their IDEA and Rehabilitation Act claims. *Everett H v. Dry Creek Joint Elementary School Dist.*, 5 F.Supp.3d 1184 (E.D. Cal. 2014).

♦   A Pennsylvania student had violent tendencies and developmental delays. He had bipolar disorder and a serious emotional disturbance. Before the student entered district schools, he attended a partial hospitalization program (PHP). Although the IEP team located a private school, the parents soon expressed dissatisfaction and sought another placement. The team did not change the placement, and it recommended an ESY program. The private school informed the parents that it would no longer provide transportation for their child due to his violent behavior. He had threatened to bring a gun on the bus and kill people. Asserting denial of a FAPE, the parents requested a due process hearing. During the hearing, the school district conceded it owed the student compensatory occupational and physical therapy services that it had failed to provide during his kindergarten school year. But a hearing officer awarded the student only 17 hours of compensatory education for occupational and physical therapy.

A state appeals panel increased the award of compensatory education to 24.5 hours, and the case reached a federal court. Although a psychologist stated the student was the most violent child he had evaluated during his 30-year career, the court found the student's teachers stated he was making social and academic progress. Like the hearing officer, the court found the placement did not deny the student a FAPE. It appeared that the student had received only one hour of instruction while attending the PHP. **A school district remained responsible for IDEA services while a student was placed in a private setting such as the PHP.** As a result, the court held the child was entitled to full days of compensatory education. Finding he had been denied 28 hours of weekly IEP services during a 15-week period, the court awarded him 420 hours of compensatory education. This would be added to awards made for the denial of services during the school year and summer, for a total of 439.5 hours. *Tyler W. v. Upper Perkiomen School Dist.*, 963 F.Supp.2d 427 (E.D. Pa. 2013).

♦   The parents of a Michigan student with autism claimed that their district failed to provide the services described in his IEP for grades one and two, and they challenged his IEP for grade three. A hearing officer conducted a 32-day hearing over a 10-month period, then issued a 141-page order finding that the district failed to properly implement the second-grade IEP and that the parents were not allowed to fully participate in the grade three IEP. **The order granted 768 hours of one-to-one compensatory education by a teacher certified to teach students with autism.** The U.S. Court of Appeals, Sixth Circuit, ultimately upheld that determination. *Woods v. Northport Public School*, 487 Fed.Appx. 968 (6th Cir. 2012).

♦   A 17-year-old special education student with ADHD was expelled for coming to school under the influence of marijuana after a multidisciplinary team determined that the incident was not a manifestation of his disability. His mother enrolled him in a private school, then filed a due process request. A hearing officer found no IDEA violation. The mother sought compensatory education about the same time that her son graduated from the private school. A federal court ruled that **the student was not entitled to compensatory education because he had already graduated**. *Fisher v. Friendship Public Charter School*, 857 F.Supp.2d 64 (D.D.C. 2012).

♦   A private evaluator found that a West Virginia student had an autism spectrum disorder, but school officials challenged that classification. A hearing officer later determined that the district violated the IDEA by rejecting her autism diagnosis and predetermining her placement. The district then insisted that a new evaluation be performed by its own candidate. When the student sought compensatory education, a federal court ruled that the district offered a deficient IEP to the student. **It failed to modify the IEP even though it was ordered to do so by the hearing officer**, and it did not provide a behavioral assessment for nearly a year after the hearing. The Fourth Circuit affirmed the award of compensatory education. *Board of Educ. of County of Nicholas v. H.A.*, 445 Fed.Appx. 660 (4th Cir. 2011).

♦   The mother of an 18-year-old Pennsylvania student with disabilities sought compensatory education for him, and a hearing officer ordered the district to provide math and reading instruction as well as emotional support services. More than halfway through the next school year, **the mother sued, claiming that the district had failed to comply with the compensatory education order**. The district claimed that the court lacked the authority to enforce the order because the mother was the prevailing party and not the aggrieved party. However, a federal court held that she was, in fact, aggrieved and thus could seek enforcement of the administrative order. *Dudley v. Lower Marion School Dist.*, 768 F.Supp.2d 779 (E.D. Pa. 2011).

♦   An Alaska school district wanted to change the setting for a student's special education writing instruction to a resource room because the student's teacher was taking family leave. The district failed to provide prior notice to his parents. The student's mother learned of the change at an IEP meeting. After the teacher returned from leave, the district kept the student in the resource room for writing instruction. The student's mother sought to move the student's writing instruction back to the general education classroom. A hearing officer ruled that the district violated the IDEA by keeping the student in the resource room after the teacher returned from leave and awarded 15 hours of compensatory writing instruction in the general education classroom. The Supreme Court of Alaska upheld that award. **The failure to return the student to the general education classroom after his teacher returned from leave justified the award.** *Madeline P. v. Anchorage School Dist.*, 265 P.3d 308 (Alaska 2011).

♦   A New York school district was found to have violated a student's rights under the IDEA. The case reached the Second Circuit, which ruled that the student still had two years of eligibility for compensatory education and that **his parents should be paid for five of the nine classes he attended at college**. It also found the reimbursement award should be reduced by the amount of financial aid and scholarships the student received. The parents were entitled to reimbursement for a laptop and reading software as well as the cost of an independent neuropsychological evaluation. *Streck v. Board of Educ. of East Greenbush Cent. School Dist.*, 408 Fed.Appx. 411 (2d Cir. 2010).

♦   The parents of an 11-year-old Pennsylvania student who had never attended public schools requested an evaluation for special education after obtaining a private evaluation. They did not sign the consent forms for a public evaluation, instead enrolling the student in a private school recommended by their evaluator. Eventually the district was able to conduct an evaluation and prepare an IEP, which the parents rejected. When they sought compensatory education for the delay, claiming that they'd asked for an evaluation during the student's kindergarten year, the Third Circuit ruled against them. It noted that **they were not entitled to compensatory education because they had no intention of placing their son in public school** and that there was no evidence they'd asked for an evaluation during kindergarten. *P.P. v. West Chester Area School Dist.*, 585 F.3d 727 (3d Cir. 2009).

♦   A deaf/hard of hearing student in California had IEPs until she entered a media arts middle school, which exited her from special education eligibility. A stay-put order kept her placement intact until she entered a media arts high school. She withdrew from school but requested another due process hearing, seeking compensatory education. The district claimed that her case became moot when she withdrew from school, but a federal court held that **compensatory education could be a remedy for failure to provide FAPE**. The court allowed her lawsuit to proceed. *Alexis R. v. High Tech Middle Media Arts School*, No. 07CV830 BTM (WMC), 2009 WL 2382429 (S.D. Cal. 8/3/09).

♦   A student was diagnosed with pervasive developmental disorder and was offered an IEP with 10 hours of 1:1 behavior and speech therapy. Near the end of the school year, it was determined that he needed more intense therapy and that he had autism. The parents sought compensatory education to make up for the less intense therapy the student had received during the school year. The case reached a New York federal court, which noted that **compensatory education ought to be available only for a gross violation of the IDEA**, resulting in a near total denial of educational services to an individual who is no longer eligible for public education due to age. Here, the student was five years old and had not been substantially excluded from school. Also, the district had provided positive behavioral interventions and supports. *J.A. and E.A. v. East Ramapo Cent. School Dist.*, 603 F.Supp.2d 684 (S.D.N.Y. 2009).

2. Beyond Age 21

In Wenger v. Canastota Cent. School Dist., *208 F.3d 204 (2d Cir. 2000), the U.S. Court of Appeals, Second Circuit, held that compensatory education is a permissible form of relief for a student over 21 years of age if there has been a gross violation of the IDEA.*

◆ A New York student with speech-language, auditory and language processing disorders was misclassified as severely cognitively impaired for nearly 10 years. Due to the misclassification and lack of a reevaluation, she was placed in a non-credit program for children with severe developmental disabilities. There, she had no access to the general curriculum and did not prepare for a high school diploma. By the time the error was realized, the student was 19 years old and had made little academic progress. A state review officer ordered the school department to provide compensatory education beyond age 21. But he declined to extend the student's eligibility or award instruction to prepare her for a high school diploma. By the time appeal reached a federal court, the student was 21 and had aged out of eligibility in New York.

The court held compensatory education is available to students over the age of 21 as a remedy for earlier educational deprivations, where there have been gross procedural violations. In this case, the deprivation of FAPE for 11 years was not just a deviation from an IEP but "a catastrophic oversight." **An award of compensatory education was held necessary to put the student in the same position she would be without a denial of FAPE.** Since any further interruption in the student's diploma track education would cause academic regression and risk losing the best chance she had at earning a diploma, the court issued an order declaring her eligible for special education. *M.W. v. New York City Dep't of Educ.*, No. 15cv5029, 2015 WL 5025368 (S.D.N.Y. 8/25/15).

◆ A Pennsylvania school district evaluated a student for speech and language therapy. His first IEP had only speech and language goals, and he did not perform at grade level. After repeating his kindergarten year, the student began to have behavior problems. Evaluations obtained by the parents indicated he had bipolar disorder, extreme visual and motor skills problems and "borderline retardation." But the district did not evaluate his cognitive abilities. During the student's second-grade year, his behavior continued to regress, and by grade three his IEP stated he was in a "seriously emotionally disturbed" category. The district placed him in a life skills support program that focused on support for mental retardation. At some point, the district mistakenly identified the student as having mental retardation. He remained in the life skills program for grades three and four. When the student's mother realized the district had improperly identified her son as mentally retarded, she withdrew him from the program.

According to the parents, the school district continued to delay evaluations. When the student was in grade eight, they moved out of the district and asked for a hearing. A hearing officer found the district denied the student appropriate services in all eight years he was in district schools. An hour of compensatory education was awarded for each hour of each school day he had attended school in the district. Later, the parents charged the district with failure to comply with the order. They sued the district in a federal court to recover the monetary equivalent of nearly 10,000 hours of compensatory education. The court dismissed the case, and appeal reached the U.S. Court of Appeals, Third Circuit. It held that while the district misdiagnosed or misclassified the student, this did not demonstrate deliberate indifference to his rights. Since the parents could not show intentional conduct or deliberate indifference by the school district, the court held for the district on the Section 504 and ADA claims. But unlike the lower court, the Third Circuit held the IDEA claims should not be dismissed. The award envisioned a fund for the parents to draw upon, but the district had refused to set one up. The district's claim that the fund was optional would have placed all the responsibility on the parents to remedy its past failures. **This was contrary to the IDEA, which requires a remedy for those who are denied appropriate services.** As a result, the IDEA claims were not dismissed. *D.E. v. Cent. Dauphin School Dist.*, 765 F.3d 260 (3d Cir. 2014).

♦   A federal court held an Ohio school district violated the IDEA by failing to provide a student who had a seizure disorder and other disabilities with adequate transition services. It was clear to the court that the district violated an IDEA mandate to invite the 16-year-old student to IEP team meetings to discuss her postsecondary goals. In addition, the district did not offer her age-appropriate assessments for postsecondary goals. After finding this conduct resulted in a denial of FAPE, the court held a conference with the parties to discuss an appropriate remedy. The parties were unable to agree, and the court provided them an opportunity to propose remedies. In reviewing Sixth Circuit authority, the court noted reservations about basing compensatory education awards on "rote hour-by-hour" calculations. While such awards are not per se inappropriate, the Sixth Circuit has warned against awards that appear punitive.

Even though the student had reached age 22, the parties agreed that the court was authorized to order compensatory services. In the court's view, neither of the parties had proposed an appropriate remedy. The student was entitled to transition services regardless of whether she was likely to attain competitive employment or achieve a high level of independence. The remedy proposed by the parents' expert appeared likely to provide her more than the district could have provided her during her high school career. As a result, the court adopted an employment goal recommended by an expert and an assessment by Goodwill Industries. The student was entitled to an award of some 600 hours of compensatory services. *Gibson v. Forest Hills School Dist.*, No. 1:11-cv-329, 2014 WL 533392 (S.D. Ohio 2/11/14).

♦ A New York student making progress under an IEP was determined not to be a district resident, and her education was disrupted. After two years away, she returned to the district. Her father then began to engage in a series of "obstructionist tactics," such as refusing to attend IEP meetings and demanding a new battery of evaluations. He also declined home education services that the district deemed necessary for the transition back to district schools. He filed a due process complaint too, but he took no action on it. Then he filed a second due process complaint requesting compensatory education. A federal court and the Second Circuit ruled against him, noting that although the school had committed several procedural violations, **the student's lack of formal education for the two-year period was due to her father's unwillingness to permit her to attend school.** Because the student had turned 21, she was not entitled to further assistance under the IDEA. *French v. New York State Dep't of Educ.*, No. 10-4298-CV, 2011 WL 5222856 (2d Cir. 11/3/11).

♦ The parents of a 21-year-old Pennsylvania student with autism asserted that she was deprived of a FAPE while in district schools. Their district set up a trust fund to pay for future educational costs for three years of compensatory education. However, the district sought to cease creating IEPs and no longer wished to serve as her local educational agency. The problem was that the private school the student attended required all students to have IEPs and required a district to serve as an LEA. The case reached the Third Circuit, which held that the student was eligible for relief despite the fact that she was now 24 years old. **The compensatory education was for the denial of FAPE while she was still IDEA-eligible**, and the trust fund by itself was not a sufficient remedy because the private school required an IEP and a district to serve as her LEA. *Ferren C. v. School Dist. of Philadelphia*, 612 F.3d 712 (3d Cir. 2010).

♦ A District of Columbia charter school entered into three settlement agreements concerning remedial education for a student with disabilities. However, his mother contended that the district failed to provide the required services. She sought compensatory education for him and was awarded more than 3,000 hours. But the D.C. Public Schools appealed and sought a stay of the award. A magistrate judge ruled against the school system, noting the student was 25 years old and **the school system was attempting to avoid paying for its failures from more than seven years prior.** *Friendship Edison Public Charter School Collegiate Campus v. Nesbitt*, 704 F.Supp.2d 50 (D.D.C. 2010).

♦ A 19-year-old Tennessee student with no hands, one foot and cerebral palsy was dropped while school district attendants were attempting to move him from his wheelchair. His parents sued for his injuries and received his complete academic record for the first time. They believed his IEPs had been inappropriate and requested a due process hearing. A hearing officer ruled for the school system, but a federal court held that the system violated the IDEA by failing to relay information from the student's previous assessments. The court also held, however, that the student received a FAPE, and it denied his request for compensatory education. After the student received a special education diploma, the Sixth Circuit reversed, ordering the district court to determine whether the case was moot in view of the issuance of a diploma. The district court then held that the student's compensatory education claim was based on his assertion that the school system had denied him a FAPE at a time when he remained eligible for services. Even though he was now 24 and had a special education diploma, **his compensatory education request involved past violations and not future ones**. The case was not moot.

The case returned to the Sixth Circuit, which affirmed the ruling for the student. The case was not moot despite the special education diploma, and the failure to share evaluations with the parents was a procedural violation of the IDEA. Further, even after the student failed to reach his IEP goals, the district did not recommend any different instructional approaches for him. *Barnett v. Memphis City Schools*, 113 Fed.Appx. 124 (6th Cir. 2004).

C. Monetary Damages

Many courts have rejected claims for monetary damages under the IDEA. In Muskrat v. Deer Creek Public Schools, *715 F.3d 775 (10th Cir. 2013), this chapter, the U.S. Court of Appeals, Tenth Circuit, found no authority showing Congress meant to funnel tort claims into the IDEA administrative regime.*

♦ The mother of an Oregon student claimed that after she filed administrative charges, claiming numerous procedural and substantive IEP deficiencies, the school district and its in-house attorney "went into litigation mode." After an administrative law judge ordered the district to provide compensatory education, but before a spot opened up with an outside service provider, the student graduated. The mother sued, but a federal court dismissed all but the retaliation charges. It awarded the mother $1 in nominal damages for the attorney's actions in trying to dissuade her from exercising her rights under the IDEA. However, the Ninth Circuit reversed, noting that **the IDEA does not permit the awarding of nominal damages**. The court held the parents of graduated students did not have standing to pursue prospective IDEA claims. *C.O. v. Portland Public Schools*, 679 F.3d 1162 (9th Cir. 2012).

♦ A Florida child with deafness and other disabilities used American Sign Language in an experimental classroom and thrived there until the district eliminated the program. His parents claimed the new program proposed for him at a new school wasn't appropriate. They also asserted that he was excluded from an aftercare program because of his disabilities. They sought due process and asserted discrimination under Section 504. The district asked a court to have the Section 504 claim dismissed, but the court refused to do so. **The parents did not have to specify the damages they were seeking at the administrative level because the hearing officer had no authority to award them.** *A.L. v. School Board of Miami-Dade County*, No. 10-24415-CV, 2011 WL 1833368 (S.D. Fla. 5/13/11).

♦ The parents of a Pennsylvania student with mental retardation brought numerous due process hearing requests over her school career. By the time she reached age 18, a hearing officer determined that her school district owed her

3,180 hours of compensatory education arising from four different school years. He required over $200,000 to be placed into a trust for her benefit. The parents then sued for compensatory damages, but a federal court and the Third Circuit ruled against them. Although the IDEA permits parents to advance claims on their own behalf, **the parents here sought only money damages, to which they were not entitled**. *Chambers v. School Dist. of Philadelphia Board of Educ.*, 587 F.3d 176 (3d Cir. 2009).

♦   Two Hawaii sisters with autism spectrum disorders were misclassified by the Hawaii Department of Education for several years. Eventually the students were classified as having autism. Their parents brought an administrative challenge, and a hearing officer found that the department had failed to provide autism services to the girls for about four years. Later, the parents sued for money damages under Section 504 and the IDEA. A federal court granted pretrial judgment to the department, but the Ninth Circuit reversed and remanded the case. It held that **the department would be liable under Section 504 if it denied the students reasonable accommodations by failing to provide access to the benefits of public education despite knowing the services were necessary and available**. Issues of fact required a trial. *Mark H. v. Hamamoto*, 620 F.3d 1090 (9th Cir. 2010).

♦   The parents of a Hawaii student with autism brought a series of administrative complaints against the state department of education for IDEA violations. The case eventually reached a federal court, which held that the student was entitled to tuition reimbursement for a defective IEP in 2005-06. **It awarded the student nearly $63,000 as compensation.** *Blake C. v. Dep't of Educ., State of Hawaii*, 593 F.Supp.2d 1199 (D. Haw. 2009).

♦   The parents of an Ohio student expressed concerns about his reading ability to his kindergarten teacher, but the district's evaluation found the student ineligible for special education. The parents obtained a private evaluation that diagnosed their son with a language-based learning disability. Eventually, the district acknowledged his eligibility for special education. The student continued to fall behind in grades three and four. When the parents ultimately sued the district and various officials, seeking emotional distress damages for the officials' intentional failure to deny their child a FAPE, a federal court ruled that the officials could not be sued. **The IDEA permits no monetary claims against individuals.** Any wrongdoing the parents might be able to show in further proceedings would be attributed to the district alone. *Doe v. Westerville City School Dist.*, No. 2:07-CV-00683, 2008 WL 2323526 (S.D. Ohio 6/2/08).

♦   The parents of a severely autistic Pennsylvania student had numerous run-ins with their school district, requesting multiple due process hearings over the student's educational career. A hearing officer eventually agreed that the district had denied the student an appropriate education for the previous three years. She ordered the district to provide 3,180 hours of compensatory education at a cost of $209,000. The parents then sued the district for $8 million for life care, pain, suffering, financial losses and compensation for loss of companionship. They claimed the student would never fully develop her communication skills. However, a federal court ruled that they could not pursue a claim against the district in their own right. **The IDEA does not confer substantive rights on the parents of disabled students.** *Ronald E. v. School Dist. of Philadelphia Board of Educ.*, No. 05-2535, 2007 WL 4225584 (E.D. Pa. 11/29/07).

♦   A New Jersey student with palsy affecting his hands and arms excelled academically, but alleged that he was not given the accommodations required under his Section 504 plan. He sued the board of education, two teachers and the principal in a state court for discrimination under various laws. After the jury was instructed that the school board was responsible for all damages, it awarded the student $500,000 against the board, $150,000 against the principal, $75,000 against his French teacher and $25,000 against his math teacher. The case reached a New Jersey Appellate Division court, which ruled that a new trial on the issue of damages was required. **The jury should not be told that the school board would be responsible for the damage awards**, as that could result in a completely arbitrary allocation of damages. *Grinbaum v. Township of Livingston Board of Educ.*, No. L-4153-01, 2007 WL 1362716 (N.J. Super. Ct. App. Div. 5/10/07).

♦   The parents of a disabled Puerto Rico student maintained that swimming was the only sport their daughter could participate in safely. However, public schools lacked swimming pools, and school officials refused to pay for private swim lessons. The parents enrolled their daughter in a private school and sought tuition reimbursement as well as money damages, which a jury awarded. The First Circuit reversed in part, noting that **personal injury damages are not available under the IDEA**. The only monetary relief available is for educational and transportation costs paid on a student's behalf. *Diaz-Fonseca v. Commw. of Puerto Rico*, 451 F.3d 13 (1st Cir. 2006).

♦   The parents of an Illinois student with a disability sued their school district's former special education director for civil rights violations under 42 U.S.C. § 1983, alleging that she was reckless in developing a defective IEP for their son. They sought money damages from her, **claiming that she had committed the same violations in a previous case and thus knew her actions violated the IDEA**. The director asked to have the lawsuit dismissed, but a federal district court refused to do so. It held that if she acted with recklessness or callous indifference to the student's IDEA rights, she could be liable for money damages. The court allowed the lawsuit to proceed. *Board of Educ. of Elmhurst Community Unit School Dist. 205 v. Daniel M.*, No. CIVA 06 C 2218, 2006 WL 2579679 (N.D. Ill. 9/5/06).

♦   A Virginia student received special education until he moved to a new district, which denied his mother's request for an evaluation. Two years later, the district finally conceded that he was eligible for special education. The mother then sued the district for violations of the IDEA and Section 504. She also sought money damages under 42 U.S.C. § 1983. The IDEA claim settled, and the other two claims reached the Fourth Circuit. The court of appeals held that **she was not entitled to money damages under Section 1983**. The IDEA established a comprehensive remedial scheme, and the student obtained all the relief he was due under that statute. However, the court held the student should be allowed to proceed with her Section 504 claim. *Duck v. Isle of Wight County School Board*, 402 F.3d 468 (4th Cir. 2005).

♦ A Florida student who had problems with grades and behavior in school was found to be ineligible for special education under the IDEA despite his mother's assertions that he had ADD. After the student was suspended for threatening to kill a teacher who gave him poor grades, his parents requested an IDEA due process hearing and copies of his grades and discipline records. The district denied the due process request and failed to provide the records within 30 days, as required by state rule. The parents then sued for money damages under Section 1983, which a jury awarded. The Eleventh Circuit reversed, noting that **there was no policy or custom of denying students access to due process or records that would justify such an award**. No other student had been denied a due process hearing, and the records delay was caused by the winter holiday. *K.M. v. School Board of Lee County, Florida*, 150 Fed.Appx. 953 (11th Cir. 2005).

IV. GOVERNMENTAL IMMUNITY

The doctrine of governmental immunity prohibits lawsuits against the government and its officials. Eleventh Amendment immunity protects states against lawsuits in federal court for money damages, not from prospective relief, like injunctions. Congress may remove a state's Eleventh Amendment protection by clearly and unambiguously abrogating it for particular and specified purposes. In the 1990 amendments to the IDEA, Congress authorized lawsuits against the states for violations of the IDEA. Generally, the Eleventh Amendment protects states or state officials in their official capacities from (a) federal court lawsuits (b) brought by individuals (c) seeking money damages.

Additionally, the Eleventh Amendment does not attach to suits brought by the federal government against a state, or lawsuits brought in state court. Nor does it protect against lawsuits that seek only injunctive relief, like court orders preventing continued harassment or discrimination.

A. Federal Cases

♦ The Kansas Supreme Court refused to review a lower court decision which held the federal Paul D. Coverdell Teacher Protection Act is not available as a defense for a school district in a negligence action by a student who reported that peers bullied him due to his "lazy eye" and height. After a classmate hit the student and fractured his jaw, his mother removed him from school. The family sued the school district, the bullies and their parents. In pretrial activity, the principal obtained judgment based on the Coverdell Act. On appeal, the Court of Appeals of Kansas noted the Coverdell Act is a No Child Left Behind Act provision that immunizes teachers and other educators from liability when they take "reasonable actions to maintain order, discipline, and an appropriate educational environment" at school. **The court held the Coverdell Act immunizes teachers, administrators and other school employees, but not school districts.** There was no basis for granting immunity because the trial court made no findings about negligence. After the court returned the case to the trial court to consider the district's potential liability, the state supreme court denied further review. *Sanchez v. Unified School Dist. 469*, 339 P.3d 399 (Kan. Ct. App. 2014, Kansas review denied, 7/22/15).

◆   A Georgia paraprofessional reportedly sprayed a special needs student with water for acting out during a class. Based on a school police officer's investigation, the principal made a child abuse complaint against the paraprofessional. A school police officer appeared before a magistrate judge to obtain an arrest warrant. According to the paraprofessional, she did this without revealing exculpatory information and falsely stated that he had admitted to the abuse. The paraprofessional was arrested and charged with simple battery and cruelty to children in the third degree. He was then fired by the school district.

In a federal court, the paraprofessional sued the school district, officer and principal for civil rights violations. The court held the officer was entitled to qualified immunity, finding there would have been probable cause for an arrest even if the exculpatory information had been included. There was probable cause for the simple battery charge, rendering the arrest valid. On appeal, the U.S. Court of Appeals, Eleventh Circuit, explained **that qualified immunity protects government officials who are engaged in discretionary functions when they are sued in their individual capacities.** Like the lower court, the Eleventh Circuit held that even if the officer omitted material evidence, there would still be probable cause to support the simple battery charge. The officer was entitled to immunity, since an arrest did not require probable cause with respect to each charge. The court held the officer did not have to resolve legal questions or investigate possible defenses. The officer had reason to doubt the paraprofessional was acting in good faith, and the court held for the officer. *Elmore v. Fulton County School Dist.*, 605 Fed.Appx. 906 (11th Cir. 2015).

◆   A Minnesota charter school special education coordinator and a teacher at the school said the charter entity knowingly submitted false documents and records to the U.S. and the state to obtain funding it was not entitled to receive. They said the charter entity manipulated school attendance and enrollment reports and overstated the special education services it provided. Although the special education coordinator spoke to school officials about the discrepancies, she said her concerns were dismissed. She said her contract was not renewed based on charges that she violated student privacy laws. In a federal court, the former special education coordinator and former teacher sued the charter entity under the federal False Claim Act (FCA) and its Minnesota counterpart.

In its defense, the charter entity claimed to be an arm of the state that was entitled to immunity. The court found state law defined "charter schools" as "school districts" for the purposes of tort liability. As a result, **the charter school entity was not entitled to immunity in this case.** The court held the complaint omitted specific facts such as the time, place and content of the false representations. Since the employees might be able to cure these deficiencies by adding specific or clearer allegations, the court granted them permission to refile their complaint. *U.S. v. Minnesota Transitions Charter Schools*, 50 F.Supp.3d 1106 (D. Minn. 2014).

♦   A severely autistic, nonverbal seven-year-old Texas student began to repeatedly slide a compact disc across a table. According to his parent, an aide grabbed the child from behind, shoved him and repeatedly kicked him. Criminal court proceedings were brought against the aide, who was placed on leave and had to surrender her teaching certificate. In a separate federal case, the parent sued the aide, principal and school district for civil rights violations. She added assault and battery claims against the aide, and negligence and emotional distress claims against the aide and principal. In pretrial activity, the court held the parent had stated a plausible claim for constitutional rights violations.

Finding the right of a student to be free from assault by a school official was clearly established at the time of the incident, the court denied the aide immunity. The court also held the parent made out viable civil rights claims against the school district and principal. The aide appealed to the U.S. Court of Appeals, Fifth Circuit. On appeal, **the court held qualified immunity shields a government official from liability in a federal civil rights action if the official's actions were objectively reasonable in light of clearly established law**. Corporal punishment in schools is a constitutional violation only when it is arbitrary, capricious or unrelated to the goal of maintaining an atmosphere conducive to learning. In this case, the court found the aide was acting to discipline the student. State civil and criminal remedies were available to redress the conduct. In fact, the aide was charged with criminal assault causing bodily harm. She was also placed on leave and required to surrender her license. As a result, the court held the aide was entitled to immunity. The judgment was reversed. *Marquez v. Garnett*, 567 Fed.Appx. 214 (5th Cir. 2014).

♦   A Wisconsin student with brittle bone disease and poor balance attended class under an IEP that called for her to be released from class separately from other students so that she wouldn't have to be in the hallways with them between classes – thereby reducing her chance for injuries. Despite that, she fell in a school hallway walking between classes and was hurt. Her parents sued the district for negligence in a state court. When the case reached the Wisconsin Court of Appeals, it ruled against them, finding that the school district was entitled to immunity. **The IEP did not impose a ministerial duty (which would mean no immunity)** on school employees because it did not eliminate discretion (which allows immunity). For example, the IEP did not state whether the student should be released from class early or late. *Edwards v. Baraboo School Dist.*, 803 N.W.2d 868 (Wis. Ct. App. 2011).

♦   A Missouri student with a learning disability tried to bring a knife to his charter school. He was arrested and admitted to a psychiatric hospital. After the school expelled him, his mother enrolled him in a public school. The superintendent knew of the knife incident and his hospitalization, but didn't inform staff members, and the IEP did not refer to the knife incident. About a year later, the student attacked a classmate with a box cutter and sliced his neck open. The victim sued the superintendent for negligence, but the Supreme Court of Missouri granted him immunity under the Coverdell Act – a provision of NCLB. **The superintendent did not have to provide notice of the student's criminal conduct because the student wasn't attending district schools at the time of the incident**, and the student's IEP made no mention of potentially violent behavior. *Dydell v. Taylor*, 332 S.W.3d 848 (Mo. 2011).

♦   A Georgia teacher often engaged in horseplay with a disabled student. One day, the teacher shoved the student's head into a trash can and then pulled him out by his legs. The student and his family sued, asserting violations of the student's constitutional rights. A federal court and the Eleventh Circuit ruled against them, noting that there was no evidence of any injury suffered by the student. Further, **the teacher did not act with malice or intent to injure**. As there was no constitutional violation, the defendants were entitled to immunity. *Mahone v. Ben Hill County School System*, 377 Fed.Appx. 913 (11th Cir. 2010).

♦   A Nevada student with tuberous sclerosis (a neurological disease that causes tumors) also suffered from autism and was non-verbal. An IDEA lawsuit was brought on his behalf against his school district and teacher. In it, he alleged that his teacher slapped him repeatedly and body-slammed him into a chair. He also claimed that school officials knew about his teacher's violent conduct but did nothing to prevent it. The teacher and district asked for qualified immunity, but the Ninth Circuit denied it. The court of appeals noted that **no reasonable special education teacher would believe it was lawful to seriously beat a disabled four-year-old**. The case was allowed to proceed. *Preschooler II v. Clark County School Board of Trustees*, 479 F.3d 1175 (9th Cir. 2007).

♦   In 1974, a Pennsylvania state school and hospital resident brought a class action suit against the school and its officials, as well as various state and local mental health administrators. The resident claimed that conditions at the institution violated Section 504 of the Rehabilitation Act, the Developmentally Disabled Assistance and Bill of Rights Act, 42 U.S.C. §§ 6001-6081 (DDABRA), Pennsylvania mental health legislation, and the Eighth and Fourteenth Amendments to the U.S. Constitution. When the case reached the U.S. Supreme Court, it reversed a decision by the Third Circuit Court of Appeals, holding that the DDABRA created no substantive rights. It then returned the case to the court of appeals. *Pennhurst State School and Hospital v. Halderman*, 451 U.S. 1, 101 S.Ct. 1531, 67 L.Ed.2d 694 (1981).

On remand, the court of appeals affirmed its previous decision. The U.S. Supreme Court again reversed and remanded the case. **It held the Eleventh Amendment prohibits federal courts from ordering state officials to conform their conduct to state laws.** *Pennhurst State School and Hospital v. Halderman*, 465 U.S. 89, 104 S.Ct. 900, 79 L.Ed.2d 67 (1984).

♦   In 1989, the U.S. Supreme Court, in *Dellmuth v. Muth*, 491 U.S. 223, 109 S.Ct. 2397, 105 L.Ed.2d 181 (1989), ruled that while school districts could be sued under the IDEA, states had Eleventh Amendment immunity in IDEA cases. Congress passed the Education of the Handicapped Act Amendments of

1990 – known as the Individuals with Disabilities Education Act, and included section 20 U.S.C. § 1403, which abrogates a state's Eleventh Amendment immunity to suit in federal court for violations of the IDEA.

B. State Statutory Immunity

Congress enacted the Federal Tort Claims Act to allow individuals to sue the federal government in limited circumstances. Many states have enacted similar legislation wherein they effectively consent to be sued in certain instances. The following cases address immunity for tort claims – which are claims for civil wrongs other than breach of contract.

♦   A Georgia paraprofessional responsible for assisting a kindergartener with her wheelchair earned immunity in a tort action for damages. According to the state court of appeals, she was using her discretion when she let go of the wheelchair to restrain another child. After the paraprofessional took her hands off the wheelchair, it rolled away and flipped over. Later, the child's parents filed a state court action against the paraprofessional. When the case reached the court of appeals, it explained that **official immunity extends to discretionary actions taken in the scope of official authority.** Finding the actions of the paraprofessional were discretionary, the court held she was entitled to immunity. *Postell v. Anderson*, 797 S.E.2d 397 (Ga. Ct. App. 2015).

♦   New Jersey's highest court will review a lower state court decision finding a school district and a school nurse were not liable to the family of a student who lost vision in one eye due to a two-year delay in reporting visual acuity test results. When the student was later diagnosed and treated for eye amblyopia (lazy eye) it was alleged that a two-year delay in notification by the school nurse resulted in a loss of sight in one of the student's eyes. **A state appellate court held the nurse was entitled to state law immunity despite failing to timely communicate the test results.** *Parsons v. Mullica Township Board of Educ.*, 2015 WL 1400996 (N.J. Super. Ct. 3/30/15. Appeal granted, 7/20/15).

♦   Arizona parents said a school employee took pornographic photos of their non-verbal special needs child. In their state court lawsuit, the school district successfully argued it did not know the employee had a prior record of inappropriate conduct. The Court of Appeals of Arizona reversed the lower court's ruling on immunity. It held immunity would not apply only if the school district had actual knowledge (rather than "constructive knowledge") of a propensity for misconduct. The trial court then issued a ruling for the school district, and the parents appealed. When the case returned to the state court of appeals, it held state law insulated a public entity from any liability for a loss caused by an employee's felony acts. The court rejected the parents' argument that "constructive knowledge" of the employee's propensity for misconduct was sufficient to apply an exception to the rule of immunity. Immunity applied unless the public entity actually knew of the propensity for misconduct. **As the parents did not suggest the school district had any actual knowledge of the employee's misconduct when he was a health care employee, the court held**

immunity had been properly granted. In addition, the district was entitled to its costs for defending the appeal. *Gallagher v. Tucson Unified School Dist.*, No. 2 CA-CV 2014-124, 2015 WL 2221657 (Ariz. Ct. App. 5/12/15).

♦   Arizona parents claimed a school employee sexually abused and exploited their child. They said he took pornographic pictures of her while she was at school. The parents sought to hold the school district liable for negligent hiring and supervision of the employee. They urged the court that a previous employer could have told the school district about the circumstances of his termination from employment. Although the district moved the court for state law immunity, the court denied it. Appeal went to the Court of Appeals of Arizona.

   The court stated that Arizona law immunizes public entities for losses arising out of (and directly attributable to) a felony by a public employee. Immunity protects an employer "unless the public entity knew of the public employee's propensity for that action." According to the parents, the immunity from this state law applied even if the public entity had only "constructive knowledge" of an employee felony. But the court said the law referred only to "knowledge." It found the legislature could have said "constructive knowledge" had it wished to apply that standard. Since nothing indicated the district had actual knowledge of the employee's propensity for felonious conduct, the court held the district was entitled to immunity. It declined to resolve the merits of the parents' claim based on "negligent failure to investigate," allowing the lower court to consider that issue. *Tucson Unified School Dist. v. Borek*, 322 P.3d 171 (Ariz. Ct. App. 2014).

♦   A Delaware parent said her autistic child fell down stairs at school while under the supervision of her teachers and paraprofessionals. She claimed the school staff should be liable for "gross, willful and wanton negligence" that caused her child to suffer serious and permanent injuries to her legs, hips and head. In her state court complaint, the parent said the school failed to properly and reasonably supervise the student, failed to provide her with an environment free from danger, hired incompetent and improperly trained and supervised staff, and did not meet the applicable standards of care. While the parent argued that the student's status as a special needs child should cause a "heightened standard of care," a state court held her complaint did not indicate facts that might show previous falls on the steps or any known safety hazards.

   According to the court, there were no facts in the complaint to adequately state a claim for gross or wanton negligence. **And while the parent asserted there had been negligent hiring and supervision by the district, these decisions were discretionary and protected by immunity.** Since she was unable to overcome the district's defense of state law immunity, the case was dismissed. *Tews v. Cape Henlopen School Dist.*, C.A. No. 12C-08158 JRJ, 2013 WL 1087580 (Del. Super. Ct. 2/14/13).

♦   An Ohio student with disabilities was assaulted on his school bus. His family sued the district for negligence, recklessness and willful or wanton misconduct, asserting that the driver operated the bus without stopping to inspect the student or protect the student from ongoing abuse. The school district asked to have the case dismissed on grounds of immunity. The state supreme court, instead, agreed with the student that since the school board was required by law to provide transportation, the function of providing it was governmental, not propriety in nature. **The court accepted, for the purpose of the dismissal motion, the premise that operation of a motor vehicle encompassed more than the mere act of driving it.** It refused to dismiss the claims against the school district or the driver. *N.A.D. v. Cleveland Metropolitan School Dist.*, No. 97195, 2012 -Ohio- 4929 (Ohio Ct. App. 10/25/12).

◆   A 22-year-old Michigan student drowned at a special needs day camp. A lifeguard noticed he was underwater and told a classmate to check on him. The student was quickly pulled from the pool, and staff tried to resuscitate him. Paramedics arrived within minutes but were unable to revive him. An autopsy indicated that the student's epilepsy was a contributing factor to his death. His estate sued his school district and day camp officials in the state court system.

Although the district and officials claimed immunity under state law, the court refused to grant it. On appeal, the Court of Appeals of Michigan explained that under state law, **a governmental agency had immunity from liability in a tort action if the agency was engaged in a "governmental function" at the time of an incident**. A governmental function, in turn, was defined as an activity mandated or authorized by the constitution, a statute, local charter, ordinance or other law. In this case, the district's special needs day camp was authorized by statute, and the court found it was an exercise of a governmental function. Although there was evidence that the camp generated a profit, the court found this did not mean the program was a "proprietary function" rather than a governmental function. Since the proprietary function exception to immunity did not apply in this case, the lower court had improperly denied immunity to the school district and officials. *Glarner v. Okemos Public Schools*, No. 308839, 2012 WL 6633980 (Mich. Ct. App. 12/20/12).

◆   A Mississippi student with a mental disability assaulted a non-disabled classmate, who then sued the district for violating her constitutional rights. She claimed that district officials knew of his propensity for violence because he had previously assaulted a teacher and another student. A federal court and the Fifth Circuit ruled against her. To create any opportunity for school liability, "the school must be aware of an immediate danger to a specific and identifiable student." Here, **the classmate was only one of many who "faced a generalized risk resulting from the school's attempt to integrate a mentally disabled child into a normal school environment."** *Dixon v. Alcorn County School Dist.*, No. 12-60515, 2012 WL 6019053 (5th Cir. 12/4/12).

◆   A six-year-old student with autism, who was nonverbal, somehow lost the tip of his finger while riding a tricycle during adapted physical education. **Two teachers and two paraeducators were present at the time of the injury, but no one witnessed the incident.** Doctors reattached the fingertip, but the student missed the rest of the semester because of complications that required multiple surgeries. When the student's parent sued the district for negligence, it claimed immunity under the Delaware State Tort Claims Act. The superior court denied immunity to the district because there was a question as to whether district employees acted with gross negligence. *Smith v. Christina School Dist.*, No. N10C-06-208 JRJ, 2011 WL 5924393 (Del. Super. Ct. 11/28/11).

♦   A Michigan school system operated a school for 18- to 26-year-old students with physical and cognitive disabilities from throughout the county. A student with cognitive impairments and a seizure disorder was practicing for a Special Olympics event in a system pool, with a lifeguard and a paraprofessional. When they turned away for a minute, he somehow drowned despite the almost immediate administration of CPR. His estate sued the school system and staff members in a state court for gross negligence. When the case reached the Court of Appeals of Michigan, it held that **the school system was entitled to immunity for hosting the Special Olympics event**. However, the court refused to grant the staff members immunity from liability without first making further findings regarding whether they were being paid by the Special Olympics or the government. *Ryan v. Lamphere Public School System*, No. 286741, 2010 WL 934243 (Mich. Ct. App. 3/16/10).

♦   According to a Michigan student with cerebral palsy and partial paralysis, a teacher's aide pushed him to a concrete floor and pushed him again when he tried to stand up. The aide later pled guilty to assault in an unrelated criminal case. When the student sued the district to recover for his injuries, the district claimed immunity, and the Michigan Court of Appeals granted it. **The aide was not acting within the course and scope of his employment when he allegedly pushed the student to the floor.** Therefore, the district was entitled to immunity for his actions. *Booker v. Detroit Public Schools*, No. 290071, 2010 WL 1052275 (Mich. Ct. App. 3/23/10).

CHAPTER TEN

Student Civil Rights

I. BULLYING AND HARASSMENT

A. Bullying

Although state anti-bullying laws and school district policies require schools to address bullying, they do not create causes of action for private lawsuits. For this reason, bullying cases are decided on tort and constitutional theories, as well as state and federal disability and anti-discrimination laws.

An August 20, 2013 "Dear Colleague" letter by the U.S. Department of Education's Office of Special Education and Rehabilitative Services (OSERS) offered guidance and an overview of school responsibilities under the IDEA to address the bullying of disabled students. The letter encouraged bullying prevention efforts embedded in comprehensive, multi-tiered behavioral frameworks to establish positive school environments. The guidance is posted at http://www2.ed.gov/policy/speced/guid/idea/memosdcltrs/index.html.

♦ New York parents said their third-grade daughter was bullied at school almost daily and that staff members did not confront the bullies. Classmates pushed and tripped her, laughed at her and called her "ugly," "stupid" and "fat." When the parents sought to raise the issue of bullying with the committee on special education, they said the principal "flatly refused to discuss the issue with them." The parents said team members told them bullying was "an inappropriate topic to consider" during an IEP meeting. They placed their child in a private school for students with learning disabilities and filed a due process

309

action against the New York City Department of Education (DOE) for private school tuition reimbursement. An impartial hearing officer (IHO) held for the department, and a review officer affirmed the decision. A federal court held for the parents, ruling that **significant, unremedied peer bullying may deny a disabled child a free appropriate public education (FAPE)**. After the case was returned to administrative levels, an IHO and review officer again held for the DOE. The trial court held for the parents, and the case reached the U.S. Court of Appeals, Second Circuit. It found the DOE denied the student a FAPE by refusing to discuss bullying with her parents, despite their reasonable concerns.

Staff members confirmed that the student was constantly teased, excluded from groups and subjected to a hostile environment. Since the DOE's persistent refusal to discuss bullying at important times in the IEP process significantly impeded the parents' participation rights, the court found a procedural denial of FAPE that justified the award of private school tuition reimbursement. *T.K. and S.K. v. New York City Dep't of Educ.*, 810 F.3d 869 (2d Cir. 2016).

♦ A Texas student endured years of bullying at school. His parents said that when they reported bullying, it often led to more misconduct and did more harm than good. By fifth grade, the student said peers assaulted him in the locker room and lavatory. He said they took his clothes from his locker and poured soap on them. Later, the student said peers took his new shoes, threw them in a toilet and urinated on them. He said a student punched him while he had tics, saying "he was trying to fix them." Nothing was done because he did not report this until the next day. Later, he reported being sprayed in the face with cleaner by a student as they cleaned tables. The principal found this was not intentional. In seventh grade, the student was involved in a locker room fight in which he said another student slammed his head against a wall. But the school determined he started the fight. After the student had "tear-away" pants ripped from him, he said the school's response was telling him "not to wear those pants anymore."

After this incident, the parents removed their son from school and sued the district for peer harassment. A federal court held the parents did not show the harassment was based on a disability and also failed to show the district was deliberately indifferent to any harassment. Appeal reached the U.S. Court of Appeals, Fifth Circuit. It held the district had not been deliberately indifferent to peer harassment. **The court found the family could not prevail under the highly deferential standard for peer harassment cases.** It also held the family did not prove discrimination by the district based on a claim that teachers sent the student out of his classroom because of behaviors caused by his disability. *Nevills v. Mart Independent School Dist.*, 608 Fed.Appx. 217 (5th Cir. 2015).

♦ A 17-year-old New York student reported being hit by a classmate without provocation. According to the parents, nobody at the school responded to their complaints and the classmate was never disciplined. Later in the school year, the student told his parents that the classmate verbally harassed and threatened to kill him and his mother. In March of the school year, the student said the classmate hit him again. According to the student's mother, the teacher did not return her calls. She said the principal directed her to stop talking to the teacher.

On a day the classmate threatened to kill the student, the mother got on a school bus and told the classmate to stay away from her son. In response, the school barred the parent from school grounds. Asserting the school did nothing to stop the harassment, the parents sued the school district for disability discrimination. **The court held a peer-based harassment claim under the ADA and Section 504 must allege that there has been some harassment based upon a disability.** While the family cited many instances of bullying by the classmate, as well as an obscenity by the bus driver, the court held they failed to show this was based on the student's disability. Finding the family's generalized harassment claims were not viable under Section 504, the ADA or the U.S. Constitution, the court dismissed the case. *Eskenazi-McGibney v. Connetquot Cent. School Dist.*, 84 F.Supp.3d 221 (E.D.N.Y. 2015).

♦ A California parent claimed his son was repeatedly bullied by peers based on his disabilities and his non-native English speaker status. He said peers forcibly restrained him, beat and kicked him, and made derogatory comments. The parent made two written incident reports detailing attacks on the student and identifying the assailants. He claimed officials did not protect him. In a state superior court, the parent sought a special order against the school district for money damages on behalf of his son and himself. In addition to bringing the case as a parent, he sued in his capacity as a California taxpayer. The parent asserted that the district did not have a comprehensive safety plan for its schools that met the requirements of California Education Code Section 32282. The court dismissed the case, holding the parent did not have standing to pursue it.

When the case reached the Court of Appeal of California, it noted the state's scheme of interrelated laws attempting to protect public school students from discrimination and harassment based on race, gender, sexual orientation or disability. **California public schools have an affirmative obligation to combat racism, sexism and other forms of bias, and a responsibility to provide equal educational opportunity to their students.** A code provision requires each school district to have comprehensive school safety plans for all of their schools. Such plans are to include a discrimination and harassment policy consistent with the prohibition on discrimination in the Education Code. As a result, the parent has standing to pursue the case both as a parent and a state taxpayer. *Hector F. v. El Centro Elementary School Dist.*, 173 Cal.Rptr.3d 413 (Cal. Ct. App. 2014).

♦ A Tennessee student with anxiety and an autism spectrum disorder qualified for a gifted student program placement. He had occasional meltdowns and had to go to a quiet place to compose himself, and he was subjected to bullying on numerous occasions. However, his classroom teacher was not made aware of the bullying or the district's strategies for preventing it. When the teacher had to leave the class for an emergency, the student and a classmate got in a fight. He received an injury that left him legally blind in one eye. His parents sued the district for negligence and were awarded $300,000. **The Tennessee Court of Appeals held that the student's social limitations and tendency to react inappropriately made a physical confrontation foreseeable.** *Phillips v. Robertson County Board of Educ.*, No. M2012–00401–COA–R3–CV, 2012 WL 3984637 (Tenn. Ct. App. 9/11/12).

♦ An eighth-grade Pennsylvania student became self-destructive and was diagnosed with bipolar disorder. Her boyfriend told classmates about her condition, and her cousin (also a classmate) began to call her "psycho," "crazy," and a "psychotic bitch." Although she had friends, she experienced harassment by a few classmates. At one point, she transferred out, but she later returned to the school and graduated. She then sued the district under the ADA and Section 504, alleging discrimination. However, a federal court and the Third Circuit ruled against her, holding that **she was not disabled because she failed to prove she had an impairment that severely restricted her in a major life activity**. *Weidow v. Scranton School Dist.*, 460 Fed.Appx. 181 (3d Cir. 2012).

♦ A Connecticut student with a learning disability, an IQ of 57 and obesity had to withdraw from school due to severe harassment by peers. He was home-schooled for a while, but his parents later sought to return him to school. That didn't happen. His parents ultimately sued their district for negligence, also **asserting civil rights claims based on the repeated harassment**. The Connecticut Superior Court ruled against them, noting that the district had immunity with respect to many of the claims. It could only be liable for harassment on school buses. Those claims failed due to insufficient evidence that harassment had occurred on buses. The Appellate Court of Connecticut affirmed the judgment. Even if the teasing and bullying were as constant as alleged, there was no evidence of negligence by the district. *Silano v. Board of Educ. of City of Bridgeport*, 21 A.3d 899 (Conn. Ct. App. 2011).

B. Peer Harassment and Sexual Assault

In peer sexual harassment cases arising under Title IX of the Education Amendments of 1972, the courts apply a "deliberate indifference" approach from Davis v. Monroe County Board of Educ., *526 U.S. 629 (1999). In* Davis, *the Supreme Court ruled school districts may be held liable under Title IX for student-on-student harassment, where school officials have actual knowledge of peer harassment, but their response is found clearly unreasonable.*

To establish school liability under Davis, *students must show 1) sexual harassment by peers; 2) deliberate indifference by school officials who have actual knowledge of the peer harassment; and 3) harassment that is so severe, pervasive and objectively offensive it deprives the student of access to educational opportunities. Federal courts have held a teacher's knowledge of peer harassment may create "actual knowledge" that triggers Title IX liability.*

♦ A Texas parent complained that a student with a disability who had previously sexually assaulted a girl and spent time in an alternative education program would soon be returning to his child's middle school. Although the parent insisted that the student with a disability go to another school, officials reassured him that other children would be protected. Midway through the school year, the disabled student and another male were accused of "T-bagging everybody." The child of the parent who complained said he had been subjected to this misconduct, and that the disabled student teased and taunted him many other times. Administrators investigated and placed the disabled student and his friend on in-school suspension. After interviewing over 50 students, administrators recommended sending the disabled student and his friend to a disciplinary alternative educational placement. Although the disabled student was transferred, the child's parent withdrew his son from the school district.

In a federal court, the parent sued the district for sexual harassment in violation of Title IX. After the court dismissed the case, he appealed to the Fifth Circuit Court of Appeals. It held that **liability under Title IX for peer-to peer sexual harassment requires proof that the school district had actual knowledge of the harassment**. But the lower court found the district had no knowledge of the harassment until the T-bagging incidents were reported. When administrators learned of the problem, they took prompt investigative and remedial action. Since the court found the school district responded promptly once it learned of the harassment, there was no Title IX violation. *Kelly v. Allen Independent School Dist.*, 602 Fed.Appx. 949 (5th Cir. 2015).

◆ A Nevada student said a classmate approached her from behind, put one hand under her chin and the other on her forehead, then pulled her head straight back, causing injuries. In a federal court, the student sued the school district for disability discrimination and negligence. But the student had not previously reported misconduct. The court analyzed the peer harassment claim under the liability standard from *Davis v. Monroe County Board of Educ.*, 526 U.S. 629 (1999). The court found the student's own statements prevented any finding that the classmate was harassing her on the basis of a disability. She did not show the school was deliberately indifferent to any misconduct. While she felt bullied by the classmate, she never reported anything to the school. **Since there was no evidence that the school knew of any discriminatory treatment of the student based on a disability, her discrimination claim failed.** A negligence claim failed because the student never reported any harassment by the classmate and admitted the teacher likely could not have prevented her injuries. The court found nothing to show the classmate's conduct was foreseeable or that the teacher acted with deliberate indifference. As a result, the school district prevailed on all the claims. *Visnovits v. White Pine County School Dist.*, No. 3:14–CV–00182, 2015 WL 1806299 (D. Nev. 4/21/15).

◆ Due to his visual impairments and severe learning disabilities, a student attended the Colorado School for Deaf and Blind as a residential student. According to his parents, a student who was a sexual predator was admitted into the school and their son's dormitory. They claimed the predatory student sexually assaulted their son. Over a year after the incident, the predatory student admitted sexually assaulting five students on school grounds. The parents said the principal then reported the assault of their child. In a federal court, the parents claimed the school failed to adopt policies to prevent sexual assault, and that it violated Title IX of the Education Amendments of 1972 by showing deliberate indifference to the sexual harassment, creating a hostile environment.

A magistrate judge found the school district was an arm of the state that had Eleventh Amendment immunity from the constitutional claims. She also found the principal should have qualified immunity and recommended dismissing the federal disability claims for failure to state a claim based on a sexually hostile environment. After months of pretrial activity, the court adopted recommendations to dismiss the constitutional claims. **In general, government agencies cannot be held liable for private acts of violence under constitutional theories.** While the constitutional claims were dismissed, claims under Title IX, Section 504 and the ADA survived for further court activity. *BPS v. Board of Trustees for Colorado School for the Deaf and Blind*, Civ. No. 12-cv-02664-RN-KLM, 2014 WL 6990331 (D. Colo. 12/10/14).

◆   A New York City student said his classmates bullied and harassed him during grade eight due to his perceived femininity and speech. He said some misconduct took place in the presence of a teacher and other employees. The student wrote a note threatening suicide, and he was hospitalized with depression. His parents stated that their child's depression worsened as the bullying continued. After the student was declared eligible for special education, an IEP was drafted that placed him in a private center. While at the center, the student reported the same harassment and abuse he had experienced in public school. Once again, he said school employees did nothing to intervene.

When the parents sought a change in placement, they said the school department told them to find a new school themselves. They requested a hearing. A hearing officer ordered the city Department of Education (DOE) to pay for a placement at an approved private school for special education. In a federal court, the parent sued the DOE and the private center. Among the claims were discrimination under Section 504 and the Americans with Disabilities Act, and harassment under Title IX. In pretrial activity, the court refused to dismiss the disability discrimination and harassment claims. While acknowledging that Title IX's "deliberate indifference" standard does not require schools to prevent or eradicate all bullying, **the court held "some effort to discourage that conduct and announce its unacceptability is required."** As a result, the disability discrimination claims would go forward against the center and DOE. For similar reasons, the Title IX claim based on gender discrimination also survived pretrial dismissal. *J.R. v. New York City Dep't of Educ.*, No. 14 Civ. 0392 (ILG) (RML), 2015 WL 5007918 (E.D.N.Y. 8/20/15).

◆   A New Jersey student with disabilities reported being sexually assaulted at school by a male student. Although she said a similar incident took place two years earlier, an investigation of that case found any sexual contact had been consensual. The parents provided the school a psychological evaluation report describing a history of taunting by peers and repeated episodes in which peers touched the student or tried to have sex with her. They sued the school board, an assistant principal and a substitute teacher who let the students in the room where the assault took place. After dismissing IDEA, Section 504, Americans with Disabilities Act and state law against discrimination claims, the family said the first incident should have put the school on notice that the student was at a heightened risk to be sexually victimized by peers. But the court held **the Constitution does not impose a duty on the states to protect individuals from harm inflicted by private actors, such as the male student in this case**.

The court rejected the student's claim that the school should have known she was at a high risk of being sexually victimized due to the prior incident.

There was little support for a claim based on failure to train or supervise staff. A claim that prior sexual assaults took place at the school did not show an inadequate training program. As there was no showing of failure to train or supervise employees in a manner that was deliberately indifferent, the constitutional claims failed. While the student would have a heavy burden at trial to meet the Title IX liability standard, the court refused to dismiss the student's Title IX claim. *Lockhart v. Willingboro High School*, Civ. No. 14-3701 (JBS/AMD), 2015 WL 1472104 (D.N.J. 3/31/15).

♦   A disabled Texas child was sexually assaulted by two boys on a school bus. After her mother learned of this, she discovered that similar assaults had taken place on the bus on previous days. School employees did not review video footage from a camera on the bus in the days leading up to the assault and thus did not learn about the prior incidents until after the child had been assaulted.

The parent sued the school district in a state court for negligence. The court refused to dismiss the action in pretrial activity, and the district appealed to the state court of appeals. There, the district argued it was entitled to immunity under the Texas Tort Claims Act (TTCA). According to the parent, the injury arose from the operation or use of a motor-driven vehicle and the district had waived its TTCA immunity. The parent alleged the failure to operate the security camera and review its footage caused the injury. But the court disagreed, finding **it was speculative that the child would not have been injured had a camera been operating**. As a result, the court held the school district did not waive its TTCA immunity. *Houston Independent School Dist. v. PERX*, No. 14-13-01115-CV, 2014 WL 4262198 (Tex. Ct. App. 8/28/14).

♦   A developmentally disabled Delaware student was led away from her private school by a classmate. He brought her to a secluded area and sexually assaulted her at knifepoint. In a state court action for negligence against the private school, the student's parents claimed the school failed to warn them of the classmate's "sexual deviance." The family also alleged the school failed to counsel, monitor, control or supervise the male student in a manner amounting to gross negligence that was an extreme departure from the ordinary standard of care. During pretrial activity, the private school brought the school district and public high school into the action, asserting negligent supervision. It claimed the public entities did not adequately supervise the female student, who was supposed to be on her bus, or the male student, who was supposed to be in detention. Although the court found the private school asserted enough facts to avoid pretrial judgment, the school district and school claimed they were entitled to state law immunity. In ruling for the private school, **the court held it could not state definitively whether the supervision of students implicated immunity**. As it was premature to make a pretrial ruling, the court denied the district and high school's motion for dismissal. *Hale v. Murphey School*, No. N13C-07-375 PRW, 2014 WL 2119652 (Del. Super. Ct. 5/20/14).

♦   A Massachusetts sixth-grader had a specific learning disability, social skills deficits and anxiety problems. During gym class, an aide observed a male student with cognitive disabilities touching her breast and crotch. A police report was filed, and the male was suspended. When he returned, he was placed in a different classroom. But for seventh grade, the two students were placed in the same classroom. The parent was not told of this, and the seventh-grade teacher was not told of the prior incident. The male student asked the female student to be his girlfriend. He twice took her to an isolated place and initiated sexual contact with her. The parent sued the school district and school officials.

A federal court explained that Title IX creates potential liability for federal funding recipients like school districts but not for individuals. It found the Title IX liability test was met in this case, as the student was subjected to severe, pervasive and offensive harassment that deprived her of educational benefits. **The school district knew of the incidents and did not take sufficient steps to separate the students.** Although the school district argued the first incident was consensual, the court found that a 12-year-old child was too young to legally consent to sexual touching. As there was ample evidence for a jury to find sexual harassment, the court held the Title IX claim against the school district should proceed. In addition, the student advanced discrimination claims against the district. However, the court dismissed them. It found the mere fact that a student with a disability was harassed did not show that the victim was targeted due to a disability. The student's due process and equal protection claims were also dismissed. *Thomas v. Springfield School Committee*, 59 F.Supp.3d 294 (D. Mass. 2014).

◆ An Iowa student with a 67 IQ left school early and met an older student at a friend's house. He raped her in the garage as the friend looked on. In a state court, the student's mother sued the school district for negligence. Her theories of liability included failing to adequately supervise her child, failing to notify her of an unauthorized absence and not acting immediately upon discovering her absence. A jury returned a verdict of $500,000 for the student, reducing it by 30% based on her own fault. Appeal reached the state supreme court.

The court held the school district had waived its argument that it had no duty to protect students from a third party after school and off school grounds. This argument had not been timely raised before the trial court. The same was true of an argument defending the failure to call the police. Generally, tort law limited liability to physical harm resulting from the risks that make an actor's conduct a tort in the first place. The court held the issue was best left to the judgment and common sense of a jury. **There was sufficient evidence in this case to generate a jury question on the issue of whether the student's injuries were among the potential harms that made the school district's conduct a tort.** The court rejected the district's argument that the off-campus location of the assault and the fact that it took place after school hours disposed of the case as a matter of law. As a result, the court held for the student. *Mitchell v. Cedar Rapids Community School Dist.*, 832 N.W.2d 689 (Iowa 2013).

◆ Texas parents of a child with blindness and autism reported bullying, threats and possible battery by his peers from his kindergarten year through grade four. They asserted they called, emailed and made in-person reports to the school about ongoing bullying about three times during these school years. In the student's fourth-grade year, he reported to his therapist that peers forced him to use the lavatory when he did not have to go. He said bullies would pull him out of the stall when his pants were down and make him stroke and fondle his penis. The student also said one of the bullies grasped his penis, stroked it and said "I will show you how to do it." Although police interviewed 15 students about the incident, no charges or juvenile proceedings were initiated.

The parents removed their son from school and requested a due process hearing. An IDEA claim was settled, with the school district agreeing to pay his private school tuition for two years. Claims filed under the Americans with Disabilities Act, Section 504 and Title IX of the Education Amendments of 1972 were referred to a federal magistrate judge, as were state tort claims. Most of those claims were eventually dismissed. According to the magistrate judge, a party seeking compensatory damages under federal laws must show more than just failure to provide a free appropriate public education. Instead, **there must be some refusal to provide reasonable accommodations that creates an inference of professional bad faith or gross misjudgment**. The school district showed that each time the parents complained, the reports were handled "quickly, appropriately and professionally." School officials did not act in bad faith or with gross misjudgment. As a result, the magistrate judge recommended dismissing the Section 504 and ADA claims. *C.L. v. Leander Independent School Dist.*, No. A-12-CA-589, 2013 WL 6837741 (W.D. Tex. 12/20/13).

◆   A Pennsylvania third-grade student with autism had behavioral issues. He was observed standing on the toilet seat in the lavatory and looking at students in other stalls. Eventually, the school decided it could no longer provide him necessary therapy or support, and the IEP team recommended a private special education school. A 15-year-old student with a prior disciplinary record attended her class and eventually initiated sexual encounters with the student. Near the end of the school year, the student's parent read his journal entries and learned of the sexual activity. She sued both the school district and private school in a federal court. It found the district retained some involvement after placing the student. **Although the parent urged the court to impose liability on the district for a "state-created danger," the court held no district action satisfied the foreseeability requirement of this theory.** The district did not have reason to suspect that sexual assaults would occur at the private school. Although the school district was entitled to judgment, the court held a jury would have to consider the punitive damage claims against the private school. *Reichert v. Pathway School*, 935 F.Supp.2d 808 (E.D. Pa. 2013).

◆   A Washington student with cognitive delays formed a relationship with an 18-year-old special education student. A teacher discovered the students were leaving class to use the lavatory at the same time. When the mother confronted her child, she learned the two students had attempted to have sex twice in the boys' lavatory. After removing her child from the school, the parent filed a police report. During her interview with a detective, the student described a consensual relationship in which she was not forced to do anything. In a state court action against the school district and officials, the mother sought damages for negligent supervision of her child. After a six-week trial, a jury found the student was not damaged by any district acts or omissions. On appeal, the mother argued that the trial court should not have admitted evidence of her child's sexual activity. Prior to the lavatory incident, she had broken off a sexual relationship because of pregnancy concerns and asked her mother for birth control pills. **But the court held the evidence was relevant to the student's understanding of the consequences of sexual activity at the time of the lavatory incidents.** Although the mother advanced other arguments, the court rejected each of them and upheld the verdict for the school district. *Patel v. Kent School Dist.*, 176 Wash.App. 1008 (Wash. Ct. App. 2013).

♦ A Michigan student with cognitive disabilities told his mother that a male classmate had grabbed his privates when he used the lavatory. After learning of the incident, the mother called the student's teacher and teacher's aide. She said the teacher expressed disbelief about the incident. A month later, the mother said her son told her the classmate had "licked his nuts" and "licked him off" and was grabbing him. After questioning the student, the school social worker began to suspect he was being abused at home. She made a report to the state Child Protective Services (CPS). In a federal court, the student's parents sued the district and school officials for sexual harassment and retaliation.

According to the court, the parent did not show the school district acted to retaliate against her. It noted the absence of any evidence that the social worker, principal or superintendent knew about the first incident. The social worker was required to report to CPS, and her report was not evidence of retaliation. The parent did not show the school district acted with the requisite culpability for a constitutional violation. In reviewing a claim for peer sexual harassment under Title IX, the court held the parent did not show the district or its employees were deliberately indifferent to the risk that her son would be assaulted in a restroom. **The court stated that harassment victims had no right to make remedial demands regarding harassers.** *Edmonds v. Detroit Public Schools*, No. 12-10023, 2013 WL 425382 (E.D. Mich. 2/4/13).

C. Sexual Assault by School Staff Members

The U.S. Supreme Court has recognized the potential for school liability under Title IX where a student is harassed by peers or staff members. In Gebser v. Lago Vista Independent School Dist., *524 U.S. 274, 118 S.Ct. 1989, 141 L.Ed.2d 277 (1998), the Supreme Court held school districts may be held liable for sexual harassment of students by teachers and other staff under Title IX.*

Damages are inappropriate in a Title IX case unless an official with the authority to address the discrimination fails to act despite actual knowledge of it, in a manner amounting to deliberate indifference.

♦ A wheelchair-bound student was denied U.S. Supreme Court review of lower court decisions denying him relief under the Rehabilitation Act for claims based on a sexual assault committed by a school employee. According to the student, an aide molested him in a school lavatory. After his mother reported the assaults, the aide confessed to the misconduct. In a federal district court, the family settled its claims against the aide. The court held for the school district on the remaining claims, and the family appealed to the U.S. Court of Appeals,

Fifth Circuit. The court held the facts did not support any of the student's claims. Two employees accompanied the student to the vast majority of his lavatory visits, and there was no showing of intentional discrimination. **Not only did the student fail to show intentional discrimination under Fifth Circuit precedents; he also failed to show the denial of a free appropriate public education.** *Estrada v. San Antonio Independent School Dist.*, 575 Fed.Appx. 541 (5th Cir. 2014, U.S. cert. denied 2/23/15).

◆   A Pennsylvania student with disabilities said an assistant principal (AP) at her school repeatedly sexually assaulted her. According to the student, her peers accused her of having sex with the AP and called her names such as "whore" and "home-wrecker." When a teacher reported the suspected relationship of the AP and student, administrators interviewed several students but found the report was not substantiated. According to the student, peers continued to harass her. Nothing was officially reported to the police until the following school year, when a school resource officer reported the relationship to municipal police.

After a brief investigation, the AP was arrested. The student transferred to another district and filed a federal case against the AP, school district and other officials. In the court's view, the constitutional claims were not viable since no violation was the result of a municipal custom, practice or policy. A "failure to intervene" claim against school administrators was dismissed, as the court held it was not shown they were deliberately indifferent to constitutional violations by the AP. **The court held the notice requirement was not satisfied based on claims of unsubstantiated rumors at the school.** It also dismissed the claims based on constitutional theories of failure to train, negligent hiring, negligent retention and failure to discipline the AP. On the other hand, the court held the student made out a valid preliminary Title IX case against the school district. As she claimed officials knew a hostile environment was created but did not respond to it, her Title IX claim was held viable. *M.S. v. Susquehanna Township School Dist.*, 43 F.Supp.3d 412 (M.D. Pa. 2014).

◆   A Massachusetts high school student was sexually harassed by her school soccer coach, but she did not reveal this for months. When her parents approached the school for help with her emotional problems, they were advised to file a child in need of services petition with a juvenile court. When the student finally told a friend she had been assaulted, her mother reported it. Another report involving the coach then surfaced. He was fired and later pled guilty to criminal charges. It was learned that throughout the fall and winter, the coach verbally harassed the student, texted her pictures of his penis, and asked for nude photos of her. After his arrest, the school held a class-wide assembly to discuss the incident and arrest. According to the parents, the student's absence was noted at the assembly, leading to speculation that she was the victim. After being admitted to a hospital, the student was evaluated for special education. Her parents placed her in a residential therapeutic school for which they sought reimbursement from the school system. After the school district found her eligible for special education, it agreed to pay for a residential placement.

The student ran away from the residential school, and the team could find no other placement for her. After a due process hearing, the parents filed a federal court case. The court held constitutional claims based on sexual abuse could proceed. **Further evidence would be heard regarding whether the school was deliberately indifferent to earlier reports of sexual relations between the coach and other students.** There was no merit to an IDEA claim, but the family raised enough evidence to avoid pretrial dismissal of their claims under Section 504 and the ADA. The court refused to dismiss a negligence claim based on failure to dismiss the coach after a reported sexual relationship. *Doe v. Bradshaw*, No. 11-11593-DPW, 2013 WL 5236110 (D. Mass. 9/16/13).

II. REASONABLE ACCOMMODATION

Rehabilitation Act Section 504 states that no otherwise qualified individual with a disability shall, "solely by reason of her or his disability," be excluded from participation in, denied the benefits of, or be subjected to discrimination under any program or activity receiving federal assistance. In school settings, a viable Section 504 claim is stated when it is alleged that a school has denied reasonable accommodations for a disabled student to receive the full benefits of the school program. The Americans with Disabilities Act of 1990 (ADA) is based upon the anti-discrimination principles of Section 504 and covers public and private entities without regard to receipt of federal funding.

Under the ADA and the Rehabilitation Act, educational facilities, as well as many other entities, are required to make reasonable accommodations for disabled individuals. This entails the reasonable modification of policies, practices or procedures when such modifications are necessary for disabled individuals to participate in programs or to benefit from services. However, modifications that would fundamentally alter the schools' programs or services, or that would result in an undue burden or hardship, are not required.

◆   A Michigan child with spastic quadriplegic cerebral palsy wished to bring a service dog to school. When the school district did not allow the dog to accompany her, the family filed a federal court action without requesting an IDEA due process hearing first. When the case reached the U.S. Court of Appeals, Sixth Circuit, it affirmed a lower court judgment dismissing the case. It held **the family should have pursued IDEA procedures before filing the action**. *Fry v. Napoleon Community Schools*, 788 F.3d 622 (6th Cir. 2015).

◆   A Florida child had cerebral palsy, a seizure disorder and other disabilities that required her to have daily living support. Her mother obtained a service dog that was trained to perform life-saving duties and to alert responders in case of a medical crisis. The school board required the mother to provide a handler for the dog, provide proof of liability insurance and proof of vaccinations mirroring those for Florida dog breeders. A health care plan was devised to address the board's responsibilities in the event that the student had a seizure, but neither the plan nor the student's IEP specified the use of a service dog. In a federal court, the mother sued the board for violating federal disability protection laws.

The court relied on 28 C.F.R. Part 35.136, a federal regulation that generally requires public entities to modify their policies so disabled persons may use their service animals. **Unless an entity could show a requested modification would fundamentally alter its program, the modification was deemed necessary to avoid discrimination.** The board did not argue that allowing the student to attend school with the service dog would fundamentally alter its program. The court held the policies requiring additional insurance and vaccinations amounted to impermissible discrimination. It also found that since the dog would be tethered to the student's wheelchair and was fully trained, there was no need for a separate handler. *Alboniga v. School Board of Broward County Florida*, 87 F.Supp.3d 1319 (S.D. Fla. 2015).

◆   Due to Klinefelter Syndrome and ADHD, a California student was eligible for Section 504 accommodations. He enrolled in an advanced placement (AP) calculus course, where he struggled and suffered from anxiety and weight loss. His mother asked for permission to drop the class, but was told the three-day window for dropping classes had passed. An assistant principal told her no exceptions could be made to the school policy. A hearing officer denied the parent's request for an order requiring the district to pay for a Section 504 evaluation and remove a failing AP calculus grade from the student's records.

A federal court held the Section 504 claim had to be dismissed. It held the student was prohibited from dropping the AP class under a general rule of the school district, not because of a disability. But the court held **the student had a plausible claim against school administrators regarding a timeline and procedure for proposing and conducting evaluations for students who might need Section 504 accommodations**. The student could refile this claim to allege he was denied a service or benefit solely due to a disability. But he could not show any deprivation of a protected interest in not being allowed to drop his AP course. A due process right is only implicated when exclusion from the entire educational process is at stake. *S.M. v. San Jose Unified School Dist.*, No. 14-CV-03613, 2015 WL 1737535 (N.D. Cal. 4/13/15).

◆   Upon enrolling her children at an Oregon school, a parent claimed she was greeted in Spanish and given Spanish-language enrollment forms even though she did not speak Spanish. She accused the school of not responding to verbal assaults of her two biracial children and said the principal "roughed up" her son. The parent said her son had oppositional defiant disorder and attention deficit hyperactivity disorder. But she said her requests to have him evaluated for a special education evaluation were rejected. After her son was expelled for behavior which she claimed was due to his disabilities, she sued the school district in a federal court. First, the court held the mother – as a non-attorney– could not sue on behalf of the children without a lawyer. But the claims on behalf of the children could be refiled with counsel, or when they reached majority. Next, the court held the constitutional claims had to be dismissed.

A race discrimination claim under Title VI of the 1964 Civil Rights Act was dismissed. As the mother did not allege any incidents of intentional discrimination, no Title VI violation was shown. **The court rejected a claim that being mistaken for Hispanic and greeted in Spanish made out a valid race discrimination claim.** But the parent was allowed to refile the claim. Last, the court agreed with the school district that the mother could not pursue an

IDEA claim based on failure to identify her son's disability without exhausting her administrative remedies. *Graham v. Portland Public School Dist. #1J*, No. 3:13-cv-00911-AC, 2015 WL 1010534 (D. Or. 3/5/15).

♦   A Pennsylvania child with autism, sleep apnea and other health conditions fell asleep on his school bus and was left there at the end of the school day. His parents later sued the school district. A federal court held the school district's knowledge about the student's disability was sufficient to establish that harm was foreseeable and fairly direct. It held the risk of harm from leaving a child unattended was foreseeable. Transportation was a daily responsibility for which the district had ample time to plan and provide for student needs. Finding the district knew of the student's medical condition and his need for special supervision, **the court found a reasonable jury could find deliberate indifference or conscience-shocking behavior based on the district's lack of relevant policies and training**. In addition, the parents made a sufficient showing that the district improperly trained its employees. *K.M. v. Chichester School Dist.*, Civ. No. 14-2131, 2015 WL 568553 (E.D. Pa. 2/10/15).

In a separate order, the court found there was no clearly established right at issue under the circumstances of the case. Since the employees were not on notice that the due process violation arose to the level of a deprivation of civil rights, they were entitled to qualified immunity. *K.M. v. Chichester School Dist.*, Civ. No. 14-2131, 2015 WL 569145 (E.D. Pa. 2/10/15).

♦   Kentucky school officials refused to place a diabetic student who needed daily insulin injections at his neighborhood school because there was no full-time nurse there. It offered a placement at another school that was staffed by a nurse. School nurses believed insulin injections were "solely a nursing function." Another request to attend the neighborhood school was denied, and the child began attending another district school that was staffed by a school nurse. The parents sued the board of education in a federal court for disability discrimination. They claimed non-medical personnel could have been trained to monitor the child and assist him. The court held for the school district. Appeal reached the U.S. Court of Appeals, Sixth Circuit, which vacated most of the judgment and sent the case back to the trial court. The trial court then noted the child could independently manipulate his insulin pump. He still needed help counting his carbohydrates, which could be done by a trained person. No evidence indicated the board had a policy to use the same assignment protocols for all diabetic children without an individual inquiry into their specific needs.

When the child became fully independent in his use of insulin pumps in grade two, he was enrolled in his neighborhood school. Moreover, the student had no unique educational needs and did not require a specialized placement. Since district schools used identical curriculums, there was no evidence that the child was denied any benefit by being required to enroll in a non-neighborhood school. **Section 504 does not require a school district to ensure a neighborhood placement.** In sum, the court found the family did not show the accommodations were unreasonable. *R.K. v. Board of Educ. of Scott County, Kentucky,* No. 5:09-CV-344-JMH, 2014 WL 4277482 (E.D. Ky. 8/28/14).

◆   An Indiana high school student began having allergic reactions to certain perfumes. His mother sought to implement a policy against the spraying of perfumes, but instead, the principal instructed staff to advise students not to spray perfume anywhere but the lavatories. After the student was hospitalized, the family sued for discrimination. A federal court ruled for the school, noting that it had made efforts to stop the spraying of perfume in hallways and classrooms. **Since there was no intentional discrimination by the school, the lawsuit had to fail.** *Zandi v. Fort Wayne Community Schools*, No. 1:10–CV–395–JVB, 2012 WL 4472006 (N.D. Ind. 9/27/12).

◆   An Illinois student with ADHD received many informal accommodations and achieved excellent grades, including in honors classes. His parents nevertheless sought Section 504 accommodations, which the district denied. When the parents sued, the district offered a Section 504 plan providing the same accommodations he had received informally. A federal court **found no evidence that the district had been deliberately indifferent to the student's Section 504 rights**. *Zachary M. v. Board of Educ. of Evanston Township High School Dist. #202*, 829 F.Supp.2d 649 (N.D Ill. 2011).

◆   A California student with a progressive genetic neurological disorder had a 3.8 grade point average, did volunteer work and joined a student club. But she was unable to use the stairs at her high school and had to wait for school staff to use the elevator to access most of her classes and the school library. She had to drop two advanced placement classes as a result. When she requested an elevator key, the district refused to give her one. She sued under Section 504 and the state's civil rights act. **A federal court agreed with the student and ordered the district to provide her with an elevator key.** *D.R. v. Antelope Valley Union High School Dist.*, 746 F.Supp.2d 1132 (C.D. Cal. 2010).

III. FEDERAL CIVIL RIGHTS REMEDIES

Section 1983 of Title 42 of the U.S. Code (42 U.S.C. Section 1983) is a federal statute that creates no rights itself, but is used to enforce rights created by federal laws and the Constitution. Section 1983 imposes liability on a school district or other government entity that has a policy or custom of violating constitutional rights. It also creates individual liability for school officials who violate clearly established constitutional rights. The IDEA expressly allows disabled students to cumulate all their available remedies under federal law.

◆   A Massachusetts student faced physical and developmental challenges attributed to his premature birth at 27 weeks. He was very small for his age and had attentional and executive function disorders. He had inappropriate social behavior and poor impulse control. The student's Section 504 plan called for counseling, supervision and the monitoring of peer conduct to protect him from abuse. According to the student's parent, he was regularly bullied and abused by peers based on his social behavior, small stature, Jewish ethnicity and religion, perceived sexual orientation and his disorders. She claimed peers mocked him, expressed a desire to kill him, made snide comments about the Holocaust and used social media to suggest he was gay. The parent sued the school district for bullying, harassment, constitutional rights violations, retaliation and state law violations. She accused teachers and administrators of engaging in abusive conduct. In pretrial activity, a federal court dismissed her negligence claims.

Because the parent did not file an IDEA due process hearing request, her Section 504 and IDEA claims were dismissed for failure to exhaust administrative remedies. The court found no due process violation. **While the parent alleged non-action by school staff, she did not assert any intentional conduct** and did not show a violation of rights that was shocking to the conscience. Not enough facts were stated to support many of the federal claims. But the court granted the parent an opportunity to refile her papers to include additional facts. Among these were an equal protection claim and a claim for retaliation under Section 504. A claim under Title VI of the Civil Rights Act of 1964 based on religious and ethnic harassment was dismissed as there was no showing that any religious harassment was severe and pervasive. *Pollard v. Georgetown School Dist.*, 139 F.Supp.3d 208 (D. Mass. 2015).

♦   The disabled mother of a Texas student who played on the junior varsity football team sued the school district for discrimination because she couldn't get into the bleachers and was forced to watch her son's game through a chain link fence in a wheelchair-accessible area. She could only see about 15% of the game from there and did not return to watch any other games. A federal court and the Fifth Circuit ruled against her, noting that the ADA did not require the district to make it possible for her to watch the game in the bleachers with the other fans. Here, **she was able to navigate the stadium, buy a ticket and concessions and view part of the game. The district's program, as a whole, was accessible to individuals with disabilities.** *Greer v. Richardson Independent School Dist.*, 472 Fed.Appx. 287 (5th Cir. 2012).

♦   A high school freshman with an IEP moved to a New York school district that was overwhelmingly white, where others threatened him and repeatedly called him "nigger." The harassment escalated over the next three years, despite frequent reports of misconduct. Near the start of his fourth year in the district, his mother allowed him to accept an IEP diploma rather than attend school further. He sued the district for race discrimination in violation of Title VI. A jury awarded him over $1 million, and the Second Circuit upheld the award. **It found abundant evidence of the district's knowledge of harassment, and its remedial responses were "little more than half-hearted measures."** *Zeno v. Pine Plains Cent. School Dist.*, 702 F.3d 655 (2d Cir. 2012).

♦   After a male student assaulted a female student with multiple disabilities, her parents sued the school district for violating Title IX and the Michigan Persons With Disabilities Civil Rights Act. The court dismissed the Title IX claim, and a jury ruled for the district on the state law discrimination claim. The Michigan Court of Appeals upheld the jury's verdict. **The student did not qualify for protection under the state discrimination law because her cognitive impairments prevented her from utilizing or benefiting from general**

educational opportunities. The law only prevented discrimination against individuals because of a disability that is unrelated to the individual's ability to use and benefit from the school's services. *Tyler v. Fowlerville Community School Dist.*, No. 295906, 2011 WL 1261828 (Mich. Ct. App. 4/5/11).

◆ Students from two different New York school districts filed complaints with the state division of human rights, claiming the districts permitted discriminatory actions against them. The districts asserted that the state human rights agency had no authority to investigate them, and the New York Court of Appeals agreed. **Students with human rights complaints can contact the state commissioner of education or seek relief under the Dignity for All Students Act.** *North Syracuse Cent. School Dist. v. New York State Division of Human Rights*, 973 N.E.2d 162 (N.Y. 2012).

◆ A Georgia school district assigned a one-on-one assistant to an aggressive autistic student for an after-school daycare program and also devised a behavior intervention plan. A custodian with a special needs son received training and served as the assistant but often had to be away to attend to his own child. On a day when the custodian was absent, the student became agitated and left the building. Eventually, several staff members placed him in his time-out room, where he hit the window and kicked the walls. A police officer handcuffed him until his father could come and pick him up. The father later sued for disability discrimination under Section 504 and the ADA, but **a federal court found no evidence of intentional discrimination against the student. At most, staff members acted negligently.** *J.D.P. v. Cherokee County, Georgia School Dist.*, 735 F.Supp.2d 1348 (N.D. Ga. 2010).

IV. DISCRIMINATION

In A.G. v. Lower Merion School Dist., *Chapter One, Section II.B., the court held that the "deliberate indifference" standard from sexual harassment and civil rights cases may also apply to disability discrimination cases under Section 504 of the Rehabilitation Act and the Americans with Disabilities Act.*

For a Section 504 violation to be discrimination in the context of education, it must be significant enough to effectively deny a disabled child a public education. For additional Section 504 and ADA cases involving claims of denial of a free appropriate public education, see Chapter One of this volume.

◆ After enrolling their child in a school district, Washington parents withdrew their consent to his special education program. They said his teacher and a co-principal blamed their child for classroom incidents in which a classmate made cruel racial remarks. The parents said the school blamed their child for other incidents and improperly decided not to question important student witnesses. When the child wrote two "disturbing essays" describing incidents in which the classmate was violently harmed, nobody told the parents about them. When the district investigated, information about one of the essays appeared in the report. As soon as the parents saw it, they asked for an immediate transfer of their son. They sued the district, and their case reached the state court of appeals. It held the school district did not follow proper investigation procedures because they did not interview all the students in the work group. The co-principal could not explain her feeling that the child's condition would affect his ability to hear a racial epithet. The essays were not shared with the parents, and the school did not take into account the discrepancy between his grades in social studies class and his other classes. In fact, the court found the school refused to consider any scenario in which the child was not to blame for conflicts with the classmate.

The school district did not appropriately discipline the classmate, despite his history of serious behavior problems. The court found the parents showed harassment that was severe, pervasive and objectively offensive and deprived their child of access to educational opportunities or benefits. In ruling for the student, **the court held school districts have a duty to promptly investigate harassment and take prompt and effective steps calculated to end it**. Finding the school district acted with deliberate indifference to the child's reports of discriminatory harassment, the court held there was a violation of state law. *Mercer Island School Dist. v. Office of Superintendent of Public Instruction*, 186 Wash.App. 939, 347 P.3d 924 (Wash. Ct. App. 2015).

◆ African-American students and their parents accused a Pennsylvania school district of intentional race discrimination in placement decisions. They claimed the district violated the IDEA in its identification and placement decisions. Some claimed they were denied opportunities to take challenging classes to prepare for college and said their classes amounted to "baby work." The court noted **Title VI of the Civil Rights Act of 1964 requires proof of intentional discrimination**. It held the statistical evidence was insufficient to prove a Title VI violation and nothing supported the discrimination claims except subjective belief. As there was no evidence of intentional discrimination by the district, the court found no Title VI violation. For similar reasons, the court found no merit to the constitutional claims. It appeared to the court that the students were simply "unhappy generally with the education they received or are receiving." On appeal, the Third Circuit Court of Appeals found the Rehabilitation Act, ADA, IDEA and Title VI claims based on discrimination were properly dismissed. With the exception of one family, these claims were properly dismissed due to the failure to exhaust IDEA administrative remedies.

The claims of some students had already been resolved in a companion case – *S.H. v. Lower Merion School Dist.*, 729 F.3d 248 (3d Cir. 2013), see Chapter One, Section II.B. In *S.H.*, the court held students who were misidentified but not eligible for IDEA services could not bring IDEA claims. As for a student who had graduated, her IDEA claims were time-barred by an IDEA limitations period. Claims against the state department of education were barred by the settlement of a separate federal case. As for claims under Title VI and the Equal Protection Clause of the Fourteenth Amendment, the students said the disproportionate placement of African-Americans in remedial classes had a discriminatory purpose based on racial bias. But the court found insufficient evidence of intentional discrimination. **Despite statistics showing minority students were overrepresented in the district's low-achievement classes, no evidence of intentional discrimination was found.** Although the students raised many additional arguments about the use of evidence by the lower court, the court rejected the challenge. As a result, the judgment for the school district was affirmed. *Blunt v. Lower Merion School Dist.*, 767 F.3d 247 (3d Cir. 2014).

♦ The parents of a Puerto Rico child with Asperger's syndrome obtained an expert's opinion recommending placement in a group of six or fewer children. The department of education's special education supervisor refused to follow the recommendation, and the parents placed the child in a private school. After attending the school for two years, the student began biomedical treatment that required him to follow a special diet. A dispute arose over the parents' request to come to school each day to feed him. Problems intensified, prompting the parents to accuse the school of discrimination. The parents tried to file a complaint against the school with the Puerto Rico Department of Education, but the department declined the request because the school was private. The parents then sued the department and school in a federal court for discrimination and retaliation. They sought relief including more than $6 million in compensatory and punitive damages. After the court dismissed the case, the parents appealed. The U.S. Court of Appeals, First Circuit **found that where a claim involves a violation of the IDEA, parties may not try to use other laws in an attempt to evade the IDEA's remedial structure**. The parents did not state a claim for discrimination or retaliation under federal law. Since they did not claim the department took action based on a disability, their discrimination claim failed. *Lebron v. Comwlth. of Puerto Rico*, 770 F.3d 25 (1st Cir. 2014).

♦ A New York child with cerebral palsy and autism was nonverbal, was not toilet trained and could not walk. Soon after she began first grade, staff members saw a paraprofessional grab her ponytail and pull her up from her stander. When they reported this to the principal, the paraprofessional was promptly removed from the classroom. After an investigation, the paraprofessional was dismissed. This action took place slightly more than one month from the day of the hair-pulling incident. The parent then sued the school department in a federal court for federal and state law claims. The case was referred to a federal magistrate judge, who found many of the claims related to placement and were thus subject to IDEA administrative exhaustion. Next, the magistrate judge found no retaliatory causal connection between allegedly adverse conduct and any protected activity. **The ponytail-pulling incident was promptly reported by staff members, and the principal removed the paraprofessional from the classroom.** Within weeks, the investigation was done and the paraprofessional was fired. As the court decided against retaining any of the federal claims, the magistrate judge recommended dismissal of the state claims in the event that the parent sought to refile them in a state court. The case returned to the court, which adopted the magistrate judge's recommendations. *M.A. v. New York Dep't of Educ.*, 1 F.Supp.3d 125 (S.D.N.Y. 2014).

♦ A New Jersey court rejected a claim by the parent of an autistic child that a neighborhood placement was assured by the state Law Against Discrimination (LAD). It rejected the argument that children were stigmatized as different by having to take smaller school buses. **Federal courts have held that if a**

328 STUDENT CIVIL RIGHTS

disabled child is not entitled to a neighborhood placement under the IDEA, there is also no entitlement under Section 504. The provision of a free appropriate public education generally rules out any federal discrimination claims. The student received an appropriate education. As there was no federal law entitlement to a neighborhood school, and as there was no LAD violation, the court dismissed the case. *J.T. v. Dumont Public Schools*, 438 N.J.Super 241, 103 A.3d 269 (N.J. Super. Ct. App. Div. 2014).

♦ A Texas student with deafness attended a school for children with disabilities. At a summer enrichment program, she had a seizure, fell into a pool and drowned. In a federal court, the student's parents sued the school district, principal and a physical education teacher under Section 504 and the ADA. After the court dismissed the case, the parents appealed to the U.S. Court of Appeals, Fifth Circuit. They claimed the district intentionally discriminated against their daughter by refusing to provide her necessary services for safe and meaningful access to the summer program. According to the court, a successful claim of discrimination against a school requires facts creating an inference of professional bad faith or gross misjudgment. **Congress did not intend Section 504 or ADA claims to create general tort liability for government entities.**

In this case, the court held the student did not show she was treated differently than others or that there was any discriminatory motivation by the school. Her parents only argued that she was denied safe and meaningful access to the program. The court found no evidence of any bad faith, gross misjudgment or intentional discrimination by the school district. **It appeared to the court that the death resulted from inclusion in the full activities of the district, rather than exclusion from them.** As a result, the court held for the school district. *Estate of A.R. v. Muzyka*, 543 Fed.Appx. 363 (5th Cir. 2013).

♦ A Texas student with a speech impairment had behavior problems. In third grade, he began throwing things and hitting classmates in class, and the teacher called the principal. The student later said the principal asked for a show of hands by classmates if they were tired of him and his behavior. He did not report this for two years and when he did so, the principal and his classroom teacher both denied it. In grade five, the student again had behavior problems. After a violent episode at home with suicidal ideation, the student was hospitalized. He was placed in homebound services. The parent informed team members for the first time of the student's charge of verbal abuse by the principal. A child abuse complaint was filed against the principal, but soon dismissed. In a federal court, the parent pursued disability discrimination claims under Section 504 and the ADA based on failure to provide a safe, non-hostile educational environment.

According to the court, the complaint did not assert the principal treated the student differently than others. At the time of the incident, she did not know the student had a behavior-related disability. **Since intentional discrimination against the student based on a behavior-related disability could not be shown, the court dismissed the ADA and Section 504 claims.** There was no showing of a district policy or custom of failing to protect students from known dangers arising from failure to correctly train and supervise staff. Even if the incident occurred in the manner portrayed by the family, the court held it was not so irrational or abusive as to violate constitutional rights. The court found no evidence of a policy or custom of intimidation by the school district. Finding none of the claims had merit, the court held for the district. *Pagan-Negron v. Seguin Independent School Dist.*, 974 F.Supp.2d 1020 (W.D. Tex. 2013).

♦   A Missouri student with perthes disease in his right hip had surgery and used a wheelchair at school. He and his mother eventually sued the school under the Americans with Disabilities Act, asserting that the school placed him in homebound instruction while he recovered from surgery and made him attend physical education classes even though he couldn't participate. However, a federal court ruled against them, noting that they should have exhausted their administrative remedies under the IDEA because the discrimination they claimed occurred related to the IEP process. Also, **the student did not qualify for protection under the ADA because his condition was temporary**. He was expected to heal within two years. *R.N. v. Cape Girardeau 63 School Dist.*, 858 F.Supp.2d 1025 (E.D. Mo. 2012).

♦   An Ohio student who engaged in behavioral outbursts and defiant absenteeism pulled a fire alarm at school and was expelled. His father, claiming the student had ADHD, sued the district and several officials for violating his rights under Section 504. A federal court dismissed the case, noting that there was no evidence of discrimination by the officials and that **neither Section 504 nor the ADA creates individual liability**. *Leonard v. Cleveland Metropolitan School Dist.*, No. 1:11-CV-01233, 2011 WL 5869606 (N.D. Ohio 11/16/11).

♦   When she was in the fifth grade, an Indiana student learned that she had been born with HIV. She discussed her condition on social media sites in sixth grade and was harassed by two students as a result. A counselor warned the harassers and met with their parent. In seventh grade, another student warned a fellow pupil not to kiss her because he could get AIDS. Again, the counselor intervened and met with the parent. In eighth grade, her soccer coach asked if she had AIDS. The principal met with the coach afterward. When the student then dropped out of school and sued for harassment, she lost. A federal court held that **the school acted immediately upon learning of the harassing incidents** and was thus not deliberately indifferent to them so as to be liable under the ADA and Section 504. *P.R. v. Metropolitan School Dist. of Washington Township*, No. 1:08-CV-1562-WTC-DML, 2010 WL 4457417 (S.D. Ind. 11/1/10).

♦   The mother of a Maine student with emotional and mental disorders claimed that their school district's IEP discriminated against her son. She sued under § 504. However, a federal court dismissed the action, noting that **Section 504 is broader in scope than the IDEA**, which limits a person's ability to pursue damage awards under other federal laws, including Section 504. Here, the mother's claim turned entirely on rights created by the IDEA, so she had no alternative but to pursue relief under that statute. *Doe v. Wells-Ogunquit Community School Dist.*, 698 F.Supp.2d 219 (D. Me. 2010).

♦   A student with oppositional defiance disorder had an IEP. She sought admission to the New Mexico Military Institute, a college preparatory school.

Her application was denied based on several factors, including behavior problems and past drug use. She sued for violations of the IDEA, Section 504 and the ADA. A federal court and the Tenth Circuit ruled against her. The institute complied with the IDEA, and she also failed to exhaust her administrative remedies under that statute. Further, even though she was IDEA-eligible, she failed to show that she was "disabled" under Section 504 and the ADA. **She could not demonstrate that she was "substantially limited in the major life activity of learning."** A person can be IDEA-eligible and not disabled under Section 504 or the ADA. *Ellenberg v. New Mexico Military Institute*, 572 F.3d 815 (10th Cir. 2009).

♦   The U.S. Supreme Court concluded that no private cause of action exists to enforce federal regulations published under Title VI of the Civil Rights Act of 1964. It dismissed a class action suit advanced by non-English speakers who claimed that Alabama's exclusive reliance on English for state driver's license examinations had a discriminatory effect based on national origin. Title VI is one of the principal federal laws preventing discrimination on the basis of race, color, or national origin. It prohibits federal funding recipients, including educational institutions, from discriminating in any covered program or activity and is commonly cited in education cases alleging discrimination. **The Supreme Court noted that Title VI prohibits only intentional discrimination** and cannot be used to enforce a disparate impact action. No private right of action existed to enforce Title VI disparate impact regulations. *Alexander v. Sandoval*, 532 U.S. 275, 121 S.Ct. 1511, 149 L.Ed.2d 517 (2001).

V.   POLICE INVOLVEMENT

Excessive force and false arrest claims by disabled students against school districts, school administrators, municipal police and school resource officers (SROs) continue to occupy federal court dockets. Jennifer A. Sughrue, Ph.D., a professor from Southeastern Louisiana University, recommends that school IEP teams consider counseling SROs in advance about students with emotional behavioral disturbance (EBD) or aggressive tendencies. Dr. Sughrue also recommends that for any student with a behavior intervention plan, the student's IEP team should include SROs in IEP team meetings.

♦   A New Mexico school resource officer (SRO) arrested and handcuffed an 11-year-old student with an emotional disturbance after she attacked a classmate and hit, scratched and kicked her teacher. The student's mother sued the SRO and county in a federal court for constitutional rights violations. Among other things, the mother argued the state Delinquency Act required the SRO to consider her child's age and mental disability before arresting her. She claimed the SRO willfully ignored state law when making the arrest. The court stated that police officers are required to investigate easily accessible evidence. But if probable cause is established, an officer is generally not required to continue searching for more evidence before an arrest. As the student had attacked a classmate and a teacher, the court held the SRO had probable cause to arrest her. The court found he had no duty to investigate whether a disability prevented her from forming criminal intent. **The court said the student's IEP did not indicate her disability prevented her from engaging in intentional conduct.** As the SRO made a lawful arrest, no Fourth Amendment violation was found. The mother then appealed to the Tenth Circuit Court of Appeals.

On appeal, the court found the SRO had probable cause to arrest the child after seeing her commit the crime of battery on a school official. It also held she did not use excessive force. In the absence of a constitutional violation by the SRO, the county could not be held liable for failing to train its officers. Even if there was a cause of action for a disabled arrestee under the ADA, the court held it would not apply in this case. The case did not involve a request for a reasonable accommodation. **The SRO observed criminal conduct and there was no "wrongful arrest," as the mother claimed.** As a result, the county prevailed. *J.H. v. Bernalillo County*, 806 F.3d 1255 (10th Cir. 2015).

◆ A Massachusetts student was interviewed by a police officer at school about materials in his school notebooks. He underwent a 45-day assessment and was suspended from school for 10 days because some of his drawings depicted guns and swords. The school district filed a due process request, seeking to place the student in a private school. After a three-day hearing, the district offered to pay the parents $11,000 per year for tuition at a private school of their choice. The parents accepted the offer but enrolled their son at a private school that did not offer special education services. A hearing officer then issued a decision that required the district to locate or create a placement for him. A federal court affirmed the decision. The parents said the school district then retracted its offer to pay tuition and requested another hearing. A hearing officer denied their requests for relief and they filed a new federal court case.

In addition to seeking review of the hearing officer's decision, the parents asserted constitutional and state law invasion of privacy claims. The court found claims that related to the student's suspensions could have been brought before the state bureau of special education appeals. Any education-related claims were now barred. But the state agency lacked authority to award relief for constitutional violations. As a result, the court held the claims pertaining to school officials were viable. While the family argued the constitutional rights claims against the district should proceed, the court held they failed to allege a violation of rights arising from a school district custom or policy. On the other hand, **the student could pursue his claims for damages arising out of the alleged unlawful seizure of his drawings**. The court held a claim under the state Privacy Act could also proceed. *E.T. v. Bureau of Special Educ. Appeals of Division of Administrative Law Appeals*, 91 F.Supp.3d 38 (D. Mass. 2015).

◆ A federal court held the parents of a child with autism showed his school committed many IDEA errors, including improper notice of a change in placement after a school meltdown. The court found the student was "on high alert because he is afraid of what is going to happen to him. Police involvement, restraints and seclusion can be frightening for any student, but more so for a student with disabilities." **Because the school district did not properly implement his IEP, the court held he should remain in general education**

settings, but with proper support. State law claims against the school district alleging emotional distress and negligence were dismissed. The same was true of a claim against the school district for punitive damages. *Troy School Dist. v. K.M.*, No. 12-CV-15413, 2015 WL 1495334 (E.D. Mich. 3/31/15).

♦ An 11-year-old California student forgot his medication for attention deficit hyperactivity disorder. He became unresponsive on the school playground. Due to fears that he would try to leave campus, a teacher called the police. When the officers arrived, she told them that the student was a "runner" who had forgotten his medication. The officers handcuffed the student and put him in a squad car. As his parents were out of town, the officers brought him to his uncle's business. In a federal court, the student's parent alleged civil rights violations. The family settled its claims against the teacher and school district.

A jury found the city and officers were not liable for excessive force and unlawful seizure. The judge found the verdict inconsistent and incomplete. Further instructions to the jury failed to clarify the inconsistency, and appeal reached the U.S. Court of Appeals, Ninth Circuit. It found the judge had failed to grasp the jurors' confusion and had further complicated things by insisting that they reach a "consistent result." The Ninth Circuit found no violation of clearly established law and held the officers had qualified immunity regarding both federal claims. But since the judge's instructions to the jury and later attempts at clarification were potentially misleading, the court found there had to be a new trial. Months later, the majority of judges of the Ninth Circuit decided to reconsider the decision. It then issued a new decision finding the chief and the police officer were entitled to qualified immunity on the unlawful seizure claim. **But the court held the officers acted unreasonably and were not entitled to immunity for keeping the student in handcuffs for about 40 minutes.** In denying immunity for this claim, the court found the student "was doing nothing more than sitting quietly and resolutely in the school playground." *C.B. v. City of Sonora*, 769 F.3d 1005 (9th Cir. 2014).

♦ An eight-year-old Tennessee student had separation problems. His father "regularly dragged him physically down the hall" and sometimes sat in the classroom for 60 to 90 minutes until the child was calm. The parents withdrew the student from school before the year was over, and he repeated kindergarten. The school offered him a "short-term, temporary Section 504 plan" for homebound services. Although the child was diagnosed with a mood disorder, he was not evaluated for special education eligibility. At a Section 504 meeting, the school created a transition plan for his return to school. But the parents did not attend the meeting and declined to obtain evaluations and testing needed for continuing Section 504 eligibility. Soon after returning to school, the student refused a teacher's instructions. He was escorted to the principal's office for threatening to "beat the crap out of her." A police officer placed the student in handcuffs for about 45 minutes before releasing him to his parents.

The parents sued the officer, board of education and school officials. **A federal court found common sense dictated that it was not reasonable to criminally charge a young child for relatively minor school misconduct.** But the court dismissed the constitutional claims against the board. The parents did not show the board acted in bad faith or exercised gross misjudgment under the Rehabilitation Act. As a result, the officer, board and school officials were all entitled to judgment. *Hoskins v. Cumberland County Board of Educ.*, No. 2:13-cv-15, 2014 WL 7238621 (M.D. Tenn. 12/17/14).

◆ A Pennsylvania student had dysthymic and attention deficit disorders. At school, he gave a friend some synthetic marijuana he had bought over the Internet. On the same day, the two were sent to detention for unrelated reasons. According to the student, he spent most of a morning with the counselor and a vice-principal in the office. The principal searched the student's cell phone and backpack. The student said he was questioned about his home life, including whether his parents used marijuana at home. When his mother arrived on campus, police officers presented her a search warrant for her residence. When the police executed the warrant, they recovered a small amount of marijuana. Later, the school board voted to expel the student for possession of contraband on school property. In a federal court, the student and mother sued the school district, superintendent, principal, vice principal, counselor and an assistant superintendent for civil rights violations, discrimination and state tort claims.

First, the court found no authority to support the family's claim that the student's rights were violated by any failure to administer the criminal rights advisory known as the *Miranda* warning. The court held the only remedy for a *Miranda* violation is to exclude unlawfully seized evidence from a criminal or juvenile prosecution. There was no evidence that the police had coerced or directed school officials and no reason to apply the *Miranda* rule. Although the student complained of due process violations, the court found the complaint did not identify any unfairness. **A claim asserting improper school cooperation with police was properly dismissed.** Legitimate safety reasons existed for the detention. State law claims for infliction of emotional distress and negligence were dismissed, as was a claim against the district for punitive damages. On the other hand, the court allowed breach of fiduciary duty and punitive damage claims against the principal, vice principal and counselor to proceed. A Section 504 claim suffered from a technical defect, but the court held it could be refiled. *K.A. v. Abington Heights School Dist.*, 28 F.Supp.3d 356 (M.D. Pa. 2014).

◆ Kentucky children had post-traumatic stress disorder and were afraid to enter their classrooms. They were eligible for special education and had IEPs intended to address behavior such as anxiety in new settings. A staff member offered to walk them to their class. Another employee suggested that the children might benefit from talking with a police officer who was occasionally called to the school. The parent agreed to the suggestion, finding it would be in line with the behavior modifications included in her children's IEPs. But when an officer arrived with the school principal, he told the parent to leave the school with her children because they were causing a disturbance. The officer told the parent he could not force her children to go to class and he asked her to leave the building. The parent stated that school staff members suggested other options, including spanking the children, seeking psychiatric care or involving child protective services. At the end of the discussion, the officer issued the parent a citation for third-degree criminal trespassing. In a federal court, the parent sued the school district and officials for IDEA violations based on refusal to provide IEP accommodations. She added a state law claim for defamation. After reciting the relevant legal standards in IDEA cases, the court found the IDEA claim had to be dismissed due to the parent's failure to exhaust her administrative remedies. Even though she claimed to be embarrassed or degraded by the comments of school staff, **the court found she did not plead specific facts to pursue her defamation claim**. As a result, the court dismissed the case. *Canders v. Jefferson County Schools*, No. 3:13-CV-01171-TBR, 2014 WL 4627273 (W.D. Ky. 9/16/14).

♦   Tennessee school officials called the local police after a student with autism repeatedly violated a school policy by using her cell phone. A police officer arrived at the school office and struggled to remove the student. In the process, he handcuffed her. After the officer brought the student to a juvenile detention center, she was charged with disorderly conduct. The charges were dropped, and the student's parents sued the school district, police officer, teacher and principal in a federal court for race discrimination and violations of state and federal law. After the court held for the district and officials, appeal reached the U.S. Court of Appeals, Sixth Circuit. It considered only the claims that the teacher and principal did not tell the officer that the student had autism.

The Sixth Circuit found no other case finding that a failure to communicate information about a person's disability to an arresting officer could be a constitutional violation. Although the Fourteenth Amendment's Due Process Clause prevents certain arbitrary and wrongful acts by the states, the court held it does not require a state to protect citizens. **Conduct attributed to a teacher and the principal did not deprive the student of a liberty interest in bodily security.** Instead, it appeared that the school resource officer called the officer to handle the situation. Failing to act was not an affirmative action that created constitutional liability. As a result, the court held for the principal and teacher. *Chigano v. City of Knoxville*, 529 Fed.Appx. 753 (6th Cir. 2013).

VI. SCHOOL ATHLETICS

Students with disabilities are often affected by state athletic eligibility rules regarding transfers or limiting participation in high school interscholastic sports to eight semesters. In Lyon v. Illinois High School Ass'n, below, a federal court held a student with a disability could not participate in wrestling for a fifth year of high school. Allowing him another year of eligibility would grant him a "privilege" that other students, disabled or not, would not enjoy.

♦   A Kentucky student with ADHD and auditory processing issues attended a school for learning disabilities in Ohio. When he entered high school, his parents selected an Ohio school because of its support program, technology platform and superior college placement and resource programs. As a freshman, the student wanted to play soccer for the high school. An Ohio High School Athletic Association (OHSAA) bylaw prohibited student-athletes whose parents do not live in Ohio from playing interscholastic sports. After the

OHSAA denied a request for a waiver, the student obtained a federal court order to enjoin the OHSAA from enforcing its residency bylaw against him.

Near the end of the school year, the parents sought a permanent order to block the OHSAA from enforcing its residency bylaw. But the court found the OHSAA bylaw did not bar him on the basis of a disability. **There was no connection between the student's disability and the reason for his ineligibility – his parents' residency.** The services provided by the Ohio school were not unique and were available at other schools in Kentucky and Ohio. Since the parents showed no connection between their child's disability and the bylaw, and they sent him to the Ohio school for reasons unrelated to a disability, the court denied their request for an order. *C.S. v. Ohio High School Athletic Ass'n*, No. 1:14-cv-525, 2015 WL 4575217 (S.D. Ohio 7/29/15).

◆ An Iowa student with disabilities reported name-calling by his peers to a teacher and bus driver. His grandmother mentioned the teasing in IEP meetings. He went out for the school football team in grade nine but said two players threw footballs at him during practices and hit him in the helmet. He reported this to coaches. During the season, the student visited the school nurse to complain of headaches and double vision. She advised him to quit football and did not report his injuries to coaches. The grandparent took the student to an emergency room. He had a hemorrhage requiring surgery and rehabilitation. Police and school officials were informed of the student's hospitalization and investigations were begun. No criminal charges were filed, and the school's investigation was inconclusive. A coach denied that the student ever reported that footballs were thrown at him, and players denied misconduct. In a federal court, the grandmother sued the district for Section 504 and constitutional violations, negligence, infliction of emotional distress and punitive damages.

The court found enough facts to support a Section 504 disability discrimination claim. There was evidence that the student was hospitalized for a head injury and had endured a yearlong period during which classmates teased him, called him names and pushed him in school hallways. But the court held a negligence claim based on failure by the nurse to provide the student a safe and nurturing educational environment should be dismissed. Nor was there sufficient evidence to support a claim for infliction of emotional distress. But the court held the student could pursue a negligence claim based on failure to remove him from football competition despite possible knowledge that he suffered a head injury. Evidence that the nurse may have destroyed notes and recreated them for the case could support a punitive damage award. *K.R.S. v. Bedford Community School Dist.*, 109 F.Supp.3d 1060 (S.D. Iowa 2015).

◆ A Louisiana private high school student's parents grew concerned over his falling grades and had him evaluated by a psychologist. He was diagnosed with an anxiety disorder. To receive accommodations that were unavailable at his school, the student transferred to another private school. This made him ineligible for interscholastic athletics for one year under a state high school association rule. After the association denied the student's request for an exemption, his parent sought a state court order to allow him to participate in interscholastic football. The court denied the order, and the student sat out of six games. The next spring, the parent sought a court order to prohibit the association from treating the student as ineligible for the first four games of the next school year. This time, he claimed the transfer was due to a disability.

After a hearing, the court granted the student an order allowing him to play football. The association appealed to the U.S. Court of Appeals, Fifth Circuit, where it argued the student did not have a qualifying disability under the ADA. The court held that to show a disability protected by the ADA, a party has to have an impairment that substantially limited one or more major life activities. While the 2008 ADA Amendments Act lowered the standard existing under prior law, the court held a party must still have a "substantial limitation" to qualify for ADA coverage. In this case, the parent did not claim the student's disorder qualified as a disability under the ADA. He instead argued that the student was a "child with a disability" under the IDEA. While ADA and IDEA standards for accommodations overlapped where both laws applied, the court held the IDEA did not require proof of an impairment that substantially limited a major life activity. **An IDEA-qualifying disability does not always implicate a substantial limit to a major life activity.** In this case, the parent and the lower court had relied exclusively on the psychiatrist's report diagnosing an anxiety disorder. The lower court had committed error by relying only on conclusory statements in the report without further analysis. A psychiatrist's diagnosis alone did not support a finding of disability under the ADA. The court returned the case to the lower court for it to determine whether the student's condition substantially limited a major life activity. *Mann v. Louisiana High School Athletic Ass'n*, 535 Fed.Appx. 405 (5th Cir. 2013).

♦ A student with an IEP to address his ADHD participated in high school wrestling for three years while attending a California high school. Due to academic problems caused by his ADHD, the student was found academically ineligible during the second semester of his junior year. His family moved to Chicago, and he repeated his junior year at a college prep school that provided him academic accommodations. Illinois High School Association (IHSA) rules limited interscholastic competition to eight semesters after enrollment in grade nine, and four years of high school competition in any sport. After the IHSA denied a waiver from both rules, the student sued the association in a federal court. An emergency hearing was held, and a federal judge issued a temporary restraining order that would allow the student to wrestle in several scheduled meets and two tournaments, including the state tournament. *Lyon v. Illinois High School Ass'n*, No. 13-CV-00173, 2013 WL 140926 (N.D. Ill. 1/10/13).

Less than two weeks after the temporary restraining order was issued, another judge evaluated the student's request for a preliminary injunction, which would have extended the duration of the temporary order. This time, the judge noted the student had already wrestled for four years at the high school level. Although he became academically ineligible during his first junior year, the student had wrestled for about four months in that school year. In the court's view, he could not show he was "otherwise qualified" as that term is defined by the ADA. He could not participate in wrestling for a fifth year of high school. **Even if the student had no disability, the four-year rule would have made him ineligible to compete in another year of wrestling.** Allowing him another year of wrestling eligibility would grant him a "privilege" that other students, disabled or not, would not enjoy. Since this belied ADA purposes, the court denied the student's request for a preliminary injunction. *Lyon v. Illinois High School Ass'n*, No. 13 C 173, 2013 WL 309205 (N.D. Ill. 1/25/13).

♦ A Mississippi student said he was subjected to bullying by students and staff on the basis of his Caucasian race and his specific learning disability. He said school employees did not stop peers from the bullying and even joined it at times. After filing a federal court complaint, the student said he was removed from the football team in retaliation. A race discrimination claim against the district failed because it did not assert any intentional discrimination. Although the student alleged he was treated differently from others in violation of the Equal Protection Clause, the court found he did not compare himself with any student who was similarly situated. This lack of a comparison group or individual defeated any possible equal protection liability. A due process claim based on the right to bodily integrity fared no better than the race discrimination claims. While the student charged the school with failing to prevent harassing and bullying conduct, Supreme Court authority made clear that schools have no duty to protect students from violence by third parties.

Claims that coaches and teachers bullied or harassed the student failed because nothing indicated any physical harm to him. But the student said he was removed from the football team only a few days after filing his federal court complaint. This proximity in time supported an inference of retaliation, and the court agreed to consider the retaliation claim. But it found no merit to a claim based on a hostile learning environment. **There can be no individual liability under Section 504 or the ADA.** On the other hand, the student asserted sufficient facts to support Section 504 and ADA claims against the district, and the court held these claims against the district could proceed. Finally, the court allowed the student and his parent to proceed with a state law claim for emotional distress. *R.S. v. Starkville School Dist.*, No. 1:12-CV-00088-SA-DAS, 2013 WL 5295685 (N.D. Miss 9/19/13).

♦ An African-American student who starred in football at a public school in Mississippi transferred to a religious school. He was not allowed to participate in sports for one year. He sued, claiming that white students who transferred were allowed to play, and that football was an integral part of his education due to his ADHD. A federal court held that he did not have a due process interest in varsity athletics participation. However, **he could proceed with his race discrimination claim**. *E.C. v. Mississippi High School Athletics Ass'n*, 868 F.Supp.2d 563 (S.D. Miss. 2012).

♦ A group of student-athletes with disabilities sued the Illinois High School Association for refusing to allow them to compete in state-sanctioned athletic events. A federal court focused on a student with lower-limb paralysis, who was among the top adaptive high school swimmers in the state, but who could not meet the existing qualifying standards set by the association for championship meets. The association argued that it was not a public entity or a place of public accommodation and so did not have to abide by the commands of the ADA,

Titles II and III. The court disagreed. **The unincorporated voluntary association of schools had to comply with the ADA.** *Illinois v. Illinois High School Ass'n*, No. 12 C 3758, 2012 WL 3581174 (N.D. Ill. 8/17/12).

♦   The parents of a disabled high school senior in New York sued their district under the Rehabilitation Act and the IDEA, asserting that the district had failed to implement their son's IEP for multiple school years, going back to middle school. A federal court largely dismissed their lawsuit, noting that most of their claims were subject to administrative exhaustion requirements or were time-barred by a three-year statute of limitations. One claim asserting **failure to implement the student's adapted P.E. program** could proceed. *Piazza v. Florida Union Free School Dist.*, 777 F.Supp.2d 669 (S.D.N.Y. 2011).

♦   The parents of a third-grader in Virginia held him back for a year despite average grades due to an auditory processing deficit. When he was in high school, he learned that because his nineteenth birthday was on July 31 rather than August 1, he would be barred from playing sports during his senior year. He sought a waiver, but the Virginia High School League denied it. He sued and lost, the court holding that **he did not have a constitutional right to play sports**. And the decision to hold him back was voluntary, and it was not made because he had a significant disability that interrupted his educational progression. *Sisson v. Virginia High School League*, No. 7:10CV00530, 2010 WL 5173264 (W.D. Va. 12/14/10).

♦   A New York student with cerebral palsy served as the football team manager. Because of minor architectural barriers, he had to take a detour to and from the school's athletic fields, costing him 20 minutes, which reduced his participation as team manager and nearly halved his time in a typical PE class. When he sued under Section 504 and the ADA, a jury ruled in his favor. On appeal, the Second Circuit found sufficient evidence that **the district denied him "meaningful access" to the school's athletic fields**. The student offered plausible, simple remedies that the district could have implemented. *Celeste v. East Meadow Union Free School Dist.*, 373 Fed.Appx. 85 (2d Cir. 2010).

CHAPTER ELEVEN

Employment

I. DISCIPLINE AND DISCHARGE

A. Misconduct

State laws establish the permissible grounds for disciplinary action against a teacher. Two frequently stated grounds for discipline are neglect of duty and conduct unbecoming a teacher. Courts that review employee suspension and discharge actions must analyze each case under applicable state laws, collective bargaining agreements, and relevant school board policies.

In Moberg v. Monterey Peninsula Unified School Dist. Board of Educ., *this chapter, a California administrative law judge explained that a teacher who sent abusive and disrespectful emails to his colleagues undercut basic program goals. She wrote: "Special education is an area where a team approach is not only desirable, but essential." Frequent emails by the teacher to colleagues indicated his inability to become a member of the special education team.*

♦ A North Carolina assistant principal (AP) and a social worker met with other school staff members and a hospital/homebound (HH) instructor to discuss a high school student who was suicidal and failing her classes. Neither the student's parent nor any special education teacher attended the meeting. Although the HH instructor said the meeting would have to be reconvened with the rest of the team present, the AP said he could drop the student from two classes so she could participate in HH programs. Believing that the mother and student attended the meeting, the chair of the exceptional children's department told a special education teacher to document placing the student in an HH program. The social worker created IEP meeting notes indicating the parent and student had attended the meeting. When the HH instructor visited the student's home, the parent learned of the action to remove her child from classes and begin an HH program. After an investigation and a hearing, the board suspended the AP for three days without pay and the social worker for one day.

Among the board's findings was that the AP knew (or should have known) there had to be a "proper IEP team meeting" in order to change the student's schedule and that the social worker intentionally falsified his meeting notes. When the case reached the North Carolina Court of Appeals, it noted testimony by the HH instructor, exceptional children's chair and other staff members indicating the AP had firsthand knowledge that the student had an IEP and had even attended one of her prior IEP meetings. **Instead of assembling the IEP team, the AP had simply dropped two of the student's classes and placed her in the HH program.** As the board found, the social worker falsified his notes to make it look like an actual IEP meeting had taken place. The employees were not entitled to a hearing before an independent hearing officer. Finding the board's decision was supported by evidence and not arbitrary, capricious or an abuse of discretion, the court of appeals held for the board. *Marisco v. New Hanover County Board of Educ.*, 776 S.E.2d 364 (Table) (N.C. Ct. App. 7/21/15; N.C. review denied, 12/15/15).

♦ An Ohio vocational agriculture teacher helped students take an online test. While his back was turned, a student choked two classmates, including a special education student. Other students did not tell the teacher what had happened and did not report the choking until later in the day. Surveillance video indicated that the special needs student became unconscious due to the choking. The board advised the teacher of an investigatory hearing and charged him with willful and persistent policy violations, such as failure to maintain a safe environment. A hearing referee found the board did not prove the teacher was previously disciplined or warned that his conduct violated board policies. Nor was he ever told he might face dismissal. No evidence of "willful and persistent violation" of relevant policies was found. But the board still voted for dismissal.

On appeal, the Court of Appeals of Ohio found **the history of providing only verbal warnings to the teacher undermined the board's claim that he had willfully violated board policies**. The court rejected a claim that the board could rely solely on the choking incident as a ground for employment termination. There were 24 students in the classroom during the relevant period, despite a state guideline suggesting vocational classes should be limited to 15. The court held for the teacher, stating the offending student's decision to commit serious misconduct while the teacher attended to other tasks should not justify dismissal. *Badertscher v. Liberty-Benton School Dist. Board of Educ.*, 29 N.E.3d 1034 (Ohio Ct. App. 2015).

♦   A New York Appellate Division Court held invalid an unsatisfactory rating that was assigned to a special education teacher based on her argument with another teacher. After forfeiting tenure in another job to obtain the special education teaching position, the teacher had a satisfactory job performance review in her first year. But she was later placed on a four-day suspension without pay after she loudly argued with a colleague in front of students. The two argued about whether students with disabilities should share space with other students in an art cluster. When the case reached the Appellate Division, it found **the incident was insufficient to support a finding of unprofessional conduct**. Moreover, the teacher's failure to admit that the conversation was an "argument" was not evidence of insubordination. Finding no rational basis for an unsatisfactory rating, the court held for the teacher. *Mendez v. New York City Dep't of Educ.*, 132 A.D.3d 533 (N.Y. App. Div. 2015).

♦   An Illinois teacher worked at a high school for 25 years and taught students with disabilities. He learned that his son had been sexually abused by a teacher from another school district. After having some drinks, the teacher went to the other teacher's house with an unloaded gun. He entered the house and screamed and yelled at the other teacher. Before leaving, he put the gun in the other teacher's mouth, threatened him and twice hit him in the face. A day later, the teacher turned himself in to the police, made a confession and was arrested for home invasion. School administrators placed him on leave pending termination. A board resolution was passed in support of his dismissal. Among the findings was that he was unfit to serve as a role model to behavior disordered students and had damaged the district's reputation. A hearing officer found the teacher pled guilty to a class three felony and was sentenced to two years' probation.

While finding the teacher had engaged in misconduct, the hearing officer found the incident was the result of a personal situation and was remediable. She reinstated the teacher to his position. After a state circuit court reversed the judgment, the case reached the Appellate Court of Illinois. **It held prior cases have held that criminal conduct by a teacher is irremediable, regardless of whether the conduct occurred in or outside of school.** Prior cases found the concept of remediable conduct was not intended to apply to criminal conduct in any case. Since well-established law allowed the board to dismiss a teacher who had engaged in criminal conduct, the court upheld his dismissal. *Board of Educ. of Township High, School Dist. 214, Cook County, Illinois v. Illinois State Board of Educ.*, No. 1-13-3808, 2014 IL App (1st) 133808-U (Ill. App. Ct. 10/7/14).

♦   A New Jersey teacher who had taught special education students for 12 years in the city of Camden hit a student with a computer cord as the student ran from the classroom. The incident was recorded by a school camera and reported to child protection authorities. Tenure charges were brought against the teacher for conduct unbecoming a teacher, unlawful corporal punishment, neglect of duty and insubordination. The case was referred to an administrative law judge (ALJ). In proceedings before the ALJ, the teacher tried to justify his actions by stating: "I work in the hood, my kids, they are – they turn out to be murderers, attempted murderers. They're gang members." He also portrayed himself as a victim of violence. Following the hearing, the ALJ upheld the dismissal based on corporal punishment and conduct unbecoming a teacher.

On appeal, a state court noted "unbecoming conduct" was a permissible ground for dismissing a tenured teacher under state law. **Physical abuse of a student was also sufficient grounds for dismissal.** The court found no basis for interfering with the ALJ's decision. The teacher's use of physical force was held inexcusable, and the court found the videotape demonstrated his actions in striking the student had been cruel, vicious and intentional. The court also found it highly disturbing for a special education teacher to describe his students as "murderers," "attempted murderers," and "gang members." And his reference to working "in the hood" connoted bigoted, stereotypical images of urban students. Finding the teacher was utterly unfit to teach and be responsible for child education and physical welfare, the court affirmed the teacher's dismissal. *Matter of Goodwater*, 2014 WL 4083197 (N.J. Super. Ct. App. Div. 8/20/14).

◆   A New Jersey school district brought formal tenure charges against a special education teacher for inappropriate conduct, including physical contact, calling her students' behavior "stupid" and referring to them as "monkeys." An administrative law judge (ALJ) considered testimony from nine witnesses. The teacher testified and disputed the charges. The ALJ found support for five of the seven charges, and the state commissioner of education affirmed the findings.

A state appellate court agreed with the ALJ that **the teacher's conduct reflected inappropriate management of the frustrations that were bound to arise when teaching children.** Since her students were mostly African-American, the commissioner found her comments were racially charged. She also gave inconsistent testimony about physical contact. Tenure charges may be upheld based upon even a single incident that is found to be "sufficiently flagrant." There was evidence that the teacher displayed great impatience with students, as well as increasing frustration and limited self-control. She admitted cursing and telling students they were acting like monkeys and her relationship with students had become adversarial. Meanwhile, the teacher expressed no regrets, and there was no indication she had accepted responsibility for her actions. *In re Watson*, 2014 WL 2480173 (N.J. Super. Ct. App. Div. 5/20/14).

◆   A West Virginia special education bus aide supervised six students on mid-day bus runs of 20 minutes to and from an off-campus work program. Videotape showed two students having sexual contact over 10-15 minute periods on two days. During both trips, videotape showed the aide talking with the driver most of the time. She talked to one student in the aisle next to her but otherwise ignored students. Toward the end of the run on the second day, the driver asked the two boys what they were doing. Only then did the aide turn around to observe them. After the board suspended the aide without pay, it held a hearing at which it upheld a recommendation for her dismissal. A grievance board held another hearing before an administrative law judge, who found the aide willfully neglected her duties. It was found that she knew her duties and what was expected of her. Since she "basically spent the entire bus trip not working," her conduct was willful neglect of duty and dismissal was held appropriate.

When the case reached the Supreme Court of Appeals of West Virginia, it described **"willful neglect of duty" as "a knowing and intentional act, rather than a negligent act."** The court found no clear error in the finding of willful neglect of duty. The aide was aware of her responsibility to supervise and care for special needs children on her bus. She abandoned her duties and chose to ignore the students in her care. While the aide claimed she was entitled to an evaluation and an opportunity to improve, the court found she was already aware of the need to visually supervise her students. Although the driver was only suspended for two days, his primary duty was to drive the bus, while the aide's sole purpose was to monitor children. As a result, the judgment for the board was affirmed. *Costello v. Board of Educ. of County of Monongalia*, No. 13-0039, 2013 WL 5967021 (W.Va. 11/8/13).

◆ A 15-year-old New Jersey student put his head down and listened to his headphones in class. His teacher began prompting him to do his work but said the student began calling him names and told him he was a bad teacher who was only there to collect a check. Without the teacher's knowledge, the student began recording the teacher with his cell phone. For a significant part of the class time, the teacher stood in front of the student's desk as the two exchanged remarks. Several times, the student said "don't call me special." At times, the teacher used profanity and threatened to "kick [the student's] ass." During the exchange, he told the student he would never return to regular education. The student withdrew from the school, saying he felt like "trash" after the incident.

Later, the school district suspended the teacher and served tenure charges on him. An ALJ found his conduct unbecoming in violation of the district's harassment, intimidation and bullying policy. Instead of termination, the ALJ sought to impose a 120-day unpaid suspension and loss of pay increments for two years. After the state commissioner of education modified the penalty to employment termination, the teacher appealed to a state appellate division court. It found the teacher had used demeaning language, profanity, threats, aggressive body language, taunting and other inappropriate behavior. The teacher's lack of judgment and control was prolonged and acute. **The teacher had engaged in bullying and badgering for an extended time period.** Finding the board's action was not arbitrary, capricious or shocking to the court's sense of fairness, the court upheld the dismissal decision. *In re Roth*, 2013 WL 3284128 (N.J. Super. Ct. 7/1/13).

◆ Before an entire class, a New York teacher made an improper remark and tossed a book at a student with disabilities. Several disciplinary charges were brought against the teacher, and the case went before a hearing officer. Although some of the charges were withdrawn or dismissed, the arbitrator found the incident occurred and imposed a $7,500 fine on the teacher. A state trial court denied a petition to annul the award, and the teacher appealed to a New York Appellate Division Court. In a brief memorandum, the court found the hearing officer's decision was entitled to deference. Although the teacher claimed the testimony of the student and an aide who had seen the events were incredible or contradictory, the court disagreed. In addition, the court found she was allowed the opportunity to call her own witnesses. Exercising its own discretion, the court found the $7,500 fine "shocks one's sense of fairness." It noted that **this had been a single incident and that while the teacher's remark was not proper, it was not of a highly inflammatory nature**. And the hearing officer had found the book did not even hit the student. It had been appropriate to decline any award of attorneys' fees, since there was some basis for the claims. As a result, award was modified. *Polito v. New York City Dep't of Educ.*, 104 A.D.3d 604, 962 N.Y.S.2d 120 (N.Y. App. Div. Ct. 2013).

◆   A California teacher was charged with numerous incidents of misconduct and making it hard for his program manager to perform her job. According to the district, the teacher did not maintain appropriate relations with other staff members, treating them "in a disrespectful and rude manner." He was charged with frequent violation of a district policy on polite employee use of email. He disregarded directives to stop sending abusive emails and was charged with not correcting classroom deficiencies, refusing to carry a district cell phone for emergencies, and transporting a medically fragile student in his own vehicle. The district charged the teacher with evident unfitness for service, persistent violation of (or refusal to obey) school laws or reasonable regulations. An ALJ held a hearing and found evidence that he never told the district that he had resigned from his previous job under an agreement requiring him to resign.

While an administrator directed the teacher to stop his abusive emails, he did not. The teacher did not provide lesson plans, failed to align student work with IEP goals, and allowed an instructional assistant to provide most of the instruction. He had difficult relationships with peers and administrators alike. After the board voted to adopt the ALJ's decision recommending dismissal, a state superior court affirmed its decision. On appeal, the state court of appeal found **the teacher's emails led to a breakdown of the team dynamics essential for a successful program**. This, along with his behavior toward staff and his deliberate, repeated neglect of teaching duties supported dismissal. The board's policy on network etiquette was a part of his contractual obligation. *Moberg v. Monterey Peninsula Unified School Dist. Board of Educ.*, No. H037865, 2013 WL 140374 (Cal. Ct. App. 1/11/13, review denied 4/10/13).

◆   A Chicago teacher instructed a special education class made up of students with behavior problems and learning disabilities. Instead of accompanying her students to the cafeteria, she went to a school office where she spent about 30-45 minutes trying to register for a class. During this time, two boys from the teacher's class took a female special needs student from another teacher's class into a closet, where they engaged in oral sex. Later in the day, two boys from the teacher's classroom went to the school auditorium, where they had sex with the same girl from the previous incident. An investigation was commenced, in which the teacher told an investigator that she had been with the students at the time of the incidents. But a teaching assistant contradicted her testimony, and surveillance records revealed she did not escort the students as she had said.

A hearing officer found the teacher was negligent and recommended reinstating her "in a warning performance status." Although the board accepted many of the hearing officer's findings, it found the teacher knowingly violated school rules and abandoned her post. This neglect, indifference and dishonesty required dismissal. After a state circuit court affirmed the dismissal, the case reached the state appellate court. It reviewed relevant Illinois statutes declaring "irremediable per se" any teacher activity that was cruel, immoral, negligent or criminal. The court found testimony and evidence showing the teacher tended to her personal needs while some students did nothing and others went off to have sex. She lied to the investigator, violated a school policy and was negligent in her oversight of students. **As the teacher's actions were found immoral and negligent, the court held they were irremediable per se and a proper basis for dismissal.** *Ball v. Board of Educ. of City of Chicago*, 2013 IL App (1st) 120136, 374 Ill.Dec. 62, 994 N.E.2d 999 (Ill. App. Ct. 2013).

♦   A New York Appellate Division Court affirmed the dismissal of a special education teacher who took two days off to extend a school holiday into a two-week break so she could take a vacation to the Dominican Republic. In the court's opinion, the teacher did not show discharge was too severe a penalty for the offense. **It found ample evidence that her absence was a well-planned event in contravention of an express order.** As a result, the dismissal was upheld. *Castle v. Maine-Endwell Cent. School Dist.*, 111 A.3d 1221, 975 N.Y.S.2d 816 (N.Y. App. Div. 2013).

♦   A Massachusetts court upheld the discharge of a teacher for verbal and physical mistreatment of students, including racial epithets and calling students "retarded." Although she claimed the discharge came in retaliation for her filing of race and age discrimination complaints with a state agency, the court found the lapse of time between the filings and her discharge was too tenuous to prove retaliation. While the teacher claimed none of the events complained of by students or parents ever occurred, **the court found "well-documented evidence" of her verbal and physical mistreatment of students**. *Joseph v. Boston School Committee*, 84 Mass.App.Ct. 1107 (Mass. App. Ct. 2013).

♦   A special education teacher refused to attend a training session about the Washington Alternative Assessment of Student (WAAS) portfolio. Another stated that she did not want to administer the WAAS because it was "ridiculous" for her severely disabled students. Despite repeated warnings, the teachers missed a key WAAS deadline. They were each suspended for 10 days without pay, and when they appealed the suspensions, the Court of Appeals of Washington upheld them. **Their insubordination and failure to give a federally mandated test was sufficient cause for the suspensions.** *Griffith v. Seattle School Dist. No. 1*, 278 P.3d 1111 (Wash. Ct. App. 2012).

♦   An Alabama school board suspended a special education teacher who forged IEP documents to indicate that a meeting was held when no meeting actually occurred. The teacher had been told that she had to complete IEPs for seven students in the first 10 days of a school year because she had failed to redo IEPs for them at the end of the preceding year. When the teacher challenged the suspension because she had already been reprimanded, a hearing officer ruled that she had been treated unfairly by being reprimanded and then suspended for the same misconduct. However, **the Court of Civil Appeals of Alabama reversed, noting that the state did not recognize the "procedural just cause" and "workplace double jeopardy" standards.** *Montgomery County Board of Educ. v. Moon-Williams*, 107 So.3d 205 (Ala. Civ. App. 2012).

B. Incompetence

In Little Lake City School Dist. v. Comm'n on Professional Competence *and* Terkosky v. Indiana Dep't of Educ., *this chapter, courts relied in part on factors identified by the California Supreme Court to determine whether a teacher is unfit to teach. In* Morrison v. State Board of Educ., *1 Cal.3d 214 (Cal. 1969), a nonexclusive list of factors was offered to assess a teacher's fitness to teach. First among them was the likelihood that a teacher's conduct has adversely affected students or colleagues. Other factors include the degree of adversity, the likelihood of a recurrence of the conduct and its timing.*

♦   **The U.S. Supreme Court denied a petition to review a New York court decision upholding a teacher's dismissal based on his inability to control the same group of special needs children for three years.** Before being assigned to a self-contained classroom, the teacher had satisfactory employment ratings for 18 years in schools operated by the New York City Department of Education. Based on his performance in the self-contained classroom, the teacher was eventually subjected to a disciplinary hearing. A hearing officer then upheld the charges for dismissal. Although a state appellate court found the termination shocking, the Court of Appeals of New York later dismissed the case. It did not find the termination "shocks the judicial conscience." *Russo v. New York City Dep't of Educ.*, 25 N.Y.3d 946, 29 N.E.3d 896 (N.Y. 2015). Without opinion, the Supreme Court refused to hear the case. *Russo v. New York City Dep't of Educ.*, No. 14-299, 136 S.Ct. 416 (cert. denied 11/2/15).

♦   A teacher accused of striking two students while she worked at a school on Chicago's South Side received another opportunity for review of a decision dismissing her from her job. In 2012, a state appeals court reversed an action dismissing the teacher, finding the board ignored factors used to determine whether a teacher's conduct was irremediable. One of the students had ADHD, and his testimony could be reexamined. When the case returned to the board, it again justified the dismissal, finding the student's testimony was more credible than that of the teacher. But when the case returned to the state appellate court, it found **the board again failed to determine whether the teacher's conduct was irremediable**. It returned the case to the board with directions to comply with its orders. *Rule v. Illinois State Board of Educ.*, No. 1-13-3685, 2015 IL App (1st) 133685-U (Ill. App. Ct. 9/15/15).

♦   A Washington special education teacher co-taught a curriculum known as Connected Mathematics Program Part 2 (CMP2) in a blended (special and general education) classroom. After the principal ended use of the blended model, she assigned the teacher to a special education math class. At a midyear review, an assistant principal rated the teacher's performance unsatisfactory in instructional skill and knowledge of subject matter. He was placed on probation under a performance improvement plan. After three observations of the teacher, the assistant principal found he did not show adequate improvement in his areas of deficiency. After the district provided the teacher notice of its intent to nonrenew his contract for failure to remediate his teaching deficiencies, a hearing officer found sufficient cause to nonrenew his employment contract.

A state superior court upheld the decision. On appeal, the Court of Appeals of Washington held **the teacher had no standing to challenge his non-renewal based on IDEA violations. He was unable to show any authority preventing a school from requiring teachers to follow a certain curriculum.** CMP2 had a specific section for special education students and could be modified to accommodate special needs students. The hearing officer did not err by finding it was the teacher's responsibility to follow the curriculum. The court found no authority supporting his other claims, and it affirmed the judgment for the school district. *Cummings v. Seattle School Dist. No. 1*, 178 Wash.App. 1027, No. 68519-8-I, 2013 WL 6835219 (Wash. Ct. App. 12/23/13).

♦   A California special education teacher was cited for unprofessionalism and failing to collaborate regularly with classroom teachers about student IEP goals. She was charged with frequent tardiness and performance issues in subject matter knowledge, student control and classroom environment. An evaluation stated she was not using required instructional strategies aligned with student instructional levels. Because the evaluation rated her teaching strategies unsatisfactory, the teacher was supposed to receive assistance from a consulting teacher. But no such assistance was provided, and she was put on a performance improvement plan. Meetings were held to discuss the teacher's progress and reprimands. New threats of employment termination were issued, and she was placed on a 90-day improvement plan. At the conclusion of the plan, the teacher's performance was found deficient, and the district placed her on leave pending dismissal. She requested a hearing, and the California Commission on Professional Competence found no cause for dismissal. A state superior court affirmed the decision, and the school district appealed. On appeal, the Court of Appeal of California found the teacher instructed a large number of students.

Due to her heavy workload, the teacher could not meet with general education teachers during the school day and was never offered a substitute on collaboration dates. The court found no testimony to support the claims of failure to collaborate and communicate with general education teachers. As for the critique of her teaching methods, the teacher stated these were general education performance measures. The court found many of the criticisms in her performance evaluations were baseless. There was no evidence that the district offered to help the teacher, and it did not show she failed to communicate with others or was frequently tardy. **The court held the teacher's performance improvement plan was unreasonable and "virtually ensured [her] failure by increasing her duties."** Substantial evidence supported the commissioner's decision. *Little Lake City School Dist. v. Comm'n on Professional Competence*, No. B244991, 2013 WL 6182625 (Cal. Ct. App. 11/26/13).

♦   After nine years as a special education teacher in a Mississippi district's alternative school, a teacher was notified of his contract termination at the end of the year due to negligence in classroom instruction, failure to complete or maintain IEPs, failure to comply with procedural safeguard policies and falsification of documentation to certain parents. After a hearing, the board of education voted to terminate his contract, and he appealed. The Court of Appeals of Mississippi noted that the superintendent complied with state law provisions permitting dismissal of any licensed school employee for incompetence, neglect of duty and other good cause. **The letter gave the teacher sufficient notice of the grounds for termination.** The district was not obligated to offer an improvement plan, and the court affirmed the judgment. *Webb v. South Panola School Dist.*, 101 So.3d 724 (Miss. Ct. App. 2012).

♦   A special education teacher in New York challenged orders by her school district to submit to a psychiatric examination to determine her fitness to work. The school district provided ample evidence of unprofessional behavior and questionable judgment, which made it suspect she was unfit to teach. A trial court dismissed the teacher's challenge to the orders, and the Supreme Court, Appellate Division, affirmed. **The teacher had to submit to the psychiatric examination.** *Seraydar v. Three Village Cent. School Dist.*, 935 N.Y.S.2d 125 (N.Y. App. Div. 2011).

C. Speech Rights and Retaliation

1. Speech Rights

♦   A Georgia special education teacher complained to her principal about the services being provided to a student. She believed a date on an IEP document was forged, and she challenged a colleague's qualifications. The teacher said her principal retaliated against her by threatening to place her on a performance development plan (PDP). She felt compelled to quit because of this threat and other conduct she claimed was retaliatory. In a federal court, the teacher asserted speech rights violations and retaliation under state law. The court held for the school district, and she appealed. The U.S. Court of Appeals, Eleventh Circuit, held that to prevail on a claim for retaliation by a government employer based on protected speech, an employee must show the speech involves the public concern. Next, the employee's interest in free speech must outweigh the employer's interest in efficient operations. **Recent Supreme Court cases have emphasized that a public employee's speech is not protected when the statements are made pursuant to official duties.** Under Eleventh Circuit case law, an employee cannot transform a personal grievance into a matter of public concern by invoking the public's interest in how a public institution is run.

In this case, the teacher did not show a serious and material change in her employment terms or conditions. She was never placed on a PDP. Although she said she was forced to quit due to her supervisor's disagreement with a change to an IEP, the court held this and other matters that she complained about did not create conditions that would force a reasonable person to resign. **The teacher did not raise these issues as a public concern, but to address issues**

that personally affected her work. The court held for the school district, determining that no reasonable jury could find her speech was protected. *Lamar v. Clayton County School Dist.*, 605 Fed.Appx. 804 (11th Cir. 2015).

♦   A Pennsylvania school district could properly dismiss a teacher who made blog entries complaining about and disparaging her students. Among the postings was a "Short Bus" sign with the comment: "I Don't Care If You Lick The Windows, Take The Special Bus Or Occasionally Pee On Yourself ... You Hang In There Sunshine, You're Friggin Special." After the teacher was dismissed, she sued the school district in a federal court. When the case reached the Third Circuit, the court found the teacher's remarks "despicable." She refused to apologize for the comments and even defended herself in the media. The court credited statements by administrators that the blog created a "ticking time bomb" at the school. Many parents said they would not allow the teacher to instruct their children, and **the court found her speech interfered with the regular operation of the school**. As a result, the school district was entitled to judgment. *Munroe v. Cent. Bucks School Dist.*, 805 F.3d 454 (3d Cir. 2015).

♦   A North Carolina school board consolidated its life skills classes. A teacher had concerns that this would cause her to have more students than she could manage competently. She emailed other staff members and the principal and verbally expressed her concerns. Near the end of the school year, the teacher wrote a letter to parents about the consolidation. Although she drafted the letter herself, she made it appear that the letter came from a group of teachers. The next fall, the principal expressed concern about her performance. Other teachers complained about the use of their names without permission, and the principal issued the teacher a letter of reprimand. As the year went on, her performance remained a concern. The principal sent the teacher another reprimand letter, then advised her she would recommend against contract renewal. The teacher resigned and joined a student in a federal lawsuit against the board of education.

The teacher claimed the board retaliated against her for trying to enforce student rights in violation of Title IX, the IDEA and her constitutional rights. First, the court rejected the student's claims. The principal promptly investigated the incident giving rise to these claims. As for the teacher, the court held she had "not offered a shred of evidence" suggesting her contract non-renewal was related to her speech. This defeated both her Title IX and Fourteenth Amendment retaliation claims. **Since Congress enacted the IDEA to benefit children, the court found it did not establish a private right of action for teachers.** Last, the teacher's First Amendment retaliation claim failed. Public employee grievances concerning their own employment issues are not a public concern. *J.W. v. Johnston County Board of Educ.*, No. 5:11-CV-707-D, 2014 WL 4771613 (E.D.N.C. 9/24/14).

♦   An Oklahoma special education teacher vigorously opposed her school's shift toward a full inclusion model. A district special services director assured her that full inclusion would comply with laws and federal guidelines and did not expose her to personal liability. But the teacher continued to voice concerns, including letters of dissent for almost all the IEPs with which she was involved.

She also contacted state agencies. A general education teacher complained about the teacher's conduct at an IEP meeting, stating that she "felt blind-sided and uninformed" about the IEP. As a result, a supervisor wrote the teacher a letter of admonishment. Near the end of the school year, the district denied her request for a job transfer and assigned her to a regular education classroom.

The case reached the U.S. Court of Appeals, Tenth Circuit, which held the letter of admonishment did not affect the teacher's work conditions. **Public employees speaking pursuant to job duties are not insulated from employer discipline.** The teacher's speech took place in the course of her official duties, which included ensuring school compliance with state and federal laws. Even if the teacher's speech was "private," she did not show the transfer was motivated by it. As a result, the court held for the school district. *Duvall v. Putnam City School Dist., Independent School Dist. No. 1 of Oklahoma County,* 530 Fed.Appx. 804 (10th Cir. 2013).

◆ A Kentucky student with diabetes attended a district school under a Section 504 plan that required a trained staff member and a nurse to be present at the school at all times. Her parents also taught at the school. At the end of her second-grade year, the district informed her parents that their contracts were not being renewed. Around that same time, the mother filed two complaints with civil rights agencies, asserting that the school was not following Section 504. Eventually the parents sued. When the district sought pretrial judgment, the **court found that a jury would have to decide whether the district discriminated against the student** and whether the parents' contracts were not renewed in retaliation for their complaints. *Nixon v. Greenup County School Dist.,* 890 F.Supp.2d 753 (E.D. Ky. 2012).

◆ A special education administrator in New York claimed that her supervisor retaliated against her for bringing a staffing issue to light. She also claimed that he engaged in behavior that created a hostile work environment on the basis of gender. She sued for discrimination and a violation of her First Amendment rights. However, the Second Circuit ruled against her. It noted that the supervisor treated everyone badly – both men and women – and that her First Amendment claim couldn't succeed because staffing issues were part of her official job duties, so **she wasn't acting as a citizen when she raised the issue**. *Jerram v. Cornwall Cent. School Dist.,* 464 Fed.Appx. 13 (2d Cir. 2012).

◆ A Michigan special education teacher's probationary contract was not renewed. The district told her that she failed to timely and appropriately complete required Medicaid and IEP reports, that she improperly delegated responsibilities to teaching assistants, and that she failed to provide students their required instructional time. She asserted that the real reason was that she complained her class size was larger than the law allowed. When she sued under the First Amendment, she lost. The Sixth Circuit noted that her complaint only went to her supervisor, and it was part of her job duties to address her caseload. Thus, **her statement was not protected under the First Amendment**. *Fox v. Traverse City Area Public Schools Board of Educ.,* 605 F.3d 345 (6th Cir. 2010).

♦   The New York City Board of Education required employees to maintain a posture of complete neutrality regarding political candidates while on duty or in contact with students. This meant that teachers were prohibited from wearing political buttons in school buildings. The board also prohibited the distribution of political material in staff mailboxes or on union bulletin boards. Several teachers and the president of a union sued, claiming that the board's regulations violated the First Amendment. **A federal court upheld the ban on political buttons**, noting that the board had legitimate pedagogical reasons for maintaining neutrality on controversial issues. However, the board could not prohibit the distribution of political material in staff mailboxes and on union bulletin boards where students were unlikely to encounter it. *Weingarten v. Board of Educ. of City of New York*, 591 F.Supp.2d 511 (S.D.N.Y. 2008).

2. Retaliation

♦   Two Connecticut special education paraprofessionals worked with non-verbal autistic children who were not toilet trained and were identified as "runners." The paraprofessionals voiced concerns to the school principal about the lack of a changing table. They also questioned safety issues related to the unfenced school playground, the failure of special education teachers to instruct the children in sign language and other matters. Both the principal and director of special education told the paraprofessionals to respect the special education teachers' expertise. An administrator said the paraprofessionals had created a "toxic environment." The paraprofessionals again raised their concerns about the students' safety issues and educational goals in response to a survey. The paraprofessionals said they were dismissed a few weeks later. Asserting they had been dismissed in retaliation for raising their concerns about students, they sued the school district. **A state court found they were not engaged in protected activity under the IDEA and did not state claims for wrongful discharge in violation of a public policy.** Regardless of whether any conduct by school administrators was considered intentional, the school district would have immunity for discretionary actions. *Bonaguide v. Regional School Dist. 6*, No. CV126007409S, 2015 WL 493455 (Conn. Super. Ct. 1/8/15).

♦   A Maryland teacher worked at the same school attended by her disabled son. Conflict arose when the principal discontinued her son's medically recommended, gluten-free diet. The teacher objected and said there had been an IEP violation. She pressed school officials to evaluate the child's needs but said the principal began retaliating against her for advocating on behalf of her son. At a meeting, the teacher was warned that her refusal to obey the principal was "borderline insubordination." She was also sent a reprimand letter. The teacher was transferred to a different school, where she continued asking about her son.
    According to the teacher, retaliation against her continued at the transfer school. She claimed she received critical, inaccurate and degrading evaluations. The district transferred the teacher to a different site, where she noticed closer supervision. She removed her child from the district and sued the board of education in a federal court. In her complaint, the teacher said the school district interfered with the IEP process, denied her access to school records, launched

an investigation about her residency and helped the child's father in his quest for child custody. Some of the claims related to employment grievances. The court held the IDEA and federal disability discrimination claims related to the son's education and were subject to administrative exhaustion. Any interference by the board in the evaluation of the student could have been addressed at a due process hearing. **But the court noted that the employment claims alleged retaliatory acts directed toward the teacher as a professional.** She alleged injuries that were professional in nature and irrelevant to any IDEA dispute. So the teacher could proceed with her employment retaliation claims. *Southard v. Wicomico County Board of Educ.*, 79 F.Supp.3d 552 (D. Md. 2015).

♦ After 20 years of service as a special education teacher in Massachusetts, a teacher developed post-traumatic stress disorder (PTSD) from repeated assaults by a violent special needs student. She said special needs students were being improperly removed from general education classes to receive IEP services. According to the teacher, some were not properly served due to scheduling conflicts created because students were being pulled out of their classes. The teacher requested reasonable accommodations for her PTSD. Within four days, the district notified her that her performance did not meet expectations. She resubmitted a reasonable accommodation request for a mentor, additional training and a "clear schedule." After citing the principal for harassing acts, being critical and giving contradictory instructions, the teacher resigned. In a federal court, she sued the school district and town, asserting discrimination and retaliation under Section 504 and the Americans with Disabilities Act.

The court held advocacy on behalf of disabled students who were not receiving IEP services could be deemed "protected activity" under federal law. At this early stage of the case, the court found the teacher's claim that she was "constructively discharged" to be plausible. She would be allowed to demonstrate that her advocacy resulted in adverse employment action. She also stated a plausible claim for denial of reasonable accommodations. But the teacher did not state a claim for a hostile work environment. *Smith v. Public Schools of Northborough-Southborough*, 133 F.Supp.3d 289 (D. Mass. 2015).

♦ A Chicago assistant principal (AP) received a report from a reading teacher that a special education teacher kicked a student who had bipolar disorder and ADHD. After speaking with the student and another staff member, the AP examined the student's head and found a small lump. He reported suspected child abuse to a state hotline and the police. According to the AP, the principal grew hostile and uncommunicative toward him, lowered his evaluations and reassigned him to a teaching position for which he was not certified. After being discharged, the AP sued the board of education in a state court for retaliatory discharge and violation of the Illinois Whistleblower Act. A jury returned a verdict in his favor on his retaliatory discharge and Whistleblower Act claims.

The court denied the board's post-trial motions, allowing a $1,000,500 award for the AP to stand. On appeal, the state appellate court found no merit to the AP's claim to employment that might extend beyond a four-year term. Since Illinois courts confine tort claims for retaliatory discharge to at-will employees, the retaliatory discharge claim failed. But the trial court did not abuse its discretion in denying post-trial motions to set aside the Whistleblower Act findings. **Evidence indicated "a continuous pattern of petty harassment by the Board in direct retaliation" for the AP's report of suspected abuse.** Since it was unclear how the damage award was applied to the AP's claims, the court held there had to be a new trial on the issue of damages. *Taylor v. Board of Educ. of City of Chicago*, 10 N.E.3d 383 (Ill. App. Ct. 2014).

♦ The U.S. Court of Appeals, Fifth Circuit, upheld a lower court ruling against a Texas special education teacher who alleged violations of the Family and Medical Leave Act (FMLA). While taking medical leave, the school district notified the teacher of her employment termination. The court noted she received her full medical leave and was paid through the end of her probationary contract. As the lower court found, the district justified the action based on performance concerns about the teacher and her use of school time to conduct a private for-profit business. **No connection was made between the employment action and the exercise of her FMLA rights.** *Henderson v. Grand Prairie Independent School Dist.*, 559 Fed.Appx. 403 (5th Cir. 2014).

♦ An Ohio employee had an excellent record working with students who had learning disabilities. In her capacity as a union representative, the employee filed a grievance against a teacher. Later, the teacher was dismissed, and the employee claimed her position was eliminated as a result. She said she was then transferred to a position working with students who had multiple disabilities who were violent and aggressive. In a state court complaint against the school board and officials, the employee claimed she was assaulted by two students and suffered severe injuries. She asserted that the teacher who was present in the classroom at the time did nothing to help her. Two board employees stated that the decision to transfer the employee had been made prior to the filing of her union grievance. Agreeing with the board, the court held in its favor.

The employee then appealed to an Ohio District Court of Appeals, where she argued she should have had an opportunity to go before a jury to attempt to prove the board acted intentionally. But the court disagreed, finding the state supreme court had recently rejected a similar argument. **The supreme court had previously held a suing party must prove a "specific" or "deliberate" intent by an employer to cause injury" under the relevant statute.** Since the Ohio General Assembly intended to limit employee tort claims to situations in which an employer acted with "specific intent to cause injury to another," the court held for the board. *Cain v. Field Local School Dist. Board of Educ.*, No 2012-P-0127, 2013 WL 1557436 (Ohio Ct. App. 4/15/13).

♦ A Georgia school district issued a letter of direction to a special education teacher who consistently failed to meet IEP deadlines. Her problems continued the next school year, and she was told to fix problems in her IEPs by a deadline. But the teacher did not meet the deadline, and she failed to submit IEPs when given a time extension. She said she had to obtain parent approval for them. Early in the next school year, the teacher was again admonished to complete her IEPs. She again said they were incomplete as she had not obtained parental consent. This time, the principal issued her a letter of redirection, citing unprofessional conduct and failure to submit timely, proper documentation. Next, the teacher was put on a professional development plan (PDP) that set expectations and provided assistance to meet goals. Despite another extension and the hiring of a substitute to cover her classes, the teacher did not meet the PDP requirements. As a result, the district pursued non-renewal of her contract. The teacher quit and filed a state professional standards commission complaint against school district administrators. After the commission found her claims unsupported, she sued the board of education for retaliation and other claims.

According to the teacher, the district retaliated against her for complaining about the use of unqualified teachers to instruct special education classes. She also complained of the lack of paraprofessional support and improper special education placements. A federal court found the letter of direction and placement of the teacher on a PDP were not "material and substantial." While the recommendation for non-renewal could be considered "adverse employment action," the court found **the teacher did not show evidence of a causal relationship between her resistance to modifying IEPs and the recommendation for non-renewal**. As she did not present evidence suggesting the district's stated reasons were a pretext for retaliation and because legitimate reasons supported dismissal, the court dismissed the case. *Edwards v. Gwinnett County School Dist.*, 977 F.Supp.2d 1322 (N.D. Ga. 2013).

♦ A Connecticut special education teacher claimed she was not rehired in retaliation for complaining about working conditions at her school. She said this led to the development of chronic asthma and other conditions. According to the teacher, school administrators refused to transfer her to a different building for over three years. When it finally did so, only one of the rooms she worked in was air conditioned, and she claimed a fan was not provided in other classrooms. The teacher filed a state court employment discrimination action. The court noted evidence that she had earned "proficient" and "basic" scores on a performance evaluation only a few months prior to receiving notice of her non-renewal. After the evaluation, the teacher had filed a complaint against the district with the state human rights office. **The court found the timing of the non-renewal action raised a question about the district's motive, and it allowed the case to proceed.** *Rivera v. Norwalk Public Schools*, No. CV 116025724S, 2013 WL 5496769 (Conn. Super. Ct. 9/13/13).

♦ When a former teacher sued a Texas school district for breach of contract and retaliation, a middle school principal testified. She claimed she was then demoted in retaliation, and she sued the district under the Texas Commission on Human Rights Act. The district asserted that she had to exhaust her internal administrative remedies before she could sue, but the court of appeals disagreed. **Since she had already filed claims under the TCHRA, she could continue the lawsuit.** *Port Arthur Independent School Dist. v. Edwards*, No. 09–11–00628–CV, 2012 WL 489052 (Tex. Ct. App. 2/16/12).

♦ A program instructor in a structured day class for students with autism or autistic-like behaviors filed a complaint against her special education director and the school psychologist with the county office of education. Despite being named in the charge, the director conducted the investigation. Following her complaint, the teacher said she was excluded from certain decisions and that aides were not provided to her, resulting in an understaffed classroom. Next, her class was transferred to a distant site. After she complained about classroom conditions, she claimed that district officials further retaliated against her. She took medical leave and later retired. When she sued the district and special education director, **a court ruled that she failed to comply with notice provisions of the California Government Claims Act (GCA)**, and dismissed her case. *Elliott v. Amador County School Dist.*, No. 2:12-cv-00117-MCE-DAD, 2012 WL 5013288 (E.D. Cal. 10/17/12).

◆   A probationary teacher in California complained about a student in her class who had severe behavior issues. Another student's parent threatened a lawsuit against her because the student was not receiving special education. The teacher had a poor relationship with her director of special education, partly due to the placement of her own child. After her contract was not renewed, she sued, asserting that she had engaged in whistleblowing activity by complaining about the education plans of students in her class. But the state court of appeal ruled against her, noting that **her complaints about unruly students were made in the context of internal personnel or administrative matters**. *Conn v. Western Placer Unified School Dist.*, 186 Cal.App.4th 1163 (Cal. Ct. App. 2010).

◆   A New York special education teacher received poor job evaluations. He claimed they were in retaliation for advocating on behalf of students, but the Second Circuit ruled against him. It cited evidence that **he was unable to teach to the level of his special needs students, even before he began to make complaints** about school policies. The negative evaluations were not causally related to his allegedly protected activity. *Valtchev v. City of New York*, 400 Fed.Appx. 586 (2d Cir. 2010).

II. EMPLOYMENT DISCRIMINATION

Congress enacted the Americans with Disabilities Act (ADA) in 1991 to extend disability protection to most employees who work for employers with at least 15 employees. The ADA Amendments Act of 2008 expanded the ADA's definition of "major life activity" to include a non-exhaustive list of physical activities. It clarified that an episodic impairment or one in remission is deemed a "disability" if it substantially limits a major life activity when active. "Mitigating measures," such as medications, are not considered when determining if a person is substantially limited in a major life activity.

Disability discrimination cases often involve claims involving health-related leaves of absence from work. For example, in Adams v. Anne Arundel County Public Schools, *this chapter, a federal appeals court found no retaliation against a Maryland school administrator based on his attempts to exercise rights under the Family and Medical Leave Act (FMLA).*

A federal regulation interpreting the FMLA (found at 29 C.F.R. Part 825.220(b)) prohibits an employer from discouraging an employee from taking leave. But another FMLA regulation allows employers to verify a claimed medical condition, assess how long an employee might be out of work, and best accommodate his or her return to work. See 29 C.F.R. Part 825.307.

A. Age and Disability Discrimination

◆ A Maryland student accused a middle school assistant principal (AP) of grabbing her arms, shaking her and pinning her against a wall. Child Protective Services conducted a child abuse investigation. The school system began an employment investigation and reassigned the AP. He took leave based on a medical opinion that he had stress, anxiety and high blood pressure. After a few days, the AP returned to school. But he said the school principal berated him, causing a panic attack. After a week of leave, the AP returned to school but again took medical leave after being reprimanded by the principal. This time, the AP was diagnosed with acute stress disorder. A pre-disciplinary conference was held while the AP was still on leave. Two weeks later, the board presented him with a formal reprimand for engaging in physical contact with the student.

During the summer break, the AP was cleared for work. In conformity with instructions by a medical professional, he was reassigned to a special academy for children with behavioral issues. The AP sued the board for violations of the FMLA and ADA. A federal court dismissed the case. On appeal, the U.S. Court of Appeals, Fourth Circuit, found the board did not interfere with the AP's FMLA leave by scheduling a pre-disciplinary conference while he was still on leave. This was a legitimate part of an ongoing investigation. **FMLA regulations permit an employer to obtain a second medical opinion (and even a third, if the first two conflict).** Reprimands did not qualify as "adverse employment action" as they did not lead to more discipline. And the transfer to the specialized school was not retaliatory. In fact, the AP's medical professional recommended a transfer to a different and less stressful school. Finding the AP could not show the board denied requested accommodations, committed retaliatory action or violated the FMLA, the court held for the school system. *Adams v. Anne Arundel County Public Schools*, 789 F.3d 422 (4th Cir. 2015).

◆ After being placed on a remediation plan, an Illinois teacher continued to earn poor employment evaluations. She was cited for playing computer games, reading shopping materials and texting. The teacher allowed student behavior problems to escalate, failed to meet deadlines and did not supply requested information. She did not prepare for IEP meetings, was often late for work, left her class unattended and failed to monitor student progress. The teacher was again placed on a remediation plan with directions for improvement. She took a medical leave and was then laid off. In a federal court, the teacher sued the school district for interfering with acts of "aiding her students with their rights" in violation of the ADA. But the court held she did not identify any action she took to protect the rights of her students. It also rejected her theory that negative employment evaluations interfered with the rights of her students to receive a free appropriate public education (FAPE). The teacher never disagreed with her supervisor's recommendations and could not show an IDEA violation or interference with her ability to teach. The court found she never raised concerns that the district tried to force her to teach in a way that violated the FAPE rights of her students. Nor did she object to any student's IEP. On the other hand, she admitted she needed to improve her job performance and that she struggled with classroom management. Finding the teacher did not engage in any activity protected by the ADA, the court held for the school district. *Frakes v. Peoria School Dist. No. 150*, No. 12-1329, 2015 WL 5050256 (C.D. Ill. 8/26/15).

◆   The U.S. Supreme Court rejected an appeal from a lower court that held a Georgia school district did not commit age discrimination by not renewing a 58-year-old teacher's contract. In prior court activity, the Eleventh Circuit found she was unable to overcome evidence of her many employment deficiencies. The board said it took action due to negative evaluations of the teacher. It cited her failure to complete student IEPs and lesson plans, her lack of classroom management skills and her failure to implement a co-teaching model. **As the teacher could not show she was not rehired because of her age, the board prevailed.** *Alexander-Igbani v. DeKalb County School Dist.*, No. 14-837, 135 S.Ct. 1893 (cert. denied 4/27/14).

◆   A 15-year veteran substitute teacher in New Mexico began to bring a service dog to school with her. The school district ordered her to stop doing so and denied a formal request to allow her to bring the dog to school. It suspended her after she brought the dog to school anyway, and she sued under the ADA and state law. A federal court and the Tenth Circuit ruled against her. **She failed to show that she suffered from severe asthma,** admitting that no doctor had ever diagnosed her as having such a condition. *Latham v. Board of Educ. of Albuquerque Public Schools*, 489 Fed.Appx. 239 (10th Cir. 2012).

◆   An Idaho special education teacher with a history of depression and bipolar disorder experienced a bout of severe depression that left her unable to take the classes necessary to prevent her teaching certification from expiring. She sought provisional certification from the school board, but it discharged her because of her lack of action over the previous five years. When she sued for disability discrimination, a federal court and the Ninth Circuit ruled against her. **She failed to show that the school board's compliance with state law certification requirements was discriminatory** in effect. She wasn't qualified within the meaning of the ADA. *Johnson v. Board of Trustees of Boundary County School Dist. No. 101*, 666 F.3d 561 (9th Cir. 2011).

◆   A Florida elementary teacher was discharged because of the continued recurrence of tuberculosis. She sued her school board in a federal court. The case reached the U.S. Supreme Court, which held tuberculosis is a disability under Section 504 because it affects the respiratory system and the ability to work, which is a "major life activity." The Court reasoned the teacher's contagion and physical impairment resulted from tuberculosis. It would be unfair to allow employers to distinguish between a disease's potential effect on others and its effect on the employee to justify discriminatory treatment. **Discrimination based on the contagious effects of a physical impairment would be inconsistent with the purpose of Section 504.** The case was returned to a lower court to determine whether the teacher was otherwise qualified for her job and if the board could reasonably accommodate her. *School Board of Nassau County v. Arline*, 480 U.S. 273, 107 S. Ct. 1123, 94 L.Ed.2d 307 (1987).

The district court then held the teacher was "otherwise qualified," as she posed no threat of transmitting tuberculosis to others. The court ordered her reinstatement or $768,724 in wages, representing her earnings until retirement. *Arline v. School Board of Nassau County*, 692 F.Supp. 1286 (M.D. Fla. 1988).

In *Bragdon v. Abbott*, 524 U.S. 624, 118 S.Ct. 2196, 141 L.Ed.2d 540 (1998), the Supreme Court held an individual with HIV was entitled to the protections of the ADA, despite the fact that she was not yet symptomatic.

♦   A Michigan school district transferred a long-time special education teacher on two occasions because of increasing budget deficits. The teacher claimed the transfers forced her retirement and asserted they were in retaliation for her opposition to discriminatory policies. However, the state court of appeals ruled against her, noting that **her earlier objection to the transfers never referenced discrimination laws**. *Rott v. Madison Dist. Public Schools*, No. 294291, 2010 WL 5175457 (Mich. Ct. App. 12/21/10).

♦   The Supreme Court held that Congress did not show a history and pattern of irrational employment discrimination by the states against individuals with disabilities when it enacted the ADA. **Since there was no pattern of unconstitutional behavior by the states, two Alabama government employees could not sue the state for money damages.** The Eleventh Amendment barred any such claims. The Court held Congress did not validly abrogate states' immunity when it enacted the ADA. *Board of Trustees of Univ. of Alabama v. Garrett*, 531 U.S. 356, 121 S.Ct. 955, 148 L.Ed.2d 866 (2001).

B.   Title VII and Related State Laws

State and federal anti-discrimination laws prohibit specific forms of employment discrimination. Title VII of the Civil Rights Act of 1964 is the primary federal law prohibiting discrimination on grounds including race, sex, national origin and religion. State civil rights acts are based upon Title VII, often directly incorporating its language and standards. Many other state and federal acts prohibit employment discrimination on the basis of other grounds.

1.   Sex Discrimination

♦   A Connecticut special education teacher estimated she spent about two-thirds of her time instructing potentially aggressive students. She asked to be excused from "restraining activities" for the students, presenting her employer a note from her doctor. The school honored the request. Six months later, while the teacher was pregnant, she asked to be excused from working closely with or having 1:1 contact with her students. This time, the request was denied, as the employer believed it involved the elimination of an essential function of her job.

Soon, the employer placed the teacher on Family and Medical Leave Act (FMLA) leave. When she declined to return to work after the expiration of this

12-week leave, the employer dismissed her. According to the teacher, the employer committed pregnancy discrimination and retaliation for seeking an extension of her leave to care for her children. In a federal court, she asserted violations of state law, the Americans with Disabilities Act (ADA), the FMLA and Title VII of the Civil Rights Act of 1964. The court held for the employer, and the teacher appealed. The U.S. Court of Appeals, Second Circuit, rejected the pregnancy discrimination claim. Neither of her two ADA disability claims was viable. **Since working closely with students was an essential job function, the employer was not required to excuse the teacher from this aspect of her job.** The employer had initiated FMLA leave in accordance with the teacher's own requests and notes from her doctor. She did not return to work upon the expiration of her 12-week FMLA leave. As there was a neutral, non-discriminatory explanation for her dismissal, the teacher's claims failed. *Turner v. Eastconn Regional Educ. Service Center*, 588 Fed.Appx. 41 (2d Cir. 2014).

♦ Before telling her principal that she was pregnant, a Tennessee teacher had good employment evaluations. Four months later, she was laid off. She was told the district would soon need fewer special education teachers. Asserting pregnancy discrimination and breach of her employment contract, the teacher sued the board of education in a federal court. In response, the board claimed it should prevail because her performance was poor and she did not hold an appropriate teaching license. The court found several reasons to deny the board's request for pretrial judgment. The teacher's evaluations at the relevant time were good. She had a waiver from teaching license requirements during the school year and could have obtained one for another year. In fact, the teacher said the principal had evaluated her as meeting required competency levels for all designated domains and had recommended that she advance to a professional license. Her employment evaluations rated her "satisfactory." But four months after announcing her pregnancy, the teacher was dismissed.

The court found evidence that the teacher was given at least three different explanations for the action on various occasions. And the principal misinformed her about how much maternity leave she could take. Finally, the court noted evidence that **the teacher's eventual replacement lacked full teaching certification and was no more qualified than she was**. Since she raised enough evidence to avoid pretrial dismissal of her discrimination and contract claims, the court denied judgment to the board. *Poling v. Cheatham County Board of Educ.*, No. 3-11-1100, 2014 WL 3697880 (M.D. Tenn. 7/24/14).

♦ New York's highest court held a school aide introduced enough evidence to avoid pretrial dismissal of her discrimination and retaliation case. In the court's view, there was sufficient evidence that her former principal's stated reason for firing her was only a pretext for discrimination. According to the court, the aide came forward with evidence that the former principal directed repeated homophobic remarks at her and reported her for misconduct in an after-school program that he did not supervise. **There was evidence that the aide did not engage in any misconduct worthy of reporting.** *Sandiford v. City of New York Dep't of Educ.*, 22 N.Y.3d 914, 999 N.E.2d 1144 (N.Y. 2013).

♦   A Louisiana special education aide worked with two disabled students, one of whom had autism and the other ADHD. She claimed that the autistic student sexually harassed her, hit her in the neck, cursed at her, kicked her, threw objects at her and threatened to kill her. The ADHD student was violent and repeatedly groped her buttocks and chest. He also made inappropriate comments. When school officials didn't address the problems to her satisfaction, she sued. A federal court dismissed most of her claims, but it considered her claim of a hostile work environment. However, it ultimately decided that **the student misconduct was not sufficient to justify a finding the school was liable**. A reasonable person would not have been detrimentally affected by the harassment, and the students' misconduct was a manifestation of their disabilities. *Dennis v. Caddo Parish School Board*, No. 09-1094, 2011 WL 3117864 (W.D. La. 7/26/11).

♦   A 63-year-old special education director in Louisiana claimed that she was demoted because of her age, race and gender, and that she was replaced by a younger man of a different race. However, the Fifth Circuit held that **the school board properly replaced her after she mishandled the reporting of her school system's special education to state authorities**. And a comment about projecting an image of youth and vitality did not amount to age bias. *Crary v. East Baton Rouge Parish School Board*, 340 Fed.Appx. 239 (5th Cir. 2009).

♦   A Nevada school employee said she was transferred to another position 20 months after being harassed during a meeting by two male coworkers. When her case reached the Supreme Court, it held no reasonable person could believe that the incident leading to the lawsuit violated Title VII. **Sexual harassment is actionable only if it is so severe or pervasive as to alter the conditions of the victim's employment** and create an abusive working environment. It found there was only "an isolated incident" that could not be considered serious. The Court found no causality between the job transfer proposed by the school district and the employee's complaint 20 months earlier. *Clark County School Dist. v. Breeden*, 532 U.S. 268, 121 S.Ct. 1508, 149 L.Ed.2d 509 (2001).

2. Race Discrimination and Affirmative Action

♦   An African-American teacher was unable to show discrimination by an Alabama board of education because she was unable to show an applicant of another race was treated more favorably than she was. After hiring the teacher, the board learned she was not yet certified to teach in Alabama. Although the board advised her to register for state-required certification tests, she did not timely register for them. As a result, a recommendation to hire the teacher was cancelled. She later sued the board for race discrimination. When the case reached the U.S. Court of Appeals, Eleventh Circuit, it found the board had relied on the same pre-employment procedures for applicants of various races. **Since the teacher did not show she was treated differently than others based on her race, the court held for the board of education**. *Bolton v. Baldwin County Public Schools*, 627 Fed.Appx. 800 (11th Cir. 2015).

♦ A California special education teacher of South African origin worked for Los Angeles Unified School District (LAUSD) for about five years before having conflicts with her principal. According to the teacher, the principal falsely said that she misbehaved during IEP meetings and ordered her to submit IEPs to him four days before IEP meetings, in violation of LAUSD policy. She said he yelled at her and fabricated student complaints about her. In a state court complaint against LAUSD and the principal, the teacher claimed he threatened her, wrote up a false report and required her to submit lesson plans. When she submitted two lesson plans in her native Zulu, she said he called it "gibberish."

After a state superior court held for LAUSD, the teacher appealed. When the case reached the Court of Appeal of California, it found that no LAUSD employee had ever disparaged the teacher's national origin or native language. It appeared that the principal did not know the first lesson plan had been written in Zulu. There was evidence that the reprimands were related to performance or unauthorized absences. It appeared that the teacher had taunted the principal in her lesson plans and wrote a plan in Zulu after being told to use English. Although the teacher claimed LAUSD and the principal committed unlawful discrimination, the court found evidence that the principal's conduct was directed at her employment deficiencies. **As LAUSD stated non-discriminatory reasons for documenting the teacher's employment deficiencies, the court held the national origin discrimination and retaliation claims were properly dismissed.** *Mnyandu v. Los Angeles Unified School Dist.*, No. B239104, 2013 WL 1820810 (Cal. Ct. App. 5/1/13).

♦ After receiving unsatisfactory performance ratings for three years, a Maryland special education teacher resigned and filed a complaint with the EEOC, alleging race discrimination, harassment and retaliation for her internal complaints of discrimination. When she later sued, a federal court ruled against her. **The performance evaluations she endured could not be construed as harassment**, and she failed to show that they were a pretext for discrimination or that they were used in retaliation for protected conduct. *Austin v. Board of Educ. of Howard County*, 2011 WL 6736724 (D. Md. 12/21/11).

♦ An African-American special education teacher in Virginia was suspended for five days after she called a referee "the n-word" at a school basketball game. **She claimed that the use of the n-word between African-Americans was culturally acceptable**, and she sued for discrimination. The Fourth Circuit ruled against her, finding no due process violations or discriminatory action. *Parker v. Albemarle County Public Schools*, 332 Fed.Appx. 111 (4th Cir. 2009).

♦ State law prohibited the California Commission for Teacher Preparation and Licensing (CTPL) from issuing credentials, permits or certificates to applicants who were unable to demonstrate reading, writing and mathematics skills in English. CTPL used a basic skills proficiency test to make this assessment. Groups representing minority educators asserted that they historically failed the test at a higher rate than Caucasians, and that the test had a disproportionately adverse impact on minorities that violated Title VII. A federal court awarded summary judgment to the state of California.

The Ninth Circuit noted that discriminatory employment tests are unlawful unless they are proven to be predictive or significantly correlated with important elements of work behavior that are relevant to the job. Here, the complaining parties successfully showed that the test requirement had a disparate impact upon minority applicants. However, **the test was properly validated in that it had a manifest relationship to school employment**. It adequately identified specific job duties to which the test could be correlated, and it established a minimum level of competence in three areas of basic education skills. Validation studies adequately considered the specific positions for which the test was required, and the skills measured by it were important elements of work behavior for employment in public schools. The state did not set passing scores at an impermissible level. For these reasons, the test requirement did not violate Title VII. *Ass'n of Mexican-American Educators v. State of California*, 231 F.3d 572 (9th Cir. 2000).

III. LABOR RELATIONS

Since collective bargaining agreements typically refer employment disputes to an arbitrator, court review of arbitration awards is sharply limited. Court review is generally limited to whether a dispute was properly before an arbitrator. Many courts employ an "essence test" to determine if an arbitration award was rationally derived from the relevant collective bargaining agreement. Absent a violation of law or public policy, courts may not disturb an award that "draws its essence" from the collective bargaining agreement.

A. Collective Bargaining and Arbitration

♦   A Vermont principal saw an instructional assistant "yank" the arm of a child with challenging behaviors. Later in the day, the principal called the assistant into his office and placed him on leave. The instructional assistant and a union representative met with the principal, who advised him that he would recommend employment termination. He then wrote a letter declaring the intent to recommend terminating the instructional assistant's employment. The instructional assistant sued the school system in a state court. The court held his sole remedy was to pursue a grievance and binding arbitration under the terms of the relevant collective bargaining agreement (CBA). On appeal, the Supreme Court of Vermont held the general rule is that employees subject to a CBA must exhaust their available CBA remedies before resorting to a lawsuit. According to the employee, he was not obligated to follow the CBA grievance policy. He accused the school system of preventing him from using the grievance policy.

But the court found the principal had formally advised the employee of his employment termination. In addition, **the principal had observed the conduct leading to discipline and the employee received a fair chance to confront him and rebut the charges**. Instead of filing a grievance, he asked to be reassigned. Not even the employee believed a grievance was filed, and the school was not responsible for his decision to forgo a grievance. Contrary to his argument, the school system did not repudiate the grievance process or prevent him from using it. As the employee knew of the terms of the CBA yet did not file a grievance, the school system prevailed. *Kingston v. Montpelier Public School System,* No. 2014-406, 2015 WL 1086184 (Vt. 3/6/15).

♦   A New Jersey teacher was supposed to provide home instruction to a special needs student no less than three times weekly. But the student's mother reported the teacher only came to the home five times during a school year. This prompted an investigation, which concluded that the teacher engaged in a pattern of falsifying district home inspection forms and failing to appear at the house to provide instruction. At a board meeting, the board voted to withhold her salary increments from a later school year based on findings that she falsified forms and engaged in conduct unbecoming a teacher. The teacher was also prohibited from providing home instruction services and declared ineligible from participating in extracurricular activities for one year. The board notice stated that it would serve as a letter of reprimand to be placed in the teacher's personnel file. Although the employee association representing teachers in the school district filed a grievance on the teacher's behalf, the board denied it.

The New Jersey Public Employment Relations Commission (PERC) held the salary increment withholding and letter of reprimand were predominantly disciplinary (and not evaluative) in nature. As a result, the PERC held the matter should proceed to arbitration. A New Jersey appeals court observed that the charges against the teacher did not require specialized educational expertise to resolve. Charges of leaving work early, falsifying time sheets and missing work are disciplinary in nature. The court agreed with the PERC that the notice to the teacher was a letter of reprimand that was disciplinary in nature. In fact, the letter was void of any evaluative comments and prescribed sanctions against the her. **Rejecting the board's claim that the action was evaluative in nature, the court held the PERC had correctly held the case should proceed to binding arbitration.** *Atlantic City Board of Educ. v. Atlantic City Educ. Ass'n,* 2015 WL 463342 (N.J. Super. Ct. App. Div. 2/5/15).

♦   Because some of its special education teachers had not attained designation as "highly qualified teachers" (HQTs), the Pittsburgh Board of Public Education laid off teachers without regard to seniority in 2012. The Pittsburgh Federation of Teachers filed a grievance on behalf of the teachers, arguing the board violated the relevant collective bargaining agreement (CBA) by failing to comply with system-seniority order during the layoff. An arbitrator held for the federation, finding the board violated the relevant CBA. After a state trial court upheld the arbitrator, appeal went to the Commonwealth Court of Pennsylvania.

On appeal, the court stated that an arbitration award must "draw its essence from the CBA." In this case, the CBA stated that "seniority shall continue to be the sole applicable seniority criterion to be applied in any layoff of a teacher." But the board laid off the special education teachers solely upon their lack of HQT status. Since the layoff based on HQT status resulted in the retention of teachers with less seniority while more senior teachers were laid off, the court held the arbitrator could properly find the issue was within the terms of the CBA. Next, the court found the award was rationally derived from the CBA. In the arbitrator's opinion, factors such as HQT status could not be considered when laying off teachers. **The court held the arbitrator correctly found the**

layoff of non-HQTs out of system seniority violated the CBA. Finding no law or public policy required teachers to have HQT status at the time of the layoff, the court upheld the arbitration award. *Pittsburgh Board of Public Educ. v. Pittsburgh Federation of Teachers*, 105 A.3d 847 (Pa. Commw. Ct. 2014).

♦   A Pennsylvania special education classroom assistant who worked with emotionally disturbed students was found unconscious in a school lavatory. She admitted wearing a Fentanyl patch that she had obtained from a friend. As she did not have a prescription for it, her use of the patch was a misdemeanor. After providing notice, the assistant's intermediate unit fired her for using and possessing a controlled substance for which she had no prescription. But an arbitrator conditionally reinstated her, finding no just cause for discharge under the state school code. He also cited her previously unblemished 23-year career.

On appeal, the Supreme Court of Pennsylvania found the arbitration award was rationally derived from the collective bargaining agreement. It returned the case to a lower court so it could decide whether the arbitration award was precluded by a public policy. When the case returned to the lower court, it found the assistant had an extensive history of abusing pain pills. Immediate reinstatement to the classroom violated public policy, and the court stated an elementary classroom was "no place for a recovering addict." By the time the employee's union appealed on the assistant's behalf, the state supreme court was considering another case involving public policy considerations. The state supreme court instructed the Commonwealth Court of Pennsylvania to reconsider the classroom assistant's case in view of the other case. When the classroom assistant's case returned to the lower court, it held **compelling public policies existed to educate children about the dangers of illegal drugs and the need to protect them from drugs and drug abuse**. As the award violated public policy, it could not be enforced. *Westmoreland Intermediate Unit #7 v. Westmoreland Intermediate Unit #7 Classroom Assistants Educ. Support Personnel Ass'n, PSEA/NEA*, 72 A.3d 755 (Pa. Commw. Ct. 2013). Further appeal was denied by the state supreme court in 2014.

♦   New Jersey supplemental teachers and therapists worked for the county special services district, providing services to eligible private schools under a state program. Their collective bargaining agreement (CBA) set a maximum workday but set no minimums. When three private schools served by the county closed, the state reduced its funding for the program by 13% for the school year. Instead of terminating individual teacher and therapist contracts, the district imposed an across-the-board reduction on their work hours of about 10%. A group of 17 teachers and therapists sought to have their work hours restored or increased. **A New Jersey appellate court found no RIF as defined by state law since there had been no guaranteed minimum hours. Moreover, the teachers and therapists were not fired and did not suffer any reduction in their compensation.** The court upheld the action. *Kourtesis v. Bergen County Special Services School Dist.*, No. 702–12/10, 2012 WL 5834395 (N.J. Super. Ct. App. Div. 11/19/12).

♦   The California Department of Education issued a legal advisory stating that trained but unlicensed employees could administer insulin to students at school if a Section 504 plan or IEP required it and no licensed person was available. A nurses' union sued, challenging the advisory as inconsistent with the state Nursing Practices Act. A court held that the advisory was invalid, and the California Court of Appeal affirmed. The courts rejected the department's assertion that invalidating the advisory would make it impossible for many students to receive required insulin injections. Despite a general shortage of nurses in the state, **school districts could locate and contract for licensed nursing services**. *American Nurses Ass'n v. O'Connell*, 185 Cal.App.4th 393 (Cal. Ct. App. 2010), *review granted* 116 Cal.Rptr.3d 194 (2010).

♦   A Connecticut board of education filed a lawsuit seeking a declaration that class size limits for special education classes contained in the teachers' collective bargaining agreement were illegal and unenforceable under the IDEA. A federal court disagreed with the board, finding that the board could comply with the class size limitations by creating additional sections for students in inclusion classes or by hiring more teachers. Further, **no evidence existed that any student was ever denied services required by an IEP as a result of the class size limitations**. *New Britain Board of Educ. v. New Britain Federation of Teachers, Local 871*, 754 F.Supp.2d 407 (D. Conn. 2010).

♦   Teachers unions in West Virginia brought a lawsuit challenging **a random, suspicionless drug testing policy for employees in "safety sensitive" positions, which included teachers**, coaches, plumbers, handymen, cabinetmakers and superintendents. A federal court struck down the policy because there was no evidence of an underlying problem with employee drug abuse. Here, there was not a sufficient safety reason for the policy. The risk of harm from impaired school employees did not approach that of an impaired worker on a train, in a customs office or at a nuclear reactor. Further, teachers and other school employees did not have a reduced expectation of privacy that would justify random, suspicionless testing. *American Federation of Teachers-West Virginia, AFL-CIO v. Kanawha County Board of Educ.*, 592 F.Supp.2d 883 (S.D. W. Va. 2009).

♦   Ohio public university regents can set standards for faculty instructional workloads in order to emphasize undergraduate instruction, according to the U.S. Supreme Court. A state law required public universities to adopt faculty workload policies and made them an inappropriate subject for collective bargaining. Any university policy prevailed over the contrary provisions of collective bargaining agreements. One university adopted a workload policy pursuant to the law and notified its professors' collective bargaining agent that it would not bargain over the policy. The professors' union filed a state court action, seeking an order that the law violated public employee equal protection rights. The Supreme Court of Ohio struck down the law. The U.S. Supreme Court then held that the Ohio state legislature could properly conclude that **collective bargaining would interfere with the legitimate goal of achieving**

uniformity in faculty workloads. The Court reversed and remanded the case. *Cent. State Univ. v. American Ass'n of Univ. Professors, Cent. State Univ. Chapter*, 526 U.S. 124, 143 L.Ed.2d 227, 119 S.Ct. 1162 (1999).

When the case returned to the Supreme Court of Ohio, it concluded that the statute did not violate either the state equal protection clause or the provision of the state constitution authorizing the legislature to pass laws regarding certain employment matters. *American Ass'n of Univ. Professors, Cent. State Univ. Chapter v. Cent. State Univ.*, 87 Ohio St. 3d 55, 717 N.E.2d 286 (Ohio 1999).

B. Unfair Labor Practices

♦   A Nebraska professional employees union represented paraprofessionals, office personnel, and operations employees. Although the collective bargaining agreements (CBAs) for these employees described the vacation time to which each employee was entitled, the CBAs did not describe how vacation time was to accrue. Each of the CBAs allowed the school district to change its policies at any time. Near the end of the 2010-11 school year, the district's board voted to change the vacation accrual policy so that vacation time would accrue over the school year instead of being granted as a lump sum at the start of a school year.

The union local asked the district not to implement the change, and two meetings were held to discuss the issue. At the time, contracts for the next school year were being negotiated. But the union did not propose any changes to the accrual policy. After CBAs for 2011-12 were signed with no changes to the policy, the union petitioned the state commission of industrial relations (CIR), asserting bad faith bargaining and unilateral action by the district. The CIR held the union had a duty to bargain over any changes to the policy and had waived its rights regarding what was otherwise a mandatory subject of collective bargaining. Appeal reached the Supreme Court of Nebraska. It held the school district acted within its authority under the CBAs to amend the policy and adopt a new one. As the CIR found, the union failed to request negotiations over the subject. **Federal labor law cases indicated that a union waived its right to bargain by failing to request bargaining or otherwise not informing an employer that its employees wished to bargain.** Finding a clear waiver by the union to bargain on the issue, the court held the CIR had properly held for the district. *Service Employees Int'l Union (AFL-CIO) Local 226 v. Douglas County School Dist. 001*, 286 Neb. 755, 839 N.W.2d 290 (Neb. 2013).

♦   A veteran Wisconsin special education teacher was charged with using excessive force on students. Her union filed a grievance, arguing there was no just cause for dismissal and seeking her reinstatement. Before the arbitrator issued a decision, Wisconsin legislators enacted 2011 Act 10, which took away many collective bargaining rights of public school employees. The act went into effect for employees covered by existing collective bargaining agreements on the day an agreement expired. After a hearing, the arbitrator found the district did not have just cause to dismiss the teacher. He ordered her to be reinstated with lost wages and benefits, reduced by an amount equal to a 30-day suspension. Among the findings was that many charges of inappropriate conduct were not credible and that most of the contact between the teacher and students was "incidental and permissible." In response, the school district filed a state court action to vacate the arbitration award. The court found the arbitration award did not disregard either state law or any public policy.

On appeal, the Court of Appeals of Wisconsin held Act 10 had no effect until the expiration of current labor agreements. Under the agreement in effect at the time of the teacher's dismissal, she had a right not to be discharged without just cause. As Act 10 took effect after the relevant facts of this case took place, the court dismissed the school district's first argument. **There was no authority for the district's claim that the use of incidental contact not authorized or required by an IEP required dismissal.** In fact, the court found Wisconsin law contemplated the necessity of contact. As the teacher had engaged in mostly permissible contact, the court found no reason to overturn the arbitration award. *School Dist. of Kewaskum v. Kewaskum Educ. Ass'n,* 351 Wis.2d 527, 840 N.W.2d 179 (Wis. Ct. App. 2013).

◆   A New Hampshire school board entered into a collective bargaining agreement with an employee association, which was made up of certified full-time teachers, librarians and guidance counselors who actively taught at least 50% of their time in the district. Later, the district hired two speech language pathologists and an occupational therapist under contracts that were identical to those of bargaining unit members. When the superintendent tried to fire a speech language pathologist, the association filed a grievance that the superintendent denied. The district then changed the contracts for the remaining speech language pathologist and occupational therapist. In the lawsuit that ensued, **the Supreme Court of New Hampshire held that the two employees were properly excluded from the bargaining unit because they were not certified full-time teachers**. *Appeal of Hollis Educ. Ass'n, NEA-New Hampshire,* 42 A.3d 863 (N.H. 2012).

◆   A Michigan school district decided to privatize occupational and physical therapy services through third-party contracts. However, the education association filed an unfair labor practice complaint over that decision. An administrative law judge found that the district had to bargain over its decision because occupational and physical therapists provided "instructional support services." The district appealed, and the Michigan Court of Appeals upheld that determination. **Here, occupational and physical therapists met with teachers and parents and attended IEP meetings, imparting knowledge to students and parents.** Although they were not certified teachers, they instructed students. *Pontiac School Dist. v. Pontiac Educ. Ass'n,* 295 Mich.App. 147 (Mich. Ct. App. 2012).

◆   A probationary Illinois teacher had performance and interpersonal relationship issues during her first three years with a special education district. During her fourth probationary year, the principal began to hold biweekly remediation meetings to develop a plan, and the teacher brought her union rep to the meetings. The principal believed that the meetings were turning into debates and excluded the rep from them. Later, the principal told the teacher her contract would end with the school year. The teacher filed an unfair labor practice charge, asserting that the union rep should not have been excluded from the meetings, but the Illinois Supreme Court ultimately held that **she was not entitled to union representation at remediation meetings under either state law or her bargaining agreement**. *SPEED Dist. 802 v. Warning*, 950 N.E.2d 1069 (Ill. 2011).

♦ A New Jersey physical education teacher of students with disabilities also served as a union representative, speaking out about student violence, drug use, smoking and inadequate discipline at school. Near the end of his career, he was accused of kicking a student – an allegation that proved to be unfounded. He later sued for retaliation, claiming he was put in danger by behavior-disordered students who weren't properly disciplined. His lawsuit failed because he could not show any retaliatory acts by school officials. **School officials were allowed to increase his class sizes under the bargaining agreement**, and the school's mission was primarily to serve emotionally disturbed children. Any injuries he suffered were caused by his students, not school officials. *Nead v. Union County Educ. Services Comm'n*, 378 Fed.Appx. 175 (3d Cir. 2010).

♦ A Connecticut teacher quit, causing the special education director to reassign his caseload. Four remaining special ed teachers had to work between 10 and 14 more hours per week. When they complained to the director, she advised them not to pursue a complaint through the union and suggested that they lie about the union's actions on their behalf. In the lawsuit that followed, the Supreme Court of Connecticut held that their work level was not substantially greater than it had been in past years, so they failed to show a unilateral change in a condition of employment. However, **the director's actions amounted to unlawful direct dealing with the teachers** to erode the union's status as their collective bargaining representative. *Board of Educ. of Region 16 v. State Board of Labor Relations*, 299 Conn. 63 (Conn. 2010).

IV. TENURE, DUE PROCESS AND OTHER RIGHTS

State tenure laws protect qualified school employees by establishing minimum procedural protections for adverse employment actions proposed by an education agency. These protections, in conjunction with existing contract rights and constitutional rights to notice and an opportunity to be heard, are referred to as due process rights.

A. Tenure and Due Process Rights

♦ Illinois legislators amended the state School Code in 2011 to make teacher performance evaluation ratings a focus in rehiring decisions following layoffs. To determine the order of layoffs, the law put teachers into four groups. Group one was made up of untenured teachers who had not received performance evaluations. Group two teachers had a performance evaluation of "needs improvement" or "unsatisfactory" in one of their last two evaluations. Group three and four teachers had some combination of "satisfactory," "proficient" or "excellent" performance evaluations in their most recent evaluations. Two special education teachers who had been classified within group two were laid off by their employer. When the case reached the Appellate Court of Illinois, it held the amended law only permitted the recall of teachers who were in groups three and four. In fact, **the district was prohibited from recalling teachers classified in groups one and two**. The court rejected the teachers' argument that a school board might subvert the rights of all tenured teachers by giving them unsatisfactory ratings. Due process protection was provided in the form of committee appointments and public hearings. The court held the school district had complied with Section 24-12. Rejecting all the teachers' arguments, the court held for the district. *Pioli v. North Chicago Community Unit School Dist. No. 187*, No. 2-13-0512, 2014 IL App. (2d) 130512-U (Ill. App. Ct. 1/13/14).

After the court issued its decision, the Supreme Court of Illinois denied a petition by the teachers to review the case. *Pioli v. North Chicago Community Unit School Dist. No. 187*, 3 N.E.3d 1053 (Table) (Ill. 2014).

◆   After a Florida teacher was charged with escalating an incident involving a child with disabilities, the district superintendent proposed terminating his employment. The teacher sought to disqualify school board members who had allowed him to teach out of his area without requiring him to gain proper certification. At a public hearing, a board member said he did not feel qualified to conduct the hearing because he had a special needs child. Another board member stated that she had a child with an IEP. A third member said she had personal experience with special education matters. Although board members expressed regrets about having to conduct the hearing, the case went forward.

The board voted to dismiss the teacher, and he appealed to a Florida District Court of Appeal. It held state law allowed a school board to conduct a hearing and did not hold elected officials to the same standards as judges. No due process issue was created based on the superintendent's dual investigatory and prosecutorial roles or the board's final adjudicative role. **A board member could be disqualified only based on bias, prejudice or interest.** A mere appearance of bias did not disqualify a board member. In any event, the court found no conduct by any board member required disqualification. **Personal experience with special needs children was no reason for disqualification.** The court held the board did not have to strictly follow court rules of evidence and procedures. While the board did not provide a model hearing, the court held it complied with due process by allowing a fair chance to challenge the reasons for the termination. *Seiden v. Adams*, 150 So.3d 1215 (Fla. Dist. Ct. App. 2014).

◆   A Connecticut teacher began posting profiles on MySpace to communicate with students. A guidance counselor learned of the profile and found pictures of naked men there, as well as "inappropriate comments" posted near student pictures. Conversations posted on the page were very peer-to-peer oriented, with students telling the teacher about their social activities and problems. After the counselor complained to the teacher, he took down the profile and created a new one that was very similar. When a number of students complained about the MySpace profile, school officials informed the teacher that his contract would not be renewed for the following year. He sought a formal hearing, at which the non-renewal decision was upheld. He then sued, claiming violations of his First and Fourteenth Amendment rights. A federal court held that **he had no due process right to continued employment because he was not tenured**. Further, school officials complied with the collective bargaining agreement by providing timely written notice of the non-renewal. Finally, there was no First Amendment violation because even though he had posted an anti-war poem, most of his MySpace postings were not of public concern, and he could not prove that the non-renewal was because of the single poem. *Spanierman v. Hughes*, 576 F.Supp.2d 292 (D. Conn. 2008).

♦ A Louisiana teacher with 18 years of experience took a job as a probationary special education teacher at a correctional center for youth. She signed two consecutive annual teaching contracts. After her second year, her contract was not renewed, but no reason was given for the action. She sued the board of education, alleging that it attempted to circumvent state law by disguising her firing as a non-renewal. The case reached the Supreme Court of Louisiana, which agreed with the teacher that **the board had to state the valid reasons for a recommendation of discharge at any time during the probationary period**, even the conclusion of a school year. A decision not to renew a contract was the same as a discharge. Since regular education teachers were entitled to the reasons for a discharge, special education teachers were entitled to the same protections. *Palmer v. Louisiana State Board of Elementary and Secondary Educ.*, 842 So.2d 363 (La. 2003).

♦ A principal's first-year evaluation expressed concerns, and she received a preliminary notice of contract non-renewal the next year. After a hearing, the board renewed her contract. At the start of the principal's third year, a district administrator developed a formal assistance plan for her. During the same school year, a group of students violently and aggressively assaulted a student. When the principal called law enforcement and suspended the students, their parents began to actively denounce her. The district administrator initially voiced support for the principal, and he recommended renewal of her contract. When a complaining parent reported that the closed board vote renewing the principal's contract violated the state open meetings law, the board rescinded its action and held a second meeting. By the time the board met again, it was bound by state law to renew the contract. However, all district employees were notified that the board had revised the principal's title and job description.

Subsequently, the principal resigned, stating that the removal of her main job duties amounted to constructive discharge. She sued the school district, school board, and district administrator in federal court. The court ruled for the board and administrator, and the Seventh Circuit affirmed. Wisconsin law and the principal's contract did not encompass any right to perform particular job duties. The district did not transfer the principal, and she retained her title and salary. **Her expectation of retaining certain job duties did not create a protectable property interest.** Accordingly, she had no constitutionally protected claims against the board, district or administrator. *Ulichny v. Merton Community School Dist.*, 249 F.3d 686 (7th Cir. 2001).

♦   A Pennsylvania state university police officer was charged with felony counts related to marijuana possession. State police notified the university about the charges, and the university immediately suspended the officer without pay pursuant to a state executive order requiring such action where a state employee is formally charged with a felony. University officials demoted the officer but did not inform him that they had obtained his confession from police records. He sued university officials contesting his suspension without pay. The U.S. Supreme Court agreed to hear the case and **held that the university did not have to suspend the officer with pay pending a hearing**. The criminal complaint established an independent basis for believing that he had committed a felony, and the suspension did not violate his due process rights. *Gilbert v. Homar*, 520 U.S. 924, 117 S.Ct. 1807, 138 L.Ed.2d 120 (1997).

B. Seniority and Reductions in Force

♦   A California school district reduced or discontinued five positions, including a full-time equivalent psychologist position. Rather than rehire two part-time psychologists for the new full-time job, the district hired a less-senior full-time psychologist. The part-time employees challenged that decision, and the case reached the California Court of Appeal, which ruled in favor of the district. School districts have broad discretion to define jobs and establish requirements, and **the district was within its rights when defining the position as full time**. *Hildebrandt v. St. Helena Unified School Dist.*, 172 Cal.App.4th 334 (Cal. Ct. App. 2009).

♦   A South Dakota school district negotiated a collective bargaining agreement that set out mandatory procedures for reductions in force. Teachers with less than full certification would be released first, followed by those without continuing contract status, then those with continuing contract status, according to "length of service." The board voted for a work force reduction and notified a teacher and a teacher/coach that they were subject to release. The teacher/coach had three years of continuous service to the district, but the other teacher had more than five years of overall service. She had worked as a substitute, taught summer school and worked as a full-time contract teacher. The board determined that because the teacher/coach would reach continuing contract status first, he had seniority. However, the state labor department held that the reduction-in-force policy measured seniority by "length of service," not "continuous service." Because the teacher's overall service was greater, the board should have retained her. The South Dakota Supreme Court agreed. The teacher's case was governed by the collective bargaining agreement, not the contract renewal statute. **The agreement enumerated the specific protocol for implementing a reduction in force.** The teacher should have been retained. *Gettysburg School Dist. 53-1 v. Larson*, 631 N.W.2d 196 (S.D. 2001).

♦   In order to fund an alternative learning center, a Kentucky school board reduced extended employment days for 46 of its 600 certified employees based on a "budget allocation." Several of the teachers sued the school board for violations of state law. The court held that the reduction in extended employment days had been accomplished according to a uniform plan in compliance with state law, and that there had been no violation of the state open meetings law. The court of appeals stated that Ky. Rev. Stat. § 161.760 provided that teacher salaries shall not be lowered unless the reduction is part of a uniform plan affecting all teachers in the entire district and there is a reduction in responsibilities. The reduction in extended employment days was a reduction of responsibilities under the law. **While a school board could adjust its budget to meet district needs, there had to be uniformity when making such adjustments so that no teacher or class of teachers was "sacrificed."** *Pigue v. Christian County Board of Educ.*, 65 S.W.3d 540 (Ky. Ct. App. 2001).

C. Certification Issues

Many courts considering whether a teacher remains fit to teach consider some or all of the factors first noted by the Supreme Court of California in Morrison v. State Board of Educ., *1 Cal.32 214, 82 Cal.Rptr. 175, 461 P.2d 375 (Cal. 1969). These include: 1) whether it is likely that the conduct at issue will be repeated; 2) any extenuating or aggravating circumstances; 3) any effects of notoriety or publicity; 4) any impairment of teacher-student relationships; 5) any disruption of the educational process; 6) the teacher's motive; and 7) the proximity or remoteness in time of the conduct.*

♦   An Ohio teacher with 25 years of experience in the same district restrained a preschool student who would not get on his school bus. She grabbed the student and dragged him on the floor, causing scratches on his lower back and buttocks. Instead of administering first aid, the teacher allowed the student to go home on his bus. As it was a Friday, her report was not given to the principal until the following Monday. The Ohio Department of Education initiated an action to permanently revoke the teacher's license for conduct unbecoming to the teaching profession. A hearing officer recommended permanent revocation and the state board of education resolved to permanently revoke her license.

In 2012, appeal reached the Court of Appeals of Ohio, which returned the case to a hearing officer. This resulted in a decision to suspend the teacher for 39 months. When the case returned to the court of appeals, it held the board was entitled to use standards from the state administrative code and the Licensure Code of Professional Conduct for Ohio Educators when interpreting the term "conduct unbecoming." The Licensure Code included acts of cruelty to children and acts of child endangerment in defining "conduct unbecoming." Also included was failure to provide appropriate supervision to students in a way that presented a risk to student health, safety and welfare. The court held it was reasonable and consistent with its 2012 decision for the board to find the conduct at issue was unbecoming. Moreover, the court found the board's resolution had been supported by reliable and substantial evidence. Finally, **the court held the penalty imposed on the teacher was appropriate and in accordance with law**. Rejecting the teacher's additional arguments, the court upheld the 39-month teaching license suspension. *Orth v. State of Ohio, Dep't of Educ.*, No. 14AP-19, 2014 -Ohio- 5353 (Ohio Ct. App. 12/4/14).

♦   A Massachusetts teacher with six continuous years of service in district schools had professional status and a right to seek a personal leave of absence of up to two years under the relevant collective bargaining agreement (CBA). Following what was described as "a great deal of miscommunication" among the teacher, state education department officials and a school district secretary, the teacher believed his application for a preliminary special education license had been denied. He received waivers from the state for the next two years and was able to continue teaching special education. The state denied the teacher's request for a third waiver from licensing requirements. This time, the district superintendent declared him ineligible for work. Although the teacher requested a year of leave to obtain a proper license, the school committee claimed it no longer had an employment relationship with him.

An arbitrator found the lack of a license or waiver did not extinguish his professional status or his rights under the CBA. Noting that the CBA provided the teacher a right to unpaid leaves of up to two years for personal reasons, the arbitrator held in his favor. On appeal, the state court of appeals noted the school committee took no steps to terminate the teacher's employment relationship in accordance with his contract, relevant state law or the CBA. Like the arbitrator, **the court held the teacher's unlicensed status did not automatically eliminate his rights**. He was still entitled to the termination processes of the teacher termination law, as well as his CBA rights. Significantly, the teacher had professional teacher status and could not be dismissed for reasons other than those listed in the termination statute. In the absence of proper proceedings under the termination statute, the employment relationship of the parties continued. Finding the arbitrator did not exceed her powers, the court held the teacher had been wrongfully denied leave to obtain a proper license. *School Committee of Marshfield v. Marshfield Educ. Ass'n*, 3 N.E.3d 602 (Mass. App. Ct. 2014).

♦   A Tennessee probationary teacher confronted a special education student who disobeyed instructions by bringing potato chips into his classroom. He stomped on the bag while telling students to get out and led the student out of the classroom by his shirt. In the following investigation, an administrator found the teacher tried to provoke students and placed two of them in choke holds. The school reported the incident to the department of children's services (DCS). Later, the DCS concluded that the teacher was a perpetrator of child abuse. In response, the board suspended the teacher. The state education department "flagged" his teaching license, making him ineligible to hold a teaching job. A hearing officer found sufficient evidence for dismissal due to unprofessional conduct. The teacher appealed to the school board, which held he should be dismissed for conduct that was unbecoming and unprofessional.

In the employment case, a trial court noted the teacher had been vindicated of the child abuse charges and found the decision not to reinstate him had been arbitrary and unsupported by evidence. On appeal, the state court of appeals found the teacher could be dismissed for both conduct unbecoming to a member of the teaching profession and disregard of the code of ethics of the state education association. **The code of ethics required teachers to make reasonable efforts to protect students from conditions harmful to learning**

or safety. Agreeing with the board, the court found that regardless of the abuse charges, there was evidence of unprofessional conduct. As the administrator noted, the teacher's conduct aggravated a volatile student situation. Since the decision to dismiss him was supported by the evidence, the court reinstated the school board's decision. *Randall v. Shelby County Unified School Board*, No. W2012-02124-COA-R3-CV, 2013 WL 3148721 (Tenn. Ct. App. 6/7/13).

◆ Two paraprofessionals reported a veteran teacher grabbed a student firmly and pulled her into a chair "a little hard." On the same day, an assistant in the teacher's class saw the teacher approach a nine-year-old student and "pop" her on the lips with her fingers. The assistant reported the incident to the school principal. When he questioned the teacher, she denied touching the student as discipline, saying she was removing an eraser from his mouth to prevent him from choking. After an investigation by the special education cooperative, the board voted to terminate the teacher's contract. Meanwhile, the state education department initiated proceedings to revoke her teaching licenses.

An ALJ considered charges of immorality and misconduct against the teacher. After a hearing, the ALJ rejected a recommendation by the state superintendent for license revocation. A two-year suspension was instead imposed. After a trial court affirmed the decision, appeal reached the state court of appeals. It found the ALJ had complied with relevant Indiana law and acted within her authority. **As a result, the court affirmed the judgment suspending the teacher's licenses for two years.** *Terkosky v. Indiana Dep't of Educ.*, 996 N.E.2d 832 (Ind. Ct. App. 2013).

◆ A Kentucky special education teacher applied for a combined special education teacher/director position, but **the school board instead hired a non-certified but otherwise qualified applicant who held an emergency certification**. The teacher sued the board in a state court, but the Kentucky Court of Appeals ruled that there was sufficient evidence that the teacher was not qualified for the job. A former employer "absolutely did not recommend him for employment," and the Education Professional Standards Board was apparently reviewing him at the time of his application. *Hicks v. Magoffin County Board of Educ.*, 292 S.W.3d 335 (Ky. Ct. App. 2009).

D. Workers' Compensation and Other Cases

◆ Utah's highest court held more consideration was due a special education teacher's unemployment compensation application after she quit because she felt she would be fired if her performance did not improve. The court explained that a worker is ineligible for unemployment benefits if he or she quits without good cause. **A worker may show good cause where the unemployment is caused by pressures so compelling that a reasonably prudent person would be justified in quitting.** In this case, the teacher consistently asserted she had quit because she feared she would fail an evaluation. During administrative proceedings, a hearing officer did not consider the reasonableness of the teacher's fears, instead finding it was possible she could have passed another evaluation if she had simply gone through with it. In the court's view, the question of whether there was good cause to quit depended upon an inquiry into whether a reasonable person facing discharge would consider resignation the only reasonable option. Since the state Department of Workforce Services had incorrectly held the teacher might have retained her job, the court returned the case to that agency for further consideration. The correct question was whether a reasonable person in the teacher's shoes would have quit based on the likelihood of dismissal and the degree to which employment termination would negatively affect her employment prospects. *Sawyer v. Dep't of Workforce Services*, 345 P.3d 1253 (Utah 2015).

◆   A Minnesota school bus driver was dismissed for twice failing to assure all special needs students exited her bus. She sought unemployment benefits. A state agency denied her request, finding she was discharged for employment misconduct. On appeal, the state court of appeals rejected her claim that she had good reason to believe others would ensure that all children had exited the bus. In the court's view, **failure by the driver to complete walk-throughs of the bus violated reasonable instructions from her supervisor**. In addition, the conduct of co-workers was not a valid defense to her misconduct. As the driver's conduct demonstrated deliberate disregard for her employer's interests and could have endangered the safety of children on her bus, the court upheld the decision that she had committed employment misconduct and was not entitled to benefits. *Johnson v. Minneapolis Special School Dist. # 001*, No. A14-0778, 2015 WL 1013646 (Minn. Ct. App. 3/9/15).

◆   A North Carolina teacher was kicked at work by an aggressive student with autism. She missed work for part of the school year due to knee surgery. At the start of the next school year, the teacher returned as a resource teacher for K-2 students. Less than halfway through the school year, she had severe pain and swelling in her knee and underwent another surgery. The doctor permanently restricted her from handling or assisting students. The school district offered the teacher a position as a resource teacher for the next year, but her doctor stated that the position was not within her work restrictions. Several months later, a digital job analysis of the resource teacher position was completed.

When the findings of the analysis were presented to the doctor, he found the position was "very safe" for the teacher. But there was no evidence that the district ever offered her the position. After consideration by the North Carolina Industrial Commission, the teacher was awarded disability benefits for temporary total disability until she returned to work, with ongoing medical treatment and benefits for post-traumatic stress, depression and anxiety. On appeal, the Court of Appeals of North Carolina rejected the district's arguments that the teacher had unjustifiably refused suitable employment. **No evidence showed the district had ever offered the teacher another job.** Evidence supported the findings that her post-traumatic stress disorder, depression and anxiety were related to her work injury. It was not unreasonable for the teacher to turn down resource room work until her doctor reviewed the digital job analysis, and the court held in her favor. *Tatum v. Cumberland County Schools*, 758 S.E.2d 707 (N.C. Ct. App. 2014).

♦ An Arkansas special education teacher was blamed for not reporting a possible inappropriate relationship between a student and a teacher. While she said she believed other school officials also knew about it, the district claimed she failed in her mandatory reporting duty. The teacher resigned prior to a board hearing to consider dismissing her and applied for unemployment benefits. Although the teacher claimed she faced certain termination, the Court of Appeals of Arkansas found she voluntarily resigned without good cause connected with her work. **The court held the teacher did not make reasonable efforts to preserve her job rights.** As she did not do so, unemployment benefits were properly denied. *Davis v. Director, Dep't of Workforce Services*, 2013 Ark.App. 515 (Ark. Ct. App. 9/18/13).

♦ A Louisiana special education teacher was repeatedly punched by a 200-pound student with autism. A few weeks later, she was bitten on the hand. A week after that, she was placed on disability leave for neck pain, for which she was eligible for "assault pay" under a state law. When she tried to return to work seven months later, she was sent home with very high blood pressure. She remained on disability leave for the next four years and then sued the school board under the ADA. The teacher claimed she suffered from PTSD and that the school board had refused to accommodate her. **A federal court ruled against her, finding that she was not disabled under the ADA because she never informed the board of her PTSD** and because she continued to receive "assault pay," which was inconsistent with her assertion that she could return to work. In a brief order, the U.S. Court of Appeals, Fifth Circuit, affirmed the judgment for the school board. *Whetstone v. Jefferson Parish Public School Board*, 529 Fed.Appx. 394 (5th Cir. 2013).

In the teacher's separate state workers' compensation case, a judge found her testimony not credible and held her claim had no merit. She appealed to the Court of Appeal of Louisiana, arguing she had a mental injury as a result of the incident. The court found the compensation judge had made it clear that the teacher was not credible. Her testimony was inconsistent, evasive and contradictory. She had a state law burden to show she suffered a mental injury resulting from sudden, unexpected and extraordinary work-related stress. But the court found no qualified expert reported she had disabling psychological problems. Two professionals had found she could return to work and was malingering. A year after the incident, the teacher's own treating physician found she could return to work. As there was no error by the workers' compensation judge, the court held for the school board and against the teacher. *Whetsone v. Jefferson Parish School Board*, 117 So.3d 566 (La. Ct. App. 2013).

♦ The Kansas Court of Appeals held a paraeducator could not pursue her unemployment benefits claim because she had untimely appealed from a state agency decision. After four years of work at a high school, her school district fired her for hosting a Halloween party where underage drinking was reported. Later, when the paraeducator applied for state unemployment benefits, she failed to follow instructions for a telephonic hearing. She then missed the deadline for an appeal by one day. A state district court held there was insufficient evidence that the paraeducator engaged in misconduct connected with her work. But on appeal, the court of appeals reversed the decision, holding **the untimely appeal deprived the lower court of power to consider the case**. *Geer-Jarvi v. Kansas Dep't of Human Resources*, 298 P.3d 1138 (Table) (Kan. Ct. App. 2013).

♦   After a Florida teacher with 31 years of experience teaching autistic and special education children restrained a child in her classroom, she was arrested and charged with felony abuse. The school board tried to fire her. Criminal charges were dropped after a hearing officer ruled that **the school board failed to prove abuse, and she was reinstated after a formal administrative hearing**. She asked the board to pay her attorneys' fees, and an appellate court held that she could pursue the claim because, although the fees arose from an administrative proceeding, the case was crucial to her criminal defense. *Silver v. Duval County School Board*, 92 So.3d 237 (Fla. Dist. Ct. App. 2012).

♦   A Texas principal's elementary school lost its exemplary rating due to low standardized test scores. She instructed her staff to contact parents of special education students to modify their children's IEPs rather than hold meetings over the matter. Only one parent refused to modify the IEP without a meeting. An assistant principal reported the matter, and the principal was placed on leave. In an attempt to sanction the principal, a hearing officer ruled largely in her favor, finding only that she did not give written notice of IEP changes to the parents. But **the Texas Court of Appeals reversed the sanction because the principal was given written notice of that charge prior to the hearing, so she had no chance to present her side of the story**. *Barton v. State Board for Educ. Certification*, 382 S.W.3d 405 (Tex. Ct. App. 2012).

♦   A Virginia physical health attendant who injured her knee while rushing to her assignment to assist an autistic student at an elementary school was denied benefits in her workers' compensation proceeding. Although she argued that the injury resulted from an "emergency," the state court of appeals disagreed. **Although the attendant was late when she rushed from her assignment with one disabled student to another, it was not an emergency.** Evidence showed the child with autism was not alone at the time, and the attendant's injury was not an "actual risk of her employment." *Gobashi v. Fairfax County Public Schools*, No. 0446-12-4, 2012 WL 6012755 (Va. Ct. App. 12/4/12).

♦   A Virginia school administrator spoke to a teacher in her classroom, then turned around and struck her knee on a wheelchair. Due to ongoing pain in her knee, she filed a claim for workers' compensation benefits, which were awarded. She received a release to return to full duty, but suffered reflex sympathetic dystrophy and used her treating physician's testimony to seek medical benefits based on a 40% impairment of her left leg. The school board's medical expert testified that her real impairment should be 2%, but **the Virginia Court of Appeals held a treating physician's opinions are entitled to great weight**. She was entitled to a 40% award. *City of Norfolk School Board v. Vaughn*, No. 1919–11–1, 2012 WL 1417772 (Va. Ct. App. 4/24/12).

♦   A Louisiana special education teacher received continuing psychotherapy treatment for post-traumatic stress disorder (PTSD) and depression after she was injured on a school bus by a student. After paying for psychotherapy treatments for some time, the school board obtained expert opinions that the teacher did not have PTSD and that the longer she continued receiving psychotherapy, the less likely she would return to work. In the lawsuit that followed, a state compensation judge held that the teacher was entitled to continuing payments for her treatment. **The state court of appeal affirmed but held that the teacher was not entitled to her attorneys' fees,** since the board did not act in an arbitrary and capricious manner. *Sider-Jeffery v. Jefferson Parish Public School System*, 105 So.3d 260 (La. Ct. App. 2012).

♦   An administrative assistant with a nonprofit educational organization that contracted with the New York City Department of Education (DOE) to provide special education services to preschool students with disabilities disclosed a conviction for first-degree robbery from when she was 17 years old. The DOE conducted a security clearance investigation and denied her application for continuing employment with the nonprofit. She challenged that decision, noting that state law required the DOE to consider eight statutory factors in determining whether she presented an unreasonable risk to the public or the nonprofit's students. However, the DOE ignored two glowing references from her current employer and cited her failure to bring in references from a prior employer, even though it never asked for any. The New York Court of Appeals ruled that **the DOE wrongfully denied her application for a security clearance by failing to consider all eight statutory factors**. *Acosta v. New York City Dep't of Educ.*, 16 N.Y.3d 309 (N.Y. 2011).

♦   A probationary nurse in Massachusetts received notice that she would not be rehired for the following school year. The notice was sent one week in advance of the June 15 deadline for notification of non-renewal. **She claimed this was actually a dismissal, not a non-renewal, and that she should have the opportunity to respond** to the effort to fire her. The Supreme Judicial Court of Massachusetts disagreed, noting that this was not a dismissal. She received all the process she was due. *Laurano v. Superintendent of Schools of Saugus*, 945 N.E.2d 933 (Mass. 2011).

CHAPTER TWELVE

School District Operations

I. BUDGET AND FINANCE

Schools that receive federal funding are required to comply with federal law. The oversight role of the federal government includes the threat of withholding funds for local noncompliance with federal requirements.

A. State and Local Educational Funding

♦ South Carolina's highest court imposed deadlines on state officials to respond to a 2014 decision finding the state's public school funding scheme as a whole violated the South Carolina Constitution. **The court held school districts must work with the state to address the violation with proposals for a House task force and a Senate special subcommittee.** The state is to submit a written statement to the court after the 2016 legislative session detailing efforts to implement a constitutional education system. The court is then to review the state's efforts and issue an order. *Abbeville County School Dist. v. State of South Carolina*, 415 S.C. 19 (S.C. 2015).

♦ A group of disabled students asserted Pennsylvania's special education funding method resulted in inequities that violated the IDEA and other federal laws. In a federal district court, they claimed an inequitable distribution of special education funding. The court reviewed a state law section specifying the apportioning of base supplement funds to school districts based on the daily membership of students in each district from the prior school year. The section made the assumption that 16% of the students in each district had a disability. According to the students, they attended school in districts where the special needs population was 17% or greater, and the market value/personal income ratio of taxpayers was a certain level. By contrast, most students in the state attended schools in districts where disabled students made up 15% or less of the student population. State special education subsidies averaged $3,326 per special education student in districts represented by the class, while the average special education subsidy in non-class districts was $4,108. An expert for the students said "IEP students" in the school districts within the class had lower math and reading scores and lower graduation rates than their counterparts in the non-class districts. But the expert did not provide evidence of any relationship between the funding disparities and any denial of a FAPE. In ruling for the state, the court found no evidence that any student's IEP was affected by a lack of funding, or that any student was denied a FAPE by the funding formula.

Any denial of FAPE was found to be related to problems with the IEPs, rather than systemic violations. On appeal, the U.S. Court of Appeals, Third Circuit, found that to prevail, the students had to prove they were treated differently than others based on a disability. But the court held they did not show they were deprived of a benefit or opportunity provided to some other group of students. **As the district court had found, the students did not show the funding formula deprived them of any program, benefit or service provided to disabled students who attended school in the non-class districts.** *CG v. Pennsylvania Dep't of Educ.*, 734 F.3d 229 (3d Cir. 2013).

◆   Pennsylvania law required the state education department to pay a share of the tuition for pupils who were enrolled in approved private schools by their public school systems in order to fulfill the obligation to provide the pupils with an appropriate education. Under Section 1376 of the state code, the department was required to set the amount for each approved private school payment. The department also approved a full-time equivalent enrollment number. When a student was placed in an approved private school, and the state approved funding, the state share of tuition was 60%, with the district responsible for the remainder. Abington School District found two resident special education students required services from approved private schools. Although state appropriations for approved private school placements had been exhausted and no department funding was available, the district enrolled them both and sought state reimbursement. The request was denied. When the school district appealed the denial of funding for the students, it argued that the eligibility for approved private school placements depended upon the appropriateness of the placement, and not the availability of department-approved spots at the schools. After the education department upheld the decision, the case came before a state court.

The court noted **the design of Section 1376 justified the practice of limiting state approval to an annual number of placements at approved private schools as set by an annual budgeting process, not by student need**. Further, the court agreed with the department that funding the placements on the basis of need would cause it to exceed its appropriation for approved private schools, which was prohibited by the state Constitution. Since the department correctly argued that funding of special education placements at approved private schools depended on the availability of department-funded slots at those schools, the court held for the department. *Abington School Dist. v. Dep't of Educ.*, 60 A.3d 201 (Pa. Commw. Ct. 2013).

♦   A group of parents sued the District of Columbia to force it to pay private special education providers in full and on time so that students wouldn't run the risk of being removed from their placements. A court issued orders requiring the district to comply. Years later, the district sought to have the orders vacated because of its new automated payment system and because no students had been threatened with displacement for many years. The **District of Columbia Circuit Court of Appeals held that the lower court improperly rejected the request without first ascertaining whether the risk of harm had been eliminated**. A lower court would have to reconsider the case. *Petties v. District of Columbia*, 662 F.3d 564 (D.C. Cir. 2011).

♦   If California underfunded some mandated programs and allowed them to go into arrears, it either had to appropriate the full amount due toward repaying local governments for the unreimbursed mandates or suspend the mandates. **California assigned the responsibility for mental health services that were formerly provided by school districts to the state and to community mental health agencies.** When it was determined that the state owed local mental health agencies more than $132 million for unfunded mental health services, the legislature tried to pay the difference. However, the governor line-item vetoed that part of the budget. The state school boards association challenged the veto, but the court of appeal upheld it. Local agencies were freed from implementing the mandate. *California School Boards Ass'n v. Brown*, 122 Cal.Rptr.3d 674 (Cal. Ct. App. 2011).

♦   A foster child in California attended a Utah residential facility under a placement approved by a juvenile court. The question of which entity had to fund that placement came before the Ninth Circuit, which ruled that **the foster parent's school district had to pay for the placement** from October of 2007 through April of 2009. For the rest of the time the student was in the Utah residential placement, the state department of education had to pay the cost. *Orange County Dep't of Educ. v. California Dep't of Educ.*, 668 F.3d 1052 (9th Cir. 2011).

♦   A New Mexico sixth-grader with autism would not go to school. His district refused to help the parents bring him to school, but it sent homework to the parents for a few weeks before dropping the student from its attendance rolls. The parents sent an informal complaint to the state department of education and spoke with a liaison officer. They filed a due process request against the district and the state. A hearing officer found that the district had denied the student a FAPE. After the district reached a settlement with the parents, the Tenth Circuit held that **the state education department did not have to provide direct services to the student while he was pursuing his due**

process action against the district. However, it could be financially liable for the district's failure to provide a FAPE. *Chavez v. New Mexico Public Educ. Dep't,* 621 F.3d 1275 (10th Cir. 2010).

♦   An alliance of school districts in Washington sued the state, asserting that it was not fully funding special education. The state provided a basic allotment as well as excess funding at 0.939 times the basic allotment and a safety net for districts that showed they needed more than the basic allotment and excess funding. The court of appeals found that the alliance failed to show the funding violated the state's constitution, and the Supreme Court of Washington affirmed. Any perceived special education deficit disappeared when the basic allotment was included in the calculations for how special education was funded. **Special education funding was in addition to the basic allotment and not in place of it.** *School Districts' Alliance for Adequate Funding of Special Educ. v. State of Washington,* 244 P.3d 1 (Wash. 2010).

♦   After the California Legislature slashed statewide funding of mental health services for special education students to $1,000, San Diego County obtained a court ruling that this was an unfunded state mandate, such that it did not have to provide the services. **The California Department of Education then required local school districts to absorb the costs of mental health services for special education students.** One school district later sued for an order that it did not have to pay the costs. However, the Court of Appeal ruled that the district should have first exhausted its administrative remedies before the Commission on State Mandates. *Grossmont Union High School Dist. v. California Dep't of Educ.,* 86 Cal.Rptr.3d 890 (Cal. Ct. App. 2008).

♦   After the New York Court of Appeals held that school districts had to make special education services available to all students residing within district boundaries even if they were attending private schools, the New York legislature enacted a statute that created a new school district whose boundaries were coterminous with a Hasidic community. Residents of the community demanded education of their children in accordance with their tradition of segregating the sexes in school. Taxpayers and an association representing New York school districts sued the state for a declaration that the statute was unconstitutional.

The U.S. Supreme Court held that a state may not delegate authority to a group chosen by religion. Although the statute did not expressly identify the Hasidic community as a recipient of governmental authority, it had clearly been passed to benefit them. The Court held the result was a purposeful and forbidden fusion of governmental and religious functions. **The creation of a school district for the religious community violated the Establishment Clause.** The legislation extended a special franchise to the Hasidic community that violated the constitutional requirement of religious neutrality by the government. The statute crossed "the line from permissible accommodation to impermissible establishment." Thus, the statute was held unconstitutional. *Board of Educ. of Kiryas Joel Village School Dist. v. Grumet,* 512 U.S. 687, 114 S.Ct. 2481, 129 L.Ed.2d 546 (1994).

♦   The New York legislature abolished the Kiryas Joel Village School District, passing two statutes that provided a mechanism for the organization of new school districts. The laws authorized school districts consisting of the entire territory of a municipality coterminous with preexisting school districts when the educational interests of the community required such action, and where certain student enrollment and property tax requirements were satisfied. The taxpayers sought a declaration that the new statutes were unconstitutional. After a lower court agreed with the taxpayers, the Court of Appeals of New York agreed to review the case. It held that despite the apparently neutral criteria in the amendments, **the Hasidic village was the only municipality that could ever avail itself of the statutory mechanism**. The legislation impermissibly favored that group. The court affirmed the judgment for the taxpayers. *Grumet v. Cuomo*, 90 N.Y.2d 57, 659 N.Y.S.2d 173, 681 N.E.2d 340 (N.Y. 1997).

In 1997, the legislature passed yet another law, but broadened its applicability to municipalities that were as yet unformed. A school district for Kiryas Joel was reconstituted under the new act, and a new challenge was mounted. The court of appeals held that while the 1997 law was facially neutral with respect to religion, its actual effect benefited only the Kiryas Joel district, and its potential benefit extended to only one other district in the state. Therefore, the law was not neutral in effect. The law violated the Establishment Clause by preferring one religion to others. *Grumet v. Pataki*, 93 N.Y.2d 677, 720 N.E.2d 66 (N.Y. 1999).

B. Federal Funding Issues

♦   After experiencing "severe and precipitous" state tax revenue reductions, South Carolina officials advised the U.S. Department of Education (DOE) of its need to reduce funding of special education by $67.4 million for the 2010 fiscal year. The state requested a waiver from the DOE from the IDEA's "maintenance of effort" condition. The DOE found the state did not treat special education in an equitable manner in comparison to other state agencies. While South Carolina had reduced its special education funding by 12.02% for 2010, the average reduction in funds for all agencies was only 7.55%. Thus, the DOE allowed a waiver of only $31.2 million. Finding the state failed to maintain financial support for special education for fiscal year 2010, the DOE reduced the state's 2012 IDEA funding by the remaining $36.2 million. South Carolina officials petitioned the U.S. Court of Appeals, Fourth Circuit, for relief.

In reviewing an IDEA provision at 20 U.S.C. § 1412, the court found that **to be eligible for a full share of annual IDEA funding, a state must not reduce the amount of its financial support for special education below the amount of the support it provided for the preceding fiscal year**. This is referred to as the "maintenance-of-effort" condition. If a state failed to meet its maintenance-of-effort in a fiscal year, the DOE secretary had to reduce federal funding under the IDEA to the state in subsequent years by the amount of the shortfall. Waivers of the maintenance-of-effort condition are allowed if this "would be equitable due to exceptional or uncontrollable circumstances such as a natural disaster or a precipitous and unforeseen decline in the financial resources of the State." The court held the denial of the request for a full waiver was a determination that South Carolina was "not eligible to receive a grant" in the amount of $36.2 million. For this reason, the DOE was required to provide South Carolina with notice and a hearing before it made a final determination about the waiver request. Meanwhile, the DOE was prohibited from reducing the state's IDEA funding for 2012 and allocating it to other states, as it sought. *South Carolina Dep't of Educ. v. Duncan*, 714 F.3d 249 (4th Cir. 2013).

◆   The Federal Impact Aid Program provides financial assistance to local school districts whose ability to finance public school education is adversely affected by a federal presence – e.g., where a significant amount of federal land is exempt from local property taxes. The statute prohibits a state from offsetting this federal aid by reducing state aid to a local district. To avoid unreasonably interfering with a state program that seeks to equalize per-pupil expenditures, the statute contains an exception permitting a state to reduce its own local funding on account of the federal aid where the Secretary of Education finds that the state program "equalizes expenditures" among local school districts. Two New Mexico school districts disputed certain calculations under the act, and the case reached the U.S. Supreme Court, which held that the Secretary of Education could identify the school districts that should be "disregarded" by looking to the number of a district's pupils as well as to the size of the district's expenditures per pupil. Thus, **the state could factor in the receipt of federal Impact Aid funds when making its own distributions of educational aid to its school districts**. *Zuni Public School Dist. No. 89 v. Dep't of Educ.*, 550 U.S. 81, 127 S.Ct. 1534, 167 L.Ed.2d 449 (2007).

◆   A group of Louisiana citizens sued the Jefferson Parish School Board for violating the First Amendment, alleging that the board improperly provided Chapter Two funds to parochial schools for the purpose of acquiring library materials and media equipment. They asserted that the funding violated the Establishment Clause, since 41 of 46 participating private schools were religiously affiliated. A federal court agreed that the funding failed the *Lemon* test from *Lemon v. Kurtzman*, 403 U.S. 602 (1971). It also found that the loan of materials to sectarian schools constituted impermissible direct government aid to the schools. Two years later, the court reversed itself in post-judgment activity, citing an intervening Supreme Court decision holding that a state could provide a sign-language interpreter on site at a parochial school. The citizens appealed to the Fifth Circuit, which held the Chapter Two grants were unconstitutional. The U.S. Supreme Court found that the use of the funds by private schools did not result in government indoctrination of religion, because eligibility was determined on a neutral basis and through private choices made by parents. Chapter Two had no impermissible content and did not define its recipients by reference to religion. Chapter Two funding in the school district did not create an improper incentive for parents to select religious schools.

A broad array of schools was eligible for assistance without regard to religious affiliation. **The program was neutral with regard to religion, and private decision-making controlled the allocation of funds to private schools.** Students who attended schools receiving Chapter Two funds were the ultimate beneficiaries of the assistance, even though the schools used them to purchase computers, software, books and other equipment. The Court upheld the board's use of Chapter Two funding. The parish did not need to exclude religious schools from the program. *Mitchell v. Helms*, 530 U.S. 793, 120 S.Ct. 2530, 147 L.Ed.2d 660 (2000).

♦ Title I of the Elementary and Secondary Education Act of 1965 provides federal funding through states to local educational agencies to provide remedial education, guidance and job counseling to at-risk students and students residing in low-income areas. Title I requires that funding be made available for all eligible students, including those attending private schools. Local agencies retain control over Title I funds and materials. The New York City Board of Education attempted to implement Title I programs at parochial schools by allowing public employees to instruct students on private school grounds during school hours. The U.S. Supreme Court agreed with a group of taxpayers that this violated the Establishment Clause in *Aguilar v. Felton*, 473 U.S. 402 (1985). In response to *Aguilar*, local education boards modified Title I programs by moving classes to remote sites, including mobile instructional units parked near sectarian schools. However, a new group of parents and parochial school students sued New York school officials in federal court.

The case reached the U.S. Supreme Court, which held that **it would no longer presume that the presence of a public school teacher on parochial school grounds creates a symbolic union between church and state**. The provision of Title I services at parochial schools resembled the provision of a sign-language interpreter under the IDEA. New York City's Title I program was constitutionally permissible because it did not result in government indoctrination, define funding recipients by reference to religion, or create excessive entanglement between education officials and religious schools. *Agostini v. Felton*, 521 U.S. 203, 138 L.Ed.2d 391, 117 S.Ct. 1997 (1997).

C. Residency Disputes

♦ Because of family circumstances, an African-American student with disabilities was sent from his grandmother's home in New York to live with family members in Maine. A school district there granted his request to enroll the student in elementary school. Because the district had no high school, it paid tuition for resident students to attend neighboring high schools. Upon entering grade nine, the student was accepted by a neighboring district as a "tuition student." He struggled in school, and his IEP was modified with a provision stating he must abide by a behavior contract or face removal from school. In the fall of the student's eleventh-grade year, he was suspended for five days for making a video of another student smoking marijuana and posting it on a social media website. When the student returned to school, the principal told him he could no longer attend. According to the student, he never had notice, a hearing or an explanation of the discipline. A federal civil rights action was filed on behalf of the student against the neighboring school district and two school officials.

According to the school district and officials, the student's claims could not proceed because he was ineligible to attend public school in Maine. This was because the student's legal guardian lived in New York and the Maine district of residence never expressly found his attendance was in the student's best interest. **But the court held it appeared that the Maine district of residence knew of the family situation when it allowed the student to enroll and attend its schools through grade eight.** When he reached high school age, the residence district paid his tuition to attend school in the neighboring district. It was reasonable to infer the superintendent of the residence district determined, explicitly or implicitly, that it was in the student's best interest to live with his uncle and go to school in Maine. For these and other reasons, the court refused to dismiss the case. It allowed the student to pursue his due process, equal protection and disability discrimination claims. *Lawhorn v. Regional School Unit 34*, No. 1:15-cv-159-NT, 2015 WL 4922293 (D. Me. 8/18/15).

♦   A California student attended a charter school. His family moved outside the school's attendance boundaries but remained in the school district. After the move, the student was readmitted by the charter school as an intra-district transfer student. While at school, he had provoking and attention-seeking behavior, among other things. The parents accused the school of trying to exclude him from outside recess and other improper discipline. They said staff harassed their son by threatening to bring charges based on his poor attendance. Relations among school staff and the parents deteriorated to the point that the principal sent the parents a letter advising them that if staff members felt they were unsafe, they had the right to call the police. The parents were told that as they now lived outside school district attendance boundaries, an application for grade two should be submitted to the child's school district of residence. The family complied, but enrollment was denied because the second-grade class was at full capacity. The family then sued the school district, charter school, principal and district superintendent in a federal court. In pretrial activity, the court dismissed most of the claims based on Eleventh Amendment immunity.

Although the parents claimed the school district violated state law by denying their child's charter school application, the court held they relied on the wrong statutory provision. The charter school in this case was a "conversion charter school." **It was appropriate for the charter school to give admission priority to resident second-grade students.** Disability discrimination laws did not protect the student, as he was "not qualified to enroll" at the charter school due to his nonresidency in the school's attendance boundaries. In reaching this result, the court rejected a claim by the parents that the residency policy had been applied to them based on their vigorous advocacy. It held for the district, charter school and the school officials. *J.C. v. Cambrian School Dist.*, No. 12-cv-03513-WHO, 2014 WL 229892 (N.D. Cal. 1/21/14).

♦   A private residential school in New York provided care for students from within and without the boundaries of a particular school district. When the school became a licensed daycare provider, it sought to have the school district pay for the education of all the out-of-district students who attended school there. When the case reached the New York Court of Appeals, it ruled that the district did not have to pay for the out-of-district students at the residential school. **According to the court, the state legislature did not intend to put the financial burden on the local school district for all of the children living at** the residential school – only those students who were residents of the district. *Board of Educ. of Garrison Union Free School Dist. v. Greek Archdiocese Institute of St. Basil,* 18 N.Y.3d 355 (N.Y. 2012).

♦   A Wisconsin county brought a child protection action against a disabled student, which led to a residential placement. The county funded the educational component of the student's placement until he turned 18, at which time the residential placement ended. The student was transferred to a community-based residential facility, and the county sought to have the school district of residence pay for the educational component of the new placement. The Wisconsin Court of Appeals agreed that **the school district had to pay for the student's education** because the student had not moved to the district to obtain education. He was there for other reasons. *Oconomowoc Area School Dist. v. Burmaster,* 747 N.W.2d 528 (Wis. Ct. App. 2008).

♦   A New Jersey student with multiple disabilities was placed in a residential program. Her parents paid $14,500 annually toward the cost of the placement, and their school district paid the remainder. Three years later, the program dismissed the student. Her father then placed her in a children's hospital in Virginia, with his insurer picking up the tab for awhile. When that funding ended, the father sought reimbursement from the district. However, the parents were divorced by now (with joint legal and physical custody), and the student's mother had moved into another district. The Third Circuit held that **because the student did not have a clear domicile, both districts should share the educational costs** of the placement. *Cumberland Regional HSD Board of Educ. v. Freehold Regional HSD Board of Educ.,* 293 Fed.Appx. 900 (3d Cir. 2008).

♦   The parents of a Massachusetts child with a disability divorced, sharing joint legal custody. Later, they placed the child with the department of social services (DSS), which then placed the child in a private residential school. Because the parents lived in separate cities, **the DSS apportioned the cost of educating the student between the two districts the parents lived in**. The mother's district appealed, but the Supreme Judicial Court of Massachusetts upheld the DSS determination. Apportioning the costs between the two districts would prevent one district from incurring unfair costs. *City of Salem v. Bureau of Special Educ. Appeals of Dep't of Educ.,* 829 N.E.2d 641 (Mass. 2005).

♦   The grandparents of a Nebraska student with developmental disabilities and behavioral problems were his legal guardians. They became unable to care for him, and he was eventually declared a ward of the state. He was placed in a group home in another county and, after he turned 19, his grandparents' county asserted that the county where he now lived should be responsible for the cost of educating him. The Supreme Court of Nebraska disagreed. It held that **the grandparents' county was responsible for the cost of educating the student because he had resided there until becoming a ward of the state**. *Board of Educ. of Jefferson County School Dist. No. 8 v. Board of Educ. of York County School Dist. No. 12,* 703 N.W.2d 257 (Neb. 2005).

♦   A Michigan parent sought to place her disabled son in a kindergarten where she worked rather than in her residential school district. However, under the state's "school of choice law," districts had to have a written agreement regarding the costs of special education prior to permitting a student to attend a public school of his or her choice. Because there was no written agreement, the student could not attend kindergarten in the mother's work district. She sued, alleging that the law violated equal protection and disability rights, but a federal court ruled against her. It found the distinction between special and general education students to be rationally based. *B.C. v. Banks*, No. 5:04-CV-155, 2005 WL 2001159 (W.D. Mich. 8/17/05).

♦   A student in the Manchester, New Hampshire, school district was left blind and severely developmentally delayed after an accident when she was three months old. Her parents placed her in a children's home in Pittsfield, New Hampshire, with the assistance of the state Division of Children and Youth Services. The parents moved and had little or no contact with the student. When they divorced, the father retained legal custody. After three years, a service provider affiliated with a state agency sought a determination of responsibility for payment of the student's educational expenses. The state department of education held that Manchester remained responsible for these costs under a law assigning liability for the educational costs of a student placed in a children's home to the district in which the student had most recently resided prior to placement. When the student's father moved to Ohio, an unsuccessful attempt was made to place the student in a residential school there. Seven years later, the student's surrogate parent became her legal guardian, and Manchester renewed its efforts to avoid liability for her educational costs. A hearing officer ruled against Manchester, and a federal court upheld that decision.

The First Circuit disagreed with Manchester's assertion that the IDEA, not state law, resolved the liability dispute. The IDEA contains no language determining which particular state agency or school district must assume financial liability for a student's education. **The state law definition of "sending district" remained the district in which the child most recently resided prior to the placement, regardless of legal residency.** Manchester remained liable for the student's educational costs. *Manchester School Dist. v. Crisman*, 306 F.3d 1 (1st Cir. 2002).

♦   During the seventh grade, the attendance of a Rhode Island student with disabilities worsened due to family disruption and her mother's cancer diagnosis. A dispute arose between the mother and the school district over the student's IEPs, and the mother enrolled the student in a Kentucky reading center at the start of her eighth-grade year. The mother requested a due process hearing, asserting IDEA procedural violations by the school committee, which alleged that the mother was living in Massachusetts. The mother admitted that she lived in Massachusetts while recuperating from brain cancer, but asserted that her residency remained in Rhode Island. A hearing officer then held that the student's 1998 and 1999 IEPs were inadequate and inappropriate but deemed the Kentucky placement inappropriate. The mother appealed to the First Circuit, which upheld the denial of tuition reimbursement, as the student did not study any subject in the Kentucky facility other than reading. Also, in order to preserve a claim for private school tuition reimbursement under the IDEA, parents must provide a school district with at least 10 days' prior written notice.

Although the mother asserted that her illness prevented her from complying with this requirement, the evidence indicated that she was able to complete application materials for the Kentucky facility during the same time period. Further, the committee did not challenge the mother's residency in retaliation for her request for due process. **Several facts indicated that the mother and student did not reside in the state.** The court affirmed the judgment for the school committee. *Rafferty v. Cranston Public School Committee*, 315 F.3d 21 (1st Cir. 2002).

◆ A New Jersey student was classified as neurologically impaired by the Somerville school system, where her parents lived before they divorced. The divorce decree provided for joint legal and shared physical custody. The mother moved into the Manville school district, while the father continued to reside in Somerville. The IEP prepared by the Somerville district placed the student in a third district, and the Somerville and Manville school boards orally agreed to split the cost. Manville then determined that it should not continue paying tuition. Somerville sued. The court held that the student was domiciled in Somerville, which should bear the costs of educating her in the future. Manville was liable only for the balance of the student's current tuition.

The New Jersey Superior Court, Appellate Division, reversed, finding that a child may be domiciled in both parental households if the evidence indicates actual residence with both parents. Fairness dictated that Manville and Somerville equally share the costs. The Manville school district appealed to the New Jersey Supreme Court, which noted that **the parties had voluntarily agreed to share the costs of educating the student and had agreed to share state and federal categorical aid on an alternating annual basis.** The district paying tuition for a given year would count the student for the purposes of receiving state and federal assistance. The parties had also agreed to share the responsibility of providing transportation. The court affirmed the appellate court's decision. *Somerville Board of Educ. v. Manville Board of Educ.*, 768 A.2d 779 (N.J. 2001).

◆ The parents of a Kansas student divorced when he was two. The student lived with his mother until age 10, then with his father, and eventually moved in with an adult sister. He attended a number of schools, some with IDEA financing and some financed by his mother. The mother moved from the Wichita school district to the Andover school district in March 1995. Eight months later, the student pled guilty to criminal charges. The court ordered him to serve 24 months of probation and complete a program at a private residential facility. The mother sought public financing from the Wichita school district. She placed him in the private facility before an IEP was prepared. Wichita refused to fund the placement. A due process hearing officer found that the student was not a resident of the Wichita district as of the time of his conviction, and therefore Wichita did not have to fund the placement. A review officer and a federal court affirmed. The student's mother appealed to the Tenth Circuit. The court of appeals noted that the student had lived within the Wichita school district boundaries all his life. The mother's residency was not relevant, as the student did not live with her and his residency controlled the case. However, **Wichita was not liable for any residential placement costs. Neither parent resided in Wichita,** and the student's adult sister was not a "person acting as a parent" within the meaning of state law. The mother's unilateral placement of her son in the residential facility was "manipulative, was not undertaken for education purposes, and essentially obstructed the IDEA process." The court affirmed the judgment for the school districts and officials. *Joshua W. v. Unified School Dist. 259 Board of Educ., Wichita Public Schools,* 211 F.3d 1278 (10th Cir. 2000) (Unpublished).

II. STUDENT RECORDS AND PRIVACY

The federal Family Educational Rights and Privacy Act (FERPA) prohibits the unauthorized release by an educational agency of personally identifiable student information without prior parental consent. State laws also impose obligations upon local educational agencies to protect student privacy. These laws occasionally come into conflict with public information disclosure acts.

In T.F. v. Fox Chapel Area School Dist., *No. 13cv166, 2013 WL 5936411 (W.D. Pa. 11/5/13), a federal court rejected a claim that a school district violated FERPA by seeking clarification from a student's doctor about his instructions. The Supreme Court has held FERPA creates no personal enforcement rights. Federal guidance permits health care providers to disclose protected student health information to school nurses, physicians or other health care providers for treatment purposes, without authorization. See http://www2.ed.gov/policy/gen/guid/fpco/doc/ferpa-hipaa-guidance.pdf.*

♦   A Massachusetts resident sought copies of agreements between a school district and the parents of disabled students regarding certain out-of-district placements. The request was denied due to the belief that this would disclose student records in violation of FERPA and state student records regulations. A state court then held the records had to be released, after the name of each child and any description of a disability was blocked out. On appeal, the Supreme Judicial Court of Massachusetts explained that any disclosure of information about a public school student is governed in part by FERPA and in part by state law. Disclosure of information on special education students is further protected by special education laws and regulations. FERPA has a two-part definition of "education records" and applies to records that "(i) contain information directly related to a student; and (ii) are maintained by an educational agency or institution or by a person acting for such agency or institution." In the court's view, the agreements contained information that was directly related to the students and maintained by the district. But a school may disclose an education record after removing personally identifiable information about a student.

Like FERPA, the state student records law and its regulations protect information, not entire documents. Any "segregable portion of the record must be disclosed," if blocking out personally identifiable information makes the information a public record. **In this case, the agreements might link student names to information about their services, programming, progress, needs, and type of disability. This information was highly personal and exempt from disclosure.** But the financial terms of out-of-district placements would not cause an unwarranted invasion of privacy. In fact, the court held the public had a right to know the financial terms of the agreements. The court held a contractual confidentiality clause did not trump the public records law. The case was returned to the trial court to review evidence about action needed to remove personally identifiable information from any records that were subject to disclosure. *Champa v. Weston Public Schools*, 39 N.E.3d 435 (Mass. 2015).

♦ A Utah court held school officials correctly denied a parent unrestricted access to surveillance video of a fight involving his son and other students. A lower court held the parent could have a copy of the video records with the images of other students blocked out. But the parent appealed instead. The state court of appeals held a surveillance recording was an "education record" under the Family Educational Rights and Privacy Act (FERPA). Unless there is written consent by parents, FERPA prohibits the release of education records maintained by a school. **FERPA guidance indicated that if student education records contained information on multiple students, the parent requesting access had a right to inspect and review only the records related to his or her own child.** If another student was depicted, the parent would not have the right to inspect and review such records. Since FERPA applied, the court held the school district correctly insisted that the parent obtain consent from all the other parents of children depicted in the records before releasing them. *Bryner v. Canyons School Dist.*, 351 P.3d 852 (Utah Ct. App. 2015).

♦ New York state audits of private preschool special education providers revealed suspect conduct. Following the audits, criminal investigations took place and certified public accountants were referred to the New York Education Department for disciplinary proceedings. A private party submitted a request to the department for disclosure of its audit guidelines and any communications with school districts and municipalities relating to program audit standards. The department denied the request, stating that the requested documents were exempt from disclosure under the state Freedom of Information Law.

A New York Appellate Division Court explained that state law exempts from disclosure records compiled for law enforcement purposes which, if disclosed, would interfere with law enforcement investigations. The court found the guidelines and related documents were compiled with law enforcement purposes in mind and were exempt from disclosure. The documents outlined the audit methods used to examine the financial behavior of preschool special education program providers. **Releasing the documents would reveal the likely form of an audit and the items investigators would scrutinize.** This could frustrate pending or prospective investigations or impede a prosecution. As the documents at issue would reveal too much about state audit techniques, the court held they were exempt from disclosure. *Madeiros v. New York State Educ. Dep't*, 133 A.D.3d 962, 18 N.Y.S.3d 782 (N.Y. App. Div. Ct. 2015).

♦   Connecticut parents believed their school had videotapes from a school bus security camera that were likely to show two other boys bullying their disabled son. They said the other students pushed their child into the windows of the bus, and the driver may have encouraged such bullying by verbally mocking their child. Claiming the school district took no precautionary measures to protect their autistic child and did not discipline the other students, the parent sought the video records from the company which operated the bus. The district denied the request, as other students on the bus were identifiable. A school attorney wrote the family that disclosure was prohibited by FERPA. The school attorney also wrote that disclosure was not required by the state Freedom of Information Act (FOIA). In addition, he noted that the student was not seen in all the requested video records. The parents filed a state court action to compel disclosure of the video records. The court rejected the school district's argument that the request arose under the FOIA. Instead, it held **the videos constituted "education records" within the meaning of FERPA**. In the court's view, an action before the commissioner would have been futile. In future proceedings, the court would balance the equities involved in the request for video records.

The court noted that in *Ragusa v. Malverne Union Free School Dist.*, 549 F.Supp.2d 288 (E.D.N.Y. 2002), a New York federal court held **a party seeking the disclosure of FERPA records must demonstrate that the need for the information outweighs the privacy interest of the other students**. FERPA required the school district to oppose the student's record request in this case, until FERPA requirements found at 20 U.S.C. § 1232g(b)(2)(B) were satisfied. While a FERPA exception permitted the release of education records pursuant to a court order, such an order could only result from a petition such as the one in this case. Parents and students who might be affected by the release of the records had to be notified in advance of the request. Such parents and students could pursue a protective action on their own behalf. Contrary to the district's argument, the student was not required to exhaust his administrative remedies before the state freedom of information commission. The court refused to dismiss the case. *Goldberg v. Regional School Dist. #18*, No. KNL-CV-146020037S, 2014 WL 6476823 (Conn. Super. Ct. 10/20/14).

♦   A New Jersey teacher used a depressed student's psychiatric evaluation as a tool to help teach students about J.D. Salinger's novel "The Catcher in the Rye." The teacher had the school's social worker black out any student names, but despite that, one of the student's friends recognized him and told his parents about the incident. The parents sued the school and various officials under 42 U.S.C. § 1983, alleging a violation of the student's due process rights. A federal court held for the school and certain officials, but ruled that **the lawsuit against the teacher and social worker could proceed because the evidence showed that they violated the student's privacy rights**. *L.S. and R.S. v. Mount Olive Board of Educ.*, 765 F.Supp.2d 648 (D.N.J. 2011).

♦   The parents of a California student with autism made a written request to the county education office for copies of all electronic mail sent or received by the agency that concerned or personally identified the student. The agency sent the parents hard copies of emails that had been printed and placed in the student's permanent file, but it refused to provide electronically formatted emails. The parents then filed a complaint with the California Department of Education, which found that the emails were not education records under FERPA and that the agency did not have to release them. When the parents sued, a federal court held that the agency's interpretation of the law was correct. **Only those emails "maintained" by the county that personally identified the student were education records.** Emails on a central mail server or in individual email inboxes were not "maintained" by the county. *S.A. v. Tulare County Office of Educ.*, No. CV F 08-1215 LJO GSA, 2009 WL 3126322 (E.D. Cal. 9/24/09).

◆   Alaska's Disability Law Center sought to investigate abuse and neglect allegations involving developmentally disabled students in the Anchorage school district. The district refused to provide contact information for student guardians or legal representatives on grounds of privacy rights under FERPA. The case reached the Ninth Circuit, which held that FERPA did not bar the release of the requested information. **The center would be duty-bound to maintain the confidentiality of any student records it received, so there was little risk of public disclosure of private student information.** And it didn't matter that the aide and teacher no longer worked at the school. *Disability Law Center of Alaska v. Anchorage School Dist.*, 581 F.3d 936 (9th Cir. 2009).

◆   A special education student in New Jersey was suspended after crossing out pictures of other students in his yearbook and stating that they were now mere memories. He also said he hoped they experienced the "pain and agony" he had. His parents placed him in a private school and sued the district under the IDEA and the Family Educational Rights and Privacy Act (FERPA). The case reached the Third Circuit, which noted that the parents had failed to exhaust their administrative remedies and that **they could not bring a private claim to enforce FERPA.** *Woodruff v. Hamilton Township Public Schools*, 305 Fed.Appx. 833 (3d Cir. 2009).

◆   A Wisconsin teacher was involved in a disciplinary grievance proceeding where she was represented by a union-appointed attorney. She provided the attorney with a copy of a student's IEP. The district reprimanded her in writing for releasing a student record to an unauthorized third party without written consent. The reprimand matter was submitted to an arbitrator, who found that the teacher could provide the IEP to her attorney. On appeal, the Wisconsin Court of Appeals noted that the disclosure violated two school board policies intended to comply with FERPA. However, an arbitration award can be overturned only if it is a "perverse misconstruction" or "manifest disregard of the law," or if it is illegal or violates public policy. Here, none of those conditions were met, and FERPA probably did not apply to individual teachers. **The teacher, therefore, could not be reprimanded for disclosing the student's IEP to her attorney.** *Madison Metropolitan School Dist. v. Madison Teachers*, 746 N.W.2d 605 (Wis. Ct. App. 2008).

◆   Connecticut's Office of Protection and Advocacy for Persons with Disabilities sought access to student records and asked to observe and interview students at an academy for students with serious emotional disturbance. The request came after parents complained of improper restraints and seclusion. The district that ran the academy cited the IDEA and FERPA in denying the request. However, the Second Circuit held that **the district had to provide access to the students as well as disclose names and contact information**. Three federal laws – the Protection and Advocacy for Individuals with Mental Illness Act, the Developmental Disabilities Assistance and Bill of Rights Act, and the Protection and Advocacy of Individual Rights Act – required the disclosure of the information to protect the students. *State of Connecticut Office of Protection and Advocacy for Persons with Disabilities v. Hartford Board of Educ.*, 464 F.3d 229 (2d Cir. 2006).

♦   A California student with a speech-language impairment received three hours of weekly behavioral support services and 30 minutes of monthly speech therapy, provided on a consulting basis. When the school district changed providers, there was a two-week gap in services. However, the new provider averaged four hours per week even though the IEP called for only three. The school district withheld the student's report card for the second and third trimesters of her eighth-grade year because she lost or defaced textbooks and her mother refused to pay for them. After a dispute between the district and the student's mother, a federal district court held that **the school district did not violate the IDEA by withholding the report cards** because it sent IEP progress reports to the mother via email. Also, the absence of the speech therapist from the IEP meeting was a harmless error because the student's resource teacher was the appropriate person to help her meet her IEP goals. *Sarah Z. v. Menlo Park City School Dist.*, No. C 06-4098 PJH, 2007 WL 1574569 (N.D. Cal. 5/30/07).

♦   A New York school district created a policy wherein a staff member who learned of a student's pregnancy "should" immediately report it to a school social worker, who would "encourage" the student to tell her parents. If she refused, the social worker, after consultation with the principal and superintendent, "should" inform the parents. When a teachers' association sued the school board over the policy, a federal court ruled it lacked standing to bring the lawsuit because it had suffered no injury. **The policy was not mandatory, and staff members faced no repercussions if they violated it.** Finally, FERPA might even require disclosure of the pregnancy to the parents. *Port Washington Teachers' Ass'n v. Board of Educ. of Port Washington Union Free School Dist.*, No. 04-CV1357TCPWDW, 2006 WL 47447 (E.D.N.Y. 1/4/06).

♦   A lawsuit arose under the Health Insurance Portability and Accountability Act (HIPAA) over whether Wyoming's Protection and Advocacy (P&A) System could access records without the authorization of the individuals to investigate abuse and neglect allegations. A federal court held HIPAA's privacy rule did not bar the state hospital and training school from disclosing protected information without the authorization of the individual so long as the disclosure was mandated by another federal law. It held the purpose of all the laws could be met by **allowing the P&A system to access incident reports with names**

withheld to make probable cause determinations. If probable cause was found, the P&A system could then seek more information. *Protection and Advocacy System v. Freudenthal*, 412 F.Supp.2d 1211 (D. Wyo. 2006).

◆   A learning disabled and speech-impaired Georgia student progressed to the fifth grade, his basic skills scores rising at least one grade level every year. His parents brought an attorney to an IEP meeting to discuss his sixth-grade IEP. The district agreed to provide extended school year services and a private psychological evaluation. The parents then claimed their son made no measurable progress in district schools. At a due process hearing, the hearing officer ruled against the parents. They appealed to a federal court, asserting that the district denied them access to 700 pages of their son's educational records. The court disagreed. **Writing samples, daily work and teachers' private notes did not constitute educational records** under FERPA or the IDEA. *K.C. v. Fulton County School Dist.*, No. 1:03-CV-3501-TWT, 2006 WL 1868348 (N.D. Ga. 6/30/06).

◆   A Minnesota student with disabilities told his mother that other students had papers with information about him and were calling him names. After learning the other students had found copies of her child's assessment summary report near the trash dumpster at their school, the mother sued the school district for violating the Minnesota Government Data Practices Act. After a trial, a jury awarded the student $140,000 in damages plus $47,000 in attorneys' fees. The state court of appeals upheld the award, noting that the act protects individuals against the inadvertent disclosure of student records and that **the school district did not have in place a policy for destroying documents**. But the attorneys' fee award had to be reconsidered. *Scott v. Minneapolis Public Schools, Special Dist. No. 1*, No. A05-649, 2006 WL 997721 (Minn. Ct. App. 4/18/06).

◆   A student who claimed that a university violated FERPA could not sue under 42 U.S.C. § 1983 to enforce his "rights" under the act. The student attended a private university in Washington, intending to teach in the state's public school system after his graduation. At the time, the state required new teachers to obtain an affidavit of good moral character from the dean of their college or university. When the university's teacher certification specialist overheard a conversation implicating the student in sexual misconduct with a classmate, she commenced an investigation of the student and reported the allegations against him to the state teacher certification agency. She later informed the student that the university would not provide him with the affidavit of good moral character required for certification. The student sued the university and the specialist under state law and under 42 U.S.C. § 1983, alleging a violation of FERPA. A jury awarded him over $1 million in damages. The case reached the U.S. Supreme Court, which ruled that **FERPA creates no personal rights that can be enforced under Section 1983**. Congress enacted FERPA to force schools to respect students' privacy with respect to educational records. It did not confer upon students enforceable rights. As a result, the Court reversed and remanded the case for further proceedings. *Gonzaga Univ. v. Doe*, 536 U.S. 273, 122 S.Ct. 2268, 153 L.Ed.2d 309 (2002).

♦   An Oklahoma mother asserted that her school district's allowance of peer grading was embarrassing to her children, one of whom received special education. She sued the school district and school administrators for violations of FERPA, the IDEA and the Constitution. A court held that the policy did not violate any constitutional privacy rights and did not involve "education records" under FERPA. Appeal reached the U.S. Supreme Court, which agreed to review whether the peer grading policy violated FERPA. It observed that FERPA defines an education record as one that is "maintained by an educational agency or institution," or by a person acting for an agency or institution. Student papers are not maintained under FERPA when students correct them or call out grades in class. The word "maintain" suggested that FERPA records were kept in files or cabinets in a "records room at the school or on a permanent secure database."

The momentary handling of assignments by students did not conform to this definition. FERPA's language implies that education records are "institutional records…, not individual assignments handled by many student graders in their separate classrooms." **The Court noted the educational benefits of peer grading, such as teaching the same material a different way, demonstrating how to assist and respect classmates and reinforcement of concepts**, and held that FERPA did not prohibit these techniques. Because Congress did not intend to intervene in drastic fashion with traditional state functions by exercising minute control over specific teaching methods, the Court reversed and remanded the decision. *Owasso Independent School Dist. No. I-011 v. Falvo*, 534 U.S. 426, 122 S.Ct. 934, 151 L.Ed.2d 896 (2002).

III. GIFTED STUDENT PROGRAMS

The IDEA does not create rights or entitlements for gifted and exceptional students. State laws may establish gifted student programs and requirements, but generally do not confer a property interest in gifted student program participation. But the Commonwealth Court of Pennsylvania has held that a gifted student was entitled to one hour of compensatory education for each school day he was denied appropriate educational services.

♦   A South Carolina parent said her child's school district violated the state gifted and talented statute. The court dismissed the case, and the family's lawyer received permission to withdraw from the case. Without the assistance of counsel, the parent appealed to the Court of Appeals of South Carolina. First, **the court found no right of action existed under the gifted and talented statute, which requires schools to provide programs for gifted and talented students to develop their unique talents**. In so ruling, the court held the law was neither enacted for the special benefit of a private party nor written to protect against a particular kind of harm. Similarly, no right of action existed under the state Parental Involvement in Their Children's Education Act. Next, the court held an equal protection claim had been properly dismissed.

The student did not claim he or other gifted and talented students at his school had been treated differently than similar students at other schools. According to the student, his due process rights were violated when his request to transfer to a different school was denied. But the court held the claim failed because he had no right to attend a specific school. In addition, he received an opportunity to be heard. Last, the court held the parent could not advance her child's case without counsel. In an IDEA case, the U.S. Supreme Court declined to rule on whether non-attorney parents could litigate claims on behalf of their children. Other courts, including the Fourth Circuit, have held non-attorney parents cannot litigate the claims of their minor children. As a result, the district prevailed. *Doe v. Board of Trustees, Richland School Dist. 2*, No. 2013-002436, 2015 WL 3885922 (S.C. Ct. App. 6/24/15).

♦ A Washington student had ADHD and sensorineural hearing loss but was accepted into an accelerated program for highly gifted students with a more advanced curriculum and faster pace than general education. In the program, his grades went from Bs and Cs to Ds and Fs. A request to limit the student's homework to two hours per night was denied. His teachers believed this would be a fundamental alteration to program standards. After placing their son in a private school, the parents requested a due process hearing and sought tuition reimbursement, arguing he was denied a FAPE. An administrative law judge held for the school district, and the parents appealed. A federal court held the parents could not prevail on their failure-to-implement claim unless there was proof of a "material failure" to implement the IEP. In this case, the school made daily progress reports, which satisfied the requirement for "periodic reports." Ample evidence showed the student's IEP goals had been implemented. Even if daily progress reports did not fully use the measurements for each goal as specified in an attachment to the IEP, the court held this was not a material failure to implement the IEP. Testimony by teachers noted that the paraeducators performed services that ranged from adequate to very good. Since the parents produced no contrary evidence, the court rejected their claim that paraprofessional services had been ineffective. Although they claimed they were not allowed to fully participate in the IEP process, the court noted they participated in IEP meetings and had frequent contacts with teachers.

Administrative exhaustion aside, the court found the parents' Section 504 and Americans with Disabilities Act claims relied on identical facts to those mentioned in the IDEA claims. **Since the request to limit homework to two hours would not have allowed the student to stay in the accelerated program, the accommodation had been properly denied.** Moreover, the parents, not the school district, had removed the student from the program. As the district had worked with them to find an appropriate placement, the court held the student was not denied access to programs based on a disability. There was no denial of FAPE, and the court held for the district. *G.B.L. v. Bellevue School Dist. #405*, No. C12-427 TSZ, 2013 WL 594289 (W.D. Wash. 2/15/13).

♦ Chicago students in a gifted education program designed a class T-shirt depicting a boy with an enormous head, misshapen teeth, a dilated pupil and a missing hand. The word "Gifties" was on the back. When the "Gifties" shirt lost in the school election, some of the gifted students protested what they thought was a rigged election and wore the shirts to school in defiance of the principal's orders. They were confined to their homerooms for a time, then allowed to wear the shirts. When they sued under the First Amendment, a federal court and the Seventh Circuit ruled against them. **The shirts did not contain a statement or symbolic message protected by the First Amendment.** *Brandt v. Board of Educ. of City of Chicago*, 480 F.3d 460 (7th Cir. 2007).

♦   The Commonwealth Court of Pennsylvania held that **a gifted student was entitled to one hour of compensatory education for each school day he was denied appropriate educational services**. The gifted IEP for one school year failed to sufficiently describe the student's present abilities or needs, lacked necessary test scores and descriptive goals, and failed to provide individualized instruction. Nevertheless, the student was not entitled to day-for-day compensatory education. *B.C. v. Penn Manor School Dist.*, 906 A.2d 642 (Pa. Commw. Ct. 2006).

♦   After a gifted student began attending UCLA at 13, his mother sued state education officials, seeking the cost of a college education. The California Court of Appeal noted that the state's free school guarantee did not mandate a K-12 education individually tailored to each student's particular needs. Also, **the gifted student was not a child with exceptional needs** so as to be eligible for a free appropriate public education under the IDEA. That statute is limited to preschool, elementary and secondary education; it does not include college education. *Levi v. O'Connell*, 144 Cal.App.4th, 50 Cal.Rptr.3d 691 (Cal. Ct. App. 2006).

♦   A Pennsylvania five-year-old with an IQ at or under 130 entered first grade a year ahead of schedule. His parents wanted him identified as gifted – IQ of 130 or higher plus multiple criteria indicating gifted ability – but the district believed that being in the first grade was enough of an enrichment given his anxiety and the way he interacted with his peers. The Pennsylvania Commonwealth Court ruled that **the district had appropriately kept the student in first grade, rather than accelerate his education further**. Although he displayed some characteristics of giftedness, the district properly considered his personality and interpersonal style. *E.N. v. M. School Dist.*, 928 A.2d 453 (Pa. Commw. Ct. 2007).

♦   A gifted student with an IQ in the 140-range also had ADHD and a learning disability. His parents rejected special education services for three years, instead opting for a Section 504 plan. After he was accepted into a private preparatory high school, the parents sought to have his placement changed. A hearing officer ruled that **the school district had offered the student FAPE**, and a New Hampshire federal court upheld that decision. The student had made academic progress and advanced from grade to grade. Also, the district was not required to seek a due process hearing when the parents rejected special education, so it did not violate the IDEA. The district did not have to maximize the student's potential. *Michael M. v. Plymouth School Dist.*, No. Civ. 01-469-M, 2004 WL 768896 (D.N.H. 4/12/04).

IV. STATE REGULATORY AUTHORITY

Cases in this section involve state law conflicts arising from the exercise of state or school district authority and the operation of state compulsory attendance and delinquency laws. Because school districts are government entities that have only the powers granted to them by state law, a reviewing court may set aside a local decision as an abuse of authority.

A. State and School District Authority

◆   New York parents submitted a letter from a pediatrician describing their child's history of adverse reactions to vaccinations. But the New York City Department of Education (DOE) denied the request, finding no medical basis for an exemption. Near this time, the parents disputed the IEP proposed for their child, and they notified the DOE of their intent to place the child in a private facility. According to the parents, the principal of the DOE school where their child was to be placed said the child needed to obtain vaccinations in order to attend school. After a hearing, the hearing officer held the vaccination issue had to be resolved by the state commissioner of education. A federal court dismissed the vaccination issue since it was not raised before the hearing officer.

The vaccination rule was a general requirement to limit contagious diseases and the child was not excluded from school solely due to his autism. When the case reached the Second Circuit, it found no error in the lower court's rulings on the evidence and reliance on testimony by DOE witnesses. Any vagueness in the IEP goals was ameliorated by the specificity and measurability of short-term goals stated in the IEP. The court noted the DOE had proposed 1:1 behavior management support for the child by a paraprofessional. On the other hand, the parents insisted upon a 1:1 student-to-teacher ratio, while the DOE proposed a 6:1:1 ratio (six students to each special education teacher and paraprofessional in the class). The court held educational policy choices deserved deference. The student's IEP called for 1:1 related services for at least 10 hours per week. This would allow the child to make meaningful educational progress in a 6:1:1 setting. **The parents could not show the child was denied access to public education based on his lack of vaccination when they unilaterally and preemptively enrolled him in a private school.** *D.A.B. v. New York City Dep't of Educ.*, 630 Fed.Appx. 73 (2d Cir. 2015).

◆   A group of deaf persons sued the Texas Education Agency (TEA) in a federal court to compel the agency to enforce the Rehabilitation Act and Americans with Disabilities Act (ADA) against private driver education schools in Texas. According to the complaining parties, individuals under age 25 cannot obtain Texas driver's licenses without submitting driver education certificates to the state Department of Public Safety (DPS). In turn, the driver education certificates were only available from private driver education schools licensed by the TEA. The complaint said TEA-licensed driver education schools would not accommodate them. The case was certified as a class action and the TEA was denied a request to dismiss the case. The case reached the U.S. Court of Appeals, Fifth Circuit. Although the TEA held the challenging parties lacked standing to pursue the case, the court disagreed. While their injuries were caused by the driver education schools, the harm was traceable to the TEA.

Multiple provisions of state law empowered the TEA to take action to redress the injuries being asserted in this case. But while the complaining parties had standing to pursue the case, the court held they could not prevail on the merits of their complaint. According to the court, **any failure of the private driver education schools to comply with the ADA or the Rehabilitation Act was not the result of a TEA policy.** As the TEA did not itself provide the program, service or activity of driver education, it was not required to ensure that driver education complied with the ADA. The court held the case should be dismissed. *Ivy v. Williams*, 781 F.3d 250 (5th Cir. 2015).

♦   A New Jersey student attended a private school under IEPs specifying her integration with regular education students in small classes with a low student-to-teacher ratio. After an on-site inspection of the school, the department of education requested assurances that nonpublic school students in the setting did not attend classes with public school students. To comply with the department's directives, the private school assured the department that it would not place any public school students with disabilities in classrooms with regular education students. The student's parents sued the department for an order to prohibit it from precluding implementation of the mainstream provisions of their child's IEP. The court issued a preliminary order for the family. On appeal, the U.S. Court of Appeals, Third Circuit, found the case was a "proceeding" under the IDEA. It held the student could remain in her placement under the IDEA stay-put provision. The nature of a "change in educational placement" under the IDEA is fact-specific. In other cases where an educational placement was held not to require attendance at a specific school, courts had found alternative locations were available that might satisfy the requirements of the student's IEP.

Transfer to a different building for fiscal or other reasons unrelated to the child is not a change in placement. **The court held the state could not wield its regulatory authority in a way that dispensed with the terms of a child's IEP.** There had been no discussion of a viable placement for the child. Since the record did not include the child's IEP, the court returned the case to the trial court for fact-finding and a review of educational alternatives. *D.M.; L.M. on behalf of E.M. v. New Jersey Dep't of Educ.*, 801 F.3d 205 (3d Cir. 2015).

♦   A New York court held a school district could not obtain court relief in a dispute over a finding by the state that its dispute resolution practices were not in compliance with state and federal law requirements. Following a state education department review of various student records and IEPs, it was found that the district's dispute resolution practices violated the law. As a result, the state education department ordered the school district to take corrective action.

The school district sued the department, but a state court dismissed the case. On appeal, the New York Supreme Court, Appellate Division, found that as a condition of federal funding, the state had to establish and maintain policies and procedures ensuring that students with disabilities receive a free appropriate public education in appropriate settings. The IDEA conditions funding upon submission by local educational agencies of a plan providing assurances to the state that its provision of services to students with disabilities complied with state policies and procedures. Nothing in the IDEA confers a private right of action to contest state regulatory and enforcement action. In the court's view, the delegation of IDEA regulatory and enforcement power to the U.S. Secretary of Education and the states (but not local educational agencies) suggested Congress intended to deny local agencies a right to challenge state compliance with the IDEA. **Since Congress did not intend to grant school districts a private right of action to challenge a state's enforcement of state and federal special education laws and regulations, the court held for the state education department.** *East Ramapo Cent. School Dist. v. King*, 130 A.D.3d 19, 11 N.Y.S.3d 284 (N.Y. App. Div. 2015).

◆ A group representing special needs students in Philadelphia schools filed an original action in the Pennsylvania Commonwealth Court, asserting the school district's long-range facilities master plan would jeopardize student educational interests. The plan sought to standardize grade configurations, increase school utilization and reduce building capacity. Programs would be relocated, personnel would be cut, 23 schools would be closed and others consolidated. According to the families, the school closings, cuts in related services and staff reductions would deprive the students of services specified in their IEPs. They asserted violations of the IDEA, Rehabilitation Act Section 504, ADA, the No Child Left Behind Act and constitutional rights. According to the commonwealth, the claims against it were barred by sovereign immunity provisions of the state constitution, which bar claims against any agency or employee for acts within their offices or employment.

Although the Pennsylvania General Assembly had waived immunity in nine areas (such as vehicle liability, care custody or control of property, highways and sidewalks), none of these areas were implicated here, and the court dismissed the claims against the state. **The assertion of system-wide deficiencies did not excuse the families from exhausting their administrative remedies under the IDEA.** As a result, the court dismissed all the IDEA-based claims. For the same reason, the court dismissed the ADA and Section 504 claims. As there is no private right of action to enforce the No Child Left Behind Act, the court held the claims filed under the act were barred. The court transferred any remaining claims against the city and the school district to a county court of common pleas. *Collins v. State of Pennsylvania*, No. 96 M.D. 2013, 2013 WL 5874770 (Pa. Commw. Ct. 10/31/13).

◆ The parents of a New Jersey student with disabilities, who had to be in a room with a temperature of at least 77 degrees Fahrenheit, objected to the home-instruction IEP proposed by their district because it only offered instruction for five hours and therapeutic services for five hours a week. They complained to the state office of special education (OSE), which determined that the district had to offer 10 hours of instruction per week. The district challenged the OSE's authority, but **an appellate court held the OSE had the authority to investigate and order the district to provide more instructional hours.** *In re New Jersey Dep't of Educ. Complaint Investigation C2012-4341*, 2012 WL 4845648 (N.J. Super. Ct. App. Div. 10/11/12).

♦   As an experiment for his doctoral dissertation, a Louisiana middle school principal got permission to create single-sex classrooms. He claimed, at the end of the year, that they resulted in significant academic improvement and a decline in behavioral problems. However, he fudged the numbers to reach that result, and he disproportionately filled coed classes with special education students. A lawsuit resulted when a parent complained, but a federal court determined that there was no intentional discrimination. However, it ordered the school board to follow a 10-step plan to implement single-sex education the following year. The Fifth Circuit then held that the lower court should oversee the implementation of the program. *Doe v. Vermilion Parish School Board*, 421 Fed.Appx. 366 (5th Cir. 2011).

♦   A Hawaii entity sought to provide intensive instructional support for students with disabilities. However, its bid was rejected because it did not meet the minimum score for consideration. It challenged the rejection of its bid administratively and then in court, but it lost. The Hawaii Court of Appeals held that the department of education had the final say in the matter and that the entity couldn't sue to challenge its decision. *Alaka'i Na Neiki, Inc. v. Hamamoto*, 257 P.3d 213 (Haw. Ct. App. 2011).

♦   The mother of an Alabama student became dissatisfied with her child's education and sued the school board, the state department of education and several officials. A federal court dismissed the department and the officials from the lawsuit, noting that the IDEA does not provide for individual liability and that **the mother failed to show any widespread systemic breakdown by the department in carrying out its mandate under the IDEA**. *B.I. v. Montgomery County Board of Educ.*, 750 F.Supp.2d 1280 (M.D. Ala. 2010).

♦   The mother of a Washington student with ADHD stopped taking care of him because of her substance abuse. She completed a treatment program and stayed sober for more than a year, but the state sought to terminate her parental rights and provided foster parent training to someone else. In the lawsuit that resulted, the Supreme Court of Washington held the state had overstepped its bounds. **The state could not terminate the mother's parental rights without at least offering to provide the same training to her that it provided to the foster parent.** *In re Welfare of C.S.*, 225 P.3d 953 (Wash. 2010).

♦   With the consent of parents, a residential school in Massachusetts used shock therapy on students when other positive and non-intrusive behavioral procedures were ineffective. The school sought to be certified by the California Department of Education as a nonpublic, nonsectarian school authorized to serve students with IEPs. The department refused to grant the certification, and the California Court of Appeal upheld that determination. **The school's written policy authorized corporal punishment, in violation of the California Education Code**, and it was not entitled to a waiver of that prohibition. *Judge Rotenberg Educ. Center v. Office of Administrative Hearings*, No. C056194, 2009 WL 162066 (Cal. Ct. App. 1/26/09).

B. Compulsory Attendance and Delinquency

State compulsory attendance and delinquency laws impose obligations on students that may be impacted by juvenile court orders. Many states have acted to create alternative placements for students who would otherwise be suspended or expelled for violation of state laws.

♦ **Wyoming's highest court held school officials have no duty to counsel a parent prior to a charge of educational neglect.** In lower court proceedings, a parent argued a state juvenile court had improperly applied child protection laws. She invoked compulsory attendance laws that required schools to provide notices and counseling to students and parents, and to investigate truancy causes. But the court held the compulsory education laws did not apply in this neglect case. Instead, the case arose under the state's child protective services statutes. The court upheld the parent's neglect conviction, finding school compliance with the compulsory attendance statutes had no bearing on the case. *In re JM*, 334 P.3d 568 (Wyo. 2014).

♦ The Supreme Court of Nebraska upheld a truancy petition despite a student's claim that her school district did not offer her services required by the state compulsory attendance law. The court rejected a claim that juvenile court authority required school compliance with Nebraska compulsory attendance statutes. **State compulsory attendance laws imposed no preconditions on juvenile court jurisdiction, so a school district did not have to comply with services described in the laws before a proceeding was initiated.** *In re Interest of Samantha C.*, 287 Neb. 644, 843 N.W.2d 665 (Neb. App. 2014).

♦ An Alabama school handbook provided for referral to an "early warning program" conducted by the county juvenile court system where a student had three unexcused absences in a semester. After a student accumulated a tenth tardy in a single semester (for a total of 40 minutes), her principal reported her to the school truant officer. The principal did not refer her to the early warning program or contact her parents, as specified in the handbook. A court adjudicated the student a child in need of supervision and placed her on probation for the rest of the school year. She appealed to the Alabama Court of Civil Appeals, admitting to being tardy on 10 occasions, but asserting that a medical condition had made it difficult for her to be on time for school. And after receiving prescription medication, she was not late for school again. The court upheld the lower court's ruling, noting that **nothing in state law required the principal to investigate the causes of the student's tardiness**. Also, the principal did not violate the student's due process rights by failing to follow the handbook's progressive discipline procedures. The handbook placed a duty on the student to provide a timely excuse for her absences. *S.H. v. State of Alabama*, 868 So.2d 1110 (Ala. Civ. App. 2003).

♦ A Massachusetts student with a long record of disruptive behavior was not identified as a student with a disability under the IDEA but was the subject of numerous school disciplinary actions. A school administrator referred him for a psycho-educational evaluation, which did not indicate the student needed special education. Three years later, a teacher observed the student participate in what appeared to be a drug transaction. The principal called the police and questioned the student in the presence of an officer. When the student emptied his pockets, he produced two homemade pipes and a wallet that contained two small packages of marijuana and cash. The student was adjudicated delinquent and sentenced to one year of probation.

The student appealed to the Massachusetts Appeals Court, where he argued that the juvenile court proceeding constituted a change of placement that violated the IDEA's stay-put provision. He claimed that the school violated the IDEA by failing to immediately provide the police with his school records. The court noted that even if the student had a disability, he was not entitled to the relief he sought. The police, not the school, had initiated the delinquency proceeding. **The IDEA does not prevent state law enforcement and judicial authorities from exercising their responsibilities when students with disabilities commit crimes.** School officials did not violate the IDEA by failing to immediately deliver his records to the police. While the IDEA requires an agency reporting a crime by a disabled student to transmit the student's educational and disciplinary records to law enforcement authorities, it does not specify when this must occur. The court affirmed the finding of delinquency. *Comwlth. of Massachusetts v. Nathaniel N.*, 764 N.E.2d 883 (Mass. App. Ct. 2002).

V. STUDENTS AND JUVENILE JUSTICE

Section 1412(a)(1)(B)(ii) of the IDEA provides that a FAPE need not be provided to children with disabilities "aged 18 through 21 to the extent that State law does not require that special education and related services under this part be provided to children with disabilities who, in the educational placement prior to their incarceration in an adult correctional facility," were not identified as a child with a disability or did not have an IEP.

Section 1412(a)(11)(C) allows states discretion as to whether they will provide services to students with disabilities who are convicted as adults under state law and subsequently incarcerated in adult prisons. As a result of these provisions, cases have arisen over exactly what obligations states have to incarcerated students with disabilities, primarily under state law. In Los Angeles Unified School Dist. v. Garcia, *this chapter, the Supreme Court of California held a parent's district of residence had the responsibility to serve the special education needs of an IDEA-eligible incarcerated adult student.*

♦   A California student pleaded guilty to misdemeanor theft and marijuana charges and was placed on probation. Within four months, he was charged with five sexual offenses against his nine-year-old niece. The student's probation was revoked, and he admitted to one count of lewd conduct. The next year, he was found unsupervised in the presence of children under 13. After admitting failure to enter a treatment program, the student was ordered to juvenile detention for 77 days and then to his mother's custody under supervision. But his probation was revoked due to absences or tardiness at school and other counts. Following revocation of his probation, the student was ordered into a "level A" placement.

On appeal, the Court of Appeal of California held the student had forfeited his claim that he had special needs because he failed to produce evidence of an IEP. While a report regarding his sexual crimes stated he had once had an IEP, his mother said he received passing grades and was "not a special education student." While there was evidence that the student had a specific learning disability, a later study reported his only identified educational need was English as a Second Language. At the conclusion of his juvenile disposition, the court found no IEP had been established. As a result, **the court had found the student was not an individual with special needs**. But the student correctly argued that the juvenile court should not have ordered him to pay $20 for each drug test. The costs of required testing cannot be made a condition of probation. *In re Jose G.*, No. C076503, 2015 WL 3814292 (Cal. Ct. App. 6/19/15).

♦   Due to specific learning deficiencies and speech and language impairments, a 15-year-old Los Angeles charter school student was eligible for special education. Before turning 16, he was charged with felonies and held in a Los Angeles juvenile facility. He received special education from the Los Angeles County Office of Education while awaiting trial. When he turned 18, he was transferred to the Los Angeles County Jail. A due process hearing was filed on behalf of the student and others like him, asserting denial of a free appropriate public education (FAPE). It was argued that no special education system existed for eligible inmates who were incarcerated in the Los Angeles County Jail.

Applying state Education Code Section 56041, an administrative law judge (ALJ) held the school districts of residence of the parents of 18- to 22-year-old eligible students bore the responsibility of providing a FAPE. A federal district court affirmed the ALJ's order and held Los Angeles Unified School District (LAUSD) was responsible for providing the student special education. While appeal was pending before the U.S. Court of Appeals, Ninth Circuit, the student pleaded guilty to several charges and was sentenced to 12 years in a state prison. Since there was no provision in state law concerning who bore the responsibility for educating a student in an adult jail, the LAUSD claimed the state had to pay for it. **The Ninth Circuit thought it likely that LAUSD would have to pay, since it was the student's last district of residence. It referred the case to the California Supreme Court for a more definitive answer.** *Los Angeles Unified School Dist. v. Garcia*, 669 F.3d 956 (9th Cir. 2012).

After accepting the question, the state supreme court noted that state and federal law generally require a state to provide FAPE to eligible students until age 22. Allocation of the responsibility for providing FAPE was left to the states and typically turned on residency. As the federal district court found, no state law provision directly resolved the question. Of the various Education Code sections regarding allocation of special education services, the court found only Section 56041 expressly referred to students aged 18 through 22. **The court found it consistent with state obligations under the IDEA to allocate the responsibility for special education to the district of residence of the parents of eligible students who were incarcerated in county jails.** This interpretation followed the state's general policy and statutory scheme. In response to the Ninth Circuit's question, the court held a parent's district of residence had to serve the class of students identified in the case. *Los Angeles Unified School Dist. v. Garcia*, 58 Cal.4th 175, 314 P.3d 767 (Cal. 2013).

The case returned to the Ninth Circuit, which affirmed a district court decision that LAUSD was responsible for providing special education to the adult student. It rejected LAUSD's claim that the county in which the jail is located should pay for the costs of special education for such adult students. *Los Angeles Unified School Dist. v. Garcia*, 741 F.3d 956 (9th Cir. 2014).

♦   An Ohio appeals court held a juvenile court improperly ordered a school district to provide special education services to an incarcerated student. Although he continued to receive the extended year services stated in his IEP while incarcerated, the services ended when summer leave began for district staff. The juvenile court then joined the district as a party to the juvenile case and ordered it to provide the student with his IEP services while he was incarcerated. Later, the state court of appeals held the student had to exhaust his available administrative remedies under the IDEA before resorting to court. **It was an abuse of discretion to join the school district to the juvenile proceeding.** *In re T.J.*, No. 98942 (Ohio Ct. App. 2/21/13).

♦   An Illinois student, while riding the school bus, hit the bus monitor on the arms. He was charged with a Class 3 felony – aggravated battery of an employee of a transportation facility for public hire. After he was found guilty, **he appealed, claiming he should only have been convicted of a misdemeanor because the bus monitor was not a "public transportation employee" under state law.** The Appellate Court of Illinois agreed. *People v. Jerome S.,* 968 N.E.2d 769 (Ill. App. Ct. 2012).

♦   A California student under juvenile court supervision was eligible for special education due to a learning disability. Three school districts in which she had resided declined to attend an IEP meeting to identify which one was responsible for her special education needs. The juvenile court found that the office of education was responsible for providing a free appropriate public education until her release from juvenile hall and placement in a residential treatment center. On appeal to the Court of Appeal of California, the county office of education argued that **the juvenile court lacked the power to determine which agency was responsible for providing special education.** The court of appeal agreed with the office of education. It held the proper course for the juvenile court was to appoint a responsible adult for the child under state law. The court returned the case to the lower court with instructions to take that action. *In re Q.N.*, 150 Cal.Rptr.3d 169 (Cal. Ct. App. 2012).

♦   A Tennessee school district, in conjunction with the sheriff's department, conducted a random canine drug sweep in the parking lot of a high school. One of the dogs alerted to the presence of drugs in a learning disabled student's car. The officers present handcuffed him and searched his vehicle, finding 10 bottles of beer. The student spent a month at an alternative school, then sued under the Fourth Amendment. A federal court held that he did not have a reasonable expectation of privacy in a parking lot accessible to the public. Further, **the dog sniff was not a "search," although it did give the officers probable cause to search his vehicle**. And the handcuffing was a reasonable seizure designed to prevent him from fleeing and to minimize risk to the officers. *Hill v. Scharber*, 544 F.Supp.2d 670 (M.D. Tenn. 2008).

♦   A 17-year-old special education student in the District of Columbia was incarcerated in Maryland and sought an order requiring the district to provide him with private special education services while he was in prison. The district agreed to provide services, but Maryland officials refused to let the private provider into the prison for security reasons. Instead, Maryland developed an IEP for him and provided him with services under that. Two years later, the student sued the district for failing to provide him with services. A federal court ruled against him. The district was unable to perform its contractual obligations because of an event not contemplated by the contract. Therefore, its duty was discharged. *Hester v. District of Columbia*, 505 F.3d 1283 (D.C. Cir. 2007).

♦   A 21-year-old Connecticut student had an IQ of 61 and was classified as educable mentally retarded. He attended a self-contained special education program at a public high school until being arrested and hospitalized. Officials helped him obtain services from the state department of children and families, and a hospital implemented his IEP. But the hospital released him and returned him to the custody of a correctional center, where he was admitted to the mental health unit. An evaluation determined that he was mentally retarded and needed a supervised, but not institutional, setting. A consultant informed the center that the student was a special education student with an IEP. The center began providing services to the student in a segregated housing unit, and an IEP team meeting was convened. The student then inflicted wounds on himself and was placed in a restrictive housing unit due to chronic disciplinary problems.

After a stalemate concerning the student's transition plan, a hearing officer awarded one year of compensatory education, and a Connecticut trial court affirmed. The special school district appealed. The court of appeals stated that the district knew the student was entitled to special education services when the center received a call from the consultant. It was the district's responsibility to comply with the IDEA, not the student's. Any delay could not be attributed to the office of protection and advocacy for educational entitlements. **The district was charged with the responsibility of identifying students with special educational needs. It was required to follow IDEA procedural requirements** and was charged with the knowledge that he had an IEP from the time of the consultant's call. The district had no IEP for the student and was required to implement a program for him. Because the district failed to provide him with a free appropriate public education, he was entitled to compensatory education, even though he was over 21. *Unified School Dist. No. 1 v. Connecticut Dep't of Educ.*, 780 A.2d 154 (Conn. App. Ct. 2001).

♦   Pennsylvania law provided that persons under age 21 who are confined to adult county correctional facilities and otherwise eligible for educational services are entitled to services to the extent expelled students are. The law differentiated between juveniles convicted as adults based on their place of incarceration, since those placed in state facilities received full education programs. Generally, juveniles sentenced to two years or less were confined in county facilities, while those sentenced to terms of five years or more were confined in state facilities. Sentences of between two and five years could be served at either type of facility. Students over age 17 in county facilities received no educational services at all, since state law did not provide for any services to expelled students. A group representing juveniles incarcerated in adult county facilities sued, asserting violation of their constitutional right to equal protection. The Third Circuit held that **the state was required only to show that the disproportionate allocation of state educational resources had some rational relationship to a legitimate end. The state had met this showing** by providing four justifications for the distinction between county and state adult corrections facilities. County correctional institutions, unlike state facilities, had space limitations. State facilities also had higher youth populations, reducing the cost of providing education there. *Brian B. v. Commw. of Pennsylvania Dep't of Educ.*, 230 F.3d 582 (3d Cir. 2000).

VI. NO CHILD LEFT BEHIND AND EVERY STUDENT SUCCEEDS

In December 2015, Congress reauthorized the Elementary and Secondary Education Act (ESEA) of 1965 by enacting the Every Student Succeeds Act (ESSA), which alters or deletes parts of the No Child Left Behind (NCLB) Act.

ESSA provisions are intended to relieve state and local educational agencies "from the more onerous provisions" of the NCLB Act. Instead of requiring states to make "adequate yearly progress," federal law will now rely upon comprehensive state-designed systems to improve the capacity of states to identify and support their struggling schools. ESSA provisions require school districts to use evidence-based models to support whole-school interventions in the lowest-performing five percent of schools. In schools where subgroups of students are persistently underperforming, school districts will be required to make targeted interventions and supports to narrow student achievement gaps.

States will submit plans outlining their accountability systems to the federal government and may choose challenging academic standards for reading and math. The U.S. government may not use mandates or incentives such as the Common Core to require particular standards. ESSA incentives aim at establishing or expanding access to high-quality, state-funded preschool education for children from low and moderate income families. Incentives patterned on the Investing in Innovation Program are intended to close the achievement gap, as are expanded incentives for teacher and administrator preparation and more resources for high-poverty neighborhoods.

As under the NCLB Act, students will participate in statewide assessments in grades 3-8 and once during high school. Testing in science is to occur three times for students in grades 3-12. But the ESSA intends to shift the focus from reliance solely upon standardized tests to the use of multiple measures of student learning and progress. States can use other indicators of student achievement and school quality to report progress such as student engagement, access to and completion of advanced coursework and school climate and safety. States will be required to improve student learning in the lowest five percent of schools and schools in which any group consistently underperforms.

A new school expenditure reporting requirement will reveal funding distributions for each school. In all, the ESSA will provide states over $15 billion per year in formula funding, with more funds for competitive grants such as the Preschool Development Grants Program to support quality access to early childhood education. School Improvement Grants as described in the NCLB Act are ended. Instead, the states will reserve Title I Part A funds to carry out statewide systems of technical assistance and support for local districts.

At end are federal mandates for teacher evaluation, professional development and recruiting. A provision of the ESSA strikes the term "teachers who are highly qualified" and inserts the term "teachers who meet the applicable State certification and licensure requirements." State agency Title I plans must be submitted to the U.S. Department of Education with meaningful, timely consultation with governors, legislators and other stakeholders.

Statewide accountability systems must include subgroups for economically disadvantaged students, students from major racial and ethnic groups and English learners. Data will be disaggregated for English language learners, migrant and homeless students, children in foster care and military-connected children and children with disabilities. As under the NCLB Act, up to one percent of students with the most significant cognitive disabilities may take alternative assessments aligned to alternate academic achievement standards.

The ESSA authorizes the Jacob K. Javits Gifted and Talented Students Education Program to build and enhance the ability of schools to identify gifted and talented students and meet their needs. A PDF file containing the full text of the Every Student Succeeds Act (114th Congress, S-1177, H.B. 5) may be found at https://www.gpo.gov/fdsys/pkg/BILLS-114s1177enr/pdf/BILLS-114s1177enr.pdf. The U.S. Department of Education has promised periodic guidance on its interpretation of the ESSA at http://www.ed.gov/ESSA.

◆ Because some of its special education teachers had not attained designation as "highly qualified teachers" (HQTs), Pittsburgh's Board of Public Education laid off teachers without regard to seniority in 2012. The Pittsburgh Federation of Teachers filed a grievance on behalf of the teachers, arguing the board violated the relevant collective bargaining agreement (CBA) by failing to comply with system-seniority order. An arbitrator held for the federation, finding the board violated the relevant CBA. After a state trial court upheld the arbitrator's decision, appeal went to the Commonwealth Court of Pennsylvania.

On appeal, the court stated that an arbitration award must "draw its essence from the CBA." In this case, the CBA stated that "seniority shall continue to be the sole applicable seniority criterion to be applied in any layoff of a teacher." But the board laid off the special education teachers solely upon their lack of HQT status. The court held the arbitrator correctly found the layoff of non-HQTs out of system-seniority violated the CBA. **Next, the court found the award did not violate either the No Child Left Behind (NCLB) Act or the IDEA.** In finding the layoff of special education teachers out of system-seniority order was premature, the arbitrator had noted there was no NCLB Act penalty for noncompliance by teachers, such as forfeiture of seniority rights. Although the board claimed it risked violating the NCLB Act's adequate yearly progress requirement, the court explained that a school district is not penalized by the NCLB Act until it fails to achieve adequate yearly progress for three consecutive years. Since the district had achieved adequate yearly progress status the previous school year, it did not face sanctions for not having 100% HQTs. The layoffs were governed solely by the CBA. As no law or public policy required teachers to have HQT status at the time of the layoff, the court upheld the arbitration award. *Pittsburgh Board of Public Educ. v. Pittsburgh Federation of Teachers*, 105 A.3d 847 (Pa. Commw. Ct. 2014).

♦   A provision of NCLB allows alternative-route teachers to become "highly qualified" without first obtaining "full state certification." A group of students, parents and nonprofits – concerned that a disproportionate number of interns were teaching in minority and low-income California schools – sued to challenge that provision. The Ninth Circuit ruled that the provision was invalid because it was inconsistent with the intent of Congress. However, **Congress then expanded the NCLB definition of "highly qualified" to include an alternative-route teacher who demonstrates satisfactory progress toward full certification**. When the case returned to the Ninth Circuit, it upheld the provision. *Renee v. Duncan*, 686 F.3d 1002 (9th Cir. 2012).

♦   Connecticut officials asked for a waiver from certain testing provisions of the NCLB. The U.S. Secretary of Education denied the waiver and sought more information while stating that a policy change for special education students was forthcoming. However, **the new policy did not permit testing of special education students at their instructional level**, even if consistent with the students' IEPs. The state then sued over the unfunded mandates provision of the act, but a federal court and the Second Circuit held that the challenges to the unfunded mandates provision could not be litigated because Connecticut was in compliance with the NCLB and continued to receive federal funds under the law. *Connecticut v. Duncan*, 612 F.3d 107 (2d Cir. 2010).

APPENDIX A

The statutory text of the Individuals with Disabilities Education Act, as amended through July, 2005, is reproduced below in its entirety. It includes the most recent amendments to the statute.

An Act

To reauthorize the Individuals with Disabilities Education Act, and for other purposes.

Be it enacted by the Senate and House of Representatives of the United States of America in Congress assembled,

SEC. 1. SHORT TITLE.

This Act may be cited as the 'Individuals with Disabilities Education Improvement Act of 2004'.

SEC. 2. ORGANIZATION OF THE ACT.

This Act is organized into the following titles:
Title I—Amendments to the Individuals With Disabilities Education Act.
Title II—National Center for Special Education Research.
Title III—Miscellaneous Provisions.

TITLE I—AMENDMENTS TO THE INDIVIDUALS WITH DISABILITIES EDUCATION ACT

SEC. 101. AMENDMENTS TO THE INDIVIDUALS WITH DISABILITIES EDUCATION ACT.

Parts A through D of the Individuals with Disabilities Education Act (20 U.S.C. 1400 et seq.) are amended to read as follows:

PART A—GENERAL PROVISIONS

SEC. 601. SHORT TITLE; TABLE OF CONTENTS; FINDINGS; PURPOSES.

(a) SHORT TITLE – This title may be cited as the 'Individuals with Disabilities Education Act'.

(b) TABLE OF CONTENTS – The table of contents for this title is as follows:

SUBPART 3—SUPPORTS TO IMPROVE RESULTS FOR CHILDREN WITH DISABILITIES

Sec. 670. Purposes.
Sec. 671. Parent training and information centers.
Sec. 672. Community parent resource centers.
Sec. 673. Technical assistance for parent training and information centers.
Sec. 674. Technology development, demonstration, and utilization; and media services.
Sec. 675. Authorization of appropriations.

SUBPART 4—GENERAL PROVISIONS

Sec. 681. Comprehensive plan for subparts 2 and 3.
Sec. 682. Administrative provisions.

(c) FINDINGS- Congress finds the following:

(1) Disability is a natural part of the human experience and in no way diminishes the right of individuals to participate in or contribute to society. Improving educational results for children with disabilities is an essential element of our national policy of ensuring equality of opportunity, full participation, independent living, and economic self-sufficiency for individuals with disabilities.

(2) Before the date of enactment of the Education for All Handicapped Children Act of 1975 (Public Law 94-142), the educational needs of millions of children with disabilities were not being fully met because—

(A) the children did not receive appropriate educational services;

(B) the children were excluded entirely from the public school system and from being educated with their peers;

(C) undiagnosed disabilities prevented the children from having a successful educational experience; or

(D) a lack of adequate resources within the public school system forced families to find services outside the public school system.

(3) Since the enactment and implementation of the Education for All Handicapped Children Act of 1975, this title has been successful in ensuring children with disabilities and the families of such children access to a free appropriate public education and in improving educational results for children with disabilities.

(4) However, the implementation of this title has been impeded by low expectations, and an insufficient focus on applying replicable research on proven methods of teaching and learning for children with disabilities.

(5) Almost 30 years of research and experience has demonstrated that the education of children with disabilities can be made more effective by—

(A) having high expectations for such children and ensuring their access to the general education curriculum in the regular classroom, to the maximum extent possible, in order to—

(i) meet developmental goals and, to the maximum extent possible, the challenging expectations that have been established for all children; and

(ii) be prepared to lead productive and independent adult lives, to the maximum extent possible;

(B) strengthening the role and responsibility of parents and ensuring that families of such children have meaningful opportunities to participate in the education of their children at school and at home;

(C) coordinating this title with other local, educational service agency, State, and Federal school improvement efforts, including improvement efforts under the Elementary and Secondary Education Act of 1965, in order to ensure that such children benefit from such efforts and that special education can become a service for such children rather than a place where such children are sent;

(D) providing appropriate special education and related services, and aids and supports in the regular classroom, to such children, whenever appropriate;

(E) supporting high-quality, intensive preservice preparation and professional development for all personnel who work with children with disabilities in order to ensure that such personnel have the skills and knowledge necessary to improve the academic achievement and functional performance of children with disabilities, including the use of scientifically based instructional practices, to the maximum extent possible;

(F) providing incentives for whole-school approaches, scientifically based early reading programs, positive behavioral interventions and supports, and early intervening services to reduce the need to label children as disabled in order to address the learning and behavioral needs of such children;

(G) focusing resources on teaching and learning while reducing paperwork and requirements that do not assist in improving educational results; and

(H) supporting the development and use of technology, including assistive technology devices and assistive technology services, to maximize accessibility for children with disabilities.

(6) While States, local educational agencies, and educational service agencies are primarily responsible for providing an education for all children with disabilities, it is in the national interest that the Federal Government have a supporting role in assisting State and local efforts to educate children with disabilities in order to improve results for such children and to ensure equal protection of the law.

(7) A more equitable allocation of resources is essential for the Federal Government to meet its responsibility to provide an equal educational opportunity for all individuals.

(8) Parents and schools should be given expanded opportunities to resolve their disagreements in positive and constructive ways.

(9) Teachers, schools, local educational agencies, and States should be relieved of irrelevant and unnecessary paperwork burdens that do not lead to improved educational outcomes.

(10)(A) The Federal Government must be responsive to the growing needs of an increasingly diverse society.

(B) America's ethnic profile is rapidly changing. In 2000, 1 of every 3 persons in the United States was a member of a minority group or was limited English proficient.

(C) Minority children comprise an increasing percentage of public school students.

(D) With such changing demographics, recruitment efforts for special education personnel should focus on increasing the participation of minorities in the teaching profession in order to provide appropriate role models with sufficient knowledge to address the special education needs of these students.

(11)(A) The limited English proficient population is the fastest growing in our Nation, and the growth is occurring in many parts of our Nation.

(B) Studies have documented apparent discrepancies in the levels of referral and placement of limited English proficient children in special education.

(C) Such discrepancies pose a special challenge for special education in the referral of, assessment of, and provision of services for, our Nation's students from non-English language backgrounds.

(12)(A) Greater efforts are needed to prevent the intensification of problems connected with mislabeling and high dropout rates among minority children with disabilities.

(B) More minority children continue to be served in special education than would be expected from the percentage of minority students in the general school population.

(C) African-American children are identified as having mental retardation and emotional disturbance at rates greater than their White counterparts.

(D) In the 1998-1999 school year, African-American children represented just 14.8 percent of the population aged 6 through 21, but comprised 20.2 percent of all children with disabilities.

(E) Studies have found that schools with predominately White students and teachers have placed disproportionately high numbers of their minority students into special education.

(13)(A) As the number of minority students in special education increases, the number of minority teachers and related services personnel produced in colleges and universities continues to decrease.

(B) The opportunity for full participation by minority individuals, minority organizations, and Historically Black Colleges and Universities in awards for grants and contracts, boards of organizations receiving assistance under this title, peer review panels, and training of professionals in the area of special education is essential to obtain greater success in the education of minority children with disabilities.

(14) As the graduation rates for children with disabilities continue to climb, providing effective transition services to promote successful post-school employment or education is an important measure of accountability for children with disabilities.

(d) PURPOSES- The purposes of this title are—

(1)(A) to ensure that all children with disabilities have available to them a free appropriate public education that emphasizes special education and related services designed to meet their unique needs and prepare them for further education, employment, and independent living;

(B) to ensure that the rights of children with disabilities and parents of such children are protected; and

(C) to assist States, localities, educational service agencies, and Federal agencies to provide for the education of all children with disabilities;

(2) to assist States in the implementation of a statewide, comprehensive, coordinated, multidisciplinary, interagency system of early intervention services for infants and toddlers with disabilities and their families;

(3) to ensure that educators and parents have the necessary tools to improve educational results for children with disabilities by supporting system improvement activities; coordinated research and personnel preparation; coordinated technical assistance, dissemination, and support; and technology development and media services; and

(4) to assess, and ensure the effectiveness of, efforts to educate children with disabilities.

SEC. 602. DEFINITIONS.

Except as otherwise provided, in this title:

(1) ASSISTIVE TECHNOLOGY DEVICE-

(A) IN GENERAL- The term 'assistive technology device' means any item, piece of equipment, or product system, whether acquired commercially off the shelf, modified, or customized, that is used to increase, maintain, or improve functional capabilities of a child with a disability.

(B) EXCEPTION- The term does not include a medical device that is surgically implanted, or the replacement of such device.

(2) ASSISTIVE TECHNOLOGY SERVICE- The term 'assistive technology service' means any service that directly assists a child with a disability in the selection, acquisition, or use of an assistive technology device. Such term includes—

(A) the evaluation of the needs of such child, including a functional evaluation of the child in the child's customary environment;

(B) purchasing, leasing, or otherwise providing for the acquisition of assistive technology devices by such child;

(C) selecting, designing, fitting, customizing, adapting, applying, maintaining, repairing, or replacing assistive technology devices;

(D) coordinating and using other therapies, interventions, or services with assistive technology devices, such as those associated with existing education and rehabilitation plans and programs;

(E) training or technical assistance for such child, or, where appropriate, the family of such child; and

(F) training or technical assistance for professionals (including individuals providing education and rehabilitation services),

employers, or other individuals who provide services to, employ, or are otherwise substantially involved in the major life functions of such child.

(3) CHILD WITH A DISABILITY-

(A) IN GENERAL- The term 'child with a disability' means a child—

(i) with mental retardation, hearing impairments (including deafness), speech or language impairments, visual impairments (including blindness), serious emotional disturbance (referred to in this title as 'emotional disturbance'), orthopedic impairments, autism, traumatic brain injury, other health impairments, or specific learning disabilities; and

(ii) who, by reason thereof, needs special education and related services.

(B) CHILD AGED 3 THROUGH 9- The term 'child with a disability' for a child aged 3 through 9 (or any subset of that age range, including ages 3 through 5), may, at the discretion of the State and the local educational agency, include a child—

(i) experiencing developmental delays, as defined by the State and as measured by appropriate diagnostic instruments and procedures, in 1 or more of the following areas: physical development; cognitive development; communication development; social or emotional development; or adaptive development; and

(ii) who, by reason thereof, needs special education and related services.

(4) CORE ACADEMIC SUBJECTS- The term 'core academic subjects' has the meaning given the term in section 9101 of the Elementary and Secondary Education Act of 1965.

(5) EDUCATIONAL SERVICE AGENCY- The term 'educational service agency'—

(A) means a regional public multiservice agency—

(i) authorized by State law to develop, manage, and provide services or programs to local educational agencies; and

(ii) recognized as an administrative agency for purposes of the provision of special education and related services provided within public elementary schools and secondary schools of the State; and

(B) includes any other public institution or agency having administrative control and direction over a public elementary school or secondary school.

(6) ELEMENTARY SCHOOL- The term 'elementary school' means a nonprofit institutional day or residential school, including a public elementary charter school,

that provides elementary education, as determined under State law.

(7) EQUIPMENT- The term 'equipment' includes—

(A) machinery, utilities, and built-in equipment, and any necessary enclosures or structures to house such machinery, utilities, or equipment; and

(B) all other items necessary for the functioning of a particular facility as a facility for the provision of educational services, including items such as instructional equipment and necessary furniture; printed, published, and audio-visual instructional materials; telecommunications, sensory, and other technological aids and devices; and books, periodicals, documents, and other related materials.

(8) EXCESS COSTS- The term 'excess costs' means those costs that are in excess of the average annual per-student expenditure in a local educational agency during the preceding school year for an elementary school or secondary school student, as may be appropriate, and which shall be computed after deducting—

(A) amounts received—

(i) under part B;

(ii) under part A of title I of the Elementary and Secondary Education Act of 1965; and

(iii) under parts A and B of title III of that Act; and

(B) any State or local funds expended for programs that would qualify for assistance under any of those parts.

(9) FREE APPROPRIATE PUBLIC EDUCATION- The term 'free appropriate public education' means special education and related services that—

(A) have been provided at public expense, under public supervision and direction, and without charge;

(B) meet the standards of the State educational agency;

(C) include an appropriate preschool, elementary school, or secondary school education in the State involved; and

(D) are provided in conformity with the individualized education program required under section 614(d).

(10) HIGHLY QUALIFIED-

(A) IN GENERAL- For any special education teacher, the term 'highly qualified' has the meaning given the term in section 9101 of the Elementary and Secondary Education Act of 1965, except that such term also—

(i) includes the requirements described in subparagraph (B); and

(ii) includes the option for teachers to meet the requirements of section 9101 of such Act by meeting the requirements of subparagraph (C) or (D).

(B) REQUIREMENTS FOR SPECIAL EDUCATION TEACHERS- When used with respect to any public elementary school or secondary school special education teacher teaching in a State, such term means that—

(i) the teacher has obtained full State certification as a special education teacher (including certification obtained through alternative routes to certification), or passed the State special education teacher licensing examination, and holds a license to teach in the State as a special education teacher, except that when used with respect to any teacher teaching in a public charter school, the term means that the teacher meets the requirements set forth in the State's public charter school law;

(ii) the teacher has not had special education certification or licensure requirements waived on an emergency, temporary, or provisional basis; and

(iii) the teacher holds at least a bachelor's degree.

(C) SPECIAL EDUCATION TEACHERS TEACHING TO ALTERNATE ACHIEVEMENT STANDARDS- When used with respect to a special education teacher who teaches core academic subjects exclusively to children who are assessed against alternate achievement standards established under the regulations promulgated under section 1111(b)(1) of the Elementary and Secondary Education Act of 1965, such term means the teacher, whether new or not new to the profession, may either—

(i) meet the applicable requirements of section 9101 of such Act for any elementary, middle, or secondary school teacher who is new or not new to the profession; or

(ii) meet the requirements of subparagraph (B) or (C) of section 9101(23) of such Act as applied to an elementary school teacher, or, in the case of instruction above the elementary level, has subject matter knowledge appropriate to the level of instruction being provided, as determined by the State, needed to effectively teach to those standards.

(D) SPECIAL EDUCATION TEACHERS TEACHING MULTIPLE SUBJECTS- When used with respect to a special education teacher who teaches 2 or more core academic subjects exclusively to children with disabilities, such term means that the teacher may either—

(i) meet the applicable requirements of section 9101 of the Elementary and Secondary Education Act of 1965 for any elementary, middle, or secondary school teacher who is new or not new to the profession;

(ii) in the case of a teacher who is not new to the profession, demonstrate competence in all the core academic subjects in which the teacher teaches in the same manner as is required for an elementary, middle, or secondary school teacher who is not new to the profession under section 9101(23)(C)(ii) of such Act, which may include a single, high objective uniform State standard of evaluation covering multiple subjects; or

(iii) in the case of a new special education teacher who teaches multiple subjects and who is highly qualified in mathematics, language arts, or science, demonstrate competence in the other core academic subjects in which the teacher teaches in the same manner as is required for an elementary, middle, or secondary school teacher under section 9101(23)(C)(ii) of such Act, which may include a single, high objective uniform State standard of evaluation covering multiple subjects, not later than 2 years after the date of employment.

(E) RULE OF CONSTRUCTION- Notwithstanding any other individual right of action that a parent or student may maintain under this part, nothing in this section or part shall be construed to create a right of action on behalf of an individual student or class of students for the failure of a particular State educational agency or local educational agency employee to be highly qualified.

(F) DEFINITION FOR PURPOSES OF THE ESEA- A teacher who is highly qualified under this paragraph shall be considered highly qualified for purposes of the Elementary and Secondary Education Act of 1965.

(11) HOMELESS CHILDREN- The term 'homeless children' has the meaning given the term 'homeless children and youths' in section 725 of the McKinney-Vento Homeless Assistance Act (42 U.S.C. 11434a).

(12) INDIAN- The term 'Indian' means an individual who is a member of an Indian tribe.

(13) INDIAN TRIBE- The term 'Indian tribe' means any Federal or State Indian tribe, band, rancheria, pueblo, colony, or community, including any Alaska Native village or regional village corporation (as defined in or established under the Alaska Native Claims Settlement Act (43 U.S.C. 1601 et seq.)).

(14) INDIVIDUALIZED EDUCATION PROGRAM; IEP- The term 'individualized education program' or 'IEP' means a written statement for each child with a disability that is developed, reviewed, and revised in accordance with section 614(d).

(15) INDIVIDUALIZED FAMILY

SERVICE PLAN- The term 'individualized family service plan' has the meaning given the term in section 636.

(16) INFANT OR TODDLER WITH A DISABILITY- The term 'infant or toddler with a disability' has the meaning given the term in section 632.

(17) INSTITUTION OF HIGHER EDUCATION- The term 'institution of higher education'—

(A) has the meaning given the term in section 101 of the Higher Education Act of 1965; and

(B) also includes any community college receiving funding from the Secretary of the Interior under the Tribally Controlled College or University Assistance Act of 1978.

(18) LIMITED ENGLISH PROFICIENT- The term 'limited English proficient' has the meaning given the term in section 9101 of the Elementary and Secondary Education Act of 1965.

(19) LOCAL EDUCATIONAL AGENCY-

(A) IN GENERAL- The term 'local educational agency' means a public board of education or other public authority legally constituted within a State for either administrative control or direction of, or to perform a service function for, public elementary schools or secondary schools in a city, county, township, school district, or other political subdivision of a State, or for such combination of school districts or counties as are recognized in a State as an administrative agency for its public elementary schools or secondary schools.

(B) EDUCATIONAL SERVICE AGENCIES AND OTHER PUBLIC INSTITUTIONS OR AGENCIES- The term includes—

(i) an educational service agency; and

(ii) any other public institution or agency having administrative control and direction of a public elementary school or secondary school.

(C) BIA FUNDED SCHOOLS- The term includes an elementary school or secondary school funded by the Bureau of Indian Affairs, but only to the extent that such inclusion makes the school eligible for programs for which specific eligibility is not provided to the school in another provision of law and the school does not have a student population that is smaller than the student population of the local educational agency receiving assistance under this title with the smallest student population, except that the school shall not be subject to the jurisdiction of any State educational agency other than the Bureau of Indian Affairs.

(20) NATIVE LANGUAGE- The term

'native language', when used with respect to an individual who is limited English proficient, means the language normally used by the individual or, in the case of a child, the language normally used by the parents of the child.

(21) NONPROFIT- The term 'nonprofit', as applied to a school, agency, organization, or institution, means a school, agency, organization, or institution owned and operated by 1 or more nonprofit corporations or associations no part of the net earnings of which inures, or may lawfully inure, to the benefit of any private shareholder or individual.

(22) OUTLYING AREA- The term 'outlying area' means the United States Virgin Islands, Guam, American Samoa, and the Commonwealth of the Northern Mariana Islands.

(23) PARENT- The term 'parent' means—

(A) a natural, adoptive, or foster parent of a child (unless a foster parent is prohibited by State law from serving as a parent);

(B) a guardian (but not the State if the child is a ward of the State);

(C) an individual acting in the place of a natural or adoptive parent (including a grandparent, stepparent, or other relative) with whom the child lives, or an individual who is legally responsible for the child's welfare; or

(D) except as used in sections 615(b)(2) and 639(a)(5), an individual assigned under either of those sections to be a surrogate parent.

(24) PARENT ORGANIZATION- The term 'parent organization' has the meaning given the term in section 671(g).

(25) PARENT TRAINING AND INFORMATION CENTER- The term 'parent training and information center' means a center assisted under section 671 or 672.

(26) RELATED SERVICES-

(A) IN GENERAL- The term 'related services' means transportation, and such developmental, corrective, and other supportive services (including speech-language pathology and audiology services, interpreting services, psychological services, physical and occupational therapy, recreation, including therapeutic recreation, social work services, school nurse services designed to enable a child with a disability to receive a free appropriate public education as described in the individualized education program of the child, counseling services, including rehabilitation counseling, orientation and mobility services, and medical services, except that such medical services shall be for diagnostic and evaluation purposes only) as may be required to assist a child with a disability to benefit from special education, and includes the early identification and assessment of disabling conditions in children.

(B) EXCEPTION- The term does not include a medical device that is surgically implanted, or the replacement of such device.

(27) SECONDARY SCHOOL- The term 'secondary school' means a nonprofit institutional day or residential school, including a public secondary charter school, that provides secondary education, as determined under State law, except that it does not include any education beyond grade 12.

(28) SECRETARY- The term 'Secretary' means the Secretary of Education.

(29) SPECIAL EDUCATION- The term 'special education' means specially designed instruction, at no cost to parents, to meet the unique needs of a child with a disability, including—

(A) instruction conducted in the classroom, in the home, in hospitals and institutions, and in other settings; and

(B) instruction in physical education.

(30) SPECIFIC LEARNING DISABILITY-

(A) IN GENERAL- The term 'specific learning disability' means a disorder in 1 or more of the basic psychological processes involved in understanding or in using language, spoken or written, which disorder may manifest itself in the imperfect ability to listen, think, speak, read, write, spell, or do mathematical calculations.

(B) DISORDERS INCLUDED- Such term includes such conditions as perceptual disabilities, brain injury, minimal brain dysfunction, dyslexia, and developmental aphasia.

(C) DISORDERS NOT INCLUDED- Such term does not include a learning problem that is primarily the result of visual, hearing, or motor disabilities, of mental retardation, of emotional disturbance, or of environmental, cultural, or economic disadvantage.

(31) STATE- The term 'State' means each of the 50 States, the District of Columbia, the Commonwealth of Puerto Rico, and each of the outlying areas.

(32) STATE EDUCATIONAL AGENCY- The term 'State educational agency' means the State board of education or other agency or officer primarily responsible for the State supervision of public elementary schools and secondary schools, or, if there is no such officer or agency, an officer or agency designated by the Governor or by State law.

(33) SUPPLEMENTARY AIDS AND SERVICES- The term 'supplementary aids and services' means aids, services, and other supports that are provided in regular education classes or other education-related settings to enable children with disabilities to be educated with nondisabled children to the maximum extent appropriate in accordance with section 612(a)(5).

(34) TRANSITION SERVICES- The term 'transition services' means a coordinated set of activities for a child with a disability that—

(A) is designed to be within a results-oriented process, that is focused on improving the academic and functional achievement of the child with a disability to facilitate the child's movement from school to post-school activities, including post-secondary education, vocational education, integrated employment (including supported employment), continuing and adult education, adult services, independent living, or community participation;

(B) is based on the individual child's needs, taking into account the child's strengths, preferences, and interests; and

(C) includes instruction, related services, community experiences, the development of employment and other post-school adult living objectives, and, when appropriate, acquisition of daily living skills and functional vocational evaluation.

(35) UNIVERSAL DESIGN- The term 'universal design' has the meaning given the term in section 3 of the Assistive Technology Act of 1998 (29 U.S.C. 3002).

(36) WARD OF THE STATE-

(A) IN GENERAL- The term 'ward of the State' means a child who, as determined by the State where the child resides, is a foster child, is a ward of the State, or is in the custody of a public child welfare agency.

(B) EXCEPTION- The term does not include a foster child who has a foster parent who meets the definition of a parent in paragraph (23).

SEC. 603. OFFICE OF SPECIAL EDUCATION PROGRAMS.

(a) ESTABLISHMENT- There shall be, within the Office of Special Education and Rehabilitative Services in the Department of Education, an Office of Special Education Programs, which shall be the principal agency in the Department for administering and carrying out this title and other programs and activities concerning the education of children with disabilities.

(b) DIRECTOR- The Office established under subsection (a) shall be headed by a Director who shall be selected by the Secretary and shall report directly to the Assistant Secretary for Special Education and Rehabilitative Services.

(c) VOLUNTARY AND UNCOMPENSATED SERVICES- Notwithstanding section 1342 of title 31, United States Code, the Secretary is authorized to accept voluntary and uncompensated services in furtherance of the purposes of this title.

SEC. 604. ABROGATION OF STATE SOVEREIGN IMMUNITY.

(a) IN GENERAL- A State shall not be immune under the 11th amendment to the Constitution of the United States from suit in Federal court for a violation of this title.

(b) REMEDIES- In a suit against a State for a violation of this title, remedies (including remedies both at law and in equity) are available for such a violation to the same extent as those remedies are available for such a violation in the suit against any public entity other than a State.

(c) EFFECTIVE DATE- Subsections (a) and (b) apply with respect to violations that occur in whole or part after the date of enactment of the Education of the Handicapped Act Amendments of 1990.

SEC. 605. ACQUISITION OF EQUIPMENT; CONSTRUCTION OR ALTERATION OF FACILITIES.

(a) IN GENERAL- If the Secretary determines that a program authorized under this title will be improved by permitting program funds to be used to acquire appropriate equipment, or to construct new facilities or alter existing facilities, the Secretary is authorized to allow the use of those funds for those purposes.

(b) COMPLIANCE WITH CERTAIN REGULATIONS- Any construction of new facilities or alteration of existing facilities under subsection (a) shall comply with the requirements of—

(1) appendix A of part 36 of title 28, Code of Federal Regulations (commonly known as the 'Americans with Disabilities Accessibility Guidelines for Buildings and Facilities'); or

(2) appendix A of subpart 101-19.6 of title 41, Code of Federal Regulations (commonly

known as the 'Uniform Federal Accessibility Standards').

SEC. 606. EMPLOYMENT OF INDIVIDUALS WITH DISABILITIES.

The Secretary shall ensure that each recipient of assistance under this title makes positive efforts to employ and advance in employment qualified individuals with disabilities in programs assisted under this title.

SEC. 607. REQUIREMENTS FOR PRESCRIBING REGULATIONS.

(a) IN GENERAL- In carrying out the provisions of this title, the Secretary shall issue regulations under this title only to the extent that such regulations are necessary to ensure that there is compliance with the specific requirements of this title.

(b) PROTECTIONS PROVIDED TO CHILDREN- The Secretary may not implement, or publish in final form, any regulation prescribed pursuant to this title that—

(1) violates or contradicts any provision of this title; or

(2) procedurally or substantively lessens the protections provided to children with disabilities under this title, as embodied in regulations in effect on July 20, 1983 (particularly as such protections related to parental consent to initial evaluation or initial placement in special education, least restrictive environment, related services, timelines, attendance of evaluation personnel at individualized education program meetings, or qualifications of personnel), except to the extent that such regulation reflects the clear and unequivocal intent of Congress in legislation.

(c) PUBLIC COMMENT PERIOD- The Secretary shall provide a public comment period of not less than 75 days on any regulation proposed under part B or part C on which an opportunity for public comment is otherwise required by law.

(d) POLICY LETTERS AND STATEMENTS- The Secretary may not issue policy letters or other statements (including letters or statements regarding issues of national significance) that—

(1) violate or contradict any provision of this title; or

(2) establish a rule that is required for compliance with, and eligibility under, this title without following the requirements of section 553 of title 5, United States Code.

(e) EXPLANATION AND ASSURANCES- Any written response by the Secretary under subsection (d) regarding a policy, question, or interpretation under part B shall include an explanation in the written response that—

(1) such response is provided as informal guidance and is not legally binding;

(2) when required, such response is issued in compliance with the requirements of section 553 of title 5, United States Code; and

(3) such response represents the interpretation by the Department of Education of the applicable statutory or regulatory requirements in the context of the specific facts presented.

(f) CORRESPONDENCE FROM DEPARTMENT OF EDUCATION DESCRIBING INTERPRETATIONS OF THIS TITLE-

(1) IN GENERAL- The Secretary shall, on a quarterly basis, publish in the Federal Register, and widely disseminate to interested entities through various additional forms of communication, a list of correspondence from the Department of Education received by individuals during the previous quarter that describes the interpretations of the Department of Education of this title or the regulations implemented pursuant to this title.

(2) ADDITIONAL INFORMATION- For each item of correspondence published in a list under paragraph (1), the Secretary shall—

(A) identify the topic addressed by the correspondence and shall include such other summary information as the Secretary determines to be appropriate; and

(B) ensure that all such correspondence is issued, where applicable, in compliance with the requirements of section 553 of title 5, United States Code.

SEC. 608. STATE ADMINISTRATION.

(a) RULEMAKING- Each State that receives funds under this title shall—

(1) ensure that any State rules, regulations, and policies relating to this title conform to the purposes of this title;

(2) identify in writing to local educational agencies located in the State and the Secretary any such rule, regulation, or policy as a State-imposed requirement that is not required by this title and Federal regulations; and

(3) minimize the number of rules, regulations, and policies to which the local educational agencies and schools located in the State are subject under this title.

(b) SUPPORT AND FACILITATION- State rules, regulations, and policies under this title shall support and facilitate local educational agency and school-level system improvement designed to enable children with disabilities to meet the challenging State student academic achievement standards.

SEC. 609. PAPERWORK REDUCTION.

(a) PILOT PROGRAM-

(1) PURPOSE- The purpose of this section is to provide an opportunity for States to identify ways to reduce paperwork burdens and other administrative duties that are directly associated with the requirements of this title, in order to increase the time and resources available for instruction and other activities aimed at improving educational and functional results for children with disabilities.

(2) AUTHORIZATION-

(A) IN GENERAL- In order to carry out the purpose of this section, the Secretary is authorized to grant waivers of statutory requirements of, or regulatory requirements relating to, part B for a period of time not to exceed 4 years with respect to not more than 15 States based on proposals submitted by States to reduce excessive paperwork and noninstructional time burdens that do not assist in improving educational and functional results for children with disabilities.

(B) EXCEPTION- The Secretary shall not waive under this section any statutory requirements of, or regulatory requirements relating to, applicable civil rights requirements.

(C) RULE OF CONSTRUCTION- Nothing in this section shall be construed to—

(i) affect the right of a child with a disability to receive a free appropriate public education under part B; and

(ii) permit a State or local educational agency to waive procedural safeguards under section 615.

(3) PROPOSAL-

(A) IN GENERAL- A State desiring to participate in the program under this section shall submit a proposal to the Secretary at such time and in such manner as the Secretary may reasonably require.

(B) CONTENT- The proposal shall include—

(i) a list of any statutory requirements of, or regulatory requirements relating to, part B that the State desires the Secretary to waive, in whole or in part; and

(ii) a list of any State requirements that the State proposes to waive or change, in whole or

in part, to carry out a waiver granted to the State by the Secretary.

(4) TERMINATION OF WAIVER- The Secretary shall terminate a State's waiver under this section if the Secretary determines that the State—

(A) needs assistance under section 616(d)(2)(A)(ii) and that the waiver has contributed to or caused such need for assistance;

(B) needs intervention under section 616(d)(2)(A)(iii) or needs substantial intervention under section 616(d)(2)(A)(iv); or

(C) failed to appropriately implement its waiver.

(b) REPORT- Beginning 2 years after the date of enactment of the Individuals with Disabilities Education Improvement Act of 2004, the Secretary shall include in the annual report to Congress submitted pursuant to section 426 of the Department of Education Organization Act information related to the effectiveness of waivers granted under subsection (a), including any specific recommendations for broader implementation of such waivers, in—

(1) reducing—

(A) the paperwork burden on teachers, principals, administrators, and related service providers; and

(B) noninstructional time spent by teachers in complying with part B;

(2) enhancing longer-term educational planning;

(3) improving positive outcomes for children with disabilities;

(4) promoting collaboration between IEP Team members; and

(5) ensuring satisfaction of family members.

SEC. 610. FREELY ASSOCIATED STATES.

The Republic of the Marshall Islands, the Federated States of Micronesia, and the Republic of Palau shall continue to be eligible for competitive grants administered by the Secretary under this title to the extent that such grants continue to be available to States and local educational agencies under this title.

PART B—ASSISTANCE FOR EDUCATION OF ALL CHILDREN WITH DISABILITIES

SEC. 611. AUTHORIZATION; ALLOTMENT; USE OF FUNDS; AUTHORIZATION OF APPROPRIATIONS.

(a) GRANTS TO STATES-

(1) PURPOSE OF GRANTS- The Secretary shall make grants to States, outlying areas, and freely associated States, and provide funds to the Secretary of the Interior, to assist them to provide special education and related services to children with disabilities in accordance with this part.

(2) MAXIMUM AMOUNT- The maximum amount of the grant a State may receive under this section—

(A) for fiscal years 2005 and 2006 is—

(i) the number of children with disabilities in the State who are receiving special education and related services—

(I) aged 3 through 5 if the State is eligible for a grant under section 619; and

(II) aged 6 through 21; multiplied by

(ii) 40 percent of the average per-pupil expenditure in public elementary schools and secondary schools in the United States; and

(B) for fiscal year 2007 and subsequent fiscal years is—

(i) the number of children with disabilities in the 2004-2005 school year in the State who received special education and related services—

(I) aged 3 through 5 if the State is eligible for a grant under section 619; and

(II) aged 6 through 21; multiplied by

(ii) 40 percent of the average per-pupil expenditure in public elementary schools and secondary schools in the United States; adjusted by

(iii) the rate of annual change in the sum of—

(I) 85 percent of such State's population described in subsection (d)(3)(A)(i)(II); and

(II) 15 percent of such State's population described in subsection (d)(3)(A)(i)(III).

(b) OUTLYING AREAS AND FREELY ASSOCIATED STATES; SECRETARY OF THE INTERIOR-

(1) OUTLYING AREAS AND FREELY ASSOCIATED STATES-

(A) FUNDS RESERVED- From the amount appropriated for any fiscal year under subsection (i), the Secretary shall reserve not more than 1 percent, which shall be used—

(i) to provide assistance to the outlying areas in accordance with their respective populations of individuals aged 3 through 21; and

(ii) to provide each freely associated State a grant in the amount that such freely associated State received for fiscal year 2003 under this part, but only if the freely associated State meets the applicable requirements of this part, as well as the requirements of section 611(b)(2)(C) as such section was in effect on the day before the date of enactment of the Individuals with Disabilities Education Improvement Act of 2004.

(B) SPECIAL RULE- The provisions of Public Law 95-134, permitting the consolidation of grants by the outlying areas, shall not apply to funds provided to the outlying areas or the freely associated States under this section.

(C) DEFINITION- In this paragraph, the term 'freely associated States' means the Republic of the Marshall Islands, the Federated States of Micronesia, and the Republic of Palau.

(2) SECRETARY OF THE INTERIOR- From the amount appropriated for any fiscal year under subsection (i), the Secretary shall reserve 1.226 percent to provide assistance to the Secretary of the Interior in accordance with subsection (h).

(c) TECHNICAL ASSISTANCE-

(1) IN GENERAL- The Secretary may reserve not more than 1/2 of 1 percent of the amounts appropriated under this part for each fiscal year to provide technical assistance activities authorized under section 616(i).

(2) MAXIMUM AMOUNT- The maximum amount the Secretary may reserve under paragraph (1) for any fiscal year is $25,000,000, cumulatively adjusted by the rate of inflation as measured by the percentage increase, if any, from the preceding fiscal year in the Consumer Price Index For All Urban Consumers, published by the Bureau of Labor Statistics of the Department of Labor.

(d) ALLOCATIONS TO STATES-

(1) IN GENERAL- After reserving funds for technical assistance, and for payments to the outlying areas, the freely associated States, and the Secretary of the Interior under subsections (b) and (c) for a fiscal year, the Secretary shall allocate the remaining amount among the States in accordance with this subsection.

(2) SPECIAL RULE FOR USE OF FISCAL YEAR 1999 AMOUNT- If a State

received any funds under this section for fiscal year 1999 on the basis of children aged 3 through 5, but does not make a free appropriate public education available to all children with disabilities aged 3 through 5 in the State in any subsequent fiscal year, the Secretary shall compute the State's amount for fiscal year 1999, solely for the purpose of calculating the State's allocation in that subsequent year under paragraph (3) or (4), by subtracting the amount allocated to the State for fiscal year 1999 on the basis of those children.

(3) INCREASE IN FUNDS- If the amount available for allocations to States under paragraph (1) for a fiscal year is equal to or greater than the amount allocated to the States under this paragraph for the preceding fiscal year, those allocations shall be calculated as follows:

(A) ALLOCATION OF INCREASE-

(i) IN GENERAL- Except as provided in subparagraph (B), the Secretary shall allocate for the fiscal year—

(I) to each State the amount the State received under this section for fiscal year 1999;

(II) 85 percent of any remaining funds to States on the basis of the States' relative populations of children aged 3 through 21 who are of the same age as children with disabilities for whom the State ensures the availability of a free appropriate public education under this part; and

(III) 15 percent of those remaining funds to States on the basis of the States' relative populations of children described in subclause (II) who are living in poverty.

(ii) DATA- For the purpose of making grants under this paragraph, the Secretary shall use the most recent population data, including data on children living in poverty, that are available and satisfactory to the Secretary.

(B) LIMITATIONS- Notwithstanding subparagraph (A), allocations under this paragraph shall be subject to the following:

(i) PRECEDING YEAR ALLOCATION- No State's allocation shall be less than its allocation under this section for the preceding fiscal year.

(ii) MINIMUM- No State's allocation shall be less than the greatest of–

(I) the sum of–

(aa) the amount the State received under this section for fiscal year 1999; and

(bb) 1/3 of 1 percent of the amount by which the amount appropriated under subsection (i) for the fiscal year exceeds the amount appropriated for this section for fiscal year 1999;

(II) the sum of-

(aa) the amount the State received under this section for the preceding fiscal year; and

(bb) that amount multiplied by the percentage by which the increase in the funds appropriated for this section from the preceding fiscal year exceeds 1.5 percent; or

(III) the sum of—

(aa) the amount the State received under this section for the preceding fiscal year; and

(bb) that amount multiplied by 90 percent of the percentage increase in the amount appropriated for this section from the preceding fiscal year.

(iii) MAXIMUM- Notwithstanding clause (ii), no State's allocation under this paragraph shall exceed the sum of—

(I) the amount the State received under this section for the preceding fiscal year; and

(II) that amount multiplied by the sum of 1.5 percent and the percentage increase in the amount appropriated under this section from the preceding fiscal year.

(C) RATABLE REDUCTION- If the amount available for allocations under this paragraph is insufficient to pay those allocations in full, those allocations shall be ratably reduced, subject to subparagraph (B)(i).

(4) DECREASE IN FUNDS- If the amount available for allocations to States under paragraph (1) for a fiscal year is less than the amount allocated to the States under this section for the preceding fiscal year, those allocations shall be calculated as follows:

(A) AMOUNTS GREATER THAN FISCAL YEAR 1999 ALLOCATIONS- If the amount available for allocations is greater than the amount allocated to the States for fiscal year 1999, each State shall be allocated the sum of—

(i) the amount the State received under this section for fiscal year 1999; and

(ii) an amount that bears the same relation to any remaining funds as the increase the State received under this section for the preceding fiscal year over fiscal year 1999 bears to the total of all such increases for all States.

(B) AMOUNTS EQUAL TO OR LESS THAN FISCAL YEAR 1999 ALLOCATIONS-

(i) IN GENERAL- If the amount available for allocations under this paragraph is equal to or less than the amount allocated to the States for fiscal year 1999, each State shall be allocated the amount the State received for fiscal year 1999.

(ii) RATABLE REDUCTION- If the amount available for allocations under this paragraph is insufficient to make the allocations described in clause (i), those allocations shall be ratably reduced.

(e) STATE-LEVEL ACTIVITIES-

(1) STATE ADMINISTRATION-

(A) IN GENERAL- For the purpose of administering this part, including paragraph (3), section 619, and the coordination of activities under this part with, and providing technical assistance to, other programs that provide services to children with disabilities—

(i) each State may reserve for each fiscal year not more than the maximum amount the State was eligible to reserve for State administration under this section for fiscal year 2004 or $800,000 (adjusted in accordance with subparagraph (B)), whichever is greater; and

(ii) each outlying area may reserve for each fiscal year not more than 5 percent of the amount the outlying area receives under subsection (b)(1) for the fiscal year or $35,000, whichever is greater.

(B) CUMULATIVE ANNUAL ADJUSTMENTS- For each fiscal year beginning with fiscal year 2005, the Secretary shall cumulatively adjust—

(i) the maximum amount the State was eligible to reserve for State administration under this part for fiscal year 2004; and

(ii) $800,000, by the rate of inflation as measured by the percentage increase, if any, from the preceding fiscal year in the Consumer Price Index For All Urban Consumers, published by the Bureau of Labor Statistics of the Department of Labor.

(C) CERTIFICATION- Prior to expenditure of funds under this paragraph, the State shall certify to the Secretary that the arrangements to establish responsibility for services pursuant to section 612(a)(12)(A) are current.

(D) PART C- Funds reserved under subparagraph (A) may be used for the administration of part C, if the State educational agency is the lead agency for the State under such part.

(2) OTHER STATE-LEVEL ACTIVITIES-

(A) STATE-LEVEL ACTIVITIES-

(i) IN GENERAL- Except as provided in clause (iii), for the purpose of carrying out State-level activities, each State may reserve for each of the fiscal years 2005 and 2006 not more than 10 percent from the amount of the State's allocation under subsection (d) for each of the fiscal years 2005 and 2006, respectively. For fiscal year 2007 and each subsequent fiscal year, the State may reserve the maximum amount the State was eligible to reserve under the preceding sentence for fiscal year 2006 (cumulatively adjusted by the rate of inflation as measured by the percentage increase, if any, from the preceding fiscal year in the Consumer Price Index For All Urban Consumers,

published by the Bureau of Labor Statistics of the Department of Labor).

(ii) SMALL STATE ADJUSTMENT- Notwithstanding clause (i) and except as provided in clause (iii), in the case of a State for which the maximum amount reserved for State administration is not greater than $850,000, the State may reserve for the purpose of carrying out State-level activities for each of the fiscal years 2005 and 2006, not more than 10.5 percent from the amount of the State's allocation under subsection (d) for each of the fiscal years 2005 and 2006, respectively. For fiscal year 2007 and each subsequent fiscal year, such State may reserve the maximum amount the State was eligible to reserve under the preceding sentence for fiscal year 2006 (cumulatively adjusted by the rate of inflation as measured by the percentage increase, if any, from the preceding fiscal year in the Consumer Price Index For All Urban Consumers, published by the Bureau of Labor Statistics of the Department of Labor).

(iii) EXCEPTION- If a State does not reserve funds under paragraph (3) for a fiscal year, then—

(I) in the case of a State that is not described in clause (ii), for fiscal year 2005 or 2006, clause (i) shall be applied by substituting 9.0 percent for 10 percent; and

(II) in the case of a State that is described in clause (ii), for fiscal year 2005 or 2006, clause (ii) shall be applied by substituting 9.5 percent for 10.5 percent.

(B) REQUIRED ACTIVITIES- Funds reserved under subparagraph (A) shall be used to carry out the following activities:

(i) For monitoring, enforcement, and complaint investigation.

(ii) To establish and implement the mediation process required by section 615(e), including providing for the cost of mediators and support personnel.

(C) AUTHORIZED ACTIVITIES- Funds reserved under subparagraph (A) may be used to carry out the following activities:

(i) For support and direct services, including technical assistance, personnel preparation, and professional development and training.

(ii) To support paperwork reduction activities, including expanding the use of technology in the IEP process.

(iii) To assist local educational agencies in providing positive behavioral interventions and supports and appropriate mental health services for children with disabilities.

(iv) To improve the use of technology in the classroom by children with disabilities to enhance learning.

(v) To support the use of technology, including technology with universal design principles and assistive technology devices, to maximize accessibility to the general education curriculum for children with disabilities.

(vi) Development and implementation of transition programs, including coordination of services with agencies involved in supporting the transition of children with disabilities to postsecondary activities.

(vii) To assist local educational agencies in meeting personnel shortages.

(viii) To support capacity building activities and improve the delivery of services by local educational agencies to improve results for children with disabilities.

(ix) Alternative programming for children with disabilities who have been expelled from school, and services for children with disabilities in correctional facilities, children enrolled in State-operated or State-supported schools, and children with disabilities in charter schools.

(x) To support the development and provision of appropriate accommodations for children with disabilities, or the development and provision of alternate assessments that are valid and reliable for assessing the performance of children with disabilities, in accordance with sections 1111(b) and 6111 of the Elementary and Secondary Education Act of 1965.

(xi) To provide technical assistance to schools and local educational agencies, and direct services, including supplemental educational services as defined in 1116(e) of the Elementary and Secondary Education Act of 1965 to children with disabilities, in schools or local educational agencies identified for improvement under section 1116 of the Elementary and Secondary Education Act of 1965 on the sole basis of the assessment results of the disaggregated subgroup of children with disabilities, including providing professional development to special and regular education teachers, who teach children with disabilities, based on scientifically based research to improve educational instruction, in order to improve academic achievement to meet or exceed the objectives established by the State under section 1111(b)(2)(G) the Elementary and Secondary Education Act of 1965.

(3) LOCAL EDUCATIONAL AGENCY RISK POOL-

(A) IN GENERAL-

(i) RESERVATION OF FUNDS- For the purpose of assisting local educational agencies (including a charter school that is a local educational agency or a consortium of local educational agencies) in addressing the needs of high need children with disabilities, each State shall have the option to reserve for each fiscal year 10 percent of the amount of funds the State reserves for State-level activities under paragraph (2)(A)—

(I) to establish and make disbursements from the high cost fund to local educational agencies in accordance with this paragraph during the first and succeeding fiscal years of the high cost fund; and

(II) to support innovative and effective ways of cost sharing by the State, by a local educational agency, or among a consortium of local educational agencies, as determined by the State in coordination with representatives from local educational agencies, subject to subparagraph (B)(ii).

(ii) DEFINITION OF LOCAL EDUCATIONAL AGENCY- In this paragraph the term 'local educational agency' includes a charter school that is a local educational agency, or a consortium of local educational agencies.

(B) LIMITATION ON USES OF FUNDS-

(i) ESTABLISHMENT OF HIGH COST FUND- A State shall not use any of the funds the State reserves pursuant to subparagraph (A)(i), but may use the funds the State reserves under paragraph (1), to establish and support the high cost fund.

(ii) INNOVATIVE AND EFFECTIVE COST SHARING- A State shall not use more than 5 percent of the funds the State reserves pursuant to subparagraph (A)(i) for each fiscal year to support innovative and effective ways of cost sharing among consortia of local educational agencies.

(C) STATE PLAN FOR HIGH COST FUND-

(i) DEFINITION- The State educational agency shall establish the State's definition of a high need child with a disability, which definition shall be developed in consultation with local educational agencies.

(ii) STATE PLAN- The State educational agency shall develop, not later than 90 days after the State reserves funds under this paragraph, annually review, and amend as necessary, a State plan for the high cost fund. Such State plan shall—

(I) establish, in coordination with representatives from local educational agencies, a definition of a high need child with a disability that, at a minimum—

(aa) addresses the financial impact a high need child with a disability has on the budget of the child's local educational agency; and

(bb) ensures that the cost of the high need

child with a disability is greater than 3 times the average per pupil expenditure (as defined in section 9101 of the Elementary and Secondary Education Act of 1965) in that State;

(II) establish eligibility criteria for the participation of a local educational agency that, at a minimum, takes into account the number and percentage of high need children with disabilities served by a local educational agency;

(III) develop a funding mechanism that provides distributions each fiscal year to local educational agencies that meet the criteria developed by the State under subclause (II); and

(IV) establish an annual schedule by which the State educational agency shall make its distributions from the high cost fund each fiscal year.

(iii) PUBLIC AVAILABILITY- The State shall make its final State plan publicly available not less than 30 days before the beginning of the school year, including dissemination of such information on the State website.

(D) DISBURSEMENTS FROM THE HIGH COST FUND-

(i) IN GENERAL- Each State educational agency shall make all annual disbursements from the high cost fund established under subparagraph (A)(i) in accordance with the State plan published pursuant to subparagraph (C).

(ii) USE OF DISBURSEMENTS- Each State educational agency shall make annual disbursements to eligible local educational agencies in accordance with its State plan under subparagraph (C)(ii).

(iii) APPROPRIATE COSTS- The costs associated with educating a high need child with a disability under subparagraph (C)(i) are only those costs associated with providing direct special education and related services to such child that are identified in such child's IEP.

(E) LEGAL FEES- The disbursements under subparagraph (D) shall not support legal fees, court costs, or other costs associated with a cause of action brought on behalf of a child with a disability to ensure a free appropriate public education for such child.

(F) ASSURANCE OF A FREE APPROPRIATE PUBLIC EDUCATION- Nothing in this paragraph shall be construed—

(i) to limit or condition the right of a child with a disability who is assisted under this part to receive a free appropriate public education pursuant to section 612(a)(1) in the least restrictive environment pursuant to section 612(a)(5); or

(ii) to authorize a State educational agency or local educational agency to establish a limit on what may be spent on the education of a child with a disability.

(G) SPECIAL RULE FOR RISK POOL AND HIGH NEED ASSISTANCE PROGRAMS IN EFFECT AS OF JANUARY 1, 2004- Notwithstanding the provisions of subparagraphs (A) through (F), a State may use funds reserved pursuant to this paragraph for implementing a placement neutral cost sharing and reimbursement program of high need, low incidence, catastrophic, or extraordinary aid to local educational agencies that provides services to high need students based on eligibility criteria for such programs that were created not later than January 1, 2004, and are currently in operation, if such program serves children that meet the requirement of the definition of a high need child with a disability as described in subparagraph (C)(ii)(I).

(H) MEDICAID SERVICES NOT AFFECTED- Disbursements provided under this paragraph shall not be used to pay costs that otherwise would be reimbursed as medical assistance for a child with a disability under the State medicaid program under title XIX of the Social Security Act.

(I) REMAINING FUNDS- Funds reserved under subparagraph (A) in any fiscal year but not expended in that fiscal year pursuant to subparagraph (D) shall be allocated to local educational agencies for the succeeding fiscal year in the same manner as funds are allocated to local educational agencies under subsection (f) for the succeeding fiscal year.

(4) INAPPLICABILITY OF CERTAIN PROHIBITIONS- A State may use funds the State reserves under paragraphs (1) and (2) without regard to—

(A) the prohibition on commingling of funds in section 612(a)(17)(B); and

(B) the prohibition on supplanting other funds in section 612(a)(17)(C).

(5) REPORT ON USE OF FUNDS- As part of the information required to be submitted to the Secretary under section 612, each State shall annually describe how amounts under this section—

(A) will be used to meet the requirements of this title; and

(B) will be allocated among the activities described in this section to meet State priorities based on input from local educational agencies.

(6) SPECIAL RULE FOR INCREASED FUNDS- A State may use funds the State reserves under paragraph (1)(A) as a result of

inflationary increases under paragraph (1)(B) to carry out activities authorized under clause (i), (iii), (vii), or (viii) of paragraph (2)(C).

(7) FLEXIBILITY IN USING FUNDS FOR PART C- Any State eligible to receive a grant under section 619 may use funds made available under paragraph (1)(A), subsection (f)(3), or section 619(f)(5) to develop and implement a State policy jointly with the lead agency under part C and the State educational agency to provide early intervention services (which shall include an educational component that promotes school readiness and incorporates preliteracy, language, and numeracy skills) in accordance with part C to children with disabilities who are eligible for services under section 619 and who previously received services under part C until such children enter, or are eligible under State law to enter, kindergarten, or elementary school as appropriate.

(f) SUBGRANTS TO LOCAL EDUCATIONAL AGENCIES-

(1) SUBGRANTS REQUIRED- Each State that receives a grant under this section for any fiscal year shall distribute any funds the State does not reserve under subsection (e) to local educational agencies (including public charter schools that operate as local educational agencies) in the State that have established their eligibility under section 613 for use in accordance with this part.

(2) PROCEDURE FOR ALLOCATIONS TO LOCAL EDUCATIONAL AGENCIES- For each fiscal year for which funds are allocated to States under subsection (d), each State shall allocate funds under paragraph (1) as follows:

(A) BASE PAYMENTS- The State shall first award each local educational agency described in paragraph (1) the amount the local educational agency would have received under this section for fiscal year 1999, if the State had distributed 75 percent of its grant for that year under section 611(d) as section 611(d) was then in effect.

(B) ALLOCATION OF REMAINING FUNDS- After making allocations under subparagraph (A), the State shall—

(i) allocate 85 percent of any remaining funds to those local educational agencies on the basis of the relative numbers of children enrolled in public and private elementary schools and secondary schools within the local educational agency's jurisdiction; and

(ii) allocate 15 percent of those remaining funds to those local educational agencies in accordance with their relative numbers of children living in poverty, as determined by the State educational agency.

(3) REALLOCATION OF FUNDS- If a State educational agency determines that a local educational agency is adequately providing a free appropriate public education to all children with disabilities residing in the area served by that local educational agency with State and local funds, the State educational agency may reallocate any portion of the funds under this part that are not needed by that local educational agency to provide a free appropriate public education to other local educational agencies in the State that are not adequately providing special education and related services to all children with disabilities residing in the areas served by those other local educational agencies.

(g) DEFINITIONS- In this section:

(1) AVERAGE PER-PUPIL EXPENDITURE IN PUBLIC ELEMENTARY SCHOOLS AND SECONDARY SCHOOLS IN THE UNITED STATES- The term 'average per-pupil expenditure in public elementary schools and secondary schools in the United States' means—

(A) without regard to the source of funds—

(i) the aggregate current expenditures, during the second fiscal year preceding the fiscal year for which the determination is made (or, if satisfactory data for that year are not available, during the most recent preceding fiscal year for which satisfactory data are available) of all local educational agencies in the 50 States and the District of Columbia; plus

(ii) any direct expenditures by the State for the operation of those agencies; divided by

(B) the aggregate number of children in average daily attendance to whom those agencies provided free public education during that preceding year.

(2) STATE- The term 'State' means each of the 50 States, the District of Columbia, and the Commonwealth of Puerto Rico.

(h) USE OF AMOUNTS BY SECRETARY OF THE INTERIOR-

(1) PROVISION OF AMOUNTS FOR ASSISTANCE-

(A) IN GENERAL- The Secretary of Education shall provide amounts to the Secretary of the Interior to meet the need for assistance for the education of children with disabilities on reservations aged 5 to 21, inclusive, enrolled in elementary schools and secondary schools for Indian children operated or funded by the Secretary of the Interior. The amount of such payment for any fiscal year shall be equal to 80 percent of the amount allotted under subsection (b)(2) for that fiscal year. Of the amount described in the preceding sentence—

(i) 80 percent shall be allocated to such schools by July 1 of that fiscal year; and

(ii) 20 percent shall be allocated to such schools by September 30 of that fiscal year.

(B) CALCULATION OF NUMBER OF CHILDREN- In the case of Indian students aged 3 to 5, inclusive, who are enrolled in programs affiliated with the Bureau of Indian Affairs (referred to in this subsection as the 'BIA') schools and that are required by the States in which such schools are located to attain or maintain State accreditation, and which schools have such accreditation prior to the date of enactment of the Individuals with Disabilities Education Act Amendments of 1991, the school shall be allowed to count those children for the purpose of distribution of the funds provided under this paragraph to the Secretary of the Interior. The Secretary of the Interior shall be responsible for meeting all of the requirements of this part for those children, in accordance with paragraph (2).

(C) ADDITIONAL REQUIREMENT- With respect to all other children aged 3 to 21, inclusive, on reservations, the State educational agency shall be responsible for ensuring that all of the requirements of this part are implemented.

(2) SUBMISSION OF INFORMATION- The Secretary of Education may provide the Secretary of the Interior amounts under paragraph (1) for a fiscal year only if the Secretary of the Interior submits to the Secretary of Education information that—

(A) demonstrates that the Department of the Interior meets the appropriate requirements, as determined by the Secretary of Education, of sections 612 (including monitoring and evaluation activities) and 613;

(B) includes a description of how the Secretary of the Interior will coordinate the provision of services under this part with local educational agencies, tribes and tribal organizations, and other private and Federal service providers;

(C) includes an assurance that there are public hearings, adequate notice of such hearings, and an opportunity for comment afforded to members of tribes, tribal governing bodies, and affected local school boards before the adoption of the policies, programs, and procedures related to the requirements described in subparagraph (A);

(D) includes an assurance that the Secretary of the Interior will provide such information as the Secretary of Education may require to

comply with section 618;

(E) includes an assurance that the Secretary of the Interior and the Secretary of Health and Human Services have entered into a memorandum of agreement, to be provided to the Secretary of Education, for the coordination of services, resources, and personnel between their respective Federal, State, and local offices and with State and local educational agencies and other entities to facilitate the provision of services to Indian children with disabilities residing on or near reservations (such agreement shall provide for the apportionment of responsibilities and costs, including child find, evaluation, diagnosis, remediation or therapeutic measures, and (where appropriate) equipment and medical or personal supplies as needed for a child to remain in school or a program); and

(F) includes an assurance that the Department of the Interior will cooperate with the Department of Education in its exercise of monitoring and oversight of this application, and any agreements entered into between the Secretary of the Interior and other entities under this part, and will fulfill its duties under this part.

(3) APPLICABILITY- The Secretary shall withhold payments under this subsection with respect to the information described in paragraph (2) in the same manner as the Secretary withholds payments under section 616(e)(6).

(4) PAYMENTS FOR EDUCATION AND SERVICES FOR INDIAN CHILDREN WITH DISABILITIES AGED 3 THROUGH 5-

(A) IN GENERAL- With funds appropriated under subsection (i), the Secretary of Education shall make payments to the Secretary of the Interior to be distributed to tribes or tribal organizations (as defined under section 4 of the Indian Self-Determination and Education Assistance Act) or consortia of tribes or tribal organizations to provide for the coordination of assistance for special education and related services for children with disabilities aged 3 through 5 on reservations served by elementary schools and secondary schools for Indian children operated or funded by the Department of the Interior. The amount of such payments under subparagraph (B) for any fiscal year shall be equal to 20 percent of the amount allotted under subsection (b)(2).

(B) DISTRIBUTION OF FUNDS- The Secretary of the Interior shall distribute the total amount of the payment under subparagraph (A) by allocating to each tribe, tribal organization, or consortium an amount based on the number of children with disabilities aged 3 through 5 residing on reservations as reported annually, divided by the total of those children served by all tribes or tribal organizations.

(C) SUBMISSION OF INFORMATION- To receive a payment under this paragraph, the tribe or tribal organization shall submit such figures to the Secretary of the Interior as required to determine the amounts to be allocated under subparagraph (B). This information shall be compiled and submitted to the Secretary of Education.

(D) USE OF FUNDS- The funds received by a tribe or tribal organization shall be used to assist in child find, screening, and other procedures for the early identification of children aged 3 through 5, parent training, and the provision of direct services. These activities may be carried out directly or through contracts or cooperative agreements with the BIA, local educational agencies, and other public or private nonprofit organizations. The tribe or tribal organization is encouraged to involve Indian parents in the development and implementation of these activities. The tribe or tribal organization shall, as appropriate, make referrals to local, State, or Federal entities for the provision of services or further diagnosis.

(E) BIENNIAL REPORT- To be eligible to receive a grant pursuant to subparagraph (A), the tribe or tribal organization shall provide to the Secretary of the Interior a biennial report of activities undertaken under this paragraph, including the number of contracts and cooperative agreements entered into, the number of children contacted and receiving services for each year, and the estimated number of children needing services during the 2 years following the year in which the report is made. The Secretary of the Interior shall include a summary of this information on a biennial basis in the report to the Secretary of Education required under this subsection. The Secretary of Education may require any additional information from the Secretary of the Interior.

(F) PROHIBITIONS- None of the funds allocated under this paragraph may be used by the Secretary of the Interior for administrative purposes, including child count and the provision of technical assistance.

(5) PLAN FOR COORDINATION OF SERVICES- The Secretary of the Interior shall develop and implement a plan for the coordination of services for all Indian children with disabilities residing on reservations covered under this title. Such plan shall provide for the coordination of services benefiting

those children from whatever source, including tribes, the Indian Health Service, other BIA divisions, and other Federal agencies. In developing the plan, the Secretary of the Interior shall consult with all interested and involved parties. The plan shall be based on the needs of the children and the system best suited for meeting those needs, and may involve the establishment of cooperative agreements between the BIA, other Federal agencies, and other entities. The plan shall also be distributed upon request to States, State educational agencies and local educational agencies, and other agencies providing services to infants, toddlers, and children with disabilities, to tribes, and to other interested parties.

(6) ESTABLISHMENT OF ADVISORY BOARD- To meet the requirements of section 612(a)(21), the Secretary of the Interior shall establish, under the BIA, an advisory board composed of individuals involved in or concerned with the education and provision of services to Indian infants, toddlers, children, and youth with disabilities, including Indians with disabilities, Indian parents or guardians of such children, teachers, service providers, State and local educational officials, representatives of tribes or tribal organizations, representatives from State Interagency Coordinating Councils under section 641 in States having reservations, and other members representing the various divisions and entities of the BIA. The chairperson shall be selected by the Secretary of the Interior. The advisory board shall—

(A) assist in the coordination of services within the BIA and with other local, State, and Federal agencies in the provision of education for infants, toddlers, and children with disabilities;

(B) advise and assist the Secretary of the Interior in the performance of the Secretary of the Interior's responsibilities described in this subsection;

(C) develop and recommend policies concerning effective inter- and intra-agency collaboration, including modifications to regulations, and the elimination of barriers to inter- and intra-agency programs and activities;

(D) provide assistance and disseminate information on best practices, effective program coordination strategies, and recommendations for improved early intervention services or educational programming for Indian infants, toddlers, and children with disabilities; and

(E) provide assistance in the preparation of information required under paragraph (2)(D).

(7) ANNUAL REPORTS-

(A) IN GENERAL- The advisory board established under paragraph (6) shall prepare and submit to the Secretary of the Interior and to Congress an annual report containing a description of the activities of the advisory board for the preceding year.

(B) AVAILABILITY- The Secretary of the Interior shall make available to the Secretary of Education the report described in subparagraph (A).

(i) AUTHORIZATION OF APPROPRIATIONS- For the purpose of carrying out this part, other than section 619, there are authorized to be appropriated—

(1) $12,358,376,571 for fiscal year 2005;

(2) $14,648,647,143 for fiscal year 2006;

(3) $16,938,917,714 for fiscal year 2007;

(4) $19,229,188,286 for fiscal year 2008;

(5) $21,519,458,857 for fiscal year 2009;

(6) $23,809,729,429 for fiscal year 2010;

(7) $26,100,000,000 for fiscal year 2011; and

(8) such sums as may be necessary for fiscal year 2012 and each succeeding fiscal year.

SEC. 612. STATE ELIGIBILITY.

(a) IN GENERAL- A State is eligible for assistance under this part for a fiscal year if the State submits a plan that provides assurances to the Secretary that the State has in effect policies and procedures to ensure that the State meets each of the following conditions:

(1) FREE APPROPRIATE PUBLIC EDUCATION-

(A) IN GENERAL- A free appropriate public education is available to all children with disabilities residing in the State between the ages of 3 and 21, inclusive, including children with disabilities who have been suspended or expelled from school.

(B) LIMITATION- The obligation to make a free appropriate public education available to all children with disabilities does not apply with respect to children—

(i) aged 3 through 5 and 18 through 21 in a State to the extent that its application to those children would be inconsistent with State law or practice, or the order of any court, respecting the provision of public education to children in those age ranges; and

(ii) aged 18 through 21 to the extent that State law does not require that special education and related services under this part be provided to children with disabilities who, in the educational placement prior to their incarceration in an adult correctional facility—

(I) were not actually identified as being a child with a disability under section 602; or

(II) did not have an individualized education program under this part.

(C) STATE FLEXIBILITY- A State that provides early intervention services in accordance with part C to a child who is eligible for services under section 619, is not required to provide such child with a free appropriate public education.

(2) FULL EDUCATIONAL OPPORTUNITY GOAL- The State has established a goal of providing full educational opportunity to all children with disabilities and a detailed timetable for accomplishing that goal.

(3) CHILD FIND-

(A) IN GENERAL- All children with disabilities residing in the State, including children with disabilities who are homeless children or are wards of the State and children with disabilities attending private schools, regardless of the severity of their disabilities, and who are in need of special education and related services, are identified, located, and evaluated and a practical method is developed and implemented to determine which children with disabilities are currently receiving needed special education and related services.

(B) CONSTRUCTION- Nothing in this title requires that children be classified by their disability so long as each child who has a disability listed in section 602 and who, by reason of that disability, needs special education and related services is regarded as a child with a disability under this part.

(4) INDIVIDUALIZED EDUCATION PROGRAM- An individualized education program, or an individualized family service plan that meets the requirements of section 636(d), is developed, reviewed, and revised for each child with a disability in accordance with section 614(d).

(5) LEAST RESTRICTIVE ENVIRONMENT-

(A) IN GENERAL- To the maximum extent appropriate, children with disabilities, including children in public or private institutions or other care facilities, are educated with children who are not disabled, and special classes, separate schooling, or other removal of children with disabilities from the regular educational environment occurs only when the nature or severity of the disability of a child is such that education in regular classes with the use of supplementary aids and services cannot be achieved satisfactorily.

(B) ADDITIONAL REQUIREMENT-

(i) IN GENERAL- A State funding mechanism shall not result in placements that violate the requirements of subparagraph (A), and a State shall not use a funding mechanism by which the State distributes funds on the basis of the type of setting in which a child is served that will result in the failure to provide a child with a disability a free appropriate public education according to the unique needs of the child as described in the child's IEP.

(ii) ASSURANCE- If the State does not have policies and procedures to ensure compliance with clause (i), the State shall provide the Secretary an assurance that the State will revise the funding mechanism as soon as feasible to ensure that such mechanism does not result in such placements.

(6) PROCEDURAL SAFEGUARDS-

(A) IN GENERAL- Children with disabilities and their parents are afforded the procedural safeguards required by section 615.

(B) ADDITIONAL PROCEDURAL SAFEGUARDS- Procedures to ensure that testing and evaluation materials and procedures utilized for the purposes of evaluation and placement of children with disabilities for services under this title will be selected and administered so as not to be racially or culturally discriminatory. Such materials or procedures shall be provided and administered in the child's native language or mode of communication, unless it clearly is not feasible to do so, and no single procedure shall be the sole criterion for determining an appropriate educational program for a child.

(7) EVALUATION- Children with disabilities are evaluated in accordance with subsections (a) through (c) of section 614.

(8) CONFIDENTIALITY- Agencies in the State comply with section 617(c) (relating to the confidentiality of records and information).

(9) TRANSITION FROM PART C TO PRESCHOOL PROGRAMS- Children participating in early intervention programs assisted under part C, and who will participate in preschool programs assisted under this part, experience a smooth and effective transition to those preschool programs in a manner consistent with section 637(a)(9). By the third birthday of such a child, an individualized education program or, if consistent with sections 614(d)(2)(B) and 636(d), an individualized family service plan, has been developed and is being implemented for the child. The local educational agency will participate in transition planning conferences arranged by the designated lead agency under section 635(a)(10).

(10) CHILDREN IN PRIVATE SCHOOLS-

(A) CHILDREN ENROLLED IN PRIVATE SCHOOLS BY THEIR PARENTS-

(i) IN GENERAL- To the extent consistent with the number and location of children with disabilities in the State who are enrolled by their parents in private elementary schools and secondary schools in the school district served by a local educational agency, provision is made for the participation of those children in the program assisted or carried out under this part by providing for such children special education and related services in accordance with the following requirements, unless the Secretary has arranged for services to those children under subsection (f):

(I) Amounts to be expended for the provision of those services (including direct services to parentally placed private school children) by the local educational agency shall be equal to a proportionate amount of Federal funds made available under this part.

(II) In calculating the proportionate amount of Federal funds, the local educational agency, after timely and meaningful consultation with representatives of private schools as described in clause (iii), shall conduct a thorough and complete child find process to determine the number of parentally placed children with disabilities attending private schools located in the local educational agency.

(III) Such services to parentally placed private school children with disabilities may be provided to the children on the premises of private, including religious, schools, to the extent consistent with law.

(IV) State and local funds may supplement and in no case shall supplant the proportionate amount of Federal funds required to be expended under this subparagraph.

(V) Each local educational agency shall maintain in its records and provide to the State educational agency the number of children evaluated under this subparagraph, the number of children determined to be children with disabilities under this paragraph, and the number of children served under this paragraph.

(ii) CHILD FIND REQUIREMENT-

(I) IN GENERAL- The requirements of paragraph (3) (relating to child find) shall apply with respect to children with disabilities in the State who are enrolled in private, including religious, elementary schools and secondary schools.

(II) EQUITABLE PARTICIPATION- The child find process shall be designed to ensure the equitable participation of parentally placed private school children with disabilities and an accurate count of such children.

(III) ACTIVITIES- In carrying out this

clause, the local educational agency, or where applicable, the State educational agency, shall undertake activities similar to those activities undertaken for the agency's public school children.

(IV) COST- The cost of carrying out this clause, including individual evaluations, may not be considered in determining whether a local educational agency has met its obligations under clause (i).

(V) COMPLETION PERIOD- Such child find process shall be completed in a time period comparable to that for other students attending public schools in the local educational agency.

(iii) CONSULTATION- To ensure timely and meaningful consultation, a local educational agency, or where appropriate, a State educational agency, shall consult with private school representatives and representatives of parents of parentally placed private school children with disabilities during the design and development of special education and related services for the children, including regarding—

(I) the child find process and how parentally placed private school children suspected of having a disability can participate equitably, including how parents, teachers, and private school officials will be informed of the process;

(II) the determination of the proportionate amount of Federal funds available to serve parentally placed private school children with disabilities under this subparagraph, including the determination of how the amount was calculated;

(III) the consultation process among the local educational agency, private school officials, and representatives of parents of parentally placed private school children with disabilities, including how such process will operate throughout the school year to ensure that parentally placed private school children with disabilities identified through the child find process can meaningfully participate in special education and related services;

(IV) how, where, and by whom special education and related services will be provided for parentally placed private school children with disabilities, including a discussion of types of services, including direct services and alternate service delivery mechanisms, how such services will be apportioned if funds are insufficient to serve all children, and how and when these decisions will be made; and

(V) how, if the local educational agency disagrees with the views of the private school officials on the provision of services or the types of services, whether provided directly or through a contract, the local educational agency shall provide to the private school officials a written explanation of the reasons why the local educational agency chose not to provide services directly or through a contract.

(iv) WRITTEN AFFIRMATION- When timely and meaningful consultation as required by clause (iii) has occurred, the local educational agency shall obtain a written affirmation signed by the representatives of participating private schools, and if such representatives do not provide such affirmation within a reasonable period of time, the local educational agency shall forward the documentation of the consultation process to the State educational agency.

(v) COMPLIANCE-

(I) IN GENERAL- A private school official shall have the right to submit a complaint to the State educational agency that the local educational agency did not engage in consultation that was meaningful and timely, or did not give due consideration to the views of the private school official.

(II) PROCEDURE- If the private school official wishes to submit a complaint, the official shall provide the basis of the noncompliance with this subparagraph by the local educational agency to the State educational agency, and the local educational agency shall forward the appropriate documentation to the State educational agency. If the private school official is dissatisfied with the decision of the State educational agency, such official may submit a complaint to the Secretary by providing the basis of the noncompliance with this subparagraph by the local educational agency to the Secretary, and the State educational agency shall forward the appropriate documentation to the Secretary.

(vi) PROVISION OF EQUITABLE SERVICES-

(I) DIRECTLY OR THROUGH CONTRACTS- The provision of services pursuant to this subparagraph shall be provided—

(aa) by employees of a public agency; or

(bb) through contract by the public agency with an individual, association, agency, organization, or other entity.

(II) SECULAR, NEUTRAL, NONIDEOLOGICAL- Special education and related services provided to parentally placed private school children with disabilities, including materials and equipment, shall be secular, neutral, and nonideological.

(vii) PUBLIC CONTROL OF FUNDS- The control of funds used to provide special education and related services under this subparagraph, and title to materials, equipment, and property purchased with those funds, shall be in a public agency for the uses and purposes provided in this title, and a public agency shall administer the funds and property.

(B) CHILDREN PLACED IN, OR REFERRED TO, PRIVATE SCHOOLS BY PUBLIC AGENCIES-

(i) IN GENERAL- Children with disabilities in private schools and facilities are provided special education and related services, in accordance with an individualized education program, at no cost to their parents, if such children are placed in, or referred to, such schools or facilities by the State or appropriate local educational agency as the means of carrying out the requirements of this part or any other applicable law requiring the provision of special education and related services to all children with disabilities within such State.

(ii) STANDARDS- In all cases described in clause (i), the State educational agency shall determine whether such schools and facilities meet standards that apply to State educational agencies and local educational agencies and that children so served have all the rights the children would have if served by such agencies.

(C) PAYMENT FOR EDUCATION OF CHILDREN ENROLLED IN PRIVATE SCHOOLS WITHOUT CONSENT OF OR REFERRAL BY THE PUBLIC AGENCY-

(i) IN GENERAL- Subject to subparagraph (A), this part does not require a local educational agency to pay for the cost of education, including special education and related services, of a child with a disability at a private school or facility if that agency made a free appropriate public education available to the child and the parents elected to place the child in such private school or facility.

(ii) REIMBURSEMENT FOR PRIVATE SCHOOL PLACEMENT- If the parents of a child with a disability, who previously received special education and related services under the authority of a public agency, enroll the child in a private elementary school or secondary school without the consent of or referral by the public agency, a court or a hearing officer may require the agency to reimburse the parents for the cost of that enrollment if the court or hearing officer finds that the agency had not made a free appropriate public education available to the child in a timely manner prior to that enrollment.

(iii) LIMITATION ON REIMBURSEMENT- The cost of reimbursement described in clause (ii) may be reduced or denied—

(I) if—

(aa) at the most recent IEP meeting that the parents attended prior to removal of the child from the public school, the parents did not inform the IEP Team that they were rejecting the placement proposed by the public agency to provide a free appropriate public education to their child, including stating their concerns and their intent to enroll their child in a private school at public expense; or

(bb) 10 business days (including any holidays that occur on a business day) prior to the removal of the child from the public school, the parents did not give written notice to the public agency of the information described in item (aa);

(II) if, prior to the parents' removal of the child from the public school, the public agency informed the parents, through the notice requirements described in section 615(b)(3), of its intent to evaluate the child (including a statement of the purpose of the evaluation that was appropriate and reasonable), but the parents did not make the child available for such evaluation; or

(III) upon a judicial finding of unreasonableness with respect to actions taken by the parents.

(iv) EXCEPTION- Notwithstanding the notice requirement in clause (iii)(I), the cost of reimbursement—

(I) shall not be reduced or denied for failure to provide such notice if—

(aa) the school prevented the parent from providing such notice;

(bb) the parents had not received notice, pursuant to section 615, of the notice requirement in clause (iii)(I); or

(cc) compliance with clause (iii)(I) would likely result in physical harm to the child; and

(II) may, in the discretion of a court or a hearing officer, not be reduced or denied for failure to provide such notice if—

(aa) the parent is illiterate or cannot write in English; or

(bb) compliance with clause (iii)(I) would likely result in serious emotional harm to the child.

(11) STATE EDUCATIONAL AGENCY RESPONSIBLE FOR GENERAL SUPERVISION-

(A) IN GENERAL- The State educational agency is responsible for ensuring that—

(i) the requirements of this part are met;

(ii) all educational programs for children with disabilities in the State, including all such programs administered by any other State agency or local agency—

(I) are under the general supervision of

individuals in the State who are responsible for educational programs for children with disabilities; and

(II) meet the educational standards of the State educational agency; and

(iii) in carrying out this part with respect to homeless children, the requirements of subtitle B of title VII of the McKinney-Vento Homeless Assistance Act (42 U.S.C. 11431 et seq.) are met.

(B) LIMITATION- Subparagraph (A) shall not limit the responsibility of agencies in the State other than the State educational agency to provide, or pay for some or all of the costs of, a free appropriate public education for any child with a disability in the State.

(C) EXCEPTION- Notwithstanding subparagraphs (A) and (B), the Governor (or another individual pursuant to State law), consistent with State law, may assign to any public agency in the State the responsibility of ensuring that the requirements of this part are met with respect to children with disabilities who are convicted as adults under State law and incarcerated in adult prisons.

(12) OBLIGATIONS RELATED TO AND METHODS OF ENSURING SERVICES-

(A) ESTABLISHING RESPONSIBILITY FOR SERVICES- The Chief Executive Officer of a State or designee of the officer shall ensure that an interagency agreement or other mechanism for interagency coordination is in effect between each public agency described in subparagraph (B) and the State educational agency, in order to ensure that all services described in subparagraph (B)(i) that are needed to ensure a free appropriate public education are provided, including the provision of such services during the pendency of any dispute under clause (iii). Such agreement or mechanism shall include the following:

(i) AGENCY FINANCIAL RESPONSIBILITY- An identification of, or a method for defining, the financial responsibility of each agency for providing services described in subparagraph (B)(i) to ensure a free appropriate public education to children with disabilities, provided that the financial responsibility of each public agency described in subparagraph (B), including the State medicaid agency and other public insurers of children with disabilities, shall precede the financial responsibility of the local educational agency (or the State agency responsible for developing the child's IEP).

(ii) CONDITIONS AND TERMS OF REIMBURSEMENT- The conditions, terms, and procedures under which a local educational agency shall be reimbursed by other agencies.

(iii) INTERAGENCY DISPUTES- Procedures for resolving interagency disputes (including procedures under which local educational agencies may initiate proceedings) under the agreement or other mechanism to secure reimbursement from other agencies or otherwise implement the provisions of the agreement or mechanism.

(iv) COORDINATION OF SERVICES PROCEDURES- Policies and procedures for agencies to determine and identify the interagency coordination responsibilities of each agency to promote the coordination and timely and appropriate delivery of services described in subparagraph (B)(i).

(B) OBLIGATION OF PUBLIC AGENCY-

(i) IN GENERAL- If any public agency other than an educational agency is otherwise obligated under Federal or State law, or assigned responsibility under State policy pursuant to subparagraph (A), to provide or pay for any services that are also considered special education or related services (such as, but not limited to, services described in section 602(1) relating to assistive technology devices, 602(2) relating to assistive technology services, 602(26) relating to related services, 602(33) relating to supplementary aids and services, and 602(34) relating to transition services) that are necessary for ensuring a free appropriate public education to children with disabilities within the State, such public agency shall fulfill that obligation or responsibility, either directly or through contract or other arrangement pursuant to subparagraph (A) or an agreement pursuant to subparagraph (C).

(ii) REIMBURSEMENT FOR SERVICES BY PUBLIC AGENCY- If a public agency other than an educational agency fails to provide or pay for the special education and related services described in clause (i), the local educational agency (or State agency responsible for developing the child's IEP) shall provide or pay for such services to the child. Such local educational agency or State agency is authorized to claim reimbursement for the services from the public agency that failed to provide or pay for such services and such public agency shall reimburse the local educational agency or State agency pursuant to the terms of the interagency agreement or other mechanism described in subparagraph (A)(i) according to the procedures established in such agreement pursuant to subparagraph (A)(ii).

(C) SPECIAL RULE- The requirements of subparagraph (A) may be met through—

(i) State statute or regulation;

(ii) signed agreements between respective agency officials that clearly identify the responsibilities of each agency relating to the provision of services; or

(iii) other appropriate written methods as determined by the Chief Executive Officer of the State or designee of the officer and approved by the Secretary.

(13) PROCEDURAL REQUIREMENTS RELATING TO LOCAL EDUCATIONAL AGENCY ELIGIBILITY- The State educational agency will not make a final determination that a local educational agency is not eligible for assistance under this part without first affording that agency reasonable notice and an opportunity for a hearing.

(14) PERSONNEL QUALIFICATIONS-

(A) IN GENERAL- The State educational agency has established and maintains qualifications to ensure that personnel necessary to carry out this part are appropriately and adequately prepared and trained, including that those personnel have the content knowledge and skills to serve children with disabilities.

(B) RELATED SERVICES PERSONNEL AND PARAPROFESSIONALS- The qualifications under subparagraph (A) include qualifications for related services personnel and paraprofessionals that—

(i) are consistent with any State-approved or State-recognized certification, licensing, registration, or other comparable requirements that apply to the professional discipline in which those personnel are providing special education or related services;

(ii) ensure that related services personnel who deliver services in their discipline or profession meet the requirements of clause (i) and have not had certification or licensure requirements waived on an emergency, temporary, or provisional basis; and

(iii) allow paraprofessionals and assistants who are appropriately trained and supervised, in accordance with State law, regulation, or written policy, in meeting the requirements of this part to be used to assist in the provision of special education and related services under this part to children with disabilities.

(C) QUALIFICATIONS FOR SPECIAL EDUCATION TEACHERS- The qualifications described in subparagraph (A) shall ensure that each person employed as a special education teacher in the State who teaches elementary school, middle school, or secondary school is highly qualified by the deadline established in section 1119(a)(2) of the Elementary and Secondary Education Act of 1965.

(D) POLICY- In implementing this section, a State shall adopt a policy that includes a requirement that local educational agencies in the State take measurable steps to recruit, hire, train, and retain highly qualified personnel to provide special education and related services under this part to children with disabilities.

(E) RULE OF CONSTRUCTION- Notwithstanding any other individual right of action that a parent or student may maintain under this part, nothing in this paragraph shall be construed to create a right of action on behalf of an individual student for the failure of a particular State educational agency or local educational agency staff person to be highly qualified, or to prevent a parent from filing a complaint about staff qualifications with the State educational agency as provided for under this part.

(15) PERFORMANCE GOALS AND INDICATORS- The State—

(A) has established goals for the performance of children with disabilities in the State that—

(i) promote the purposes of this title, as stated in section 601(d);

(ii) are the same as the State's definition of adequate yearly progress, including the State's objectives for progress by children with disabilities, under section 1111(b)(2)(C) of the Elementary and Secondary Education Act of 1965;

(iii) address graduation rates and dropout rates, as well as such other factors as the State may determine; and

(iv) are consistent, to the extent appropriate, with any other goals and standards for children established by the State;

(B) has established performance indicators the State will use to assess progress toward achieving the goals described in subparagraph (A), including measurable annual objectives for progress by children with disabilities under section 1111(b)(2)(C)(v)(II)(cc) of the Elementary and Secondary Education Act of 1965; and

(C) will annually report to the Secretary and the public on the progress of the State, and of children with disabilities in the State, toward meeting the goals established under subparagraph (A), which may include elements of the reports required under section 1111(h) of the Elementary and Secondary Education Act of 1965.

(16) PARTICIPATION IN ASSESSMENTS-

(A) IN GENERAL- All children with disabilities are included in all general State and districtwide assessment programs, including assessments described under section 1111 of the Elementary and Secondary Education Act of 1965, with appropriate accommodations and alternate assessments where necessary and as indicated in their respective individualized education programs.

(B) ACCOMMODATION GUIDELINES- The State (or, in the case of a districtwide assessment, the local educational agency) has developed guidelines for the provision of appropriate accommodations.

(C) ALTERNATE ASSESSMENTS-

(i) IN GENERAL- The State (or, in the case of a districtwide assessment, the local educational agency) has developed and implemented guidelines for the participation of children with disabilities in alternate assessments for those children who cannot participate in regular assessments under subparagraph (A) with accommodations as indicated in their respective individualized education programs.

(ii) REQUIREMENTS FOR ALTERNATE ASSESSMENTS- The guidelines under clause (i) shall provide for alternate assessments that—

(I) are aligned with the State's challenging academic content standards and challenging student academic achievement standards; and

(II) if the State has adopted alternate academic achievement standards permitted under the regulations promulgated to carry out section 1111(b)(1) of the Elementary and Secondary Education Act of 1965, measure the achievement of children with disabilities against those standards.

(iii) CONDUCT OF ALTERNATE ASSESSMENTS- The State conducts the alternate assessments described in this subparagraph.

(D) REPORTS- The State educational agency (or, in the case of a districtwide assessment, the local educational agency) makes available to the public, and reports to the public with the same frequency and in the same detail as it reports on the assessment of nondisabled children, the following:

(i) The number of children with disabilities participating in regular assessments, and the number of those children who were provided accommodations in order to participate in those assessments.

(ii) The number of children with disabilities participating in alternate assessments described in subparagraph (C)(ii)(I).

(iii) The number of children with disabilities participating in alternate assessments described in subparagraph (C)(ii)(II).

(iv) The performance of children with disabilities on regular assessments and on alternate assessments (if the number of children with disabilities participating in those assessments is sufficient to yield statistically reliable information and reporting that information will not reveal personally identifiable information about an individual student), compared with the achievement of all children, including children with disabilities, on those assessments.

(E) UNIVERSAL DESIGN- The State educational agency (or, in the case of a districtwide assessment, the local educational agency) shall, to the extent feasible, use universal design principles in developing and administering any assessments under this paragraph.

(17) SUPPLEMENTATION OF STATE, LOCAL, AND OTHER FEDERAL FUNDS-

(A) EXPENDITURES- Funds paid to a State under this part will be expended in accordance with all the provisions of this part.

(B) PROHIBITION AGAINST COMMINGLING- Funds paid to a State under this part will not be commingled with State funds.

(C) PROHIBITION AGAINST SUPPLANTATION AND CONDITIONS FOR WAIVER BY SECRETARY- Except as provided in section 613, funds paid to a State under this part will be used to supplement the level of Federal, State, and local funds (including funds that are not under the direct control of State or local educational agencies) expended for special education and related services provided to children with disabilities under this part and in no case to supplant such Federal, State, and local funds, except that, where the State provides clear and convincing evidence that all children with disabilities have available to them a free appropriate public education, the Secretary may waive, in whole or in part, the requirements of this subparagraph if the Secretary concurs with the evidence provided by the State.

(18) MAINTENANCE OF STATE FINANCIAL SUPPORT-

(A) IN GENERAL- The State does not reduce the amount of State financial support for special education and related services for children with disabilities, or otherwise made available because of the excess costs of educating those children, below the amount of that support for the preceding fiscal year.

(B) REDUCTION OF FUNDS FOR FAILURE TO MAINTAIN SUPPORT- The Secretary shall reduce the allocation of funds under section 611 for any fiscal year following the fiscal year in which the State fails to comply with the requirement of subparagraph (A) by the same amount by which the State fails to meet the requirement.

(C) WAIVERS FOR EXCEPTIONAL OR UNCONTROLLABLE CIRCUMSTANCES- The Secretary may waive the requirement of subparagraph (A) for a State, for 1 fiscal year at a time, if the Secretary determines that—

(i) granting a waiver would be equitable due to exceptional or uncontrollable circumstances such as a natural disaster or a precipitous and unforeseen decline in the financial resources of the State; or

(ii) the State meets the standard in paragraph (17)(C) for a waiver of the requirement to supplement, and not to supplant, funds received under this part.

(D) SUBSEQUENT YEARS- If, for any year, a State fails to meet the requirement of subparagraph (A), including any year for which the State is granted a waiver under subparagraph (C), the financial support required of the State in future years under subparagraph (A) shall be the amount that would have been required in the absence of that failure and not the reduced level of the State's support.

(19) PUBLIC PARTICIPATION- Prior to the adoption of any policies and procedures needed to comply with this section (including any amendments to such policies and procedures), the State ensures that there are public hearings, adequate notice of the hearings, and an opportunity for comment available to the general public, including individuals with disabilities and parents of children with disabilities.

(20) RULE OF CONSTRUCTION- In complying with paragraphs (17) and (18), a State may not use funds paid to it under this part to satisfy State-law mandated funding obligations to local educational agencies, including funding based on student attendance or enrollment, or inflation.

(21) STATE ADVISORY PANEL-

(A) IN GENERAL- The State has established and maintains an advisory panel for the purpose of providing policy guidance with respect to special education and related services for children with disabilities in the State.

(B) MEMBERSHIP- Such advisory panel shall consist of members appointed by the Governor, or any other official authorized under State law to make such appointments, be representative of the State population, and be composed of individuals involved in, or concerned with, the education of children with disabilities, including—

(i) parents of children with disabilities (ages birth through 26);

(ii) individuals with disabilities;

(iii) teachers;

(iv) representatives of institutions of higher education that prepare special education and related services personnel;

(v) State and local education officials, including officials who carry out activities under subtitle B of title VII of the McKinney-Vento Homeless Assistance Act (42 U.S.C. 11431 et seq.);

(vi) administrators of programs for children with disabilities;

(vii) representatives of other State agencies involved in the financing or delivery of related services to children with disabilities;

(viii) representatives of private schools and public charter schools;

(ix) not less than 1 representative of a vocational, community, or business organization concerned with the provision of transition services to children with disabilities;

(x) a representative from the State child welfare agency responsible for foster care; and

(xi) representatives from the State juvenile and adult corrections agencies.

(C) SPECIAL RULE- A majority of the members of the panel shall be individuals with disabilities or parents of children with disabilities (ages birth through 26).

(D) DUTIES- The advisory panel shall—

(i) advise the State educational agency of unmet needs within the State in the education of children with disabilities;

(ii) comment publicly on any rules or regulations proposed by the State regarding the education of children with disabilities;

(iii) advise the State educational agency in developing evaluations and reporting on data to the Secretary under section 618;

(iv) advise the State educational agency in developing corrective action plans to address findings identified in Federal monitoring reports under this part; and

(v) advise the State educational agency in developing and implementing policies relating to the coordination of services for children with disabilities.

(22) SUSPENSION AND EXPULSION RATES-

(A) IN GENERAL- The State educational agency examines data, including data disaggregated by race and ethnicity, to determine if significant discrepancies are occurring in the rate of long-term suspensions and expulsions of children with disabilities—

(i) among local educational agencies in the State; or

(ii) compared to such rates for nondisabled children within such agencies.

(B) REVIEW AND REVISION OF POLICIES- If such discrepancies are occurring, the State educational agency reviews and, if appropriate, revises (or requires the affected State or local educational agency to revise) its policies, procedures, and practices relating to the development and implementation of IEPs, the use of positive behavioral interventions and supports, and procedural safeguards, to ensure that such policies, procedures, and practices comply with this title.

(23) ACCESS TO INSTRUCTIONAL MATERIALS-

(A) IN GENERAL- The State adopts the National Instructional Materials Accessibility Standard for the purposes of providing instructional materials to blind persons or other persons with print disabilities, in a timely manner after the publication of the National Instructional Materials Accessibility Standard in the Federal Register.

(B) RIGHTS OF STATE EDUCATIONAL AGENCY- Nothing in this paragraph shall be construed to require any State educational agency to coordinate with the National Instructional Materials Access Center. If a State educational agency chooses not to coordinate with the National Instructional Materials Access Center, such agency shall provide an assurance to the Secretary that the agency will provide instructional materials to blind persons or other persons with print disabilities in a timely manner.

(C) PREPARATION AND DELIVERY OF FILES- If a State educational agency chooses to coordinate with the National Instructional Materials Access Center, not later than 2 years after the date of enactment of the Individuals with Disabilities Education Improvement Act of 2004, the agency, as part of any print instructional materials adoption process, procurement contract, or other practice or instrument used for purchase of print instructional materials, shall enter into a written contract with the publisher of the print instructional materials to—

(i) require the publisher to prepare and, on or before delivery of the print instructional materials, provide to the National Instructional Materials Access Center electronic files containing the contents of the print instructional materials using the National Instructional Materials Accessibility Standard;

or

(ii) purchase instructional materials from the publisher that are produced in, or may be rendered in, specialized formats.

(D) ASSISTIVE TECHNOLOGY- In carrying out this paragraph, the State educational agency, to the maximum extent possible, shall work collaboratively with the State agency responsible for assistive technology programs.

(E) DEFINITIONS- In this paragraph:

(i) NATIONAL INSTRUCTIONAL MATERIALS ACCESS CENTER- The term 'National Instructional Materials Access Center' means the center established pursuant to section 674(e).

(ii) NATIONAL INSTRUCTIONAL MATERIALS ACCESSIBILITY STANDARD- The term National Instructional Materials Accessibility Standard' has the meaning given the term in section 674(e)(3)(A).

(iii) SPECIALIZED FORMATS- The term 'specialized formats' has the meaning given the term in section 674(e)(3)(D).

(24) OVERIDENTIFICATION AND DISPROPORTIONALITY- The State has in effect, consistent with the purposes of this title and with section 618(d), policies and procedures designed to prevent the inappropriate overidentification or disproportionate representation by race and ethnicity of children as children with disabilities, including children with disabilities with a particular impairment described in section 602.

(25) PROHIBITION ON MANDATORY MEDICATION-

(A) IN GENERAL- The State educational agency shall prohibit State and local educational agency personnel from requiring a child to obtain a prescription for a substance covered by the Controlled Substances Act (21 U.S.C. 801 et seq.) as a condition of attending school, receiving an evaluation under subsection (a) or (c) of section 614, or receiving services under this title.

(B) RULE OF CONSTRUCTION- Nothing in subparagraph (A) shall be construed to create a Federal prohibition against teachers and other school personnel consulting or sharing classroom-based observations with parents or guardians regarding a student's academic and functional performance, or behavior in the classroom or school, or regarding the need for evaluation for special education or related services under paragraph (3).

(b) STATE EDUCATIONAL AGENCY AS PROVIDER OF FREE APPROPRIATE PUBLIC EDUCATION OR DIRECT SERVICES- If the State educational agency provides free appropriate public education to children with disabilities, or provides direct services to such children, such agency—

(1) shall comply with any additional requirements of section 613(a), as if such agency were a local educational agency; and

(2) may use amounts that are otherwise available to such agency under this part to serve those children without regard to section 613(a)(2)(A)(i) (relating to excess costs).

(c) EXCEPTION FOR PRIOR STATE PLANS-

(1) IN GENERAL- If a State has on file with the Secretary policies and procedures that demonstrate that such State meets any requirement of subsection (a), including any policies and procedures filed under this part as in effect before the effective date of the Individuals with Disabilities Education Improvement Act of 2004, the Secretary shall consider such State to have met such requirement for purposes of receiving a grant under this part.

(2) MODIFICATIONS MADE BY STATE- Subject to paragraph (3), an application submitted by a State in accordance with this section shall remain in effect until the State submits to the Secretary such modifications as the State determines necessary. This section shall apply to a modification to an application to the same extent and in the same manner as this section applies to the original plan.

(3) MODIFICATIONS REQUIRED BY THE SECRETARY- If, after the effective date of the Individuals with Disabilities Education Improvement Act of 2004, the provisions of this title are amended (or the regulations developed to carry out this title are amended), there is a new interpretation of this title by a Federal court or a State's highest court, or there is an official finding of noncompliance with Federal law or regulations, then the Secretary may require a State to modify its application only to the extent necessary to ensure the State's compliance with this part.

(d) APPROVAL BY THE SECRETARY-

(1) IN GENERAL- If the Secretary determines that a State is eligible to receive a grant under this part, the Secretary shall notify the State of that determination.

(2) NOTICE AND HEARING- The Secretary shall not make a final determination that a State is not eligible to receive a grant under this part until after providing the State—

(A) with reasonable notice; and

(B) with an opportunity for a hearing.

(e) ASSISTANCE UNDER OTHER FEDERAL PROGRAMS- Nothing in this title permits a State to reduce medical and other assistance available, or to alter eligibility, under titles V and XIX of the Social Security Act with respect to the provision of a free appropriate public education for children with disabilities in the State.

(f) BY-PASS FOR CHILDREN IN PRIVATE SCHOOLS-(1) IN GENERAL- If, on the date of enactment of the Education of the Handicapped Act Amendments of 1983, a State educational agency was prohibited by law from providing for the equitable participation in special programs of children with disabilities enrolled in private elementary schools and secondary schools as required by subsection (a)(10)(A), or if the Secretary determines that a State educational agency, local educational agency, or other entity has substantially failed or is unwilling to provide for such equitable participation, then the Secretary shall, notwithstanding such provision of law, arrange for the provision of services to such children through arrangements that shall be subject to the requirements of such subsection.

(2) PAYMENTS-

(A) DETERMINATION OF AMOUNTS- If the Secretary arranges for services pursuant to this subsection, the Secretary, after consultation with the appropriate public and private school officials, shall pay to the provider of such services for a fiscal year an amount per child that does not exceed the amount determined by dividing—

(i) the total amount received by the State under this part for such fiscal year; by

(ii) the number of children with disabilities served in the prior year, as reported to the Secretary by the State under section 618.

(B) WITHHOLDING OF CERTAIN AMOUNTS- Pending final resolution of any investigation or complaint that may result in a determination under this subsection, the Secretary may withhold from the allocation of the affected State educational agency the amount the Secretary estimates will be necessary to pay the cost of services described in subparagraph (A).

(C) PERIOD OF PAYMENTS- The period under which payments are made under subparagraph (A) shall continue until the Secretary determines that there will no longer be any failure or inability on the part of the State educational agency to meet the requirements of subsection (a)(10)(A).

(3) NOTICE AND HEARING-

(A) IN GENERAL- The Secretary shall not take any final action under this subsection until the State educational agency affected by such action has had an opportunity, for not less than 45 days after receiving written notice thereof, to submit written objections and to appear before the Secretary or the Secretary's designee to show cause why such action should not be taken.

(B) REVIEW OF ACTION- If a State educational agency is dissatisfied with the Secretary's final action after a proceeding under subparagraph (A), such agency may, not later than 60 days after notice of such action, file with the United States court of appeals for the circuit in which such State is located a petition for review of that action. A copy of the petition shall be forthwith transmitted by the clerk of the court to the Secretary. The Secretary thereupon shall file in the court the record of the proceedings on which the Secretary based the Secretary's action, as provided in section 2112 of title 28, United States Code.

(C) REVIEW OF FINDINGS OF FACT- The findings of fact by the Secretary, if supported by substantial evidence, shall be conclusive, but the court, for good cause shown, may remand the case to the Secretary to take further evidence, and the Secretary may thereupon make new or modified findings of fact and may modify the Secretary's previous action, and shall file in the court the record of the further proceedings. Such new or modified findings of fact shall likewise be conclusive if supported by substantial evidence.

(D) JURISDICTION OF COURT OF APPEALS; REVIEW BY UNITED STATES SUPREME COURT- Upon the filing of a petition under subparagraph (B), the United States court of appeals shall have jurisdiction to affirm the action of the Secretary or to set it aside, in whole or in part. The judgment of the court shall be subject to review by the Supreme Court of the United States upon certiorari or certification as provided in section 1254 of title 28, United States Code.

SEC. 613. LOCAL EDUCATIONAL AGENCY ELIGIBILITY.

(a) IN GENERAL- A local educational agency is eligible for assistance under this part for a fiscal year if such agency submits a plan that provides assurances to the State educational agency that the local educational agency meets each of the following conditions:

(1) CONSISTENCY WITH STATE POLICIES- The local educational agency, in providing for the education of children with disabilities within its jurisdiction, has in effect policies, procedures, and programs that are consistent with the State policies and procedures established under section 612.

(2) USE OF AMOUNTS-

(A) IN GENERAL- Amounts provided to the local educational agency under this part shall be expended in accordance with the applicable provisions of this part and—

(i) shall be used only to pay the excess costs of providing special education and related services to children with disabilities;

(ii) shall be used to supplement State, local, and other Federal funds and not to supplant such funds; and

(iii) shall not be used, except as provided in subparagraphs (B) and (C), to reduce the level of expenditures for the education of children with disabilities made by the local educational agency from local funds below the level of those expenditures for the preceding fiscal year.

(B) EXCEPTION- Notwithstanding the restriction in subparagraph (A)(iii), a local educational agency may reduce the level of expenditures where such reduction is attributable to—

(i) the voluntary departure, by retirement or otherwise, or departure for just cause, of special education personnel;

(ii) a decrease in the enrollment of children with disabilities;

(iii) the termination of the obligation of the agency, consistent with this part, to provide a program of special education to a particular child with a disability that is an exceptionally costly program, as determined by the State educational agency, because the child—

(I) has left the jurisdiction of the agency;

(II) has reached the age at which the obligation of the agency to provide a free appropriate public education to the child has terminated; or

(III) no longer needs such program of special education; or

(iv) the termination of costly expenditures for long-term purchases, such as the acquisition of equipment or the construction of school facilities.

(C) ADJUSTMENT TO LOCAL FISCAL EFFORT IN CERTAIN FISCAL YEARS-

(i) AMOUNTS IN EXCESS- Notwithstanding clauses (ii) and (iii) of subparagraph (A), for any fiscal year for which the allocation received by a local educational agency under section 611(f) exceeds the amount the local educational agency received for the previous fiscal year, the local educational agency may reduce the level of expenditures otherwise required by subparagraph (A)(iii) by not more than 50 percent of the amount of such excess.

(ii) USE OF AMOUNTS TO CARRY OUT ACTIVITIES UNDER ESEA- If a local educational agency exercises the authority under clause (i), the agency shall use an amount of local funds equal to the reduction in expenditures under clause (i) to carry out activities authorized under the Elementary and Secondary Education Act of 1965.

(iii) STATE PROHIBITION- Notwithstanding clause (i), if a State educational agency determines that a local educational agency is unable to establish and maintain programs of free appropriate public education that meet the requirements of subsection (a) or the State educational agency has taken action against the local educational agency under section 616, the State educational agency shall prohibit the local educational agency from reducing the level of expenditures under clause (i) for that fiscal year.

(iv) SPECIAL RULE- The amount of funds expended by a local educational agency under subsection (f) shall count toward the maximum amount of expenditures such local educational agency may reduce under clause (i).

(D) SCHOOLWIDE PROGRAMS UNDER TITLE I OF THE ESEA- Notwithstanding subparagraph (A) or any other provision of this part, a local educational agency may use funds received under this part for any fiscal year to carry out a schoolwide program under section 1114 of the Elementary and Secondary Education Act of 1965, except that the amount so used in any such program shall not exceed—

(i) the number of children with disabilities participating in the schoolwide program; multiplied by

(ii)(I) the amount received by the local educational agency under this part for that fiscal year; divided by

(II) the number of children with disabilities in the jurisdiction of that agency.

(3) PERSONNEL DEVELOPMENT- The local educational agency shall ensure that all personnel necessary to carry out this part are appropriately and adequately prepared, subject to the requirements of section 612(a)(14) and section 2122 of the Elementary and Secondary Education Act of 1965.

(4) PERMISSIVE USE OF FUNDS-

(A) USES- Notwithstanding paragraph (2)(A) or section 612(a)(17)(B) (relating to commingled funds), funds provided to the local educational agency under this part may be used for the following activities:

(i) SERVICES AND AIDS THAT ALSO BENEFIT NONDISABLED CHILDREN- For the costs of special education and related services, and supplementary aids and services, provided in a regular class or other education-related setting to a child with a disability in accordance with the individualized education program of the child, even if 1 or more nondisabled children benefit from such services.

(ii) EARLY INTERVENING SERVICES- To develop and implement coordinated, early intervening educational services in accordance with subsection (f).

(iii) HIGH COST EDUCATION AND RELATED SERVICES- To establish and implement cost or risk sharing funds, consortia, or cooperatives for the local educational agency itself, or for local educational agencies working in a consortium of which the local educational agency is a part, to pay for high cost special education and related services.

(B) ADMINISTRATIVE CASE MANAGEMENT- A local educational agency may use funds received under this part to purchase appropriate technology for recordkeeping, data collection, and related case management activities of teachers and related services personnel providing services described in the individualized education program of children with disabilities, that is needed for the implementation of such case management activities.

(5) TREATMENT OF CHARTER SCHOOLS AND THEIR STUDENTS- In carrying out this part with respect to charter schools that are public schools of the local educational agency, the local educational agency—

(A) serves children with disabilities attending those charter schools in the same manner as the local educational agency serves children with disabilities in its other schools, including providing supplementary and related services on site at the charter school to the same extent to which the local educational agency has a policy or practice of providing such services on the site to its other public schools; and

(B) provides funds under this part to those charter schools—

(i) on the same basis as the local educational agency provides funds to the local educational agency's other public schools, including proportional distribution based on relative enrollment of children with disabilities; and

(ii) at the same time as the agency distributes other Federal funds to the agency's other public schools, consistent with the State's charter school law.

(6) PURCHASE OF INSTRUCTIONAL MATERIALS-

(A) IN GENERAL- Not later than 2 years after the date of enactment of the Individuals with Disabilities Education Improvement Act of 2004, a local educational agency that chooses to coordinate with the National Instructional Materials Access Center, when purchasing print instructional materials, shall acquire the print instructional materials in the same manner and subject to the same conditions as a State educational agency acquires print instructional materials under section 612(a)(23).

(B) RIGHTS OF LOCAL EDUCATIONAL AGENCY- Nothing in this paragraph shall be construed to require a local educational agency to coordinate with the National Instructional Materials Access Center. If a local educational agency chooses not to coordinate with the National Instructional Materials Access Center, the local educational agency shall provide an assurance to the State educational agency that the local educational agency will provide instructional materials to blind persons or other persons with print disabilities in a timely manner.

(7) INFORMATION FOR STATE EDUCATIONAL AGENCY- The local educational agency shall provide the State educational agency with information necessary to enable the State educational agency to carry out its duties under this part, including, with respect to paragraphs (15) and (16) of section 612(a), information relating to the performance of children with disabilities participating in programs carried out under this part.

(8) PUBLIC INFORMATION- The local educational agency shall make available to parents of children with disabilities and to the general public all documents relating to the eligibility of such agency under this part.

(9) RECORDS REGARDING MIGRATORY CHILDREN WITH DISABILITIES- The local educational agency shall cooperate in the Secretary's efforts under section 1308 of the Elementary and Secondary Education Act of 1965 to ensure the linkage of records pertaining to migratory children with a disability for the purpose of electronically exchanging, among the States, health and educational information regarding such children.

(b) EXCEPTION FOR PRIOR LOCAL PLANS-

(1) IN GENERAL- If a local educational agency or State agency has on file with the State educational agency policies and procedures that demonstrate that such local educational agency, or such State agency, as the case may be, meets any requirement of subsection (a), including any policies and procedures filed under this part as in effect before the effective date of the Individuals with Disabilities Education Improvement Act of 2004, the State educational agency shall consider such local educational agency or State agency, as the case may be, to have met such requirement for purposes of receiving assistance under this part.

(2) MODIFICATION MADE BY LOCAL EDUCATIONAL AGENCY- Subject to paragraph (3), an application submitted by a local educational agency in accordance with this section shall remain in effect until the local educational agency submits to the State educational agency such modifications as the local educational agency determines necessary.

(3) MODIFICATIONS REQUIRED BY STATE EDUCATIONAL AGENCY- If, after the effective date of the Individuals with Disabilities Education Improvement Act of 2004, the provisions of this title are amended (or the regulations developed to carry out this title are amended), there is a new interpretation of this title by Federal or State courts, or there is an official finding of noncompliance with Federal or State law or regulations, then the State educational agency may require a local educational agency to modify its application only to the extent necessary to ensure the local educational agency's compliance with this part or State law.

(c) NOTIFICATION OF LOCAL EDUCATIONAL AGENCY OR STATE AGENCY IN CASE OF INELIGIBILITY- If the State educational agency determines that a local educational agency or State agency is not eligible under this section, then the State educational agency shall notify the local educational agency or State agency, as the case may be, of that determination and shall provide such local educational agency or State agency with reasonable notice and an opportunity for a hearing.

(d) LOCAL EDUCATIONAL AGENCY COMPLIANCE-

(1) IN GENERAL- If the State educational agency, after reasonable notice and an opportunity for a hearing, finds that a local educational agency or State agency that has been determined to be eligible under this

section is failing to comply with any requirement described in subsection (a), the State educational agency shall reduce or shall not provide any further payments to the local educational agency or State agency until the State educational agency is satisfied that the local educational agency or State agency, as the case may be, is complying with that requirement.

(2) ADDITIONAL REQUIREMENT- Any State agency or local educational agency in receipt of a notice described in paragraph (1) shall, by means of public notice, take such measures as may be necessary to bring the pendency of an action pursuant to this subsection to the attention of the public within the jurisdiction of such agency.

(3) CONSIDERATION- In carrying out its responsibilities under paragraph (1), the State educational agency shall consider any decision made in a hearing held under section 615 that is adverse to the local educational agency or State agency involved in that decision.

(e) JOINT ESTABLISHMENT OF ELIGIBILITY-

(1) JOINT ESTABLISHMENT-

(A) IN GENERAL- A State educational agency may require a local educational agency to establish its eligibility jointly with another local educational agency if the State educational agency determines that the local educational agency will be ineligible under this section because the local educational agency will not be able to establish and maintain programs of sufficient size and scope to effectively meet the needs of children with disabilities.

(B) CHARTER SCHOOL EXCEPTION- A State educational agency may not require a charter school that is a local educational agency to jointly establish its eligibility under subparagraph (A) unless the charter school is explicitly permitted to do so under the State's charter school law.

(2) AMOUNT OF PAYMENTS- If a State educational agency requires the joint establishment of eligibility under paragraph (1), the total amount of funds made available to the affected local educational agencies shall be equal to the sum of the payments that each such local educational agency would have received under section 611(f) if such agencies were eligible for such payments.

(3) REQUIREMENTS- Local educational agencies that establish joint eligibility under this subsection shall—

(A) adopt policies and procedures that are consistent with the State's policies and procedures under section 612(a); and

(B) be jointly responsible for implementing programs that receive assistance under this part.

(4) REQUIREMENTS FOR EDUCATIONAL SERVICE AGENCIES-

(A) IN GENERAL- If an educational service agency is required by State law to carry out programs under this part, the joint responsibilities given to local educational agencies under this subsection shall—

(i) not apply to the administration and disbursement of any payments received by that educational service agency; and

(ii) be carried out only by that educational service agency.

(B) ADDITIONAL REQUIREMENT- Notwithstanding any other provision of this subsection, an educational service agency shall provide for the education of children with disabilities in the least restrictive environment, as required by section 612(a)(5).

(f) EARLY INTERVENING SERVICES-

(1) IN GENERAL- A local educational agency may not use more than 15 percent of the amount such agency receives under this part for any fiscal year, less any amount reduced by the agency pursuant to subsection (a)(2)(C), if any, in combination with other amounts (which may include amounts other than education funds), to develop and implement coordinated, early intervening services, which may include interagency financing structures, for students in kindergarten through grade 12 (with a particular emphasis on students in kindergarten through grade 3) who have not been identified as needing special education or related services but who need additional academic and behavioral support to succeed in a general education environment.

(2) ACTIVITIES- In implementing coordinated, early intervening services under this subsection, a local educational agency may carry out activities that include—

(A) professional development (which may be provided by entities other than local educational agencies) for teachers and other school staff to enable such personnel to deliver scientifically based academic instruction and behavioral interventions, including scientifically based literacy instruction, and, where appropriate, instruction on the use of adaptive and instructional software; and

(B) providing educational and behavioral evaluations, services, and supports, including scientifically based literacy instruction.

(3) CONSTRUCTION- Nothing in this subsection shall be construed to limit or create

a right to a free appropriate public education under this part.

(4) REPORTING- Each local educational agency that develops and maintains coordinated, early intervening services under this subsection shall annually report to the State educational agency on—

(A) the number of students served under this subsection; and

(B) the number of students served under this subsection who subsequently receive special education and related services under this title during the preceding 2-year period.

(5) COORDINATION WITH ELEMENTARY AND SECONDARY EDUCATION ACT OF 1965- Funds made available to carry out this subsection may be used to carry out coordinated, early intervening services aligned with activities funded by, and carried out under, the Elementary and Secondary Education Act of 1965 if such funds are used to supplement, and not supplant, funds made available under the Elementary and Secondary Education Act of 1965 for the activities and services assisted under this subsection.

(g) DIRECT SERVICES BY THE STATE EDUCATIONAL AGENCY-

(1) IN GENERAL- A State educational agency shall use the payments that would otherwise have been available to a local educational agency or to a State agency to provide special education and related services directly to children with disabilities residing in the area served by that local educational agency, or for whom that State agency is responsible, if the State educational agency determines that the local educational agency or State agency, as the case may be—

(A) has not provided the information needed to establish the eligibility of such local educational agency or State agency under this section;

(B) is unable to establish and maintain programs of free appropriate public education that meet the requirements of subsection (a);

(C) is unable or unwilling to be consolidated with 1 or more local educational agencies in order to establish and maintain such programs; or

(D) has 1 or more children with disabilities who can best be served by a regional or State program or service delivery system designed to meet the needs of such children.

(2) MANNER AND LOCATION OF EDUCATION AND SERVICES- The State educational agency may provide special education and related services under paragraph (1) in such manner and at such locations (including regional or State centers) as the State educational agency considers appropriate. Such education and services shall be provided in accordance with this part.

(h) STATE AGENCY ELIGIBILITY- Any State agency that desires to receive a subgrant for any fiscal year under section 611(f) shall demonstrate to the satisfaction of the State educational agency that—

(1) all children with disabilities who are participating in programs and projects funded under this part receive a free appropriate public education, and that those children and their parents are provided all the rights and procedural safeguards described in this part; and

(2) the agency meets such other conditions of this section as the Secretary determines to be appropriate.

(i) DISCIPLINARY INFORMATION- The State may require that a local educational agency include in the records of a child with a disability a statement of any current or previous disciplinary action that has been taken against the child and transmit such statement to the same extent that such disciplinary information is included in, and transmitted with, the student records of nondisabled children. The statement may include a description of any behavior engaged in by the child that required disciplinary action, a description of the disciplinary action taken, and any other information that is relevant to the safety of the child and other individuals involved with the child. If the State adopts such a policy, and the child transfers from 1 school to another, the transmission of any of the child's records shall include both the child's current individualized education program and any such statement of current or previous disciplinary action that has been taken against the child.

(j) STATE AGENCY FLEXIBILITY-

(1) ADJUSTMENT TO STATE FISCAL EFFORT IN CERTAIN FISCAL YEARS- For any fiscal year for which the allotment received by a State under section 611 exceeds the amount the State received for the previous fiscal year and if the State in school year 2003-2004 or any subsequent school year pays or reimburses all local educational agencies within the State from State revenue 100 percent of the non-Federal share of the costs of special education and related services, the State educational agency, notwithstanding paragraphs (17) and (18) of section 612(a) and section 612(b), may reduce the level of expenditures from State sources for the

education of children with disabilities by not more than 50 percent of the amount of such excess.

(2) PROHIBITION- Notwithstanding paragraph (1), if the Secretary determines that a State educational agency is unable to establish, maintain, or oversee programs of free appropriate public education that meet the requirements of this part, or that the State needs assistance, intervention, or substantial intervention under section 616(d)(2)(A), the Secretary shall prohibit the State educational agency from exercising the authority in paragraph (1).

(3) EDUCATION ACTIVITIES- If a State educational agency exercises the authority under paragraph (1), the agency shall use funds from State sources, in an amount equal to the amount of the reduction under paragraph (1), to support activities authorized under the Elementary and Secondary Education Act of 1965 or to support need based student or teacher higher education programs.

(4) REPORT- For each fiscal year for which a State educational agency exercises the authority under paragraph (1), the State educational agency shall report to the Secretary the amount of expenditures reduced pursuant to such paragraph and the activities that were funded pursuant to paragraph (3).

(5) LIMITATION- Notwithstanding paragraph (1), a State educational agency may not reduce the level of expenditures described in paragraph (1) if any local educational agency in the State would, as a result of such reduction, receive less than 100 percent of the amount necessary to ensure that all children with disabilities served by the local educational agency receive a free appropriate public education from the combination of Federal funds received under this title and State funds received from the State educational agency.

SEC. 614. EVALUATIONS, ELIGIBILITY DETERMINATIONS, INDIVIDUALIZED EDUCATION PROGRAMS, AND EDUCATIONAL PLACEMENTS.

(a) EVALUATIONS, PARENTAL CONSENT, AND REEVALUATIONS-

(1) INITIAL EVALUATIONS-

(A) IN GENERAL- A State educational agency, other State agency, or local educational agency shall conduct a full and individual initial evaluation in accordance with this paragraph and subsection (b), before the initial provision of special education and related services to a child with a disability under this part.

(B) REQUEST FOR INITIAL EVALUATION- Consistent with subparagraph (D), either a parent of a child, or a State educational agency, other State agency, or local educational agency may initiate a request for an initial evaluation to determine if the child is a child with a disability.

(C) PROCEDURES-

(i) IN GENERAL- Such initial evaluation shall consist of procedures—

(I) to determine whether a child is a child with a disability (as defined in section 602) within 60 days of receiving parental consent for the evaluation, or, if the State establishes a timeframe within which the evaluation must be conducted, within such timeframe; and

(II) to determine the educational needs of such child.

(ii) EXCEPTION- The relevant timeframe in clause (i)(I) shall not apply to a local educational agency if—

(I) a child enrolls in a school served by the local educational agency after the relevant timeframe in clause (i)(I) has begun and prior to a determination by the child's previous local educational agency as to whether the child is a child with a disability (as defined in section 602), but only if the subsequent local educational agency is making sufficient progress to ensure a prompt completion of the evaluation, and the parent and subsequent local educational agency agree to a specific time when the evaluation will be completed; or

(II) the parent of a child repeatedly fails or refuses to produce the child for the evaluation.

(D) PARENTAL CONSENT-

(i) IN GENERAL-

(I) CONSENT FOR INITIAL EVALUATION- The agency proposing to conduct an initial evaluation to determine if the child qualifies as a child with a disability as defined in section 602 shall obtain informed consent from the parent of such child before conducting the evaluation. Parental consent for evaluation shall not be construed as consent for placement for receipt of special education and related services.

(II) CONSENT FOR SERVICES- An agency that is responsible for making a free appropriate public education available to a child with a disability under this part shall seek to obtain informed consent from the parent of such child before providing special education and related services to the child.

(ii) ABSENCE OF CONSENT-

(I) FOR INITIAL EVALUATION- If the

parent of such child does not provide consent for an initial evaluation under clause (i)(I), or the parent fails to respond to a request to provide the consent, the local educational agency may pursue the initial evaluation of the child by utilizing the procedures described in section 615, except to the extent inconsistent with State law relating to such parental consent.

(II) FOR SERVICES- If the parent of such child refuses to consent to services under clause (i)(II), the local educational agency shall not provide special education and related services to the child by utilizing the procedures described in section 615.

(III) EFFECT ON AGENCY OBLIGATIONS- If the parent of such child refuses to consent to the receipt of special education and related services, or the parent fails to respond to a request to provide such consent—

(aa) the local educational agency shall not be considered to be in violation of the requirement to make available a free appropriate public education to the child for the failure to provide such child with the special education and related services for which the local educational agency requests such consent; and

(bb) the local educational agency shall not be required to convene an IEP meeting or develop an IEP under this section for the child for the special education and related services for which the local educational agency requests such consent.

(iii) CONSENT FOR WARDS OF THE STATE-

(I) IN GENERAL- If the child is a ward of the State and is not residing with the child's parent, the agency shall make reasonable efforts to obtain the informed consent from the parent (as defined in section 602) of the child for an initial evaluation to determine whether the child is a child with a disability.

(II) EXCEPTION- The agency shall not be required to obtain informed consent from the parent of a child for an initial evaluation to determine whether the child is a child with a disability if—

(aa) despite reasonable efforts to do so, the agency cannot discover the whereabouts of the parent of the child;

(bb) the rights of the parents of the child have been terminated in accordance with State law; or

(cc) the rights of the parent to make educational decisions have been subrogated by a judge in accordance with State law and consent for an initial evaluation has been given

by an individual appointed by the judge to represent the child.

(E) RULE OF CONSTRUCTION- The screening of a student by a teacher or specialist to determine appropriate instructional strategies for curriculum implementation shall not be considered to be an evaluation for eligibility for special education and related services.

(2) REEVALUATIONS-

(A) IN GENERAL- A local educational agency shall ensure that a reevaluation of each child with a disability is conducted in accordance with subsections (b) and (c)—

(i) if the local educational agency determines that the educational or related services needs, including improved academic achievement and functional performance, of the child warrant a reevaluation; or

(ii) if the child's parents or teacher requests a reevaluation.

(B) LIMITATION- A reevaluation conducted under subparagraph (A) shall occur—

(i) not more frequently than once a year, unless the parent and the local educational agency agree otherwise; and

(ii) at least once every 3 years, unless the parent and the local educational agency agree that a reevaluation is unnecessary.

(b) EVALUATION PROCEDURES-

(1) NOTICE- The local educational agency shall provide notice to the parents of a child with a disability, in accordance with subsections (b)(3), (b)(4), and (c) of section 615, that describes any evaluation procedures such agency proposes to conduct.

(2) CONDUCT OF EVALUATION- In conducting the evaluation, the local educational agency shall—

(A) use a variety of assessment tools and strategies to gather relevant functional, developmental, and academic information, including information provided by the parent, that may assist in determining—

(i) whether the child is a child with a disability; and

(ii) the content of the child's individualized education program, including information related to enabling the child to be involved in and progress in the general education curriculum, or, for preschool children, to participate in appropriate activities;

(B) not use any single measure or assessment as the sole criterion for determining whether a child is a child with a disability or determining an appropriate educational program for the child; and

(C) use technically sound instruments that

may assess the relative contribution of cognitive and behavioral factors, in addition to physical or developmental factors.

(3) ADDITIONAL REQUIREMENTS- Each local educational agency shall ensure that—

(A) assessments and other evaluation materials used to assess a child under this section—

(i) are selected and administered so as not to be discriminatory on a racial or cultural basis;

(ii) are provided and administered in the language and form most likely to yield accurate information on what the child knows and can do academically, developmentally, and functionally, unless it is not feasible to so provide or administer;

(iii) are used for purposes for which the assessments or measures are valid and reliable;

(iv) are administered by trained and knowledgeable personnel; and

(v) are administered in accordance with any instructions provided by the producer of such assessments;

(B) the child is assessed in all areas of suspected disability;

(C) assessment tools and strategies that provide relevant information that directly assists persons in determining the educational needs of the child are provided; and

(D) assessments of children with disabilities who transfer from 1 school district to another school district in the same academic year are coordinated with such children's prior and subsequent schools, as necessary and as expeditiously as possible, to ensure prompt completion of full evaluations.

(4) DETERMINATION OF ELIGIBILITY AND EDUCATIONAL NEED- Upon completion of the administration of assessments and other evaluation measures—

(A) the determination of whether the child is a child with a disability as defined in section 602(3) and the educational needs of the child shall be made by a team of qualified professionals and the parent of the child in accordance with paragraph (5); and

(B) a copy of the evaluation report and the documentation of determination of eligibility shall be given to the parent.

(5) SPECIAL RULE FOR ELIGIBILITY DETERMINATION- In making a determination of eligibility under paragraph (4)(A), a child shall not be determined to be a child with a disability if the determinant factor for such determination is—

(A) lack of appropriate instruction in reading, including in the essential components

of reading instruction (as defined in section 1208(3) of the Elementary and Secondary Education Act of 1965);

(B) lack of instruction in math; or

(C) limited English proficiency.

(6) SPECIFIC LEARNING DISABILITIES-

(A) IN GENERAL- Notwithstanding section 607(b), when determining whether a child has a specific learning disability as defined in section 602, a local educational agency shall not be required to take into consideration whether a child has a severe discrepancy between achievement and intellectual ability in oral expression, listening comprehension, written expression, basic reading skill, reading comprehension, mathematical calculation, or mathematical reasoning.

(B) ADDITIONAL AUTHORITY- In determining whether a child has a specific learning disability, a local educational agency may use a process that determines if the child responds to scientific, research-based intervention as a part of the evaluation procedures described in paragraphs (2) and (3).

(c) ADDITIONAL REQUIREMENTS FOR EVALUATION AND REEVALUATIONS-

(1) REVIEW OF EXISTING EVALUATION DATA- As part of an initial evaluation (if appropriate) and as part of any reevaluation under this section, the IEP Team and other qualified professionals, as appropriate, shall—

(A) review existing evaluation data on the child, including—

(i) evaluations and information provided by the parents of the child;

(ii) current classroom-based, local, or State assessments, and classroom-based observations; and

(iii) observations by teachers and related services providers; and

(B) on the basis of that review, and input from the child's parents, identify what additional data, if any, are needed to determine—

(i) whether the child is a child with a disability as defined in section 602(3), and the educational needs of the child, or, in case of a reevaluation of a child, whether the child continues to have such a disability and such educational needs;

(ii) the present levels of academic achievement and related developmental needs of the child;

(iii) whether the child needs special education and related services, or in the case of a reevaluation of a child, whether the child continues to need special education and related services; and

(iv) whether any additions or modifications to the special education and related services are needed to enable the child to meet the measurable annual goals set out in the individualized education program of the child and to participate, as appropriate, in the general education curriculum.

(2) SOURCE OF DATA- The local educational agency shall administer such assessments and other evaluation measures as may be needed to produce the data identified by the IEP Team under paragraph (1)(B).

(3) PARENTAL CONSENT- Each local educational agency shall obtain informed parental consent, in accordance with subsection (a)(1)(D), prior to conducting any reevaluation of a child with a disability, except that such informed parental consent need not be obtained if the local educational agency can demonstrate that it had taken reasonable measures to obtain such consent and the child's parent has failed to respond.

(4) REQUIREMENTS IF ADDITIONAL DATA ARE NOT NEEDED- If the IEP Team and other qualified professionals, as appropriate, determine that no additional data are needed to determine whether the child continues to be a child with a disability and to determine the child's educational needs, the local educational agency—

(A) shall notify the child's parents of—

(i) that determination and the reasons for the determination; and

(ii) the right of such parents to request an assessment to determine whether the child continues to be a child with a disability and to determine the child's educational needs; and

(B) shall not be required to conduct such an assessment unless requested to by the child's parents.

(5) EVALUATIONS BEFORE CHANGE IN ELIGIBILITY-

(A) IN GENERAL- Except as provided in subparagraph (B), a local educational agency shall evaluate a child with a disability in accordance with this section before determining that the child is no longer a child with a disability.

(B) EXCEPTION-

(i) IN GENERAL- The evaluation described in subparagraph (A) shall not be required before the termination of a child's eligibility under this part due to graduation from secondary school with a regular diploma, or due to exceeding the age eligibility for a free appropriate public education under State law.

(ii) SUMMARY OF PERFORMANCE-

For a child whose eligibility under this part terminates under circumstances described in clause (i), a local educational agency shall provide the child with a summary of the child's academic achievement and functional performance, which shall include recommendations on how to assist the child in meeting the child's postsecondary goals.

(d) INDIVIDUALIZED EDUCATION PROGRAMS-

(1) DEFINITIONS- In this title:

(A) INDIVIDUALIZED EDUCATION PROGRAM-

(i) IN GENERAL- The term 'individualized education program' or 'IEP' means a written statement for each child with a disability that is developed, reviewed, and revised in accordance with this section and that includes—

(I) a statement of the child's present levels of academic achievement and functional performance, including—

(aa) how the child's disability affects the child's involvement and progress in the general education curriculum;

(bb) for preschool children, as appropriate, how the disability affects the child's participation in appropriate activities; and

(cc) for children with disabilities who take alternate assessments aligned to alternate achievement standards, a description of benchmarks or short-term objectives;

(II) a statement of measurable annual goals, including academic and functional goals, designed to—

(aa) meet the child's needs that result from the child's disability to enable the child to be involved in and make progress in the general education curriculum; and

(bb) meet each of the child's other educational needs that result from the child's disability;

(III) a description of how the child's progress toward meeting the annual goals described in subclause (II) will be measured and when periodic reports on the progress the child is making toward meeting the annual goals (such as through the use of quarterly or other periodic reports, concurrent with the issuance of report cards) will be provided;

(IV) a statement of the special education and related services and supplementary aids and services, based on peer-reviewed research to the extent practicable, to be provided to the child, or on behalf of the child, and a statement of the program modifications or supports for school personnel that will be provided for the child—

(aa) to advance appropriately toward

attaining the annual goals;

(bb) to be involved in and make progress in the general education curriculum in accordance with subclause (I) and to participate in extracurricular and other nonacademic activities; and

(cc) to be educated and participate with other children with disabilities and nondisabled children in the activities described in this subparagraph;

(V) an explanation of the extent, if any, to which the child will not participate with nondisabled children in the regular class and in the activities described in subclause (IV)(cc);

(VI)(aa) a statement of any individual appropriate accommodations that are necessary to measure the academic achievement and functional performance of the child on State and districtwide assessments consistent with section 612(a)(16)(A); and

(bb) if the IEP Team determines that the child shall take an alternate assessment on a particular State or districtwide assessment of student achievement, a statement of why—

(AA) the child cannot participate in the regular assessment; and

(BB) the particular alternate assessment selected is appropriate for the child;

(VII) the projected date for the beginning of the services and modifications described in subclause (IV), and the anticipated frequency, location, and duration of those services and modifications; and

(VIII) beginning not later than the first IEP to be in effect when the child is 16, and updated annually thereafter—

(aa) appropriate measurable postsecondary goals based upon age appropriate transition assessments related to training, education, employment, and, where appropriate, independent living skills;

(bb) the transition services (including courses of study) needed to assist the child in reaching those goals; and

(cc) beginning not later than 1 year before the child reaches the age of majority under State law, a statement that the child has been informed of the child's rights under this title, if any, that will transfer to the child on reaching the age of majority under section 615(m).

(ii) RULE OF CONSTRUCTION- Nothing in this section shall be construed to require—

(I) that additional information be included in a child's IEP beyond what is explicitly required in this section; and

(II) the IEP Team to include information under 1 component of a child's IEP that is already contained under another component of such IEP.

(B) INDIVIDUALIZED EDUCATION PROGRAM TEAM- The term 'individualized education program team' or 'IEP Team' means a group of individuals composed of—

(i) the parents of a child with a disability;

(ii) not less than 1 regular education teacher of such child (if the child is, or may be, participating in the regular education environment);

(iii) not less than 1 special education teacher, or where appropriate, not less than 1 special education provider of such child;

(iv) a representative of the local educational agency who—

(I) is qualified to provide, or supervise the provision of, specially designed instruction to meet the unique needs of children with disabilities;

(II) is knowledgeable about the general education curriculum; and

(III) is knowledgeable about the availability of resources of the local educational agency;

(v) an individual who can interpret the instructional implications of evaluation results, who may be a member of the team described in clauses (ii) through (vi);

(vi) at the discretion of the parent or the agency, other individuals who have knowledge or special expertise regarding the child, including related services personnel as appropriate; and

(vii) whenever appropriate, the child with a disability.

(C) IEP TEAM ATTENDANCE-

(i) ATTENDANCE NOT NECESSARY- A member of the IEP Team shall not be required to attend an IEP meeting, in whole or in part, if the parent of a child with a disability and the local educational agency agree that the attendance of such member is not necessary because the member's area of the curriculum or related services is not being modified or discussed in the meeting.

(ii) EXCUSAL- A member of the IEP Team may be excused from attending an IEP meeting, in whole or in part, when the meeting involves a modification to or discussion of the member's area of the curriculum or related services, if—

(I) the parent and the local educational agency consent to the excusal; and

(II) the member submits, in writing to the parent and the IEP Team, input into the development of the IEP prior to the meeting.

(iii) WRITTEN AGREEMENT AND CONSENT REQUIRED- A parent's agreement under clause (i) and consent under clause (ii) shall be in writing.

(D) IEP TEAM TRANSITION- In the case

of a child who was previously served under part C, an invitation to the initial IEP meeting shall, at the request of the parent, be sent to the part C service coordinator or other representatives of the part C system to assist with the smooth transition of services.

(2) REQUIREMENT THAT PROGRAM BE IN EFFECT-

(A) IN GENERAL- At the beginning of each school year, each local educational agency, State educational agency, or other State agency, as the case may be, shall have in effect, for each child with a disability in the agency's jurisdiction, an individualized education program, as defined in paragraph (1)(A).

(B) PROGRAM FOR CHILD AGED 3 THROUGH 5- In the case of a child with a disability aged 3 through 5 (or, at the discretion of the State educational agency, a 2-year-old child with a disability who will turn age 3 during the school year), the IEP Team shall consider the individualized family service plan that contains the material described in section 636, and that is developed in accordance with this section, and the individualized family service plan may serve as the IEP of the child if using that plan as the IEP is—

(i) consistent with State policy; and

(ii) agreed to by the agency and the child's parents.

(C) PROGRAM FOR CHILDREN WHO TRANSFER SCHOOL DISTRICTS-

(i) IN GENERAL-

(I) TRANSFER WITHIN THE SAME STATE- In the case of a child with a disability who transfers school districts within the same academic year, who enrolls in a new school, and who had an IEP that was in effect in the same State, the local educational agency shall provide such child with a free appropriate public education, including services comparable to those described in the previously held IEP, in consultation with the parents until such time as the local educational agency adopts the previously held IEP or develops, adopts, and implements a new IEP that is consistent with Federal and State law.

(II) TRANSFER OUTSIDE STATE- In the case of a child with a disability who transfers school districts within the same academic year, who enrolls in a new school, and who had an IEP that was in effect in another State, the local educational agency shall provide such child with a free appropriate public education, including services comparable to those described in the previously held IEP, in consultation with the parents until such time as the local educational agency conducts an evaluation pursuant to subsection (a)(1), if determined to be necessary by such agency, and develops a new IEP, if appropriate, that is consistent with Federal and State law.

(ii) TRANSMITTAL OF RECORDS- To facilitate the transition for a child described in clause (i)—

(I) the new school in which the child enrolls shall take reasonable steps to promptly obtain the child's records, including the IEP and supporting documents and any other records relating to the provision of special education or related services to the child, from the previous school in which the child was enrolled, pursuant to section 99.31(a)(2) of title 34, Code of Federal Regulations; and

(II) the previous school in which the child was enrolled shall take reasonable steps to promptly respond to such request from the new school.

(3) DEVELOPMENT OF IEP-

(A) IN GENERAL- In developing each child's IEP, the IEP Team, subject to subparagraph (C), shall consider—

(i) the strengths of the child;

(ii) the concerns of the parents for enhancing the education of their child;

(iii) the results of the initial evaluation or most recent evaluation of the child; and

(iv) the academic, developmental, and functional needs of the child.

(B) CONSIDERATION OF SPECIAL FACTORS- The IEP Team shall—

(i) in the case of a child whose behavior impedes the child's learning or that of others, consider the use of positive behavioral interventions and supports, and other strategies, to address that behavior;

(ii) in the case of a child with limited English proficiency, consider the language needs of the child as such needs relate to the child's IEP;

(iii) in the case of a child who is blind or visually impaired, provide for instruction in Braille and the use of Braille unless the IEP Team determines, after an evaluation of the child's reading and writing skills, needs, and appropriate reading and writing media (including an evaluation of the child's future needs for instruction in Braille or the use of Braille), that instruction in Braille or the use of Braille is not appropriate for the child;

(iv) consider the communication needs of the child, and in the case of a child who is deaf or hard of hearing, consider the child's language and communication needs, opportunities for direct communications with peers and professional personnel in the child's language and communication mode, academic level, and full range of needs, including opportunities for direct instruction in the child's language and communication mode; and

(v) consider whether the child needs assistive technology devices and services.

(C) REQUIREMENT WITH RESPECT TO REGULAR EDUCATION TEACHER- A regular education teacher of the child, as a member of the IEP Team, shall, to the extent appropriate, participate in the development of the IEP of the child, including the determination of appropriate positive behavioral interventions and supports, and other strategies, and the determination of supplementary aids and services, program modifications, and support for school personnel consistent with paragraph (1)(A)(i)(IV).

(D) AGREEMENT- In making changes to a child's IEP after the annual IEP meeting for a school year, the parent of a child with a disability and the local educational agency may agree not to convene an IEP meeting for the purposes of making such changes, and instead may develop a written document to amend or modify the child's current IEP.

(E) CONSOLIDATION OF IEP TEAM MEETINGS- To the extent possible, the local educational agency shall encourage the consolidation of reevaluation meetings for the child and other IEP Team meetings for the child.

(F) AMENDMENTS- Changes to the IEP may be made either by the entire IEP Team or, as provided in subparagraph (D), by amending the IEP rather than by redrafting the entire IEP. Upon request, a parent shall be provided with a revised copy of the IEP with the amendments incorporated.

(4) REVIEW AND REVISION OF IEP-

(A) IN GENERAL- The local educational agency shall ensure that, subject to subparagraph (B), the IEP Team—

(i) reviews the child's IEP periodically, but not less frequently than annually, to determine whether the annual goals for the child are being achieved; and

(ii) revises the IEP as appropriate to address—

(I) any lack of expected progress toward the annual goals and in the general education curriculum, where appropriate;

(II) the results of any reevaluation conducted under this section;

(III) information about the child provided to, or by, the parents, as described in subsection (c)(1)(B);

(IV) the child's anticipated needs; or

(V) other matters.

(B) REQUIREMENT WITH RESPECT TO REGULAR EDUCATION TEACHER- A regular education teacher of the child, as a member of the IEP Team, shall, consistent with paragraph (1)(C), participate in the review and revision of the IEP of the child.

(5) MULTI-YEAR IEP DEMONSTRATION-

(A) PILOT PROGRAM-

(i) PURPOSE- The purpose of this paragraph is to provide an opportunity for States to allow parents and local educational agencies the opportunity for long-term planning by offering the option of developing a comprehensive multi-year IEP, not to exceed 3 years, that is designed to coincide with the natural transition points for the child.

(ii) AUTHORIZATION- In order to carry out the purpose of this paragraph, the Secretary is authorized to approve not more than 15 proposals from States to carry out the activity described in clause (i).

(iii) PROPOSAL-

(I) IN GENERAL- A State desiring to participate in the program under this paragraph shall submit a proposal to the Secretary at such time and in such manner as the Secretary may reasonably require.

(II) CONTENT- The proposal shall include—

(aa) assurances that the development of a multi-year IEP under this paragraph is optional for parents;

(bb) assurances that the parent is required to provide informed consent before a comprehensive multi-year IEP is developed;

(cc) a list of required elements for each multi-year IEP, including—

(AA) measurable goals pursuant to paragraph (1)(A)(i)(II), coinciding with natural transition points for the child, that will enable the child to be involved in and make progress in the general education curriculum and that will meet the child's other needs that result from the child's disability; and

(BB) measurable annual goals for determining progress toward meeting the goals described in subitem (AA); and

(dd) a description of the process for the review and revision of each multi-year IEP, including—

(AA) a review by the IEP Team of the child's multi-year IEP at each of the child's natural transition points;

(BB) in years other than a child's natural transition points, an annual review of the child's IEP to determine the child's current levels of progress and whether the annual goals for the child are being achieved, and a requirement to amend the IEP, as appropriate, to enable the child to continue to meet the measurable goals set out in the IEP;

(CC) if the IEP Team determines on the basis of a review that the child is not making sufficient progress toward the goals described in the multi-year IEP, a requirement that the local educational agency shall ensure that the IEP Team carries out a more thorough review of the IEP in accordance with paragraph (4) within 30 calendar days; and

(DD) at the request of the parent, a requirement that the IEP Team shall conduct a review of the child's multi-year IEP rather than or subsequent to an annual review.

(B) REPORT- Beginning 2 years after the date of enactment of the Individuals with Disabilities Education Improvement Act of 2004, the Secretary shall submit an annual report to the Committee on Education and the Workforce of the House of Representatives and the Committee on Health, Education, Labor, and Pensions of the Senate regarding the effectiveness of the program under this paragraph and any specific recommendations for broader implementation of such program, including—

(i) reducing—

(I) the paperwork burden on teachers, principals, administrators, and related service providers; and

(II) noninstructional time spent by teachers in complying with this part;

(ii) enhancing longer-term educational planning;

(iii) improving positive outcomes for children with disabilities;

(iv) promoting collaboration between IEP Team members; and

(v) ensuring satisfaction of family members.

(C) DEFINITION- In this paragraph, the term 'natural transition points' means those periods that are close in time to the transition of a child with a disability from preschool to elementary grades, from elementary grades to middle or junior high school grades, from middle or junior high school grades to secondary school grades, and from secondary school grades to post-secondary activities, but in no case a period longer than 3 years.

(6) FAILURE TO MEET TRANSITION OBJECTIVES- If a participating agency, other than the local educational agency, fails to provide the transition services described in the IEP in accordance with paragraph (1)(A)(i)(VIII), the local educational agency shall reconvene the IEP Team to identify alternative strategies to meet the transition objectives for the child set out in the IEP.

(7) CHILDREN WITH DISABILITIES IN ADULT PRISONS-

(A) IN GENERAL- The following requirements shall not apply to children with disabilities who are convicted as adults under State law and incarcerated in adult prisons:

(i) The requirements contained in section 612(a)(16) and paragraph (1)(A)(i)(VI) (relating to participation of children with disabilities in general assessments).

(ii) The requirements of items (aa) and (bb) of paragraph (1)(A)(i)(VIII) (relating to transition planning and transition services), do not apply with respect to such children whose eligibility under this part will end, because of such children's age, before such children will be released from prison.

(B) ADDITIONAL REQUIREMENT- If a child with a disability is convicted as an adult under State law and incarcerated in an adult prison, the child's IEP Team may modify the child's IEP or placement notwithstanding the requirements of sections 612(a)(5)(A) and paragraph (1)(A) if the State has demonstrated a bona fide security or compelling penological interest that cannot otherwise be accommodated.

(e) EDUCATIONAL PLACEMENTS- Each local educational agency or State educational agency shall ensure that the parents of each child with a disability are members of any group that makes decisions on the educational placement of their child.

(f) ALTERNATIVE MEANS OF MEETING PARTICIPATION- When conducting IEP team meetings and placement meetings pursuant to this section, section 615(e), and section 615(f)(1)(B), and carrying out administrative matters under section 615 (such as scheduling, exchange of witness lists, and status conferences), the parent of a child with a disability and a local educational agency may agree to use alternative means of meeting participation, such as video conferences and conference calls.

SEC. 615. PROCEDURAL SAFEGUARDS.

(a) ESTABLISHMENT OF PROCEDURES- Any State educational agency, State agency, or local educational agency that receives assistance under this part shall establish and maintain procedures in accordance with this section to ensure that children with disabilities and their parents are guaranteed procedural safeguards with respect to the provision of a free appropriate public education by such agencies.

(b) TYPES OF PROCEDURES- The procedures required by this section shall include the following:

(1) An opportunity for the parents of a child with a disability to examine all records relating to such child and to participate in meetings with respect to the identification, evaluation, and educational placement of the child, and the provision of a free appropriate public education to such child, and to obtain an independent educational evaluation of the child.

(2)(A) Procedures to protect the rights of the child whenever the parents of the child are not known, the agency cannot, after reasonable efforts, locate the parents, or the child is a ward of the State, including the assignment of an individual to act as a surrogate for the parents, which surrogate shall not be an employee of the State educational agency, the local educational agency, or any other agency that is involved in the education or care of the child. In the case of—

(i) a child who is a ward of the State, such surrogate may alternatively be appointed by the judge overseeing the child's care provided that the surrogate meets the requirements of this paragraph; and

(ii) an unaccompanied homeless youth as defined in section 725(6) of the McKinney-Vento Homeless Assistance Act (42 U.S.C. 11434a(6)), the local educational agency shall appoint a surrogate in accordance with this paragraph.

(B) The State shall make reasonable efforts to ensure the assignment of a surrogate not more than 30 days after there is a determination by the agency that the child needs a surrogate.

(3) Written prior notice to the parents of the child, in accordance with subsection (c)(1), whenever the local educational agency—

(A) proposes to initiate or change; or

(B) refuses to initiate or change,the identification, evaluation, or educational placement of the child, or the provision of a free appropriate public education to the child.

(4) Procedures designed to ensure that the notice required by paragraph (3) is in the native language of the parents, unless it clearly is not feasible to do so.

(5) An opportunity for mediation, in accordance with subsection (e).

(6) An opportunity for any party to present a complaint—

(A) with respect to any matter relating to the identification, evaluation, or educational placement of the child, or the provision of a free appropriate public education to such child; and

(B) which sets forth an alleged violation that occurred not more than 2 years before the date the parent or public agency knew or should have known about the alleged action that forms the basis of the complaint, or, if the State has an explicit time limitation for presenting such a complaint under this part, in such time as the State law allows, except that the exceptions to the timeline described in subsection (f)(3)(D) shall apply to the timeline described in this subparagraph.

(7)(A) Procedures that require either party, or the attorney representing a party, to provide due process complaint notice in accordance with subsection (c)(2) (which shall remain confidential)—

(i) to the other party, in the complaint filed under paragraph (6), and forward a copy of such notice to the State educational agency; and

(ii) that shall include—

(I) the name of the child, the address of the residence of the child (or available contact information in the case of a homeless child), and the name of the school the child is attending;

(II) in the case of a homeless child or youth (within the meaning of section 725(2) of the McKinney-Vento Homeless Assistance Act (42 U.S.C. 11434a(2)), available contact information for the child and the name of the school the child is attending;

(III) a description of the nature of the problem of the child relating to such proposed initiation or change, including facts relating to such problem; and

(IV) a proposed resolution of the problem to the extent known and available to the party at the time.

(B) A requirement that a party may not have a due process hearing until the party, or the attorney representing the party, files a notice that meets the requirements of subparagraph (A)(ii).

(8) Procedures that require the State educational agency to develop a model form to assist parents in filing a complaint and due process complaint notice in accordance with paragraphs (6) and (7), respectively.

(c) NOTIFICATION REQUIREMENTS-

(1) CONTENT OF PRIOR WRITTEN NOTICE- The notice required by subsection (b)(3) shall include—

(A) a description of the action proposed or refused by the agency;

(B) an explanation of why the agency proposes or refuses to take the action and a description of each evaluation procedure, assessment, record, or report the agency used as a basis for the proposed or refused action;

(C) a statement that the parents of a child with a disability have protection under the procedural safeguards of this part and, if this notice is not an initial referral for evaluation, the means by which a copy of a description of the procedural safeguards can be obtained;

(D) sources for parents to contact to obtain assistance in understanding the provisions of this part;

(E) a description of other options considered by the IEP Team and the reason why those options were rejected; and

(F) a description of the factors that are relevant to the agency's proposal or refusal.

(2) DUE PROCESS COMPLAINT NOTICE-

(A) COMPLAINT- The due process complaint notice required under subsection (b)(7)(A) shall be deemed to be sufficient unless the party receiving the notice notifies the hearing officer and the other party in writing that the receiving party believes the notice has not met the requirements of subsection (b)(7)(A).

(B) RESPONSE TO COMPLAINT-

(i) LOCAL EDUCATIONAL AGENCY RESPONSE-

(I) IN GENERAL- If the local educational agency has not sent a prior written notice to the parent regarding the subject matter contained in the parent's due process complaint notice, such local educational agency shall, within 10 days of receiving the complaint, send to the parent a response that shall include—

(aa) an explanation of why the agency proposed or refused to take the action raised in the complaint;

(bb) a description of other options that the IEP Team considered and the reasons why those options were rejected;

(cc) a description of each evaluation procedure, assessment, record, or report the agency used as the basis for the proposed or refused action; and

(dd) a description of the factors that are relevant to the agency's proposal or refusal.

(II) SUFFICIENCY- A response filed by a local educational agency pursuant to subclause (I) shall not be construed to preclude such local educational agency from asserting that the parent's due process complaint notice was insufficient where appropriate.

(ii) OTHER PARTY RESPONSE- Except as provided in clause (i), the non-complaining party shall, within 10 days of receiving the complaint, send to the complaint a response that specifically addresses the issues raised in the complaint.

(C) TIMING- The party providing a hearing officer notification under subparagraph (A) shall provide the notification within 15 days of receiving the complaint.

(D) DETERMINATION- Within 5 days of receipt of the notification provided under subparagraph (C), the hearing officer shall make a determination on the face of the notice of whether the notification meets the requirements of subsection (b)(7)(A), and shall immediately notify the parties in writing of such determination.

(E) AMENDED COMPLAINT NOTICE-

(i) IN GENERAL- A party may amend its due process complaint notice only if—

(I) the other party consents in writing to such amendment and is given the opportunity to resolve the complaint through a meeting held pursuant to subsection (f)(1)(B); or

(II) the hearing officer grants permission, except that the hearing officer may only grant such permission at any time not later than 5 days before a due process hearing occurs.

(ii) APPLICABLE TIMELINE- The applicable timeline for a due process hearing under this part shall recommence at the time the party files an amended notice, including the timeline under subsection (f)(1)(B).

(d) PROCEDURAL SAFEGUARDS NOTICE-

(1) IN GENERAL-

(A) COPY TO PARENTS- A copy of the procedural safeguards available to the parents of a child with a disability shall be given to the parents only 1 time a year, except that a copy also shall be given to the parents—

(i) upon initial referral or parental request for evaluation;

(ii) upon the first occurrence of the filing of a complaint under subsection (b)(6); and

(iii) upon request by a parent.

(B) INTERNET WEBSITE- A local educational agency may place a current copy of the procedural safeguards notice on its Internet website if such website exists.

(2) CONTENTS- The procedural safeguards notice shall include a full explanation of the procedural safeguards, written in the native language of the parents (unless it clearly is not feasible to do so) and written in an easily understandable manner,

available under this section and under regulations promulgated by the Secretary relating to—

(A) independent educational evaluation;

(B) prior written notice;

(C) parental consent;

(D) access to educational records;

(E) the opportunity to present and resolve complaints, including—

(i) the time period in which to make a complaint;

(ii) the opportunity for the agency to resolve the complaint; and

(iii) the availability of mediation;

(F) the child's placement during pendency of due process proceedings;

(G) procedures for students who are subject to placement in an interim alternative educational setting;

(H) requirements for unilateral placement by parents of children in private schools at public expense;

(I) due process hearings, including requirements for disclosure of evaluation results and recommendations;

(J) State-level appeals (if applicable in that State);

(K) civil actions, including the time period in which to file such actions; and

(L) attorneys' fees.

(e) MEDIATION-

(1) IN GENERAL- Any State educational agency or local educational agency that receives assistance under this part shall ensure that procedures are established and implemented to allow parties to disputes involving any matter, including matters arising prior to the filing of a complaint pursuant to subsection (b)(6), to resolve such disputes through a mediation process.

(2) REQUIREMENTS- Such procedures shall meet the following requirements:

(A) The procedures shall ensure that the mediation process—

(i) is voluntary on the part of the parties;

(ii) is not used to deny or delay a parent's right to a due process hearing under subsection (f), or to deny any other rights afforded under this part; and

(iii) is conducted by a qualified and impartial mediator who is trained in effective mediation techniques.

(B) OPPORTUNITY TO MEET WITH A DISINTERESTED PARTY- A local educational agency or a State agency may establish procedures to offer to parents and schools that choose not to use the mediation process, an opportunity to meet, at a time and location convenient to the parents, with a disinterested party who is under contract with—

(i) a parent training and information center or community parent resource center in the State established under section 671 or 672; or

(ii) an appropriate alternative dispute resolution entity, to encourage the use, and explain the benefits, of the mediation process to the parents.

(C) LIST OF QUALIFIED MEDIATORS- The State shall maintain a list of individuals who are qualified mediators and knowledgeable in laws and regulations relating to the provision of special education and related services.

(D) COSTS- The State shall bear the cost of the mediation process, including the costs of meetings described in subparagraph (B).

(E) SCHEDULING AND LOCATION- Each session in the mediation process shall be scheduled in a timely manner and shall be held in a location that is convenient to the parties to the dispute.

(F) WRITTEN AGREEMENT- In the case that a resolution is reached to resolve the complaint through the mediation process, the parties shall execute a legally binding agreement that sets forth such resolution and that—

(i) states that all discussions that occurred during the mediation process shall be confidential and may not be used as evidence in any subsequent due process hearing or civil proceeding;

(ii) is signed by both the parent and a representative of the agency who has the authority to bind such agency; and

(iii) is enforceable in any State court of competent jurisdiction or in a district court of the United States.

(G) MEDIATION DISCUSSIONS- Discussions that occur during the mediation process shall be confidential and may not be used as evidence in any subsequent due process hearing or civil proceeding.

(f) IMPARTIAL DUE PROCESS HEARING-

(1) IN GENERAL-

(A) HEARING- Whenever a complaint has been received under subsection (b)(6) or (k), the parents or the local educational agency involved in such complaint shall have an opportunity for an impartial due process hearing, which shall be conducted by the State educational agency or by the local educational agency, as determined by State law or by the State educational agency.

(B) RESOLUTION SESSION-

(i) PRELIMINARY MEETING- Prior to the opportunity for an impartial due process hearing under subparagraph (A), the local educational agency shall convene a meeting with the parents and the relevant member or members of the IEP Team who have specific knowledge of the facts identified in the complaint—

(I) within 15 days of receiving notice of the parents' complaint;

(II) which shall include a representative of the agency who has decisionmaking authority on behalf of such agency;

(III) which may not include an attorney of the local educational agency unless the parent is accompanied by an attorney; and

(IV) where the parents of the child discuss their complaint, and the facts that form the basis of the complaint, and the local educational agency is provided the opportunity to resolve the complaint, unless the parents and the local educational agency agree in writing to waive such meeting, or agree to use the mediation process described in subsection (e).

(ii) HEARING- If the local educational agency has not resolved the complaint to the satisfaction of the parents within 30 days of the receipt of the complaint, the due process hearing may occur, and all of the applicable timelines for a due process hearing under this part shall commence.

(iii) WRITTEN SETTLEMENT AGREEMENT- In the case that a resolution is reached to resolve the complaint at a meeting described in clause (i), the parties shall execute a legally binding agreement that is—

(I) signed by both the parent and a representative of the agency who has the authority to bind such agency; and

(II) enforceable in any State court of competent jurisdiction or in a district court of the United States.

(iv) REVIEW PERIOD- If the parties execute an agreement pursuant to clause (iii), a party may void such agreement within 3 business days of the agreement's execution.

(2) DISCLOSURE OF EVALUATIONS AND RECOMMENDATIONS-

(A) IN GENERAL- Not less than 5 business days prior to a hearing conducted pursuant to paragraph (1), each party shall disclose to all other parties all evaluations completed by that date, and recommendations based on the offering party's evaluations, that the party intends to use at the hearing.

(B) FAILURE TO DISCLOSE- A hearing officer may bar any party that fails to comply with subparagraph (A) from introducing the relevant evaluation or recommendation at the hearing without the consent of the other party.

(3) LIMITATIONS ON HEARING-

(A) PERSON CONDUCTING HEARING- A hearing officer conducting a hearing pursuant to paragraph (1)(A) shall, at a minimum—

(i) not be—

(I) an employee of the State educational agency or the local educational agency involved in the education or care of the child; or

(II) a person having a personal or professional interest that conflicts with the person's objectivity in the hearing;

(ii) possess knowledge of, and the ability to understand, the provisions of this title, Federal and State regulations pertaining to this title, and legal interpretations of this title by Federal and State courts;

(iii) possess the knowledge and ability to conduct hearings in accordance with appropriate, standard legal practice; and

(iv) possess the knowledge and ability to render and write decisions in accordance with appropriate, standard legal practice.

(B) SUBJECT MATTER OF HEARING- The party requesting the due process hearing shall not be allowed to raise issues at the due process hearing that were not raised in the notice filed under subsection (b)(7), unless the other party agrees otherwise.

(C) TIMELINE FOR REQUESTING HEARING- A parent or agency shall request an impartial due process hearing within 2 years of the date the parent or agency knew or should have known about the alleged action that forms the basis of the complaint, or, if the State has an explicit time limitation for requesting such a hearing under this part, in such time as the State law allows.

(D) EXCEPTIONS TO THE TIMELINE- The timeline described in subparagraph (C) shall not apply to a parent if the parent was prevented from requesting the hearing due to—

(i) specific misrepresentations by the local educational agency that it had resolved the problem forming the basis of the complaint; or

(ii) the local educational agency's withholding of information from the parent that was required under this part to be provided to the parent.

(E) DECISION OF HEARING OFFICER-

(i) IN GENERAL- Subject to clause (ii), a decision made by a hearing officer shall be made on substantive grounds based on a determination of whether the child received a free appropriate public education.

(ii) PROCEDURAL ISSUES- In matters

alleging a procedural violation, a hearing officer may find that a child did not receive a free appropriate public education only if the procedural inadequacies—

(I) impeded the child's right to a free appropriate public education;

(II) significantly impeded the parents' opportunity to participate in the decisionmaking process regarding the provision of a free appropriate public education to the parents' child; or

(III) caused a deprivation of educational benefits.

(iii) RULE OF CONSTRUCTION- Nothing in this subparagraph shall be construed to preclude a hearing officer from ordering a local educational agency to comply with procedural requirements under this section.

(F) RULE OF CONSTRUCTION- Nothing in this paragraph shall be construed to affect the right of a parent to file a complaint with the State educational agency.

(g) APPEAL-

(1) IN GENERAL- If the hearing required by subsection (f) is conducted by a local educational agency, any party aggrieved by the findings and decision rendered in such a hearing may appeal such findings and decision to the State educational agency.

(2) IMPARTIAL REVIEW AND INDEPENDENT DECISION- The State educational agency shall conduct an impartial review of the findings and decision appealed under paragraph (1). The officer conducting such review shall make an independent decision upon completion of such review.

(h) SAFEGUARDS- Any party to a hearing conducted pursuant to subsection (f) or (k), or an appeal conducted pursuant to subsection (g), shall be accorded—

(1) the right to be accompanied and advised by counsel and by individuals with special knowledge or training with respect to the problems of children with disabilities;

(2) the right to present evidence and confront, cross-examine, and compel the attendance of witnesses;

(3) the right to a written, or, at the option of the parents, electronic verbatim record of such hearing; and

(4) the right to written, or, at the option of the parents, electronic findings of fact and decisions, which findings and decisions—

(A) shall be made available to the public consistent with the requirements of section 617(b) (relating to the confidentiality of data, information, and records); and

(B) shall be transmitted to the advisory panel established pursuant to section 612(a)(21).

(i) ADMINISTRATIVE PROCEDURES-

(1) IN GENERAL-

(A) DECISION MADE IN HEARING- A decision made in a hearing conducted pursuant to subsection (f) or (k) shall be final, except that any party involved in such hearing may appeal such decision under the provisions of subsection (g) and paragraph (2).

(B) DECISION MADE AT APPEAL- A decision made under subsection (g) shall be final, except that any party may bring an action under paragraph (2).

(2) RIGHT TO BRING CIVIL ACTION-

(A) IN GENERAL- Any party aggrieved by the findings and decision made under subsection (f) or (k) who does not have the right to an appeal under subsection (g), and any party aggrieved by the findings and decision made under this subsection, shall have the right to bring a civil action with respect to the complaint presented pursuant to this section, which action may be brought in any State court of competent jurisdiction or in a district court of the United States, without regard to the amount in controversy.

(B) LIMITATION- The party bringing the action shall have 90 days from the date of the decision of the hearing officer to bring such an action, or, if the State has an explicit time limitation for bringing such action under this part, in such time as the State law allows.

(C) ADDITIONAL REQUIREMENTS- In any action brought under this paragraph, the court—

(i) shall receive the records of the administrative proceedings;

(ii) shall hear additional evidence at the request of a party; and

(iii) basing its decision on the preponderance of the evidence, shall grant such relief as the court determines is appropriate.

(3) JURISDICTION OF DISTRICT COURTS; ATTORNEYS' FEES-

(A) IN GENERAL- The district courts of the United States shall have jurisdiction of actions brought under this section without regard to the amount in controversy.

(B) AWARD OF ATTORNEYS' FEES-

(i) IN GENERAL- In any action or proceeding brought under this section, the court, in its discretion, may award reasonable attorneys' fees as part of the costs—

(I) to a prevailing party who is the parent of a child with a disability;

(II) to a prevailing party who is a State educational agency or local educational agency against the attorney of a parent who files a complaint or subsequent cause of action that is frivolous, unreasonable, or without foundation, or against the attorney of a parent who continued to litigate after the litigation clearly became frivolous, unreasonable, or without foundation; or

(III) to a prevailing State educational agency or local educational agency against the attorney of a parent, or against the parent, if the parent's complaint or subsequent cause of action was presented for any improper purpose, such as to harass, to cause unnecessary delay, or to needlessly increase the cost of litigation.

(ii) RULE OF CONSTRUCTION- Nothing in this subparagraph shall be construed to affect section 327 of the District of Columbia Appropriations Act, 2005.

(C) DETERMINATION OF AMOUNT OF ATTORNEYS' FEES- Fees awarded under this paragraph shall be based on rates prevailing in the community in which the action or proceeding arose for the kind and quality of services furnished. No bonus or multiplier may be used in calculating the fees awarded under this subsection.

(D) PROHIBITION OF ATTORNEYS' FEES AND RELATED COSTS FOR CERTAIN SERVICES-

(i) IN GENERAL- Attorneys' fees may not be awarded and related costs may not be reimbursed in any action or proceeding under this section for services performed subsequent to the time of a written offer of settlement to a parent if—

(I) the offer is made within the time prescribed by Rule 68 of the Federal Rules of Civil Procedure or, in the case of an administrative proceeding, at any time more than 10 days before the proceeding begins;

(II) the offer is not accepted within 10 days; and

(III) the court or administrative hearing officer finds that the relief finally obtained by the parents is not more favorable to the parents than the offer of settlement.

(ii) IEP TEAM MEETINGS- Attorneys' fees may not be awarded relating to any meeting of the IEP Team unless such meeting is convened as a result of an administrative proceeding or judicial action, or, at the discretion of the State, for a mediation described in subsection (e).

(iii) OPPORTUNITY TO RESOLVE COMPLAINTS- A meeting conducted pursuant to subsection (f)(1)(B)(i) shall not be considered—

(I) a meeting convened as a result of an administrative hearing or judicial action; or

(II) an administrative hearing or judicial action for purposes of this paragraph.

(E) EXCEPTION TO PROHIBITION ON ATTORNEYS' FEES AND RELATED COSTS- Notwithstanding subparagraph (D), an award of attorneys' fees and related costs may be made to a parent who is the prevailing party and who was substantially justified in rejecting the settlement offer.

(F) REDUCTION IN AMOUNT OF ATTORNEYS' FEES- Except as provided in subparagraph (G), whenever the court finds that—

(i) the parent, or the parent's attorney, during the course of the action or proceeding, unreasonably protracted the final resolution of the controversy;

(ii) the amount of the attorneys' fees otherwise authorized to be awarded unreasonably exceeds the hourly rate prevailing in the community for similar services by attorneys of reasonably comparable skill, reputation, and experience;

(iii) the time spent and legal services furnished were excessive considering the nature of the action or proceeding; or

(iv) the attorney representing the parent did not provide to the local educational agency the appropriate information in the notice of the complaint described in subsection (b)(7)(A), the court shall reduce, accordingly, the amount of the attorneys' fees awarded under this section.

(G) EXCEPTION TO REDUCTION IN AMOUNT OF ATTORNEYS' FEES- The provisions of subparagraph (F) shall not apply in any action or proceeding if the court finds that the State or local educational agency unreasonably protracted the final resolution of the action or proceeding or there was a violation of this section.

(j) MAINTENANCE OF CURRENT EDUCATIONAL PLACEMENT- Except as provided in subsection (k)(4), during the pendency of any proceedings conducted pursuant to this section, unless the State or local educational agency and the parents otherwise agree, the child shall remain in the then-current educational placement of the child, or, if applying for initial admission to a public school, shall, with the consent of the parents, be placed in the public school program until all such proceedings have been completed.

(k) PLACEMENT IN ALTERNATIVE EDUCATIONAL SETTING-

(1) AUTHORITY OF SCHOOL PERSONNEL-

(A) CASE-BY-CASE DETERMINATION- School personnel may consider any unique circumstances on a case-by-case basis when determining whether to order a change in placement for a child with a disability who violates a code of student conduct.

(B) AUTHORITY- School personnel under this subsection may remove a child with a disability who violates a code of student conduct from their current placement to an appropriate interim alternative educational setting, another setting, or suspension, for not more than 10 school days (to the extent such alternatives are applied to children without disabilities).

(C) ADDITIONAL AUTHORITY- If school personnel seek to order a change in placement that would exceed 10 school days and the behavior that gave rise to the violation of the school code is determined not to be a manifestation of the child's disability pursuant to subparagraph (E), the relevant disciplinary procedures applicable to children without disabilities may be applied to the child in the same manner and for the same duration in which the procedures would be applied to children without disabilities, except as provided in section 612(a)(1) although it may be provided in an interim alternative educational setting.

(D) SERVICES- A child with a disability who is removed from the child's current placement under subparagraph (G) (irrespective of whether the behavior is determined to be a manifestation of the child's disability) or subparagraph (C) shall—

(i) continue to receive educational services, as provided in section 612(a)(1), so as to enable the child to continue to participate in the general education curriculum, although in another setting, and to progress toward meeting the goals set out in the child's IEP; and

(ii) receive, as appropriate, a functional behavioral assessment, behavioral intervention services and modifications, that are designed to address the behavior violation so that it does not recur.

(E) MANIFESTATION DETERMINATION-

(i) IN GENERAL- Except as provided in subparagraph (B), within 10 school days of any decision to change the placement of a child with a disability because of a violation of a code of student conduct, the local educational agency, the parent, and relevant members of the IEP Team (as determined by the parent and the local educational agency) shall review all relevant information in the student's file, including the child's IEP, any teacher observations, and any relevant information provided by the parents to determine—

(I) if the conduct in question was caused by, or had a direct and substantial relationship to, the child's disability; or

(II) if the conduct in question was the direct result of the local educational agency's failure to implement the IEP.

(ii) MANIFESTATION- If the local educational agency, the parent, and relevant members of the IEP Team determine that either subclause (I) or (II) of clause (i) is applicable for the child, the conduct shall be determined to be a manifestation of the child's disability.

(F) DETERMINATION THAT BEHAVIOR WAS A MANIFESTATION- If the local educational agency, the parent, and relevant members of the IEP Team make the determination that the conduct was a manifestation of the child's disability, the IEP Team shall—

(i) conduct a functional behavioral assessment, and implement a behavioral intervention plan for such child, provided that the local educational agency had not conducted such assessment prior to such determination before the behavior that resulted in a change in placement described in subparagraph (C) or (G);

(ii) in the situation where a behavioral intervention plan has been developed, review the behavioral intervention plan if the child already has such a behavioral intervention plan, and modify it, as necessary, to address the behavior; and

(iii) except as provided in subparagraph (G), return the child to the placement from which the child was removed, unless the parent and the local educational agency agree to a change of placement as part of the modification of the behavioral intervention plan.

(G) SPECIAL CIRCUMSTANCES- School personnel may remove a student to an interim alternative educational setting for not more than 45 school days without regard to whether the behavior is determined to be a manifestation of the child's disability, in cases where a child—

(i) carries or possesses a weapon to or at school, on school premises, or to or at a school function under the jurisdiction of a State or local educational agency;

(ii) knowingly possesses or uses illegal drugs, or sells or solicits the sale of a controlled substance, while at school, on school premises, or at a school function under the jurisdiction of a State or local educational agency; or

(iii) has inflicted serious bodily injury upon another person while at school, on school premises, or at a school function under the jurisdiction of a State or local educational agency.

(H) NOTIFICATION- Not later than the date on which the decision to take disciplinary action is made, the local educational agency shall notify the parents of that decision, and of all procedural safeguards accorded under this section.

(2) DETERMINATION OF SETTING- The interim alternative educational setting in subparagraphs (C) and (G) of paragraph (1) shall be determined by the IEP Team.

(3) APPEAL-

(A) IN GENERAL- The parent of a child with a disability who disagrees with any decision regarding placement, or the manifestation determination under this subsection, or a local educational agency that believes that maintaining the current placement of the child is substantially likely to result in injury to the child or to others, may request a hearing.

(B) AUTHORITY OF HEARING OFFICER-

(i) IN GENERAL- A hearing officer shall hear, and make a determination regarding, an appeal requested under subparagraph (A).

(ii) CHANGE OF PLACEMENT ORDER- In making the determination under clause (i), the hearing officer may order a change in placement of a child with a disability. In such situations, the hearing officer may—

(I) return a child with a disability to the placement from which the child was removed; or

(II) order a change in placement of a child with a disability to an appropriate interim alternative educational setting for not more than 45 school days if the hearing officer determines that maintaining the current placement of such child is substantially likely to result in injury to the child or to others.

(4) PLACEMENT DURING APPEALS- When an appeal under paragraph (3) has been requested by either the parent or the local educational agency—

(A) the child shall remain in the interim alternative educational setting pending the decision of the hearing officer or until the expiration of the time period provided for in paragraph (1)(C), whichever occurs first, unless the parent and the State or local educational agency agree otherwise; and

(B) the State or local educational agency shall arrange for an expedited hearing, which shall occur within 20 school days of the date the hearing is requested and shall result in a determination within 10 school days after the hearing.

(5) PROTECTIONS FOR CHILDREN NOT YET ELIGIBLE FOR SPECIAL EDUCATION AND RELATED SERVICES-

(A) IN GENERAL- A child who has not been determined to be eligible for special education and related services under this part and who has engaged in behavior that violates a code of student conduct, may assert any of the protections provided for in this part if the local educational agency had knowledge (as determined in accordance with this paragraph) that the child was a child with a disability before the behavior that precipitated the disciplinary action occurred.

(B) BASIS OF KNOWLEDGE- A local educational agency shall be deemed to have knowledge that a child is a child with a disability if, before the behavior that precipitated the disciplinary action occurred—

(i) the parent of the child has expressed concern in writing to supervisory or administrative personnel of the appropriate educational agency, or a teacher of the child, that the child is in need of special education and related services;

(ii) the parent of the child has requested an evaluation of the child pursuant to section 614(a)(1)(B); or

(iii) the teacher of the child, or other personnel of the local educational agency, has expressed specific concerns about a pattern of behavior demonstrated by the child, directly to the director of special education of such agency or to other supervisory personnel of the agency.

(C) EXCEPTION- A local educational agency shall not be deemed to have knowledge that the child is a child with a disability if the parent of the child has not allowed an evaluation of the child pursuant to section 614 or has refused services under this part or the child has been evaluated and it was determined that the child was not a child with a disability under this part.

(D) CONDITIONS THAT APPLY IF NO BASIS OF KNOWLEDGE-

(i) IN GENERAL- If a local educational agency does not have knowledge that a child is a child with a disability (in accordance with subparagraph (B) or (C)) prior to taking disciplinary measures against the child, the child may be subjected to disciplinary measures applied to children without disabilities who engaged in comparable behaviors consistent with clause (ii).

(ii) LIMITATIONS- If a request is made for an evaluation of a child during the time period in which the child is subjected to disciplinary measures under this subsection, the evaluation shall be conducted in an expedited manner. If the child is determined to be a child with a disability, taking into consideration information from the evaluation conducted by the agency and information provided by the parents, the agency shall provide special education and related services in accordance with this part, except that, pending the results of the evaluation, the child shall remain in the educational placement determined by school authorities.

(6) REFERRAL TO AND ACTION BY LAW ENFORCEMENT AND JUDICIAL AUTHORITIES-

(A) RULE OF CONSTRUCTION- Nothing in this part shall be construed to prohibit an agency from reporting a crime committed by a child with a disability to appropriate authorities or to prevent State law enforcement and judicial authorities from exercising their responsibilities with regard to the application of Federal and State law to crimes committed by a child with a disability.

(B) TRANSMITTAL OF RECORDS- An agency reporting a crime committed by a child with a disability shall ensure that copies of the special education and disciplinary records of the child are transmitted for consideration by the appropriate authorities to whom the agency reports the crime.

(7) DEFINITIONS- In this subsection:

(A) CONTROLLED SUBSTANCE- The term 'controlled substance' means a drug or other substance identified under schedule I, II, III, IV, or V in section 202(c) of the Controlled Substances Act (21 U.S.C. 812(c)).

(B) ILLEGAL DRUG- The term 'illegal drug' means a controlled substance but does not include a controlled substance that is legally possessed or used under the supervision of a licensed health-care professional or that is legally possessed or used under any other authority under that Act or under any other provision of Federal law.

(C) WEAPON- The term 'weapon' has the meaning given the term 'dangerous weapon' under section 930(g)(2) of title 18, United States Code.

(D) SERIOUS BODILY INJURY- The term 'serious bodily injury' has the meaning given the term 'serious bodily injury' under paragraph (3) of subsection (h) of section 1365 of title 18, United States Code.

(l) RULE OF CONSTRUCTION- Nothing in this title shall be construed to restrict or limit the rights, procedures, and remedies available under the Constitution, the Americans with Disabilities Act of 1990, title V of the Rehabilitation Act of 1973, or other Federal laws protecting the rights of children with disabilities, except that before the filing of a civil action under such laws seeking relief that is also available under this part, the procedures under subsections (f) and (g) shall be exhausted to the same extent as would be required had the action been brought under this part.

(m) TRANSFER OF PARENTAL RIGHTS AT AGE OF MAJORITY-

(1) IN GENERAL- A State that receives amounts from a grant under this part may provide that, when a child with a disability reaches the age of majority under State law (except for a child with a disability who has been determined to be incompetent under State law)—

(A) the agency shall provide any notice required by this section to both the individual and the parents;

(B) all other rights accorded to parents under this part transfer to the child;

(C) the agency shall notify the individual and the parents of the transfer of rights; and

(D) all rights accorded to parents under this part transfer to children who are incarcerated in an adult or juvenile Federal, State, or local correctional institution.

(2) SPECIAL RULE- If, under State law, a child with a disability who has reached the age of majority under State law, who has not been determined to be incompetent, but who is determined not to have the ability to provide informed consent with respect to the educational program of the child, the State shall establish procedures for appointing the parent of the child, or if the parent is not available, another appropriate individual, to represent the educational interests of the child throughout the period of eligibility of the child under this part.

(n) ELECTRONIC MAIL- A parent of a child with a disability may elect to receive notices required under this section by an electronic mail (e-mail) communication, if the agency makes such option available.

(o) SEPARATE COMPLAINT- Nothing in this section shall be construed to preclude a parent from filing a separate due process complaint on an issue separate from a due process complaint already filed.

SEC. 616. MONITORING, TECHNICAL ASSISTANCE, AND ENFORCEMENT.

(a) FEDERAL AND STATE MONITORING-

(1) IN GENERAL- The Secretary shall—

(A) monitor implementation of this part

through—

(i) oversight of the exercise of general supervision by the States, as required in section 612(a)(11); and

(ii) the State performance plans, described in subsection (b);

(B) enforce this part in accordance with subsection (e); and

(C) require States to—

(i) monitor implementation of this part by local educational agencies; and

(ii) enforce this part in accordance with paragraph (3) and subsection (e).

(2) FOCUSED MONITORING- The primary focus of Federal and State monitoring activities described in paragraph (1) shall be on—

(A) improving educational results and functional outcomes for all children with disabilities; and

(B) ensuring that States meet the program requirements under this part, with a particular emphasis on those requirements that are most closely related to improving educational results for children with disabilities.

(3) MONITORING PRIORITIES- The Secretary shall monitor the States, and shall require each State to monitor the local educational agencies located in the State (except the State exercise of general supervisory responsibility), using quantifiable indicators in each of the following priority areas, and using such qualitative indicators as are needed to adequately measure performance in the following priority areas:

(A) Provision of a free appropriate public education in the least restrictive environment.

(B) State exercise of general supervisory authority, including child find, effective monitoring, the use of resolution sessions, mediation, voluntary binding arbitration, and a system of transition services as defined in sections 602(34) and 637(a)(9).

(C) Disproportionate representation of racial and ethnic groups in special education and related services, to the extent the representation is the result of inappropriate identification.

(4) PERMISSIVE AREAS OF REVIEW- The Secretary shall consider other relevant information and data, including data provided by States under section 618.

(b) STATE PERFORMANCE PLANS-

(1) PLAN-

(A) IN GENERAL- Not later than 1 year after the date of enactment of the Individuals with Disabilities Education Improvement Act of 2004, each State shall have in place a performance plan that evaluates that State's efforts to implement the requirements and purposes of this part and describes how the State will improve such implementation.

(B) SUBMISSION FOR APPROVAL- Each State shall submit the State's performance plan to the Secretary for approval in accordance with the approval process described in subsection (c).

(C) REVIEW- Each State shall review its State performance plan at least once every 6 years and submit any amendments to the Secretary.

(2) TARGETS-

(A) IN GENERAL- As a part of the State performance plan described under paragraph (1), each State shall establish measurable and rigorous targets for the indicators established under the priority areas described in subsection (a)(3).

(B) DATA COLLECTION-

(i) IN GENERAL- Each State shall collect valid and reliable information as needed to report annually to the Secretary on the priority areas described in subsection (a)(3).

(ii) RULE OF CONSTRUCTION- Nothing in this title shall be construed to authorize the development of a nationwide database of personally identifiable information on individuals involved in studies or other collections of data under this part.

(C) PUBLIC REPORTING AND PRIVACY-

(i) IN GENERAL- The State shall use the targets established in the plan and priority areas described in subsection (a)(3) to analyze the performance of each local educational agency in the State in implementing this part.

(ii) REPORT-

(I) PUBLIC REPORT- The State shall report annually to the public on the performance of each local educational agency located in the State on the targets in the State's performance plan. The State shall make the State's performance plan available through public means, including by posting on the website of the State educational agency, distribution to the media, and distribution through public agencies.

(II) STATE PERFORMANCE REPORT- The State shall report annually to the Secretary on the performance of the State under the State's performance plan.

(iii) PRIVACY- The State shall not report to the public or the Secretary any information on performance that would result in the disclosure of personally identifiable information about individual children or where the available data is insufficient to yield statistically reliable information.

(c) APPROVAL PROCESS-

(1) DEEMED APPROVAL- The Secretary shall review (including the specific provisions described in subsection (b)) each performance plan submitted by a State pursuant to subsection (b)(1)(B) and the plan shall be deemed to be approved by the Secretary unless the Secretary makes a written determination, prior to the expiration of the 120-day period beginning on the date on which the Secretary received the plan, that the plan does not meet the requirements of this section, including the specific provisions described in subsection (b).

(2) DISAPPROVAL- The Secretary shall not finally disapprove a performance plan, except after giving the State notice and an opportunity for a hearing.

(3) NOTIFICATION- If the Secretary finds that the plan does not meet the requirements, in whole or in part, of this section, the Secretary shall—

(A) give the State notice and an opportunity for a hearing; and

(B) notify the State of the finding, and in such notification shall—

(i) cite the specific provisions in the plan that do not meet the requirements; and

(ii) request additional information, only as to the provisions not meeting the requirements, needed for the plan to meet the requirements of this section.

(4) RESPONSE- If the State responds to the Secretary's notification described in paragraph (3)(B) during the 30-day period beginning on the date on which the State received the notification, and resubmits the plan with the requested information described in paragraph (3)(B)(ii), the Secretary shall approve or disapprove such plan prior to the later of—

(A) the expiration of the 30-day period beginning on the date on which the plan is resubmitted; or

(B) the expiration of the 120-day period described in paragraph (1).

(5) FAILURE TO RESPOND- If the State does not respond to the Secretary's notification described in paragraph (3)(B) during the 30-day period beginning on the date on which the State received the notification, such plan shall be deemed to be disapproved.

(d) SECRETARY'S REVIEW AND DETERMINATION-

(1) REVIEW- The Secretary shall annually review the State performance report submitted pursuant to subsection (b)(2)(C)(ii)(II) in accordance with this section.

(2) DETERMINATION-

(A) IN GENERAL- Based on the information provided by the State in the State performance report, information obtained through monitoring visits, and any other public information made available, the Secretary shall determine if the State—

(i) meets the requirements and purposes of this part;

(ii) needs assistance in implementing the requirements of this part;

(iii) needs intervention in implementing the requirements of this part; or

(iv) needs substantial intervention in implementing the requirements of this part.

(B) NOTICE AND OPPORTUNITY FOR A HEARING- For determinations made under clause (iii) or (iv) of subparagraph (A), the Secretary shall provide reasonable notice and an opportunity for a hearing on such determination.

(e) ENFORCEMENT-

(1) NEEDS ASSISTANCE- If the Secretary determines, for 2 consecutive years, that a State needs assistance under subsection (d)(2)(A)(ii) in implementing the requirements of this part, the Secretary shall take 1 or more of the following actions:

(A) Advise the State of available sources of technical assistance that may help the State address the areas in which the State needs assistance, which may include assistance from the Office of Special Education Programs, other offices of the Department of Education, other Federal agencies, technical assistance providers approved by the Secretary, and other federally funded nonprofit agencies, and require the State to work with appropriate entities. Such technical assistance may include—

(i) the provision of advice by experts to address the areas in which the State needs assistance, including explicit plans for addressing the area for concern within a specified period of time;

(ii) assistance in identifying and implementing professional development, instructional strategies, and methods of instruction that are based on scientifically based research;

(iii) designating and using distinguished superintendents, principals, special education administrators, special education teachers, and other teachers to provide advice, technical assistance, and support; and

(iv) devising additional approaches to providing technical assistance, such as collaborating with institutions of higher education, educational service agencies, national centers of technical assistance supported under part D, and private providers of scientifically based technical assistance.

(B) Direct the use of State-level funds under section 611(e) on the area or areas in which the State needs assistance.

(C) Identify the State as a high-risk grantee and impose special conditions on the State's grant under this part.

(2) NEEDS INTERVENTION- If the Secretary determines, for 3 or more consecutive years, that a State needs intervention under subsection (d)(2)(A)(iii) in implementing the requirements of this part, the following shall apply:

(A) The Secretary may take any of the actions described in paragraph (1).

(B) The Secretary shall take 1 or more of the following actions:

(i) Require the State to prepare a corrective action plan or improvement plan if the Secretary determines that the State should be able to correct the problem within 1 year.

(ii) Require the State to enter into a compliance agreement under section 457 of the General Education Provisions Act, if the Secretary has reason to believe that the State cannot correct the problem within 1 year.

(iii) For each year of the determination, withhold not less than 20 percent and not more than 50 percent of the State's funds under section 611(e), until the Secretary determines the State has sufficiently addressed the areas in which the State needs intervention.

(iv) Seek to recover funds under section 452 of the General Education Provisions Act.

(v) Withhold, in whole or in part, any further payments to the State under this part pursuant to paragraph (5).

(vi) Refer the matter for appropriate enforcement action, which may include referral to the Department of Justice.

(3) NEEDS SUBSTANTIAL INTERVENTION- Notwithstanding paragraph (1) or (2), at any time that the Secretary determines that a State needs substantial intervention in implementing the requirements of this part or that there is a substantial failure to comply with any condition of a State educational agency's or local educational agency's eligibility under this part, the Secretary shall take 1 or more of the following actions:

(A) Recover funds under section 452 of the General Education Provisions Act.

(B) Withhold, in whole or in part, any further payments to the State under this part.

(C) Refer the case to the Office of the Inspector General at the Department of Education.

(D) Refer the matter for appropriate enforcement action, which may include referral to the Department of Justice.

(4) OPPORTUNITY FOR HEARING-

(A) WITHHOLDING FUNDS- Prior to withholding any funds under this section, the Secretary shall provide reasonable notice and an opportunity for a hearing to the State educational agency involved.

(B) SUSPENSION- Pending the outcome of any hearing to withhold payments under subsection (b), the Secretary may suspend payments to a recipient, suspend the authority of the recipient to obligate funds under this part, or both, after such recipient has been given reasonable notice and an opportunity to show cause why future payments or authority to obligate funds under this part should not be suspended.

(5) REPORT TO CONGRESS- The Secretary shall report to the Committee on Education and the Workforce of the House of Representatives and the Committee on Health, Education, Labor, and Pensions of the Senate within 30 days of taking enforcement action pursuant to paragraph (1), (2), or (3), on the specific action taken and the reasons why enforcement action was taken.

(6) NATURE OF WITHHOLDING-

(A) LIMITATION- If the Secretary withholds further payments pursuant to paragraph (2) or (3), the Secretary may determine—

(i) that such withholding will be limited to programs or projects, or portions of programs or projects, that affected the Secretary's determination under subsection (d)(2); or

(ii) that the State educational agency shall not make further payments under this part to specified State agencies or local educational agencies that caused or were involved in the Secretary's determination under subsection (d)(2).

(B) WITHHOLDING UNTIL RECTIFIED- Until the Secretary is satisfied that the condition that caused the initial withholding has been substantially rectified—

(i) payments to the State under this part shall be withheld in whole or in part; and

(ii) payments by the State educational agency under this part shall be limited to State agencies and local educational agencies whose actions did not cause or were not involved in the Secretary's determination under subsection (d)(2), as the case may be.

(7) PUBLIC ATTENTION- Any State that has received notice under subsection (d)(2) shall, by means of a public notice, take such measures as may be necessary to bring the

pendency of an action pursuant to this subsection to the attention of the public within the State.

(8) JUDICIAL REVIEW-

(A) IN GENERAL- If any State is dissatisfied with the Secretary's action with respect to the eligibility of the State under section 612, such State may, not later than 60 days after notice of such action, file with the United States court of appeals for the circuit in which such State is located a petition for review of that action. A copy of the petition shall be transmitted by the clerk of the court to the Secretary. The Secretary thereupon shall file in the court the record of the proceedings upon which the Secretary's action was based, as provided in section 2112 of title 28, United States Code.

(B) JURISDICTION; REVIEW BY UNITED STATES SUPREME COURT- Upon the filing of such petition, the court shall have jurisdiction to affirm the action of the Secretary or to set it aside, in whole or in part. The judgment of the court shall be subject to review by the Supreme Court of the United States upon certiorari or certification as provided in section 1254 of title 28, United States Code.

(C) STANDARD OF REVIEW- The findings of fact by the Secretary, if supported by substantial evidence, shall be conclusive, but the court, for good cause shown, may remand the case to the Secretary to take further evidence, and the Secretary may thereupon make new or modified findings of fact and may modify the Secretary's previous action, and shall file in the court the record of the further proceedings. Such new or modified findings of fact shall be conclusive if supported by substantial evidence.

(f) STATE ENFORCEMENT- If a State educational agency determines that a local educational agency is not meeting the requirements of this part, including the targets in the State's performance plan, the State educational agency shall prohibit the local educational agency from reducing the local educational agency's maintenance of effort under section 613(a)(2)(C) for any fiscal year.

(g) RULE OF CONSTRUCTION- Nothing in this section shall be construed to restrict the Secretary from utilizing any authority under the General Education Provisions Act to monitor and enforce the requirements of this title.

(h) DIVIDED STATE AGENCY RESPONSIBILITY- For purposes of this section, where responsibility for ensuring that the requirements of this part are met with respect to children with disabilities who are convicted as adults under State law and incarcerated in adult prisons is assigned to a public agency other than the State educational agency pursuant to section 612(a)(11)(C), the Secretary, in instances where the Secretary finds that the failure to comply substantially with the provisions of this part are related to a failure by the public agency, shall take appropriate corrective action to ensure compliance with this part, except that—

(1) any reduction or withholding of payments to the State shall be proportionate to the total funds allotted under section 611 to the State as the number of eligible children with disabilities in adult prisons under the supervision of the other public agency is proportionate to the number of eligible individuals with disabilities in the State under the supervision of the State educational agency; and

(2) any withholding of funds under paragraph (1) shall be limited to the specific agency responsible for the failure to comply with this part.

(i) DATA CAPACITY AND TECHNICAL ASSISTANCE REVIEW- The Secretary shall—

(1) review the data collection and analysis capacity of States to ensure that data and information determined necessary for implementation of this section is collected, analyzed, and accurately reported to the Secretary; and

(2) provide technical assistance (from funds reserved under section 611(c)), where needed, to improve the capacity of States to meet the data collection requirements.

SEC. 617. ADMINISTRATION.

(a) RESPONSIBILITIES OF SECRETARY- The Secretary shall—

(1) cooperate with, and (directly or by grant or contract) furnish technical assistance necessary to, a State in matters relating to—

(A) the education of children with disabilities; and

(B) carrying out this part; and

(2) provide short-term training programs and institutes.

(b) PROHIBITION AGAINST FEDERAL MANDATES, DIRECTION, OR CONTROL- Nothing in this title shall be construed to authorize an officer or employee of the Federal Government to mandate, direct, or control a State, local educational agency, or school's specific instructional content, academic achievement standards and assessments, curriculum, or program of instruction.

(c) CONFIDENTIALITY- The Secretary shall take appropriate action, in accordance with section 444 of the General Education Provisions Act, to ensure the protection of the confidentiality of any personally identifiable data, information, and records collected or maintained by the Secretary and by State educational agencies and local educational agencies pursuant to this part.

(d) PERSONNEL- The Secretary is authorized to hire qualified personnel necessary to carry out the Secretary's duties under subsection (a), under section 618, and under subpart 4 of part D, without regard to the provisions of title 5, United States Code, relating to appointments in the competitive service and without regard to chapter 51 and subchapter III of chapter 53 of such title relating to classification and general schedule pay rates, except that no more than 20 such personnel shall be employed at any time.

(e) MODEL FORMS- Not later than the date that the Secretary publishes final regulations under this title, to implement amendments made by the Individuals with Disabilities Education Improvement Act of 2004, the Secretary shall publish and disseminate widely to States, local educational agencies, and parent and community training and information centers—

(1) a model IEP form;

(2) a model individualized family service plan (IFSP) form;

(3) a model form of the notice of procedural safeguards described in section 615(d); and

(4) a model form of the prior written notice described in subsections (b)(3) and (c)(1) of section 615 that is consistent with the requirements of this part and is sufficient to meet such requirements.

SEC. 618. PROGRAM INFORMATION.

(a) IN GENERAL- Each State that receives assistance under this part, and the Secretary of the Interior, shall provide data each year to the Secretary of Education and the public on the following:

(1)(A) The number and percentage of children with disabilities, by race, ethnicity, limited English proficiency status, gender, and disability category, who are in each of the following separate categories:

(i) Receiving a free appropriate public education.

(ii) Participating in regular education.

(iii) In separate classes, separate schools or facilities, or public or private residential facilities.

(iv) For each year of age from age 14 through 21, stopped receiving special education and related services because of program completion (including graduation with a regular secondary school diploma), or other reasons, and the reasons why those children stopped receiving special education and related services.

(v)(I) Removed to an interim alternative educational setting under section 615(k)(1).

(II) The acts or items precipitating those removals.

(III) The number of children with disabilities who are subject to long-term suspensions or expulsions.

(B) The number and percentage of children with disabilities, by race, gender, and ethnicity, who are receiving early intervention services.

(C) The number and percentage of children with disabilities, by race, gender, and ethnicity, who, from birth through age 2, stopped receiving early intervention services because of program completion or for other reasons.

(D) The incidence and duration of disciplinary actions by race, ethnicity, limited English proficiency status, gender, and disability category, of children with disabilities, including suspensions of 1 day or more.

(E) The number and percentage of children with disabilities who are removed to alternative educational settings or expelled as compared to children without disabilities who are removed to alternative educational settings or expelled.

(F) The number of due process complaints filed under section 615 and the number of hearings conducted.

(G) The number of hearings requested under section 615(k) and the number of changes in placements ordered as a result of those hearings.

(H) The number of mediations held and the number of settlement agreements reached through such mediations.

(2) The number and percentage of infants and toddlers, by race, and ethnicity, who are at risk of having substantial developmental delays (as defined in section 632), and who are receiving early intervention services under part C.

(3) Any other information that may be required by the Secretary.

(b) DATA REPORTING-

(1) PROTECTION OF IDENTIFIABLE DATA- The data described in subsection (a) shall be publicly reported by each State in a manner that does not result in the disclosure of data identifiable to individual children.

(2) SAMPLING- The Secretary may permit States and the Secretary of the Interior to obtain the data described in subsection (a) through sampling.

(c) TECHNICAL ASSISTANCE- The Secretary may provide technical assistance to States to ensure compliance with the data collection and reporting requirements under this title.

(d) DISPROPORTIONALITY-

(1) IN GENERAL- Each State that receives assistance under this part, and the Secretary of the Interior, shall provide for the collection and examination of data to determine if significant disproportionality based on race and ethnicity is occurring in the State and the local educational agencies of the State with respect to—

(A) the identification of children as children with disabilities, including the identification of children as children with disabilities in accordance with a particular impairment described in section 602(3);

(B) the placement in particular educational settings of such children; and

(C) the incidence, duration, and type of disciplinary actions, including suspensions and expulsions.

(2) REVIEW AND REVISION OF POLICIES, PRACTICES, AND PROCEDURES- In the case of a determination of significant disproportionality with respect to the identification of children as children with disabilities, or the placement in particular educational settings of such children, in accordance with paragraph (1), the State or the Secretary of the Interior, as the case may be, shall—

(A) provide for the review and, if appropriate, revision of the policies, procedures, and practices used in such identification or placement to ensure that such policies, procedures, and practices comply with the requirements of this title;

(B) require any local educational agency identified under paragraph (1) to reserve the maximum amount of funds under section 613(f) to provide comprehensive coordinated early intervening services to serve children in the local educational agency, particularly children in those groups that were significantly overidentified under paragraph (1); and

(C) require the local educational agency to publicly report on the revision of policies, practices, and procedures described under subparagraph (A).

SEC. 619. PRESCHOOL GRANTS.

(a) IN GENERAL- The Secretary shall provide grants under this section to assist States to provide special education and related services, in accordance with this part—

(1) to children with disabilities aged 3 through 5, inclusive; and

(2) at the State's discretion, to 2-year-old children with disabilities who will turn 3 during the school year.

(b) ELIGIBILITY- A State shall be eligible for a grant under this section if such State—

(1) is eligible under section 612 to receive a grant under this part; and

(2) makes a free appropriate public education available to all children with disabilities, aged 3 through 5, residing in the State.

(c) ALLOCATIONS TO STATES-

(1) IN GENERAL- The Secretary shall allocate the amount made available to carry out this section for a fiscal year among the States in accordance with paragraph (2) or (3), as the case may be.

(2) INCREASE IN FUNDS- If the amount available for allocations to States under paragraph (1) for a fiscal year is equal to or greater than the amount allocated to the States under this section for the preceding fiscal year, those allocations shall be calculated as follows:

(A) ALLOCATION-

(i) IN GENERAL- Except as provided in subparagraph (B), the Secretary shall—

(I) allocate to each State the amount the State received under this section for fiscal year 1997;

(II) allocate 85 percent of any remaining funds to States on the basis of the States' relative populations of children aged 3 through 5; and

(III) allocate 15 percent of those remaining funds to States on the basis of the States' relative populations of all children aged 3 through 5 who are living in poverty.

(ii) DATA- For the purpose of making grants under this paragraph, the Secretary shall use the most recent population data, including data on children living in poverty, that are available and satisfactory to the Secretary.

(B) LIMITATIONS- Notwithstanding subparagraph (A), allocations under this paragraph shall be subject to the following:

(i) PRECEDING YEARS- No State's allocation shall be less than its allocation under this section for the preceding fiscal year.

(ii) MINIMUM- No State's allocation shall

be less than the greatest of—

(I) the sum of—

(aa) the amount the State received under this section for fiscal year 1997; and

(bb) 1/3 of 1 percent of the amount by which the amount appropriated under subsection (j) for the fiscal year exceeds the amount appropriated for this section for fiscal year 1997;

(II) the sum of—

(aa) the amount the State received under this section for the preceding fiscal year; and

(bb) that amount multiplied by the percentage by which the increase in the funds appropriated under this section from the preceding fiscal year exceeds 1.5 percent; or

(III) the sum of—

(aa) the amount the State received under this section for the preceding fiscal year; and

(bb) that amount multiplied by 90 percent of the percentage increase in the amount appropriated under this section from the preceding fiscal year.

(iii) MAXIMUM- Notwithstanding clause (ii), no State's allocation under this paragraph shall exceed the sum of—

(I) the amount the State received under this section for the preceding fiscal year; and

(II) that amount multiplied by the sum of 1.5 percent and the percentage increase in the amount appropriated under this section from the preceding fiscal year.

(C) RATABLE REDUCTIONS- If the amount available for allocations under this paragraph is insufficient to pay those allocations in full, those allocations shall be ratably reduced, subject to subparagraph (B)(i).

(3) DECREASE IN FUNDS- If the amount available for allocations to States under paragraph (1) for a fiscal year is less than the amount allocated to the States under this section for the preceding fiscal year, those allocations shall be calculated as follows:

(A) ALLOCATIONS- If the amount available for allocations is greater than the amount allocated to the States for fiscal year 1997, each State shall be allocated the sum of—

(i) the amount the State received under this section for fiscal year 1997; and

(ii) an amount that bears the same relation to any remaining funds as the increase the State received under this section for the preceding fiscal year over fiscal year 1997 bears to the total of all such increases for all States.

(B) RATABLE REDUCTIONS- If the amount available for allocations is equal to or less than the amount allocated to the States for fiscal year 1997, each State shall be allocated the amount the State received for fiscal year 1997, ratably reduced, if necessary.

(d) RESERVATION FOR STATE ACTIVITIES-

(1) IN GENERAL- Each State may reserve not more than the amount described in paragraph (2) for administration and other State-level activities in accordance with subsections (e) and (f).

(2) AMOUNT DESCRIBED- For each fiscal year, the Secretary shall determine and report to the State educational agency an amount that is 25 percent of the amount the State received under this section for fiscal year 1997, cumulatively adjusted by the Secretary for each succeeding fiscal year by the lesser of—

(A) the percentage increase, if any, from the preceding fiscal year in the State's allocation under this section; or

(B) the percentage increase, if any, from the preceding fiscal year in the Consumer Price Index For All Urban Consumers published by the Bureau of Labor Statistics of the Department of Labor.

(e) STATE ADMINISTRATION-

(1) IN GENERAL- For the purpose of administering this section (including the coordination of activities under this part with, and providing technical assistance to, other programs that provide services to children with disabilities) a State may use not more than 20 percent of the maximum amount the State may reserve under subsection (d) for any fiscal year.

(2) ADMINISTRATION OF PART C- Funds described in paragraph (1) may also be used for the administration of part C.

(f) OTHER STATE-LEVEL ACTIVITIES- Each State shall use any funds the State reserves under subsection (d) and does not use for administration under subsection (e)—

(1) for support services (including establishing and implementing the mediation process required by section 615(e)), which may benefit children with disabilities younger than 3 or older than 5 as long as those services also benefit children with disabilities aged 3 through 5;

(2) for direct services for children eligible for services under this section;

(3) for activities at the State and local levels to meet the performance goals established by the State under section 612(a)(15);

(4) to supplement other funds used to develop and implement a statewide coordinated services system designed to improve results for children and families, including children with

disabilities and their families, but not more than 1 percent of the amount received by the State under this section for a fiscal year;

(5) to provide early intervention services (which shall include an educational component that promotes school readiness and incorporates preliteracy, language, and numeracy skills) in accordance with part C to children with disabilities who are eligible for services under this section and who previously received services under part C until such children enter, or are eligible under State law to enter, kindergarten; or

(6) at the State's discretion, to continue service coordination or case management for families who receive services under part C.

(g) SUBGRANTS TO LOCAL EDUCATIONAL AGENCIES-

(1) SUBGRANTS REQUIRED- Each State that receives a grant under this section for any fiscal year shall distribute all of the grant funds that the State does not reserve under subsection (d) to local educational agencies in the State that have established their eligibility under section 613, as follows:

(A) BASE PAYMENTS- The State shall first award each local educational agency described in paragraph (1) the amount that agency would have received under this section for fiscal year 1997 if the State had distributed 75 percent of its grant for that year under section 619(c)(3), as such section was then in effect.

(B) ALLOCATION OF REMAINING FUNDS- After making allocations under subparagraph (A), the State shall—

(i) allocate 85 percent of any remaining funds to those local educational agencies on the basis of the relative numbers of children enrolled in public and private elementary schools and secondary schools within the local educational agency's jurisdiction; and

(ii) allocate 15 percent of those remaining funds to those local educational agencies in accordance with their relative numbers of children living in poverty, as determined by the State educational agency.

(2) REALLOCATION OF FUNDS- If a State educational agency determines that a local educational agency is adequately providing a free appropriate public education to all children with disabilities aged 3 through 5 residing in the area served by the local educational agency with State and local funds, the State educational agency may reallocate any portion of the funds under this section that are not needed by that local educational agency to provide a free appropriate public education

to other local educational agencies in the State that are not adequately providing special education and related services to all children with disabilities aged 3 through 5 residing in the areas the other local educational agencies serve.

(h) PART C INAPPLICABLE- Part C does not apply to any child with a disability receiving a free appropriate public education, in accordance with this part, with funds received under this section.

(i) STATE DEFINED- In this section, the term 'State' means each of the 50 States, the District of Columbia, and the Commonwealth of Puerto Rico.

(j) AUTHORIZATION OF APPROPRIATIONS- There are authorized to be appropriated to carry out this section such sums as may be necessary.

PART C—INFANTS AND TODDLERS WITH DISABILITIES

SEC. 631. FINDINGS AND POLICY.

(a) FINDINGS- Congress finds that there is an urgent and substantial need—

(1) to enhance the development of infants and toddlers with disabilities, to minimize their potential for developmental delay, and to recognize the significant brain development that occurs during a child's first 3 years of life;

(2) to reduce the educational costs to our society, including our Nation's schools, by minimizing the need for special education and related services after infants and toddlers with disabilities reach school age;

(3) to maximize the potential for individuals with disabilities to live independently in society;

(4) to enhance the capacity of families to meet the special needs of their infants and toddlers with disabilities; and

(5) to enhance the capacity of State and local agencies and service providers to identify, evaluate, and meet the needs of all children, particularly minority, low-income, inner city, and rural children, and infants and toddlers in foster care.

(b) POLICY- It is the policy of the United States to provide financial assistance to States—

(1) to develop and implement a statewide, comprehensive, coordinated, multidisciplinary, interagency system that provides early intervention services for infants and toddlers

with disabilities and their families;

(2) to facilitate the coordination of payment for early intervention services from Federal, State, local, and private sources (including public and private insurance coverage);

(3) to enhance State capacity to provide quality early intervention services and expand and improve existing early intervention services being provided to infants and toddlers with disabilities and their families; and

(4) to encourage States to expand opportunities for children under 3 years of age who would be at risk of having substantial developmental delay if they did not receive early intervention services.

SEC. 632. DEFINITIONS.

In this part:

(1) AT-RISK INFANT OR TODDLER- The term 'at-risk infant or toddler' means an individual under 3 years of age who would be at risk of experiencing a substantial developmental delay if early intervention services were not provided to the individual.

(2) COUNCIL- The term 'council' means a State interagency coordinating council established under section 641.

(3) DEVELOPMENTAL DELAY- The term 'developmental delay', when used with respect to an individual residing in a State, has the meaning given such term by the State under section 635(a)(1).

(4) EARLY INTERVENTION SERVICES- The term 'early intervention services' means developmental services that—

(A) are provided under public supervision;

(B) are provided at no cost except where Federal or State law provides for a system of payments by families, including a schedule of sliding fees;

(C) are designed to meet the developmental needs of an infant or toddler with a disability, as identified by the individualized family service plan team, in any 1 or more of the following areas:

(i) physical development;

(ii) cognitive development;

(iii) communication development;

(iv) social or emotional development; or

(v) adaptive development;

(D) meet the standards of the State in which the services are provided, including the requirements of this part;

(E) include—

(i) family training, counseling, and home visits;

(ii) special instruction;

(iii) speech-language pathology and audiology services, and sign language and cued language services;

(iv) occupational therapy;

(v) physical therapy;

(vi) psychological services;

(vii) service coordination services;

(viii) medical services only for diagnostic or evaluation purposes;

(ix) early identification, screening, and assessment services;

(x) health services necessary to enable the infant or toddler to benefit from the other early intervention services;

(xi) social work services;

(xii) vision services;

(xiii) assistive technology devices and assistive technology services; and

(xiv) transportation and related costs that are necessary to enable an infant or toddler and the infant's or toddler's family to receive another service described in this paragraph;

(F) are provided by qualified personnel, including—

(i) special educators;

(ii) speech-language pathologists and audiologists;

(iii) occupational therapists;

(iv) physical therapists;

(v) psychologists;

(vi) social workers;

(vii) nurses;

(viii) registered dietitians;

(ix) family therapists;

(x) vision specialists, including ophthalmologists and optometrists;

(xi) orientation and mobility specialists; and

(xii) pediatricians and other physicians;

(G) to the maximum extent appropriate, are provided in natural environments, including the home, and community settings in which children without disabilities participate; and

(H) are provided in conformity with an individualized family service plan adopted in accordance with section 636.

(5) INFANT OR TODDLER WITH A DISABILITY- The term 'infant or toddler with a disability'—

(A) means an individual under 3 years of age who needs early intervention services because the individual—

(i) is experiencing developmental delays, as measured by appropriate diagnostic instruments and procedures in 1 or more of the areas of cognitive development, physical development, communication development, social or emotional development, and adaptive development; or

(ii) has a diagnosed physical or mental condition that has a high probability of resulting in developmental delay; and

(B) may also include, at a State's discretion—

(i) at-risk infants and toddlers; and

(ii) children with disabilities who are eligible for services under section 619 and who previously received services under this part until such children enter, or are eligible under State law to enter, kindergarten or elementary school, as appropriate, provided that any programs under this part serving such children shall include—

(I) an educational component that promotes school readiness and incorporates pre-literacy, language, and numeracy skills; and

(II) a written notification to parents of their rights and responsibilities in determining whether their child will continue to receive services under this part or participate in preschool programs under section 619.

SEC. 633. GENERAL AUTHORITY.

The Secretary shall, in accordance with this part, make grants to States (from their allotments under section 643) to assist each State to maintain and implement a statewide, comprehensive, coordinated, multidisciplinary, interagency system to provide early intervention services for infants and toddlers with disabilities and their families.

SEC. 634. ELIGIBILITY.

In order to be eligible for a grant under section 633, a State shall provide assurances to the Secretary that the State—

(1) has adopted a policy that appropriate early intervention services are available to all infants and toddlers with disabilities in the State and their families, including Indian infants and toddlers with disabilities and their families residing on a reservation geographically located in the State, infants and toddlers with disabilities who are homeless children and their families, and infants and toddlers with disabilities who are wards of the State; and

(2) has in effect a statewide system that meets the requirements of section 635.

SEC. 635. REQUIREMENTS FOR STATEWIDE SYSTEM.

(a) IN GENERAL- A statewide system described in section 633 shall include, at a minimum, the following components:

(1) A rigorous definition of the term 'developmental delay' that will be used by the State in carrying out programs under this part in order to appropriately identify infants and toddlers with disabilities that are in need of services under this part.

(2) A State policy that is in effect and that ensures that appropriate early intervention services based on scientifically based research, to the extent practicable, are available to all infants and toddlers with disabilities and their families, including Indian infants and toddlers with disabilities and their families residing on a reservation geographically located in the State and infants and toddlers with disabilities who are homeless children and their families.

(3) A timely, comprehensive, multidisciplinary evaluation of the functioning of each infant or toddler with a disability in the State, and a family-directed identification of the needs of each family of such an infant or toddler, to assist appropriately in the development of the infant or toddler.

(4) For each infant or toddler with a disability in the State, an individualized family service plan in accordance with section 636, including service coordination services in accordance with such service plan.

(5) A comprehensive child find system, consistent with part B, including a system for making referrals to service providers that includes timelines and provides for participation by primary referral sources and that ensures rigorous standards for appropriately identifying infants and toddlers with disabilities for services under this part that will reduce the need for future services.

(6) A public awareness program focusing on early identification of infants and toddlers with disabilities, including the preparation and dissemination by the lead agency designated or established under paragraph (10) to all primary referral sources, especially hospitals and physicians, of information to be given to parents, especially to inform parents with premature infants, or infants with other physical risk factors associated with learning or developmental complications, on the availability of early intervention services under this part and of services under section 619, and procedures for assisting such sources in disseminating such information to parents of

infants and toddlers with disabilities.

(7) A central directory that includes information on early intervention services, resources, and experts available in the State and research and demonstration projects being conducted in the State.

(8) A comprehensive system of personnel development, including the training of paraprofessionals and the training of primary referral sources with respect to the basic components of early intervention services available in the State that—

(A) shall include—

(i) implementing innovative strategies and activities for the recruitment and retention of early education service providers;

(ii) promoting the preparation of early intervention providers who are fully and appropriately qualified to provide early intervention services under this part; and

(iii) training personnel to coordinate transition services for infants and toddlers served under this part from a program providing early intervention services under this part and under part B (other than section 619), to a preschool program receiving funds under section 619, or another appropriate program; and

(B) may include—

(i) training personnel to work in rural and inner-city areas; and

(ii) training personnel in the emotional and social development of young children.

(9) Policies and procedures relating to the establishment and maintenance of qualifications to ensure that personnel necessary to carry out this part are appropriately and adequately prepared and trained, including the establishment and maintenance of qualifications that are consistent with any State-approved or recognized certification, licensing, registration, or other comparable requirements that apply to the area in which such personnel are providing early intervention services, except that nothing in this part (including this paragraph) shall be construed to prohibit the use of paraprofessionals and assistants who are appropriately trained and supervised in accordance with State law, regulation, or written policy, to assist in the provision of early intervention services under this part to infants and toddlers with disabilities.

(10) A single line of responsibility in a lead agency designated or established by the Governor for carrying out—

(A) the general administration and supervision of programs and activities receiving assistance under section 633, and the monitoring of programs and activities used by the State to carry out this part, whether or not such programs or activities are receiving assistance made available under section 633, to ensure that the State complies with this part;

(B) the identification and coordination of all available resources within the State from Federal, State, local, and private sources;

(C) the assignment of financial responsibility in accordance with section 637(a)(2) to the appropriate agencies;

(D) the development of procedures to ensure that services are provided to infants and toddlers with disabilities and their families under this part in a timely manner pending the resolution of any disputes among public agencies or service providers;

(E) the resolution of intra- and interagency disputes; and

(F) the entry into formal interagency agreements that define the financial responsibility of each agency for paying for early intervention services (consistent with State law) and procedures for resolving disputes and that include all additional components necessary to ensure meaningful cooperation and coordination.

(11) A policy pertaining to the contracting or making of other arrangements with service providers to provide early intervention services in the State, consistent with the provisions of this part, including the contents of the application used and the conditions of the contract or other arrangements.

(12) A procedure for securing timely reimbursements of funds used under this part in accordance with section 640(a).

(13) Procedural safeguards with respect to programs under this part, as required by section 639.

(14) A system for compiling data requested by the Secretary under section 618 that relates to this part.

(15) A State interagency coordinating council that meets the requirements of section 641.

(16) Policies and procedures to ensure that, consistent with section 636(d)(5)—

(A) to the maximum extent appropriate, early intervention services are provided in natural environments; and

(B) the provision of early intervention services for any infant or toddler with a disability occurs in a setting other than a natural environment that is most appropriate, as determined by the parent and the individualized family service plan team, only when early intervention cannot be achieved satisfactorily for the infant or toddler in a natural environment.

(b) POLICY- In implementing subsection (a)(9), a State may adopt a policy that includes making ongoing good-faith efforts to recruit and hire appropriately and adequately trained personnel to provide early intervention services to infants and toddlers with disabilities, including, in a geographic area of the State where there is a shortage of such personnel, the most qualified individuals available who are making satisfactory progress toward completing applicable course work necessary to meet the standards described in subsection (a)(9).

(c) Flexibility To Serve Children 3 Years of Age Until Entrance Into Elementary School-

(1) IN GENERAL- A statewide system described in section 633 may include a State policy, developed and implemented jointly by the lead agency and the State educational agency, under which parents of children with disabilities who are eligible for services under section 619 and previously received services under this part, may choose the continuation of early intervention services (which shall include an educational component that promotes school readiness and incorporates preliteracy, language, and numeracy skills) for such children under this part until such children enter, or are eligible under State law to enter, kindergarten.

(2) REQUIREMENTS- If a statewide system includes a State policy described in paragraph (1), the statewide system shall ensure that—

(A) parents of children with disabilities served pursuant to this subsection are provided annual notice that contains—

(i) a description of the rights of such parents to elect to receive services pursuant to this subsection or under part B; and

(ii) an explanation of the differences between services provided pursuant to this subsection and services provided under part B, including—

(I) types of services and the locations at which the services are provided;

(II) applicable procedural safeguards; and

(III) possible costs (including any fees to be charged to families as described in section 632(4)(B)), if any, to parents of infants or toddlers with disabilities;

(B) services provided pursuant to this subsection include an educational component that promotes school readiness and incorporates preliteracy, language, and numeracy skills;

(C) the State policy will not affect the right of any child served pursuant to this subsection to instead receive a free appropriate public education under part B;

(D) all early intervention services outlined in the child's individualized family service plan under section 636 are continued while any eligibility determination is being made for services under this subsection;

(E) the parents of infants or toddlers with disabilities (as defined in section 632(5)(A)) provide informed written consent to the State, before such infants or toddlers reach 3 years of age, as to whether such parents intend to choose the continuation of early intervention services pursuant to this subsection for such infants or toddlers;

(F) the requirements under section 637(a)(9) shall not apply with respect to a child who is receiving services in accordance with this subsection until not less than 90 days (and at the discretion of the parties to the conference, not more than 9 months) before the time the child will no longer receive those services; and

(G) there will be a referral for evaluation for early intervention services of a child who experiences a substantiated case of trauma due to exposure to family violence (as defined in section 320 of the Family Violence Prevention and Services Act).

(3) REPORTING REQUIREMENT- If a statewide system includes a State policy described in paragraph (1), the State shall submit to the Secretary, in the State's report under section 637(b)(4)(A), a report on the number and percentage of children with disabilities who are eligible for services under section 619 but whose parents choose for such children to continue to receive early intervention services under this part.

(4) AVAILABLE FUNDS- If a statewide system includes a State policy described in paragraph (1), the policy shall describe the funds (including an identification as Federal, State, or local funds) that will be used to ensure that the option described in paragraph (1) is available to eligible children and families who provide the consent described in paragraph (2)(E), including fees (if any) to be charged to families as described in section 632(4)(B).

(5) RULES OF CONSTRUCTION-

(A) SERVICES UNDER PART B- If a statewide system includes a State policy described in paragraph (1), a State that provides services in accordance with this subsection to a child with a disability who is eligible for services under section 619 shall not be required to provide the child with a free appropriate public education under part B for the period of time in which the child is receiving services under this part.

(B) SERVICES UNDER THIS PART- Nothing in this subsection shall be construed to require a provider of services under this part to provide a child served under this part with a free appropriate public education.

SEC. 636. INDIVIDUALIZED FAMILY SERVICE PLAN.

(a) ASSESSMENT AND PROGRAM DEVELOPMENT- A statewide system described in section 633 shall provide, at a minimum, for each infant or toddler with a disability, and the infant's or toddler's family, to receive—

(1) a multidisciplinary assessment of the unique strengths and needs of the infant or toddler and the identification of services appropriate to meet such needs;

(2) a family-directed assessment of the resources, priorities, and concerns of the family and the identification of the supports and services necessary to enhance the family's capacity to meet the developmental needs of the infant or toddler; and

(3) a written individualized family service plan developed by a multidisciplinary team, including the parents, as required by subsection (e), including a description of the appropriate transition services for the infant or toddler.

(b) PERIODIC REVIEW- The individualized family service plan shall be evaluated once a year and the family shall be provided a review of the plan at 6-month intervals (or more often where appropriate based on infant or toddler and family needs).

(c) PROMPTNESS AFTER ASSESSMENT- The individualized family service plan shall be developed within a reasonable time after the assessment required by subsection (a)(1) is completed. With the parents' consent, early intervention services may commence prior to the completion of the assessment.

(d) CONTENT OF PLAN- The individualized family service plan shall be in writing and contain—

(1) a statement of the infant's or toddler's present levels of physical development, cognitive development, communication development, social or emotional development, and adaptive development, based on objective criteria;

(2) a statement of the family's resources, priorities, and concerns relating to enhancing the development of the family's infant or toddler with a disability;

(3) a statement of the measurable results or outcomes expected to be achieved for the infant or toddler and the family, including pre-literacy and language skills, as developmentally appropriate for the child, and the criteria, procedures, and timelines used to determine the degree to which progress toward achieving the results or outcomes is being made and whether modifications or revisions of the results or outcomes or services are necessary;

(4) a statement of specific early intervention services based on peer-reviewed research, to the extent practicable, necessary to meet the unique needs of the infant or toddler and the family, including the frequency, intensity, and method of delivering services;

(5) a statement of the natural environments in which early intervention services will appropriately be provided, including a justification of the extent, if any, to which the services will not be provided in a natural environment;

(6) the projected dates for initiation of services and the anticipated length, duration, and frequency of the services;

(7) the identification of the service coordinator from the profession most immediately relevant to the infant's or toddler's or family's needs (or who is otherwise qualified to carry out all applicable responsibilities under this part) who will be responsible for the implementation of the plan and coordination with other agencies and persons, including transition services; and

(8) the steps to be taken to support the transition of the toddler with a disability to preschool or other appropriate services.

(e) PARENTAL CONSENT- The contents of the individualized family service plan shall be fully explained to the parents and informed written consent from the parents shall be obtained prior to the provision of early intervention services described in such plan. If the parents do not provide consent with respect to a particular early intervention service, then only the early intervention services to which consent is obtained shall be provided.

SEC. 637. STATE APPLICATION AND ASSURANCES.

(a) APPLICATION- A State desiring to receive a grant under section 633 shall submit an application to the Secretary at such time and in such manner as the Secretary may reasonably require. The application shall contain—

(1) a designation of the lead agency in the State that will be responsible for the administration of funds provided under section 633;

(2) a certification to the Secretary that the arrangements to establish financial responsibility for services provided under this part pursuant to section 640(b) are current as of the date of submission of the certification;

(3) information demonstrating eligibility of the State under section 634, including—

(A) information demonstrating to the Secretary's satisfaction that the State has in effect the statewide system required by section 633; and

(B) a description of services to be provided to infants and toddlers with disabilities and their families through the system;

(4) if the State provides services to at-risk infants and toddlers through the statewide system, a description of such services;

(5) a description of the uses for which funds will be expended in accordance with this part;

(6) a description of the State policies and procedures that require the referral for early intervention services under this part of a child under the age of 3 who—

(A) is involved in a substantiated case of child abuse or neglect; or

(B) is identified as affected by illegal substance abuse, or withdrawal symptoms resulting from prenatal drug exposure;

(7) a description of the procedure used to ensure that resources are made available under this part for all geographic areas within the State;

(8) a description of State policies and procedures that ensure that, prior to the adoption by the State of any other policy or procedure necessary to meet the requirements of this part, there are public hearings, adequate notice of the hearings, and an opportunity for comment available to the general public, including individuals with disabilities and parents of infants and toddlers with disabilities;

(9) a description of the policies and procedures to be used—

(A) to ensure a smooth transition for toddlers receiving early intervention services under this part (and children receiving those services under section 635(c)) to preschool, school, other appropriate services, or exiting the program, including a description of how—

(i) the families of such toddlers and children will be included in the transition plans required by subparagraph (C); and

(ii) the lead agency designated or established under section 635(a)(10) will—

(I) notify the local educational agency for the area in which such a child resides that the child will shortly reach the age of eligibility for preschool services under part B, as determined in accordance with State law;

(II) in the case of a child who may be eligible for such preschool services, with the approval of the family of the child, convene a conference among the lead agency, the family, and the local educational agency not less than 90 days (and at the discretion of all such parties, not more than 9 months) before the child is eligible for the preschool services, to discuss any such services that the child may receive; and

(III) in the case of a child who may not be eligible for such preschool services, with the approval of the family, make reasonable efforts to convene a conference among the lead agency, the family, and providers of other appropriate services for children who are not eligible for preschool services under part B, to discuss the appropriate services that the child may receive;

(B) to review the child's program options for the period from the child's third birthday through the remainder of the school year; and

(C) to establish a transition plan, including, as appropriate, steps to exit from the program;

(10) a description of State efforts to promote collaboration among Early Head Start programs under section 645A of the Head Start Act, early education and child care programs, and services under part C; and

(11) such other information and assurances as the Secretary may reasonably require.

(b) ASSURANCES- The application described in subsection (a)—

(1) shall provide satisfactory assurance that Federal funds made available under section 643 to the State will be expended in accordance with this part;

(2) shall contain an assurance that the State will comply with the requirements of section 640;

(3) shall provide satisfactory assurance that the control of funds provided under section 643, and title to property derived from those funds, will be in a public agency for the uses and purposes provided in this part and that a public agency will administer such funds and property;

(4) shall provide for—

(A) making such reports in such form and containing such information as the Secretary may require to carry out the Secretary's functions under this part; and

(B) keeping such reports and affording such access to the reports as the Secretary may find necessary to ensure the correctness and verification of those reports and proper disbursement of Federal funds under this part;

(5) provide satisfactory assurance that Federal funds made available under section 643 to the State—

(A) will not be commingled with State funds; and

(B) will be used so as to supplement the level of State and local funds expended for infants and toddlers with disabilities and their families and in no case to supplant those State and local funds;

(6) shall provide satisfactory assurance that such fiscal control and fund accounting procedures will be adopted as may be necessary to ensure proper disbursement of, and accounting for, Federal funds paid under section 643 to the State;

(7) shall provide satisfactory assurance that policies and procedures have been adopted to ensure meaningful involvement of underserved groups, including minority, low-income, homeless, and rural families and children with disabilities who are wards of the State, in the planning and implementation of all the requirements of this part; and

(8) shall contain such other information and assurances as the Secretary may reasonably require by regulation.

(c) STANDARD FOR DISAPPROVAL OF APPLICATION- The Secretary may not disapprove such an application unless the Secretary determines, after notice and opportunity for a hearing, that the application fails to comply with the requirements of this section.

(d) SUBSEQUENT STATE APPLICATION- If a State has on file with the Secretary a policy, procedure, or assurance that demonstrates that the State meets a requirement of this section, including any policy or procedure filed under this part (as in effect before the date of enactment of the Individuals with Disabilities Education Improvement Act of 2004), the Secretary shall consider the State to have met the requirement for purposes of receiving a grant under this part.

(e) MODIFICATION OF APPLICATION- An application submitted by a State in accordance with this section shall remain in effect until the State submits to the Secretary such modifications as the State determines necessary. This section shall apply to a modification of an application to the same

extent and in the same manner as this section applies to the original application.

(f) MODIFICATIONS REQUIRED BY THE SECRETARY- The Secretary may require a State to modify its application under this section, but only to the extent necessary to ensure the State's compliance with this part, if—

(1) an amendment is made to this title, or a Federal regulation issued under this title;

(2) a new interpretation of this title is made by a Federal court or the State's highest court; or

(3) an official finding of noncompliance with Federal law or regulations is made with respect to the State.

SEC. 638. USES OF FUNDS.

In addition to using funds provided under section 633 to maintain and implement the statewide system required by such section, a State may use such funds—

(1) for direct early intervention services for infants and toddlers with disabilities, and their families, under this part that are not otherwise funded through other public or private sources;

(2) to expand and improve on services for infants and toddlers and their families under this part that are otherwise available;

(3) to provide a free appropriate public education, in accordance with part B, to children with disabilities from their third birthday to the beginning of the following school year;

(4) with the written consent of the parents, to continue to provide early intervention services under this part to children with disabilities from their 3rd birthday until such children enter, or are eligible under State law to enter, kindergarten, in lieu of a free appropriate public education provided in accordance with part B; and

(5) in any State that does not provide services for at-risk infants and toddlers under section 637(a)(4), to strengthen the statewide system by initiating, expanding, or improving collaborative efforts related to at-risk infants and toddlers, including establishing linkages with appropriate public or private community-based organizations, services, and personnel for the purposes of—

(A) identifying and evaluating at-risk infants and toddlers;

(B) making referrals of the infants and toddlers identified and evaluated under subparagraph (A); and

(C) conducting periodic follow-up on each

such referral to determine if the status of the infant or toddler involved has changed with respect to the eligibility of the infant or toddler for services under this part.

SEC. 639. PROCEDURAL SAFEGUARDS.

(a) MINIMUM PROCEDURES- The procedural safeguards required to be included in a statewide system under section 635(a)(13) shall provide, at a minimum, the following:

(1) The timely administrative resolution of complaints by parents. Any party aggrieved by the findings and decision regarding an administrative complaint shall have the right to bring a civil action with respect to the complaint in any State court of competent jurisdiction or in a district court of the United States without regard to the amount in controversy. In any action brought under this paragraph, the court shall receive the records of the administrative proceedings, shall hear additional evidence at the request of a party, and, basing its decision on the preponderance of the evidence, shall grant such relief as the court determines is appropriate.

(2) The right to confidentiality of personally identifiable information, including the right of parents to written notice of and written consent to the exchange of such information among agencies consistent with Federal and State law.

(3) The right of the parents to determine whether they, their infant or toddler, or other family members will accept or decline any early intervention service under this part in accordance with State law without jeopardizing other early intervention services under this part.

(4) The opportunity for parents to examine records relating to assessment, screening, eligibility determinations, and the development and implementation of the individualized family service plan.

(5) Procedures to protect the rights of the infant or toddler whenever the parents of the infant or toddler are not known or cannot be found or the infant or toddler is a ward of the State, including the assignment of an individual (who shall not be an employee of the State lead agency, or other State agency, and who shall not be any person, or any employee of a person, providing early intervention services to the infant or toddler or any family member of the infant or toddler) to act as a surrogate for the parents.

(6) Written prior notice to the parents of the infant or toddler with a disability whenever the State agency or service provider proposes to initiate or change, or refuses to initiate or change, the identification, evaluation, or placement of the infant or toddler with a disability, or the provision of appropriate early intervention services to the infant or toddler.

(7) Procedures designed to ensure that the notice required by paragraph (6) fully informs the parents, in the parents' native language, unless it clearly is not feasible to do so, of all procedures available pursuant to this section.

(8) The right of parents to use mediation in accordance with section 615, except that—

(A) any reference in the section to a State educational agency shall be considered to be a reference to a State's lead agency established or designated under section 635(a)(10);

(B) any reference in the section to a local educational agency shall be considered to be a reference to a local service provider or the State's lead agency under this part, as the case may be; and

(C) any reference in the section to the provision of a free appropriate public education to children with disabilities shall be considered to be a reference to the provision of appropriate early intervention services to infants and toddlers with disabilities.

(b) SERVICES DURING PENDENCY OF PROCEEDINGS- During the pendency of any proceeding or action involving a complaint by the parents of an infant or toddler with a disability, unless the State agency and the parents otherwise agree, the infant or toddler shall continue to receive the appropriate early intervention services currently being provided or, if applying for initial services, shall receive the services not in dispute.

SEC. 640. PAYOR OF LAST RESORT.

(a) NONSUBSTITUTION- Funds provided under section 643 may not be used to satisfy a financial commitment for services that would have been paid for from another public or private source, including any medical program administered by the Secretary of Defense, but for the enactment of this part, except that whenever considered necessary to prevent a delay in the receipt of appropriate early intervention services by an infant, toddler, or family in a timely fashion, funds provided under section 643 may be used to pay the provider of services pending reimbursement from the agency that has ultimate responsibility for the payment.

(b) OBLIGATIONS RELATED TO AND METHODS OF ENSURING SERVICES-

(1) ESTABLISHING FINANCIAL RESPONSIBILITY FOR SERVICES-

(A) IN GENERAL- The Chief Executive Officer of a State or designee of the officer shall ensure that an interagency agreement or other mechanism for interagency coordination is in effect between each public agency and the designated lead agency, in order to ensure—

(i) the provision of, and financial responsibility for, services provided under this part; and

(ii) such services are consistent with the requirements of section 635 and the State's application pursuant to section 637, including the provision of such services during the pendency of any such dispute.

(B) CONSISTENCY BETWEEN AGREEMENTS OR MECHANISMS UNDER PART B- The Chief Executive Officer of a State or designee of the officer shall ensure that the terms and conditions of such agreement or mechanism are consistent with the terms and conditions of the State's agreement or mechanism under section 612(a)(12), where appropriate.

(2) REIMBURSEMENT FOR SERVICES BY PUBLIC AGENCY-

(A) IN GENERAL- If a public agency other than an educational agency fails to provide or pay for the services pursuant to an agreement required under paragraph (1), the local educational agency or State agency (as determined by the Chief Executive Officer or designee) shall provide or pay for the provision of such services to the child.

(B) REIMBURSEMENT- Such local educational agency or State agency is authorized to claim reimbursement for the services from the public agency that failed to provide or pay for such services and such public agency shall reimburse the local educational agency or State agency pursuant to the terms of the interagency agreement or other mechanism required under paragraph (1).

(3) SPECIAL RULE- The requirements of paragraph (1) may be met through—

(A) State statute or regulation;

(B) signed agreements between respective agency officials that clearly identify the responsibilities of each agency relating to the provision of services; or

(C) other appropriate written methods as determined by the Chief Executive Officer of the State or designee of the officer and approved by the Secretary through the review and approval of the State's application pursuant to section 637.

(c) REDUCTION OF OTHER BENEFITS-

Nothing in this part shall be construed to permit the State to reduce medical or other assistance available or to alter eligibility under title V of the Social Security Act (relating to maternal and child health) or title XIX of the Social Security Act (relating to medicaid for infants or toddlers with disabilities) within the State.

SEC. 641. STATE INTERAGENCY COORDINATING COUNCIL.

(a) ESTABLISHMENT-

(1) IN GENERAL- A State that desires to receive financial assistance under this part shall establish a State interagency coordinating council.

(2) APPOINTMENT- The council shall be appointed by the Governor. In making appointments to the council, the Governor shall ensure that the membership of the council reasonably represents the population of the State.

(3) CHAIRPERSON- The Governor shall designate a member of the council to serve as the chairperson of the council, or shall require the council to so designate such a member. Any member of the council who is a representative of the lead agency designated under section 635(a)(10) may not serve as the chairperson of the council.

(b) COMPOSITION-

(1) IN GENERAL- The council shall be composed as follows:

(A) PARENTS- Not less than 20 percent of the members shall be parents of infants or toddlers with disabilities or children with disabilities aged 12 or younger, with knowledge of, or experience with, programs for infants and toddlers with disabilities. Not less than 1 such member shall be a parent of an infant or toddler with a disability or a child with a disability aged 6 or younger.

(B) SERVICE PROVIDERS- Not less than 20 percent of the members shall be public or private providers of early intervention services.

(C) STATE LEGISLATURE- Not less than 1 member shall be from the State legislature.

(D) PERSONNEL PREPARATION- Not less than 1 member shall be involved in personnel preparation.

(E) AGENCY FOR EARLY INTERVENTION SERVICES- Not less than 1 member shall be from each of the State agencies involved in the provision of, or payment for, early intervention services to infants and toddlers with disabilities and their families and shall have sufficient authority to engage in policy planning and implementation on behalf of such agencies.

(F) AGENCY FOR PRESCHOOL SERVICES- Not less than 1 member shall be from the State educational agency responsible for preschool services to children with disabilities and shall have sufficient authority to engage in policy planning and implementation on behalf of such agency.

(G) STATE MEDICAID AGENCY- Not less than 1 member shall be from the agency responsible for the State medicaid program.

(H) HEAD START AGENCY- Not less than 1 member shall be a representative from a Head Start agency or program in the State.

(I) CHILD CARE AGENCY- Not less than 1 member shall be a representative from a State agency responsible for child care.

(J) AGENCY FOR HEALTH INSURANCE- Not less than 1 member shall be from the agency responsible for the State regulation of health insurance.

(K) OFFICE OF THE COORDINATOR OF EDUCATION OF HOMELESS CHILDREN AND YOUTH- Not less than 1 member shall be a representative designated by the Office of Coordinator for Education of Homeless Children and Youths.

(L) STATE FOSTER CARE REPRESENTATIVE- Not less than 1 member shall be a representative from the State child welfare agency responsible for foster care.

(M) MENTAL HEALTH AGENCY- Not less than 1 member shall be a representative from the State agency responsible for children's mental health.

(2) OTHER MEMBERS- The council may include other members selected by the Governor, including a representative from the Bureau of Indian Affairs (BIA), or where there is no BIA-operated or BIA-funded school, from the Indian Health Service or the tribe or tribal council.

(c) MEETINGS- The council shall meet, at a minimum, on a quarterly basis, and in such places as the council determines necessary. The meetings shall be publicly announced, and, to the extent appropriate, open and accessible to the general public.

(d) MANAGEMENT AUTHORITY- Subject to the approval of the Governor, the council may prepare and approve a budget using funds under this part to conduct hearings and forums, to reimburse members of the council for reasonable and necessary expenses for attending council meetings and performing council duties (including child care for parent representatives), to pay compensation to a member of the council if the member is not employed or must forfeit wages from other employment when performing official council business, to hire staff, and to obtain the services of such professional, technical, and clerical personnel as may be necessary to carry out its functions under this part.

(e) FUNCTIONS OF COUNCIL-

(1) DUTIES- The council shall—

(A) advise and assist the lead agency designated or established under section 635(a)(10) in the performance of the responsibilities set forth in such section, particularly the identification of the sources of fiscal and other support for services for early intervention programs, assignment of financial responsibility to the appropriate agency, and the promotion of the interagency agreements;

(B) advise and assist the lead agency in the preparation of applications and amendments thereto;

(C) advise and assist the State educational agency regarding the transition of toddlers with disabilities to preschool and other appropriate services; and

(D) prepare and submit an annual report to the Governor and to the Secretary on the status of early intervention programs for infants and toddlers with disabilities and their families operated within the State.

(2) AUTHORIZED ACTIVITY- The council may advise and assist the lead agency and the State educational agency regarding the provision of appropriate services for children from birth through age 5. The council may advise appropriate agencies in the State with respect to the integration of services for infants and toddlers with disabilities and at-risk infants and toddlers and their families, regardless of whether at-risk infants and toddlers are eligible for early intervention services in the State.

(f) CONFLICT OF INTEREST- No member of the council shall cast a vote on any matter that is likely to provide a direct financial benefit to that member or otherwise give the appearance of a conflict of interest under State law.

SEC. 642. FEDERAL ADMINISTRATION.

Sections 616, 617, and 618 shall, to the extent not inconsistent with this part, apply to the program authorized by this part, except that—

(1) any reference in such sections to a State

educational agency shall be considered to be a reference to a State's lead agency established or designated under section 635(a)(10);

(2) any reference in such sections to a local educational agency, educational service agency, or a State agency shall be considered to be a reference to an early intervention service provider under this part; and

(3) any reference to the education of children with disabilities or the education of all children with disabilities shall be considered to be a reference to the provision of appropriate early intervention services to infants and toddlers with disabilities.

SEC. 643. ALLOCATION OF FUNDS.

(a) RESERVATION OF FUNDS FOR OUTLYING AREAS-

(1) IN GENERAL- From the sums appropriated to carry out this part for any fiscal year, the Secretary may reserve not more than 1 percent for payments to Guam, American Samoa, the United States Virgin Islands, and the Commonwealth of the Northern Mariana Islands in accordance with their respective needs for assistance under this part.

(2) CONSOLIDATION OF FUNDS- The provisions of Public Law 95-134, permitting the consolidation of grants to the outlying areas, shall not apply to funds those areas receive under this part.

(b) PAYMENTS TO INDIANS-

(1) IN GENERAL- The Secretary shall, subject to this subsection, make payments to the Secretary of the Interior to be distributed to tribes, tribal organizations (as defined under section 4 of the Indian Self-Determination and Education Assistance Act), or consortia of the above entities for the coordination of assistance in the provision of early intervention services by the States to infants and toddlers with disabilities and their families on reservations served by elementary schools and secondary schools for Indian children operated or funded by the Department of the Interior. The amount of such payment for any fiscal year shall be 1.25 percent of the aggregate of the amount available to all States under this part for such fiscal year.

(2) ALLOCATION- For each fiscal year, the Secretary of the Interior shall distribute the entire payment received under paragraph (1) by providing to each tribe, tribal organization, or consortium an amount based on the number of infants and toddlers residing on the reservation, as determined annually, divided by the total of such children served by all tribes, tribal

organizations, or consortia.

(3) INFORMATION- To receive a payment under this subsection, the tribe, tribal organization, or consortium shall submit such information to the Secretary of the Interior as is needed to determine the amounts to be distributed under paragraph (2).

(4) USE OF FUNDS- The funds received by a tribe, tribal organization, or consortium shall be used to assist States in child find, screening, and other procedures for the early identification of Indian children under 3 years of age and for parent training. Such funds may also be used to provide early intervention services in accordance with this part. Such activities may be carried out directly or through contracts or cooperative agreements with the Bureau of Indian Affairs, local educational agencies, and other public or private nonprofit organizations. The tribe, tribal organization, or consortium is encouraged to involve Indian parents in the development and implementation of these activities. The above entities shall, as appropriate, make referrals to local, State, or Federal entities for the provision of services or further diagnosis.

(5) REPORTS- To be eligible to receive a payment under paragraph (2), a tribe, tribal organization, or consortium shall make a biennial report to the Secretary of the Interior of activities undertaken under this subsection, including the number of contracts and cooperative agreements entered into, the number of infants and toddlers contacted and receiving services for each year, and the estimated number of infants and toddlers needing services during the 2 years following the year in which the report is made. The Secretary of the Interior shall include a summary of this information on a biennial basis to the Secretary of Education along with such other information as required under section 611(h)(3)(E). The Secretary of Education may require any additional information from the Secretary of the Interior.

(6) PROHIBITED USES OF FUNDS- None of the funds under this subsection may be used by the Secretary of the Interior for administrative purposes, including child count, and the provision of technical assistance.

(c) STATE ALLOTMENTS-

(1) IN GENERAL- Except as provided in paragraphs (2) and (3), from the funds remaining for each fiscal year after the reservation and payments under subsections (a), (b), and (e), the Secretary shall first allot to each State an amount that bears the same ratio to the amount of such remainder as the number

of infants and toddlers in the State bears to the number of infants and toddlers in all States.

(2) MINIMUM ALLOTMENTS- Except as provided in paragraph (3), no State shall receive an amount under this section for any fiscal year that is less than the greater of—

(A) 1/2 of 1 percent of the remaining amount described in paragraph (1); or

(B) $500,000.

(3) RATABLE REDUCTION-

(A) IN GENERAL- If the sums made available under this part for any fiscal year are insufficient to pay the full amounts that all States are eligible to receive under this subsection for such year, the Secretary shall ratably reduce the allotments to such States for such year.

(B) ADDITIONAL FUNDS- If additional funds become available for making payments under this subsection for a fiscal year, allotments that were reduced under subparagraph (A) shall be increased on the same basis the allotments were reduced.

(4) DEFINITIONS- In this subsection—

(A) the terms 'infants' and 'toddlers' mean children under 3 years of age; and

(B) the term 'State' means each of the 50 States, the District of Columbia, and the Commonwealth of Puerto Rico.

(d) REALLOTMENT OF FUNDS- If a State elects not to receive its allotment under subsection (c), the Secretary shall reallot, among the remaining States, amounts from such State in accordance with such subsection.

(e) RESERVATION FOR STATE INCENTIVE GRANTS-

(1) IN GENERAL- For any fiscal year for which the amount appropriated pursuant to the authorization of appropriations under section 644 exceeds $460,000,000, the Secretary shall reserve 15 percent of such appropriated amount to provide grants to States that are carrying out the policy described in section 635(c) in order to facilitate the implementation of such policy.

(2) AMOUNT OF GRANT-

(A) IN GENERAL- Notwithstanding paragraphs (2) and (3) of subsection (c), the Secretary shall provide a grant to each State under paragraph (1) in an amount that bears the same ratio to the amount reserved under such paragraph as the number of infants and toddlers in the State bears to the number of infants and toddlers in all States receiving grants under such paragraph.

(B) MAXIMUM AMOUNT- No State shall receive a grant under paragraph (1) for any fiscal year in an amount that is greater than 20 percent of the amount reserved under such paragraph for the fiscal year.

(3) CARRYOVER OF AMOUNTS-

(A) FIRST SUCCEEDING FISCAL YEAR- Pursuant to section 421(b) of the General Education Provisions Act, amounts under a grant provided under paragraph (1) that are not obligated and expended prior to the beginning of the first fiscal year succeeding the fiscal year for which such amounts were appropriated shall remain available for obligation and expenditure during such first succeeding fiscal year.

(B) SECOND SUCCEEDING FISCAL YEAR- Amounts under a grant provided under paragraph (1) that are not obligated and expended prior to the beginning of the second fiscal year succeeding the fiscal year for which such amounts were appropriated shall be returned to the Secretary and used to make grants to States under section 633 (from their allotments under this section) during such second succeeding fiscal year.

SEC. 644. AUTHORIZATION OF APPROPRIATIONS.

For the purpose of carrying out this part, there are authorized to be appropriated such sums as may be necessary for each of the fiscal years 2005 through 2010.

PART D—NATIONAL ACTIVITIES TO IMPROVE EDUCATION OF CHILDREN WITH DISABILITIES

SEC. 650. FINDINGS.

Congress finds the following:

(1) The Federal Government has an ongoing obligation to support activities that contribute to positive results for children with disabilities, enabling those children to lead productive and independent adult lives.

(2) Systemic change benefiting all students, including children with disabilities, requires the involvement of States, local educational agencies, parents, individuals with disabilities and their families, teachers and other service providers, and other interested individuals and organizations to develop and implement comprehensive strategies that improve educational results for children with disabilities.

(3) State educational agencies, in partnership with local educational agencies,

parents of children with disabilities, and other individuals and organizations, are in the best position to improve education for children with disabilities and to address their special needs.

(4) An effective educational system serving students with disabilities should—

(A) maintain high academic achievement standards and clear performance goals for children with disabilities, consistent with the standards and expectations for all students in the educational system, and provide for appropriate and effective strategies and methods to ensure that all children with disabilities have the opportunity to achieve those standards and goals;

(B) clearly define, in objective, measurable terms, the school and post-school results that children with disabilities are expected to achieve; and

(C) promote transition services and coordinate State and local education, social, health, mental health, and other services, in addressing the full range of student needs, particularly the needs of children with disabilities who need significant levels of support to participate and learn in school and the community.

(5) The availability of an adequate number of qualified personnel is critical—

(A) to serve effectively children with disabilities;

(B) to assume leadership positions in administration and direct services;

(C) to provide teacher training; and

(D) to conduct high quality research to improve special education.

(6) High quality, comprehensive professional development programs are essential to ensure that the persons responsible for the education or transition of children with disabilities possess the skills and knowledge necessary to address the educational and related needs of those children.

(7) Models of professional development should be scientifically based and reflect successful practices, including strategies for recruiting, preparing, and retaining personnel.

(8) Continued support is essential for the development and maintenance of a coordinated and high quality program of research to inform successful teaching practices and model curricula for educating children with disabilities.

(9) Training, technical assistance, support, and dissemination activities are necessary to ensure that parts B and C are fully implemented and achieve high quality early intervention, educational, and transitional results for

children with disabilities and their families.

(10) Parents, teachers, administrators, and related services personnel need technical assistance and information in a timely, coordinated, and accessible manner in order to improve early intervention, educational, and transitional services and results at the State and local levels for children with disabilities and their families.

(11) Parent training and information activities assist parents of a child with a disability in dealing with the multiple pressures of parenting such a child and are of particular importance in—

(A) playing a vital role in creating and preserving constructive relationships between parents of children with disabilities and schools by facilitating open communication between the parents and schools; encouraging dispute resolution at the earliest possible point in time; and discouraging the escalation of an adversarial process between the parents and schools;

(B) ensuring the involvement of parents in planning and decisionmaking with respect to early intervention, educational, and transitional services;

(C) achieving high quality early intervention, educational, and transitional results for children with disabilities;

(D) providing such parents information on their rights, protections, and responsibilities under this title to ensure improved early intervention, educational, and transitional results for children with disabilities;

(E) assisting such parents in the development of skills to participate effectively in the education and development of their children and in the transitions described in section 673(b)(6);

(F) supporting the roles of such parents as participants within partnerships seeking to improve early intervention, educational, and transitional services and results for children with disabilities and their families; and

(G) supporting such parents who may have limited access to services and supports, due to economic, cultural, or linguistic barriers.

(12) Support is needed to improve technological resources and integrate technology, including universally designed technologies, into the lives of children with disabilities, parents of children with disabilities, school personnel, and others through curricula, services, and assistive technologies.

Subpart 1—State Personnel Development Grants

SEC. 651. PURPOSE; DEFINITION OF PERSONNEL; PROGRAM AUTHORITY.

(a) PURPOSE- The purpose of this subpart is to assist State educational agencies in reforming and improving their systems for personnel preparation and professional development in early intervention, educational, and transition services in order to improve results for children with disabilities.

(b) DEFINITION OF PERSONNEL- In this subpart the term 'personnel' means special education teachers, regular education teachers, principals, administrators, related services personnel, paraprofessionals, and early intervention personnel serving infants, toddlers, preschoolers, or children with disabilities, except where a particular category of personnel, such as related services personnel, is identified.

(c) COMPETITIVE GRANTS-

(1) IN GENERAL- Except as provided in subsection (d), for any fiscal year for which the amount appropriated under section 655, that remains after the Secretary reserves funds under subsection (e) for the fiscal year, is less than $100,000,000, the Secretary shall award grants, on a competitive basis, to State educational agencies to carry out the activities described in the State plan submitted under section 653.

(2) PRIORITY- In awarding grants under paragraph (1), the Secretary may give priority to State educational agencies that—

(A) are in States with the greatest personnel shortages; or

(B) demonstrate the greatest difficulty meeting the requirements of section 612(a)(14).

(3) MINIMUM AMOUNT- The Secretary shall make a grant to each State educational agency selected under paragraph (1) in an amount for each fiscal year that is—

(A) not less than $500,000, nor more than $4,000,000, in the case of the 50 States, the District of Columbia, and the Commonwealth of Puerto Rico; and

(B) not less than $80,000 in the case of an outlying area.

(4) INCREASE IN AMOUNT- The Secretary may increase the amounts of grants under paragraph (4) to account for inflation.

(5) FACTORS- The Secretary shall determine the amount of a grant under paragraph (1) after considering—

(A) the amount of funds available for making the grants;

(B) the relative population of the State or outlying area;

(C) the types of activities proposed by the State or outlying area;

(D) the alignment of proposed activities with section 612(a)(14);

(E) the alignment of proposed activities with the State plans and applications submitted under sections 1111 and 2112, respectively, of the Elementary and Secondary Education Act of 1965; and

(F) the use, as appropriate, of scientifically based research activities.

(d) FORMULA GRANTS-

(1) IN GENERAL- Except as provided in paragraphs (2) and (3), for the first fiscal year for which the amount appropriated under section 655, that remains after the Secretary reserves funds under subsection (e) for the fiscal year, is equal to or greater than $100,000,000, and for each fiscal year thereafter, the Secretary shall allot to each State educational agency, whose application meets the requirements of this subpart, an amount that bears the same relation to the amount remaining as the amount the State received under section 611(d) for that fiscal year bears to the amount of funds received by all States (whose applications meet the requirements of this subpart) under section 611(d) for that fiscal year.

(2) MINIMUM ALLOTMENTS FOR STATES THAT RECEIVED COMPETITIVE GRANTS-

(A) IN GENERAL- The amount allotted under this subsection to any State educational agency that received a competitive multi-year grant under subsection (c) for which the grant period has not expired shall be not less than the amount specified for that fiscal year in the State educational agency's grant award document under that subsection.

(B) SPECIAL RULE- Each such State educational agency shall use the minimum amount described in subparagraph (A) for the activities described in the State educational agency's competitive grant award document for that year, unless the Secretary approves a request from the State educational agency to spend the funds on other activities.

(3) MINIMUM ALLOTMENT- The amount of any State educational agency's allotment under this subsection for any fiscal year shall not be less than—

(A) the greater of $500,000 or 1/2 of 1 percent of the total amount available under this subsection for that year, in the case of each of the 50 States, the District of Columbia, and the Commonwealth of Puerto Rico; and

(B) $80,000, in the case of an outlying area.

(4) DIRECT BENEFIT- In using grant funds allotted under paragraph (1), a State educational agency shall, through grants, contracts, or cooperative agreements, undertake activities that significantly and directly benefit the local educational agencies in the State.

(e) CONTINUATION AWARDS-

(1) IN GENERAL- Notwithstanding any other provision of this subpart, from funds appropriated under section 655 for each fiscal year, the Secretary shall reserve the amount that is necessary to make a continuation award to any State educational agency (at the request of the State educational agency) that received a multi-year award under this part (as this part was in effect on the day before the date of enactment of the Individuals with Disabilities Education Improvement Act of 2004), to enable the State educational agency to carry out activities in accordance with the terms of the multi-year award.

(2) PROHIBITION- A State educational agency that receives a continuation award under paragraph (1) for any fiscal year may not receive any other award under this subpart for that fiscal year.

SEC. 652. ELIGIBILITY AND COLLABORATIVE PROCESS.

(a) ELIGIBLE APPLICANTS- A State educational agency may apply for a grant under this subpart for a grant period of not less than 1 year and not more than 5 years.

(b) PARTNERS-

(1) IN GENERAL- In order to be considered for a grant under this subpart, a State educational agency shall establish a partnership with local educational agencies and other State agencies involved in, or concerned with, the education of children with disabilities, including—

(A) not less than 1 institution of higher education; and

(B) the State agencies responsible for administering part C, early education, child care, and vocational rehabilitation programs.

(2) OTHER PARTNERS- In order to be considered for a grant under this subpart, a State educational agency shall work in partnership with other persons and organizations involved in, and concerned with, the education of children with disabilities, which may include—

(A) the Governor;

(B) parents of children with disabilities ages birth through 26;

(C) parents of nondisabled children ages birth through 26;

(D) individuals with disabilities;

(E) parent training and information centers or community parent resource centers funded under sections 671 and 672, respectively;

(F) community based and other nonprofit organizations involved in the education and employment of individuals with disabilities;

(G) personnel as defined in section 651(b);

(H) the State advisory panel established under part B;

(I) the State interagency coordinating council established under part C;

(J) individuals knowledgeable about vocational education;

(K) the State agency for higher education;

(L) public agencies with jurisdiction in the areas of health, mental health, social services, and juvenile justice;

(M) other providers of professional development that work with infants, toddlers, preschoolers, and children with disabilities; and

(N) other individuals.

(3) REQUIRED PARTNER- If State law assigns responsibility for teacher preparation and certification to an individual, entity, or agency other than the State educational agency, the State educational agency shall—

(A) include that individual, entity, or agency as a partner in the partnership under this subsection; and

(B) ensure that any activities the State educational agency will carry out under this subpart that are within that partner's jurisdiction (which may include activities described in section 654(b)) are carried out by that partner.

SEC. 653. APPLICATIONS.

(a) IN GENERAL-

(1) SUBMISSION- A State educational agency that desires to receive a grant under this subpart shall submit to the Secretary an application at such time, in such manner, and including such information as the Secretary may require.

(2) STATE PLAN- The application shall include a plan that identifies and addresses the State and local needs for the personnel

preparation and professional development of personnel, as well as individuals who provide direct supplementary aids and services to children with disabilities, and that—

(A) is designed to enable the State to meet the requirements of section 612(a)(14) and section 635(a) (8) and (9);

(B) is based on an assessment of State and local needs that identifies critical aspects and areas in need of improvement related to the preparation, ongoing training, and professional development of personnel who serve infants, toddlers, preschoolers, and children with disabilities within the State, including—

(i) current and anticipated personnel vacancies and shortages; and

(ii) the number of preservice and inservice programs; and

(C) is integrated and aligned, to the maximum extent possible, with State plans and activities under the Elementary and Secondary Education Act of 1965, the Rehabilitation Act of 1973, and the Higher Education Act of 1965.

(3) REQUIREMENT- The State application shall contain an assurance that the State educational agency will carry out each of the strategies described in subsection (b)(4).

(b) ELEMENTS OF STATE PERSONNEL DEVELOPMENT PLAN- Each State personnel development plan under subsection (a)(2) shall—

(1) describe a partnership agreement that is in effect for the period of the grant, which agreement shall specify—

(A) the nature and extent of the partnership described in section 652(b) and the respective roles of each member of the partnership, including the partner described in section 652(b)(3) if applicable; and

(B) how the State educational agency will work with other persons and organizations involved in, and concerned with, the education of children with disabilities, including the respective roles of each of the persons and organizations;

(2) describe how the strategies and activities described in paragraph (4) will be coordinated with activities supported with other public resources (including part B and part C funds retained for use at the State level for personnel and professional development purposes) and private resources;

(3) describe how the State educational agency will align its personnel development plan under this subpart with the plan and application submitted under sections 1111 and 2112, respectively, of the Elementary and Secondary Education Act of 1965;

(4) describe those strategies the State educational agency will use to address the professional development and personnel needs identified under subsection (a)(2) and how such strategies will be implemented, including—

(A) a description of the programs and activities to be supported under this subpart that will provide personnel with the knowledge and skills to meet the needs of, and improve the performance and achievement of, infants, toddlers, preschoolers, and children with disabilities; and

(B) how such strategies will be integrated, to the maximum extent possible, with other activities supported by grants funded under section 662;

(5) provide an assurance that the State educational agency will provide technical assistance to local educational agencies to improve the quality of professional development available to meet the needs of personnel who serve children with disabilities;

(6) provide an assurance that the State educational agency will provide technical assistance to entities that provide services to infants and toddlers with disabilities to improve the quality of professional development available to meet the needs of personnel serving such children;

(7) describe how the State educational agency will recruit and retain highly qualified teachers and other qualified personnel in geographic areas of greatest need;

(8) describe the steps the State educational agency will take to ensure that poor and minority children are not taught at higher rates by teachers who are not highly qualified; and

(9) describe how the State educational agency will assess, on a regular basis, the extent to which the strategies implemented under this subpart have been effective in meeting the performance goals described in section 612(a)(15).

(c) PEER REVIEW-

(1) IN GENERAL- The Secretary shall use a panel of experts who are competent, by virtue of their training, expertise, or experience, to evaluate applications for grants under section 651(c)(1).

(2) COMPOSITION OF PANEL- A majority of a panel described in paragraph (1) shall be composed of individuals who are not employees of the Federal Government.

(3) PAYMENT OF FEES AND EXPENSES OF CERTAIN MEMBERS- The Secretary may use available funds appropriated to carry out this subpart to pay the expenses and fees of panel members who are not

employees of the Federal Government.

(d) REPORTING PROCEDURES- Each State educational agency that receives a grant under this subpart shall submit annual performance reports to the Secretary. The reports shall—

(1) describe the progress of the State educational agency in implementing its plan;

(2) analyze the effectiveness of the State educational agency's activities under this subpart and of the State educational agency's strategies for meeting its goals under section 612(a)(15); and

(3) identify changes in the strategies used by the State educational agency and described in subsection (b)(4), if any, to improve the State educational agency's performance.

SEC. 654. USE OF FUNDS.

(a) PROFESSIONAL DEVELOPMENT ACTIVITIES- A State educational agency that receives a grant under this subpart shall use the grant funds to support activities in accordance with the State's plan described in section 653, including 1 or more of the following:

(1) Carrying out programs that provide support to both special education and regular education teachers of children with disabilities and principals, such as programs that—

(A) provide teacher mentoring, team teaching, reduced class schedules and case loads, and intensive professional development;

(B) use standards or assessments for guiding beginning teachers that are consistent with challenging State student academic achievement and functional standards and with the requirements for professional development, as defined in section 9101 of the Elementary and Secondary Education Act of 1965; and

(C) encourage collaborative and consultative models of providing early intervention, special education, and related services.

(2) Encouraging and supporting the training of special education and regular education teachers and administrators to effectively use and integrate technology—

(A) into curricula and instruction, including training to improve the ability to collect, manage, and analyze data to improve teaching, decisionmaking, school improvement efforts, and accountability;

(B) to enhance learning by children with disabilities; and

(C) to effectively communicate with parents.

(3) Providing professional development

activities that—

(A) improve the knowledge of special education and regular education teachers concerning—

(i) the academic and developmental or functional needs of students with disabilities; or

(ii) effective instructional strategies, methods, and skills, and the use of State academic content standards and student academic achievement and functional standards, and State assessments, to improve teaching practices and student academic achievement;

(B) improve the knowledge of special education and regular education teachers and principals and, in appropriate cases, paraprofessionals, concerning effective instructional practices, and that—

(i) provide training in how to teach and address the needs of children with different learning styles and children who are limited English proficient;

(ii) involve collaborative groups of teachers, administrators, and, in appropriate cases, related services personnel;

(iii) provide training in methods of—

(I) positive behavioral interventions and supports to improve student behavior in the classroom;

(II) scientifically based reading instruction, including early literacy instruction;

(III) early and appropriate interventions to identify and help children with disabilities;

(IV) effective instruction for children with low incidence disabilities;

(V) successful transitioning to postsecondary opportunities; and

(VI) using classroom-based techniques to assist children prior to referral for special education;

(iv) provide training to enable personnel to work with and involve parents in their child's education, including parents of low income and limited English proficient children with disabilities;

(v) provide training for special education personnel and regular education personnel in planning, developing, and implementing effective and appropriate IEPs; and

(vi) provide training to meet the needs of students with significant health, mobility, or behavioral needs prior to serving such students;

(C) train administrators, principals, and other relevant school personnel in conducting effective IEP meetings; and

(D) train early intervention, preschool, and related services providers, and other relevant school personnel, in conducting effective individualized family service plan (IFSP) meetings.

(4) Developing and implementing initiatives to promote the recruitment and retention of highly qualified special education teachers, particularly initiatives that have been proven effective in recruiting and retaining highly qualified teachers, including programs that provide—

(A) teacher mentoring from exemplary special education teachers, principals, or superintendents;

(B) induction and support for special education teachers during their first 3 years of employment as teachers; or

(C) incentives, including financial incentives, to retain special education teachers who have a record of success in helping students with disabilities.

(5) Carrying out programs and activities that are designed to improve the quality of personnel who serve children with disabilities, such as—

(A) innovative professional development programs (which may be provided through partnerships that include institutions of higher education), including programs that train teachers and principals to integrate technology into curricula and instruction to improve teaching, learning, and technology literacy, which professional development shall be consistent with the definition of professional development in section 9101 of the Elementary and Secondary Education Act of 1965; and

(B) the development and use of proven, cost effective strategies for the implementation of professional development activities, such as through the use of technology and distance learning.

(6) Carrying out programs and activities that are designed to improve the quality of early intervention personnel, including paraprofessionals and primary referral sources, such as—

(A) professional development programs to improve the delivery of early intervention services;

(B) initiatives to promote the recruitment and retention of early intervention personnel; and

(C) interagency activities to ensure that early intervention personnel are adequately prepared and trained.

(b) OTHER ACTIVITIES- A State educational agency that receives a grant under this subpart shall use the grant funds to support activities in accordance with the State's plan described in section 653, including 1 or more of the following:

(1) Reforming special education and regular education teacher certification (including recertification) or licensing requirements to ensure that—

(A) special education and regular education teachers have—

(i) the training and information necessary to address the full range of needs of children with disabilities across disability categories; and

(ii) the necessary subject matter knowledge and teaching skills in the academic subjects that the teachers teach;

(B) special education and regular education teacher certification (including recertification) or licensing requirements are aligned with challenging State academic content standards; and

(C) special education and regular education teachers have the subject matter knowledge and teaching skills, including technology literacy, necessary to help students with disabilities meet challenging State student academic achievement and functional standards.

(2) Programs that establish, expand, or improve alternative routes for State certification of special education teachers for highly qualified individuals with a baccalaureate or master's degree, including mid-career professionals from other occupations, paraprofessionals, and recent college or university graduates with records of academic distinction who demonstrate the potential to become highly effective special education teachers.

(3) Teacher advancement initiatives for special education teachers that promote professional growth and emphasize multiple career paths (such as paths to becoming a career teacher, mentor teacher, or exemplary teacher) and pay differentiation.

(4) Developing and implementing mechanisms to assist local educational agencies and schools in effectively recruiting and retaining highly qualified special education teachers.

(5) Reforming tenure systems, implementing teacher testing for subject matter knowledge, and implementing teacher testing for State certification or licensing, consistent with title II of the Higher Education Act of 1965.

(6) Funding projects to promote reciprocity of teacher certification or licensing between or among States for special education teachers, except that no reciprocity agreement developed under this paragraph or developed using funds provided under this subpart may lead to the weakening of any State teaching certification

or licensing requirement.

(7) Assisting local educational agencies to serve children with disabilities through the development and use of proven, innovative strategies to deliver intensive professional development programs that are both cost effective and easily accessible, such as strategies that involve delivery through the use of technology, peer networks, and distance learning.

(8) Developing, or assisting local educational agencies in developing, merit based performance systems, and strategies that provide differential and bonus pay for special education teachers.

(9) Supporting activities that ensure that teachers are able to use challenging State academic content standards and student academic achievement and functional standards, and State assessments for all children with disabilities, to improve instructional practices and improve the academic achievement of children with disabilities.

(10) When applicable, coordinating with, and expanding centers established under, section 2113(c)(18) of the Elementary and Secondary Education Act of 1965 to benefit special education teachers.

(c) CONTRACTS AND SUBGRANTS- A State educational agency that receives a grant under this subpart—

(1) shall award contracts or subgrants to local educational agencies, institutions of higher education, parent training and information centers, or community parent resource centers, as appropriate, to carry out its State plan under this subpart; and

(2) may award contracts and subgrants to other public and private entities, including the lead agency under part C, to carry out the State plan.

(d) USE OF FUNDS FOR PROFESSIONAL DEVELOPMENT- A State educational agency that receives a grant under this subpart shall use—

(1) not less than 90 percent of the funds the State educational agency receives under the grant for any fiscal year for activities under subsection (a); and

(2) not more than 10 percent of the funds the State educational agency receives under the grant for any fiscal year for activities under subsection (b).

(e) GRANTS TO OUTLYING AREAS- Public Law 95-134, permitting the consolidation of grants to the outlying areas, shall not apply to funds received under this subpart.

SEC. 655. AUTHORIZATION OF APPROPRIATIONS.

There are authorized to be appropriated to carry out this subpart such sums as may be necessary for each of the fiscal years 2005 through 2010.

Subpart 2—Personnel Preparation, Technical Assistance, Model Demonstration Projects, and Dissemination of Information

SEC. 661. PURPOSE; DEFINITION OF ELIGIBLE ENTITY.

(a) PURPOSE- The purpose of this subpart is—

(1) to provide Federal funding for personnel preparation, technical assistance, model demonstration projects, information dissemination, and studies and evaluations, in order to improve early intervention, educational, and transitional results for children with disabilities; and

(2) to assist State educational agencies and local educational agencies in improving their education systems for children with disabilities.

(b) DEFINITION OF ELIGIBLE ENTITY-

(1) IN GENERAL- In this subpart, the term eligible entity' means—

(A) a State educational agency;

(B) a local educational agency;

(C) a public charter school that is a local educational agency under State law;

(D) an institution of higher education;

(E) a public agency not described in subparagraphs (A) through (D);

(F) a private nonprofit organization;

(G) an outlying area;

(H) an Indian tribe or a tribal organization (as defined under section 4 of the Indian Self-Determination and Education Assistance Act); or

(I) a for-profit organization, if the Secretary finds it appropriate in light of the purposes of a particular competition for a grant, contract, or cooperative agreement under this subpart.

(2) SPECIAL RULE- The Secretary may limit which eligible entities described in paragraph (1) are eligible for a grant, contract, or cooperative agreement under this subpart to 1 or more of the categories of eligible entities described in paragraph (1).

SEC. 662. PERSONNEL DEVELOPMENT TO IMPROVE SERVICES AND RESULTS FOR CHILDREN WITH DISABILITIES.

(a) IN GENERAL- The Secretary, on a competitive basis, shall award grants to, or enter into contracts or cooperative agreements with, eligible entities to carry out 1 or more of the following objectives:

(1) To help address the needs identified in the State plan described in section 653(a)(2) for highly qualified personnel, as defined in section 651(b), to work with infants or toddlers with disabilities, or children with disabilities, consistent with the qualifications described in section 612(a)(14).

(2) To ensure that those personnel have the necessary skills and knowledge, derived from practices that have been determined, through scientifically based research, to be successful in serving those children.

(3) To encourage increased focus on academics and core content areas in special education personnel preparation programs.

(4) To ensure that regular education teachers have the necessary skills and knowledge to provide instruction to students with disabilities in the regular education classroom.

(5) To ensure that all special education teachers are highly qualified.

(6) To ensure that preservice and in-service personnel preparation programs include training in—

(A) the use of new technologies;

(B) the area of early intervention, educational, and transition services;

(C) effectively involving parents; and

(D) positive behavioral supports.

(7) To provide high-quality professional development for principals, superintendents, and other administrators, including training in—

(A) instructional leadership;

(B) behavioral supports in the school and classroom;

(C) paperwork reduction;

(D) promoting improved collaboration between special education and general education teachers;

(E) assessment and accountability;

(F) ensuring effective learning environments; and

(G) fostering positive relationships with parents.

(b) PERSONNEL DEVELOPMENT; ENHANCED SUPPORT FOR BEGINNING SPECIAL EDUCATORS-

(1) IN GENERAL- In carrying out this section, the Secretary shall support activities—

(A) for personnel development, including activities for the preparation of personnel who will serve children with high incidence and low incidence disabilities, to prepare special education and general education teachers, principals, administrators, and related services personnel (and school board members, when appropriate) to meet the diverse and individualized instructional needs of children with disabilities and improve early intervention, educational, and transitional services and results for children with disabilities, consistent with the objectives described in subsection (a); and

(B) for enhanced support for beginning special educators, consistent with the objectives described in subsection (a).

(2) PERSONNEL DEVELOPMENT- In carrying out paragraph (1)(A), the Secretary shall support not less than 1 of the following activities:

(A) Assisting effective existing, improving existing, or developing new, collaborative personnel preparation activities undertaken by institutions of higher education, local educational agencies, and other local entities that incorporate best practices and scientifically based research, where applicable, in providing special education and general education teachers, principals, administrators, and related services personnel with the knowledge and skills to effectively support students with disabilities, including—

(i) working collaboratively in regular classroom settings;

(ii) using appropriate supports, accommodations, and curriculum modifications;

(iii) implementing effective teaching strategies, classroom-based techniques, and interventions to ensure appropriate identification of students who may be eligible for special education services, and to prevent the misidentification, inappropriate overidentification, or underidentification of children as having a disability, especially minority and limited English proficient children;

(iv) effectively working with and involving parents in the education of their children;

(v) utilizing strategies, including positive behavioral interventions, for addressing the conduct of children with disabilities that impedes their learning and that of others in the classroom;

(vi) effectively constructing IEPs, participating in IEP meetings, and implementing IEPs;

(vii) preparing children with disabilities to participate in statewide assessments (with or without accommodations) and alternate assessments, as appropriate, and to ensure that all children with disabilities are a part of all accountability systems under the Elementary and Secondary Education Act of 1965; and

(viii) working in high need elementary schools and secondary schools, including urban schools, rural schools, and schools operated by an entity described in section 7113(d)(1)(A)(ii) of the Elementary and Secondary Education Act of 1965, and schools that serve high numbers or percentages of limited English proficient children.

(B) Developing, evaluating, and disseminating innovative models for the recruitment, induction, retention, and assessment of new, highly qualified teachers to reduce teacher shortages, especially from groups that are underrepresented in the teaching profession, including individuals with disabilities.

(C) Providing continuous personnel preparation, training, and professional development designed to provide support and ensure retention of special education and general education teachers and personnel who teach and provide related services to children with disabilities.

(D) Developing and improving programs for paraprofessionals to become special education teachers, related services personnel, and early intervention personnel, including interdisciplinary training to enable the paraprofessionals to improve early intervention, educational, and transitional results for children with disabilities.

(E) In the case of principals and superintendents, providing activities to promote instructional leadership and improved collaboration between general educators, special education teachers, and related services personnel.

(F) Supporting institutions of higher education with minority enrollments of not less than 25 percent for the purpose of preparing personnel to work with children with disabilities.

(G) Developing and improving programs to train special education teachers to develop an expertise in autism spectrum disorders.

(H) Providing continuous personnel preparation, training, and professional development designed to provide support and improve the qualifications of personnel who provide related services to children with disabilities, including to enable such personnel to obtain advanced degrees.

(3) ENHANCED SUPPORT FOR BEGINNING SPECIAL EDUCATORS- In carrying out paragraph (1)(B), the Secretary shall support not less than 1 of the following activities:

(A) Enhancing and restructuring existing programs or developing preservice teacher education programs to prepare special education teachers, at colleges or departments of education within institutions of higher education, by incorporating an extended (such as an additional 5th year) clinical learning opportunity, field experience, or supervised practicum into such programs.

(B) Creating or supporting teacher-faculty partnerships (such as professional development schools) that—

(i) consist of not less than—

(I) 1 or more institutions of higher education with special education personnel preparation programs;

(II) 1 or more local educational agencies that serve high numbers or percentages of low-income students; or

(III) 1 or more elementary schools or secondary schools, particularly schools that have failed to make adequate yearly progress on the basis, in whole and in part, of the assessment results of the disaggregated subgroup of students with disabilities;

(ii) may include other entities eligible for assistance under this part; and

(iii) provide—

(I) high-quality mentoring and induction opportunities with ongoing support for beginning special education teachers; or

(II) inservice professional development to beginning and veteran special education teachers through the ongoing exchange of information and instructional strategies with faculty.

(c) LOW INCIDENCE DISABILITIES; AUTHORIZED ACTIVITIES-

(1) IN GENERAL- In carrying out this section, the Secretary shall support activities, consistent with the objectives described in subsection (a), that benefit children with low incidence disabilities.

(2) AUTHORIZED ACTIVITIES- Activities that may be carried out under this subsection include activities such as the following:

(A) Preparing persons who—

(i) have prior training in educational and

other related service fields; and

(ii) are studying to obtain degrees, certificates, or licensure that will enable the persons to assist children with low incidence disabilities to achieve the objectives set out in their individualized education programs described in section 614(d), or to assist infants and toddlers with low incidence disabilities to achieve the outcomes described in their individualized family service plans described in section 636.

(B) Providing personnel from various disciplines with interdisciplinary training that will contribute to improvement in early intervention, educational, and transitional results for children with low incidence disabilities.

(C) Preparing personnel in the innovative uses and application of technology, including universally designed technologies, assistive technology devices, and assistive technology services—

(i) to enhance learning by children with low incidence disabilities through early intervention, educational, and transitional services; and

(ii) to improve communication with parents.

(D) Preparing personnel who provide services to visually impaired or blind children to teach and use Braille in the provision of services to such children.

(E) Preparing personnel to be qualified educational interpreters, to assist children with low incidence disabilities, particularly deaf and hard of hearing children in school and school related activities, and deaf and hard of hearing infants and toddlers and preschool children in early intervention and preschool programs.

(F) Preparing personnel who provide services to children with significant cognitive disabilities and children with multiple disabilities.

(G) Preparing personnel who provide services to children with low incidence disabilities and limited English proficient children.

(3) DEFINITION- In this section, the term 'low incidence disability' means—

(A) a visual or hearing impairment, or simultaneous visual and hearing impairments;

(B) a significant cognitive impairment; or

(C) any impairment for which a small number of personnel with highly specialized skills and knowledge are needed in order for children with that impairment to receive early intervention services or a free appropriate public education.

(4) SELECTION OF RECIPIENTS- In selecting eligible entities for assistance under this subsection, the Secretary may give preference to eligible entities submitting applications that include 1 or more of the following:

(A) A proposal to prepare personnel in more than 1 low incidence disability, such as deafness and blindness.

(B) A demonstration of an effective collaboration between an eligible entity and a local educational agency that promotes recruitment and subsequent retention of highly qualified personnel to serve children with low incidence disabilities.

(5) PREPARATION IN USE OF BRAILLE- The Secretary shall ensure that all recipients of awards under this subsection who will use that assistance to prepare personnel to provide services to visually impaired or blind children that can appropriately be provided in Braille, will prepare those individuals to provide those services in Braille.

(d) LEADERSHIP PREPARATION; AUTHORIZED ACTIVITIES-

(1) IN GENERAL- In carrying out this section, the Secretary shall support leadership preparation activities that are consistent with the objectives described in subsection (a).

(2) AUTHORIZED ACTIVITIES- Activities that may be carried out under this subsection include activities such as the following:

(A) Preparing personnel at the graduate, doctoral, and postdoctoral levels of training to administer, enhance, or provide services to improve results for children with disabilities.

(B) Providing interdisciplinary training for various types of leadership personnel, including teacher preparation faculty, related services faculty, administrators, researchers, supervisors, principals, and other persons whose work affects early intervention, educational, and transitional services for children with disabilities, including children with disabilities who are limited English proficient children.

(e) APPLICATIONS-

(1) IN GENERAL- An eligible entity that wishes to receive a grant, or enter into a contract or cooperative agreement, under this section shall submit an application to the Secretary at such time, in such manner, and containing such information as the Secretary may require.

(2) IDENTIFIED STATE NEEDS-

(A) REQUIREMENT TO ADDRESS IDENTIFIED NEEDS- An application for assistance under subsection (b), (c), or (d) shall include information demonstrating to the satisfaction of the Secretary that the activities described in the application will address needs identified by the State or States the eligible entity proposes to serve.

(B) COOPERATION WITH STATE EDUCATIONAL AGENCIES- An eligible entity that is not a local educational agency or a State educational agency shall include in the eligible entity's application information demonstrating to the satisfaction of the Secretary that the eligible entity and 1 or more State educational agencies or local educational agencies will cooperate in carrying out and monitoring the proposed project.

(3) ACCEPTANCE BY STATES OF PERSONNEL PREPARATION REQUIREMENTS- The Secretary may require eligible entities to provide in the eligible entities' applications assurances from 1 or more States that such States intend to accept successful completion of the proposed personnel preparation program as meeting State personnel standards or other requirements in State law or regulation for serving children with disabilities or serving infants and toddlers with disabilities.

(f) SELECTION OF RECIPIENTS-

(1) IMPACT OF PROJECT- In selecting eligible entities for assistance under this section, the Secretary shall consider the impact of the proposed project described in the application in meeting the need for personnel identified by the States.

(2) REQUIREMENT FOR ELIGIBLE ENTITIES TO MEET STATE AND PROFESSIONAL QUALIFICATIONS- The Secretary shall make grants and enter into contracts and cooperative agreements under this section only to eligible entities that meet State and professionally recognized qualifications for the preparation of special education and related services personnel, if the purpose of the project is to assist personnel in obtaining degrees.

(3) PREFERENCES- In selecting eligible entities for assistance under this section, the Secretary may give preference to eligible entities that are institutions of higher education that are—

(A) educating regular education personnel to meet the needs of children with disabilities in integrated settings;

(B) educating special education personnel to work in collaboration with regular educators in integrated settings; and

(C) successfully recruiting and preparing individuals with disabilities and individuals from groups that are underrepresented in the profession for which the institution of higher education is preparing individuals.

(g) SCHOLARSHIPS- The Secretary may include funds for scholarships, with necessary stipends and allowances, in awards under subsections (b), (c), and (d).

(h) SERVICE OBLIGATION-

(1) IN GENERAL- Each application for assistance under subsections (b), (c), and (d) shall include an assurance that the eligible entity will ensure that individuals who receive a scholarship under the proposed project agree to subsequently provide special education and related services to children with disabilities, or in the case of leadership personnel to subsequently work in the appropriate field, for a period of 2 years for every year for which the scholarship was received or repay all or part of the amount of the scholarship, in accordance with regulations issued by the Secretary.

(2) SPECIAL RULE- Notwithstanding paragraph (1), the Secretary may reduce or waive the service obligation requirement under paragraph (1) if the Secretary determines that the service obligation is acting as a deterrent to the recruitment of students into special education or a related field.

(3) SECRETARY'S RESPONSIBILITY- The Secretary—

(A) shall ensure that individuals described in paragraph (1) comply with the requirements of that paragraph; and

(B) may use not more than 0.5 percent of the funds appropriated under subsection (i) for each fiscal year, to carry out subparagraph (A), in addition to any other funds that are available for that purpose.

(i) AUTHORIZATION OF APPROPRIATIONS- There are authorized to be appropriated to carry out this section such sums as may be necessary for each of the fiscal years 2005 through 2010.

SEC. 663. TECHNICAL ASSISTANCE, DEMONSTRATION PROJECTS, DISSEMINATION OF INFORMATION, AND IMPLEMENTATION OF SCIENTIFICALLY BASED RESEARCH.

(a) IN GENERAL- The Secretary shall make competitive grants to, or enter into contracts or cooperative agreements with, eligible entities to provide technical assistance, support model demonstration projects, disseminate useful information, and implement activities that are supported by scientifically based research.

(b) REQUIRED ACTIVITIES- Funds received under this section shall be used to support activities to improve services provided under this title, including the practices of professionals and others involved in providing such services to children with disabilities, that promote academic achievement and improve results for children with disabilities through—

(1) implementing effective strategies for addressing inappropriate behavior of students with disabilities in schools, including strategies to prevent children with emotional and behavioral problems from developing emotional disturbances that require the provision of special education and related services;

(2) improving the alignment, compatibility, and development of valid and reliable assessments and alternate assessments for assessing adequate yearly progress, as described under section 1111(b)(2)(B) of the Elementary and Secondary Education Act of 1965;

(3) providing training for both regular education teachers and special education teachers to address the needs of students with different learning styles;

(4) disseminating information about innovative, effective, and efficient curricula designs, instructional approaches, and strategies, and identifying positive academic and social learning opportunities, that—

(A) provide effective transitions between educational settings or from school to post school settings; and

(B) improve educational and transitional results at all levels of the educational system in which the activities are carried out and, in particular, that improve the progress of children with disabilities, as measured by assessments within the general education curriculum involved; and

(5) applying scientifically based findings to facilitate systemic changes, related to the provision of services to children with disabilities, in policy, procedure, practice, and the training and use of personnel.

(c) AUTHORIZED ACTIVITIES- Activities that may be carried out under this section include activities to improve services provided under this title, including the practices of professionals and others involved in providing such services to children with disabilities, that promote academic achievement and improve results for children with disabilities through—

(1) applying and testing research findings in typical settings where children with disabilities

receive services to determine the usefulness, effectiveness, and general applicability of such research findings in such areas as improving instructional methods, curricula, and tools, such as textbooks and media;

(2) supporting and promoting the coordination of early intervention and educational services for children with disabilities with services provided by health, rehabilitation, and social service agencies;

(3) promoting improved alignment and compatibility of general and special education reforms concerned with curricular and instructional reform, and evaluation of such reforms;

(4) enabling professionals, parents of children with disabilities, and other persons to learn about, and implement, the findings of scientifically based research, and successful practices developed in model demonstration projects, relating to the provision of services to children with disabilities;

(5) conducting outreach, and disseminating information, relating to successful approaches to overcoming systemic barriers to the effective and efficient delivery of early intervention, educational, and transitional services to personnel who provide services to children with disabilities;

(6) assisting States and local educational agencies with the process of planning systemic changes that will promote improved early intervention, educational, and transitional results for children with disabilities;

(7) promoting change through a multistate or regional framework that benefits States, local educational agencies, and other participants in partnerships that are in the process of achieving systemic-change outcomes;

(8) focusing on the needs and issues that are specific to a population of children with disabilities, such as providing single-State and multi-State technical assistance and in-service training—

(A) to schools and agencies serving deaf-blind children and their families;

(B) to programs and agencies serving other groups of children with low incidence disabilities and their families;

(C) addressing the postsecondary education needs of individuals who are deaf or hard-of-hearing; and

(D) to schools and personnel providing special education and related services for children with autism spectrum disorders;

(9) demonstrating models of personnel preparation to ensure appropriate placements

and services for all students and to reduce disproportionality in eligibility, placement, and disciplinary actions for minority and limited English proficient children; and

(10) disseminating information on how to reduce inappropriate racial and ethnic disproportionalities identified under section 618.

(d) BALANCE AMONG ACTIVITIES AND AGE RANGES- In carrying out this section, the Secretary shall ensure that there is an appropriate balance across all age ranges of children with disabilities.

(e) LINKING STATES TO INFORMATION SOURCES- In carrying out this section, the Secretary shall support projects that link States to technical assistance resources, including special education and general education resources, and shall make research and related products available through libraries, electronic networks, parent training projects, and other information sources, including through the activities of the National Center for Education Evaluation and Regional Assistance established under part D of the Education Sciences Reform Act of 2002.

(f) APPLICATIONS-

(1) IN GENERAL- An eligible entity that wishes to receive a grant, or enter into a contract or cooperative agreement, under this section shall submit an application to the Secretary at such time, in such manner, and containing such information as the Secretary may require.

(2) STANDARDS- To the maximum extent feasible, each eligible entity shall demonstrate that the project described in the eligible entity's application is supported by scientifically valid research that has been carried out in accordance with the standards for the conduct and evaluation of all relevant research and development established by the National Center for Education Research.

(3) PRIORITY- As appropriate, the Secretary shall give priority to applications that propose to serve teachers and school personnel directly in the school environment.

SEC. 664. STUDIES AND EVALUATIONS.

(a) STUDIES AND EVALUATIONS-

(1) DELEGATION- The Secretary shall delegate to the Director of the Institute of Education Sciences responsibility to carry out this section, other than subsections (d) and (f).

(2) ASSESSMENT- The Secretary shall, directly or through grants, contracts, or cooperative agreements awarded to eligible entities on a competitive basis, assess the progress in the implementation of this title, including the effectiveness of State and local efforts to provide—

(A) a free appropriate public education to children with disabilities; and

(B) early intervention services to infants and toddlers with disabilities, and infants and toddlers who would be at risk of having substantial developmental delays if early intervention services were not provided to the infants and toddlers.

(b) ASSESSMENT OF NATIONAL ACTIVITIES-

(1) IN GENERAL- The Secretary shall carry out a national assessment of activities carried out with Federal funds under this title in order—

(A) to determine the effectiveness of this title in achieving the purposes of this title;

(B) to provide timely information to the President, Congress, the States, local educational agencies, and the public on how to implement this title more effectively; and

(C) to provide the President and Congress with information that will be useful in developing legislation to achieve the purposes of this title more effectively.

(2) SCOPE OF ASSESSMENT- The national assessment shall assess activities supported under this title, including—

(A) the implementation of programs assisted under this title and the impact of such programs on addressing the developmental needs of, and improving the academic achievement of, children with disabilities to enable the children to reach challenging developmental goals and challenging State academic content standards based on State academic assessments;

(B) the types of programs and services that have demonstrated the greatest likelihood of helping students reach the challenging State academic content standards and developmental goals;

(C) the implementation of the professional development activities assisted under this title and the impact on instruction, student academic achievement, and teacher qualifications to enhance the ability of special education teachers and regular education teachers to improve results for children with disabilities; and

(D) the effectiveness of schools, local educational agencies, States, other recipients of assistance under this title, and the Secretary in achieving the purposes of this title by—

(i) improving the academic achievement of children with disabilities and their performance on regular statewide assessments as compared to nondisabled children, and the performance of children with disabilities on alternate assessments;

(ii) improving the participation of children with disabilities in the general education curriculum;

(iii) improving the transitions of children with disabilities at natural transition points;

(iv) placing and serving children with disabilities, including minority children, in the least restrictive environment appropriate;

(v) preventing children with disabilities, especially children with emotional disturbances and specific learning disabilities, from dropping out of school;

(vi) addressing the reading and literacy needs of children with disabilities;

(vii) reducing the inappropriate overidentification of children, especially minority and limited English proficient children, as having a disability;

(viii) improving the participation of parents of children with disabilities in the education of their children; and

(ix) resolving disagreements between education personnel and parents through alternate dispute resolution activities, including mediation.

(3) INTERIM AND FINAL REPORTS- The Secretary shall submit to the President and Congress—

(A) an interim report that summarizes the preliminary findings of the assessment not later than 3 years after the date of enactment of the Individuals with Disabilities Education Improvement Act of 2004; and

(B) a final report of the findings of the assessment not later than 5 years after the date of enactment of such Act.

(c) STUDY ON ENSURING ACCOUNTABILITY FOR STUDENTS WHO ARE HELD TO ALTERNATIVE ACHIEVEMENT STANDARDS- The Secretary shall carry out a national study or studies to examine—

(1) the criteria that States use to determine—

(A) eligibility for alternate assessments; and

(B) the number and type of children who take those assessments and are held accountable to alternative achievement standards;

(2) the validity and reliability of alternate assessment instruments and procedures;

(3) the alignment of alternate assessments and alternative achievement standards to State academic content standards in reading, mathematics, and science; and

(4) the use and effectiveness of alternate assessments in appropriately measuring student progress and outcomes specific to individualized instructional need.

(d) ANNUAL REPORT- The Secretary shall provide an annual report to Congress that—

(1) summarizes the research conducted under part E of the Education Sciences Reform Act of 2002;

(2) analyzes and summarizes the data reported by the States and the Secretary of the Interior under section 618;

(3) summarizes the studies and evaluations conducted under this section and the timeline for their completion;

(4) describes the extent and progress of the assessment of national activities; and

(5) describes the findings and determinations resulting from reviews of State implementation of this title.

(e) AUTHORIZED ACTIVITIES- In carrying out this section, the Secretary may support objective studies, evaluations, and assessments, including studies that—

(1) analyze measurable impact, outcomes, and results achieved by State educational agencies and local educational agencies through their activities to reform policies, procedures, and practices designed to improve educational and transitional services and results for children with disabilities;

(2) analyze State and local needs for professional development, parent training, and other appropriate activities that can reduce the need for disciplinary actions involving children with disabilities;

(3) assess educational and transitional services and results for children with disabilities from minority backgrounds, including—

(A) data on—

(i) the number of minority children who are referred for special education evaluation;

(ii) the number of minority children who are receiving special education and related services and their educational or other service placement;

(iii) the number of minority children who graduated from secondary programs with a regular diploma in the standard number of years; and

(iv) the number of minority children who drop out of the educational system; and

(B) the performance of children with disabilities from minority backgrounds on

State assessments and other performance indicators established for all students;

(4) measure educational and transitional services and results for children with disabilities served under this title, including longitudinal studies that—

(A) examine educational and transitional services and results for children with disabilities who are 3 through 17 years of age and are receiving special education and related services under this title, using a national, representative sample of distinct age cohorts and disability categories; and

(B) examine educational results, transition services, postsecondary placement, and employment status for individuals with disabilities, 18 through 21 years of age, who are receiving or have received special education and related services under this title; and

(5) identify and report on the placement of children with disabilities by disability category.

(f) STUDY- The Secretary shall study, and report to Congress regarding, the extent to which States adopt policies described in section 635(c)(1) and on the effects of those policies.

SEC. 665. INTERIM ALTERNATIVE EDUCATIONAL SETTINGS, BEHAVIORAL SUPPORTS, AND SYSTEMIC SCHOOL INTERVENTIONS.

(a) PROGRAM AUTHORIZED- The Secretary may award grants, and enter into contracts and cooperative agreements, to support safe learning environments that support academic achievement for all students by—

(1) improving the quality of interim alternative educational settings; and

(2) providing increased behavioral supports and research-based, systemic interventions in schools.

(b) AUTHORIZED ACTIVITIES- In carrying out this section, the Secretary may support activities to—

(1) establish, expand, or increase the scope of behavioral supports and systemic interventions by providing for effective, research-based practices, including—

(A) training for school staff on early identification, prereferral, and referral procedures;

(B) training for administrators, teachers, related services personnel, behavioral specialists, and other school staff in positive behavioral interventions and supports, behavioral intervention planning, and classroom and student management techniques;

(C) joint training for administrators, parents, teachers, related services personnel, behavioral specialists, and other school staff on effective strategies for positive behavioral interventions and behavior management strategies that focus on the prevention of behavior problems;

(D) developing or implementing specific curricula, programs, or interventions aimed at addressing behavioral problems;

(E) stronger linkages between school-based services and community-based resources, such as community mental health and primary care providers; or

(F) using behavioral specialists, related services personnel, and other staff necessary to implement behavioral supports; or

(2) improve interim alternative educational settings by—

(A) improving the training of administrators, teachers, related services personnel, behavioral specialists, and other school staff (including ongoing mentoring of new teachers) in behavioral supports and interventions;

(B) attracting and retaining a high quality, diverse staff;

(C) providing for referral to counseling services;

(D) utilizing research-based interventions, curriculum, and practices;

(E) allowing students to use instructional technology that provides individualized instruction;

(F) ensuring that the services are fully consistent with the goals of the individual student's IEP;

(G) promoting effective case management and collaboration among parents, teachers, physicians, related services personnel, behavioral specialists, principals, administrators, and other school staff;

(H) promoting interagency coordination and coordinated service delivery among schools, juvenile courts, child welfare agencies, community mental health providers, primary care providers, public recreation agencies, and community-based organizations; or

(I) providing for behavioral specialists to help students transitioning from interim alternative educational settings reintegrate into their regular classrooms.

(c) DEFINITION OF ELIGIBLE ENTITY- In this section, the term eligible entity' means—

(1) a local educational agency; or

(2) a consortium consisting of a local educational agency and 1 or more of the following entities:

(A) Another local educational agency.

(B) A community-based organization with a demonstrated record of effectiveness in helping children with disabilities who have behavioral challenges succeed.

(C) An institution of higher education.

(D) A community mental health provider.

(E) An educational service agency.

(d) APPLICATIONS- Any eligible entity that wishes to receive a grant, or enter into a contract or cooperative agreement, under this section shall—

(1) submit an application to the Secretary at such time, in such manner, and containing such information as the Secretary may require; and

(2) involve parents of participating students in the design and implementation of the activities funded under this section.

(e) REPORT AND EVALUATION- Each eligible entity receiving a grant under this section shall prepare and submit annually to the Secretary a report on the outcomes of the activities assisted under the grant.

SEC. 667. AUTHORIZATION OF APPROPRIATIONS.

(a) IN GENERAL- There are authorized to be appropriated to carry out this subpart (other than section 662) such sums as may be necessary for each of the fiscal years 2005 through 2010.

(b) RESERVATION- From amounts appropriated under subsection (a) for fiscal year 2005, the Secretary shall reserve $1,000,000 to carry out the study authorized in section 664(c). From amounts appropriated under subsection (a) for a succeeding fiscal year, the Secretary may reserve an additional amount to carry out such study if the Secretary determines the additional amount is necessary.

Subpart 3—Supports To Improve Results for Children With Disabilities

SEC. 670. PURPOSES.

The purposes of this subpart are to ensure that—

(1) children with disabilities and their parents receive training and information designed to assist the children in meeting developmental and functional goals and challenging academic achievement goals, and in preparing to lead productive independent adult lives;

(2) children with disabilities and their parents receive training and information on their rights, responsibilities, and protections under this title, in order to develop the skills necessary to cooperatively and effectively participate in planning and decision making relating to early intervention, educational, and transitional services;

(3) parents, teachers, administrators, early intervention personnel, related services personnel, and transition personnel receive coordinated and accessible technical assistance and information to assist such personnel in improving early intervention, educational, and transitional services and results for children with disabilities and their families; and

(4) appropriate technology and media are researched, developed, and demonstrated, to improve and implement early intervention, educational, and transitional services and results for children with disabilities and their families.

SEC. 671. PARENT TRAINING AND INFORMATION CENTERS.

(a) PROGRAM AUTHORIZED-

(1) IN GENERAL- The Secretary may award grants to, and enter into contracts and cooperative agreements with, parent organizations to support parent training and information centers to carry out activities under this section.

(2) DEFINITION OF PARENT ORGANIZATION- In this section, the term parent organization' means a private nonprofit organization (other than an institution of higher education) that—

(A) has a board of directors—

(i) the majority of whom are parents of children with disabilities ages birth through 26;

(ii) that includes—

(I) individuals working in the fields of special education, related services, and early intervention; and

(II) individuals with disabilities; and

(iii) the parent and professional members of which are broadly representative of the population to be served, including low-income parents and parents of limited English proficient children; and

(B) has as its mission serving families of

children with disabilities who—

(i) are ages birth through 26; and

(ii) have the full range of disabilities described in section 602(3).

(b) REQUIRED ACTIVITIES- Each parent training and information center that receives assistance under this section shall—

(1) provide training and information that meets the needs of parents of children with disabilities living in the area served by the center, particularly underserved parents and parents of children who may be inappropriately identified, to enable their children with disabilities to—

(A) meet developmental and functional goals, and challenging academic achievement goals that have been established for all children; and

(B) be prepared to lead productive independent adult lives, to the maximum extent possible;

(2) serve the parents of infants, toddlers, and children with the full range of disabilities described in section 602(3);

(3) ensure that the training and information provided meets the needs of low-income parents and parents of limited English proficient children;

(4) assist parents to—

(A) better understand the nature of their children's disabilities and their educational, developmental, and transitional needs;

(B) communicate effectively and work collaboratively with personnel responsible for providing special education, early intervention services, transition services, and related services;

(C) participate in decisionmaking processes and the development of individualized education programs under part B and individualized family service plans under part C;

(D) obtain appropriate information about the range, type, and quality of—

(i) options, programs, services, technologies, practices and interventions based on scientifically based research, to the extent practicable; and

(ii) resources available to assist children with disabilities and their families in school and at home;

(E) understand the provisions of this title for the education of, and the provision of early intervention services to, children with disabilities;

(F) participate in activities at the school level that benefit their children; and

(G) participate in school reform activities;

(5) in States where the State elects to contract with the parent training and information center, contract with State educational agencies to provide, consistent with subparagraphs (B) and (D) of section 615(e)(2), individuals who meet with parents to explain the mediation process to the parents;

(6) assist parents in resolving disputes in the most expeditious and effective way possible, including encouraging the use, and explaining the benefits, of alternative methods of dispute resolution, such as the mediation process described in section 615(e);

(7) assist parents and students with disabilities to understand their rights and responsibilities under this title, including those under section 615(m) upon the student's reaching the age of majority (as appropriate under State law);

(8) assist parents to understand the availability of, and how to effectively use, procedural safeguards under this title, including the resolution session described in section 615(e);

(9) assist parents in understanding, preparing for, and participating in, the process described in section 615(f)(1)(B);

(10) establish cooperative partnerships with community parent resource centers funded under section 672;

(11) network with appropriate clearinghouses, including organizations conducting national dissemination activities under section 663 and the Institute of Education Sciences, and with other national, State, and local organizations and agencies, such as protection and advocacy agencies, that serve parents and families of children with the full range of disabilities described in section 602(3); and

(12) annually report to the Secretary on—

(A) the number and demographics of parents to whom the center provided information and training in the most recently concluded fiscal year;

(B) the effectiveness of strategies used to reach and serve parents, including underserved parents of children with disabilities; and

(C) the number of parents served who have resolved disputes through alternative methods of dispute resolution.

(c) OPTIONAL ACTIVITIES- A parent training and information center that receives assistance under this section may provide information to teachers and other professionals to assist the teachers and professionals in improving results for children with disabilities.

(d) APPLICATION REQUIREMENTS- Each application for assistance under this section shall identify with specificity the special efforts that the parent organization will undertake—

(1) to ensure that the needs for training and information of underserved parents of children with disabilities in the area to be served are effectively met; and

(2) to work with community based organizations, including community based organizations that work with low-income parents and parents of limited English proficient children.

(e) DISTRIBUTION OF FUNDS-

(1) IN GENERAL- The Secretary shall—

(A) make not less than 1 award to a parent organization in each State for a parent training and information center that is designated as the statewide parent training and information center; or

(B) in the case of a large State, make awards to multiple parent training and information centers, but only if the centers demonstrate that coordinated services and supports will occur among the multiple centers.

(2) SELECTION REQUIREMENT- The Secretary shall select among applications submitted by parent organizations in a State in a manner that ensures the most effective assistance to parents, including parents in urban and rural areas, in the State.

(f) QUARTERLY REVIEW-

(1) MEETINGS- The board of directors of each parent organization that receives an award under this section shall meet not less than once in each calendar quarter to review the activities for which the award was made.

(2) CONTINUATION AWARD- When a parent organization requests a continuation award under this section, the board of directors shall submit to the Secretary a written review of the parent training and information program conducted by the parent organization during the preceding fiscal year.

SEC. 672. COMMUNITY PARENT RESOURCE CENTERS.

(a) PROGRAM AUTHORIZED-

(1) IN GENERAL- The Secretary may award grants to, and enter into contracts and cooperative agreements with, local parent organizations to support community parent resource centers that will help ensure that underserved parents of children with disabilities, including low income parents, parents of limited English proficient children, and parents with disabilities, have the training and information the parents need to enable the parents to participate effectively in helping

their children with disabilities—

(A) to meet developmental and functional goals, and challenging academic achievement goals that have been established for all children; and

(B) to be prepared to lead productive independent adult lives, to the maximum extent possible.

(2) DEFINITION OF LOCAL PARENT ORGANIZATION- In this section, the term local parent organization' means a parent organization, as defined in section 671(a)(2), that—

(A) has a board of directors the majority of whom are parents of children with disabilities ages birth through 26 from the community to be served; and

(B) has as its mission serving parents of children with disabilities who—

(i) are ages birth through 26; and

(ii) have the full range of disabilities described in section 602(3).

(b) REQUIRED ACTIVITIES- Each community parent resource center assisted under this section shall—

(1) provide training and information that meets the training and information needs of parents of children with disabilities proposed to be served by the grant, contract, or cooperative agreement;

(2) carry out the activities required of parent training and information centers under paragraphs (2) through (9) of section 671(b);

(3) establish cooperative partnerships with the parent training and information centers funded under section 671; and

(4) be designed to meet the specific needs of families who experience significant isolation from available sources of information and support.

SEC. 673. TECHNICAL ASSISTANCE FOR PARENT TRAINING AND INFORMATION CENTERS.

(a) PROGRAM AUTHORIZED-

(1) IN GENERAL- The Secretary may, directly or through awards to eligible entities, provide technical assistance for developing, assisting, and coordinating parent training and information programs carried out by parent training and information centers receiving assistance under section 671 and community parent resource centers receiving assistance under section 672.

(2) DEFINITION OF ELIGIBLE ENTITY- In this section, the term eligible entity' has the meaning given the term in section 661(b).

(b) AUTHORIZED ACTIVITIES- The Secretary may provide technical assistance to a parent training and information center or a community parent resource center under this section in areas such as—

(1) effective coordination of parent training efforts;

(2) dissemination of scientifically based research and information;

(3) promotion of the use of technology, including assistive technology devices and assistive technology services;

(4) reaching underserved populations, including parents of low-income and limited English proficient children with disabilities;

(5) including children with disabilities in general education programs;

(6) facilitation of transitions from—

(A) early intervention services to preschool;

(B) preschool to elementary school;

(C) elementary school to secondary school; and

(D) secondary school to postsecondary environments; and

(7) promotion of alternative methods of dispute resolution, including mediation.

(c) COLLABORATION WITH THE RESOURCE CENTERS- Each eligible entity receiving an award under subsection (a) shall develop collaborative agreements with the geographically appropriate regional resource center and, as appropriate, the regional educational laboratory supported under section 174 of the Education Sciences Reform Act of 2002, to further parent and professional collaboration.

SEC. 674. TECHNOLOGY DEVELOPMENT, DEMONSTRATION, AND UTILIZATION; MEDIA SERVICES; AND INSTRUCTIONAL MATERIALS.

(a) PROGRAM AUTHORIZED-

(1) IN GENERAL- The Secretary, on a competitive basis, shall award grants to, and enter into contracts and cooperative agreements with, eligible entities to support activities described in subsections (b) and (c).

(2) DEFINITION OF ELIGIBLE ENTITY- In this section, the term eligible entity' has the meaning given the term in section 661(b).

(b) TECHNOLOGY DEVELOPMENT, DEMONSTRATION, AND USE-

(1) IN GENERAL- In carrying out this section, the Secretary shall support activities to promote the development, demonstration, and use of technology.

(2) AUTHORIZED ACTIVITIES- The following activities may be carried out under this subsection:

(A) Conducting research on and promoting the demonstration and use of innovative, emerging, and universally designed technologies for children with disabilities, by improving the transfer of technology from research and development to practice.

(B) Supporting research, development, and dissemination of technology with universal design features, so that the technology is accessible to the broadest range of individuals with disabilities without further modification or adaptation.

(C) Demonstrating the use of systems to provide parents and teachers with information and training concerning early diagnosis of, intervention for, and effective teaching strategies for, young children with reading disabilities.

(D) Supporting the use of Internet-based communications for students with cognitive disabilities in order to maximize their academic and functional skills.

(c) EDUCATIONAL MEDIA SERVICES-

(1) IN GENERAL- In carrying out this section, the Secretary shall support—

(A) educational media activities that are designed to be of educational value in the classroom setting to children with disabilities;

(B) providing video description, open captioning, or closed captioning, that is appropriate for use in the classroom setting, of—

(i) television programs;

(ii) videos;

(iii) other materials, including programs and materials associated with new and emerging technologies, such as CDs, DVDs, video streaming, and other forms of multimedia; or

(iv) news (but only until September 30, 2006);

(C) distributing materials described in subparagraphs (A) and (B) through such mechanisms as a loan service; and

(D) providing free educational materials, including textbooks, in accessible media for visually impaired and print disabled students in elementary schools and secondary schools, postsecondary schools, and graduate schools.

(2) LIMITATION- The video description, open captioning, or closed captioning described in paragraph (1)(B) shall be provided only when the description or captioning has not been previously provided by the producer or distributor, or has not been fully funded by other sources.

(d) APPLICATIONS-

(1) IN GENERAL- Any eligible entity that wishes to receive a grant, or enter into a contract or cooperative agreement, under subsection (b) or (c) shall submit an application to the Secretary at such time, in such manner, and containing such information as the Secretary may require.

(2) SPECIAL RULE- For the purpose of an application for an award to carry out activities described in subsection (c)(1)(D), such eligible entity shall—

(A) be a national, nonprofit entity with a proven track record of meeting the needs of students with print disabilities through services described in subsection (c)(1)(D);

(B) have the capacity to produce, maintain, and distribute in a timely fashion, up-to-date textbooks in digital audio formats to qualified students; and

(C) have a demonstrated ability to significantly leverage Federal funds through other public and private contributions, as well as through the expansive use of volunteers.

(e) NATIONAL INSTRUCTIONAL MATERIALS ACCESS CENTER-

(1) IN GENERAL- The Secretary shall establish and support, through the American Printing House for the Blind, a center to be known as the National Instructional Materials Access Center' not later than 1 year after the date of enactment of the Individuals with Disabilities Education Improvement Act of 2004.

(2) DUTIES- The duties of the National Instructional Materials Access Center are the following:

(A) To receive and maintain a catalog of print instructional materials prepared in the National Instructional Materials Accessibility Standard, as established by the Secretary, made available to such center by the textbook publishing industry, State educational agencies, and local educational agencies.

(B) To provide access to print instructional materials, including textbooks, in accessible media, free of charge, to blind or other persons with print disabilities in elementary schools and secondary schools, in accordance with such terms and procedures as the National Instructional Materials Access Center may prescribe.

(C) To develop, adopt and publish procedures to protect against copyright infringement, with respect to the print instructional materials provided under sections 612(a)(23) and 613(a)(6).

(3) DEFINITIONS- In this subsection:

(A) BLIND OR OTHER PERSONS WITH PRINT DISABILITIES- The term blind or other persons with print disabilities' means children served under this Act and who may qualify in accordance with the Act entitled An Act to provide books for the adult blind', approved March 3, 1931 (2 U.S.C. 135a; 46 Stat. 1487) to receive books and other publications produced in specialized formats.

(B) NATIONAL INSTRUCTIONAL MATERIALS ACCESSIBILITY STANDARD- The term National Instructional Materials Accessibility Standard' means the standard established by the Secretary to be used in the preparation of electronic files suitable and used solely for efficient conversion into specialized formats.

(C) PRINT INSTRUCTIONAL MATERIALS- The term print instructional materials' means printed textbooks and related printed core materials that are written and published primarily for use in elementary school and secondary school instruction and are required by a State educational agency or local educational agency for use by students in the classroom.

(D) SPECIALIZED FORMATS- The term specialized formats' has the meaning given the term in section 121(d)(3) of title 17, United States Code.

(4) APPLICABILITY- This subsection shall apply to print instructional materials published after the date on which the final rule establishing the National Instructional Materials Accessibility Standard was published in the Federal Register.

(5) LIABILITY OF THE SECRETARY- Nothing in this subsection shall be construed to establish a private right of action against the Secretary for failure to provide instructional materials directly, or for failure by the National Instructional Materials Access Center to perform the duties of such center, or to otherwise authorize a private right of action related to the performance by such center, including through the application of the rights of children and parents established under this Act.

(6) INAPPLICABILITY- Subsections (a) through (d) shall not apply to this subsection.

SEC. 675. AUTHORIZATION OF APPROPRIATIONS.

There are authorized to be appropriated to carry out this subpart such sums as may be necessary for each of the fiscal years 2005 through 2010.

Subpart 4—General Provisions

SEC. 681. COMPREHENSIVE PLAN FOR SUBPARTS 2 AND 3.

(a) COMPREHENSIVE PLAN-

(1) IN GENERAL- After receiving input from interested individuals with relevant expertise, the Secretary shall develop and implement a comprehensive plan for activities carried out under subparts 2 and 3 in order to enhance the provision of early intervention services, educational services, related services, and transitional services to children with disabilities under parts B and C. To the extent practicable, the plan shall be coordinated with the plan developed pursuant to section 178(c) of the Education Sciences Reform Act of 2002 and shall include mechanisms to address early intervention, educational, related service and transitional needs identified by State educational agencies in applications submitted for State personnel development grants under subpart 1 and for grants under subparts 2 and 3.

(2) PUBLIC COMMENT- The Secretary shall provide a public comment period of not less than 45 days on the plan.

(3) DISTRIBUTION OF FUNDS- In implementing the plan, the Secretary shall, to the extent appropriate, ensure that funds awarded under subparts 2 and 3 are used to carry out activities that benefit, directly or indirectly, children with the full range of disabilities and of all ages.

(4) REPORTS TO CONGRESS- The Secretary shall annually report to Congress on the Secretary's activities under subparts 2 and 3, including an initial report not later than 12 months after the date of enactment of the Individuals with Disabilities Education Improvement Act of 2004.

(b) ASSISTANCE AUTHORIZED- The Secretary is authorized to award grants to, or enter into contracts or cooperative agreements with, eligible entities to enable the eligible entities to carry out the purposes of such subparts in accordance with the comprehensive plan described in subsection (a).

(c) SPECIAL POPULATIONS-

(1) APPLICATION REQUIREMENT- In making an award of a grant, contract, or cooperative agreement under subpart 2 or 3, the Secretary shall, as appropriate, require an eligible entity to demonstrate how the eligible entity will address the needs of children with disabilities from minority backgrounds.

(2) REQUIRED OUTREACH AND TECHNICAL ASSISTANCE- Notwithstanding any other provision of this title, the Secretary shall reserve not less than 2 percent of the total amount of funds appropriated to carry out subparts 2 and 3 for either or both of the following activities:

(A) Providing outreach and technical assistance to historically Black colleges and universities, and to institutions of higher education with minority enrollments of not less than 25 percent, to promote the participation of such colleges, universities, and institutions in activities under this subpart.

(B) Enabling historically Black colleges and universities, and the institutions described in subparagraph (A), to assist other colleges, universities, institutions, and agencies in improving educational and transitional results for children with disabilities, if the historically Black colleges and universities and the institutions of higher education described in subparagraph (A) meet the criteria established by the Secretary under this subpart.

(d) PRIORITIES- The Secretary, in making an award of a grant, contract, or cooperative agreement under subpart 2 or 3, may, without regard to the rulemaking procedures under section 553 of title 5, United States Code, limit competitions to, or otherwise give priority to—

(1) projects that address 1 or more—

(A) age ranges;

(B) disabilities;

(C) school grades;

(D) types of educational placements or early intervention environments;

(E) types of services;

(F) content areas, such as reading; or

(G) effective strategies for helping children with disabilities learn appropriate behavior in the school and other community based educational settings;

(2) projects that address the needs of children based on the severity or incidence of their disability;

(3) projects that address the needs of—

(A) low achieving students;

(B) underserved populations;

(C) children from low income families;

(D) limited English proficient children;

(E) unserved and underserved areas;

(F) rural or urban areas;

(G) children whose behavior interferes with their learning and socialization;

(H) children with reading difficulties;

(I) children in public charter schools;

(J) children who are gifted and talented; or

(K) children with disabilities served by local educational agencies that receive payments under title VIII of the Elementary and Secondary Education Act of 1965;

(4) projects to reduce inappropriate identification of children as children with disabilities, particularly among minority children;

(5) projects that are carried out in particular areas of the country, to ensure broad geographic coverage;

(6) projects that promote the development and use of technologies with universal design, assistive technology devices, and assistive technology services to maximize children with disabilities' access to and participation in the general education curriculum; and

(7) any activity that is authorized in subpart 2 or 3.

(e) ELIGIBILITY FOR FINANCIAL ASSISTANCE- No State or local educational agency, or other public institution or agency, may receive a grant or enter into a contract or cooperative agreement under subpart 2 or 3 that relates exclusively to programs, projects, and activities pertaining to children aged 3 through 5, inclusive, unless the State is eligible to receive a grant under section 619(b).

SEC. 682. ADMINISTRATIVE PROVISIONS.

(a) APPLICANT AND RECIPIENT RESPONSIBILITIES-

(1) DEVELOPMENT AND ASSESSMENT OF PROJECTS- The Secretary shall require that an applicant for, and a recipient of, a grant, contract, or cooperative agreement for a project under subpart 2 or 3—

(A) involve individuals with disabilities or parents of individuals with disabilities ages birth through 26 in planning, implementing, and evaluating the project; and

(B) where appropriate, determine whether the project has any potential for replication and adoption by other entities.

(2) ADDITIONAL RESPONSIBILITIES- The Secretary may require a recipient of a grant, contract, or cooperative agreement under subpart 2 or 3 to—

(A) share in the cost of the project;

(B) prepare any findings and products from the project in formats that are useful for specific audiences, including parents, administrators, teachers, early intervention personnel, related services personnel, and individuals with disabilities;

(C) disseminate such findings and products; and

(D) collaborate with other such recipients in carrying out subparagraphs (B) and (C).

(b) APPLICATION MANAGEMENT-

(1) STANDING PANEL-

(A) IN GENERAL- The Secretary shall establish and use a standing panel of experts who are qualified, by virtue of their training, expertise, or experience, to evaluate each application under subpart 2 or 3 that requests more than $75,000 per year in Federal financial assistance.

(B) MEMBERSHIP- The standing panel shall include, at a minimum—

(i) individuals who are representatives of institutions of higher education that plan, develop, and carry out high quality programs of personnel preparation;

(ii) individuals who design and carry out scientifically based research targeted to the improvement of special education programs and services;

(iii) individuals who have recognized experience and knowledge necessary to integrate and apply scientifically based research findings to improve educational and transitional results for children with disabilities;

(iv) individuals who administer programs at the State or local level in which children with disabilities participate;

(v) individuals who prepare parents of children with disabilities to participate in making decisions about the education of their children;

(vi) individuals who establish policies that affect the delivery of services to children with disabilities;

(vii) individuals who are parents of children with disabilities ages birth through 26 who are benefiting, or have benefited, from coordinated research, personnel preparation, and technical assistance; and

(viii) individuals with disabilities.

(C) TERM- No individual shall serve on the standing panel for more than 3 consecutive years.

(2) PEER-REVIEW PANELS FOR PARTICULAR COMPETITIONS-

(A) COMPOSITION- The Secretary shall ensure that each subpanel selected from the standing panel that reviews an application under subpart 2 or 3 includes—

(i) individuals with knowledge and expertise on the issues addressed by the activities described in the application; and

(ii) to the extent practicable, parents of children with disabilities ages birth through 26, individuals with disabilities, and persons from diverse backgrounds.

(B) FEDERAL EMPLOYMENT LIMITATION- A majority of the individuals on each subpanel that reviews an application under subpart 2 or 3 shall be individuals who are not employees of the Federal Government.

(3) USE OF DISCRETIONARY FUNDS FOR ADMINISTRATIVE PURPOSES-

(A) EXPENSES AND FEES OF NON-FEDERAL PANEL MEMBERS- The Secretary may use funds available under subpart 2 or 3 to pay the expenses and fees of the panel members who are not officers or employees of the Federal Government.

(B) ADMINISTRATIVE SUPPORT- The Secretary may use not more than 1 percent of the funds appropriated to carry out subpart 2 or 3 to pay non-Federal entities for administrative support related to management of applications submitted under subpart 2 or 3, respectively.

(c) PROGRAM EVALUATION- The Secretary may use funds made available to carry out subpart 2 or 3 to evaluate activities carried out under subpart 2 or 3, respectively.

(d) MINIMUM FUNDING REQUIRED-

(1) IN GENERAL- Subject to paragraph (2), the Secretary shall ensure that, for each fiscal year, not less than the following amounts are provided under subparts 2 and 3 to address the following needs:

(A) $12,832,000 to address the educational, related services, transitional, and early intervention needs of children with deaf-blindness.

(B) $4,000,000 to address the postsecondary, vocational, technical, continuing, and adult education needs of individuals with deafness.

(C) $4,000,000 to address the educational, related services, and transitional needs of children with an emotional disturbance and those who are at risk of developing an emotional disturbance.

(2) RATABLE REDUCTION- If the sum of the amount appropriated to carry out subparts 2 and 3, and part E of the Education Sciences Reform Act of 2002 for any fiscal year is less than $130,000,000, the amounts listed in paragraph (1) shall be ratably reduced for the fiscal year.'.

TITLE II—NATIONAL CENTER FOR SPECIAL EDUCATION RESEARCH

SEC. 201. NATIONAL CENTER FOR SPECIAL EDUCATION RESEARCH.

(a) AMENDMENT- The Education Sciences Reform Act of 2002 (20 U.S.C. 9501 et seq.) is amended—

(1) by redesignating part E as part F; and

(2) by inserting after part D the following:

PART E—NATIONAL CENTER FOR SPECIAL EDUCATION RESEARCH

SEC. 175. ESTABLISHMENT.

(a) ESTABLISHMENT- There is established in the Institute a National Center for Special Education Research (in this part referred to as the Special Education Research Center').

(b) MISSION- The mission of the Special Education Research Center is—

(1) to sponsor research to expand knowledge and understanding of the needs of infants, toddlers, and children with disabilities in order to improve the developmental, educational, and transitional results of such individuals;

(2) to sponsor research to improve services provided under, and support the implementation of, the Individuals with Disabilities Education Act (20 U.S.C. 1400 et seq.); and

(3) to evaluate the implementation and effectiveness of the Individuals with Disabilities Education Act in coordination with the National Center for Education Evaluation and Regional Assistance.

(c) Applicability of Education Sciences Reform Act of 2002- Parts A and F, and the standards for peer review of applications and for the conduct and evaluation of research under sections 133(a) and 134, respectively, shall apply to the Secretary, the Director, and the Commissioner in carrying out this part.

SEC. 176. COMMISSIONER FOR SPECIAL EDUCATION RESEARCH.

The Special Education Research Center shall be headed by a Commissioner for Special Education Research (in this part referred to as the Special Education Research Commissioner') who shall have substantial knowledge of the Special Education Research Center's activities, including a high level of expertise in the fields of research, research management, and the education of children with disabilities.

SEC. 177. DUTIES.

(a) GENERAL DUTIES- The Special Education Research Center shall carry out research activities under this part consistent with the mission described in section 175(b), such as activities that—

(1) improve services provided under the Individuals with Disabilities Education Act in order to improve—

(A) academic achievement, functional outcomes, and educational results for children with disabilities; and

(B) developmental outcomes for infants or toddlers with disabilities;

(2) identify scientifically based educational practices that support learning and improve academic achievement, functional outcomes, and educational results for all students with disabilities;

(3) examine the special needs of preschool aged children, infants, and toddlers with disabilities, including factors that may result in developmental delays;

(4) identify scientifically based related services and interventions that promote participation and progress in the general education curriculum and general education settings;

(5) improve the alignment, compatibility, and development of valid and reliable assessments, including alternate assessments, as required by section 1111(b) of the Elementary and Secondary Education Act of 1965 (20 U.S.C. 6311(b));

(6) examine State content standards and alternate assessments for students with significant cognitive impairment in terms of academic achievement, individualized instructional need, appropriate education settings, and improved post-school results;

(7) examine the educational, developmental, and transitional needs of children with high incidence and low incidence disabilities;

(8) examine the extent to which overidentification and underidentification of children with disabilities occurs, and the causes thereof;

(9) improve reading and literacy skills of children with disabilities;

(10) examine and improve secondary and postsecondary education and transitional outcomes and results for children with disabilities;

(11) examine methods of early intervention for children with disabilities, including children with multiple or complex developmental delays;

(12) examine and incorporate universal design concepts in the development of standards, assessments, curricula, and instructional methods to improve educational and transitional results for children with disabilities;

(13) improve the preparation of personnel, including early intervention personnel, who provide educational and related services to children with disabilities to increase the academic achievement and functional performance of students with disabilities;

(14) examine the excess costs of educating a child with a disability and expenses associated with high cost special education and related services;

(15) help parents improve educational results for their children, particularly related to transition issues;

(16) address the unique needs of children with significant cognitive disabilities; and

(17) examine the special needs of limited English proficient children with disabilities.

(b) STANDARDS- The Special Education Research Commissioner shall ensure that activities assisted under this section—

(1) conform to high standards of quality, integrity, accuracy, validity, and reliability;

(2) are carried out in accordance with the standards for the conduct and evaluation of all research and development established by the National Center for Education Research; and

(3) are objective, secular, neutral, and nonideological, and are free of partisan political influence, and racial, cultural, gender, regional, or disability bias.

(c) PLAN- The Special Education Research Commissioner shall propose to the Director a research plan, developed in collaboration with the Assistant Secretary for Special Education and Rehabilitative Services, that—

(1) is consistent with the priorities and mission of the Institute and the mission of the

Special Education Research Center;

(2) is carried out, updated, and modified, as appropriate;

(3) is consistent with the purposes of the Individuals with Disabilities Education Act;

(4) contains an appropriate balance across all age ranges and types of children with disabilities;

(5) provides for research that is objective and uses measurable indicators to assess its progress and results; and

(6) is coordinated with the comprehensive plan developed under section 681 of the Individuals with Disabilities Education Act.

(d) GRANTS, CONTRACTS, AND COOPERATIVE AGREEMENTS-

(1) IN GENERAL- In carrying out the duties under this section, the Director may award grants to, or enter into contracts or cooperative agreements with, eligible applicants.

(2) ELIGIBLE APPLICANTS- Activities carried out under this subsection through contracts, grants, or cooperative agreements shall be carried out only by recipients with the ability and capacity to conduct scientifically valid research.

(3) APPLICATIONS- An eligible applicant that wishes to receive a grant, or enter into a contract or cooperative agreement, under this section shall submit an application to the Director at such time, in such manner, and containing such information as the Director may require.

(e) DISSEMINATION- The Special Education Research Center shall—

(1) synthesize and disseminate, through the National Center for Education Evaluation and Regional Assistance, the findings and results of special education research conducted or supported by the Special Education Research Center; and

(2) assist the Director in the preparation of a biennial report, as described in section 119.

(f) AUTHORIZATION OF APPROPRIATIONS- There are authorized to be appropriated to carry out this part such sums as may be necessary for each of fiscal years 2005 through 2010.'.

(b) CONFORMING AMENDMENTS-

(1) AMENDMENTS TO THE TABLE OF CONTENTS- The table of contents in section 1 of the Act entitled An Act to provide for improvement of Federal education research, statistics, evaluation, information, and dissemination, and for other purposes', approved November 5, 2002 (116 Stat. 1940; Public Law 107-279), is amended—

(A) by redesignating the item relating to part E as the item relating to part F; and

(B) by inserting after the item relating to section 174 the following:

Part E—National Center for Special Education Research

SEC. 175. ESTABLISHMENT

SEC. 176. COMMISSIONER FOR SPECIAL EDUCATION RESEARCH.

SEC. 177. DUTIES.

(2) EDUCATION SCIENCES REFORM ACT OF 2002- The Education Sciences Reform Act of 2002 (20 U.S.C. 9501 et seq.) is amended—

(A) in section 111(b)(1)(A) (20 U.S.C. 9511(b)(1)(A)), by inserting and special education' after early childhood education';

(B) in section 111(c)(3) (20 U.S.C. 9511(c)(3))—

(i) in subparagraph (B), by striking and' after the semicolon;

(ii) in subparagraph (C), by striking the period and inserting ; and'; and

(iii) by adding at the end the following:

(D) the National Center for Special Education Research (as described in part E).';

(C) in section 115(a) (20 U.S.C. 9515(a)), by striking including those' and all that follows through such as' and inserting including those associated with the goals and requirements of the Elementary and Secondary Education Act of 1965 (20 U.S.C. 6301 et seq.), the Individuals with Disabilities Education Act (20 U.S.C. 1400 et seq.), and the Higher Education Act of 1965 (20 U.S.C. 1001 et seq.), such as'; and

(D) in section 116(c)(4)(A)(ii) (20 U.S.C. 9516(c)(4)(A)(ii), by inserting special education experts,' after early childhood experts,'.

(3) ELEMENTARY AND SECONDARY EDUCATION ACT OF 1965- Section 1117(a)(3) of the Elementary and Secondary Education Act of 1965 (20 U.S.C. 6317(a)(3)) is amended by striking part E' and inserting part D'.

SEC. 202. NATIONAL BOARD FOR EDUCATION SCIENCES.

Section 116(c)(9) of the Education Sciences Reform Act of 2002 (20 U.S.C. 9516(c)(9)) is amended by striking the third sentence and inserting the following: Meetings of the Board are subject to section 552b of title 5, United States Code (commonly referred to as the Government in the Sunshine Act).'.

SEC. 203. REGIONAL ADVISORY COMMITTEES.

Section 206(d)(3) of the Educational Technical Assistance Act of 2002 (20 U.S.C. 9605(d)(3)) is amended by striking Academy' and inserting Institute'.

TITLE III— MISCELLANEOUS PROVISIONS

SEC. 301. AMENDMENT TO CHILDREN'S HEALTH ACT OF 2000.

Section 1004 of the Children's Health Act of 2000 (42 U.S.C. 285g note) is amended—

(1) in subsection (b), by striking Agency' and inserting Agency, and the Department of Education'; and

(2) in subsection (c)—

(A) in paragraph (2), by striking and' after the semicolon;

(B) in paragraph (3), by striking the period at the end and inserting ; and'; and

(C) by adding at the end the following:

(4) be conducted in compliance with section 444 of the General Education Provisions Act (20 U.S.C. 1232g), including the requirement of prior parental consent for the disclosure of any education records, except without the use of authority or exceptions granted to authorized representatives of the Secretary of Education for the evaluation of Federally-supported education programs or in connection with the enforcement of the Federal legal requirements that relate to such programs.

SEC. 302. EFFECTIVE DATES.

(a) Parts A, B, and C, and subpart 1 of part D-

(1) IN GENERAL- Except as provided in paragraph (2), parts A, B, and C, and subpart 1

of part D, of the Individuals with Disabilities Education Act, as amended by title I, shall take effect on July 1, 2005.

(2) HIGHLY QUALIFIED DEFINITION- Subparagraph (A), and subparagraphs (C) through (F), of section 602(10) of the Individuals with Disabilities Education Act, as amended by title I, shall take effect on the date of enactment of this Act for purposes of the Elementary and Secondary Education Act of 1965.

(b) SUBPARTS 2, 3, AND 4 OF PART D- Subparts 2, 3, and 4 of part D of the Individuals with Disabilities Education Act, as amended by title I, shall take effect on the date of enactment of this Act.

(c) Education Sciences Reform Act of 2002-

(1) NATIONAL CENTER FOR SPECIAL EDUCATION RESEARCH- Sections 175, 176, and 177 (other than section 177(c)) of the Education Sciences Reform Act of 2002, as enacted by section 201(a)(2) of this Act, shall take effect on the date of enactment of this Act.

(2) PLAN- Section 177(c) of the Education Sciences Reform Act of 2002, as enacted by section 201(a)(2) of this Act, shall take effect on October 1, 2005.

SEC. 303. TRANSITION.

(a) ORDERLY TRANSITION-

(1) IN GENERAL- The Secretary of Education (in this section referred to as the Secretary') shall take such steps as are necessary to provide for the orderly transition from the Individuals with Disabilities Education Act, as such Act was in effect on the day preceding the date of enactment of this Act, to the Individuals with Disabilities Education Act and part E of the Education Sciences Reform Act of 2002, as amended by this Act.

(2) LIMITATION- The Secretary's authority in paragraph (1) shall terminate 1 year after the date of enactment of this Act.

(b) MULTI-YEAR AWARDS- Notwithstanding any other provision of law, the Secretary may use funds appropriated under part D of the Individuals with Disabilities Education Act to make continuation awards for projects that were funded under section 618, and part D, of the Individuals with Disabilities Education Act (as such section and part were in effect on September 30, 2004), in accordance with the terms of the original awards.

(c) RESEARCH- Notwithstanding section 302(b) or any other provision of law, the Secretary may award funds that are appropriated under the Department of Education Appropriations Act, 2005 for special education research under either of the headings SPECIAL EDUCATION' or INSTITUTE OF EDUCATION SCIENCES' in accordance with sections 672 and 674 of the Individuals with Disabilities Education Act, as such sections were in effect on October 1, 2004.

SEC. 304. REPEALER.

Section 644 of the Individuals with Disabilities Education Act, as such section was in effect on the day before the enactment of this Act, is repealed.

SEC. 305. IDEA TECHNICAL AMENDMENTS TO OTHER LAWS.

(a) Title 10- Section 2164(f) of title 10, United States Code is amended—

(1) in paragraph (1)(B)—

(A) by striking infants and toddlers' each place the term appears and inserting infants or toddlers';

(B) by striking part H' and inserting part C'; and

.   (C) by striking 1471' and inserting 1431'; and

(2) in paragraph (3)—

(A) in subparagraph (A)—

(i) by striking 602(a)(1)' and inserting 602'; and

(ii) by striking 1401(a)(1)' and inserting 1401';

(B) by striking subparagraph (B);

(C) by redesignating subparagraph (C) as subparagraph (B); and

(D) in subparagraph (B) (as so redesignated)—

(i) by striking and toddlers' and inserting or toddlers';

(ii) by striking 672(1)' and inserting 632'; and

(iii) by striking 1472(1)' and inserting 1432'.

(b) Defense Dependents Education Act of 1978- Section 1409(c)(2) of the Defense Dependents Education Act of 1978 (20 U.S.C. 927(c)(2)) is amended—

(1) by striking 677' and inserting 636'; and

(2) by striking part H' and inserting part C'.

(c) Higher Education Act of 1965- The Higher Education Act of 1965 (20 U.S.C. 1001 et seq.) is amended—

(1) in section 465(a)(2)(C) (20 U.S.C. 1087ee(a)(2)(C), by striking Individuals With'

and inserting Individuals with' and;

(2) in section 469(c) (20 U.S.C. 1087ii(c)), by striking 602(a)(1) and 672(1)' and inserting 602 and 632'.

(d) EDUCATION OF THE DEAF ACT-The matter preceding subparagraph (A) of section 104(b)(2) of the Education of the Deaf Act (20 U.S.C. 4304(b)(2)) is amended by striking 618(a)(1)(A)' and inserting 618(a)(1)'.

(e) Goals 2000: Educate America Act-Section 3(a)(9) of the Goals 2000: Educate America Act (20 U.S.C. 5802(a)(9)) is amended by striking 602(a)(17)' and inserting 602'.

(f) School-to-Work Opportunities Act of 1994- Section 4(15) of the School-to-Work Opportunities Act of 1994 (20 U.S.C. 6103(15)) is amended—

(1) by striking 602(a)(17)' and inserting 602'; and

(2) by striking 1401(17)' and inserting 1401'.

(g) Elementary and Secondary Education Act of 1965- The Elementary and Secondary Education Act of 1965 (20 U.S.C. 6301 et seq.) is amended—

(1) in section 1111(b)(2)(I)(ii) (20 U.S.C. 6311(b)(2)(I)(ii)), by striking 612(a)(17)(A)' and inserting 612(a)(16)(A)';

(2) in section 5208 (20 U.S.C. 7221g), by striking 602(11)' and inserting 602'; and

(3) in section 5563(b)(8)(C) (20 U.S.C. 7273b(b)(8)(C)), by striking 682' and inserting 671'.

(h) Rehabilitation Act of 1973- The Rehabilitation Act of 1973 (29 U.S.C. 701 et seq.) is amended—

(1) in section 101(a)(11)(D)(ii) (29 U.S.C. 721(a)(11)(D)(ii)), by striking (as added by section 101 of Public Law 105-17)';

(2) in section 105(b)(1)(A)(ii) (29 U.S.C. 725(b)(1)(A)(ii)), by striking 682(a) of the Individuals with Disabilities Education Act (as added by section 101 of the Individuals with Disabilities Education Act Amendments of 1997; Public Law 105-17)' and inserting 671 of the Individuals with Disabilities Education Act';

(3) in section 105(c)(6) (29 U.S.C. 725(c)(6))—

(A) by striking 612(a)(21)' and inserting 612(a)(20)';

(B) by striking Individual with' and inserting Individuals with'; and

(C) by striking (as amended by section 101 of the Individuals with Disabilities Education Act Amendments of 1997; Public Law 105-17)';

(4) in section 302(f)(1)(D)(ii) (29 U.S.C. 772 (f)(1)(D)(ii)), by striking (as amended by section 101 of the Individuals with Disabilities Education Act Amendments of 1997 (Public Law 105-17))';

(5) in section 303(c)(6) (29 U.S.C. 773(c)(6))—

(A) by striking 682(a)' and inserting 671'; and

(B) by striking (as added by section 101 of the Individuals with Disabilities Education Act Amendments of 1997; Public Law 105-17)'; and

(6) in section 303(c)(4)(A)(ii) (29 U.S.C. 773(c)(4)(A)(ii)), by striking 682(a) of the Individuals with Disabilities Education Act (as added by section 101 of the Individuals with Disabilities Education Act Amendments of 1997; Public Law 105-17)' and inserting 671 of the Individuals with Disabilities Education Act'.

(i) PUBLIC HEALTH SERVICE ACT- The Public Health Service Act (42 U.S.C. 201 et seq.) is amended—

(1) in section 399A(f) (42 U.S.C. 280d(f), by striking part H' and inserting part C';

(2) in section 399(n)(3) (42 U.S.C. 280c-6(n)(3)), by striking part H' and inserting part C';

(3) in section 399A(b)(8) (42 U.S.C. 280d(b)(8)), by striking part H' and inserting part C';

(4) in section 562(d)(3)(B) (42 U.S.C. 290ff-1(d)(3)(B)), by striking and H' and inserting and C'; and

(5) in section 563(d)(2) (42 U.S.C. 290ff-2(d)(2)), by striking 602(a)(19)' and inserting 602'.

(j) SOCIAL SECURITY ACT- The Social Security Act (42 U.S.C. 301 et seq.) is amended—

(1) in section 1903(c) (42 U.S.C. 1396b(c)), by striking part H' and inserting part C'; and

(2) in section 1915(c)(5)(C)(i) (42 U.S.C. 1396n(c)(5)(C)(i)), by striking (as defined in section 602(16) and (17) of the Education of the Handicapped Act (20 U.S.C. 1401(16), (17))' and inserting (as such terms are defined in section 602 of the Individuals with Disabilities Education Act (20 U.S.C. 1401))'.

(k) Domestic Volunteer Service Act of 1973- Section 211(a) of the Domestic Volunteer Service Act of 1973 (42 U.S.C. 5011(a)) is amended—

(1) by striking part H' and inserting part C'; and

(2) by striking 1471' and inserting 1431'.

(l) HEAD START ACT- The Head Start Act (42 U.S.C. 9831 et seq.) is amended—

(1) in section 640(a)(5)(C)(iv) (42 U.S.C. 9835(a)(5)(C)(iv)), by striking 1445' and inserting 1444';

(2) in section 640(d) (42 U.S.C. 9835(d))—

(A) by striking U.S.C' and inserting U.S.C.'; and

(B) by striking 1445' and inserting 1444';

(3) in section 641(d)(3) (42 U.S.C. 9836(d)(3)), by striking U.S.C 1431-1445' and inserting U.S.C. 1431-1444'; and

(4) in section 642(c) (42 U.S.C. 9837(c)), by striking 1445' and inserting 1444'.

(m) National and Community Service Act of 1990- Section 101(21)(B) of the National and Community Service Act of 1990 (42 U.S.C. 12511(21)(B)) is amended—

(1) by striking 602(a)(1)' and inserting 602'; and

(2) by striking 1401(a)(1)' and inserting 1401'.

(n) Developmental Disabilities Assistance and Bill of Rights Act of 2000- The Developmental Disabilities Assistance and Bill of Rights Act of 2000 (42 U.S.C. 15001 et seq.) is amended—

(1) in section 125(c)(5)(G)(i) (42 U.S.C. 15025(c)(5)(G)(i)), by striking subtitle C' and inserting part C'; and

(2) in section 154(a)(3)(E)(ii)(VI) (42 U.S.C. 15064(a)(3)(E)(ii)(VI))—

(A) by striking 682 or 683' and inserting 671 or 672'; and

(B) by striking (20 U.S.C. 1482, 1483)'.

(o) District of Columbia School Reform Act of 1995- The District of Columbia School Reform Act of 1995 (Public Law 104-134) is amended—

(1) in section 2002(32)—

(A) by striking 602(a)(1)' and inserting 602'; and

(B) by striking 1401(a)(1)' and inserting 1401';

(2) in section 2202(19), by striking Individuals With' and inserting Individuals with'; and

(3) in section 2210—

(A) in the heading for subsection (c), by striking WITH DISABILITIES' and inserting WITH DISABILITIES'; and

(B) in subsection (c), by striking Individuals With' and inserting Individuals with'.

SEC. 306. COPYRIGHT.

Section 121 of title 17, United States Code, is amended—

(1) by redesignating subsection (c) as

subsection (d);

(2) by inserting after subsection (b) the following:

(c) Notwithstanding the provisions of section 106, it is not an infringement of copyright for a publisher of print instructional materials for use in elementary or secondary schools to create and distribute to the National Instructional Materials Access Center copies of the electronic files described in sections 612(a)(23)(C), 613(a)(6), and section 674(e) of the Individuals with Disabilities Education Act that contain the contents of print instructional materials using the National Instructional Material Accessibility Standard (as defined in section 674(e)(3) of that Act), if—

(1) the inclusion of the contents of such print instructional materials is required by any State educational agency or local educational agency;

(2) the publisher had the right to publish such print instructional materials in print formats; and

(3) such copies are used solely for reproduction or distribution of the contents of such print instructional materials in specialized formats; and

(3) in subsection (d), as redesignated by this section—

(A) in paragraph (2), by striking 'and' after the semicolon; and

(B) by striking paragraph (3) and inserting the following:

(3) 'print instructional materials' has the meaning given under section 674(e)(3)(C) of the Individuals with Disabilities Education Act; and

(4) 'specialized formats' means—

(A) braille, audio, or digital text which is exclusively for use by blind or other persons with disabilities; and

(B) with respect to print instructional materials, includes large print formats when such materials are distributed exclusively for use by blind or other persons with disabilities.

Go to *www.gpo.gov/fdsys/pkg/FR-2006-08-14/pdf/06-6656.pdf* to view the Federal Regulations Implementing The 2006 IDEA Amendments.

APPENDIX B

Table of Special Education Cases
Decided by the U.S. Supreme Court

Title and Citation (in chronological order)

Southeastern Community College v. Davis, 442 U.S. 397, 99 S.Ct. 2361, 60 L.Ed.2d 980 (1979).

Univ. of Texas v. Camenisch, 451 U.S. 390, 101 S.Ct. 1830, 68 L.Ed.2d 175 (1981).

Pennhurst State School and Hospital v. Halderman, 451 U.S. 1, 101 S.Ct. 1531, 67 L.Ed.2d 694 (1981) (*Pennhurst I*).

Board of Educ. v. Rowley, 458 U.S. 176, 102 S.Ct. 3034, 73 L.Ed.2d 690 (1982).

Pennhurst State School and Hospital v. Halderman, 465 U.S. 89, 104 S.Ct. 900, 79 L.Ed.2d 67 (1984) (*Pennhurst II*).

Irving Independent School Dist. v. Tatro, 468 U.S. 883, 104 S.Ct. 3371, 82 L.Ed.2d 664 (1984).

Smith v. Robinson, 468 U.S. 992, 104 S.Ct. 3457, 82 L.Ed.2d 746 (1984).

Honig v. Students of California School for the Blind, 471 U.S. 148, 105 S.Ct. 1820, 85 L.Ed.2d 114 (1985).

Burlington School Committee v. Dep't of Educ. of Massachusetts, 471 U.S. 359, 105 S.Ct. 1996, 85 L.Ed.2d 385 (1985).

City of Cleburne, Texas v. Cleburne Living Center, 473 U.S. 432, 105 S.Ct. 3249, 87 L.Ed.2d 313 (1985).

Witters v. Washington Dep't of Services for the Blind, 474 U.S. 481, 106 S.Ct. 748, 88 L.Ed.2d 846 (1986).

School Board of Nassau County v. Arline, 480 U.S. 273, 107 S.Ct. 1123, 94 L.Ed.2d 307 (1987).

Honig v. Doe, 484 U.S. 305, 108 S.Ct. 592, 98 L.Ed.2d 686 (1988).

Traynor v. Turnage, 485 U.S. 535, 108 S.Ct. 1372, 99 L.Ed.2d 618 (1988).

Dellmuth v. Muth, 491 U.S. 223, 109 S.Ct. 2397, 105 L.Ed.2d 181 (1989).

Zobrest v. Catalina Foothills School Dist., 509 U.S. 1, 113 S.Ct. 2462, 125 L.Ed.2d 1 (1993).

Florence County School Dist. Four v. Carter, 510 U.S. 7, 114 S.Ct. 361, 126 L.Ed.2d 284 (1993).

Board of Educ. of Kiryas Joel Village School Dist. v. Grumet, 512 U.S. 687, 114 S.Ct. 2481, 129 L.Ed.2d 546 (1994).

Cedar Rapids Community School Dist. v. Garret F., 526 U.S. 66, 119 S.Ct. 992, 143 L.Ed.2d 154 (1999).

Owasso Independent School Dist. No. I-011 v. Falvo, 534 U.S. 426, 122 S.Ct. 934, 151 L.Ed.2d 896 (2002).

Locke v. Davey, 540 U.S. 712, 124 S.Ct. 1307, 158 L.Ed.2d 1 (2004).

Schaffer v. Weast, 546 U.S. 49, 126 S.Ct. 528, 163 L.Ed.2d 387 (2005).

Arlington Cent. School Dist. Board of Educ. v. Murphy, 548 U.S. 291, 126 S.Ct. 2455, 165 L.Ed.2d 526 (2006).

Winkelman v. Parma City School Dist., 550 U.S. 516, 127 S.Ct. 1994, 167 L.Ed.2d 904 (2007).

Fitzgerald v. Barnstable School Committee, 555 U.S. 246, 129 S.Ct. 788, 172 L.Ed.2d 582 (2009).

Ysursa v. Pocatello Educ. Ass'n, 555 U.S. 353, 129 S.Ct. 1093, 172 L.Ed.2d 770 (2009).

Forest Grove School Dist. v. T.A., 557 U.S. 230, 129 S.Ct. 2484, 174 L.Ed.2d 168 (2009).

THE JUDICIAL SYSTEM

In order to allow you to determine the relative importance of a judicial decision, the cases included in *Students with Disabilities and Special Education Law* identify the particular court from which a decision has been issued. For example, a case decided by a state supreme court generally will be of greater significance than a state circuit court case. Hence, a basic knowledge of the structure of our judicial system is important to an understanding of school law.

Almost all the reports in this volume are taken from appellate court decisions. Although most education law decisions occur at trial court and administrative levels, appellate court decisions have the effect of binding lower courts and administrators so that appellate court decisions have the effect of law within their court systems.

State and federal court systems generally function independently of each other. Each court system applies its own law according to statutes and the determinations of its highest court. However, judges at all levels often consider opinions from other court systems to settle issues which are new or arise under unique fact situations. Similarly, lawyers look at the opinions of many courts to locate authority that supports their clients' cases.

Once a lawsuit is filed in a particular court system, that system retains the matter until its conclusion. Unsuccessful parties at the administrative or trial court level generally have the right to appeal unfavorable determinations of law to appellate courts within the system. When federal law issues or constitutional grounds are present, lawsuits may be appropriately filed in the federal court system. In those cases, the lawsuit is filed initially in the federal district court for that area.

On rare occasions, the U.S. Supreme Court considers appeals from the highest courts of the states if a distinct federal question exists and at least four justices agree on the question's importance. The federal courts occasionally send cases to state courts for application of state law. These situations are infrequent and, in general, the state and federal court systems should be considered separate from each other.

The most common system, used by nearly all states and also the federal judiciary, is as follows: a legal action is commenced in district court (sometimes called trial court, county court, common pleas court or superior court) where a decision is initially reached. The case may then be appealed to the court of appeals (or appellate court), and, in turn, this decision may be appealed to the supreme court.

Several states, however, do not have a court of appeals; lower court decisions are appealed directly to the state's supreme court. Additionally, some states have labeled their courts in a nonstandard fashion.

In Maryland, the highest state court is called the Court of Appeals. In the state of New York, the trial court is called the Supreme Court. Decisions of this court may be appealed to the Supreme Court, Appellate Division. The highest court in New York is the Court of Appeals. Pennsylvania has perhaps the most complex court system. The lowest state court is the Court of Common Pleas. Depending on the circumstances of the case, appeals may be taken to either the Commonwealth Court or the Superior Court. In certain instances the Commonwealth Court functions as a trial court as well as an appellate court. The Superior Court, however, is strictly an intermediate appellate court. The highest court in Pennsylvania is the Supreme Court.

While supreme court decisions are generally regarded as the last word in legal matters, it is important to remember that trial and appeals court decisions also create important legal precedents. For the hierarchy of typical state and federal court systems, please see the diagram below.

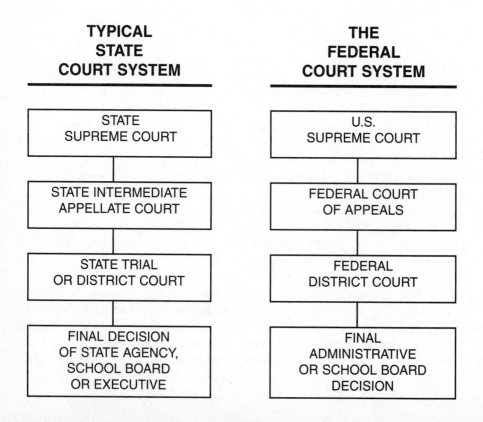

Federal courts of appeals hear appeals from the district courts that are located in their circuits. Below is a list of states matched to the federal circuits in which they are located.

First Circuit	— Puerto Rico, Maine, New Hampshire, Massachusetts, Rhode Island
Second Circuit	— New York, Vermont, Connecticut
Third Circuit	— Pennsylvania, New Jersey, Delaware, Virgin Islands
Fourth Circuit	— West Virginia, Maryland, Virginia, North Carolina, South Carolina
Fifth Circuit	— Texas, Louisiana, Mississippi
Sixth Circuit	— Ohio, Kentucky, Tennessee, Michigan
Seventh Circuit	— Wisconsin, Indiana, Illinois
Eighth Circuit	— North Dakota, South Dakota, Nebraska, Arkansas, Missouri, Iowa, Minnesota
Ninth Circuit	— Alaska, Washington, Oregon, California, Hawaii, Arizona, Nevada, Idaho, Montana, Northern Mariana Islands, Guam
Tenth Circuit	— Wyoming, Utah, Colorado, Kansas, Oklahoma, New Mexico
Eleventh Circuit	— Alabama, Georgia, Florida
District of Columbia Circuit	— Hears cases from the U.S. District Court for the District of Columbia.
Federal Circuit	— Sitting in Washington, D.C., the U.S. Court of Appeals, Federal Circuit hears patent and trade appeals and certain appeals on claims brought against the federal government and its agencies.

HOW TO READ A CASE CITATION

Generally, court decisions can be located in case reporters at law school or governmental law libraries. Some cases can also be located on the Internet through legal websites or official court websites.

Each case summary contains the citation, or legal reference, to the full text of the case. The diagram below illustrates how to read a case citation.

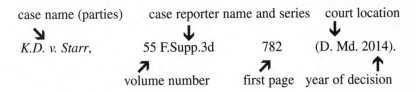

Some cases may have two or three reporter names such as U.S. Supreme Court cases and cases reported in regional case reporters as well as state case reporters. For example, a U.S. Supreme Court case usually contains three case reporter citations.

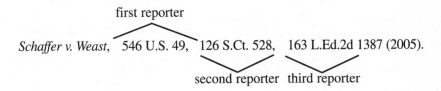

The citations are still read in the same manner as if only one citation has been listed.

Occasionally, a case may contain a citation which does not reference a case reporter. For example, a citation may contain a reference such as:

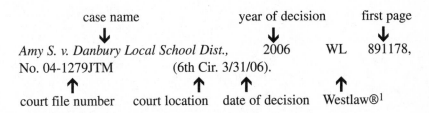

[1] Westlaw® is a computerized database of court cases available for a fee.

The court file number indicates the specific number assigned to a case by the particular court system deciding the case. In our example, the Sixth Circuit Court has assigned the case of *Amy S. v. Danbury Local School District* the case number of "No. 04-1279JTM," which will serve as the reference number for the case and any matter relating to the case. Locating a case on the Internet generally requires either the case name and date of the decision, and/or the court file number.

Below, we have listed the full names of the regional reporters. As mentioned previously, many states have individual state reporters. The names of those reporters may be obtained from a reference law librarian.

P.   **Pacific Reporter**
Alaska, Arizona, California, Colorado, Hawaii, Idaho, Kansas, Montana, Nevada, New Mexico, Oklahoma, Oregon, Utah, Washington, Wyoming

A.   **Atlantic Reporter**
Connecticut, Delaware, District of Columbia, Maine, Maryland, New Hampshire, New Jersey, Pennsylvania, Rhode Island, Vermont

N.E.   **Northeastern Reporter**
Illinois, Indiana, Massachusetts, New York, Ohio

N.W.   **Northwestern Reporter**
Iowa, Michigan, Minnesota, Nebraska, North Dakota, South Dakota, Wisconsin

So.   **Southern Reporter**
Alabama, Florida, Louisiana, Mississippi

S.E.   **Southeastern Reporter**
Georgia, North Carolina, South Carolina, Virginia, West Virginia

S.W.   **Southwestern Reporter**
Arkansas, Kentucky, Missouri, Tennessee, Texas

F.   **Federal Reporter**
The thirteen federal judicial circuits courts of appeals decisions. See *The Judicial System*, p. 513, for specific state circuits.

F.Supp.   **Federal Supplement**
The thirteen federal judicial circuits district court decisions.

Fed.Appx.   **Federal Appendix**
Contains unpublished opinions of the U.S. Circuit Courts of Appeal. See *The Judicial System*, p. 513, for specific state circuits.

U.S.   **United States Reports**
S.Ct.   **Supreme Court Reporter**   U.S. Supreme Court Decisions
L.Ed.   **Lawyers' Edition**

GLOSSARY

Age Discrimination in Employment Act (ADEA) - The ADEA, 29 U.S.C. § 621 *et seq.*, is part of the Fair Labor Standards Act. It prohibits discrimination against persons who are at least 40 years old, and applies to employers that have 20 or more employees and that affect interstate commerce.

Americans with Disabilities Act (ADA) - Key provisions of the ADA, 42 U.S.C. § 12101 *et seq.*, went into effect on July 26, 1992. Among other things, it prohibits discrimination against a qualified individual with a disability because of that person's disability with respect to job application procedures, the hiring, advancement or discharge of employees, employee compensation, job training, and other terms, conditions and privileges of employment.

Bona Fide - Latin term meaning "good faith." Generally used to note a party's lack of bad intent or fraudulent purpose.

Class Action Suit - Federal Rule of Civil Procedure 23 allows members of a class to sue as representatives on behalf of the whole class provided that the class is so large that joinder of all parties is impractical, there are questions of law or fact common to the class, the claims or defenses of the representatives are typical of the claims or defenses of the class, and the representative parties will adequately protect the interests of the class. In addition, there must be some danger of inconsistent verdicts or adjudications if the class action were prosecuted as separate actions. Most states also allow class actions under the same or similar circumstances.

Collateral Estoppel - Also known as issue preclusion. The idea that once an issue has been litigated, it may not be re-tried. Similar to the doctrine of *Res Judicata* (see below).

Due Process Clause - The clauses of the Fifth and Fourteenth Amendments to the Constitution that guarantee the citizens of the United States "due process of law" (see below). The Fifth Amendment's Due Process Clause applies to the federal government, and the Fourteenth Amendment's Due Process Clause applies to the states.

Due Process of Law - The idea of "fair play" in the government's application of law to its citizens, guaranteed by the Fifth and Fourteenth Amendments. Substantive due process is just plain *fairness*, and procedural due process is accorded when the government utilizes adequate procedural safeguards for the protection of an individual's liberty or property interests.

Education for All Handicapped Children Act (EAHCA) - See Individuals with Disabilities Education Act (IDEA).

Education of the Handicapped Act (EHA) - See Individuals with Disabilities Education Act (IDEA).

Enjoin - See Injunction.

Equal Pay Act - Federal legislation which is part of the Fair Labor Standards Act. It applies to discrimination in wages that is based on gender. For race discrimination, employees paid unequally must utilize Title VII or 42 U.S.C. § 1981. Unlike many labor statutes, there is no minimum number of employees necessary to invoke the act's protection.

Equal Protection Clause - The clause of the Fourteenth Amendment that prohibits a state from denying any person within its jurisdiction equal protection of its laws. Also, the Due Process Clause of the Fifth Amendment that pertains to the federal government. This has been interpreted by the Supreme Court to grant equal protection even though there is no explicit grant in the Constitution.

Establishment Clause - The clause of the First Amendment that prohibits Congress from making "any law respecting an establishment of religion." This clause has been interpreted as creating a "wall of separation" between church and state. The test now used to determine whether government action violates the Establishment Clause, referred to as the *Lemon* test, asks whether the action has a secular purpose, whether its primary effect promotes or inhibits religion, and whether it requires excessive entanglement between church and state.

Fair Labor Standards Act (FLSA) - Federal legislation that mandates the payment of minimum wages and overtime compensation to covered employees. The overtime provisions require employers to pay at least time-and-one-half to employees who work more than 40 hours per week.

Federal Tort Claims Act - Federal legislation that determines the circumstances under which the United States waives its sovereign immunity (see below) and agrees to be sued in court for money damages. The government retains its immunity in cases of intentional torts committed by its employees or agents, and where the tort is the result of a "discretionary function" of a federal employee or agency. Many states have similar acts.

42 U.S.C. §§ 1981, 1983 - Section 1983 of the federal Civil Rights Act prohibits any person acting under color of state law from depriving any other person of rights protected by the Constitution or by federal laws. A vast majority of lawsuits claiming constitutional violations are brought under § 1983. Section 1981 provides that all persons enjoy the same right to make and enforce contracts as "white citizens." Section 1981 applies to employment contracts. Further, unlike § 1983, § 1981 applies even to private actors. It is not limited to those acting under color of state law. These sections do not apply to the federal government, though the government may be sued directly under the Constitution for any violations.

Free Appropriate Public Education (FAPE) - The IDEA requires local educational agencies to provide students with disabilities with a free appropriate public education. Under the federal FAPE standard, a student receives a FAPE through an individually developed education program that allows the student to receive educational benefit. States can enact higher standards under the IDEA, but at a minimum must comply with the federal standard governing the provision of a FAPE.

Free Exercise Clause - The clause of the First Amendment that prohibits Congress from interfering with citizens' rights to the free exercise of their religion. Through the Fourteenth Amendment, it has also been made applicable to the states and their sub-entities. The Supreme Court has held that laws of general applicability that have an incidental effect on persons' free exercise rights are not violative of the Free Exercise Clause.

Handicapped Children's Protection Act (HCPA) - (See also Individuals with Disabilities Education Act (IDEA).) The HCPA, enacted as an amendment to the EHA, provides for the payment of attorneys' fees to a prevailing parent or guardian in a lawsuit brought under the EHA (IDEA).

Hearing Officer - Also known as an administrative law judge. The hearing officer decides disputes that arise *at the administrative level*, and has the power to administer oaths, take testimony, rule on evidentiary questions, and make determinations of fact.

Immunity (Sovereign Immunity) - Federal, state and local governments are free from liability for torts committed except in cases in which they have consented to be sued (by statute or by court decisions).

Incorporation Doctrine - By its own terms, the Bill of Rights applies only to the federal government. The Incorporation Doctrine states that the Fourteenth Amendment makes the Bill of Rights applicable to the states.

Individuals with Disabilities Education Act (IDEA) - Also known as the Education of the Handicapped Act (EHA), the Education for All Handicapped Children Act (EAHCA), and the Handicapped Children's Protection Act (HCPA). Originally enacted as the EHA, the IDEA is the federal legislation that provides for the free appropriate public education of all children with disabilities.

Individualized Education Program (IEP) - The IEP is designed to give children with disabilities a free appropriate education. It is updated annually, with the participation of the child's parents or guardian.

Injunction - An equitable remedy (see Remedies) wherein a court orders a party to do or refrain from doing some particular action.

Issue Preclusion - Also known as collateral estoppel, the legal rule that prohibits a court from reconsideration of a particular issue in litigation arising from the same set of facts, involving the same parties and requesting similar relief to a matter previously heard by the court.

Jurisdiction - The power of a court to determine cases and controversies. The Supreme Court's jurisdiction extends to cases arising under the Constitution and under federal law. Federal courts have the power to hear cases where there is diversity of citizenship or where a federal question is involved.

Least Restrictive Environment/Mainstreaming - Part of what is required for a free appropriate education is that each child with a disability be educated in the "least restrictive environment." To the extent that disabled children are educated with non-disabled children in regular education classes, those children are being mainstreamed.

Negligence per se - Negligence on its face. Usually, the violation of an ordinance or statute will be treated as negligence per se because no careful person would have been guilty of it.

Per Curiam - Latin phrase meaning "by the court." Used in court reports to note an opinion written by the court rather than by a single judge or justice.

Placement - A special education student's placement must be appropriate (as well as responsive to the particular child's needs). Under the IDEA's "stay-put" provision, school officials may not remove a special education child from his or her "then current placement" over the parents' objections until the completion of administrative or judicial review proceedings.

Preemption Doctrine - Doctrine which states that when federal and state law attempt to regulate the same subject matter, federal law prevents the state law from operating. Based on the Supremacy Clause of Article VI, Clause 2, of the Constitution.

Pro Se - A party appearing in court, without the benefit of an attorney, is said to be appearing pro se.

Rehabilitation Act - Section 504 of the Rehabilitation Act prohibits employers who receive federal financial assistance from discriminating against otherwise qualified individuals with handicaps solely because of their handicaps. An otherwise qualified individual is one who can perform the "essential functions" of the job with "reasonable accommodation."

Related Services - As part of the free appropriate education due to children with disabilities, school districts may have to provide related services such as transportation, physical and occupational therapy, and medical services that are for diagnostic or evaluative purposes relating to education.

Remand - The act of an appellate court in returning a case to the court from which it came for further action.

Remedies - There are two general categories of remedies, or relief: legal remedies, which consist of money damages, and equitable remedies, which consist of a court mandate that a specific action be prohibited or required. For example, a claim for compensatory and punitive damages seeks a legal remedy; a claim for an injunction seeks an equitable remedy. Equitable remedies are generally unavailable unless legal remedies are inadequate to address the harm.

Res Judicata - The judicial notion that a claim or action may not be tried twice or re-litigated, or that all causes of action arising out of the same set of operative facts should be tried at one time. Also known as claim preclusion.

Section 1981 & Section 1983 - (see 42 U.S.C. §§ 1981, 1983).

Sovereign Immunity - The idea that the government cannot be sued without its consent. It stems from the English notion that "the King can do no wrong." This immunity from suit has been abrogated in most states and by the federal government through legislative acts known as "tort claims acts."

Standing - The judicial doctrine which states that in order to maintain a lawsuit a party must have some real interest at stake in the outcome of the trial.

Statute of Limitations - A statute of limitation provides the time period in which a specific cause of action may be brought.

Summary Judgment - Federal Rule of Civil Procedure 56 provides for the summary adjudication of a case before trial if either party can show that there is no genuine issue as to any material fact and that, given the facts agreed upon, the party is entitled to judgment as a matter of law. In general, summary judgment is used to dispose of claims which do not support a legally recognized claim.

Supremacy Clause - Clause in Article VI of the Constitution, which states that federal legislation is the supreme law of the land. This clause is used to support the Preemption Doctrine (see above).

Title VII, Civil Rights Act of 1964 (Title VII) - Title VII prohibits discrimination in employment based upon race, color, sex, national origin, or religion. It applies to any employer having fifteen or more employees. Under Title VII, where an employer intentionally discriminates, employees may obtain money damages unless the claim is for race discrimination. For those claims, monetary relief is available under 42 U.S.C. § 1981.

Tort - A tort is a civil wrong, other than breach of contract. Torts include negligence, assault, battery, trespass, defamation, infliction of emotional distress and wrongful death.

U.S. Equal Employment Opportunity Commission (EEOC) - The EEOC is the government entity that is empowered to enforce Title VII (see above) and other federal laws against discrimination through investigation and/or lawsuits. Private individuals alleging discrimination must pursue administrative remedies within the EEOC before they are allowed to file suit under Title VII.

Vacate - The act of annulling the judgment of a court either by an appellate court or by the court itself. The Supreme Court will generally vacate a lower court's judgment without deciding the case itself, and remand the case to the lower court for further consideration in light of some recent controlling decision.

Writ of Certiorari - The device used by the Supreme Court to transfer cases from the appellate court's docket to its own. Since the Supreme Court's appellate jurisdiction is largely discretionary, it need only issue such a writ when it desires to rule in the case.

INDEX